T0367668

Capabilities, Gender, Equality

Questions of gender, injustice and equality pervade all our lives, and as such, the capabilities or "human development" approach to understanding well-being and basic political entitlements continues to be debated. In this thought-provoking book, a range of authors provides unique reflections on the capabilities approach and, specifically, Martha C. Nussbaum's contributions to issues of gender, equality and political liberalism. Moreover, the authors tackle a broad range of development issues, including those of religion, ecological and environmental justice, social justice, child care, disability, and poverty. This is the first book to examine Nussbaum's work in political philosophy in such depth, bringing together a group of distinguished experts with diverse disciplinary perspectives. It also features a unique contribution from Nussbaum herself, in which she offers reactions to the discussion and her latest thoughts on the capabilities approach. *Capabilities, Gender, Equality* will interest a wide range of readers and policy-makers interested in new human development policies.

FLAVIO COMIM is an Associate Professor of Economics at the Federal University of Rio Grande do Sul (UFRGS), Brazil. He is also an Affiliated Lecturer for the Department of Land Economy and the Centre of Development Studies and a Von Hugel Research Associate at the University of Cambridge. He has published widely in areas such as history of economic thought, economic methodology, development ethics, and the capability approach.

MARTHA C. NUSSBAUM is the Ernst Freund Distinguished Service Professor of Law and Ethics at the University of Chicago, appointed in the Law School and the Philosophy Department. Over the years, Nussbaum has extended and developed the capabilities approach, and she has received numerous awards for her work.

Capabilities, Gender, Equality

Towards Fundamental Entitlements

Edited by

Flavio Comim and Martha C. Nussbaum

CAMBRIDGE
UNIVERSITY PRESS

CAMBRIDGE
UNIVERSITY PRESS

University Printing House, Cambridge CB2 8BS, United Kingdom

Cambridge University Press is part of the University of Cambridge.

It furthers the University's mission by disseminating knowledge in the pursuit of education, learning and research at the highest international levels of excellence.

www.cambridge.org
Information on this title: www.cambridge.org/9781107015692

© Cambridge University Press 2014

First published 2014

A catalogue record for this publication is available from the British Library

Library of Congress Cataloging-in-Publication Data
Capabilities, gender, equality : towards fundamental entitlements / edited by Flavio Comim and Martha C. Nussbaum.
    pages cm
Includes index.
ISBN 978-1-107-01569-2 (Hardback)
1. Economic development–Developing countries. 2. Equality–Developing countries. 3. Social planning–Developing countries. I. Comim, Flavio. II. Nussbaum, Martha Craven, 1947–
HC59.7.C3137 2013
330.9172′4001–dc23   2013014367

ISBN 978-1-107-01569-2 Hardback

Contents

Figures

Tables

Contributors

JOHN M. ALEXANDER Professor of Business Ethics, Loyola Institute of Business Administration, Loyola College, Chennai, India

JEREMY BENDIK-KEYMER Elmer G. Beamer – Hubert H. Schneider Professor in Ethics and Associate Professor of Philosophy, Department of Philosophy, Case Western Reserve University

HILDE BOJER Associate Professor Emerita, Department of Economics, University of Oslo

HARRY BRIGHOUSE Professor, Philosophy Department and Affiliate Professor of Educational Policy Studies, University of Wisconsin–Madison

FLAVIO COMIM Associate Professor, UFRGS, Brazil and Affiliated Lecturer in Human Development and Ecosystems, Department of Land Economy and the Centre of Development Studies, University of Cambridge.

MARC FLEURBAEY Robert E. Kuenne Professor of Economics and Humanistic Studies, Woodrow Wilson School and University Center for Human Values, Princeton University

DES GASPER Professor of Human Development, Development Ethics and Public Policy, International Institute of Social Studies, Erasmus University Rotterdam

MURIEL GILARDONE Associate Professor, Normandie Université, UCBN, CREM (UMR CNRS 6211)

IAN GOUGH Visiting Professor, London School of Economics and Political Science, Centre for the Analysis of Social Exclusion (CASE) and Centre for the Study of Global Governance; Emeritus Professor of Social Policy, University of Bath

ISABELLE GUÉRIN Research Fellow, Institut de Recherche pour le Développement, Paris School of Economics

BREENA HOLLAND Associate Professor, Political Science Department and the Environmental Initiative, Lehigh University

ULRIKE KNOBLOCH PostDoc and Lecturer in Gender, Economics and Ethics, Department of Social Sciences, University of Fribourg, Switzerland

SANTOSH MEHROTRA Director-General Institute of Applied Manpower Research, Planning Commission, Government of India

MARTHA C. NUSSBAUM Ernst Freund Distinguished Service Professor of Law and Ethics, The Law School, The University of Chicago

JANE PALIER Research Fellow, Centre Walras, University Lumière Lyon 2; Research Scholar, Institut de Recherche pour le Développement

HENRY S. RICHARDSON Professor, Department of Philosophy and Senior Research Scholar, Kennedy Institute of Ethics, Georgetown University

PATRICIA WELCH SALEEBY Assistant Professor, School of Social Work, Southern Illinois University Carbondale

ELAINE UNTERHALTER Professor of Education and International Development, Faculty of Policy and Society, Institute of Education, University of London

MELANIE WALKER National Research Foundation Chair in Higher Education and Human Development, University of the Free State, South Africa

JONATHAN WARNER Professor and Tutor in Economics, Quest University Canada

Preface

Professor Martha C. Nussbaum is one of the most distinguished and influential philosophers of our times, a towering figure in philosophy and the social sciences. Her work has inspired a generation of philosophers, economists, sociologists, educators, anthropologists, psychologists, social scientists, policy-makers, planners and development practitioners to reflect upon issues of justice, gender, human rights, political liberalism, religion, education, disability, among many others. This book delves into key elements of her work from a critical perspective and explores future challenges for the capabilities approach.

The origin of this book lies in a conference entitled 'Promoting Women's Capabilities: examining Nussbaum's Capabilities Approach', convened by the Von Hügel Institute of St Edmund's College, Cambridge in September 2002. The conference brought interdisciplinary scholars from around the world to discuss the work of Professor Nussbaum and it closed with a riveting debate between Professor Nussbaum and Professor Sen on their work on capabilities. In 2001 a conference at St Edmund's College had examined the work of Professor Amartya Sen. These two conferences were followed by the Pavia Conferences in 2003 and 2004 and the founding of the Human Development and Capability Association (HDCA). Not enough could be said of the inspirational leadership of the late Father Frank Carey, then Director of the Von Hügel Institute, in the realization of the Cambridge Conferences. His compassion and love for humanity and his faith in the fight against injustices were defining of these two special moments for capabilities scholars.

The contributions to this book include a number of papers based on the conference and also invited papers. The preparation process, in addition to two rounds of peer reviewing, benefited from comments from Professor Nussbaum on the conference papers and, following the publication of her *tour de force*, *Frontiers of Justice*, in 2006 and of *Creating Capabilities* in 2011, authors had the opportunity to further elaborate their papers.

This book examines, from an interdisciplinary perspective, several aspects of Professor Nussbaum's work, with focus on gender, equality and foundational issues of her approach. While her research and writings cover a much wider universe, the book themes are strategic in her work and key for understanding the impact of her capabilities approach on political philosophy and human development.

To a large extent, Professor Nussbaum's work is revolutionary. She invites her readers to reinterpret the contribution of John Rawls and the meaning of political liberalism. She presents new views on transnational justice, disability and justice to non-human animals, new perspectives on gender discrimination, new challenges to educational policies, and new policies for considering the role of art, public spaces, emotions, the workplace and the government in the promotion of human development and global justice. Professor Nussbaum's work enriches our understanding of the 'human' in human development. Her capabilities approach provides a solid foundation for tackling complex issues. The present book offers a reflection on core aspects of her magnificent contribution to philosophy, political and social sciences.

Flavio Comim

Introduction
Capabilities, challenges, and the omnipresence of political liberalism

Martha C. Nussbaum

The chapters in this volume cover such a wide range of topics and engage in such intricate debates with my work that it would be impossible to respond to them all with the level of rigor and detail that they invite, and it would be rude and disrespectful to respond to only some of them. I shall therefore use this Introduction to do two things. First, I shall lay out some future challenges for the capabilities approach that the chapters, as a group, suggest – both by what they say and by what they omit. I shall then delve into just one issue that currently engages me a good deal, closely connected to the recent paper on political liberalism that is reprinted in the present volume: the question of whether the idea of political liberalism is applicable to all the democracies of the world, and to the global political order itself, insofar as there is one. That issue is not addressed in the reprinted article, but it urgently needs addressing.

Challenges for the capabilities approach
Confronting alternative theories

Political justification, as I conceive it (accepting John Rawls's account of how we pursue reflective equilibrium), is a matter both of repeated testing against people's considered judgments and of confronting alternative theories.[1] In *Women and Human Development* I confronted informed-desire Utilitarianism, trying to show how the capabilities approach (CA) is superior. In *Frontiers of Justice* I did something similar with theories of the social contract. It is a matter of intricate philosophical work to confront such theories, especially the best and deepest, and

---

[1] See Nussbaum, *Women and Human Development* (Cambridge University Press, 2000), Chapter 2, for a detailed account. One should also take note of my "On hearing women's voices: a reply to Susan Okin," *Philosophy and Public Affairs* 32 (2004), 193–205, where I correct a common misreading: listening to the voices of poor people is, for me, not a part of political justification but rather a part of self-education, to make sure that the theory responds to reality. Gough's paper (Chapter 14, below) has this misreading, or so I believe.

I view my engagement with John Rawls's great theory as an ongoing conversation. For that reason I particularly welcome Henry Richardson's eloquent defense of a reformulated Original Position (OP). Responding to him in the *Journal of Ethics*, I have said that the changes he proposes in Rawls's formulation satisfy the most urgent of my objections.[2] But since Richardson focused on the question of disability, not the equally important questions of transnational justice and justice to non-human animals, there is more work to be done in this regard, and I look forward to engaging with him further in the future.

Similarly inviting is the alternative theory articulated by Mark Fleurbaey. Just as Richardson modifies Rawlsian contractarianism to meet my objections, so Fleurbaey modifies preference-based Utilitarianism in a quite attractive way that invites full-scale treatment. I think he has gone a long way to removing some of the biggest objections to preference-based approaches, and I also agree with him that one should not make choice the be-all and end-all of political principles. Where I would want to engage further, however, would be in the area of fundamental political principles that express equal respect for all. It seems to me that our interest in having equal voting rights, equal rights of conscience, etc. does not derive from individual preferences in any direct way. We want our nation to show respect for each and every person by giving them equal voting rights even if they don't care about voting, as many Americans don't. It's an objective statement of the equal worth of persons, and we make that statement because we think the worth of persons is equal, period. Indeed, I have defended equal voting rights for people with severely impaired cognitive capabilities, who could not possibly understand or care about voting, just on the grounds that this is required by a deep idea of equal respect.[3] I think Fleurbaey's otherwise attractive proposal runs into serious difficulty dealing with people whose cognitive disabilities are severe, given its emphasis on rankings of lives, which many such people can't do, and on autonomy, which they cannot attain. The next step in our dialog would be to explore all of these issues.

The Gough–Doyal approach to basic needs is another that needs extensive discussion, although I think Gough (Chapter 14) is correct that it dovetails in many respects with my own. Still, the approach is more subjective than mine. First, it attaches considerable weight to actual consensus, whereas

---

[2] Nussbaum, "Replies," *Journal of Ethics* 10 (2006), 463–506.
[3] Nussbaum, "The capabilities of people with cognitive disabilities," *Metaphilosophy* 40 (2009), 331–351. Reprinted in *Cognitive Disability and its Challenge to Moral Philosophy*, ed. Eva Kittay and Licia Carlson (Malden, MA: Wiley-Blackwell, 2010), 75–96.

I follow Rawls in making consensus only a possible goal. Second, the approach defines serious harm as "fundamental disablement in the pursuit of one's vision of the good." I am not sure how this makes room for the lives of people with severe cognitive disabilities, nor even for the problem of adaptive preferences. On those areas we'd need further dialog. Finally, since Gough concludes that the "foundations" of my theory are "shaky," I would want to point out that, with Rawls, I reject any type of foundationalism in political justification: if one looks for foundations, one will not find them, because I think justification is and should be holistic and ongoing, reaching toward an endpoint of reflective equilibrium that is not yet attained by any theory. Detailed confrontation between Gough's theory and mine would be part of that search.

Finally, although nobody mentions it here, Amartya Sen's challenge to all ideal theories of justice, in *The Idea of Justice*,[4] raises a fundamental issue for my theory as much as for Rawls's, since my theory is more like Rawls's than like the non-ideal theory advanced by Sen, in its overall aims and nature. I have said a good deal about other differences between Sen's theory and my own,[5] but that large difference remains to be explored – not necessarily by me!

Animals and the environment

The chapters by Bendik-Keymer and Holland represent very welcome statements about how the capabilities approach may possibly help us to address urgent issues of environmental quality and non-human life, and what dividends we might expect from its application there. They represent, however, just the first steps in a larger theoretical project. Holland applies the capabilities approach entirely within the context of an anthropocentric account of capabilities. That's one good thing to do, but we need to ask, at a deeper level, whose capabilities count as goals. In *Frontiers of Justice* I have offered some reasons for thinking of non-human animals as subjects of political justice, but I (so far) resist the inclusion of plants (except instrumentally), and I retain the principle that individuals are ends, thus refusing to make ecosystems ends in themselves, though they are surely important for the ends of animals and humans. Others will take the dialog further. Bendik-Keymer, emphasizing the depth and multifacetedness of the notion of dignity, gives us a good start.

---

[4] Sen, *The Idea of Justice* (Cambridge, MA: Harvard University Press, 2009).
[5] In Nussbaum, *Creating Capabilities: The Human Development Approach* (Cambridge, MA: Harvard University Press, 2009).

Emotions

Although quite a few of the chapters (especially, perhaps, Comim's eloquent one) mention the emotions and their role in my work, none focuses on their political role. As I mentioned at the conclusion of *Frontiers of Justice*, that is my next, and current, project. Imagining a demanding political goal that demands sacrifice of self-interest requires imagining how people can be led to care about it. We cannot justify it without showing that it can be stable over time, and for the right reasons. John Rawls understood this, and he supplied a sketch of how a public psychology of emotion might underwrite a just society. But it remained both too sketchy and too abstract, in my view, too little connected to the uneven, quirky emotions of real people. So that is the task that has been occupying me for the past ten years, and in 2013 my book *Political Emotions: Why Love Matters for Justice* appeared.[6] Suffice it to say that themes of gender are at the very heart of the project.

Law and public choice

Nobody in the present volume takes up my contention that the capabilities are a template for constitution-making or for implicit constitutional entitlements in nations without a written constitution.[7] My own writing on this focuses on the US Constitution and the Indian Constitution, but it would be great to have much more work on this topic from a variety of legal traditions. One issue that is illuminated thereby is the constantly vexing issue of measurement. How do we measure the presence of a capability? People usually search for some quantifiable something. But if they thought about the history of a constitutional principle, such as free speech, or freedom of religion, they would see that the way we typically measure how far it is present in a society is more discursive and historical: we study the history of case law, for example, seeing what sorts of litigants bring their grievances before the courts, and how their complaints are adjudicated.[8] Especially where gender equality is concerned, this would be a very fruitful approach.

---

[6] Martha C. Nussbaum, *Political Emotions: Why Love Matters for Justice* (Cambridge, MA: Harvard University Press, 2013).

[7] I say this everywhere, but the idea is developed at greatest length in Nussbaum, "Constitutions and capabilities: 'perception' against lofty formalism," Supreme Court Foreword, *Harvard Law Review* 121 (2007), 4–97.

[8] I wrote a longish book about just one principle: *Liberty of Conscience: In Defense of America's Tradition of Religious Equality* (New York: Basic Books, 2008); that entire book is what I take to be a measurement, in the case of one nation and one principle.

Another invitation I've repeatedly issued is for more work on the institutional structure of the capabilities approach. Iris Marion Young often criticized me for not saying anything about this, and I said to her that she could do it far better than I could. But, tragically, she will not address that or any other further issue. I, however, still feel that I don't know enough. I have made an effort to study public choice theory, with the aid of a superb class taught by my colleague, Saul Levmore, but this showed me two things: first, that the literature contains intense debate rather than settled consensus; second, that my type of mind is not the type that is going to make creative contributions in this area. So I really wish that some formally trained scholars would take this on. I know there is much to be learned here.

Political liberalism: omnipresent and transnational

In "Perfectionist liberalism and political liberalism," reprinted in this volume, I make an argument for a norm of Rawlsian political liberalism at the domestic level.[9] It might be thought, since my discussion begins from Rawls, that I intend the argument to apply only to Europe and North America, since Rawls (apparently) so limits it. Indeed, John Alexander's chapter in the present volume argues that I have no warrant for exporting it to the nations of the developing world, since Rawls did not so apply his own concept. I did once make an argument that the norm of political liberalism applied to transnational norms, as well as to norms internal to non-Western societies, but that argument (written for my article "Rawls and feminism" in *The Cambridge Companion to Rawls*) was excised for reasons of space and because other sections of the article were deemed more immediately pertinent to feminism.[10] Here I shall not reproduce that older argument, but shall begin from the ground up, so to speak, although I shall incorporate elements of a little-known paper of mine, "Political liberalism and respect: a response to Linda Barclay."[11]

I shall argue for several claims in this brief discussion, which should be read as a crucial addendum to the *Philosophy and Public Affairs* (*PAPA*) article:[12]

---

[9] See John Rawls, *Political Liberalism*, expanded paper edition (New York: Columbia University Press, 1986). Hereafter *PL*.

[10] Nussbaum, "Rawls and feminism," in *The Cambridge Companion to Rawls*, ed. Samuel Freeman (Cambridge University Press, 2003), 488–520. Some of the material from the excised section will appear in Nussbaum, "Rawls, *Political Liberalism: A Reassessment*," to be published in a volume of essays on *PL* edited by Thom Brooks and Martha C. Nussbaum (Columbia University Press, 2014).

[11] In *SATS: A Nordic Journal of Philosophy* 4 (2003), 25–44.

[12] Reprinted as Chapter 1 of this book.

(1) That John Rawls, although he did apparently restrict the application of political liberalism to the European and American nations, did not advance compelling reasons for so doing.

(2) That the same issues that make political liberalism a normatively good position for a Western domestic society are reasons present in every existing democratic state.

(3) That these same reasons are not only not undercut but actually acquire additional force when we move from the domestic sphere to that of international relations.

Rawls's restriction

It is actually quite difficult to know why Rawls decided to restrict the application of his doctrine of political liberalism and overlapping consensus to Western countries that have a legacy of thought deriving from the experience of the Wars of Religion.[13] Indeed, he does not exactly say that he views that legacy as a necessary condition for the application of the doctrine; what he says seems compatible with the idea that he takes no stand one way or the other regarding its extension to other cultures.

Before we go further, we need to know what Rawls thinks needs to be the case if we are to apply these ideas to a society. Clearly, he does not think that we need to be able to show that most citizens in a nation currently hold these views. For Rawls clearly thinks his ideas applicable to the United States, where he knows and repeatedly states that they face strong opposition of one type or another.[14] Nor, apparently – since he adopts positions on economic redistribution and campaign finance that he is well aware were minority positions in 1986, when the paper edition of *PL* was published – do we even need to show that these positions are majority positions. On another front, Rawls's account of religious liberty and equality is probably incompatible with the views and practices of a majority of Europeans.[15] So, actual consensus or even majority support are not necessary. Nor does he claim that he has proven that such a consensus "would eventually form" around his ideas.[16] The chapter on overlapping consensus, indeed, shows us that he believes that all that is required – at most – is that we be able to demonstrate a

---

[13] For pertinent comments, see *PL*, xxvi, xxxi

[14] Consider the discussions of free speech and campaign finance in *PL*, where he uses US legal materials to apply his basic ideas.

[15] See Nussbaum, *The New Religious Intolerance: Overcoming the Politics of Fear in an Anxious Age* (Cambridge, MA: Harvard University Press, 2012).

[16] *PL*, xlvii–xlviii: "PL makes no attempt to prove, or to show, that such a consensus would eventually form around a reasonable political conception of justice."

plausible path from where we currently are to an overlapping consensus, over quite a lot of time. From a mere *modus vivendi*, we can see how we might advance to a constitutional consensus; and from there we can imagine how we might advance to the overlapping consensus. He does not tell us where he thinks particular nations currently are on this spectrum. (Kurt Baier argued that a constitutional consensus is sufficient for political stability, and that the US is already at the stage of constitutional consensus, although it would appear that he was thinking about political and civil liberty, not about economic justice.[17]) This transition, Rawls holds, is made possible by the looseness in most people's comprehensive doctrines: they are not all of a piece, and new ideas can lodge in part of a doctrine that will ultimately cause the revision, even radical revision, of other parts.[18]

It is abundantly clear from that important chapter[19] that a nation that right now has at best a *modus vivendi* on crucial matters can be a full and unproblematic candidate for the application of Rawls's doctrines. Indeed, by continuing to include the US and Europe, although no country in the group has even a *modus vivendi* on the full range of issues that Rawls's theory addresses (the US not on economic matters, Europe not on religious liberty and religious establishment), he strongly suggests that we usually begin further back, with an unsettled debate in which the normative ideas of the political doctrine he defends are but one voice among many. All that's needed is the not utterly unreasonable hope that these ideas could over time follow the type of trajectory he imagines, and a plausible story about how that transition might go. Indeed, by suggesting a parallel between our current situation and the situation of liberal intellectuals in Weimar Germany (who failed to provide a compelling abstract defense of their norms, a mistake that Rawls intends to help us not make today), Rawls strongly suggests that the values he defends may at present be those of a severely embattled minority.[20] At the conclusion of the Introduction, moreover, he emphasizes that even the idea that human beings have a moral nature of the sort that could eventually accept the principles of justice is not advanced as a fact, but only as a Kantian practical postulate, which we accept because the alternative would leave us wondering "whether it is worthwhile for human beings to live on the earth."[21]

---

[17] Kurt Baier, "Justice and the aims of political philosophy," *Ethics* 99 (1989), 771–790. Rawls discusses Baier's article in *PL*, 149 and n. 15, noting that he is not claiming that a true overlapping consensus is necessary for political stability: Baier might be right that constitutional consensus is enough.

[18] See *PL*, 159.   [19] *PL*, 133–172.   [20] *PL*, lxi–lxii.   [21] *PL*, lxii.

Why, then, does Rawls believe that the ideas apply only or primarily to the US and Europe? Certainly not because he ignores the existence of illiberal ideas in those political cultures and their history: indeed, the eloquent preface to the paper edition of *PL* couches the whole project as a response to fascism. He says virtually nothing. But let us imagine his most likely response (given his emphasis on the Wars of Religion). It is that the experience of the Wars of Religion gave European nations (and their colonial offshoots in North America) an idea of how wrong it is to oppress people and how important liberty of conscience is. Even if such ideas did not immediately prevail, they struck deep roots, and stuck around. At the same time, the experience of the Wars of Religion gave those nations experience of a fact that Rawls makes fundamental to his account of the "burdens of judgment": namely, that under conditions of liberty people do not come into agreement in their comprehensive ethical and religious doctrines. And seeing that lack of agreement, combined with the importance of conscience, people would reasonably find attractive the ideas of political liberalism.

This is plausible enough, but note that it took a very long time for anyone in North America or Europe to find this inference plausible. Westphalia was not an agreement in favor of liberty of conscience and respectful pluralism. Domestically, people kept trying to oppress minorities, just as the former dissenters, who ought to have known better, did in North America – with the shining early exceptions of Rhode Island and Pennsylvania. So Rawls can't mean that this experience is a sufficient condition for people coming to find political liberalism attractive.

Does he think it a necessary condition, and, if he does, why does he? Now first of all, I think we really should be asking not "What is required for people to want to apply a normative concept to themselves?" but rather "What is required in order for a normative concept to be correctly applied to them?" There are all sorts of reasons why people fail to apply normative concepts to themselves (concepts such as racial equality and gender equality, to name only two) – reasons including ignorance, greed, and selfish partiality. Rawls, as a Kantian, is fully aware of this. The Original Position has its roots in normative ideas of impartiality that do exist in people's minds, but along with a lot of other stuff that works against impartiality: that's why it takes the veil of ignorance, which renders that other stuff inoperative, to extract its implications. So Rawls does not hold that a concept is applicable to people only if they already have it and apply it to themselves. At most he holds that the concept has roots in some things that people believe, even if for the most part they act in accordance with other things they believe.

So it seems that he ought to conclude that the normative concepts of political liberalism, concepts such as equal respect and overlapping consensus, and the impartiality of the OP itself, are applicable to people whenever there is something in the thought of that group, and of many individuals in the group, that could reasonably ground the development of such concepts.

Rawls clearly thinks that the experience of the Wars of Religion helped people get these ideas – although, as I have mentioned, it certainly took a long time. Does he think that other ethical traditions of the world – Buddhism, Islam, and Hinduism, for example – do not contain these grounding experiences and the associated concepts, while the religions of the West and the history of the West do better? He certainly does not say this, and he would have been ill advised to do so, since so far as I know he never devoted study to those nations and traditions. We certainly see prominent recognition of ideas of human equality and equal respect in the independence movements and the subsequent constitutional traditions of both India and South Africa, two of the largest and most prominent non-Western democracies.

Did they borrow these ideas from the West? Even if they did, it would still be important to insist that this does not entail that the ideas must be applied only there. All human beings are ingenious borrowers of ideas. The West got all of its mathematics from the East, and the Enlightenment could not have taken place without that borrowing; nonetheless, we do not consider that we have no right to claim those ideas. Similarly, even were it true that the ideas of political equality, democracy, human dignity, and toleration were basically Western Enlightenment notions, this would not prevent and has not prevented many other nations and peoples of the world from putting them into their constitutions, from fighting and dying for them, and so forth. Such a deliberate staking of one's future on the ideas would seem to make the ideas theirs even more firmly than they are ours, who got them by habit. If, moreover, we were to adopt the principle that the ideas of a people are only the oldest ideas in their tradition, we ourselves would have to go back to Homeric Greece, perhaps, where none of the Rawlsian ideas can be found in anything like their modern form, as Rawls himself stressed.[22] (Not to mention the fact that many of "us" would trace our origins back to Africa, China, India, the shtetls of Eastern Europe, etc., all with their different ideas.) Why do we allow ourselves and not others the ability to change and to borrow?

[22] *PL*, xxiv.

Second, the historical record of any culture is the record, largely, of its most powerful voices; we have little record of what poor, illiterate people have thought about the world they live in, or what women of any social class have thought of their lives. So to the extent that we defer to what appears to be the entrenched tradition of a distant society, allowing that tradition to delimit what we expect of it, we are simply agreeing to entrench sexism and class hierarchy, without fully hearing the voices of those who suffer from them. For many women, for example, the ideas of feminism are more intimately theirs, more their tradition, than whatever it was that oppressed them.

We should not, however, concede that the ideas that provide the materials for Rawls's conception are "Western," even in the sense of their historical origin. Is it plausible to suppose that Gandhi and Mandela, when what they saw of "the West" every day was brutality and utter disregard for human rights, together with the most obtuse and virulent racism, would have thought that they should go to "the West" to pick up those ideas? Of course, both of these men admired parts of Western civilization, but both considered that it had failed, as Gandhi's famous remark about Western civilization ("I think it would be a good idea") shows with characteristic pithiness and humor. But both also found deep roots of these ideas in their own traditions. Gandhi, of course, had work to do to find human equality in Hinduism, but he energetically undertook this reconstruction of what he took to be the religion's core, with some assistance from India's Buddhist traditions, which were much admired by Nehru, and which were so deeply admired by B. R. Ambedkar, chief architect of India's Constitution, that, a dalit, he converted to Buddhism. And Buddhism was no recent import: it had been teaching human equality since the time of Ashoka in the third to second centuries BCE. Islam, present in India since at least the eighth century CE, has deep traditions of equality, and in its own historical context was a revolutionary egalitarian movement. Of course, no religion has done well with gender equality until recently, but that's a general story, and certainly the Wars of Religion did not shed light on that important value. As for condemnation of selfishness and greed, that is a staple of all the major religions, not peculiar to those of the West.

What about the ideas most immediately at issue in the debate between political and comprehensive liberalism: the idea of the "burdens of judgment" and the persistence of religious and ethical pluralism under conditions of liberty? Did the experiences of non-Western nations contain experiences that would give thoughtful people such ideas? (We can quickly agree that most people all round the world don't automatically have them.) Well, if we just look at India, we will see that the history of that nation includes deep division and bloody struggles over religion – between Buddhist and Hindu, already in Ashoka's empire of the third to second centuries BCE, leading him to promulgate the remarkable edicts that would appear to contain the world's first doctrine of religious toleration; between Hindu and Hindu, and then Hindu and Muslim, throughout the medieval period, leading to Akbar's (seventeenth-century) policies of state syncretism and toleration. (I note that Akbar was well known in Renaissance Britain, and his doctrines were highly influential as Englishmen worked on the topic for the first time: they turned to India as a nation that had more and deeper experience with the topic.) Ashoka's ideas of religious toleration were extremely important to Jawaharlal Nehru, who gives them a central place in his marvelous *The Discovery of India*,[23] an account of India's traditions written from a British jail. So important was Ashoka that his Buddhist symbol, the wheel of law, occupies a central place in the Indian flag.

We can say much the same of South Africa. Although Hindus and Muslims were categorized more by race than by religion, they certainly knew very well the ways in which people disagree and the bitter disputes to which this can lead.

So, if Rawls had studied this history, I think he would have had to agree that the ideas in question had roots as adequate in other cultures as in those that were his focus. Indeed, in the case of religious pluralism in India, they were older and more generally disseminated than similar ideas in Europe until at least the late eighteenth century, if then. (We should remember that Britain was much slower than the US to extend full civil rights to Jews and atheists.)

In any case, it is probably not necessary to say that history has given a people the specific set of experiences contained in the "burdens of judgment" – the concepts of political liberalism are applicable to them, I believe, just in case the weaker condition I mentioned above is fulfilled: ideas of human equality and impartiality are lurking somewhere in the mess of opinions that people hold, and we can tell a plausible story about how they might prevail.

Political liberalism is for every nation

The ideas of political liberalism, as I argued, don't require any esoteric experience to ground them. What is necessary to make them have a significant place is a plurality of reasonable comprehensive doctrines,

---

[23] Jawaharlal Nehru, *The Discovery of India* (New York: Oxford University Press, 1998 [1946]).

which has not converged to agreement under conditions of freedom. The word "reasonable," as in "Perfectionist liberalism and political liberalism," I understand to mean "held by people who are capable of respecting their fellow citizens as equals." In other words, "reasonable" in my usage (and I think Rawls should have, and in part did, say this) has nothing to say about the internal shape or content of the doctrine. Most comprehensive doctrines contain contradictions, as well as vagueness, indeterminacy, and flat-out irrationality.

So, among nations in which people are capable of understanding and being swayed by norms of equal respect, which is to say in modern democratic societies (not that they always live by ideas of equal respect, but they understand the meaning of these ideas), is there any that does not contain a plurality of religions and other comprehensive doctrines? Indubitably, in today's world, the answer is "no." I am inclined to believe that it always has been "no," only we haven't always listened to a wide enough range of voices (those of women and the poor, and lower castes, for example). I'm also inclined to believe that there is no *family* that has a homogeneous and single comprehensive doctrine, perhaps not even a family of one. Certainly Fred Kniss's elegant study of value differences in Mennonite communities has exploded the idea that there are idyllic face-to-face cultural groups which all agree about all the important matters.[24] Indeed, the more often people see one another, the more likely differences are to appear.

Even if people agree in all important matters today, they may not do so tomorrow, as the settlers of New England colonies soon discovered: fantasizing that they would found a normatively homogeneous "City on the Hill," the founders of the Massachusetts Bay Colony, for example, soon found out that there were differences aplenty, whether they had been there all along or whether they appeared as individuals sought the truth for themselves. Banishment and punishment for heresy quickly became a way of life. So, even if there were no different doctrines to be equally respected, we ought to govern using the ideas of political liberalism, since differences can always arise, and we need to have respectful ways of dealing with them.

But we do not need to reach these subtleties and niceties. For all the world is, today, basically alike in the sense that every nation contains all the major religions, whether they suppress them or allow them to flourish; it's only the numbers that differ. The US has lots of Buddhists, Muslims, Confucianists and Hindus, as well as Christians and Jews and Native Americans, and also numerous agnostics and atheists and a handful of

---

[24] Fred Kniss, *Disquiet in the Land: Cultural Conflict in American Mennonite Communities* (New Brunswick, NJ: Rutgers University Press, 1997).

Parsis. It's difficult to get numbers, since the census does not ask about religion, but the Pew survey on religion shows that only 78.4 percent of US residents are Christian – and this includes Mormons, both Orthodox and Roman Catholics, and many types of Protestants.[25] Moreover, 28 percent of Americans have changed religion, and 44 percent have done so if we count movement among different Christian groups. Sixteen percent say they do not consider themselves religious. Europe would like to think of itself as Christian, but of course it has had Jews for a long time, and it has many Muslims, Hindus and Buddhists today. In India, where the census does ask about religion, we know that Hindus are around 80 percent, Muslims around 13 percent, Christians around 2.3 percent, Sikhs around 2 percent, with Buddhists, Jains, Parsis, Jews, and others in smaller numbers. (Atheists and agnostics aren't counted, since people are classified into a religious system at birth regardless of what they believe.[26] But they are very numerous, in my experience.) In short, all the same groups turn up everywhere, so we're just arguing about the numbers. (And we haven't even mentioned non-religious comprehensive doctrines, such as Marxism and some types of feminism, which are also widely instantiated.) In short, the situations of all modern democracies are similar, so far as the problems giving rise to political liberalism are concerned.

Thus, the main lines of the argument of my "Perfectionist liberalism" apply to every modern democracy: they should prefer political liberalism to perfectionist liberalism (a view that bases political principles on a single comprehensive doctrine, whether religious or secular), on grounds of equal respect. These arguments resemble, and are an extension of, familiar Madisonian arguments against the establishment of religion. As Madison said, when a given doctrine is the official government doctrine, all citizens do not enter the polity "on equal conditions."

Is there ever a good justification for a state that is perfectionist in the sense of making a single doctrine – whether a traditional religion or a secular ethical doctrine such as Joseph Raz's doctrine of autonomy (the target of "Perfectionist liberalism") – the basis of its political principles? I believe there are cases in which that sort of choice is the best we can do, for the time being, in a difficult situation. I have made this case for the plural establishments in India in my recent paper "Personal laws and Equality: the case of India."[27] No doubt there are other such cases.

[25] www.pewforum.org/Religion-News/Study-Finds-Americans-Fluid-in-Their-Religious-Affiliation.aspx.
[26] Thus, only 0.1 percent fail to name a religious affiliation.
[27] In Tom Ginsburg, ed., *Comparative Constitutional Design* (Cambridge University Press, 2012), 266–293.

But in such a case, where there is a non-ideal solution that threatens equal respect, it is all the more incumbent upon the majority to bend over backwards to treat minorities scrupulously and fairly. This condition is not always fulfilled.

I have spoken so far only of democratic nations, and it's clear that I'm talking about nations that are concerned enough about equal respect for persons that it makes sense to delve into the niceties of the choice between perfectionist and political liberalism. I believe that it would be a good idea if dictatorships also accepted the ideas of political liberalism, but obviously there is a lot more wrong with them than that. When Madison criticized the establishment of religion in Virginia, he was making a subtle point about equal respect against the background of a general respect for rights and liberties. That is the type of point I am making in my *PAPA* article. To apply it to dictatorships is thus several steps ahead of where they currently are. First, they would have to become legitimate, which in my view requires a reasonable degree of respect for all citizens' rights and political equality, and then we could go into the details. Often, during the difficult transition from dictatorship to democracy, a perfectionist type of liberalism is needed, and that was, I believe, the case of India in its transition from the Raj to its current state. Today, things have moved along well enough that it would be best to get rid of the systems of religious personal law, although nobody can quite figure out how to achieve that.

Global political liberalism

Let us now consider the political principles we are going to seek across national boundaries, to ground cooperation among nations, and common goals. I have argued in *Frontiers of Justice*[28] that the capabilities can provide international dealings with an attractive set of goals, which would then be implemented primarily by individual nations, but also through a thin system of international agencies and agreements, whatever seems to work at a given time. We begin with the goal, and then work backward to the policies that seem to move us closer to that goal, while being decently respectful of national sovereignty.

So, looking at the world, do we have reason to think the ideas of political liberalism appealing? What might the alternatives be? Well, perfectionist liberalism, on the one side, in the form of the ascendancy of one particular religious or secular comprehensive doctrine; on the

[28] Nussbaum, *Frontiers of Justice: Disability, Nationality, Species Membership* (Cambridge, MA: Harvard University Press, 2006).

other, an account of the goal that appears to have no ethical content, such as gross domestic product (GDP) per capita. If people think that the ethical norms of respect and pluralism embodied in political liberalism are not applicable to the common pursuits of nations, they will probably choose one of the alternatives.

But the world is just like a nation, only more so. It contains all the comprehensive doctrines that nations do, and in case any nation has no representatives of some of them (as, I suppose, a nation might utterly lack Parsis, or devotees of Native American religion), well, the world has that one, too. In addition, the world contains a diversity of political cultures, which might themselves be counted as comprehensive doctrines for this purpose; at least someone might argue that they ought to count. So there are far greater reasons to express the norms abstemiously and non-metaphysically. Indeed, that is why I have built abstractness and thinness into the capabilities paradigm, in part to give the diverse nations, with their diverse political histories, room to specify the norms differently at a concrete level.[29]

In other words, the world contains all the comprehensive doctrines, but it is plural in a further way, containing a diversity of national cultures. Since I defend a strong role for national sovereignty,[30] a requirement of fully equal respect for persons, for me, is respect for national sovereignty, which means (at least regarding nations that pass a threshold of legitimacy) a respect for national diversity. So that constitutes yet a further reason why the transnational goal should not be specified in perfectionist terms, and should be specified in accordance with political liberal values.

---

[29] Here, note, there is an asymmetry between the domestic and the transnational: in the domestic case, political liberalism does not encourage the different groups to write a separate constitution, and overlapping consensus means accepting the constitution as interpreted. In the transnational case, different nations are encouraged to write their own constitutions, embodying but further specifying the ideas of the capabilities goal.

[30] See *Frontiers of Justice*, Chapter 5.

Part I

The capabilities approach

1 Perfectionist liberalism and political liberalism*

Martha C. Nussbaum

Two types of liberalism

The views of Isaiah Berlin are an influential example, in the philosophical literature, of what we might call perfectionist liberalism, a type of liberal political view that spells out a set of controversial metaphysical and ethical doctrines concerning the nature of value and the good life, and then goes on to recommend political principles built upon these values. Berlin's formulations, though influential, are characteristically compressed and allusive, but Joseph Raz has developed a closely related set of ideas with great explicitness and clarity. For Raz, the key personal and political value is autonomy, a power of self-direction and self-government. To this (and here is the connection to Berlin) he links the acceptance of moral pluralism: to see why only a relatively extensive range of options adequately supports autonomy, one must grasp the fact that there are many incompatible ways of living, all of which are morally good and valuable. Thus Raz's doctrine of autonomy – as he states – requires the acceptance of moral pluralism and uses that idea to support its account of adequate options. Religious and secular toleration, he argues, should be based on an acceptance of the ideal of autonomy and the truth of moral pluralism. Thus Raz espouses a two-part ideal: the central value is autonomy, but, as he understands that idea, it requires the acceptance of another controversial doctrine about value, namely pluralism.

* This article was first written for a conference on Isaiah Berlin at Harvard University, September 2009. I am grateful for the very helpful comments of Erin Kelly and Thomas Scanlon on that occasion. The main ideas originated in a discussion following Joseph Raz's presentation to the Law–Philosophy Workshop at the University of Chicago in November 2008 and published on the University of Chicago Law School faculty blog. I am grateful to Raz for discussion on that occasion. For discussion of these issues over the years I am grateful to Charles Larmore, and for comments on a draft I am grateful to Daniel Brudney, Agnes Callard, Rosalind Dixon, Aziz Huq, Andrew Koppelman, Brian Leiter, Micah Lott, and Henry Richardson. Finally, I am extremely grateful to the editors of *Philosophy & Public Affairs* for their painstaking and extremely valuable comments.

The major liberal alternative to Berlin's and Raz's perfectionist liberalism, in the recent Anglo–American philosophical literature,[1] is the view called "political liberalism." This view was developed first by Charles Larmore in *Patterns of Moral Complexity* and *The Morals of Modernity*,[2] with explicit reference to Berlin, but in most detail by John Rawls in his great book *Political Liberalism* (*PL*).[3] I, too, hold a view of this type, having been convinced by the arguments of Larmore and Rawls.[4] It seems worth exploring the reasons that led the three of us to prefer political liberalism to a view of Raz's type.

I begin by outlining the views of Berlin and Raz. I then turn to Larmore's critique and Rawls's restatement of that critique, which I accept in most respects. I then discuss a crucial ambiguity in the formulation of a key notion in political liberalism: that of "reasonable disagreement" (in the case of Larmore), or "reasonable comprehensive doctrines" (in the case of Rawls). Having resolved that ambiguity in favor of the version of the view that I find most appealing, I then argue that political liberalism is superior to perfectionist liberalism as a basis for political principles in a pluralistic society. In a concluding section, I address the issue of stability.

Let us begin with a working definition of perfectionist liberalism;[5] what political liberalism is and requires will emerge in the course of confronting its opposite number. Perfectionist liberalism is defined by Larmore, who initiated this debate, as a family of views that bases political principles on "ideals claiming to shape our overall conception of the good life, and not just our role as citizens"; elsewhere he says that these views involve

---

[1] One could reasonably think of this debate as extending to continental Europe, since Rawls's work is widely discussed throughout Europe, and since Larmore writes in French, publishes in France before publishing in other countries, and has had a major influence on the French debate.

[2] Charles Larmore, *Patterns of Moral Complexity* (Cambridge University Press, 1987); *The Morals of Modernity* (Cambridge University Press, 1996).

[3] John Rawls, *Political Liberalism*, expanded paper ed. (New York: Columbia University Press, 1986). Page references to this work will be given in parentheses inside the text. Another important contribution to the development of the idea of political liberalism is Thomas Nagel, "Moral conflict and political legitimacy," *Philosophy & Public Affairs* 16 (1987): 215–240, and *Equality and Partiality* (New York: Oxford University Press, 1995). Nagel's account of the relevant distinctions is different from that of Rawls, relying on a notion of two "standpoints" within the person; it therefore requires separate consideration, and, despite its interest and importance, I shall discuss it no further here.

[4] See Martha C. Nussbaum, *Women and Human Development: The Capabilities Approach* (Cambridge University Press, 2000); *Frontiers of Justice: Disability, Nationality, Species Membership* (Cambridge, MA: Harvard University Press, 2006); and *Creating Capabilities: The Human Development Approach* (Cambridge, MA: Harvard University Press, 2011).

[5] Raz describes his view as perfectionist and as opposed to "anti-perfectionism": see, for example, his "Autonomy, toleration, and the harm principle," in *Issues in Contemporary Legal Philosophy*, ed. Ruth Gavison (New York and Oxford: Oxford University Press, 1987), pp. 313–333, at pp. 331–332.

controversial ideals of the good life, or views about "the ultimate nature of the human good."[6] As I define perfectionist liberalism, following Larmore, it is a species of a genus of liberal views that might be called "comprehensive liberalisms," liberalisms that base political principles on some comprehensive doctrine about human life that covers not only the political domain but also the domain of human conduct generally.

Most forms of comprehensive liberalism are perfectionist, involving a doctrine about the good life and the nature of value. But a doctrine can be comprehensive without being perfectionist. Some comprehensive doctrines that have had great influence in the past have been deterministic or fatalistic, thus closing off the space for striving toward a specific ideal of the good life. So astrology, which controlled policy in some times and places, could hardly be described as perfectionism, since it held that our fates are all fixed by our stars and that it makes no sense to think of ourselves as pursuing a good life. More pertinently for contemporary thought, the type of comprehensive liberalism advocated by Ronald Dworkin may be non-perfectionistic, in that its ideal of state neutrality, though explicitly defended as a comprehensive and not a political form of liberalism, deliberately refrains from advocating any specific doctrine of the good life.[7] From now on, I leave those comprehensive but non-perfectionistic doctrines to one side to focus on perfectionism. Perfectionistic forms of comprehensive liberalism (whether utilitarian or Hegelian, or based on a picture of neo-Aristotelian virtue, or on Christian doctrines, or on one of many other possible views) have been immensely influential historically and remain so today. The Raz/Berlin position, avowedly perfectionist in Larmore's sense, remains a particularly interesting and attractive liberal view, which (along with its various relatives) deserves continued scrutiny. The subtle relationship between political liberalism and Dworkin's comprehensive view must remain a topic for another occasion.[8]

Why go over this ground again? Rawls and Larmore have both said quite a lot in favor of the form of liberalism they support, and it might

---

[6] Larmore, "Political liberalism," in *The Morals of Modernity*, pp. 122, 132.

[7] See Ronald Dworkin, *Sovereign Virtue* (Cambridge, MA: Harvard University Press, 2000), pp. 154–155: however, one could also argue that by emphasizing a continuity between valuable lives and liberal political institutions (a theme clearly emphasized in Dworkin's *Justice for Hedgehogs* (Cambridge, MA: Harvard University Press, 2011) but already present in the earlier work), the view moves toward perfectionism.

[8] Another important distinction is that between perfectionism with respect to content and perfectionism with respect to grounds, or modes of justification: see the important discussion of different types of neutrality in Peter DeMarneffe, "Liberalism, liberty, and neutrality," *Philosophy & Public Affairs* 19 (1990): 253–274. Rawls and Larmore do not invoke this distinction, which would have been helpful to their arguments. As I discuss their views below, I shall attempt to introduce it.

seem otiose to revisit the issue. However, reconsideration is needed, for two reasons. First, the views of Rawls and Larmore contain crucial but insufficiently noticed ambiguities; sorting them out will prove illuminating. Second, although Rawls's *Theory of Justice* is widely known, and frequently discussed in the literature on welfarism and utilitarianism, such is not the case with his great later book. The concept of political liberalism is simply ignored in a large proportion of discussions of welfare and social policy, as are the challenges Rawls poses to thinkers who would base politics on a single comprehensive normative view.[9] Many

---

[9] This is true to some extent even in philosophical utilitarianism: Peter Singer, for example, has never, to my knowledge, addressed the challenge that political liberalism raises for his comprehensive view. It is ubiquitously true in philosophically informed areas of welfarist economics. Thus, in the special issue of *Feminist Economics* devoted to the work of Amartya Sen (9, no. 2–3 [2003]), Sen is specifically asked whether he accepts the idea of political liberalism (see Nussbaum, "Capabilities as fundamental entitlements: Sen and social justice," pp. 33–50, at pp. 49–50), but he does not address this question in his reply. (These issues of the journal have been reprinted as Amartya Sen's *Work and Ideas: A Gender Perspective*, ed. Bina Agarwal, Jane Humphries, and Ingrid Robeyns (New York: Routledge, 2005).) Nor does the idea of political liberalism play any role in Sen's extensive treatment of Rawls in *The Idea of Justice* (Cambridge, MA: Harvard University Press, 2009). Similarly, Sen's *Identity and Violence: The Illusion of Destiny* (New York: Norton, 2006) fails to ask what respect for persons requires when people have deep attachments to their ethnic or religious identities, suggesting that there is a correct, plural view of identity that politics can legitimately endorse. Influential philosophically concerned economists in law who write extensively on welfare, proposing political principles for a pluralistic society, and yet do not confront the issue of political liberalism, are Louis Kaplow and Steven Shavell, *Fairness Versus Welfare* (Cambridge, MA: Harvard University Press, 2002); Eric Posner, "Human welfare, not human rights," *Columbia Law Review* 108 (2008), 1758–1802; and Matthew D. Adler, *Well-Being and Equity: A Framework for Policy Analysis*, draft prior to final copy edit (New York: Oxford University Press, 2011). Both Posner and Adler defend a plural-valued type of consequentialism for political purposes, without taking sides one way or the other on whether this political doctrine is comprehensive, or partial and political; Kaplow and Shavell are comprehensive welfarists, without confronting the challenge political liberalism raises for their view. On the policy side, where such distinctions make a real difference to people's lives, the philosophically informed and generally admirable Sen/Stiglitz/Fitoussi report on quality of life commissioned by President Sarkozy of France similarly is totally silent about the comprehensive/political distinction: see J. E. Stiglitz, Amartya Sen, and Jean-Paul Fitoussi, "Report of the Commission on the Measurement of Economic Performance and Social Progress," at www.stiglitz-sen-fitoussi.fr/ (2010).

On the side of non-welfarist political philosophy, the distinction between political and comprehensive is neglected by Anthony Appiah in *The Ethics of Identity* (Princeton University Press, 2005), although it lies right at the heart of his philosophical project (to articulate a form of liberalism that is compatible with pluralism), and although he discusses Rawls in some detail: see my review-discussion in *Journal of Social Philosophy* 37 (2006), 301–313. It is also neglected in the excellent book *Disadvantage* by Jonathan Wolff and Avner De-Shalit (New York: Oxford University Press, 2007), where it does seem quite germane to their enterprise of establishing general welfare principles for ethnically and economically divided societies, though the authors build on philosophical work of mine on capabilities that emphasizes the distinction.

theorists influenced by various forms of normative utilitarianism have simply not attended to the issues of respect raised by their commitment to a comprehensive normative ethical doctrine as the basis for political principles and policy choices. It is certainly possible for consequentialist and welfarist views to be reformulated as forms of political liberalism. It also might be possible for them to defend their perfectionist doctrines against Rawlsian challenges. But the failure of their proponents to confront the issue head on means that this work has not yet been done. It is my hope that the challenge contained in this chapter may stimulate this further work.

Berlin's pluralism, Raz's pluralism

Berlin's pluralism is the target of Larmore's critique and Rawls's reformulation of that critique, so we must attempt to characterize it, despite the allusive and cryptic nature of Berlin's discussion.[10] For Berlin, pluralism is the denial of monism about the ultimate sources of value.[11] Observing that many political doctrines have been monistic about value, he tells us that we should not accept monism, for reasons both practical and theoretical. In practical terms, suggests Berlin, monism has been a source of tyranny and bigotry: it is no accident that "The Pursuit of the Ideal" opens with a catalog of atrocities perpetrated during the twentieth century in the name of some monistic ideal. But the more important argument made by Berlin is that monism is false, and pluralism is true. Monism is the doctrine that there is just "one true answer and one only" to questions about the ultimate sources of value (PI, p. 5).[12] Pluralism, by contrast, is the view "that there are many different ends that men may seek and still be fully rational, fully men, capable of understanding each other" (PI, p. 9). In a later essay collected in *The Crooked Timber of Humanity*, he elaborates. Pluralism asks us:

To look upon life as affording a plurality of values, equally genuine, equally ultimate, above all equally objective; incapable, therefore, of being ordered in a timeless hierarchy, or judged in terms of some one absolute standard.[13]

---

[10] In order to move on to the primary issue, the critique of Berlin by Larmore and Rawls, I focus on the texts that Larmore relies on to characterize the position he criticizes. I do not purport to offer a comprehensive exegesis of Berlin's views on liberalism.

[11] Here I agree with Larmore, "Pluralism and reasonable disagreement," in *The Morals of Modernity*, especially pp. 155–163.

[12] I cite the essay, referred to in this article as PI, in the version given in Isaiah Berlin, *The Proper Study of Mankind* (New York: Farrar, Straus and Giroux, 1997), pp. 1–16.

[13] Berlin, *The Crooked Timber of Humanity* (New York: Knopf, 1991), p. 79.

Pluralism, then, is a thesis about values and their objective status, and a thesis that is supposed to be true.

How are the practical and the theoretical theses connected? Clearly the truth of the thesis of pluralism is understood to give support to political principles based on it, but exactly how does its truth figure in the argument for liberal political principles? Berlin does not make this clear, but it appears that the truth of the theoretical thesis is a necessary prop for the liberal doctrine of toleration and non-interference. If only one view were true, it is not clear whether any independent reasons would lead Berlin to favor liberal non-interference with the views that have been found to be false.[14]

From now on, like Raz,[15] I distinguish pluralism of the sort relevant to Berlin and Raz from what I shall call internal pluralism, a view that both Berlin and Larmore do not clearly distinguish from pluralism of the sort on which they focus.[16] Because the distinction is philosophically

[14] Thus at PI, p. 15, Berlin favors putting some views off limits, on the grounds that they conflict with "common" values that are accepted by all the diverse forms of life that pluralism supports. Those views (including Nazism and views that advocate torture for pleasure) are not to be tolerated.

[15] See Raz, "Autonomy, toleration, and the harm principle," p. 316, where Raz defines the type of pluralism that interests him as "the view that there are various forms and styles of life which exemplify different virtues and which are incompatible," and then observes that "[t]here is nothing to stop a person from being both an ideal teacher and an ideal family person," thus distinguishing pluralism of his sort from what I call "internal pluralism." Raz, of course, does not assert, implausibly, that there would never be difficult conflicts in the life of someone who is both a teacher and a family person; the point is that the life is one that can be lived, because the two ideals do not make demands that are in principle incompatible.

[16] Nor does Larmore make this distinction, when he states, in *The Morals of Modernity*, that pluralism is a characteristically modern position. Internal pluralism is ubiquitous in the Ancient Greek and Roman world, the Indian world, and no doubt in many other ancient cultures. The form of pluralism with which Larmore is most concerned – the idea that there are several "reasonable" comprehensive views of how to live – appears to be older in India than in the West: an edict of the emperor Ashoka (around the third and second centuries BCE) says that "the sects of other people all deserve reverence for one reason or another." But a similar idea is on the scene at least in the Roman world, and Cicero's correspondence with his Epicurean friend Atticus shows us an interesting version of it. Cicero, who certainly does not like Epicureanism, and who has a very different comprehensive doctrine, says, in a letter of 61 BCE, that he and Atticus are so close that nothing separates them "apart from our choices of an overall mode of life" (*praeter voluntatem institutae vitae*). He then says that his friend was led to his choice by *minime reprehendenda ratio* (a hardly exceptionable course of reasoning). See *Letters to Atticus*, Loeb Classical Library edition, ed. David Shackleton Bailey, vol. I. (This is my own translation: Shackleton Bailey overtranslates, I think, when he writes an "entirely justifiable way of thinking," something Cicero would never say about the Epicurean doctrine.) The larger context makes his meaning clear: in these perilous times, we can understand why an honorable man would seek retirement from public life (*honestum otium*), and then Cicero admits that his own choice to serve the Republic is motivated by "what one might call ambition."

important and largely ignored in this debate, apart from a brief remark by Raz, we must pause briefly to discuss it.

Internal pluralism tells us that there are several distinct, intrinsically valuable elements that can be combined in a single, reasonably unified picture of a good human life. The internal pluralist undertakes to organize these plural sources of value as best she can. Most cultures are internal-pluralist: that is, they recommend a range of interrelated goods, holding that several of these have intrinsic value; they propose some way of organizing them all. Ancient Greek culture did this through the polytheism of Greek religion: the sources of value (worship) are plural, and each member of the culture is supposed to honor them all, although this can be rather difficult at times. Loyalty to the gods of the family and loyalty to the state can clash in extreme circumstances, as they do in Sophocles's *Antigone*. The duty to honor Demeter (goddess of marital fertility) and the duty to honor Aphrodite (goddess of erotic love) are likely to clash at some point in many lives. The overall picture, though, is of a single religion with multiple domains, not of divergent and incompatible overall forms of life.[17] Similarly, ancient Hindu culture recognized plural sources and, like Greek culture, tried to organize them into a more or less cohesive cultural whole.[18] But pluralism is not confined to polytheism. Most religious and cultural views, for example, have held that love of one's children and friends has intrinsic value, while also recognizing that the loyalties involved may at times be quite difficult to render harmonious. Internal pluralism is just a feature of any reasonably sane cultural view. It is difficult indeed to think of a morality that is genuinely monistic, reducing all the values to one, unless it be Benthamite utilitarianism, and we know how quickly the plausible arguments of John Stuart Mill transformed that view into a cohesive internal-pluralist doctrine.

What concerns Berlin – and, as we shall see, Raz – however, is not internal pluralism, even with profound tensions. It is incompatibility among overall doctrines of life, the impossibility of living as, say, both an Ancient Greek and a utilitarian, or a Nietzschean and a Christian: the impossibility of living with utterly incompatible leading values and

---

[17] There are limiting cases: for example, the requirements of Dionysian religion involve such a degree of tension with the standard requirements of the civic religion that it is unclear whether a coherent unitary life can be made out of the two; this case bleeds into pluralism of Berlin's type. For a revealing discussion of different types of conflict, see Henry S. Richardson, *Practical Reasoning about Final Ends* (New York: Cambridge University Press, 1994), pp. 144–151.

[18] Or, really, many wholes, since Hinduism contains large regional differences: see Wendy Doniger, *The Hindus: An Alternative History* (New York and London: Penguin, 2009).

outlooks. Berlin's pluralism, then, is the doctrine that there exists a plurality of overall accounts of how one should live, all of which are valid or objectively correct.

In *The Morality of Freedom* (MF) and in his important paper "Autonomy, toleration, and the harm principle,"[19] Joseph Raz argues in favor of a version of liberalism that is perfectionistic in two ways. First, and most centrally, Raz defends a controversial doctrine of autonomy as the key to what makes lives valuable in general, and he urges that this value ought to be the core value in a liberal society. Raz's autonomy is a controversial perfectionist norm that would be rejected, for example, by believers in authoritarian religions. Second, Raz makes a further perfectionist move when he argues that liberal societies, in order to support autonomy, must accept a doctrine of pluralism that is closely related to Berlin's pluralism. Let us now examine this connection.

Raz's argument in "Autonomy" has a different starting point from Berlin's: the central moral ideal is autonomy, and pluralism enters the picture in explaining what autonomy requires: it is only in the light of autonomy that we comprehend why an adequate range of options means a plural and, indeed, an extensive range. Why does autonomy require a belief in pluralism? Autonomy, for Raz, is not good independently of the choices it makes possible; its goodness is conditional on the worth of those choices. "Autonomous life is valuable only if it is spent in the pursuit of acceptable and valuable projects and relationships. The autonomy principle permits and even requires governments to create morally valuable opportunities and to eliminate repugnant ones."[20] This understanding of autonomy means that if only one form of life had been morally valuable, government would not have needed to create plural options, all the others being objectionable. So it is only because Raz believes pluralism to be true that he can conclude that autonomy requires government to create plural options and, indeed, an extensive menu of options (though, he emphasizes, no particular option need be on the list).

In *The Morality of Freedom*, Raz makes this same argument at greater length. He uses the effective example of "The Hounded Woman" to show that government undermines well-being if almost all the choices it offers require a person to sacrifice her goal.[21] Government, then, must

---

[19] Joseph Raz, *The Morality of Freedom* (Oxford: Clarendon Press, 1986), hereafter MF; "Autonomy, toleration, and the harm principle," (see note 5). The two contemporaneous texts treat the same set of problems from slightly different perspectives, and I shall treat the two texts as of equal authority.

[20] Raz, "Autonomy," p. 173; see also p. 168: government is not required to create repugnant or evil options so that people may freely avoid them.

[21] MF, pp. 373–376.

offer people an "adequate range of options" if it is to foster autonomy. These options must, however, be genuinely valuable: autonomy has no value qua autonomy when it is used in the pursuit of evil or worthless ends, and the availability of such options is "not a requirement of respect for autonomy."[22]

Because Raz holds that not all goals are valuable, and that the autonomy principle does not require government to protect the non-valuable goals as options, he then must offer an account of why it is, after all, so bad to offer only a single option. "Autonomy requires that many morally acceptable options be available to a person."[23] But to see why these options must be "many," we must appreciate the fact that the genuinely valuable forms of life are, in fact, plural. The autonomy-based principle of toleration is the view that pluralism about value is true, and that people should believe in the truth of pluralism so that they happily extend autonomy to others, even though they pursue ends that the person herself does not value. Raz thinks that it is not only permissible but also urgently required for governments to promote toleration by building political principles based on the truth of pluralism.[24] Thus government will be in the business of ranking and ordering comprehensive doctrines, both by saying that these are genuinely valuable and those are not, and by asserting that a plurality of doctrines has moral worth.

Why do Berlin and Raz think that belief in the truth of pluralism is necessary for toleration? Berlin appears to be motivated by the following thought: if people don't think that their neighbor's view of life is objectively true, they will always want to interfere with them and bring them around to their own view, and they won't support policies that extend to people a wide range of opportunities for choice. Raz argues somewhat differently: autonomy requires toleration because it requires the state to provide an adequate range of options, and an adequate range is an extensive range (requiring toleration of mutually repugnant lifestyles) only because pluralism is true. If it had not been true, then nothing, including autonomy, would require us to tolerate what we don't like in the lifestyle of others: the autonomous murderer is, if anything, worse than the non-autonomous murderer.[25] Closing off bad options is just

---

[22] MF, pp. 380–381.   [23] MF, p. 378.

[24] A key element of such a politics will, he argues, be endorsement of Mill's "harm principle"; here he and the political liberal can agree. But Raz's reasons for endorsing the harm principle will be different from those that Rawls would favor: for Raz, the truth of plural valuable options; for Rawls (who, however, does not discuss this example), the idea that respect for persons requires government not to take a stand on the truth of people's comprehensive doctrines one way or the other.

[25] MF, p. 380.

fine, so if a society is to be tolerant, protecting a plurality of options, even though many citizens do not like many of them, that practice must be undergirded by a public recognition that there are plural genuinely good options. For neither Berlin nor Raz is the principle of pluralism merely strategic: both give it strong endorsement as true in its own right.

An important historical antecedent for Raz and Berlin is Rousseau, who insisted that the good society must teach a principle of theological toleration that at least prevented people from believing that their neighbors (holding different religions) were damned. "It is impossible to live in peace with those one believes to be damned," Rousseau concludes.[26] Berlin, looking at the horrors of Nazism and Stalinism, suggests, similarly, that we have reason to believe that Rousseau's claim is true: so long as people think their neighbors are fundamentally in error, there will be no end to their attempts at repression and coercion.[27] For Rousseau, the importance of a widespread acceptance of pluralism about value is primarily psychological and motivational: people will not cease to persecute others unless they believe the truth of pluralism. Berlin appears to be moved by similar psychological considerations, although not by these alone.[28] Where Raz is concerned, it is abundantly clear that pluralism is not merely a psychological thesis about how to motivate people toward toleration: the objective truth of plural options is necessary both to the justification of state policies making an extensive range of options available and to the justification of toleration as an appropriate attitude to foster toward the things we dislike in the lives of our fellows.

How demanding is Raz's principle of pluralism? Very much so, it turns out. Moral pluralism, as Raz defines it in *The Morality of Freedom*, involves two claims, both of which Berlin also endorses: first, "that incompatible forms of life are morally acceptable," and second, "that they display distinct virtues, each capable of being pursued for its own sake" (p. 396). Whatever form of life one is pursuing, "[t]here are virtues which elude one because they are available only to people pursuing alternative and incompatible forms of life" (p. 396). Raz then distinguishes "weak" from "strong" pluralism: to the criteria given above, which define "weak" pluralism, we may add "one or more" of the

---

[26] Jean-Jacques Rousseau, On the Social Contract, in *The Basic Political Writings*, trans. Donald A. Cress (Indianapolis: Hackett, 1987), Book 4, Chapter 8, p. 226.
[27] See PI, pp. 12–14: monism is "dangerous," because it teaches that there is an "ultimate solution to the problems of society" (the comparison to Hitler is explicit in the text), and "the millions slaughtered in wars or revolutions – gas chambers, gulag, genocide, all the monstrosities for which our century will be remembered – are the price men must pay for the felicity of future generations."
[28] He describes his own route to the realization of this "truth" in PI, pp. 6–10.

following three, to make the form of pluralism "strong": first, "the incompatible virtues are not completely ranked relative to each individual." Second, "the incompatible virtues are not completely ranked by some impersonal criteria of moral worth." Third, "the incompatible virtues exemplify diverse fundamental concerns" (pp. 396–397). Raz believes that he has proven that valuing autonomy requires us to endorse the strong form of pluralism (p. 398), but he relies only on the weaker form in running his argument (p. 398). The weak form, however, still requires the view that a plurality of incompatible forms of life is to be endorsed as morally acceptable. By requiring this endorsement, valuing autonomy "establishes the necessity for toleration" (pp. 406–407). Weak pluralism is a doctrine that the major religious and secular comprehensive doctrines in most modern societies will refuse to endorse; "strong" pluralism is even more clearly incompatible with all but a small number of such doctrines.

Thus Raz espouses perfectionism in a double sense. Like Berlin, he endorses a principle of pluralism that is unacceptable to many citizens; unlike Berlin, he deploys this principle in the service of an equally controversial comprehensive ideal of autonomy.

Larmore, Rawls: reasonable disagreement, political liberalism

In "Pluralism and reasonable disagreement," Charles Larmore begins by pointing out, correctly, that the principle of pluralism is controversial. Many, if not most, religious believers do not believe that there are many objectively correct routes to salvation, or, more generally, many objectively correct ways of leading a good life. Pluralist religious views have become somewhat more common today than they were formerly,[29] but even the most tolerant religions typically exclude atheists and agnostics from the group of the "saved"; many include only other monotheists and exclude polytheists and members of non-theistic religions, as well as atheists and agnostics. And while many agnostics and atheists are happy to accept the validity of at least some forms of theism, there are many who think that all religion is just a large error, and certainly not objectively true. To base liberalism on pluralism, then, is to base it on a principle that most religious believers, and many other people, cannot accept without converting to a different doctrine.

---

[29] In October 1995, Pope John Paul II endorsed a limited form of pluralism, granting that there were plural routes to salvation. Particularly striking was his inclusion of polytheistic Hinduism among those routes.

Very different is the view that Larmore now defends. He argues that disagreements about value under conditions of freedom persist and do not appear to resolve themselves, unlike most scientific disagreements. Like Rawls in the important section of *Political Liberalism* entitled "The burdens of judgment" (pp. 54–58), Larmore tentatively suggests some reasons why this may be true of value: difficulties of weighting and ordering, differences of life experience, and so on. But this is tangential: the main thing we should understand, says Larmore, is that people tend to disagree on these matters, and their disagreements are not caused by anything so obvious that we could easily remove it (a mistake of fact, for example). Moreover, people who think that their view is right and that other views are wrong can still accept this fact of "reasonable disagreement."

If they do accept it, then, says Larmore, they will see that they cannot base political principles on their own view (which they think true) without doing violence to the convictions of others; they will therefore seek to found political morality on "a core morality that reasonable people can accept despite their natural tendency to disagree about comprehensive visions of the nature of value and so in particular about the merits of pluralism and monism."[30] The choice to favor such a thin core morality and to ground political principles in it (the view that Larmore dubs "political liberalism") can be shared by monists and pluralists alike, so long as they admit the existence of reasonable disagreement. Larmore insists that the view does have definite moral content and is justified by some definite moral values; nonetheless, it is sufficiently abstemious, both in content and in grounding,[31] to avoid controversial ideas of the type that divide citizens who reasonably disagree.

Rawls develops this idea much more fully. Like Larmore, he insists that the persistence of disagreements about value under conditions of political freedom should be taken as evidence that these disagreements are not based on anything like an easily identifiable mistake. He may initially seem to be accepting something like the Raz/Berlin position, but that is not so: his view is that, without taking any stand one way or another on questions of truth or adequacy, we can see that the factors that lead people to differ are complicated, difficult, and deeply rooted in their search for the meaning of life, in such a way that they are unlikely to go away without government coercion. Many different comprehensive doctrines that citizens hold are in that sense reasonable. (We shall

---

[30] Larmore, "Pluralism and reasonable disagreement," p. 167.

[31] Here I am invoking DeMarneffe's distinction (see note 8) to flesh out what Larmore's discussion clearly suggests.

analyze that important and slippery notion in the next section, and we shall see that, understood in one way, it does come uncomfortably close to the Raz/Berlin position; there is, however, another way of interpreting it that does not have this problem.) If we accept the burdens of judgment, then we have reason to try to ground our political principles in a set of "freestanding" moral ideas that can be accepted by citizens with a wide range of different views concerning the ultimate sources of value. Principles will be acceptable in this way only if their framers practice a "method of avoidance," refusing to ground them in controversial metaphysical, religious, or epistemological doctrines, and not even in comprehensive ethical doctrines. Instead, they will seek a freestanding ethical justification for the principles that will ultimately form one part of the comprehensive doctrines of all of them, like a "module" (*PL*, p. 12), says Rawls, that attaches to doctrines of many different kinds.[32] Thus Rawls, like Larmore, thinks of political liberalism in terms of both limited content (it is a "module" rather than a comprehensive ideal) and limited types of grounding (it is justified in a "freestanding" way, without invoking controversial metaphysical or epistemological doctrines).[33]

Rawls suggests a deeper reason why citizens will endorse political liberalism and its method of avoidance, even though they may believe their own doctrine to be correct and the others incorrect. The reason is that they respect their fellow citizens, and respect them as equals.[34] Their reasonableness is an ethical reasonableness: respecting their fellow

---

[32] This is how doctrines would ultimately need to be defended. Rawls's later discussions of civility add the "proviso" that one may, without violating the ethical duty of civility, invoke one's comprehensive doctrine to defend political principles, "provided that in due course public reasons, given by a reasonable political conception, are presented sufficient to support whatever the comprehensive doctrines are introduced to support" (*PL*, pp. li–lii; and see the similar statement in "The idea of public reason revisited," hereafter IPRR, in *John Rawls: Collected Papers*, ed. Samuel Freeman (Cambridge, MA: Harvard University Press, 1999), pp. 573–615, at pp. 591–594).

[33] Once again, however, it has determinate ethical content and is justified by determinate ethical notions, so it is not fully neutral in either of DeMarneffe's two senses.

[34] For the idea of citizens as free and equal persons, and the related idea of reciprocity, see *PL*, pp. 18–19 and passim; the idea that citizens' freedom and equality require fair treatment of their varied comprehensive doctrines is fundamental to both *PL* and Rawls, *A Theory of Justice* (Cambridge, MA: Harvard University Press, 1971), for example, in its reasoning about the priority of religious liberty. It is given a particularly extensive treatment in "Fairness to goodness," in *Collected Papers*, pp. 267–285. At *TJ*, p. 586, Rawls says that ideas of equal human dignity and respect are given a definite content by the principles of justice: to respect persons is to recognize an "inviolability founded on justice" that is expressed in the two principles. As Larmore observes, the idea of respect for persons, though nowhere subjected to extensive analysis on its own, "shape[s] [his] thought at the deepest level": see Charles Larmore, "Public reason," in *The Cambridge Companion to Rawls*, ed. Samuel Freeman (New York: Cambridge University Press, 2003), pp. 368–393, at p. 391.

citizens, they want to give them plenty of space to search in their own way, even though they may believe that the conclusions most people come to are wrong. Respect is for persons, not directly for the doctrines they hold, and yet respect for persons leads to the conclusion that they ought to have liberty to pursue commitments that lie at the core of their identity, provided that they do not violate the rights of others and that no other compelling state interest intervenes.[35] Larmore does not explicitly ground political liberalism in exactly this way in his earlier work, but in interpreting Rawls he has characteristically drawn attention to the centrality of the idea of respect in Rawls's theory, and he has recently emphasized the centrality of respect in his own political views.[36] It seems to me that reference to respect is necessary at this point: for why otherwise would the confident monist not be ready to go ahead and coerce fellow citizens into salvation? Just noticing that people don't agree about such matters without coercion does not, all by itself, supply a reason against forcing them to agree.

As I (along with both Rawls and Larmore) use the idea of respect, respect for persons is not a subjective, emotional state, such as a feeling of admiration. It is a way of regarding and treating persons, closely related to the Kantian idea of treating humanity as an end and never as a mere means.[37] Respect is thus closely linked to the idea of dignity, to the idea that humanity has worth and not merely a price.[38] Equal respect would then be respect that appropriately acknowledges the equal dignity and worth that persons have as ends. Although this idea has a definite ethical content, it has long been recognized (for example, in the framing of the Universal Declaration of Human Rights) that one may endorse it for political purposes without thereby endorsing a comprehensive Kantian doctrine or any other specific comprehensive doctrine: thus one may

---

[35] See my discussion of Roger Williams's view and its relationship to Rawls's in *Liberty of Conscience: In Defense of America's Tradition of Religious Equality* (New York: Basic Books, 2008), Chapter 2. Rawls does not discuss the "compelling state interest" requirement apropos of the Religion clauses of the First Amendment, but he does discuss it with reference to the Speech clause, arguing that only a danger of the utter collapse of the constitutional system can justify limiting political speech.

[36] See Larmore, "Public reason," and "Respect for persons," *The Hedgehog Review* 7 (2005), 66–76.

[37] See Larmore, "Respect for persons": respect is incompatible with conduct that treats "persons merely as means, as objects of coercion, and not also as ends, engaging directly their distinctive capacity as persons."

[38] See Rawls, *A Theory of Justice*, p. 586, on dignity: he argues, convincingly, that it has little determinate content which needs to be defined in connection with a group of other ideas and principles. See my discussion in "Human dignity and political entitlements," in *Human Dignity and Bioethics: Essays Commissioned by the President's Council on Bioethics* (Washington, DC, 2008), pp. 351–380.

endorse it while believing a form of religious doctrine that Kant would not accept, or while holding a view about freedom of the will that is not Kant's.[39] Equal respect is a political, not a comprehensive, value; thus one might in principle accept it while continuing to believe that persons do not deserve equal respect in religious or metaphysical respects, although such a view will contain tensions that may be difficult to negotiate.[40]

Notice that this is a rather different grounding for political liberalism than the grounding supplied by alluding to the special difficulty of getting to an adequate view on matters of value. For one might think it as easy as pie to get the correct view in religious matters and yet believe that every citizen ought to have plenty of space to figure this out on his or her own. Indeed, I can't see why someone with an authoritarian religion would think that it is terribly difficult to get the truth: all you need to do is to listen to the right authority. So it is not very surprising that some formulations of political liberalism have preferred a grounding in respect rather than in difficulty. Jacques Maritain, for example (one might call him the first political liberal, for his work on the Universal Declaration of Human Rights), writes:

There is real and genuine tolerance only when a man is firmly and absolutely convinced of a truth, or of what he holds to be a truth, and when he at the same time recognizes the right of those who deny this truth to exist, and to contradict him, and to speak their own mind, not because they are free from truth but because they seek truth in their own way, and because he respects in them human nature and human dignity and those very resources and living springs of the intellect and of conscience which make them potentially capable of attaining the truth he loves.[41]

---

[39] See Maritain, cited in note 41, below. Rawls, too, insists on the distinction between an appropriation of Kantian ethical notions for political purposes and the use of a controversial comprehensive Kantian doctrine, and he insisted on the importance of not using or even suggesting that one was using a comprehensive Kantian doctrine. Thus, in a 1998 letter about planned revisions to *PL* on file with the author and with Columbia University Press, he announced his intention to change the terms "practical reason" and "principles of practical reason," because they suggest a Kantian doctrine of reason, which he calls "a serious mistake."

[40] See discussion in note 63, below and text at that point.

[41] Jacques Maritain, "Truth and human fellowship," in *On the Use of Philosophy: Three Essays* (Princeton University Press, 1961). Maritain's own views anticipate Rawls's in many respects. Describing the practical political agreement that produced the Universal Declaration of Human Rights, the drafting of which Maritain worked on with thinkers from, among others, Egypt and China, he makes it evident that he thinks the agreement prescinds from sectarian metaphysical commitments precisely in order to arrive at a mutually respectful agreement among people who differ in their comprehensive doctrines. See Maritain, *Man and the State* (University of Chicago Press, 1951),

I am not denying that a Catholic might also accept the burdens of judgment, if he or she thought that authority pronounced only on some matters, that is, that the scope of papal infallibility is narrow enough that it doesn't answer many of life's questions. What I want to emphasize is that one can get to political liberalism through respect alone, without alluding to the special difficulties of judgment. Of course, one will then require some account of why respect for persons leads us to give people lots of space in matters of value, but not in mathematical or scientific matters. But we can develop, I believe, an account of the human centrality of searching for ultimate meaning that would deal with that question, namely, why it is especially violative of persons to impose a scheme of value upon them, but not violative to impose upon them the truth of $2 + 2 = 4$. I do not propose to attempt that here. But in my own appropriation of the Rawlsian idea of political liberalism, I focus on the core idea of respect for persons rather than on the burdens of judgment.[42]

Why, one might ask, should we suppose that respect for persons supports political principles that do not endorse the truth of any particular comprehensive doctrine of the good? Don't we take people seriously and treat them as ends in themselves when, in conversation, we do insist on the truth of views that we believe we can defend? Sometimes, indeed, it may be more respectful to lay our cards on the table rather than avoiding confrontation. Here we may give two responses, both pointing to features of political life. First, in the case of personal friendship, it will always be a delicate contextual matter when, and to what extent, and how to insist on the truth of one's own comprehensive doctrine. Some ways of doing this are compatible with respecting that person as an equal, some are not. But it seems likely that the boundaries of acceptability cannot be given in advance: perceiving them requires a delicate sense of context and relationship. In the political domain, of course, this nuanced appreciation of particular relationships is not available when government sends a message.

Second, and more importantly, when it is government that sends the message, that changes the message, because government defines one's life opportunities in a pervasive and fundamental way. So if government endorses the view that Christianity (say) is best, that sends a message that

Chapters 4 and 5, especially 4.1, entitled "Men mutually opposed in their theoretical conceptions can come to a merely practical agreement regarding a list of human rights," p. 76. For a fine account of the work that led to the framing of the Universal Declaration, see Mary Ann Glendon, *A World Made New: Eleanor Roosevelt and the Universal Declaration of Human Rights* (New York: Random House, 2002).

[42] In *Women and Human Development, Frontiers of Justice*, and *Creating Capabilities* (see note 4); see also *Liberty of Conscience*.

the framework of liberties and opportunities shaping all citizens' lives will have the superiority of Christianity woven through it, in a way that marginalizes or demotes other views. This, of course, would not usually be the case when a Christian attempts to convince a friend of the superiority of the Christian way of life. Thus the argument for political liberalism depends, in part, on an appreciation of the deep and pervasive role of the political in all citizens' lives.

At this point we can conclude that there is a route to liberal ideas of toleration and religious freedom that does not require the acceptance of a controversial and religiously divisive principle of pluralism. Whether that route takes the form of accepting "burdens of judgment" or the form of developing a doctrine of respect for conscience, or whether it combines the two ideas in some way, the conclusion can plainly be reached without accepting anything like the Berlin/Raz principle of pluralism.

Traditional historical forms of liberalism have not seen the problem involved in perfectionist liberalism. Neither utilitarianism nor the Hegelian/Aristotelian perfectionist liberalism of T. H. Green makes any gesture in the direction of respect for diverse comprehensive doctrines. In large part, this has happened because liberal thinkers have been strongly opposed to traditional religion, and have seen their own liberal doctrine as a replacement for religion. Bentham and Mill were atheists who would have viewed the demise of organized religion with no regret at all, and who thought it was perfectly proper for the state to encourage its demise by favoring a secular alternative, though not by interfering with individual freedom of choice.[43] Green's perfectionist neo-Aristotelian doctrine was intended, similarly, as a replacement for doctrines that, in his view, were less adequate. I think we see more clearly today, and we understand that respect for one's fellow citizens as equals requires not building the state on the ascendancy of any one particular comprehensive doctrine of

---

[43] Mill repeatedly expresses enthusiasm for Auguste Comte's idea that an atheistic doctrine of extensive sympathy (given extensive state sponsorship, although not coercively enforced) would come to replace existing religions: see, in particular, Mill, *Auguste Comte and Positivism* (London: Kegan Paul, 1891; reprinted from original of 1861); "The utility of religion," in Mill, *Three Essays on Religion* (Amherst, NY: Prometheus Books, 1998); Mill, "Utilitarianism," Chapter 3 in John Stuart Mill and Jeremy Bentham, *Utilitarianism and Other Essays*, ed. Alan Ryan (New York and London: Penguin, 1987). Mill criticizes many specifics of the Comtean program, but he considers Positivism (whose central tenet is that humanity has reached a postreligious age) a philosophical achievement on a par with the work of Descartes and Leibniz (see *Auguste Comte and Positivism*, p. 200). One might argue that in other writings Mill expresses ideas that are more compatible with political liberalism; that exegetical issue will not occupy me here. Both Rawls and Larmore treat Kant as the holder of a comprehensive perfectionist doctrine, but, once again, that is a controversial exegetical claim that is irrelevant to the argument of this chapter.

the purpose and meaning of life, however excellent. Of course, it remains the case that respect is for persons, not for their doctrines. But these doctrines are so deeply a part of people's search for the meaning of life that public governmental denigration of those doctrines puts those people at a disadvantage, suggesting that they are less worthy than other citizens, and in effect not treating them as fully equal ends in themselves. Liberals do not need to make such denigrating statements.

Rawls: reasonable citizens, reasonable comprehensive doctrines

At this point, we have a highly abstract idea, but we do not yet know how to formulate political principles embodying it for societies in which many different comprehensive doctrines exist. Both Rawls and Larmore insist that political principles for such a society are not neutral, inasmuch as they have a definite moral content (given in large part by the central commitment to equal respect as a political value). The "overlapping consensus" that Rawls hopes may ultimately be achieved is thus a substantive moral consensus, not just any chance kind of overlap. Indeed, he argues plausibly that no consensus would be stable if it did not rest on substantive moral notions in this way. But this moral ideal means that not every comprehensive doctrine anyone might happen to hold will participate in the overlapping consensus. At this point, both Rawls and Larmore introduce a notion of the "reasonable" to divide comprehensive doctrines into two groups, those that will and those that will not become participants in the hoped-for consensus, affirming the society's basic political principles.

We must now pause to explore what "reasonable" means, as applied to comprehensive doctrines, since much hangs on this, and it is here, as we shall see, that a difficulty lurks. For Larmore, the distinction between "reasonable" disagreements and other disagreements has considerable importance in motivating the structure of the view. Similarly, an important feature of Rawls's analysis in *PL* is his distinction between "reasonable" and "unreasonable" comprehensive doctrines. In both cases, there is a hidden difficulty that we must confront. I begin with Rawls, since it is no easy matter to clarify his view. I shall later turn more briefly to Larmore. In each case I shall recommend a preferred alternative of my own that is one possible reading of Rawls's text, though probably not of Larmore's.

Rawls's account of the "burdens of judgment" emphasizes the fact that people disagree about matters of ultimate value and adhere to different comprehensive doctrines not simply on account of irrationality or sloppy thinking but on account of factors that make the disputes between them cases of "reasonable disagreement." To say this is to recognize "the many hazards involved in the correct (and conscientious) exercise of our powers of reason and judgment in the ordinary course of political life" (*PL*, p. 56). The sources of reasonable disagreement mentioned by Rawls (pp. 56–57) include the complexity and difficulty of the relevant evidence; the fact that the evidence by itself does not tell us how to assign weight to different considerations; the indeterminacy of central concepts in hard cases; the fact that assessment and weighting of evidence are shaped by different life experiences; the existence of normative considerations on both sides of an issue; and the need for any social system to select from the full range of human values that might be realized. People who differ on account of these factors differ reasonably; or, to put it another way, reasonable citizens can, and do, disagree for such reasons. "This pluralism is not seen as disaster but rather as the natural outcome of the activities of human reason under enduring free institutions. To see reasonable pluralism as a disaster is to see the exercise of reason under the conditions of freedom itself as a disaster" (pp. xxvi–xxvii). Many comprehensive doctrines can be reasonable in this sense (p. 129).

Rawls recognizes that there are also unreasonable comprehensive doctrines and unreasonable disagreements, doctrines that cannot form part of the "overlapping consensus" because they do not accept some of its central ideas (such as the equality of persons). Some unreasonable doctrines may be silly and innocuous. But Rawls recognizes that there are doctrines that are "not only irrational but mad and aggressive" (p. 144). Among them are doctrines that "reject one or more democratic freedoms" (p. 64, n. 19). Such doctrines do not form part of the overlapping consensus. Rawls's highly protective doctrine of free political speech suggests that their speech may be limited only in the sort of emergency that amounts to a constitutional crisis. Nonetheless, the constitutional order will have entrenched the major liberties, and thus doctrines that propose the elimination of one or more of these liberties cannot come up as simple legislative proposals. In general, the job of a liberal society must be one "of containing [such doctrines] – like war and disease – so that they do not overturn political justice" (p. 64, n. 19).

It is clear enough, then, that the distinction between reasonable and unreasonable comprehensive doctrines is central to Rawls. But the reader is left with several difficult questions. The first pertains to Rawls's way of articulating the distinction. Throughout the book, including the section on "the burdens of judgment," the term "reasonable" is used in an ethical sense: "reasonable" persons are those who are willing "to propose fair terms of cooperation and to abide by them provided others do."[44] A second aspect is a willingness to recognize the burdens of judgment and "to accept their consequences for the use of public reason in directing the legitimate course of political power in a constitutional regime" (p. 54). (Rawls appears to assume that these two descriptions do not come apart: people who are willing to propose fair terms of cooperation are also ready to accept the burdens of judgment.) This second aspect is also ethical: the reasonable citizen does not try to enforce her own comprehensive doctrine through law, out of a recognition of the burdens of judgment and a related respect for her fellow citizens. Both aspects of the reasonable appear to be closely connected with the idea of respect, whose centrality in Rawls's whole enterprise is clear. More generally, throughout the text, in contrasting the "reasonable" with the "rational," Rawls clearly uses "reasonable" in this ethical sense; although, as Samuel Freeman has convincingly argued, there are "epistemic elements" in this usage, and Rawls relies on these "to some degree."[45] But that does not yet settle the issue of how Rawls uses "reasonable" as applied to comprehensive doctrines, and here I agree, once again, with Freeman, who concludes that "Rawls defines 'reasonable comprehensive doctrines' epistemically, as doctrines that are responsive to evidence and possess certain other theoretical features."[46] Let us investigate this textual issue more closely: it is very complex.

At times, Rawls connects the idea of a reasonable comprehensive doctrine very closely to the idea of the reasonable citizen: reasonable comprehensive doctrines are "the doctrines that reasonable citizens affirm" (p. 36). But Rawls later suggests that he does not intend this characterization as a definition, or at least not as a complete definition, of reasonable comprehensive doctrines. On page 59, having already assumed that "reasonable persons affirm only reasonable comprehensive doctrines," he then states: "Now we need a definition of such doctrines." His definition includes three features, all of them theoretical rather than ethical. First, a reasonable doctrine is "an exercise of theoretical reason" that "covers the major religious, philosophical, and moral aspects of human life in a more or less consistent and coherent manner. It organizes and characterizes recognized values so that they are compatible with one another and express an intelligible view of the world." Second, the doctrine is also an "exercise of practical reason" that gives instruction on how to weigh values and what to do when they conflict. Third, such a

---

[44] On the importance of the notion of "fair terms of cooperation" for Rawls, see Larmore, "Public reason," p. 391.
[45] Samuel Freeman, *Rawls* (New York: Routledge, 2007), p. 346.
[46] Ibid. Freeman does not, however, discuss the difficulties to which this shift gives rise.

doctrine, while not necessarily fixed and unchanging, "normally belongs to, or draws upon, a tradition of thought and doctrine" and therefore tends to evolve "slowly in the light of what from its point of view ... it sees [as] good and sufficient reasons" (p. 59). Rawls explicitly distinguishes these sources of disagreement from a variety of sources of "unreasonable disagreement" (p. 58).

This "definition" may be intended by Rawls as a way of elaborating the second aspect of the "reasonable" in the ethical sense, namely, "the willingness to recognize the burdens of judgment and to accept their consequences for the use of public reason." Nonetheless, it incorporates some fairly strong theoretical criteria, however vaguely stated, that are not obviously entailed by this second very general idea as originally stated. The theoretical criteria raise some troublesome questions. As we shall see, they carry Rawls uncomfortably close to the Raz/Berlin position, adding an unnecessary element, or at least risk, of perfectionism to Rawls's view.

The problem with Rawls's formulation is that there would appear to be many doctrines affirmed by reasonable citizens (in the ethical sense, respectful of one another) that do not meet these rather exacting theoretical standards. Worldviews based on astrology, New Age religion, and many other pictures of the world that many Americans affirm probably fail to satisfy all three criteria: some may lack coherence and comprehensiveness, some may be impervious to evidence (as many ancient thinkers held concerning astrology), some may be too fanciful or piecemeal to contain what we could call an "intelligible" view of the world. (Much, clearly, depends on how we further interpret Rawls's criteria.) Many Americans hold even weirder doctrines: a large proportion believe that aliens have invaded, and this somehow forms part of their view of life. Rawls might well be willing to call all such antiscientific doctrines unreasonable, given his view that the major conclusions of science form part of public reason. That would already raise difficult questions, since citizens who affirm an antiscientific doctrine can still be reasonable in the ethical sense.

But if we look closely at some key doctrines of many of the major religions, they too generate problems, which we may fail to notice only because the doctrines look so familiar. The Christian doctrine of the Trinity seems straightforward enough; and yet, as numerous Christian philosophers emphasize, it asks the believing Christian to believe a contradiction. Dante, in *Paradiso*, vividly depicts this doctrine as a way of humbling the arrogant aspirations of the intellect. As Dante contemplates the Trinity and tries to hold this idea in his mind, he compares himself to a geometrician who tries to square the circle and finds that he

cannot. The human intellect simply cannot encompass the mystery.[47]
The doctrine of the Trinity may be interpreted in ways that soften this
problem, but central strands of Christianity, at any rate, emphasize the
importance of departing from the most fundamental axiom of reason.
Nor is this a case that one might easily isolate from the rest of Christian
doctrine: it is a premise in most concrete arguments that the believer will
make or learn. It would be implausible, then, to describe this doctrine as
"more or less consistent and coherent." Indeed, its whole purpose is to
violate consistency and coherence in order to humble reason. In other
words, it is not just from the point of view of a non-believer that a key
doctrine of Christianity looks irrational: its irrationality is absolutely key
to its theological meaning and purpose. Modern Christians often forget
how radical a doctrine this humbling of the intellect is, because they are
used to the idea of the Trinity and find it easy to pay lip service to it
without trying to grasp something that the human mind is not equipped
to grasp.

Another locus of irrationality in traditional Christianity is the doctrine
of grace: for in at least some standard accounts (for example, Augustine's), God's grace is not based upon any reasons at all, and yet must be
acknowledged to be just.[48] Once again, it would be difficult to shoehorn
this Augustinian view into the theoretical account of the reasonable, as
Rawls articulates it. It appears to violate both the first and the second
criteria of (theoretical) reasonableness, on any plausible interpretation. If
these problems exist in fitting Rawls's criteria to the scholastic strand in
Roman Catholicism, which is the most rationalistic strand of traditional
Christianity, they exist all the more when we contemplate Christianity in
its Protestant and evangelical forms, especially those that ask the believer
to defer to the biblical text, which it would be most implausible to
describe as a coherent and consistent whole; moreover, fundamentalist
Christians (unlike believers in other eras) do not propose strategies of
non-literal interpretation that soften or remove inconsistencies.

Traditional Judaism, while to some extent more rationalistic than
Christianity, similarly contains the demand to accept a mystery that is
in principle not graspable by reason. The end of the *Book of Job*, for
example, contains a vivid repudiation of the aspirations of Hellenic

---

[47] *Paradiso*, canto 23; compare *Purgatorio* canto 31, lines 13–21, where Dante compares
himself to a bow drawn too tight and therefore broken, using Aristotle's metaphor for
intellectual aspiration to show that this aspiration to understanding must be humbled
before Christian love.

[48] See Peter Brown's interpretation of the Ad Simplicianum de Diversis Quaetionibus in
Augustine of Hippo (Berkeley and Los Angeles: University of California Press, 1967), pp.
155ff.

rationalism, which has given rise to a prominent mystical strand in Judaism, exemplified by Gershom Scholem and the Hasidic rabbis. Moreover, many forms of Judaism contain a principle of autonomy that causes them to run afoul of Rawls's second doctrine: there are no in-advance instructions for hard cases, precisely because each person must figure out what to do for him- or herself – the law is not in heaven but on earth (Deut. 30:12–14). Reform Judaism has augmented the scope of that principle, so that autonomy altogether trumps dogma, and we might say that in the end Reform Judaism has no doctrines (perhaps not even theism, although this is disputed), only the core idea of the moral law, which each believer must interpret and apply to the world in his or her own way. For religious doctrine to provide any theoretical structure seems to Reform Jews to violate autonomy.[49] This still looks like a comprehensive doctrine, but it does not count as a reasonable one, according to Rawls's definition. It does not even instruct believers to develop consistent and coherent solutions of their own that satisfy Rawls's first and second criteria; and it actively repudiates the third (tradition-based) criterion, assigning to tradition no moral weight at all.

One could multiply examples. What is clear, then, is that Rawls has introduced a massive difficulty by defining reasonable doctrines in terms of these theoretical criteria, a difficulty that pertains not only to doctrines that he might be willing to disparage as unreasonable (although I think he shouldn't) but also to doctrines that are central to his whole motivation and purpose. Moreover, his definition seems to run afoul of one of the core ideas of the text, the idea of respect for reasonable citizens. So long as people are reasonable in the ethical sense, why should the political conception denigrate them because they believe in astrology, or crystals, or the Trinity? Why not let them, and their beliefs, alone? Indeed, the theoretical interpretation of the reasonable, while not equivalent to the Raz/Berlin position, moves too close to it for comfort, allowing public denigration of a group of comprehensive doctrines that, from the point of view of the ethical aims of the political conception, is unproblematic.

It is revealing, and a sign of the depth of the problem, that an interpreter who worked especially closely with Rawls, in a lecture whose aim was to describe clearly the key ideas of *PL*, ascribes to Rawls the doctrine that I have just suggested he ought to hold:

A reasonable comprehensive doctrine can be irrational – you can be like Tertullian and say, "I believe because it is absurd." All a comprehensive

---

[49] For discussion of some key historical texts, see Martha C. Nussbaum, "Judaism and the love of reason," in *Philosophy, Feminism, Faith*, ed. Marya Bower and Ruth Groenhout (Bloomington: Indiana University Press, 2003), pp. 9–39.

doctrine has to do to be reasonable is to endorse a liberal political conception. But outside of that it can hold anything it wants.[50]

Burton Dreben, who gets Rawls right on every other issue, so far as I can see, plainly is at odds with some key portions of the text on this one (and Freeman's close study of the text concurs). But he is not at odds, I suggest, with the deeper spirit of Rawls's project and the centrality of the notion of respect in it. Perhaps Rawls really should have used the notion of the reasonable citizen to define reasonable comprehensive doctrines: reasonable doctrines are just those doctrines (however piece-meal or ridden with inconsistency) that reasonable citizens affirm. The burdens of judgment might then still enter into the thinking of such citizens when they consider why they should not insist on the truth of their doctrine in the public realm. But that is enough use for them: reasonable citizens should not be in the business of looking over the shoulders of their fellow citizens to ask whether their doctrines contain an acceptably comprehensive and coherent exercise of theoretical reason. Such scrutiny, besides inviting the *tu quoque* that the New Ager or the friend of astrology might rightly give to a mainstream Christian, is a kind of invidious interference that has no place in respectful political liberalism.

Of course, it is perfectly clear that citizens in Rawls's Well-Ordered Society will be welcome to criticize other people's comprehensive doctrines, religious or secular, in the many discussions that take place within the "background culture" (civil society and informal personal interactions). They do not even have a political duty to be civil when they do so; Rawls's "duty of civility" pertains only to discussions of "constitutional essentials and matters of basic justice" that take place within the framework of certain key political roles (e.g., those of judge, legislator, and voter). Thus citizens have a moral duty not to vote against someone because they don't like that person's religion, but even that is a non-enforceable moral duty. What Rawls wishes to rule out is that the state would make statements (or incorporate principles) deni-grating one religion or doctrine and preferring another, so long as the doctrine in question is "reasonable." "Unreasonable" doctrines may be denigrated, and the state is permitted, perhaps required, to incorporate principles that denigrate them. What I am saying here is that this is fine, so long as the definition of the reasonable is the ethical one, thus licensing the state to criticize, for example, doctrines that believe in

---

[50] Burton Dreben, "On Rawls and political liberalism," in *The Cambridge Companion to Rawls*, ed. Samuel Freeman (New York: Cambridge University Press, 2003), p. 326.

slavery or the political subordination of women. What seems very problematic, however, is to license the state to criticize doctrines that are "unreasonable" in the theoretical sense. If I want to believe something silly, or to subordinate my judgment to that of some irrational authority, it is not the business of a pluralistic society to state that I am in any sense inferior for so doing.

Why did Rawls include the theoretical criteria in his definition of the notion of reasonableness? Like every point in Rawls concerning which one might think him mistaken, this one has deep roots in his thought and good arguments in its favor. Rawls plainly thinks that the kind of respect on which liberal democracy depends requires, or is at least greatly aided by, distinguishing between doctrines that are just silly or in some obvious way irrational and doctrines that are not; holders of doctrines in the latter group do not agree because of the burdens of judgment, problems of reason common to all human beings under conditions of freedom, and thus problems that do not compromise mutual respect.[51] Holders of doctrines in the latter group will feel differently, he suggests, about holders of doctrines in the first group: they will think that if these people had corrected the errors in their reasoning, they would be maintaining the same thing that we maintain. (And then what: would they become inclined not to treat them with equal respect?) Rawls does not devote much discussion to the large number of real people, reasonable in the ethical sense, who hold doctrines that he himself would probably rank in this category, such as New Ageism or astrology. Perhaps if he did discuss these cases he would be willing to maintain that citizens who affirm them are unreasonable, thus sticking to the theoretical criteria he has advanced; but one might well feel that such a judgment shows too little respect for reasonable citizens (in the ethical sense). What dooms the whole project of offering theoretical criteria for reasonableness, however, so far as I can see, is the fact that the major religions, his central cases, and the ones whose adherents he most wants to persuade, fail to meet them, and fail for reasons that, in the case of Christianity, go deep: a repudiation of theoretical reason that lies at the heart of that religion's account of faith, in at least some central instances.

Were Rawls to adopt the suggestion I have made, he would probably need to articulate his account of the burdens of judgment as a series of historical or sociological observations about modernity, rather than as a basis for the normative distinction between reasonable and unreasonable

---

[51] Similarly, the idea that it is very difficult to arrive at the correct view in such matters, even using one's reason in the best possible way, is fundamental to at least one strand in Locke's defense of toleration.

doctrines.[52] He could simply say, then, that we must all recognize that disagreement is sometimes the result of free institutions, and that we should all recognize that we can engage in respectful social cooperation without reaching agreement on religious matters.[53] That would be a high price for him to pay, in terms of the theoretical ambitions of the program he and Charles Larmore share, because it would drop the pivotal distinction between mere error and more respect-worthy sources of disagreement. I myself feel that it is not too high a price: for by paying that price we purchase a wider and more inclusive notion of respect. It just doesn't seem right for citizens to be looking into other citizens' religions and asking how reasonable they are, provided that the doctrines they hold are reasonable in the ethical sense that is involved in the public political conception.

Rawls appears to make a decisive move in the direction I favor in the section discussing overlapping consensus; here he states that one way the movement from a mere *modus vivendi* to an overlapping consensus takes place is through the fact that citizens typically have "a certain looseness in [their] comprehensive views" (p. 159): "Most people's religious, philosophical, and moral comprehensive doctrines are not seen by them as fully general and comprehensive", and this fact allows for "slippage," as citizens come to endorse the political conception, often "without seeing any particular connection, one way or the other, between those principles and their other views" (p. 160). These important observations are not applied back to the account of the burdens of judgment or to the distinction between reasonable and unreasonable comprehensive doctrines, but they do at least indicate that Rawls is prepared to interpret his theoretical criteria very loosely. At any rate, readers must sort this out for themselves.

Larmore's text contains a similar problem, which I shall treat more briefly. Like Rawls, Larmore plainly thinks that it is important to distinguish reasonable disagreements from other sorts of disagreements.[54] He offers an account of the "burdens of reason" that is similar to Rawls's,

---

[52] And so it is also not clear whether the account of "reasonable" persons would need to be correspondingly revised: it might be that only the condition having to do with fair terms of cooperation would survive, and that having to do with the burdens of judgment would drop out. For illuminating discussion on this point, I am grateful to Erin Kelly.

[53] Rawls appears to take this line in IPRR, his latest statement on this question: see pp. 573–574; a plurality of conflicting doctrines is "the normal result" of a culture of free institutions, and "[c]itizens realize that they cannot reach agreement or even approach mutual understanding on the basis of their irreconcilable comprehensive doctrines."

[54] For Larmore, this is the pivotal distinction; unlike Rawls, he does not focus theoretical attention on the distinction between reasonable and unreasonable comprehensive doctrines, although he would very likely consider this a closely related distinction.

listing a variety of factors that may prevent people from arriving at agreement. He notes that we do not yet have an account of why disagreement in matters of value should be so pervasive, while scientific disagreement is less ubiquitous. He says that he does not have an explanation of this difference.[55] But he insists that it is important to distinguish reasonable disagreement from skepticism: the parties to disagreement may be able to offer reasons for their views, and those reasons may satisfy a high standard. It is not because people don't have good arguments for their views that they do not agree. In particular, Larmore is determined to reject the idea that people stick to their views in the face of disagreement because of "faith." "Our allegiance [to our view] may be much more than a matter of faith."[56] Shortly thereafter, he says that we do not need to consider these allegiances "as but an article of faith." So it would seem that a disagreement counts as reasonable for Larmore only if both parties base their allegiance on arguments and not simply on faith.

I think that this demand for a particular sort of grounding for a view is disrespectful to religious citizens who think that faith is a very good basis for their views, in fact the best basis. While attempting to articulate a version of liberalism that does not rest on controversial metaphysical or epistemological doctrines, Larmore imports just such a doctrine into the very statement of the view. Rawls is at least torn in this matter; Larmore seems not to be at all torn. He clearly thinks faith a lesser source for a view than reasoned argument, and he seems not to think this a problem for a political view that wishes to show equal respect for all people.

My solution to this problem is that we remember that respect in political liberalism is, first and foremost, respect for persons, not respect for the doctrines they hold, for the grounding of those doctrines, or for anything else about them. It is because we respect persons that we think that their comprehensive doctrines deserve space to unfold themselves, and deserve respectful, non-derogatory treatment from government (whatever treatment they receive from citizens in the "background culture").

---

[55] Larmore, "Pluralism and reasonable disagreement," p. 171. In his 2005 article "Respect for persons" (cited in note 36), Larmore explicitly states that for him "reasonable," as applied to comprehensive doctrines, is not a notion that flows directly from the notion of equal respect; he casts aspersions on that sort of view, saying, "naturally little is accomplished by definitional maneuvers." His own definition of "reasonable" there is "rather abstract," involving "exercising the basic capacities of reason and conversing with others in good faith." An earlier account is "thinking and conversing in good faith and applying, as best we can, the general capacities of reason that pertain to every domain of inquiry." Thus he would seem to favor a definition that is at least partly theoretical, and only minimally ethical.

[56] Larmore, "Pluralism and reasonable disagreement," p. 173.

For a public official in a leading role to say "X's doctrine is not as well grounded as Y's" is, inevitably, to denigrate X, and we want our political principles to show equal respect to X and Y. We must, then, avoid defining "reasonable" in a way that denigrates the grounds of some people's doctrines: to do otherwise is to violate the very abstemiousness toward controversial epistemological and metaphysical doctrines that political liberalism rightly asks us to insist upon.

Therefore, let's stick with the ethical definition of "reasonable." A "reasonable" citizen is one who respects other citizens as equals. A "reasonable" comprehensive doctrine is one endorsed by such a reasonable citizen, that is, including a serious commitment to the value of equal respect for persons as a political value. Beyond that, it is just nosy and impertinent for the state or its agents to inquire into the basis of people's religious adherence. Whether it be tradition-based, authority-based, argument-based, faith-based, or based in nothing but its allure, a religious doctrine deserves to be called "reasonable" if and only if it is the sort of doctrine that can be endorsed by a reasonable citizen. The object of respect is the person and the person's faculties (conscience, for example). We need say nothing much about the differences among the comprehensive doctrines (apart from ruling out some as incompatible with equal respect), and we certainly should avoid a ranking of the type that Larmore, and at times Rawls, seem to suggest.

The case for political liberalism

Consider the many religious and secular views of life that exist in modern societies. Many if not most of them cannot accept Raz's idea that autonomy, understood as Raz understands it, ought to be a moral ideal. Some religions allow their adherents more autonomy and some less, but very few valorize it as Raz does. (Moreover, as we've said, few religions accept Berlin's moral pluralism, a view that Raz thinks presupposed by the morality of autonomy.) As for secular views of the good life, most of those are not terribly pluralistic either. Many Marxists do not think that non-Marxist views should even be tolerated, although this point is contested; certainly a serious Marxist cannot grant that the major religions and the comprehensive ethical doctrines of bourgeois morality are all objectively true.[57] Utilitarians typically hold that

---

[57] Is Marxism a reasonable comprehensive doctrine in Rawls's sense? Not if it requires endorsing the legitimate use of violence and the suspension of political liberties; but there are versions of Marxism, both in philosophy (G. A. Cohen, Jon Elster) and in politics (the Marxist parties of India and some parts of Europe) that do seem to qualify as reasonable.

Kantian and Aristotelian views are not even acceptable, and they certainly do not believe them objectively true. Many holders of secular views do not think of religious views as acceptable, and they certainly do not think them true. Ditto with the view religious believers take of secular doctrines.

Raz, then, and to all appearances Berlin want to build liberal society on a set of views that virtually none of its members actually holds. In Berlin's case, one can see what he is reacting against: the danger to human liberty that comes from excessive dogmatism about one's own ideal. But he does not appear to realize that his own pluralist alternative, espoused as a political principle, would have equally dangerous consequences. In the section of *The Social Contract* entitled "Of the civil religion," Rousseau creates a state religion that contains something like Berlin's pluralism, in the form of a doctrine of "theological toleration": one cannot hold that one religion is correct and others incorrect. Rousseau believes that civil peace requires such a theological belief, and it may be that Berlin holds something like this. Both, in the service of toleration, as they understand toleration, require of all citizens something that virtually none of them can believe without abandoning their religion. Rousseau knows very well that his civil religion will prove unacceptable to Roman Catholics and to many, if not most, varieties of Protestantism. He is prepared to banish adherents to such views if they will not drop them in favor of the civil religion. Raz and Berlin make no such draconian proposal, but they do insist on building the state on principles that a large proportion of its citizens cannot accept.

That is a strategic problem, clearly. It is difficult to see how a liberalism of that sort could remain stable, unless religious citizens really do something like what Rousseau wants, dropping their religion in favor of the liberal state doctrine. It's not surprising that Rousseau foresees a large role for banishment in his society. The problem, however, is graver yet: it is a problem of respect. When the institutions that pervasively govern your life are built on a view that in all conscience you cannot endorse, that means that you are, in effect, in a position of second-class citizenship. Even if you are tolerated (and it is not too clear from Raz's paper to what extent the major religions would be tolerated), government will state, every day, that a different view, incompatible with yours, is the correct view, and that yours is wrong. Moreover, as Raz explicitly said in discussion of his paper,[58] government will be licensed to try to convert

---

[58] Law-Philosophy Workshop, The University of Chicago, 2008. Even though Raz does not state this in MF, it seems to be a natural consequence of the theoretical importance he gives to the broad acceptance of these views.

you to the correct view. This is what I would call "expressive subordination," subordination that consists in being publicly ranked beneath others.[59]

Expressive subordination is a form of religious establishment. The fact that Raz's view is secular makes no difference to that conclusion. And it is wrong for the reason that religious establishment is always wrong: it offends against the equality of citizens. It tells them, to quote James Madison, that they do not all enter the public square "on equal conditions."[60] This conclusion apparently does not trouble Raz: if they do not accept the fact of pluralism and the ideal of autonomy, it is fine to treat them unequally. But it troubles me, as it troubled Larmore and Rawls. It is because many people think that Raz's sort of comprehensive liberalism is the only viable form of liberalism that they also think that liberalism is not neutral about the good life but is a form of religion in its own right.

But Raz's liberalism, as we've seen, is not the only form of liberalism. For one may develop a form of liberalism that begins from the idea of equal respect for persons. One then reasons that equal respect requires not setting up any one of the available forms of life as the ideal but instead requires prescinding from any such ranking of lives. Seeing how, under conditions of freedom, people do not agree about values, we ought to show respect for those "reasonable disagreements" by basing our political principles on a thin and abstemious view, one that abstains from controversial metaphysical, epistemological, and comprehensive ethical claims. The view will have a moral content, clearly: but the hope is that its moral content will be acceptable to all the major comprehensive doctrines, a kind of "module," as Rawls puts it, that they can all attach to their own views of life. It is thus the object of an "overlapping consensus" among all the major views. This hope can be realized only if we (when speaking in a political role) carefully avoid making perfectionist claims in the manner that Raz does, or even – I think – claims about reasons in the way that Larmore and, at times, Rawls do. We will not say that autonomy makes lives go better in general, and we will not endorse moral pluralism. We will also not say that it is better to offer

---

[59] Of course, on the view I hold, individual citizens and groups of citizens in the "background culture" will be free to try to convert others to their view: the phobia about conversion that has led some Indian states to restrict proselytizing has no place in political liberalism. The point is rather that government cannot be the agent of this process without establishing a hierarchy.

[60] Madison, "Memorial and remonstrance against religious assessments," 1785, in *Religion and the Constitution*, 2nd ed., ed. Michael McConnell, John H. Garvey, and Thomas C. Berg (New York: Aspen, 2006), p. 50.

arguments for your view than to hold it out of faith. But we will show respect for citizens by creating and protecting spaces in which they can live according to their own views.

Rawls and I would insist that there is a cousin of autonomy that must figure in such a view: for real freedom to live according to one's own view also requires protecting the spaces in which people may leave one view and opt for another, and also the spaces in which children learn about options so that they can really live their own lives. That sort of thing Rawls calls "political autonomy."[61] It is not, however, the same thing as Raz's autonomy, because no announcement is made by the state that lives lived under one's own direction are better than lives lived in submission to some form of religious or cultural or military authority.[62] Of course, in Rawls's state no cultural authority is allowed to coerce people, and they must always be free to enjoy their fully equal rights as citizens, including the free choice of occupation and freedom of religion. But the Roman Catholic, or the member of the Old Order Amish, can still feel that the political view, by protecting spaces within which they claim authority, respects them and does not denigrate them, as would not be the case with Raz's comprehensive view of autonomy. Political autonomy is not entirely neutral: it has a definite view about the ingredients of good political life, including a respect for argument and the public exchange of reasons. In that sense, it does not aim at the type of politics that some of the comprehensive doctrines might favor for themselves, were they to establish a theocracy with no internal pluralism. Such, however, is not the condition of modernity, and believers are aware of this. Given that they share a common political life with others who differ, they can see the requirements of political autonomy as respectful of them, understanding the political as a realm of difference governed by mutual respect, whereas they could not accept autonomy of Raz's sort, prescribed as a comprehensive value. It might be that citizens who grow up with political autonomy might in time long for autonomy in the rest of their lives: thus, as Rawls mentions, it is possible that his ideal will put more strain on some doctrines than on others. But here we should agree with Rawls: showing that all doctrines will have an equally easy time gaining adherents over time is not required to show that the political view is one that respects citizens as

---

[61] *PL*, pp. xliv–xlv.

[62] No state really says this, because every state needs military defense, and presumably Raz would not deny this. His state, then, would have to say, "It is fine to subordinate your autonomy to the service of your country, but not to religious authority," a statement even more problematic than a blanket condemnation of all non-autonomous lives.

equals.[63] (Moreover, the sociological/psychological speculation may prove untrue: political autonomy might make at least some people long for control and intellectual security in other parts of their lives.)

It has become evident by now that the major religions can in fact accept Rawlsian political liberalism, though they cannot accept Raz's perfectionist liberalism. Roman Catholics, for example, can agree with Rawls that we must ground toleration in a view of equal respect for persons. Such a person will still think that her religion is true and others false; but respect for persons requires protecting the space in which each lives by her own lights. So we get wide toleration, but without expressive subordination.

Political liberalism does not avoid stating that some ethical and religious doctrines are unacceptable, as we have seen. For its political principles do have a moral content, prominently including the equality of citizens and the importance of equal respect. Such ideas will be deeply entrenched in a society's constitution. So the proponent of slavery, or gender hierarchy, will not get equal treatment in that society: the life he wants to lead offends fundamental constitutional norms, so he would have to amend the constitution to be able to live it. Nonetheless, Rawls holds that such a person will enjoy wide liberty to speak and act, so long as he is not violating the rights of others.[64]

Why might one prefer Raz's view to Rawls's? One reason, which seems to be that of both Berlin and Raz, is a deep conviction that their moral ideal is correct and important, and that any good society should recognize this fact. I have argued that they pay too high a price for what we might ironically call their "pursuit of the ideal": the price of denigrating and expressively subordinating many citizens who are willing to live with others on terms of equality and reciprocity.

Another reason for preferring perfectionism (although it is not that of Berlin and Raz) might be a deep rationalism. To some people – and it appears that Kant and Mill were among them[65] – the main thing that has been wrong with most societies is that they have based their political principles on irrational deference to tradition or authority; the right thing

---

[63] See *PL*, p. 199: "Political liberalism is unjustly biased against certain comprehensive conceptions only if, say, individualistic ones alone can endure in a liberal society, or they so predominate that associations affirming values of religion or community cannot flourish, and moreover the conditions leading to this outcome are themselves unjust, in view of present and foreseeable circumstances."

[64] *PL*, pp. 340–356. In such a case, the person would be unreasonable in the ethical sense, as would her doctrine; but the state will take no action, provided that she is not violating the rights of others or causing a threat of upheaval.

[65] Although, once again, exegetical controversies about the interpretation of Kant and Mill are irrelevant to my argument here.

to do, in order to correct this baneful tendency, is to ground political principles in a comprehensive rationalism. To such people it just seems unacceptable that the state should limit itself to saying that rational argument is central in political life: surely faith is always and everywhere worse than argument. Such people will acknowledge that Rawlsian politics puts evidence and rational argument in the driver's seat in the political realm,[66] but the failure to recommend reason over faith more globally seems like a large failure. Can it really be the case, for example, that teachers in public schools (who are therefore agents of government) can recommend argument over faith only for the purposes of citizenship, and not as the best way to approach life's problems in general? That seems to the rationalist intolerable.

I have been confronting this opponent throughout this chapter by pointing to the connection between equal respect for persons, on the part of the state, and a refusal to endorse any one comprehensive doctrine. And I think that the reply to the outraged question is "yes": teachers in public schools should not say that argument is better than faith as a general way of solving all problems in life.[67] To say that is to denigrate students who are members of non-rationalist religions. They may certainly say that in contexts where citizens of many different views debate about fundamental matters, rational argument is crucial. They may also commend it as part and parcel of a particular enterprise, such as scientific proof. But they should not say, "Live your life by reason and not by faith." Secular rationalists would not agree, but I am not sure how to envisage the next stage of the argument here.

There is another argument that leads back to comprehensive liberalism, and I believe that it is stronger than the rationalist argument. One might reasonably believe, and argue, that most of the views around in most societies are racist or sexist, or hierarchical in some other way, and that only a comprehensive perfectionist view, accepted as the basis of the state, could really get rid of their baneful political influence. The objector

---

[66] On the delicate question of how the political conception will advance a norm of objectivity without becoming a comprehensive doctrine, see Nussbaum, "Political objectivity," *New Literary History* 32 (2001), 883–906, interpreting and defending Rawls's view.

[67] It is not clear whether Rawlsian duties of civility apply to such people: one could argue that they do; given the pervasive influence of public education on all of one's life as a citizen, schools are part of the basic structure. But even if one should resist this idea, and thus hold that it is morally permissible for teachers to make statements defending comprehensive rationalism, one should certainly insist that the teacher point out that the nation in which pupils and teacher live is not built upon the truth of comprehensive rationalism, so that teacher is simply arguing from her own comprehensive doctrine, not from public values.

would try to show that hierarchical views are typically irrational, based on stereotypes that cannot stand the light of rational argument. They flourish when deprived of that light, but wither when exposed to it. Thus, in societies that promote tradition and authority over reason, they are likely to prove strong, whereas a comprehensively rationalist society can effectively combat them.

This view, too, was apparently held by Mill. In *The Subjection of Women*, he argues that the stereotypes about gender difference that keep women subordinated just won't stand up to the test of evidence and argument. Thus they will wither away when exposed to argument. Mill knows that it will be hard enough for argument to prevail against traditional opinion, but he then deplores the fact that his society is losing the confidence in reason that characterized eighteenth-century society. "For the apotheosis of Reason," he writes, "we have substituted that of Instinct; and we call everything instinct which we find in ourselves and for which we cannot trace any rational foundation."[68] Thus, even if good arguments are made against stereotypes, they will fail to get a hearing in a culture that is generally dismissive of argument.[69]

The late Susan Moller Okin, a distinguished feminist political theorist, and an editor of Mill's *Subjection*, rejected Rawls's political liberalism for such reasons. She thought most religions and traditional cultures were sexist to the core, so the only way to make progress was to do away with them, insofar as we could, by public persuasion.[70] Since freedom of

---

[68] John Stuart Mill, *The Subjection of Women*, ed. Susan Moller Okin (Indianapolis, IN: Hackett, 1988), p. 4.

[69] Mill certainly wants both culture and law to change; how far he believes it right for government to promulgate a comprehensive doctrine of women's equality – by contrast with specific political reforms that he evidently favors – remains unclear, and therefore I do not address it further here.

[70] Susan Moller Okin, "Political liberalism, justice and gender," *Ethics* 105 (1994), 23–43; *Is Multiculturalism Bad for Women?* ed. Joshua Cohen, Matthew Howard, and Martha C. Nussbaum (Princeton University Press, 1999), pp. 9–24, and the longer version, "Feminism and multiculturalism: some tensions," *Ethics* 108 (1998), 661–684. Okin's central discussion concerns the "founding myths" of ancient Greco-Roman religion, Christianity, Judaism, and Islam, but her theoretical claim is much more sweeping: "Much of most cultures is about controlling women and maintaining gender roles" ("Feminism and multiculturalism," p. 667). A similar statement appears in the shorter version: "Most cultures have as one of their principal aims the control of women by men" (*Is Multiculturalism Bad for Women?* p. 13). As the *Ethics* paper unfolds and she engages with theorists who discuss examples from other religions (e.g., Kymlicka's discussions of the religious practices of indigenous minorities and Kukathas's general reference to "immigrant cultures"), she similarly broadens the scope of her critique. (The book version, similarly, discusses native practices in Peru and in traditional African religion.) In "Feminism and multiculturalism," n. 17, she explicitly endorses a claim by two feminist scholars that "[t]raditions have always been a double-edged sword for women. Subordinate economic and social status, and restrictions on women's activity

speech would not be suppressed, the only way to give public discourage-
ment to religion would seem to be the endorsement of a comprehensive
perfectionist doctrine including, prominently, women's equality in every
sphere of life, not simply in the public culture. Okin thought that Rawls
asked too little of the religions when he simply asked them to accept the
full equality of women as citizens, but did not ask them, for example, to
accept the theological or eschatological equality of women. I see her
point. Although I do not accept her argument, and although I believe
she misunderstands Rawls at some points,[71] her argument seems to me
the best one against Rawls's form of liberalism. One should insist that the
political realm (including the public schools) will itself be entitled to use
rational argument to undermine demeaning stereotypes. But one should
probably concede that in the absence of thoroughgoing culture reform,
this intervention is likely to achieve its results more slowly and with
greater difficulty. I think that the best line of defense for Raz would be
to focus on such cases.

I do not think Okin is correct about religion: I think by now most of
them have participated in debates about sex equality and movements
toward sex equality on a par with the rest of their cultures, shifting their
comprehensive doctrines in keeping with the shift in the views about
public culture that they share with their fellow citizens. Few have shown
more resistance to change than the cultures that surround them.[72] (So,
too, with most secular comprehensive doctrines, which have also been
sexist.) Some have even been in advance of their surrounding cultures.
More importantly, though, I also think that politics has no business
talking about the afterlife or who should be a priest. (Political liberalism
is closely related to Locke's idea about the proper jurisdiction of the civil
realm. The relationship between these two doctrines deserves further
study.) However, I see enough force in the considerations raised by Okin
(and Mill) that I think that the debate between political and comprehensive liberalism is a deep one, and it ought to continue until we understand all the options and issues as well as we can. We should therefore all

---

and mobility are embedded in most traditional cultures." While Okin usually does not
distinguish between religion and culture, her lengthy discussions of the four religious
"founding myths" place an emphasis on religion as a medium of control.

[71] See Nussbaum, "Rawls and feminism," in *Cambridge Companion to Rawls*, pp. 488–520.

[72] Even in those cases where a religious hierarchy still espouses overtly sexist doctrines – as,
for example, with the refusal of the Roman Catholic Church to ordain women – the laity
and large parts of the clergy, in the United States at any rate, favor change, so it should
not even be said that the Roman Catholic religion is per se opposed to sex equality.
Clearly, however, the centralized and international character of the Roman Catholic
Church poses special difficulties for change, since the public cultures of the nations from
which many of its members are drawn do not fully support the equality of women.

be immensely grateful to Raz and Berlin for giving us a version of the perfectionist alternative that is as clear and thorough as any that we are likely to see for some time.

Political liberalism: an example

Berlin suggests that perfectionist liberalism is necessary because the comprehensive doctrines that do not accept liberal principles of toleration and autonomy will destabilize liberal society. Raz argues that perfectionism is necessary for toleration, which he describes as involving the curbing of hostile or negative tendencies: so he too raises questions of stability.[73] I have suggested that perfectionist liberalism of the sort they advocate is disrespectful, and that political liberalism can prove stable, provided that the holders of the various comprehensive doctrines care sufficiently about respect for persons. It helps, then, to see that there are forms of political liberalism that exist and that hold viable democracies together. Of course, none exists in a Rawlsian Well-Ordered Society where the two principles of justice are fully implemented; but both might be said to be at the stage of "constitutional consensus" that Rawls sees as a station on the road to overlapping consensus.[74]

There are quite a few examples one might give. The constitutions of both India and South Africa provide very interesting examples of how a commitment to respect for persons can be translated into a constitutional scheme that is "freestanding" in Rawls's sense, that is, grounded in no divisive religious or metaphysical doctrine, but only in a working practical commitment to human dignity and human rights. For the sake of illustration, however, let me focus on just one example, the treatment of religion under US constitutional law.[75]

The American colonists were all too familiar with the fact that differing ideals, and each group's "pursuit of the ideal," frequently led to the subordination of others: to banishment, to punishment, to exclusion from political office. They were therefore moved not only to defend religious liberty in the new nation, guaranteeing all citizens the "free exercise" of their religion, but also, as time went on, to oppose all religious establishments. Establishments were worst when they threatened liberty, penalizing people for non-orthodox worship, or forcing them to affirm orthodox sentiments that they might not believe, or attaching conditions of religious orthodoxy to a person's civil rights or

---

[73] See MF, pp. 401–402.
[74] See *PL,* pp. 158–163, for the idea of a "constitutional consensus."
[75] I have treated this example extensively in *Liberty of Conscience.*

ability to hold office. It was quickly understood, however, that even an apparently benign establishment fosters inequality by making a statement that the government of the nation endorses a particular brand of religion. This endorsement is at the same time, inevitably, a disendorsement, creating an in-group and an out-group. Madison said, we recall, that "all men are to be considered as entering into Society on equal conditions," and he believed that even a non-coercive establishment violates that equality. Madison was speaking, in 1785, in opposition to a proposal to tax all citizens of Virginia for the support of the established Anglican Church. According to the exceedingly mild proposal, citizens who were not Anglicans would be permitted to divert their tax payments to their own churches. Nonetheless, Madison thought that the bare announcement that the Anglican Church was the state church created ranks and orders of citizens. In 1984, discussing the US Constitution's ban on religious establishment, Justice Sandra Day O'Connor recapitulated the long Madisonian tradition:

The Establishment Clause prohibits government from making adherence to a religion relevant in any way to a person's standing in the political community... Endorsement sends a message to non-adherents that they are outsiders, not full members of the political community, and an accompanying message to adherents that they are insiders, favored members of the political community. Disapproval sends the opposite message. (*Lynch* v. *Donnelly*, 1984)

According to Justice O'Connor's very helpful analysis, the right question to ask of any potentially problematic policy in the area of religious establishment is the following one: would an objective observer, acquainted with all the relevant historical and contextual facts, view the policy in question as one that makes a public statement of endorsement or disapproval, sending a message of inequality?[76]

Although there are many accounts of the purpose and meaning of the Establishment Clause, I believe (and have argued) that the Madison/O'Connor formulation goes to the heart of the matter.[77] Fundamentally, the clause is about equality, the equal standing of all persons in the political realm. It expresses equal respect. It says that no comprehensive doctrine gives one person claim to respect that another does not have. The Establishment Clause, then, sets up a form of political liberalism.

---

[76] By "sends the ... message," O'Connor presumably means that the policy in question, by communicating government's approval of a particular comprehensive doctrine selected among others, is reasonably understood to make a statement that this doctrine is preferred by government, and that its adherents, therefore, by living the life that government prefers, are a privileged in-group of citizens.

[77] Nussbaum, *Liberty of Conscience*, Chapter 6.

Raz could not accept it because he would like to establish controversial sectarian principles of a perfectionist nature, principles that would not be acceptable to believing members of most existing religions. The religious would exist in the very condition of expressive subordination described by Madison and O'Connor: they would be an out-group, told by the statements of their government and its leaders that theirs is a disfavored view.

Of course, no such idea can develop utterly without political and interpretive controversy. But on the whole, this idea of non-subordination, and the concomitant idea of non-endorsement, have exerted a powerful influence on both law and politics more generally, and have allowed the members of diverse doctrines to live together without having to think that the political principles of the nation in which they live either endorse or deny their religious doctrines. It gives those who pursue the ideal in their own different ways a meeting place that denigrates none of them; and it offers this same meeting place to the secular humanist who holds a comprehensive doctrine of autonomy, as does Raz. It does seem to give the people of an overwhelmingly religious nation such as the United States a basis for attachment to core political principles that would not have been provided by any form of perfectionism: for any perfectionism would either establish one religion at the expense of others or would establish a secular principle (such as Bentham's utilitarianism or Raz's autonomy) at the expense of the doctrines held by a vast majority of this nation's people.

Berlin clearly felt the need for some meeting ground that could hold together people of a diverse society. Given his endorsement of the metaphysical, and controversial, principle of pluralism, however, he was able to give only a very thin account of this common ground, in the form of "a minimum without which societies could scarcely survive" (PI, p. 15). He mentions only a few such propositions: the wrongfulness of slavery and ritual murder, of "the Nazi gas chambers or the torture of human beings for pleasure or profit or even political good – or the duty of children to denounce their parents ... or mindless killing" (p. 15). I think this ground is so minimal that it is dubious that it can provide an account of stability for a liberal society. To my mind, political liberalism's account of the common ground is superior, because it incorporates much more substantive and organizing ethical notions, such as that of equal respect, and the political principles that flow from that.

If political liberalism is superior to perfectionist liberalism on ethical grounds, as I have argued, and if it does better even on the issue of stability, we can have no reason not to prefer it overall.

2 Rawlsian social-contract theory and the severely disabled*

Henry S. Richardson

An issue needing to be addressed

In a series of powerfully argued recent works, Martha C. Nussbaum claims that the social-contract device that John Rawls employs, the Original Position (OP), is ill suited to generating acceptable principles of justice pertaining to the treatment of humans with physical and mental disabilities.[1] Rawls makes no effort to generate such principles himself, she recognizes; instead, he attempts to work out principles for an idealized world in which "all citizens are fully cooperating members of a society over a complete life" (*CP* 332).[2] His motivation for idealizing so radically in this respect seems to rest – as also in the case of his idealizing assumption that the society to which principles are to apply is closed

* This chapter is based on the article "Rawlsian social-contract theory and the severely disabled" by Henry S. Richardson in *The Journal of Ethics*, Volume 10, December 2006, Issue 4, pp 419–462"; © Springer Netherlands, Dordrecht; with kind permission from Springer Science+Business Media B.V. For illuminating discussion of earlier drafts I am grateful to Robert Leider and the other members of my seminar on Rawls, to participants in the University of Pennsylvania's Law and Philosophy Workshop, and to Rainer Forst and the members of his Kolloquium at the Goethe-Universität, Frankfurt. I have benefited from thoughtful written comments from Leif Wenar and Thomas Schramme, as well as from Martha C. Nussbaum, who was generous enough to make available her forthcoming book and to discuss it with me.

[1] Martha C. Nussbaum, "Capabilities and Disabilities: Justice for Mentally Disabled Citizens," *Philosophical Topics* 2 (2002): 133–65; Martha C. Nussbaum, "Beyond the Social Contract: Toward Global Justice," in *Tanner Lectures in Human Values, Vol. 25* (Salt Lake City: University of Utah Press, 2004), 413–507; Martha C. Nussbaum, *Frontiers of Justice: Disability, Nationality, Species Membership* (Cambridge, Mass.: Harvard University Press, 2005). Parenthetical page numbers in the text with no other designation will refer to the last of these.

[2] Parenthetical references to Rawls's work in the text make use of the following abbreviations:
CP: John Rawls, *Collected Papers*, ed. Samuel Freeman (Cambridge, Mass.: Harvard University Press, 1999).
PL: John Rawls, *Political Liberalism* (New York: Columbia University Press, 1996).
R: John Rawls, *Justice as Fairness: A Restatement*, ed. Erin Kelly (Cambridge, Mass.: Harvard University Press, 2001).
TJ: John Rawls, *A Theory of Justice*, rev. ed. (Cambridge, Mass.: Harvard University Press, 1999).

and isolated – on the hope that "once we have a sound theory for this case, the remaining problems of justice will prove more tractable in the light of it. With suitable modifications such a theory should provide the key for some of these other questions" (*TJ* 7; *PL* 183). He recognizes that "care for those with [unusual and costly medical requirements] is a pressing practical question" (*PL* 332). Although one must admire Rawls's attempt to carve out a workable problem, this verbal recognition of the practically pressing nature of issues about disability does not satisfy Nussbaum, nor should it satisfy us. There are too many general reasons to suspect that confronting the issue of care for those with serious disabilities will require us radically to rethink some of our basic ideas about justice.

Among the general reasons against postponement that Nussbaum adduces are the following:[3]

1. *The pervasiveness of dependence and disability:* each of us enters life as a dependent infant lacking the capabilities of a fully cooperating member of society, almost all of us get seriously ill at some point, and many of us will be infirm and dependent again in old age (87–8).
2. *The universality of care:* correspondingly, care-giving work by parents (most often mothers), doctors and nurses, and by one's children or the state, is an essential feature of human life (218–20).[4]
3. *The continuum of disability:* each of us has capabilities that are defective in one way or another. There is a continuum (although not a clearly ordered one) in this regard (99, 125–6).
4. *The moral imperative to avoid drawing a dichotomy between the disabled and the non-disabled:* given the appalling history of social treatment of those with serious disabilities, it would be wrong to approach these issues with an "us" and "them" mentality (192–4).

For all these reasons, Nussbaum argues, it is a mistake to postpone the difficult questions about justice and disability.

Nussbaum also argues that there are more specific reasons why Rawls's postponement is misguided. She doubts that a suitable modification of his social-contract thought experiment could well address the core issues pertaining to justice and disability, arguing that this omission would be "not easy to rectify" (18). Her specific reasons for doubt are powerful and articulate. She argues that Rawls's social-contract framework cannot yield suitable principles that apply to all persons, no matter

[3] The labeling is mine.
[4] See Eva Feder Kittay, *Love's Labor: Essays on Women, Equality, and Dependency* (New York: Routledge, 1999).

how disabled. In this chapter, I accept the general reasons for not postponing this issue, and so plunge into it; but rather than take up one by one her specific reasons for thinking Rawls's principles and framework cannot be suitably modified to deal with the issue, I have opted simply to work with the framework and see where it might take us. I hope to show how it can be suitably modified to address this difficult issue in a fruitful fashion.

One of Rawls's original insights about the idea of a social contract is that the idealized initial choice situation (ICS) can serve as a basis for comparing alternative principles of justice. The OP is his favored interpretation of the ICS, but there are many possible variations. Because different versions of the ICS would lead to the choice of different sets of principles, the contractarian idea provides one illuminating way to compare different sets of principles. As Rawls put it:

> We may conjecture that for each traditional conception of justice there exists an interpretation of the initial situation in which its principles are the preferred solution. Thus, for example, there are interpretations that lead to the classical as well as the average principle of utility... The procedure of contract theories provides, then, a general analytic method for the comparative study of conceptions of justice. (*TJ* 105)

For instance, in the OP, Rawls endows the parties with a "thin" theory of the good, in which the "primary goods" (rights, liberties, opportunities, income, wealth, and the social basis of self-respect) are organized by reference to the "highest-order interests" in freely framing and pursuing a conception of the good and in developing and acting from a sense of justice. Because the parties are defined as caring about rights and liberties, and because they are also defined as organizing their pursuits on the basis of a highest-order interest in freely framing a conception of the good, they have reason to give priority to liberty. This, in turn, leads them to favor Rawls's two principles over utilitarianism, as the First Principle gives priority to the basic liberties.

Here, since we are in the business of considering whether Rawls's theory of justice may be plausibly extended to address issues of disability, I will similarly extend his conjecture about the usefulness of the ICS as a comparative and diagnostic device. I believe that we may utilize the idea of the ICS as a comparative and analytic tool, not only for the traditional theories of justice but also for new proposals about justice regarding disability. At any rate, that is how I will use the device here. Such an enterprise is, of course, Rawls's paradigm case of the need to work toward reflective equilibrium. In putting forward an interpretation of an ICS such that we can have some confidence that the principles the hypothetical parties would choose are just, what we must do is find ways to build or "model" into that interpretation a number of crucial – and presumably rather general – considered judgments that "we do in fact accept" (*TJ* 19). When we then look at the principles that the parties to our ICS would prefer, we might be appalled. If so, we are forced back to the drawing board. As Rawls puts it,

> In searching for the most favored description of [the initial choice] situation we work from both ends ... By going back and forth, sometimes altering the conditions of the contractual circumstances, at others withdrawing our judgments and conforming them to principle, I assume that eventually we shall find a description of the initial situation that both expresses reasonable conditions and yields principles which match our considered judgments duly pruned and adjusted. This state of affairs I refer to as reflective equilibrium. (*TJ* 18)

In *A Theory of Justice*, of course, Rawls never presents us with a chronology of his attempts to work out his own favored interpretation of the ICS – the OP – complete with all the detours and bumps along the way. Here, by contrast, my own ideas about justice and disability being in a relatively primitive state, I invite you to follow me on an off-road journey complete with just such dead-ends and obstacles and leaving off still in the midst of the wilderness.

In particular, I will not attempt to show that the principles covering disability that emerge from the best-supported interpretation of the ICS are principles that, on due reflection, we can accept. These principles are quite generous toward those with serious disabilities, to an extent that raises questions about the feasibility of arranging society in accordance with them. Perhaps they go too far. In putting them forward, I am guided more by Nussbaum's proposals than by any independent sense of what ought to be done. Her own proposals are also quite generous toward those with serious disabilities; and her critical claim about Rawls – the one I am examining here – is that his social-contract framework cannot be extended to generate any such principles. Here I show how it can be. Further work on the subject may show that both Nussbaum's principles and the alternative ones defended here are more generous than we can afford to be, but that would not affect the philosophical point about the usefulness of Rawlsian social-contract analysis.

It bears emphasizing that the usefulness of Rawls's initial choice situation is not *confined* to the comparative and diagnostic. Rawls's OP powerfully unites some fundamental convictions we have about morality, justice, and the appropriate constraints on developing principles. Its veil of ignorance represents a vivid way of combining common-sense thoughts about being in someone else's shoes with a kind of impartiality that neutralizes arbitrary inequalities of advantage. Its combination of the veil with the mutually disinterested rationality of the parties aims to express something of the spirit of universal benevolence, but with more definite results (*TJ* 128, 166). Because it captures ideals of empathy, impartiality, equality, rationality, and benevolence in these ways, the OP represents a morally compelling viewpoint for us to consider as we begin to tackle the challenging issue of justice regarding disability.

Taking from Nussbaum my initial fix on which principles are acceptable regarding disability, my intention is to lay more emphasis on the principles-to-ICS direction of reflective equilibration than does Rawls's order of exposition (NB: not the same as his order of justification), which tends instead to work down from the ICS to the principles. I will begin the constructive part of my argument by laying out alternative sets of principles of justice that apply to the most as well as to the least disabled among us. Among these alternatives will be several that might plausibly claim to capture the intention of Nussbaum's capabilities approach, as applied to the issue of disability, as well as some that stick closer to Rawls's two principles. These alternative sets of principles will be the "menu options" faced by the parties in the ICS. Once these are on the table, the next question will be, for each alternative: What would be the interpretation of the ICS that would lead the parties to prefer *these* principles? Finally, we may then examine which of these interpretations of the ICS seems most reasonable as a basis for choosing principles of justice that extend to those with serious disabilities. By proceeding in this way, my hope is we may gain some analytic insight on these difficult issues. Of course, this is only one possible way of comparing alternative principles of justice regarding disability, but it will prove a useful one. Before I can get to the constructive part of my argument, however, I must first address an apparently fundamental obstacle to extending the Rawlsian framework to address the severely disabled, namely the centrality, in his conception of justice, of the ideal of reciprocity.

Distributive justice guided by the ideal of reciprocity

The "fundamental organizing idea" that Rawls works up into a full-blown conception of social justice is the idea of fair cooperation among free and equal citizens (*PL* 15). However one interprets this idea, it is clear that some of the severely disabled – especially those with severe mental disabilities – are not capable of cooperating as free and equal citizens. Yet the ability so to cooperate seems essential for Rawls's most fundamental idea of distributive justice to apply, namely the idea of reciprocal benefit. "Fair terms of cooperation," he writes, "articulate an idea of reciprocity and mutuality: all who cooperate must benefit, or share in common burdens, in some appropriate fashion judged by a suitable benchmark of comparison" (*PL* 300). To address the claims of the severely disabled within the category of justice, some adjustment to the basic orienting ideas is clearly needed. Nussbaum makes important modifications to the guiding ideas of reciprocity, inviolability, and human dignity – shifting to an Aristotelian interpretation from a Kantian one – with the result that, she believes, the whole idea of a Rawlsian initial choice situation is rendered inapt (176–7). Here, my approach will instead involve a reassessment of the role of reciprocity in Rawls's arguments.

One possible response to the fact that the severely disabled cannot be reciprocally cooperating citizens would be to limit the discussion to those whom Rawls describes as "above the line." In *Political Liberalism*, Rawls draws the line in question in a brief statement of how he might address the issue of disability. He distinguishes four types of variation, and, with regard to each, asks "whether a variation places people above or below the line: that is, whether it leaves them with more or less than the minimum essential capabilities required to be a normal cooperating member of society" (*PL* 183). As to "moral and intellectual capacities and skills," he takes it that his simplifying assumption that all are fully cooperating members of society entails that the only variations range "above the line." Regarding "physical capacities and skills," he considers only the case of those who temporarily fall below the line: these people we might realistically try to restore to cooperative membership in society. One might build on Rawls's discussion by similarly confining the discussion to those whose disabilities leave them "above the line" or with the possibility of getting back above it. The term "the severely disabled," as I shall use it, refers to those permanently below the line.

There are three reasons, however, not to confine our inquiry in this way. Two of them emerge directly from Nussbaum's reasons against postponing the general issue of disability. There is the fact that capabilities vary along a continuum, making any attempt at line-drawing apt to be arbitrary. Further, the moral reasons we have to avoid drawing a dichotomy between the disabled and the non-disabled also cast this talk of persons being "above or below the line" under a pall of suspicion. But the most decisive reason not to limit ourselves to those "above the line" arises from the dialectic between Rawls and Nussbaum. Nussbaum's challenge to Rawls is that his sort of social-contract theory cannot adequately address the issues of justice posed by severe disabilities.[5] That is the challenge that I aim here to address, not duck.

A theory of justice that addresses those with all levels of disability clearly cannot literally demand reciprocal contributions from all persons. Will loosening the commitment to reciprocity so as to widen the scope of the Rawlsian theory destroy its intuitive appeal? This is an eminently disputable question. I am inclined to think that it will not: here I can only sketch my reasons. Consider, to begin with, the play that already exists in Rawls's formulations of the ideal of reciprocity, such as the statement already quoted at the outset of this section: "Fair terms of cooperation articulate an idea of reciprocity and mutuality: all who cooperate must benefit, or share in common burdens, in some appropriate fashion judged by a suitable benchmark of comparison." My goal will be to widen the scope of the theory without literally disagreeing with this statement.[6] Note, first, that it does not say that *only* those who cooperate may benefit. More broadly, the aim of the extended theory can be to find terms of cooperation that articulate a mode of reciprocity and mutuality that is *generally*, albeit not universally, applicable in society. Because Rawls's is a theory directed at the basic structure of society rather than at each individual or at each transaction, this loosened structural interpretation of social cooperation, which forbears from demanding universal participation, marks no great departure from his view.

I am also persuaded that Rawls's arguments making use of the device of the OP do not essentially depend on any reciprocity premise. This matter is again controversial. It is connected with the question of the ways in which Rawls's is and is not a social-contract view. Again, I cannot

---

[5] Nussbaum also draws a line, namely between individuals genetically human – such as those in a persistent vegetative state – whose life is "just not a human life at all" (Nussbaum, *Frontiers*, 181) and those who are living a human life. The "severely disabled" on whom my chapter focuses most of its attention are those – and there are many – who are above Nussbaum's line but below Rawls's. I am grateful to Rainer Forst for discussion of this issue.

[6] There are doubtless other statements of Rawls's about reciprocity that are less amenable to the line I take. One is the following characterization of the aim of "property-owning democracy," a regime that Rawls never claims is required by justice, but to which he is obviously drawn: "the aim is to realize in the basic institutions the idea of society as a fair system of cooperation between citizens regarded as free and equal. To do this, those institutions must, from the outset, put in the hand of citizens generally, and not only of a few, sufficient productive means for them to be fully cooperating members of society on a footing of equality" [Rawls, *Restatement*, 140]. Here, plainly, Rawls is again abstracting from the possibility that some persons are sufficiently disabled that they will remain unable to be fully cooperating members of society no matter how many "productive means" they have. I thank Peter Niesen for discussion of this point.

go over the issues in detail here. Jean Hampton carefully reconstructed Rawls's arguments from the OP with this question in mind, concluding that considerations of reciprocity were not playing an essential role.[7] Her arguments do not convince me that Rawls's is not a social-contract theory – though I here simply concentrate on Rawls's device of an ICS in which principles are to be chosen, and leave for another day the question of what it takes to qualify some use of that device as a social-contract theory. Hampton's arguments *do* convince me, however, that an appeal to the idea of reciprocity is not essential to Rawls's argument.[8] To be sure, mention of reciprocity remains quite prominent in Rawls's writings, but many of the passages use the term to characterize the *content* of the principles of Justice as Fairness, Rawls's preferred view, not to make arguments for that view. The relatively few passages in the text treating reciprocity as a premise of the argument for those principles I would regard as vestigial survivals of a very early version of his argument, as articulated in "Justice as Reciprocity" (*CP* 190–224). This paper, although published only in 1971, was written in 1960, so at a time previous to Rawls's adoption of the veil of ignorance, which fundamentally changed his characterization of the ICS (*CP* x). The incorporation of the veil of ignorance, Hampton suggested, fundamentally alters the argument, radically reducing its reliance on reciprocity.

Qualifying reciprocity in the way made inevitable by including the seriously disabled among the set of persons to whom the principles apply raises a still deeper issue, which concerns the reasons for thinking of the claims of the disabled as raising issues of justice. If someone is so disabled as to be incapable of social cooperation, why do we owe that person any of the fruits of social cooperation as a matter of justice? Why should we not instead think of our duties toward him or her as duties of charity? To this question, Nussbaum's alternative view presents a compelling answer, which appeals to her more Aristotelian conception of the idea of human dignity, which, unlike Rawls's more Kantian conception, is not built around the higher-order powers of reasonableness and rationality, capacities that the severely disabled lack (that is what

---

[7] Jean Hampton, "Contracts and Choices: Does Rawls Have a Social Contract Theory?" *Journal of Philosophy* 77 (1980): 315–38.

[8] Samuel Freeman, "Reason and Agreement in Social Contract Views," *Philosophy & Public Affairs* 19 (1990): 145–46, effectively rebuts Hampton's claim that the distinctness of the parties plays no role in Rawls's argument. That they are distinct – minimally, as representatives of distinct persons – is necessary, Freeman argues, to making sense of Rawls's appeal to the "strains of commitment" (Rawls, *A Theory of Justice*, 153–54) and, more generally, of his social-contract idea. These points, about which I take it that Freeman is correct, do not undercut Hampton's further claim that the normative demand for reciprocity plays no role in the mature argument from the OP.

keeps them "below the line"). While Nussbaum may be right about the implications for the severely disabled of these two conceptions of human dignity, we should note that their claims of justice need not hinge on the idea of dignity. The fundamental moral reasons why social justice applies to those of all levels of disability might instead be articulated in terms of the ideals of empathy, impartiality, and equality – some of the moral notions that, as we have seen, find expression in the OP. That principles applicable to those of all levels of disability are principles of *justice* might follow, not from the nature of their grounds but from their being – like all of the principles discussed here – constitutional principles that direct and limit the collective use of force.[9]

Someone approaching social-contract theory from a more Hobbesian angle might be puzzled by this.[10] Why would self-interested contractors agree to extend principles of justice to those of all levels of disability? Why would they enter into the social contract at all if it does not offer the prospect of reciprocal benefit? Within Rawlsian social-contract theory, however, these questions are ill formed. The *parties* are not asked whether they wish to enter society, nor are they asked to compare the merits of society to that of a "state of nature." (*We* can think about the point of justice, and in so doing may arrive, like Rawls, at the Humean characterization that social justice addresses circumstances of moderate scarcity and diverse belief, and we can stipulate that the parties keep these circumstances in mind, but that is another matter.) What corresponds to the state of nature in Rawls's theory, he says, is the Original Position itself (*TJ* 11), which is not an arena in which lives are lived. The task given to the parties, accordingly, is not to decide whether to "enter" society but to choose principles of justice *for* society. Whether those of all levels of disability are to be addressed by the principles is, similarly, not a choice for the parties to make; rather, it is settled by the theorist, who either accepts or rejects a simplifying assumption like Rawls's.

In the remainder of this chapter, then, I will develop variants of the OP that seem called for by various reasonable approaches to social justice for those of all levels of disability. In so doing, I will not be giving up on the ideal of reciprocity, but neither will I be deploying it as rigidly as would someone who thinks the ideal of reciprocity is irrelevant to those who cannot cooperate. The question in the case of each variant ICS will be: What principles covering those of all levels of disability would be chosen by someone guided by the ideal of fair social cooperation, taken

---

[9] I am grateful to Paul Guyer for discussion of this issue.
[10] Here I am grateful for discussion with Claire Finkelstein and her students.

as a regulative ideal? Each variant of the OP that I will consider will retain the elements that suit it as an heuristic for answering this question. Most importantly, each will extend the veil of ignorance by dropping the assumption that no one is disabled. In order now to begin to generate these variously interpreted initial choice situations, I must first set out some alternative principles to be considered therein.

Alternative principles of justice extended to cover disability

In generating alternative principles of justice applicable to the more and the less disabled, I make no effort to be original. Instead, I use as my guides Rawls's two principles, on the one hand, and Nussbaum's capabilities approach (CA), on the other. Rawls's principles, in fact, I will take over verbatim, though extending them to cover the disabled obviously alters their practical import. In Nussbaum's case, I will concentrate on her principle of minimum justice, which has been at the core of her capabilities approach. In so doing, I will be largely ignoring some of her most recent thoughts about the inequalities that may persist once minimum justice is assured (291–5). Especially once these further thoughts are factored in, her principles actually come to resemble Rawls's fairly closely (179). In addition to Rawls's principles of basic justice and Nussbaum's principle of minimum justice, attractive combined views are possible – indeed, one was once off-handedly suggested by Rawls. Another intermediate possibility may be defined that is closer to Nussbaum's view.

Before spelling out any of these alternatives, I need to make clear what the range of problems is to which they are addressed. Nussbaum's work has focused our critical attention on whether Rawls's view can be extended to address issues of justice pertaining to disability. This is not the only question of extension that we must face here, however, for the core of Nussbaum's view is also expressly put forward as a partial theory of justice, not a complete one. In order to bring the two views fairly into contact, I need to adjust each of them so that they address the same subject matter. As each of them presents their views, they are addressed to somewhat different questions. Oversimplifying to telegraph the contrast: Rawls's theory addresses *basic* justice, whereas the part of Nussbaum's theory to be discussed here addresses *minimum* justice. To explain: Rawls's aim is to generate principles to govern the basic structure of society (*TJ* sec. 2), establishing just parameters for its "constitutional essentials" (*CP* 425, 575n.). Nussbaum does not limit her concern to constitutional essentials, and instead defends a principle of minimum justice that must be satisfied by a society if it is to count as "decent" (84). The central principle of justice she defends is the following:

(CA): Governments have responsibility, as a matter of justice, to see to it that each citizen reaches a threshold level of capability in each of the ten basic types of human capability, as listed by the theory. (70–71)[11]

This principle, as she explicitly notes, does not exhaust the requirements of justice, not even of distributive justice, but it does set a minimum below which governments must not fall.

In order to compare their sets of principles, I will maintain Rawls's focus on the basic structure, but insist that minimum justice also be addressed. Defining the subject matter for the principles this way truncates the intended scope of Nussbaum's principle, for she apparently intends it to govern legislation and policy as well as the constitutional essentials (155). I do not believe this makes for an unfair comparison, however, as she plainly means her principle to govern the constitutional essentials as well. She presents (CA) as characterizing a paramount responsibility of governments, one that ought to be enshrined in the constitution of every nation. Rawls, for his part, as we shall see, seems to have neglected the issue of minimum justice in framing his two principles.[12] Accordingly, we shall have to see whether they can be supplemented so as to address minimum justice adequately, or whether, instead, Nussbaum's capabilities approach generates a better overall alternative, once issues of minimum justice are taken into account. For the purposes of this chapter, then, the aspect of justice to which the principles of justice under discussion are addressed is the basic structure of society, including any constitutional essentials, and including any needed provisions of minimum justice.

Rawls's reasons for "postponing" issues pertaining to disability presuppose that there is at least one other stage at which principles of justice are to be elaborated and selected, beyond the OP. In fact, he assumes, and stipulates that the parties assume, that there are three more stages: constitutional, legislative, and judicial. Section 31 of *A Theory of Justice* describes a "four-stage sequence," offered as "a schema for sorting out the complications that must be faced" (*TJ* 172). These stages remain

---

[11] One of the great strengths of Nussbaum's view is its comprehensive list of central human capabilities; see Martha C. Nussbaum, *Women and Human Development* (Cambridge University Press, 2000). I will discuss some of the details of this list, below. At this initial level, however, we may abstract from their content.

[12] As Leif Wenar has pointed out to me, one might look beyond Rawls's two principles to his account of political legitimacy, as spelled out in *Political Liberalism*, for Rawls's account of minimum justice.

hypothetical or virtual, and hence idealized. Each is governed by the preceding stage. Importantly, the veil of ignorance persists until the final stage, being progressively lifted. In the OP proper, the veil blocks all particular information from the parties, including not only information about the particular persons they represent (their talents, social position, or conception of the good) but also information about their society ("its natural circumstances and resources, its level of economic advance and political culture, and so on" (*TJ* 172–3). The parties to the second stage, the virtual constitutional convention, still do not know the particulars about the persons they represent, but they *do* know the pertinent facts about their society. In the third stage, the virtual legislative stage, the participants know all this and a little bit more. This stipulated informational difference between the OP and the next two stages of the four-stage sequence stands behind Rawls's proposal to postpone questions about justice and disability. What he says is that "variations [in physical capacities and skills] that put some citizens below the [level of capabilities required to be a normal cooperating member of society] can be dealt with ... at the legislative stage when the prevalence and kinds of these misfortunes are known and the costs of treating them can be ascertained and balanced along with total government expenditure" (*PL* 184). This is a credible reason for allocating these issues to the legislative stage, for there is no doubt that a just response to the issue of disability will make considerable demands on the public treasury. In addressing those demands, therefore, one might well want to know the natural circumstances of the society in question, including its level of development. Nonetheless, as we saw at the outset, there are strong reasons not to delegate the matter to a virtual legislature. Accordingly, we will override Rawls on the point. I will, however, retain the full veil of ignorance in each interpretation of the ICS that I consider. The upshot, then, is that the parties are ignorant of the level of disability of the persons they represent. In making this move, we must remain mindful of the fact that this deprives the parties of much information that might be relevant to whether it is feasible or appropriate to undertake certain highly costly commitments. Working within this restriction puts a limit on the complexity and the definiteness of the principles that the parties would find attractive.

To accommodate this focus on the basic structure and the parties' ignorance about their own society, we need to reframe Nussbaum's principle slightly. Governments operate legislatively or via non-legislative policy decisions, and *within* a constitution. The basic structure, or constitutional essentials, of a society is not something under the ordinary control of a government. As Rawls sees things, at least, once a just basic structure has been assured by a permanent constitution, the government ought presumably to leave the constitution alone in going about its business. Accordingly, the following is a counterpart to Nussbaum's principle (CA), adjusted so as to apply to the basic structure and not to other matters:

Basic capabilities approach (CAB): The basic institutions of society are to be arranged so as to assure, so far as reasonably possible, that each citizen reaches a threshold level of capability in each of the ten basic types of human capability.

The hedge embodied in the clause about what is "reasonably possible," in this principle, seems the price we have to pay, within Rawls's contractarian scheme, for refusing to postpone issues about disability to the legislative stage in which the parties know the level of resources of the society in which the persons they represent reside. Of course, principles by themselves cannot assure any such thing. In stating the principle this way, we accordingly must continue to assume or imagine that this principle will control a four-stage sequence in a well-ordered society and accordingly will be duly implemented via constitutional and legislative provisions that work it out for each particular society. Although (CAB) is thus explicitly hedged in a way that (CA) is not, no doubt Nussbaum intends (CA) to be applied in ways that similarly respect the limits of what is reasonably possible.

In order fairly to compare alternative principles of justice for the basic structure, Rawls invokes the idea of a "well-ordered society." This idealizing stipulation helps provide a level playing field for comparing alternative principles. Ultimately, what the persons for whom the parties are "trustees" care about is how their lives go and how society works.[13] Principles shape lives only indirectly – and if the principles are ignored, then their effect will be negligible. In comparing principles from a contractarian point of view, accordingly, there is a great danger that one will end up comparing one's own principles, as well implemented, with one's rival's principles, as poorly implemented. Rawls invokes the idea of a "well-ordered society" in part in order to avoid stacking the deck in this kind of way. It helps hold constant the degree to which the alternative principles being considered by the parties are in force in the hypothetical society guided by them. The full idea of the well-ordered society is highly complex, at one point summarized by Rawls in terms of twelve propositions (*CP* 233–5). The ones of main interest to us here are the first two, which I modify in order to account for the existence of the severely disabled:

---

[13] See Rawls, *Political Liberalism*, 75: "We stipulate that the parties evaluate the available principles by estimating how well they secure the primary goods essential to realize the higher-order interests of the person for whom each acts as a trustee." See also *ibid.*, p. 106.

1. Insofar as anyone accepts any principles of justice, everyone accepts the same principles (the same conception) of justice, and this fact is generally known.
2. Basic social institutions and their arrangement into one scheme (the basic structure of society) satisfy, and are with reason generally believed to satisfy, these principles.

These two assumptions are essential to the choice faced by Rawls's parties, for in choosing principles, their task is, by stipulation, to compare the well-ordered society that would result under one set of principles with the well-ordered society that would result under another set. In keeping with Rawls's later attempt to take more seriously the plurality of religious and moral doctrines prevalent in every modern society, one may need to add an explanatory gloss to point (1), noting that the conception of political justice may be shared in an overlapping consensus that nests it within the citizens' various comprehensive views, but I do not think it needs to be dropped.[14] In each version of the ICS I will consider, I will retain this layer, at least, of the well-ordered society stipulation.

With these preliminaries in place, I can now go on to state the other sets of principles I will consider as rivals to the modified Nussbaum principle, (CAB). To begin with, there are Rawls's own principles, the two principles of Justice as Fairness (JF). Here they are as stated in *PL* (5–6):

(JF)

1. Each person has an equal claim to a fully adequate scheme of equal basic rights and liberties, which scheme is compatible with the same scheme for all; and in this scheme the equal political liberties, and only those liberties, are to be guaranteed their fair value [the "First Principle"].
2. Social and economic inequalities are to satisfy two conditions:
   (a) First, they are to be attached to positions and offices open to all under conditions of fair equality of opportunity [the "equal opportunity" principle].
   (b) Second, they are to be to the greatest benefit of the least advantaged members of society [the "difference principle"].

---

[14] In Rawls, *Political Liberalism*, xlii, Rawls writes that his assumptions in *A Theory of Justice* included the premise "that in the well-ordered society of justice as fairness, citizens hold the same comprehensive doctrine," an approach he later came to believe was inconsistent with recognizing the "fact of reasonable pluralism" (*ibid.*, 36). I take it, though, that it is not the first proposition from the list in the "Reply to Alexander and Musgrave" (the assumption that all are known to accept the same principles of justice) that entails this problematic assumption, but rather the ones he there lists as (4)–(6), which invoke the Kantian ideal of citizens as free and equal: Rawls, *Collected Papers*, 233.

Priority rule (*TJ* 266): these principles and conditions are to be ranked in lexical order, with highest priority to the First Principle, then the equal opportunity principle, and finally the difference principle.

Just two remarks about how we should understand (JF) in the present context. First, since our aim is to consider principles that address the more as well as the less disabled, we will assume that (JF) has such a range of application. Obviously, this will affect the way in which we interpret such clauses as "open to all" in the equal opportunity principle and "least advantaged" in the difference principle. Second, in characterizing the idea of "a fully adequate scheme of equal basic rights and liberties," Rawls takes it that we may draw up the list of the relevant basic rights and liberties by reference to historically accepted understandings and by reference to the political conception of the person, including the idea of the two highest-order interests (*PL* 293). So as not to short-circuit the current discussion, however, let us assume that whatever is involved in such a "fully adequate scheme," it does not by definition involve a fully adequate resolution of the demands on justice made by disability. Let us take it, instead, to be limited to the kinds of rights and liberties actually enshrined, for instance, in the US Bill of Rights.

As I have mentioned, Nussbaum is more focused than is Rawls on the question of minimum justice. At one place in *Political Liberalism*, however, Rawls does advert to the question, if only for ulterior reasons. Although he does not develop the point, he does note that "important aspects of the principles are left out in the brief statement" of them which I have just quoted. "In particular," he writes,

the first principle covering the equal basic rights and liberties may easily be preceded by a lexically prior principle requiring that citizens' basic needs be met, at least insofar as their being met is necessary for citizens to understand and to be able fruitfully to exercise those rights and liberties. Certainly any such principle must be assumed in applying the first principle. (*PL* 7)[15]

I will use this off-handed remark of Rawls's as the basis for generating two alternatives that are, in an obvious way, intermediate between (CAB) and (JF). What will distinguish these two intermediate alternatives is the

---

[15] Some explanation of the cryptic assertion of the final sentence in the quote appears in Rawls, *Restatement*, 44 n.7: the principles "may be preceded by a lexically prior principle requiring that basic needs be met, at least insofar as their being met is a necessary condition for citizens to understand and to be able fruitfully to exercise their basic rights and liberties." Given this remark, it is fair to say that the two intermediate alternatives shortly to be defined in the text, (NPG) and (NC), probably go beyond what Rawls had in mind.

way in which they interpret the idea of basic needs. One will stick closer to Rawls's own interpretation of (JF), and employ his idea of primary goods to state the lexically prior principle pertaining to basic needs. The other will instead employ Nussbaum's notion of capabilities to interpret the idea of basic needs.

In order to develop an idea of basic needs based on Rawls's account of the primary goods, should we think in terms of all of them, or only some? They are, again: rights, liberties, opportunities, income, wealth, and the social basis of self-respect. Since (JF) has a top-priority principle devoted to the basic rights and liberties, and we are now considering modifying (JF) by adding a principle addressed to needs, it makes sense to concentrate on the remaining four types of primary good: opportunities, income, wealth, and self-respect. Accordingly, the first intermediate possibility we will consider is the following:

(NPG):

1. The basic institutions of society are to be arranged so that, so far as reasonably possible, each citizen is assured a decent minimum of opportunity, income, wealth, and self-respect.
2. [The First Principle: see above.]
3. [The equal opportunity principle: see above.]
4. [The difference principle: see above.]

Priority rule: these principles are lexically ranked in the order stated.

The second intermediate alternative has the same structure as (NPG) but substitutes a different interpretation of basic needs that is drawn from Nussbaum's view. Indeed, it represents one possible way of attempting to combine her view with Rawls's:

(NC):

1. The basic institutions of society are to be arranged so as to assure, so far as reasonably possible, that each citizen reaches a threshold level of capability in each of the ten basic types of human capability.
2. [The First Principle: see above.]
3. [The equal opportunity principle: see above.]
4. [The difference principle: see above.]

Priority rule: these principles are lexically ranked in the order stated.

Given Nussbaum's stress on the fact that her view is put forward as a partial theory of justice focused on the issues of minimum justice, it is not even clear that she would prefer (CAB) to (NC). For his part, Rawls might find (NC) more congenial than we would expect. When he recommends postponing issues pertaining to justice and disability, he notes that, were he to address such issues, he would "follow the general idea of

the much further worked out view of Norman Daniels" (*PL* 184 n.).
Central to Daniels's approach is the suggestion that by "needs" we
understand the prerequisites of achieving or maintaining "species-typical
functioning."[16] Something like this Aristotelian idea also underlies Nussbaum's conception of the basic human capabilities: each of them is
defined as a capability to engage in a fundamental mode of species-
typical functioning. Having such a capability is obviously *one* crucial kind
of prerequisite to engaging in the functioning.[17] To be sure, Nussbaum's
characterization of the capabilities is moralized, all the way down, in a
way that Daniels's more naturalistic account is not. Nussbaum has also,
to my knowledge, developed these Aristotelian ideas of capability and
functioning more fully than has Daniels. Even so, it is striking to find
Rawls draws to Daniels's view when he turned his attention, however
fleetingly, to the idea of basic needs.

Obviously, we might continue to generate alternatives to consider.
One might, for instance, generate variants of the lower-priority difference principle that explicitly defined the least-advantaged by reference
to the ten basic capabilities rather than by reference to the primary
goods of income and wealth – which are the primary goods, apart from
self-respect, that are not addressed by higher-priority principles. This
matter of how the least advantaged are defined is certainly a central
point of Nussbaum's critique of Rawls (166–8).[18] Given the limited
space I have available, however, I have thought it best to concentrate on
the differences at the level of the highest-priority principles. Another
possibility that would be worth considering would be to adopt Norman
Daniels's suggestion that health-care needs might be addressed by
means of an expanded version of the equal opportunity principle.[19]

---

[16] Norman Daniels, "Health Care Needs and Distributive Justice," *Philosophy and Public Affairs* 10 (1981): 153; Norman Daniels, *Just Health Care* (Cambridge University Press, 1985), 28.

[17] In Henry S. Richardson, "Some Limitations of Nussbaum's Capabilities," *Quinnipiac Law Review* 19 (2000): 309–32, I argue that, given that Nussbaum's focus on the capabilities derives from a theory of the human good that identifies living a good life with *functioning* in certain ways, she actually ought not entirely shift over from the language of functioning to that of capability when developing a social and political theory. The hybrid view, (NC), offers an interesting perspective on this issue, for Nussbaum's principal reason for insisting on talking about capabilities rather than functionings is to secure the place of freedom. If, however, the capabilities-minimum principle were part of a broader political view that, like (NC), included an independent, high-priority principle protecting the equal basic liberties, it would become less worrisome to give the functionings a place in the theory.

[18] Although the difference principle as stated in (JF) is non-committal as to the basis of indexing expectations, I will presume that Rawls's indexing in terms of income and wealth is retained.

[19] Daniels, *Just Health Care*.

Daniels's case for focusing specially on health centers on the normative importance of addressing people's needs for opportunities for species-typical functioning. In order to accommodate this concern within Rawls's framework, he suggests amending the equal opportunity principle to account for this. In my own view, however, once the capabilities principles are on the table – whether in the form of (CAB) or of (NC) – these provide an attractive, alternative way of taking account of opportunities for species-typical function. Indeed, that is how the basic capabilities are cast, at least in Nussbaum's version of the capabilities approach. Further, to address such needs via a guarantee of some kind of basic minimum is to take them seriously as *needs* in a way that assimilating them to the other conditions of fair competition does not.

While there is a lot more to be said about the merits of Daniels's proposal, for present purposes I will restrict the discussion to the following four alternatives: Nussbaum's view as adapted to basic justice (CAB), and Rawls's principles by themselves (JF), as combined with a highest-order basic-needs principle defined in terms of the primary goods (NPG), or as combined with Nussbaum's principle (NC). I now turn to considering how to vary the interpretation of the ICS so as to favor each of these alternatives.

Versions of the initial choice situation corresponding to the alternative principles

In order sensibly to discuss varying the interpretation of the ICS, we need to know what is being kept constant. I have mentioned a number of general features of Rawls's OP. Before proceeding to develop alternative interpretations of the ICS that support the different sets of principles we have before us, let me recapitulate the general features of the initial choice situations that I will assume in each case, as holding in common among all these different interpretations. I begin with ten stipulations that also apply to Rawls's OP. The first seven of these, to which I have already alluded, are the following:

(a) *Purely hypothetical:* each ICS is to be viewed as a hypothetical perspective, a "device of construction" for analytically approaching the articulation of principles of justice.
(b) *Defined parties:* as entities that are elements of a theoretically defined hypothetical situation, the parties in each ICS are defined, in each case, stipulatively. They may or may not resemble actual human beings.

(c) *Choice from a menu of principles:* the parties are presented with a small, finite list of possible sets of principles among which to choose; for present purposes, they will be, in each case, the four alternatives set out in the previous section: CAB, JF, NPG, and NC.

(d) *The basic structure as subject:* The parties are to choose principles intended to govern the basic structure of society, including its constitutional essentials.

(e) *Well-ordered societies as a device of comparison:* in comparing the alternative sets of principles, the parties are to consider how each would work out in a well-ordered society in which those principles form the basis of the publicly accepted conception of justice.

(f) *The veil of ignorance:* the parties know all general facts about human society, but they know no particular facts either about the persons they represent or about the society those persons inhabit.

(g) *The four-stage sequence:* the parties are to assume that the principles they select are to be implemented via a constitution and legislative provisions that are settled upon under the idealized conditions (including a gradually lifting veil of ignorance) described by Rawls.

These first seven stipulations settle the main shape and task of a Rawlsian ICS.

Because stipulation (f), the veil of ignorance, marks such a radical difference between the defined parties and actual persons, three further stipulations are needed that, again, all my versions of the ICS share with the OP. This radical difference implies that no party to an ICS could be an actual person and no actual person could be a party to an ICS. What relationship holds, then, between the parties and the persons on whose behalf they choose? Adopting Rawls's language, cited above, we stipulate the following answer to this question:

(h) *The parties as trustees:* the parties choose as trustees on behalf of the (unknown) persons they represent (consider *PL* 76, 106).

Spelling out this point is crucial to applying the ICS to issues of justice pertaining to the severely disabled.

The severely mentally disabled, of course, cannot reason about principles of justice, but *no* human being can either be wholly ignorant of particular facts or totally informed about all general facts about the workings of society. Again, no actual person could be a party to an ICS; rather, these are theoretically designed entities which will, by stipulation, reason in a certain way. Since the veil of ignorance blocks the parties knowing which person they represent, this means that the theory must supply the parties with a motivation or a conception of the good.

In fact, I will use different motivational assumptions to generate the three variant interpretations of the ICS that I will consider. Each of them will, however, retain the following Rawlsian stipulation about the parties' motivational structure:

(i) *Mutually disinterested rationality:* each party cares only about, and rationally promotes, the goods attained, achieved, or enjoyed by the person it represents: each pursues those goods in a way wholly uncomplicated by altruism, self-abnegation, envy, or spite.

Finally, we should add a tenth Rawlsian stipulation, which is necessary because the veil otherwise bars the parties from knowing anything about the particular society to which the principles are to apply. This is the stipulation that the parties may at least assume that the society is characterized by the "circumstances of justice," as follows:

(j) *The circumstances of justice:* the parties are to assume that the society to which the principles are to apply is characterized by (a) moderate scarcity, (b) a permanent, reasonable pluralism of religious and ethical conceptions, and (c) "a more or less self-sufficient scheme of social cooperation for mutual good."[20]

Note that there are two sides to the final clause's simplification: one is the postponement of difficult issues of global justice – another topic that Nussbaum takes on – but another is the abstraction, in the domestic case, from the ways in which foreign interference and domination can mess up a society's basic structure. The parties are to assume that there are no excuses for what would otherwise count as injustice that flow from dependence on other, potentially unjust, societies. Hence, while on the one hand this means that any principles generated will not be directly applicable to a nation such as Bolivia, which is heavily dependent on its exports of natural gas, it also means, on the other hand, that the parties are not in a position to adopt compromise principles that accept this kind of dependence on other nations as a given.

---

[20] These three clauses correspond to the three propositions that, according to Rawls, *Collected Papers*, 235 ["Reply to Alexander and Musgrave"], "characterize the circumstances of justice." The final one is quoted from *ibid.*, p. 234. He there makes no mention of the assumption, included in the characterization of the circumstances of justice in *A Theory of Justice*, that persons in the society "are roughly similar in physical and mental powers; or at any rate, their capacities are comparable in that no one among them can dominate the rest" (*TJ* 109–10). Since, as Nussbaum notes in *Frontiers* (147), this additional assumption would prevent the principles from applying to the more disabled, our purposes here require that we leave it out, in any case. In the context of this discussion of disability, we must of course read "mutual good" loosely, just as we read "reciprocity" loosely.

To these ten Rawlsian stipulations, we need to add three more that reflect our aim to extend the principles of justice to cover the more and the less disabled. The first, and most basic, is the following:

(k) *The inclusion of those with all levels of disability:* the parties are to assume that the persons they represent include persons of all levels of ability and disability, in such proportions as general knowledge about humans and human society would indicate.

Together with (f), the veil, stipulation (k) implies that each of the parties is ignorant about the level of disability of the person on whose behalf it is to choose. (Indeed, the veil would imply this in any case were the theorist not to add a stipulation like Rawls's that assumes away the existence of the disabled.) In addition, we should assume that the parties recognize each of the four fundamental reasons, noted at the outset of this chapter, for not simply postponing issues about disability. The first three of these, which are presumably special cases of the general facts otherwise already assumed to be known by the parties, we may lump together:

(l) *The fundamental facts regarding disability:* the parties are to assume that disability is a pervasive and unavoidable feature of human life; that care-giving work is an essential feature of human life; and that all humans have capabilities that are defective in some regard, there being a continuum of disability.

Finally, the remaining reason against postponement was a moral conclusion:

(m) *The wrongness of dichotomous treatment:* the parties are to assume that it would be wrong for principles of basic justice to invoke a simple dichotomy between "the disabled" and "the non-disabled."

This final stipulation will tend to rule out any alternatives that address one set of principles to the disabled and another to the non-disabled. Note that none of the four alternatives we are looking at here does that.

With the three disability-related stipulations in place, it seems unlikely that any version of the ICS that included these stipulations would end up supporting any counterpart of the four alternatives considered here that left out or assumed away serious disabilities. Looking at the matter from the other direction, it is plain that adding these stipulations to each ICS will radically affect the interpretation of each of the principles. In particular, (JF), as stated above, is verbally identical to Rawls's two principles of justice. If (JF) were adopted in an ICS featuring stipulations *(k)–(m)*, however, that would mean that these principles are to be applied to humans of all ranges of disability. Since providing equal opportunity for the more disabled is relatively difficult, and since the more disabled are likely to be among the least advantaged members of society, this interpretive shift has radical practical implications. By subtracting the Rawlsian idealization that had served to postpone the issue, adding in these three stipulations generates principles more sweeping in their practical import.

These thirteen stipulations *(a)–(m)* define the common ground among the different interpretations of the ICS to be explored here. With four alternative sets of principles extending justice to all levels of disability, there are in principle six pairwise comparisons to consider. I cannot in an exhaustive way determine which set would come out on top under which variant of the ICS. Instead, I will group the sets of principles in terms of their most salient differences in order to reduce our problem to looking at three fundamental comparisons, as follows:[21]

> *First Fundamental Comparison:* the simple Rawlsian approach (JF) as compared to the mixed conceptions (either NPG or NC).
> *Second Fundamental Comparison:* the simple Nussbaumian approach (CAB) as compared to the mixed conceptions (either NPG or NC).
> *Third Fundamental Comparison:* the mixed conception interpreting needs in terms of primary goods (NPG) as compared to the mixed conception interpreting needs in terms of capabilities (NC).

In each case, my aim will be to distinguish interpretations of the ICS that support one of these sets of principles over the other. In each case, given the thirteen stipulated features of the ICS that will remain constant, the main variable we have to work with is the conception of the good defined into the parties.

The First Fundamental Comparison: the simple Rawlsian view vs. mixed views

The mixed conceptions add to (JF) a highest-order principle addressed to basic needs. What motivational stipulation about the parties would lead them to prefer (JF) to either mixed conception? In addressing this question, we need to keep in mind that (JF) has been effectively radicalized by extending its application to people of all ranges of disability. Since

---

[21] This procedure imitates Rawls's; but whereas his fundamental comparisons all employ the same interpretation of the ICS, namely the OP, in our case we are searching for plausible interpretations of the ICS that would support a given set of principles over the relevant rivals.

we may safely assume that the least advantaged in any society will be people who are severely disabled, this means that the difference principle, so applied, permits inequalities only if they raise the expectations of the severely disabled. We have not modified Rawls's indexing of expectations, however: we leave in place his suggestion that, for the purposes of the lower-priority difference principle, expectations are to be indexed on the basis of income and wealth.[22] Accordingly, while the practical implications of this broader implication are fairly radical, they are not so radical as a principle that would require maximizing the *capabilities* of the least advantaged. The latter possibility, as I have mentioned, I set aside for present purposes. So (JF)'s difference principle means maximizing the expected income and wealth, over a complete life, of the severely disabled. Since the severely disabled are presumably not earning an income, we are probably talking about maximizing transfer payments to them – quite a generous proposal. But because the parties, by virtue of the veil, do not know the level of development of their society, they cannot be sure what the resulting minimum income level would achieve in terms of allowing a severely disabled person to function.

Another point to consider is the interpretation of self-respect, now that we have broadened the problem to include people of all disability levels. Rawls treats the primary good of "the social basis of self-respect" – or of self-respect, insofar as it is affected by social arrangements – in a way that is strongly colored by his simplifying assumption that every person is a "fully cooperating member of society." The sort of socially affected self-respect on which he focuses we might call *the self-respect of the equal citizen*. For instance, in explaining one reason why "the well-ordered society of [or corresponding to] justice as fairness is a good," he revealingly glosses "mutual self-respect":

A second reason political society [within this well-ordered society] is a good for citizens is that it secures for them the good of justice and the social bases of self-respect. Thus, in securing the equal rights and liberties, fair equality of opportunity, and the like, political society guarantees the essentials of persons' public recognition as free and equal citizens. (*PL* 202–3)

Plainly enough, the self-respect of the equal citizen is not available to those with severe mental disabilities. Indeed, in another passage explaining the importance of self-respect, Rawls invokes his simplifying assumption:

[22] Indexing overall primary-good expectations on the basis solely of income and wealth is, of course, less plausible when we expand our attention to include people of all levels of disability. Cf. Rawls, *Political Liberalism*, 180 n.8 on the importance of his simplifying assumptions, more generally, to defending this mode of indexing expectations.

Self-respect is rooted in our self-confidence as a fully cooperating member of society capable of pursuing a worthwhile conception of the good over a complete life. Thus self-respect presupposes the development and exercise of both moral powers and therefore an effective sense of justice. (*PL* 318)

The mental and moral powers presupposed by this conception of self-respect clearly put it out of reach of many with severe mental disabilities.

One of Nussbaum's great achievements in her work on disability has been to articulate a broader conception of self-respect. This arises in connection with her fundamental appeal to the notion of human dignity (167). As her case studies of relatively disabled people make plain, a valuable type of dignity and self-respect can reside even in people whose mental capacities are so limited that they will never be able to join in the mutual recognition of citizens as equals. This more fundamental sort of self-respect has a psychological importance that, oddly enough, is noted by Rawls in the sentences immediately following those just quoted:

The importance of self-respect is that it provides a secure sense of our own value, a firm conviction that our determinate conception of the good is worth carrying out. Without self-respect nothing may seem worth doing, and if some things have value for us, we lack the will to pursue them. (*PL* 318)

In order to articulate what we might call *fundamental self-respect*, then, what we need to do is to separate that layer which is necessary for all people, no matter what their level of ability or disability, to have a sense that their life is worth living, from the more ambitious political recognition that Rawls has in mind. For almost everyone but the nearly comatose or the most severely autistic, a modicum of mutual recognition seems necessary and useful for supporting one's reasonable sense that one's life is worth living.[23]

These observations put us in a position to differentiate the versions of the ICS that would support (JF) over mixed conceptions from those that would do the opposite. To construct an ICS in which the parties prefer (JF), we should define them by means of the following motivational assumption:

(M1) The parties are motivated by the Rawlsian primary goods: rights, liberties, opportunities, income, wealth, and the social basis of self-respect, understood as the self-respect of the equal citizen.

---

[23] As Nussbaum notes (187), it may be necessary to decide that some people, such as perhaps those in a persistent vegetative state, are so severely disabled as to wholly lack the capacity for a dignified human life. In her development of her threshold principle, (CA), she limits its reach to those who do have the capacity to live a dignified human life. This limit does not violate the ban on drawing a dichotomy between the abled and the disabled, as there are many severely disabled people who, as she persuasively argues, do have the capacity to live a dignified human life.

This is the motivational assumption that Rawls employs in the OP. If this is all that the parties care about, then they will not be daunted by the possibility that if the society for which they are choosing principles is relatively poor, the minimum income expectation protected by the difference principle may not guarantee everyone a decent level of capability. Similarly, if the only aspect of self-respect that they care about is the self-respect of the equal citizen, they will not intrinsically prefer principles that aim to protect fundamental self-respect. Their positive reason for not wanting to add a basic-needs principle would come from their rational pursuit of the primary goods. This last point, especially, requires some explanation.

With only those motivations given them by stipulation, the parties to Rawls's ICS will act as if they were attempting to maximize the satisfaction of those motivations on behalf of the persons they represent. Given this, Rawls's argument for the difference principle has long been the object of criticism by those who wondered why rational, mutually disinterested parties would opt for such a seemingly risk-averse principle, rather than opting, instead, for the seemingly more risk-neutral option represented by the utilitarian principle. Rawls's answer, roughly, is that, given the vast uncertainty that the parties face, when choosing under the veil, they are not in a position meaningfully to maximize the expected share of primary goods to be enjoyed by the persons for whom they are acting as trustees. They are, however, in a position to determine, Rawls argues, that the well-ordered society corresponding to justice as fairness would be at least satisfactory for all, whereas the one corresponding to utilitarianism might well not be.[24] When we now extend the problem to include the issue of disability, parties whose motivation is defined by (M1) would still, I think, come to a similar conclusion. The First Principle secures their basic rights and liberties, the equal opportunity principle their opportunities, and the difference principle maximizes the minimum lifetime expectation of income and wealth. There is nothing else such parties care about, aside from self-respect, which (M1) interprets narrowly. From their point of view, then, adding an extra, basic-needs provision unnecessarily constrains their rational promotion of their stipulated motives. Accordingly, as least as far as this first pairwise comparison goes, it looks as if parties characterized by (M1) would favor the Rawlsian principles over a mixed conception, even now that the problem of justice has been extended to cover the relatively disabled and the disability-related stipulations have been added.

---

[24] See the revised statement of the argument in Rawls, *Restatement*, sec. 28.

On the basis of these arguments, it is easy enough to see how to modify the motivational assumption so that the parties would, instead, prefer a mixed conception. Indeed, there are several plausible motivational assumptions that would do the trick. Anticipating the second fundamental comparison, as well as some additional considerations that will arise only in the following section, I suggest that we consider the following motivational assumption:

(M2) The parties are motivated by rights, liberties, opportunities, income, and wealth; by fundamental self-respect; and by the capabilities.[25]

While some may doubt this motivational assumption's coherence or its compatibility with a liberal response to pluralism, I postpone such questions about the philosophical suitability of the assumption to the following section: here we are simply locating the interpretations of the ICS that would favor one or another of the alternative principles we have identified.

Given our other twelve stipulations, parties characterized by (M2) would not find (JF) satisfactory. Since they care about fundamental self-respect, they would rightly worry that (JF) would fail to protect the self-respect, or dignity, of the seriously disabled, and so would conclude that (JF) does not reasonably guarantee them a satisfactory minimum. Since they care also about the capabilities Nussbaum lists, they would not be mollified by the fact that the difference principle would maximize the minimum expectation of income and wealth. They would not want to be in the position of a severely disabled person with ample income but lacking adequate social bases of self-respect. For the severely disabled, the self-respect of the fully cooperative citizen is out of reach, but that does not mean that they must be viewed as "objects of our charity and compassion" (R 129).[26] Rather, fundamental self-respect may be protected by building provision for everyone's basic needs into the constitutional essentials of society. How to avoid expressing potentially disparaging attitudes of charitableness is a delicate question, to which I return below.

In addition to this argument from fundamental self-respect, there is a simpler reason that parties characterized by (M2) would find (JF)

---

[25] If we assume Nussbaum's specific list of capabilities, this list of what motivates the parties in (M2) is actually redundant, for she already includes the social bases of self-respect and, as we shall shortly see, at least some of the crucial basic liberties.

[26] Rawls there develops the contrast between reciprocal cooperation among fully cooperative agents and charity for the unfortunate. I am grateful to Nien-Hê Hsieh for drawing my attention to this passage, which he illuminatingly discusses in Nien-Hê Hsieh, "Rawlsian Justice and Workplace Republicanism," Social Theory and Practice 31 (2005): 1–28.

unsatisfactory. On account of their uncertainty about the level of development of the society in which the principles will be applied, they will rightly worry that maximizing the minimum income-and-wealth expectation will do too little for the severely disabled. At low levels of development, even a strictly equal distribution of income and wealth might leave the severely disabled in a bad way. Accordingly, to forestall such possibilities, the parties will want basic needs specially addressed. They will prefer a mixed conception to (JF).

The Second Fundamental Comparison: the simple Nussbaumian view vs. mixed views

The second pairwise comparison is between a simple Nussbaumian approach and a mixed conception (whether NPG or NC). Considering the component principles of the mixed conceptions in priority order, the most salient difference, in this case, concerns whether or not there is a principle securing equal basic liberties. This difference is less significant than would be possible to glean from my exposition so far, as I have not laid out Nussbaum's account of the ten central human capabilities. Some of these make a place for basic liberties. For instance, one aspect of the basic capability to "use the senses, to imagine, think, and reason," as she interprets it, is "being able to use one's mind in ways protected by guarantees of freedom of expression with respect to both political and artistic speech, and freedom of religious exercise" (76). That the basic capabilities are, in Nussbaum's account, specified in normative ways should not surprise us: this is part and parcel of her approach, which singles out the *valuable* human capabilities for protection. This aspect of the capability of thinking and reasoning is supplemented by the capacity for practical reasoning – "being able to form a conception of the good and to engage in critical reflection about the planning of one's life" – which, as she comments, "entails protection for the liberty of conscience" (77). Further protection of free speech enters as part of her interpretation of the basic capability of control over one's (political) environment. In addition to these ways of building a link to the basic liberties into the interpretation of the capabilities, Nussbaum builds an equal opportunity aspect into the basic capability of control over one's (work) environment. As she interprets that capability, it includes "having the right to seek employment on an equal basis with others." Accordingly, the difference between a mixed conception and a simple Nussbaumian one such as (CAB) is considerably narrower than one might have expected, had one not had in mind her full account of the basic human capabilities.

With regard to the basic liberties, the principal difference between these two broad alternatives boils down to whether or not the view insists on a fully adequate scheme of equal basic liberties. The mixed conceptions do insist on this, so long as basic needs have been taken care of; (CAB) does not.[27] This difference might emerge prominently in a relatively well-off society. Consider, for instance, Rawls's insistence that a fully adequate scheme of equal liberties must include a guarantee of the "fair value" of the equal political liberties. (This provision is spelled out as part of Rawls's full statement of the First Principle, quoted above in stating (JF).) This guarantee "means that the worth of the political liberties to all citizens, whatever their social or economic position, must be approximately equal, or at least sufficiently equal, in the sense that everyone has a fair opportunity to hold political office and to influence the outcome of political decisions" (*PL* 327). In a relatively well-off capitalist democracy, at least, ensuring the fair value of the political liberties will presumably require structural measures such as public financing of political campaigns and restrictions on corporate political advertising.[28] Although Nussbaum's capability list, as currently worded, includes the capability to "participate effectively in political choices that govern one's life" (77), this does not seem to entail the *equal* influence of the fair-value guarantee. To be sure, nothing would prevent Nussbaum from adding that guarantee of equality into her list.[29] If she opted to do that with the fair-value guarantee and with all other aspects of having a "fully adequate" set of equal basic liberties, then the difference between her view and the mixed conceptions (or at any rate NC) would become quite difficult to discern. The capabilities view would, in effect, amount to (NC) minus the priority rules. For purposes of discussion, I will assume that the interpretation of the relevant capabilities does not build in a fair-value guarantee.

This last observation suggests one reason why Nussbaum might do better to refrain from building full adequacy of the scheme of equal basic liberties into the definitions in her list of central human capabilities. The principal strategy of (CA) and (CAB), as we have seen, is to focus on *minimum* justice. What is demanded is that each citizen be secured a minimum threshold in each capability. Nussbaum puts forward no priority rules and no suggestions about trade-offs among the different capabilities, as the suggestion is that there is to be no compromise: we

---

[27] As I have mentioned, however, Nussbaum separately addresses questions of equality, and in particular equal basic liberty, in Nussbaum, *Frontiers*, 292–93.

[28] See Rawls's criticism of *Buckley* v. *Valeo*, the US Supreme Court case that held corporate political advertising to be protected as free speech, in Rawls, *Political Liberalism*, 359–63.

[29] As I have noted, *Frontiers* 291–95 moves in this direction.

must not rest until each citizen is secured this minimum level of capability in each of the ten central respects. If any of the capabilities on the list are interpreted in *too* demanding a fashion, however, then either that demanding aspect will have to be dropped out again when it comes time to specify the minimum thresholds (a matter that Nussbaum recognizes requires some independent work: 180) or else trade-offs will become inescapable. Since her view does not provide us with any guidance for coping with such trade-offs, it seems wise for it to avoid interpreting the capability set so as, in effect, to build *full* justice into minimal justice.

Having located this central difference between the simple Nussbaumian alternatives and the mixed conceptions, it is simple enough to construct motivational assumptions that favor one alternative or the other. Motivational assumptions that would favor the mixed conceptions would stipulate that the parties care about their basic rights and liberties, as such. Both (M1) and (M2), the motivational assumptions articulated so far, do stipulate this. Hence, on each of these, the parties would prefer a mixed conception. One motivational assumption that would favor the simple Nussbaumian conception (CAB) is the following:

(M3) The parties are motivated by the capabilities.

While parties motivated solely by (M3) might conceivably prefer to (CAB) some other capabilities principle that went beyond minimum justice, they have no clear reason to prefer an alternative that singles out the equal basic liberties.

The Third Fundamental Comparison: (NPG) v. (NC)

If we confine our attention to a pairwise choice between (NPG) and (NC), which differ only in how basic needs are specified, the issues are essentially the same as those we have already discussed in looking at the choice between (JF) and the mixed conceptions. Parties that care only about the primary goods, as per (M1), will prefer (NPG), which spells out the principle addressing basic needs in precisely the terms they care about. Parties that care about capabilities – whether only about capabilities as in (M3) or also about capabilities as in (M2) – will prefer (NC). As we saw in the earlier discussion, this preference by parties who care about capabilities will be heightened by their consideration of the facts of disability. Just as a guaranteed minimum income may be of insufficient help to a severely disabled person, so too with a guarantee that his or her income needs will be met. A severely disabled person is likely to have far more urgent needs for care, loving attention, and being included in some kind of social life. Parties that care only about capabilities as in (M3) might prefer an amendment of (NC) that somehow interpreted the difference principle in capability terms; but as always the argument deals only with those principles on the menu.

Alternative interpretations of the ICS corresponding to each set of principles

Consolidating these results, we can see that these three motivational assumptions generate three different interpretations of the ICS, each of which favors one of the alternative sets of principles we have defined. Using subscripts to indicate an ICS involving all thirteen common stipulations plus the motivational one indicated in the subscript, and expanding the comparisons now to include all four of the alternatives we have defined, we can summarize our main results as follows:[30]

1. Parties in ICS_{M1} will choose (JF);
2. Parties in ICS_{M2} will choose (NC);
3. Parties in ICS_{M3} will choose (CAB).

Our fundamental comparisons did not elicit a motivational assumption that would most favor (NPG) among these four alternatives. I do not think that this is an accident. As the facts of disability highlight, it does not seem plausible to interpret basic needs in terms of the primary goods. Accordingly, in relation to the motivational assumption, (NPG) stands at an unstable point, attempting to recognize basic needs without drawing on an account of central human capabilities. If the capabilities approach is steadfastly excluded from the motivational assumption, as by (M1), then the parties will, as we have seen, no longer have reason to add *any* basic-needs provision to (JF). If, however, motivation by the capabilities is added in at all, as by (M2), then, as I have argued, the parties will have reason to prefer the capabilities-based needs principle in (NC).

The philosophically favored ICS for extending principles to disabilities issues

In Rawls's well-known simile, the ICS serves as a fulcrum or "Archimedean point" that allows us, in thought, to stand outside the actual basic

---

[30] In fact, we have seen that parties in ICS_{M1} will rank (JF) first, (NPG) second, (NC) third, and (CAB) fourth; that parties in ICS_{M2} will rank (NC) first, (NPG) second, and the other two views lower; and – adding the observation that parties who care about capabilities will care about basic needs – that parties in ICS_{M3} will rank (CAB) first, (NC) second, (NPG) third, and (JF) fourth.

structure of society – which otherwise exerts an almost suffocating control on our thinking – and consider what would be required for a society
to be basically just (*TJ* 230). When we use this leverage to turn over
rocks, we should not be surprised that what we find underneath is
sometimes messy. The point is that doing this will enable us to look
critically at aspects of society that otherwise escape our gaze, not that it
will spare us the labor of reflection. It is *we* who must reflect, considering
whether our tentative articulation of ideals of social cooperation yields
palatable results and whether our concrete convictions are well explained
and supported by our broader ideals. The parties to the ICS lack the
ability to reflect in this way: It is we who must redefine them if their
choices are unacceptable.[31] And now we find that the same necessity for
reflection holds when we work from the opposite end of the lever, starting
from some general observations about the urgency of addressing the
rights of the seriously disabled and using the device of the ICS to reflect
on what fundamental constraints we ought to impose on the choice of
principles of justice. It is easy enough to identify the different motivational assumptions that will end up leading the parties to favor different
principles, but which of these motivational assumptions ought to be built
into the ICS? There is no simply obvious answer, and no escape from
open-ended philosophical reflection on the matter.

Simplifying somewhat, we can say that under (M1) the parties care
only about primary goods, under (M3) they care only about the capabilities, and under (M2) they care about both. If both classes of goods
simply *do* matter, then that would make a prima facie case for (M2),
which makes the parties sensitive to both. Rawls never claims, however,
that the primary goods matter in themselves. Rather, he presented them
initially as all-purpose means, "things that every rational man is presumed to want," no matter what his life plan, but not necessarily to want
for their own sakes (*TJ* 54). In his later work, he provides a different
account of the primary goods, one that casts them as necessary means to
realizing the two highest-order moral powers of framing and pursuing
one's own conception of the good and forming and acting on a sense of
justice. Because of the general usefulness of the capabilities Nussbaum
identifies, and because, as we have seen, they include aspects of basic
liberty and opportunity, it seems that the capabilities, too, could be
linked in this way to the two highest-order moral powers – either in
addition to the primary goods or instead of them. There may be deep
issues about this link that I am missing, but for present purposes, at least,

---

[31] Rawls does of course retain the ideal of full, mutually aware, reflective acceptance at
another level: that of what he calls "public justification": Rawls, *Political Liberalism*, 387.

I will assume that Rawls's conception of the two highest-order moral powers themselves (as opposed to his detailed attempts to link them to the primary goods) does not strongly favor one of our three motivational assumptions over the others.

The capabilities have a better case to represent goods that simply *do* matter. At least, the functionings that are realized when people act on their capabilities are each put forward by Nussbaum as elements of a good human life. In contrast to the primary goods, which are put forward merely as generally useful means, the capabilities are intrinsically related to what are purported to be the intrinsic goods of human life. Insofar as this roughly Aristotelian account of a good human life is convincing, the capabilities have the following claim to our theoretical consideration: they represent constitutively necessary means to living a good human life. While here I obviously cannot enter into debates about the general nature of the good, I take it that this consideration at least generates a prima facie case for including the capabilities among those items that the parties care about. Why would one refrain from doing so?

The facts of pluralism appear to generate three kinds of reason for limiting the goods recognized in the ICS to something like the primary goods: justificational, legitimacy-involving, and expressive. While neither of the first two is decisive, I go over the issues involved because many readers will have this concern. I will argue that while the third, expressive reason does not suffice to show that it would be inappropriate for the parties to be motivated by the capabilities, it does suggest that they should not be motivated *solely* by the capabilities.

The justificational reason is simply that, in the end, one hopes that the entire conception of justice, including the arguments developed via the ICS, could become the object of an overlapping consensus in which all the diverse, reasonable members of society came publicly to accept the conception. By remaining rather "thin" or pared down, the account of primary goods may avoid invoking some substantive commitment anathema to some reasonable comprehensive view. The hope embodied in this strategy is strengthened by Rawls's account in *Political Liberalism*, which gives the rationale for the primary goods in terms of the higher-order powers. These powers, in turn, he connects, definitionally, with the idea of a reasonable comprehensive doctrine.

The legitimacy-based reason for steering clear of a thicker conception of the good is closely related to this. Because a theory of justice addressed to the basic structure of society concerns the nature and limits of "the coercive machinery of government," it must work within what Rawls calls "the liberal principle of legitimacy":

Our exercise of political power is fully proper only when it is exercised in accordance with a constitution the essentials of which all citizens as free and equal may reasonably be expected to endorse in light of principles and ideals acceptable to their common human reason (*PL* 137).[32]

Rawls has consistently suggested that, given the conditions of pluralism, this principle makes it illegitimate to appeal to "perfectionist" standards that rank the comparative worth of different individuals' way of life (consider *TJ* 289). A second reason for sticking with primary goods, then, is to avoid breaching this principle of legitimacy.

Finally, one might distinguish from this an expressivist reason for restraint. This third reason is implicit in Rawls's critique of perfectionism and in his argument that, in the well-ordered society corresponding to justice as fairness, the public affirmation and recognition of everyone's status as free and equal citizens provide a secure basis for everyone's self-respect (*TJ* 477). The point has been more fully developed, however, by Elizabeth S. Anderson. Anderson highlights the disrespectful message potentially conveyed by egalitarian theories that gear themselves toward compensating for inequalities of fortune, the so-called "luck-egalitarians" who attempt to compensate those with the ill fortune to have been born unintelligent, untalented, or ugly. "What do luck egalitarians have to say to those cursed by such defects in their internal assets?" Anderson asks. Well:

Suppose their compensation checks arrived in the mail along with a letter signed by the State Equality Board explaining the reasons for their compensation. Imagine what these letters would say. "To the disabled [for instance]: Your defective native endowments or current disabilities, alas, make your life less worth living than the lives of normal people. To compensate for this misfortune, we, the able ones, will give you extra resources."[33]

Such a statement seems an affront to the recipients' dignity. In response to Anderson's expressivist critique, one erstwhile luck-egalitarian has pointed out that if one is in possession of "an objective scale of well-being," then any compensation can be based on that scale, and "not intrinsically [on] any [invidious] comparison between" the worth any two people's lives.[34] But an objective scale of well-being or worth is precisely what Rawls assumes that the facts of pluralism put out of reach of a public conception of justice. Taking pluralism seriously means taking this expressivist challenge seriously: since

[32] Rawls, *Political Liberalism*, 137.
[33] Elizabeth S. Anderson, "What is the Point of Equality?" *Ethics* 109 (1999): 305.
[34] Richard J. Arneson, "Luck Egalitarianism and Prioritarianism," *Ethics* 110 (2000): 343.

redistributive efforts cannot rest on uncontroversial *facts* about comparative well-being, one must take care about the *judgments* they express.

In sum, the fact of reasonable pluralism seems to generate three strong reasons for sticking to a quite thin theory of the good, such as that embodied by the primary goods, for the purposes of developing principles of basic justice, rather than moving to a thicker theory such as that exemplified by the capabilities approach: (i) the thin theory seems to afford a less controversial basis for justifying principles of justice, yielding an approach (ii) more likely to satisfy the liberal principle of legitimacy, and (iii) less likely to express offensive judgments about people's lives.

The question, however, is whether Nussbaum's capabilities account really offends against any of these considerations. Having adopted Rawls's hope of finding an overlapping consensus around a political conception of justice, she has devoted considerable effort to establishing that each of the central capabilities on her list is accepted as important and valuable by each of the major world cultures (8). Although her list of ten capabilities is more contentful than is Rawls's list of primary goods, neither account pretends to total neutrality about the good.[35] Nussbaum highlights six ways in which her account builds in respect for pluralism: it is open-ended and subject to revision; it avowedly remains rather general and abstract, allowing room for different jurisdictions to specify it differently; it is put forward, like Rawls's mature theory, as a "freestanding" view that does not depend on any comprehensive conception; it stresses capabilities rather than evaluating lives on the basis, directly, of functioning; it includes aspects of the basic liberties, as we have seen; and it does not entail that government measures be taken to maximize the capabilities at every opportunity (78–80). So there seems to be a good chance that Nussbaum's capabilities approach, like Rawls's thin theory of the good, may meet the demands of public justification under conditions of pluralism. If it has particularly controversial features that would block this possibility, perhaps the account could be revised so as to abstract from them. If Nussbaum's capabilities approach, in some guise, can meet these justificational demands then, by the same token, it can satisfy the liberal criterion of legitimacy. And indeed, that each of the central capabilities is important to living well seems to be an ideal that might well be acceptable to all in light of common human reason.

---

[35] For Rawls's disavowal of neutrality, see Rawls, *Political Liberalism*, Lect. V.

What about the expressivist concern Anderson raises? This is obviously a delicate matter once the theory of basic justice is extended to address issues of relative disability. Anderson's critique of luck-egalitarians presumes that they need to rank people's lives in terms of overall well-being or in terms of the worthiness of living that life but, with Rawls, also presumes that there is no publicly acceptable way of doing that under conditions of pluralism. Accordingly, she lends her support to a Rawlsian style of egalitarian theory built around the mutual recognition of citizens as free and equal, a status defined in terms of the political values of a freestanding liberal conception. How does Nussbaum's view stand in this respect? If we confine our attention to her conception of minimum justice, as stated in (CA) or (CAB), then, it seems to me that her view is closer to a Rawlsian view in this respect than it is to the luck-egalitarians' view. Neither (CA) nor (CAB) has any need of ranking lives according to the degree of well-being or human dignity that someone enjoys. We have seen, rather, that she argues that the demand of justice that each person be secured a minimum level of capability in each of the ten central categories can be grounded in the equal human dignity of all persons, no matter what their level of ability or disability. Accordingly, her standard of minimum justice does not require her to rank the worth of different individuals' lives.

We may conclude then, that while conditions of pluralism do indeed restrict the conception of the good it is plausible to attribute to parties in an ICS, Nussbaum's capabilities meet that restriction about as well as do Rawls's primary goods. And since, as I have suggested, the capabilities have a better claim to capturing goods that really do matter, there is a strong case for including them among the items that the parties care about. In other words, there is some philosophical reason to favor (M2) or (M3) over (M1), which limits their motivations to the primary goods.

Let us now turn things around and ask whether there is any reason to suppose that parties care about the primary goods at all. In particular, let us assume that the parties care about the capabilities. Given that, is there any general reason to characterize them as also caring about the primary goods? Why would it not be redundant to think of them as caring also about the primary goods? What do the primary goods capture that the capabilities do not?

There are two general commitments that the addition of the primary goods would serve. One of these was foreshadowed by our discussion of the comparison between (CAB) and the mixed conceptions. The parties would have reason to prefer the mixed conceptions, I argued, if they cared independently about their basic rights and liberties. Now, at the level of considering the alternative characterizations of the ICS, the question is what reason we might have so to represent the parties. The most basic reason to do so, as suggested not only by Rawls's work but also by that of Amartya Sen – the co-originator, with Nussbaum, of the capabilities approach – is that we need to recognize that our freedom as agents has a moral importance that is independent of, and irreducible to, our well-being.[36] Accordingly, there are two grounds for caring about basic liberties, and not just one. One ground, as captured in the capabilities list, is that living freely is a constituent element of living a good human life. Another ground, however, is that, as a political matter, we believe it important to protect individuals' basic rights and liberties, no matter what their conception of the good (at least so long at it is reasonable). Rawls insists that one important way to think of the parties to the OP as free is to represent them as knowing that it is possible for the persons they represent to undergo "a profound and pervasive shift, or reversal, in [their] final ends and commitments ... On the road to Damascus Saul of Tarsus becomes Paul the Apostle. Yet such a conversion implies no change in [their] public or institutional identity" (*PL* 31). In Rawls's OP, a commitment to the kind of political freedom expressed in these statements is represented in two ways: by extending the veil of ignorance to conceptions of the good, which prevents the parties from building such commitments into public political principles, and by including the basic rights and liberties among what the parties care about. So this kind of philosophical recognition of the moral importance of freedom as a matter independent of well-being provides a strong reason at least to include the primary goods that Rawls lists first: rights and liberties.

The second general commitment supports adding the primary goods about which Nussbaum is most skeptical: income and wealth. The argument here derives from the expressivist considerations raised by Anderson. In defending (CAB) against Anderson's challenge, I relied on the fact that (CAB) is restricted to minimum justice. Yet basic justice, as we have seen, extends beyond minimum justice; and, per stipulation (d), the task of the parties is to select principles of basic justice. In particular, there remains a valid concern of basic distributive justice that is independent of the securing of any minimum threshold for everyone. There is a valid question of justice about whether the inequalities in people's expectations and life chances that result from a given basic structure are fair. (A commitment to fairness also provides reason to

---

[36] See Amartya Sen, "Well-Being, Agency and Freedom: The Dewey Lectures 1984," *Journal of Philosophy* 82, no. 4 (April 1985): 169–221.

characterize the parties as caring about the primary good, opportunities, independently of well-being.) If we are to provide the parties in the ICS with a way of pursuing this question compatibly with pluralism, we need to find a way of doing so without inviting them to engage in the kind of invidious ranking that Anderson sees in the luck-egalitarian approach. For this purpose, the capabilities are ill-suited by their plurality. With ten central categories of capability to work with, there seems no workable way in principle, with or without regard to the constraints of pluralism, to use the capabilities list directly to generate all-things-considered comparisons of the lifetime expectations of different people: indeed, the very idea of doing so is perhaps incoherent. Accordingly, any priority ranking among the capabilities strong enough to *convert* the list of ten into a single index would surely violate the constraints of pluralism and express perfectionist commitments not equally respectful of everyone's dignity. Hence, the capabilities do not seem to be a good basis for assessing comparative lifetime expectations. By using income and wealth as a proxy measure for people's expectations, Rawls's approach well avoids these difficulties. The point is not that everyone values money for its own sake. Rather, it is the reverse: as Aristotle noted, no one rightly values money for its own sake; but it is useful for many other things and supportive to most any lifestyle of someone engaged with the public institutions regulated by the constitution. It is an imperfect proxy measure of expectations, but it is a serviceable one, and one that, because so obviously a proxy, avoids the expressivist concern. In a theory of justice addressed to persons of all levels of disability, relying on this simplified index of expectations would yield unacceptable results were persons' basic needs not also given a place in the view; but we are considering whether to *add* concern for income and wealth to parties already motivated by the capabilities. Describing them as caring about the capabilities secures a place in the view for basic needs; if they also care about income and wealth, they will want to adopt a distributive principle for going beyond this minimum. A distributive principle that, like the difference principle, indexes expectations in terms of income and wealth can do so without threatening equality of respect.

These general commitments to freedom and fairness, then, support adding rights and liberties, opportunities, income, and wealth to the list of what the parties care about. Since we have previously concluded that they ought to be represented as caring about the capabilities, what emerges from the considerations canvassed here as the philosophically favored interpretation of the ICS is the one that adopts (M2), according to which the parties care about both the primary goods (with self-respect broadly interpreted) and about the capabilities. There is nothing incoherent in the mixed motivation (M2), though admittedly merely constructing parties that care about both primary goods and capabilities obviously does little to synthesize Rawls's and Nussbaum's approaches.[37] That work must be done elsewhere – for example, in the formulation of principles to put on the menu: (NPG) and (NC) are highly modest efforts in this direction. If ICS_{M2} is the philosophically favored interpretation of the ICS for present purposes, then it follows from the discussion in the last section that, among the alternative sets of principles we have considered, these philosophical considerations most favor (NC). Taking account of freedom and fairness as well as basic needs, and focusing on issues of justice for those of all levels of disability, we ought to prefer this combination of Nussbaum and Rawls's principles to either of their principles taken alone.

Concluding reflections

Should this conclusion have been obvious to us all along? Perhaps it was to those with clearer vision than I. For those less clairvoyant, the intermediate device of the ICS serves as a useful means of putting together all the many conditions we must juggle in developing a theory of basic justice: recall the thirteen stipulations held constant across the different interpretations of the ICS. Some of these, to be sure, go to articulating the idea of a hypothetical social contract; but many of them express conditions we think appropriate to impose on the articulation of principles of justice. We saw that there is no problem in adapting such a hypothetical device to the problem of justice for those of all levels of disability. We have also seen how Rawls's use of the device of an ICS can function, in that context, as well, as a basis for analytically comparing different principles. My discussion of this analysis has not reached reflective equilibrium, for it has proceeded really in only one direction, from relatively concrete observations about the pressingness of problems of justice involving disability towards more abstract considerations about the kinds of commitment (to meeting basic needs, to fairness, and to freedom) that matter in a theory of justice. I have not looked back in the other direction, to consider whether the principles that seem favored by our relatively abstract ideals are feasible in a concrete situation such as ours or consistent with our relatively concrete considered judgments. One would want to return to more concrete matters of constitutional design and consider a wide range of more practical issues about implementing the principles discussed here. Even in the first direction, as

---

[37] I am grateful to Martin Saar for discussion of this point.

I have admitted, I have not pressed as far as possible, for I have not explored the alternative conceptions of fair social cooperation that might be invoked to support the alternative versions of the ICS considered here. A more thorough examination would have to proceed back and forth, as Rawls says, duly pruning and adjusting at both ends. Here, my only purpose has been to illustrate how the Rawlsian device of the initial choice situation can facilitate analytic progress on the difficult issues pertaining to justice and disability.

3 Logos, pathos and ethos in Martha C. Nussbaum's capabilities approach to human development*

Des Gasper

Introduction: elements in an approach to human development

Three areas for constructive work on human development are much discussed: what are the values which should define and guide human development; what are causes and barriers for human development; and how can we operationalize a theorized approach (a package of concepts, values and explanatory theories) in terms of measurement, instruments and policy priorities. There are also three less discussed but essential counterpart areas of work. First, operationalization requires not just measurement but institutionalization, including establishing and sustaining a programme of research for action, and attracting and keeping the support of a body of researchers and potential users. Second, an ongoing research and policy programme of human development, and action on its findings, requires a basis of widespread public commitment and concern. Lastly, without rich observation and evidence, each of the required commitment, concern, ethical theory and positive theory is likely to be weak and insufficient. Table 3.1 highlights these two sets of areas: the left-hand column lists the already much discussed areas, and the right-hand column presents the less discussed but equally essential counterparts.

A theory of human development needs thus to be more than only a theory in welfare economics or ethics. Amartya Sen's capability approach arose in response to the question of what is the appropriate space for evaluating people's advantage and the distribution of advantages ('equality of what?'). A human development theory or approach has further purposes besides evaluation and so requires additional types of information. Sen has extended his capability approach considerably, notably in *Development as Freedom* (1999), but it retains a welfare economics imprint. A human development theory should preferably be helpful in

* My thanks to Flavio Comim, seminar audiences in Cambridge, and several anonymous referees for helpful feedback on earlier versions.

Table 3.1 *Essential areas for work on human development*

Much discussed areas	Vital additional areas
Ethical theory	Mobilization and sustaining of public and private concern and commitment
Positive knowledge on: • Causes • Requisites • Constraints • Effects	Rich observation and evidence (including of the lives and thoughts of deliberating human subjects, in their diverse concreteness, complexity and individual specificity)
'Operationalization': • Measurement • Prioritization • Implementation	Institutionalization, including through stimulating and maintaining a research and policy programme(s) • Cooperative network of researchers and users, with resources and morale • Sustained by judicious strategy and tactics

other roles, too: including for understanding behaviour and explaining agency and satisfactions; for mobilization of attention, concern and commitment; and for guidance in the processes of formulating, making and implementing public choices.

Martha C. Nussbaum's special quality has been to give an overall vision of human development which adds depth in most of these connected areas, not only the evaluation and measurement of advantages and their distribution. We will see how she enriches attention to the 'human' in thinking about 'human development', through her treatments of the centrality of human emotions, affiliations and communication. Her publications since 1999 considerably strengthen and enrich her contribution, though retaining some perhaps questionable features. I will look especially at her formulations in *Women and Human Development* (2000a) and *Creating Capabilities* (2011), but with supplementary reference to *Sex and Social Justice* (1999a), *Upheavals of Thought* (2001a) and *The Clash Within* (2007), as well as at *Poetic Justice*'s (1995c) statement of her methodological perspective, since these other books remain neglected in the international development studies literature.

This chapter has the following main parts. A short first part addresses the relationship between purposes and methods in ethics. It distinguishes various foci or arenas in ethical and ethics-related discourse, and examines some corresponding methods. This sets the stage.

The second part presents Nussbaum's work in ethical theory, including her priority capabilities list, as part of an overall approach to development ethics, including ethics-related observation and practice. We will look at each of the major areas we highlight in Table 3.1, not only at abstracted theoretical ethics. We make a detailed comparison with Sen's capability approach, and see its somewhat different purposes and correspondingly different methods. We identify and review major debates around Nussbaum's capabilities approach, and look at how the revised and deepened version published since 1999 responds to earlier comments.

The chapter's third and fourth parts examine Nussbaum's recommended methods. Centrally, we consider her advocacy of the use of imaginative and other idiographic literature, including for deepening understanding and building concern and sympathy for persons; and of the analysis and use of emotions, with special reference to compassion. We consider also the broader principles, of engagement with a wide range of evidence, including personalized accounts, and of 'internal criticism', i.e. conversation with a cultural tradition by drawing on its own internal resources. We will consider the methods' rationales, how far Nussbaum follows the principles, and how far she could open up to further types of evidence, collaboration and interaction.

In effect, the chapter examines logos, ethos and pathos – the three elements of persuasion recognized by classical Greek rhetoric: *logos* (reasoning), *pathos* (the felt experience which a discourse draws on and the feelings it evokes) and *ethos* (including the degree of confidence, mutual respect and authority which the author establishes in relation to the audience) – in Nussbaum's work on human development.

Diverse stages in practical discourse require diverse methods

The more types of purpose one has, the more types of evidence, conceptualization and theorization one must use. Consider a series of stages or foci in practical ethics: exposure to real cases; trying to grasp and interpret them using readily available 'everyday' ideas; trying to build general concepts or theory, if and when felt necessary; returning to analyze real cases using such tools from theory; and making and acting on practical choices. More simply, we might refer to three broad stages: induction, theorization and decision-making/action. These different purposes and stages of thought are found to involve different styles of case-use and argumentation (Gasper 2000a).

Induction involves reflecting on experiences of real people, preferably through striking, absorbing, accessible examples. Cases can sensitize people to situations, issues and ethical claims, build fellow-feeling, and convey notions about what is good. To do this they must be vivid, engrossing and typically about real or plausible people. 'Constitutive narratives', for example, says Benner (1991: 2), are stories which 'exemplify positive notions about what is good', they convey core values within an area of practice and help to motivate and sustain its practitioners.

The immediacy and force of a story, a real case, outdo any general statement. It contextualizes and adds personal flavour and credibility. Anecdotes, too, not only thick rich narratives, may do part of this, and do so with great economy. Brief anecdotes give no answers, at least no reliable ones, but they can establish a felt connection and help to open hearts and minds. The *Voices of the Poor* study (e.g. Narayan *et al.* 2000) lacks holistic narratives – people's comments were processed and pigeonholed – but some of its quotations pierce like a knife.

Theorizing, whether theory-building or the 'modelling' of a particular case, typically calls for more abstracted thought, with exclusions and simplifications to allow systematic analysis of or with the remaining factors. Often excluded will be details about people which could distract the analyzer and distort her analysis. Sometimes the cases considered are wholly imaginary.

The cases which are looked at to support decision-making and action should typically again be real and often detailed, to convey the complexity of contexts and to show, in 'learning narratives' (Benner 1991), the skills needed to act on values. Such stories bring emotions which are remembered, too, which helps in later recall and activation of the skills, in action. We change our moral views especially by experiences which strongly involve our emotions, says Nussbaum. Ideally, such emotions and stories, sometimes of inspiring personal exemplars, help to build commitment as well as skills.

This general principle that ethics and practical discourse include a variety of activities, which have distinct purposes and different appropriate methods, informs Nussbaum's work. It lends the work unusual richness and insight. Her capabilities approach thus involves much more than a list of specific priorities in or for human lives. In a preliminary description, one could say that it also involves the following:

- A *wide-angle but focused vision*, looking at the content and potentials in key aspects of people's lives, all people's lives. Her list of priority capabilities fits here.
- A way of looking, within the field of vision, with *openness and sympathy*. The list of priority capabilities embodies a basic theme: insistence on *respect for all persons*, as our starting point, from which culturally diverse interpretations and historically specific negotiations will proceed, rather than starting our public reasoning from whatever biased cultural and historical orderings hold sway.

- Use of a wider *range of evidence*, including richer sources – fiction, poetry, autobiographies, and now also interviews and open-ended observation – than those used in economics and much other work on living standards.
- A deeper *way of understanding*: using rich pictures of mind, personhood, emotions and language, and a richer *style of presentation*, that seeks to explore the human content of evidence, including its emotional content, to build concern both for persons and for particular aspects of life.

Should all this be included when we consider Nussbaum's capabilities approach? Yes, if we are interested in what are the essential working parts of her approach to the ethics of human development. Furthermore, we can see linkages within this set which suggest that it forms an interconnected package, not a priority capabilities list plus a bunch of quite separate features. While the other features are not ones that could only accompany a capabilities list, to specify and discuss her capabilities approach without them is artificial and misleading.

'The capabilities approach' is an imperfect title, then, for this overall perspective on human development. 'Capability approach' was a fair description of Sen's proposal for welfare economics: to adopt an alternative primary space for the accounting of well-being or advantage, an alternative to utility or real income. When extending his work beyond welfare accounting, Sen has employed other titles: 'development as freedom' or UNDP's 'human development'. Nussbaum used the label 'Aristotelian social democracy' in her earlier work, but outgrew that. 'Cosmopolitan humanism' might fit now, with perhaps 'the capabilities approach' as a secondary label to indicate the disaggregated perspective on people's lives and the respect for their freedoms.[1] Or one might focus on what the approach approaches and speak of Nussbaum's approach to the ethics of human development. Here, however, just as Alkire (2002) uses the label 'capability approach' to refer to Sen's entire system, we may for simplicity refer to Nussbaum's overall approach as her 'capabilities approach'.[2]

Nussbaum's approach attends to issues not covered in Sen's, while his in turn contains purposes and aspects, such as measurement, not covered in hers. Sen has a stronger planning orientation or relevance; Nussbaum

---

[1] *Creating Capabilities* rejects a designation as cosmopolitan (p. 92), since here Nussbaum employs an extreme 'comprehensive' (p. 93) definition of political cosmopolitanism: primary loyalty to humanity as a whole, as if a citizen of a world-state. In contrast, the usage of cosmopolitan in this chapter does fit Nussbaum's position: acceptance of the Stoic principles of equal dignity and substantial ethical concern for all of humanity, as in support for an extensive universal set of human rights.

[2] *Creating Capabilities* notes concern for capabilities of non-human animals as an additional reason for this label.

a stronger orientation to devising basic constitutional principles, as seen for example in *Women and Human Development*, and to citizen education, as in *Poetic Justice*, *Cultivating Humanity* (1997), *The Clash Within* and *Not for Profit* (2010).

Mapping Nussbaum's capabilities approach

The evolution of Nussbaum's capabilities approach since the early 1990s

The WIDER research programme that was led by Sen and Nussbaum in the late 1980s and early 1990s led to two noteworthy volumes, *The Quality of Life* (Nussbaum and Sen 1993) and *Women, Culture, and Development* (Nussbaum and Glover 1995). They consolidated and extended ideas on what we should mean by improvement in the life of a person or group, and on how far answers to such questions are culturally relative. Nussbaum and Sen have espoused somewhat different positions. Some people find attractions in Nussbaum's neo-Aristotelian capabilities ethic, compared with Sen's thinner, more Kantian approach. Nussbaum gives a rich picture of what is a full human life; talks more in terms of real people, real life, not abstractions; and may thus be more able to reach wider or different ranges of people than only economists and analytic philosophers (Gasper 1997: 299). Yet Nussbaum's work from that period (1988, 1992, 1993, 1995a, 1995b) often raised misgivings: 'a "top-table", still too disciplinary, and emphatically Aristotelian style might bring not just substantive intellectual shortcomings, but antagonize others and thus short-circuit the debate it sought to advance' (Gasper 1997: 300).

Nussbaum's subsequent work, notably in *Women and Human Development* (*WHD*), has taken up the challenges voiced by many commentators. *WHD* gave a deeper, more measured, integrated and practical statement than in the earlier papers, which she rightly declared now to be superseded (e.g. 2000b: 103). Some major new areas of exposure and thought became apparent: an absorption in the hard, practical reasoning of law, especially after her move from a department of classics to a law school; her adoption of a Rawlsian political liberalism which provides space for various comprehensive ethics rather than tries to enforce any one; and equally important, regular visits to India, partnered by considerable associated study.

Nussbaum's approach takes human unity as the default case in ethics and adds variation where there is reason to do so, rather than starting by presuming difference and requiring us to prove commonality. She demonstrates in detail, by theory and by examples, how there is scope for cultural variation in operationalizing stipulated central capabilities and in life beyond them. She notes a series of channels for this (2000b: 132): (i) the stipulation is of only a limited core set of priority capabilities, beyond which there can be diversity; (ii) the core set includes liberties and choice; (iii) these priorities are stated only in general terms, and are (iv) to be then operationalized by local democratic processes; and (v) they are stated in terms of ensuring capabilities (as opportunities) rather than insisting on the corresponding functionings. Feature (i) marks the move away from her earlier advocacy for public policy of a more extensive and individualistic ethic. She now effectively incorporates insights from communitarianism, while avoiding relativism.

She thus makes clear her support for a 'political' rather than 'comprehensive' liberalism, and for an 'overlapping consensus' model (as argued for by many basic needs theorists: Braybrooke 1987, Gasper 1996, 2004). She focuses on specifying criteria of 'a decent social minimum' (2000a: 75) rather than a comprehensive list of proposed requirements for human flourishing; and on a limited set of more basic capabilities, not a long list of required functionings. Her early 1990s' version had instead propounded criteria for, first, a life deemed 'human' rather than sub-human, and second, a life deemed a good human life. The newer version has a more useful intermediate focus, consistent with the advice of various commentators.

The 'top table', Aristotelian, combative, Northern feel has considerably declined. Aristotle remains a major influence, for reasons eloquently summarized in *Creating Capabilities* (2011: 125ff.) but no longer dominant. The primary self-designation as Aristotelian has gone, reflecting awareness of its dangers and of her other affiliations, new and old, including to the Enlightenment and its aims of liberty and 'a life enlightened by the critical use of reason' (1999b: 2; see also 2000b: 103).

General orientation and elements of Sen's and Nussbaum's capability approaches

To try to understand Nussbaum's capabilities approach we can compare it with Sen's work, with special reference to their mature versions, in *Women and Human Development* and in Sen's synthetic statement *Development as Freedom*.[3] Tables 3.2 and 3.3 offer a multi-part comparison, which can be outlined as follows:

[3] WHD offered a comparison (pp. 11–15), but this was written prior to the appearance of *Development as Freedom* and drew some excessive contrasts. A powerful later paper by Nussbaum (2003) in effect compares the two books, with primary reference to the issue of specification of priority capabilities. Chapter 4 of *Creating Capabilities* adds further remarks.

Table 3.2 *First three parts of a comparison of the capabilities ethics of Sen and Nussbaum*

	Sen	Nussbaum
A. Orientation		
Main audience	Economists, analytical philosophers, UNDP, World Bank	Literary philosophers, humanists, feminists, lawyers, civil society
Style	Politically safe: 'cautious boldness, seeking a wide, mainstream audience with terms, tones and topics that will appeal [to] and engage them' (Gasper 2000b: 996)	Bold (though cautious in *WHD* on issues in India – e.g. Shah Bano case; but not so in *The Clash Within*)
Attention to culture	Limited	Extensive
Multi-cultural	Yes	Has become multi-cultural (in relation to the contemporary world; was already so for literary and past worlds)
Universalist/relativist in ethics	Universalist, with much space for variation	Universalist, with much space for variation Head-on critique of relativism
B. Background perspectives		
Normative individualism	Yes	Yes, '*Principle of each person's capability*': no one is expendable (Nussbaum 2000a:12), each should be treated as an end
Theory of the person	Less content: his picture includes reason and desires (plus 'sympathy' and 'commitment') but has less on meanings, or on the skills in reasoning, valuing, operating and cooperating. People are seen as reasoning choosers more than as full actors	Richer picture of thought, including emotions and the influences on them. Stronger than Sen on interpreting meanings and action, including on uses of emotions
Emphasis on freedom	Very high. Includes stress on the instrumental value of freedom, in addition to its independent value and its constructive value (i.e. role in building validated moral conclusions). Emphasis on freedom as choice and on 'development as freedom'. Strong focus also on justice. Relatively little on care	High.* Less focus on behaviour in markets; more stress than Sen on law, emotional development, etc. Emphasis on freedom as self-mastery? 'Development as human decency and human flourishing'. Strong focus on justice. Substantial attention also to care

103

Table 3.2 (*cont.*)

	Sen	Nussbaum
C. Capability approach components		
1. Broad informational base	Yes. A wide field of vision, looking at the contents of (all) people's lives	Yes, even wider
2. A language (family of terms)	Its main creator	Partly shares this language, but partly modifies it
2a. Notion of functioning	Highly generalized and abstract treatment	More concrete, with attention to experiential content of some central functionings
2b. Notion of 'capability' / 'capabilities'	Undifferentiated, micro-economics influenced, theory-derived conception of 'capability': as opportunities	Experience-derived, plural, phenomenological notions of 'capabilities': as potentials, as skills, as opportunities
2c. Well-being/agency	Extensive use of this distinction, since he centrally argues with and against utilitarians	Prefers categories less based on arguing with utilitarians (and which thus might sometimes half adopt their biases; Nussbaum 2000a:14, 2011: 197 ff.)
2d. 'Sympathy'/ 'commitment'	These distinctions exemplify a well-being/agency distinction, but Sen does not do much with them	A major focus. Goes far deeper than Sen in this area, using more and other terms
3a. Moral priority to capabilities, in valuation	Yes; proposed as the key 'space' for evaluation. Choice is presumed not to become oppressive	Yes
3b. Moral priority to liberty	Yes	Yes, in that liberty is not to be traded away for more of other goods (2000a: 12)
4. Priority to capability, as a policy rule	Yes [One can accept #4 without accepting #3, but not vice versa]	Yes. This is consistent with Nussbaum's focus on legal constitutions
5 and 6: how to prioritize, including among capabilities	5: by having 'reason to value'. 6: Sen points to public processes, calls for participation	5: Same as for Sen. 6: Nussbaum focuses on processes in both the political and legal systems

7a. Priority capabilities list	No explicit list. No clear 'Marxian/Aristotelian idea of truly human functioning' (Nussbaum 2000a: 13). Sen is ambiguous here	Yes – but increasingly has presented own list as indicative of a prioritization procedure and as open to local interpretation
7b. Link to human rights framework	Now quite strongly linked (e.g. in Human Development Report 2000), but with doubts about treating rights as hard side constraints (Nussbaum 2000a: 14)	Capabilities approach as explicitly a human rights approach (Nussbaum 2006), 'a basis for central constitutional principles' (2000a: 12). Basic rights are to threshold levels for priority capabilities
7c. Thresholds (prescriptive basic needs)	Nussbaum suggests 'Sen nowhere uses the idea of a threshold' (2000a: 12). Rather, he sometimes uses it, but does not specify thresholds unilaterally	Priority goes to achieving basic threshold levels. This ranks above the expansion of opportunities beyond those levels for richer others
7d. Security	Required for priority capabilities (CHS 2003)	Required for priority capabilities (Nussbaum 2011: 145)

* Nussbaum can be as strong as Sen in the degree of normative priority she declares for capabilities (*WHD*, p. 63, calls capabilities 'the' not 'a' relevant space for comparisons of quality of life; see also pp. 87–8). This priority to capabilities is more plausible for prescription, and less often so for evaluation, where the case for attention to functionings is often high. She exaggerates the case against requiring certain functionings (such requirements are widespread, e.g. in road use, p. 88), but elsewhere does note cases where mandatory functioning is justified (often for children, health, safety and various duties; 2000b: 130–1). Her principle of equal capability applies only up to the level of the decent minimum. Like Sen, she certainly gives weight to other distributive principles too, as seen in her discussions of cases.

Table 3.3 *Sen and Nussbaum's capability concepts and labels*

	Concept 1: An undeveloped human potential, skill, capacity	Concept 2: A developed human potential, skill, capacity	Concept 3: The attainable (set of valued) functioning(s), given a person's skills and external conditions	Concept 4: A priority for attainable (and/or achieved) functioning
Sen's label		Capability (informal usage)	Capability (formal usage)	Basic capability (occasional usage)
Nussbaum's label (2000a: 84)	Basic capability; innate	Internal capability	Combined capability (earlier: external capability)	Central capability. (Basic capability – an occasional usage, e.g. 1999a: 87)
Alternative label (Gasper 1997)	P-capability (P for potential)	S-capability (S for skill)	O-capability, or option (O for option)	Priority capability/ basic need or basic right

A. General orientation: Sen and Nussbaum have substantially different audiences and so engage in different conversations.

B. In terms of the intellectual tools they bring, Nussbaum employs a more elaborate theory of personhood.

C. This difference is reflected in some of the elements of their capability approaches proper, including their concepts of capability, as we will see shortly.[4] They differ, too, on the need for an indicative list of priority capabilities. We will see that this relates to the different sets of roles identified and adopted for their approaches.

D. Concerning roles, both Nussbaum and Sen impressively span from review of experience, through building theoretical frameworks, to forging proposals for action. Nussbaum is more oriented to the additional roles of building engagement, concern and motivation. For questioning consumerism in rich countries, Nussbaum's approach offers more, too.

E. Nussbaum uses a different, on the whole wider and richer, methodological 'palette', corresponding to her different conceptions of audience, personhood and roles.

Some elements in the comparison will be familiar to many readers of Sen and Nussbaum and their major commentators (e.g. Alkire 2002, Crocker

---

[4] 2C's comparison uses the classification of components which I used in Gasper (2002, 2007a) to characterize Sen's approach.

2008; see also Gasper 1997, 2002, 2007a), especially within the first three aspects, and I will not attempt to discuss all the elements in detail here. The main purpose of the tables is instead to organize the comparison and to bring out some less familiar elements. Several of these concern roles and method, and will be presented in Table 3.4.

Concepts of capability A merit of Nussbaum's version compared with that of Sen has been the distinctions she makes between types of capability, even though her labels may be questioned (Gasper 1997, 2002). She uses 'basic capability' to refer to undeveloped potentials. The label 'basic' is, however, ambiguous and is often used by others normatively rather than, as here, positively. She uses 'internal capability' for developed skills, but 'basic' capabilities too are internal to people. Earlier she used the label of 'external capability' for the attainable options which people have (plain 'capabilities' in Sen's informal usage) given their 'internal capabilities' and the relevant external conditions. Her newer label, 'combined capability', captures the relevance of both sets of factors but could bring misleading connotations, too. And she uses 'central capability' for a priority-status attainable option, though again 'central' is an ambiguous term. The adjective 'priority' could be more transparent. Nussbaum does, of course, make a claim for the instrumental and normative centrality of the key capabilities that she lists. They are held to be valued in themselves, necessary features of being fully human, and instrumentally central for any life (2000a: 74). Table 3.3 sums up this set of terms, in comparison with Sen's terms, everyday language, and a possible alternative set of labels. Whatever the labels are, Nussbaum helps us to think more clearly about four importantly different concepts.

The proposed list of priority capabilities

Nussbaum's exercise in theory building aims to identify a largely consensual or persuasive list of universal priority (opportunity) capabilities. Why? She notes that the list is permanently open to debate and re-making, and to local interpretation and threshold setting – for example, thresholds are 'set by internal political processes in each nation, often with the contribution of a process of judicial review' (2001a: 418). So why try to personally specify such a list? The answers implied seem to be that without a highlighted indicative set of candidate entrenched priorities we leave too much open to self-interested interpretation by the powerful, and that Nussbaum seeks to convey a method of thinking, with principles of procedure and selection, for developing such a priority set. Rather than being an exercise in monological elite rule, such a priority list will suggest a starting point and ground for a bill of rights, part of a legal constitution. 'Human rights are, in effect, justified claims to such basic capabilities or opportunities' (1999a: 87). Nussbaum's greater emphasis previously on Aristotelianism rather than on the Universal Declaration of Human Rights, plus other aspects of her earlier style, contributed to the still recurrent charges of elitism.

Her list highlights capacities and opportunities to choose. Some critics propose that it is illiberal to *insist* that people must have choice and the capacities for choice. But choice includes the option to choose a way of life which is without choice (within a religious order, for example). She provides examples of well-educated women who choose to wear a burka although not obliged to, and of some who make that choice after a period living without the burka, but who do not insist that others should be deprived of the choice and obliged to wear the burka (e.g. 2000a: 153). Similarly, she gives striking examples of people celebrating their increased field of choice, such as thanks to literacy.

Nussbaum sometimes evinces optimism about convergence on a consensus core set of capabilities and is surprisingly optimistic about the impacts of oppression on preferences and acceptance (e.g. 'regimes that fail to deliver health, or basic security, or liberty are unstable' – 2000a: 155). Are her views and proposed priorities really a wide consensus? While Gayatri Spivak (1999) for one suggests not, the priorities seem compatible with the huge *Voices of the Poor* study (Narayan *et al.* 2000). But her list in any case rests not primarily on current opinion polls but on a proposed criterion of prioritization and on the expectation that its results will converge with those from use of a criterion of informed and educated desire.

While Nussbaum does carefully apply a criterion – what constitutes a decent human life? – it remains somewhat vague and its application intuitive. Her preference for the Mosaic length of ten makes the resulting list a little contrived. In contrast, Doyal and Gough's *A Theory of Need* (1991) uses sharper criteria. – first, what are the requirements for physical and mental health and for autonomy of agency? and second, what are those for higher levels of flourishing, including critical autonomy? – and a more explicit and structured method of application, which proceeds back down a chain of causation from desirable functionings to required capabilities to commodity characteristics to specific satisfiers to implied societal preconditions (see also Gasper 1996; Gough 2000, 2013). Nussbaum lacks this structure and thus her list becomes a more personal selection of priorities from across several of these levels.

So, Nussbaum's work can be seen as justifying a bill of rights, but is less rigorous and elaborated than Doyal and Gough's parallel work, which corroborates but upgrades the approach behind her list. Why, then, has

Nussbaum's work had more attention and impact? Part of the reason is that Nussbaum more strongly embeds her means of prioritization into a larger humanistic project. While her prioritization methods may be less refined, she has elaborated additional methods which address much else of what we require in human development ethics, as we will see later.

The theory needs refinement in some other respects, too. Any theory faces difficult boundary cases. Nussbaum's requires qualification for cases beyond its core focus of the adult householder citizen, such as the seriously disabled or 'differently abled' for whom some capabilities are out of reach (see Nussbaum 2006), and for the half of humankind who are children or infirm. Nussbaum provides some of these qualifications, in a practical style enriched by her legal studies. She considers the case of religious celibates, who seem to reject that 'it is always rational to want [all the specified core human capabilities] whatever else one wants' (2000a: 88) and argues that they rationally would want the sexual and other opportunities whose use they reject, for only thus does their sexual and other abstinence acquire meaning. Many hermits may disagree. She argues that hermits in fact seek affiliation to others, by praying for others or indirectly promoting universal spiritual upliftment. But some hermits seek no societal affiliation, no human betterment, only an affiliation to some notion of the divine.

Nussbaum has here two ways forward open to her, and these are not mutually exclusive. She could take the main path followed by Doyal and Gough: identifying and promoting fulfilment of the needs implied by a more restricted, sharper normative criterion. She can then avoid insisting that hermits want or logically should want sexual opportunities. Second, if she wishes to continue to work with the more extensive and vaguer criterion of human decency or dignity – less extensive and vague than the 'good life' criterion expounded in her early 1990s' work but still not likely to give a tidy list of ten – then the theory requires fuzzier specification. The international human rights tradition and the global ethics movement of Hans Küng and others help to convey how a fuzzy theory can still valuably structure ongoing areas of debate, guide choices, and respect and face differences. Nussbaum already identifies two of her central capabilities – affiliation and practical reason – as more central than others, and comparably there can be some marginal cases and the list will have no sharp end point. Some of the proposed priority capabilities might be better seen as important desiderata than as absolute require-ments (Crocker 1995; Gasper 1997). In this second option the list could be presented as an exemplar of a methodology which offers a framework for dialogical investigation and practical specification (consider Alkire 2002). Otherwise it arouses fears in some people of a preemptive bid to capture the ear of metropolitan power-holders.

A list should be theorized and relativized by identifying and high-lighting the roles it is meant to serve. Nussbaum has argued that a list is important not only as a counterweight to power in distribution pro-cesses within an established political community but also more gener-ally that it can promote sympathetic recognition of and attention to other humans. If we see the list as a method, or part of a method or family of methods, within an approach, then we can think about its functions and then about how to construct and use it. The list is a means, not an end; if we focus on the ends we can sometimes find suitable alternative or supplementary or modified means. The many valuable aspects in the overall capabilities approach should not be obscured by reduction of the approach to a quest for one specification of this one element.

Roles and methods

Roles more broadly. A conscious role of Sen's capability approach is to increase the range of types of information which we use, in order to provide a more adequate evaluative accounting. Sen later highlighted a second role: to provide underpinnings for conceptions of human rights. Nussbaum shares these aims. She highlights a sister to the role of mobilizing more relevant information, namely to provide a relevant language to express people's own multi-faceted concerns better than do measures of income and utility (2000b: 138–9). Next, the evaluative accounter, not merely his present accounting, can be affected by the choice of language. Two more roles of Nussbaum's approach are thus to make observers more open, through this enriched perception of the content of lives, and, it is hoped, to build sympathy and commitment. Imaginatively 'standing in other people's shoes' can change you, not only your information set.

Nussbaum – who was an actress in an early stage of her career – is more conscious or explicit than Sen about these later roles. While Sen rightly points out that goodwill exists, contrary to the assumptions and influence of much economics, he considers less the methods by which it might be fostered and defended. Yet it often exists only as a thing of rags and tatters. He has advanced a hypothesis that public information in a democracy prevents famines, but this presumes that the informed major-ity will care about a threatened minority. The hypothesis therefore fails in some cases intra-nationally, as well as, of course, inter-nationally.

Table 3.4 extends our comparison of Sen and Nussbaum into these areas of roles and methods. It uses the criteria which we mentioned earlier.

Table 3.4 *Final two parts of a comparison of the capabilities ethics of Sen and Nussbaum*

	Sen	Nussbaum
D. Roles		
Multi-modal (witness, theory, policy)	Yes. A source of his effectiveness	Yes, her policy orientation has grown, with a distinctive focus on fundamental entitlements and constitutional principles
To direct attention to a wide range of information and make observers more open	Yes	Yes, even more so than Sen
To provide a language to express people's concerns	Less so	More so
To help build observers' concern and sympathy, including globally	Yes, though this has received less emphasis than the knowledge roles of having a wider range of information	Yes, more than in Sen. To build sensitivity both for persons and for particular aspects of life. Explicitly cosmopolitan, universal
To provide a basis for action	Effective with audiences who are already committed. Limited with others?	Greater attention than Sen to the motivational requirements for action
Action on what? Consumerism?	Is consumerism discussed? ('he sidelines how the acquisition of commodities can sometimes be at the cost of much human freedom', Gasper 2000b: 996)	Attention to consumerism is readily compatible with Nussbaum's richer picture of human needs and motives
E. On method		
Way of looking	Broad informational base, plus vivid illustrations	A way of looking with openness and concern
Range of types of evidence	Mostly official statistics and historiography. Some use of testimony and personal witness, and of mythology	A wider range of evidence, including richer sources – fiction, poetry, biography and autobiography, now sometimes also interviews, direct observation
Way of understanding	Humane social scientist	A deeper way of understanding, using richer pictures of self, mind, emotions and language
Style of presentation	Humane committed social scientist	A richer style of presentation, that explores the human content of evidence, including its emotional content, to build concern and commitment

Table 3.4 (*cont.*)

	Sen	Nussbaum
Type of cases	Often uses artificial cases, simplified 'situations'	Rich cases, often real cases
Rhetorical repertoire (logos, pathos, ethos)	Attends to and is effective in all three of these rhetorical dimensions, including by adapting his style for different audiences. This is an important source of his influence, including in analytic philosophy and economics	Attends powerfully to each aspect, but with occasional lapses in ethos. Has great power for some audiences, but lesser accessibility, credibility or meaningfulness to most economists

Table 3.5 *Comparison of Sen and Nussbaum's attention to stages and cases*

	Sen	Nussbaum
FIRST STAGE Exposure to experience	High attention by economics standards, still low for humanities. Compared with previous welfare economics, his capability approach leads one to consider the substantive contents of lives. Considers anecdotes and situations (Gasper 2000a)	Much more attention than in Sen, including to thoughts, intentions, feelings, life histories, and thus to particularized individuals as well as selected functionings. Considers histories and rich fiction (Gasper 2000a)
SECOND STAGE Theorization	Intensive formal analysis of somewhat simplified, abstracted situations, often imagined ones	Theorizing here is less separated from the study of cases. Gives substantial but less detailed attention than Sen to formal analysis; has less apparatus for doing such analysis
THIRD STAGE Prescribing for action	Substantial attention, especially jointly with Jean Drèze (see Gasper 2008, 2009)	As intensive as Sen, but with a different focus: on individual legal cases, specific legislation and legal constitutions

Methods, in relation to purposes. While Nussbaum's works from *Sex and Social Justice* (1999) onwards clarify the objectives of her capabilities approach, its foreground components and their justification, her special strengths of methodological richness and in conceptualization of personhood are longerstanding. They deserve equal or greater attention in discussing her approach to human development, and have changed much less since the mid 1990s.

The method components overlap and mutually reinforce each other, but each deserves separate specification, as in Table 3.4. A broad informational base and rich detail in presentation can contribute to empathy, being able to understand others' feelings, and to sympathy, seeing with concern, caring. However, 'Whether such empathy will promote compassion on the part of insiders or outsiders...will depend on our judgements of seriousness, responsibility, and appropriate concern' (Nussbaum 2001a: 440). And whether compassion leads to caring action depends also on will, and on views about transjurisdictional duties and the respective roles of different bodies.

Nussbaum's universalistic language focuses on what we share as human beings: it aims to give respect to what deserves respect, not to morally irrelevant features such as (typically) race and gender and (sometimes) nationality. Her modulated cosmopolitanism (Nussbaum 1994, 2006), in which she advocates concentric circles of decreasingly intense affiliation, is linked to her method. To look at the detailed contents of people's lives is considered a way of strengthening not just recognition of what we share behind the circumstantial details but also the emotional acceptance of this shared humanity.

What is the relationship between stages, purposes and methods in Sen and Nussbaum's work? Table 3.5 elaborates upon the picture of possible purposes given in Table 3.4's 'multi-modal' row (witness, theory, policy), while using the abbreviated classification of stages in ethics: exposure and induction, theorization, and prescribing for action. It then indicates how even upon the same stage the two approaches differ, reflecting their creators' different disciplines and background perspectives. Sen's central focus is as a theorist, whose work is enriched by and enriches empirical observation and policy analysis (Gasper 2008). Nussbaum's list is an attempt to ensure that such empirical and policy work attends to key dimensions of human existence. Her methodology centres on detailed reflection on 'life-size' cases which involve recognizably real people, whether truly real or literary creations. In the Aristotelian tradition such extended treatment of cases is held to foster ethical discernment (Nussbaum 1999b). Her work across the three stages is not tri-partite: her reflection on a case often spans all three. And her methods include close textual analysis, with all the surprises and learning that this can generate.

The stylized comparison above of Sen and Nussbaum has brought out in particular that Nussbaum's approach not only contains arguments against ethical relativism and for a universal priorities list but has a range of purposes and corresponding methods which demand examination as central to her project. The second half of the chapter explores this agenda and discusses how Nussbaum uses her declared methods.

Nussbaum and ethics methodology: of stories and emotions

Nussbaum advocates a wide but focused vision that covers key aspects of people's lives and devotes attention to the human significance of evidence, including its emotional content. She proposes empathy and shows how it links to compassion. In all these respects she in large part does what she advocates. But one also encounters repeatedly expressed dissatisfactions with her range of evidence, range of interlocutors and style of debate.

A full discussion would assess each of Nussbaum's proposals on method, including in relation to her purposes, and assess her practice against her theories. We would look at her investigation of emotions less comforting than sympathy, but equally fundamental: fear, disgust and shame. Here we must be selective. We will consider her examination and application of the key emotion of compassion, and her use of rich human narratives; the extent of her intellectual sources, including her relatively limited field exposure and collaborations; and an occasionally still over-confrontational argumentative style.

Sympathy and commitment, compassion and mercy

An enormous virtue of Nussbaum's work lies in its attention to emotions, including to their roles in ethical judgement and ethical action. She considers, too, their dangers, distortions and determinants. Emotions figure as central capability no. 5 in her list (2011: 33–4) and are involved in items 7–9: affiliation, play and relations with other species.[5] To describe and explain, and to persuade and act effectively, we need to understand, employ and influence much besides 'utility' and 'preference'. Not least, we need more attention to the realms of care, besides the realms of freedom and of justice (van Staveren 2001), and to issues touched on by Sen in the 1970s under the labels 'sympathy' and 'commitment' (Sen 2005; Gasper 2007b). Nussbaum has gone much further in this direction, drawing on wider sources.

Sen stressed the presence and importance of motives other than self-interest. In his usage, 'sympathy' meant felt satisfaction which is derived from seeing or contributing to the well-being of others, and 'commitment' meant the willingness to act towards goals other than the agent's own

---

[5] Nussbaum sometimes defines emotions too narrowly: as related to things outside a person's control which have great importance for the person's *own* flourishing (2001a: 4, 22). Our own goals and our own flourishing must be distinguished, Sen would say, for we can sacrifice ourselves for others and for ideals.

well-being, including the well-being of others, even though this will not raise and might diminish the agent's well-being. Sen's distinctions perhaps still reflected the mould of utilitarianism: only one type of felt satisfaction was recognized. A concern for others which did not make the agent happy was then not seen as sympathy, even though the word's parts (sym-pathy) suggest feeling-with. 'Commitment' remained a disconnected, somewhat mysterious category. Nussbaum points out that 'one cannot fully articulate Sen's own more complex predictive and normative theory of reasoning without prominently including the emotions in which parts of that reasoning are embodied' (2001a: 392).

Compassion (Nussbaum's preferred term for sympathy) has a central role in moral, and thus all social, life. While Elster's treatise on the emotions mentions it only briefly (1999: 68–70), as pity, Nussbaum examines it on an appropriate scale. '[A] basic sort of compassion for suffering individuals, built on meanings learnt in childhood' appears virtually universal and quasi-natural, and often survives even massive counterforces of ideology and socialization (2001a: 389). 'By contrast, an abstract moral theory uninhabited by those connections of imagination and sympathy can easily be turned to evil ends, because its human meaning is unclear' (pp. 389–90). Emotion is certainly not a sufficient guide in ethics, she emphasizes, but it is a necessary component, and emotions can be educated.

Nussbaum distinguishes empathy, the ability to imagine the experience of another person, from compassion, seen as concern ('a painful emotion') 'at another person's undeserved misfortune' (2001a: 301). She takes sympathy to be coterminous with compassion, or a mild version of it, and avoids the term pity, deeming it now tainted by condescension. Aristotle described compassion as concern for the misfortune of another person, arising when that misfortune is seen by the observer as (1) major, (2) undeserved and (3) of a type which could happen to himself. Nussbaum endorses the first two posited parts, but gives good reasons to consider the third a relevant contributory factor but not a necessary feature. She replaces it with (3*): the misfortune happens to someone (or some being) who figures within the observer's universe of concern. The re-specification seems meant as an empirical description; it is not argued like a typical definition, in terms of convention, etymology or logic, but on the basis of cases of real or imagined feelings. The diagnosis helps Nussbaum find impediments to compassion: fear of acquiring duties to help (2001b: xxxvii), and envy, shame and disgust, which belittle others' sufferings or exclude them from one's universe of concern (2001a: 423). It also implies ways to try to promote appropriate compassion, by spreading more adequate theories of (1) ethical importance, (2) causation and desert and (3) the scope of ethical community.

We can question Aristotle's second component too, the idea that compassion does not apply to deserved misfortune. In this case the component is stipulated by Nussbaum as part of her definition, but that seems to exceed most ordinary usage. The term 'compassion' – to feel with or for another's suffering; 'pity inclining one to help or be merciful' (*Oxford Dictionary*) – does not by etymology or convention imply that the suffering must be undeserved (see also Comte-Sponville 2002: 106 ff.), though that is certainly a reinforcing factor, as in the case of children in very poor countries. Nussbaum refines her stipulation in two important ways: if the misfortune is excessive compared with the misdemeanour, or if the misdemeanour is related to factors beyond the agent's control, then compassion can arise.

Compassion is for a victim, mercy is for a culprit, says Nussbaum. Mercy is benevolence towards a culpable but partly condonable wrong-doer. But in effect we can extend compassion to a culprit if we see damage which he has suffered earlier. He may be held only partially blameworthy and hence deserving of compassion if he has been punished as if fully responsible. In a fine essay on 'Equity and mercy' (1999a: Chapter 6), Nussbaum relates mercy to an attention to the particular circumstances and detailed histories of persons, such as provided in rich, realistic novels, depth journalism and humanistic anthropology. We come to see the forces, complexities and chances, often beyond the control of individuals, which contribute to misfortunes and misdemeanours. Whether one factor forms grounds for mitigation or for the opposite depends on its combination with the other factors, so: 'Telling the whole story, with all the particulars, is the only way to get at that' (1999a: 177). Further, punishment is not determined exclusively by the degree of mitigation but also by concerns such as deterrence and the other effects and costs; and compassion does not logically imply that we must act to remedy a situation, for that depends also on the likely effects and costs of the attempt. The implication is that we may not need to be so wary of feeling compassion. We can show compassion to those whom we consider in error. Nussbaum's explorations of imaginative literature help to show how.

Ethical insights from thick-textured humanist narratives

In *Poetic Justice* Nussbaum memorably argues:

A novel like [Dickens's] *Hard Times* is a paradigm of such [needs/capabilities based] assessment [of people's quality of life]. Presenting the life of a population with a rich variety of qualitative distinctions, and complex individual descriptions of functioning and impediments to functioning, using a general notion of human need and human functioning in a highly concrete context, it provides the sort of information required to assess quality of life, and involves its reader in the task of making the assessment. (Nussbaum 1995c: 52)

The novel *Hard Times* is shown to have both a critical and a constructive role. It brings to life, in the person of Gradgrind, a narrow perspective from routine economic thought, that insists that ordinary people's motives are simple, self-interest alone, and that everything important can be measured, compared and aggregated in a single calculation which establishes a tidy, correct solution. The novel refutes that perspective, through Gradgrind's story and that of his family. Thus what is called 'sophisticated economics of the Gradgrind sort is a bad novel' (1995c: 34): it tells poor (inaccurate, unreliable, misleading) stories and is potentially useful only when it makes clear that it is a reductionist, as-if exercise.

Constructively, good novels like *Hard Times* do the following, Nussbaum shows:

- They present 'a style of human relating in which. . .moral attitudes are made more generous by the play of the imagination' (1998: 234), thus contributing to a habit of considering that the other 'has a complex inner life, in some ways mysterious, in some ways like [one's] own' (1995c: 38). This reaching behind surfaces contributes to more adequate explanations of life and to better societies. Lack of such imaginative entry to others' minds brings 'psychological narcissism, of citizens who have difficulty connecting to other human beings with a sense of the human significance of the issues at stake' (2001a: 426).
- They show the joy and value of some things – including play and fun – in themselves, not merely as items for use.
- They cross the boundaries between cultures: 'works of imaginative literature are frequently far more supple and versatile [tools] across cultural boundaries than are philosophical treatises with their time-bound and culture-bound terms of art, their frequent lack of engagement with common hopes and fears' (1998: 242).
- They promote a shareable perspective on 'the human being': a recognition of 'human needs that transcend boundaries of time, place, class, religion and ethnicity, and [make] the focus of [our] moral deliberation the question of their adequate fulfilment' (1995c: 45); and that thus embody 'the Enlightenment ideal of the equality and dignity of all human life, not of uncritical traditionalism' (1995c: 46).
- At the same time, they insist on the 'diverse concreteness' (1995c: 20) of 'deliberating subjects' (p. 34), 'the complexity of the lives of individuals and the salience of individual differences' (p. 34). 'A story of

human life quality, without stories of individual human actors, would...be too indeterminate to show how resources actually work in promoting various types of human functioning' (p. 71).

In sum, Nussbaum claims that imaginative literature 'provides insights that should play a role (though not as uncriticized foundations) in the construction of an adequate moral and political theory; second, that it develops moral capacities without which citizens will not succeed in making reality out of the normative conclusions of any moral or political theory, however excellent' (1995c: 12). It can, not least, 'contribute to the dismantling of the stereotypes that support group hatred' (p. 92).

Some literary theorists suggest that imaginative literature is potentially uniquely good in these roles. They see 'literature as a distinctive mode of thought about being human' (Haines 1998: 21). Whether 'literature' extends beyond novels, poems and plays to essays, biography, travelogues and literary criticism is debated. For development ethics, real narratives are vital, probably even more so than fiction. Consider, for example, the impact of works of biography and autobiography from China, such as *Wild Swans* (Chang 1991) and *Son of the Revolution* (Heng and Shapiro 1983). However, Nussbaum's main focus and that of much of the related discussion is on imaginative writing, with a claim that this has special features. It takes us into a variety of other minds, in ways that other forms – even perhaps poly-vocal reportage – may be less able to.

The thick language of literature 'expresses our moral intuitions in a way that the "thin" language [of much philosophy] does not', argues Parker (1998: 10), drawing on Charles Taylor's *Sources of the Self*. Restriction to the thin languages of philosophy leads us to talk about something else than our real moral thoughts. In reaction to the sixteenth and seventeenth centuries' Wars of Religion in Europe, Enlightenment ethics chose to proceed with a conception of persons as individual reasoners only, neglecting their other features and capacities, even their processes of maturation as persons. 'The abstract moral deliberator has no capacities that can be shown only through their development', unlike in the richer moral psychology seen in the Bildungsroman (Diamond 1998: 52). Various philosophers now make such points at a general level. Nussbaum is 'a distinguished exception' in providing also in-depth readings of literature, remarks Haines (1998: 30). This adds weight to her view on whether imaginative literature can be a substitute for philosophical ethics. She concludes rather that the two provide complementary ways of thinking ethically and that literary criticism mediates between the two (p. 32).

Pictures provide a sister route by which sympathy is aroused or withheld. Pictures have a special power but also a simplicity and, by virtue of the very openness and underspecification which can stimulate our imaginations, a proneness to distorted interpretation. Our facility in mentally inventing scenarios often brings the danger that we think we understand when in fact we don't (Becker 1998). Written accounts call forth images too but try to inform our interpretation more. Novels typically elaborate the linking scenarios more carefully, to ensure that we understand with more care and depth. They try to not just show a process in their characters but to induce its counterpart in the reader. Building a sense of real people through evocative detail, recounting situations and events in which we could imagine ourselves, and drawing out their unforeseen consequences can engage our sympathy for those described.

Wayne Booth argued in *The Rhetoric of Fiction* that sympathy 'is technically produced and controlled by the devices of access, closeness and distance' (Nair 2000: 114). First, 'We are more likely to sympathise with people when we have a lot of information about their inner lives, motivation, fears, etc.' (p. 110). This is the method eschewed by economics (and by pictures from afar), whose analyses strictly ration the requirements for both information and sympathy, following Sir Dennis Robertson's premise that nothing is scarcer, relative to requirements, than love for one's fellow man (Robertson 1956). Second, 'We sympathise with people when we see other people who do not share our access to their inner lives [DG: e.g. sometimes external economists] judging them harshly or incorrectly. In life we get this kind of information through intimacy and friendship. In fiction we get it through the narrator...or through direct access to the minds of the characters' (Nair 2000: 110–11). Third, 'Information alone cannot necessarily elicit a sympathetic response. Sometimes it is the careful control of the flow of information, which controls a reader's judgement' (p. 111). When a reader shares information that he knows one character has and another lacks, it tends to place him in the former's shoes and on their side. A third-person narrator may present events to us but through the protagonist's eyes, thus making us see her with both distance and involvement.

Novels can cast particular light on how 'the self comes into being as a dialogic process' (Hillis Miller, cited by Parker 1998: 13) rather than being inherent like the kernel of a nut. Identity can be seen, says Nair, first as derived from the relationships between persons, 'the system of differences through which individuality is constructed/structured', and second 'as a narrative. The only way to explain who we are is to tell our own story' (Nair 2000: 109). This takes us beyond Sen's picture of identity as simply multi-dimensional (Sen 2006) to reflect on how persons' valuations in those dimensions arise and evolve within systems of social relationships which also evolve.

Nussbaum proposes that 'there are some moral views which can be adequately expressed only through novels', thanks to novels' scale and style of investigation (Diamond 1998: 39). The central moral payoff from novels is not only from following what the characters experience and how they choose but, says Nussbaum, even more from following how the novelist reflects on this. The reflection comes not as formal general arguments, although those are what most philosophers search for from literature, often impervious to its ambiguities, warn Diamond, Nussbaum and others. Literature offers no propositional systems but builds our sensitivity and imagination – our heart and soul (Adamson 1998: 89). Philosophers in practical ethics sometimes use cases intensively, but only as illustrations, for building general classifications, guidelines and codes. To protect anonymity and to abstract sufficiently in order to try to establish general principles, they 'routinely alter [cases'] setting and culture, supposing that this leaves the "essential" aspects of the case untouched' (Wiltshire 1998: 188). Yet the particular details may be central to the meaning of the case. Wiltshire argues that given the situational specificity and complexity of cases, and the prevalence of vital aspects which are not tidily commensurable, we should not rely on general rulebooks but on educated judgement based on deep immersion and the use of educated emotions. Personal narratives written by participants, for example those involved in 'complex emergencies', can offer such immersion and education. They tell real histories, not anecdotes or reductive simplifications or momentary situation reports, with attention to the emotions involved and the context of whole lives. The narratives illustrate conflicting viewpoints, real time pressures, unforeseen events and undesired effects, and the transformation of perspectives in the face of extreme experiences (Wiltshire 1998: 188–9). They fulfil most of the functions which Nussbaum identifies as required in ethics, and with more realism than in nearly all fiction. Her own work presents various narratives, real and fictional, which essay these tasks.

Adamson fears that Nussbaum is overly prone to impose a lucid order, find a ready answer, rather than sometimes live with indeterminacy. Nussbaum repeatedly declares she is open to that (e.g. 2001b: 14) and insists that a literary work be read as a whole, not dipped into for selected illustrations. Literature maintains our awareness that there is more in life than we know or understand, whereas so much ethics is narrowly, overconfidently knowing (Diamond 1998: 51). So, literature can help build sensitivity and imagination, as well as help us to respond and act (e.g. Nussbaum 2001b: xvii, Chapter 7). It can generate questions, perception of possibilities and, says Adamson, a sense of people's lives – rather than by itself give answers to 'How should we live?', let alone a full and adequate general conception of 'Life' (1998: 104). Nussbaum concurs.

Caveats: ethos, compassion, building a research movement

Range of sources

Sen, Nussbaum and the UN Human Development Reports conclude that not all things of major importance are commensurable, neither when we think of life as a whole nor when we discuss public policy. We therefore need to evaluate by using diverse sets of information. Nussbaum goes further, since alongside evaluation she adds purposes of explanation and persuasion. She mobilizes a range of types of material in addition to those conventional in philosophy and economics. Her longstanding and enlightening examination of imaginative literature – classical Greek, Hellenistic, Roman and modern European – has steadily extended to cover less exclusively Northern, bourgeois or fictional sources. She draws also from law and psychology, and thoughtfully treats the practical choices faced by judges and (other) policy-makers, including issues of balancing, feasibility and timing. Her post-1994 work has engaged much more with varied modern realities of livelihood and politics. Her limited but intense research trips to India in March 1997 and December 1998 influenced *WHD* strongly and are part of what has grown into a much more extensive engagement.

Both field visits to India were a matter of a few weeks: active, tightly programmed, but still a matter of weeks; the second occurred shortly before finalization of *WHD's* Preface. 'What was Kant's or Rawls's field exposure?' and 'Literature is the perfect substitute', one might say in defence. Philosophers must primarily base themselves on the field studies done by others. But credibility and image problems arise for social philosophers of global human development if they work in isolation and without varied experience of the globe. How reliably can they interpret what they read? Credit goes to Nussbaum for exposing herself more directly. At the age of fifty she experienced 'days that were different from any days I had ever spent' (*WHD*, p. ix), but did not pause there to reflect on the possible impact of months, and years, of such exposure.

The extent and quality of one's range of interlocutors is a vital potential compensation for the inevitable limits of one's own experience. Nussbaum disciplines her ideas by reference to contemporary cases, the situations of ordinary people and the views of colleagues from many countries, including a number in India, as well as to Proust, the Greek tragedies and Henry James. The balance remains somewhat towards a 'Northern highbrow' mix. While she has added substantial, modern, non-European cases and coverage, in *WHD* those cases remained relatively few and in the style of literary cameos, indeed sometimes taken from literature (notably a story by Tagore). *WHD* makes intensive and good use of the cases of two modern Indian women – Vasanti in Ahmedabad and Jayamma in Trivandrum. These cases open the book and are regularly referred to in its later stages (and again in *Creative Capabilities*). Yet they seem rather thin in number (two) and depth (perhaps even from single meetings reliant on interpreters) for Nussbaum's ambitious purposes. Nussbaum promised a later fuller book, but appeared to have fuller theoretical coverage in mind, not a much fuller experiential base or collaboration with a Southern author or authors. *The Clash Within* reflects several more years of involvement with India, but misses the benefit of an Indian co-author. The gaps here can be taken as spaces for further work by others, including both social scientists and philosophers, especially in cross-disciplinary and multi-national collaborations.

Rhetorical strategy, tact and tactics

Nussbaum reaches out to a variety of audiences through a variety of media – books and lectures, magazine articles and TV discussions – on a series of striking topics which she shows to be interconnected. Her rhetorical strengths include great lucidity sustained across extensive and intricate argumentation, exploration of emotions and meanings through use of a wide range of revealing examples, and very evident intense reflection and sincerity.

In terms of reasoning, while *Women and Human Development* and *Creating Capabilities* explicitly do not present Nussbaum's full philosophical defence of her approach, they buttress the approach in several ways. One is by comparison with theoretical alternatives, which strengthens audience confidence. For example, *WHD* gives an impressive refutation of pure proceduralism, the idea that principles of justice can be established without any substantive ideas about the nature of the agents whom these principles are meant to concern (e.g. p. 139). Conclusions could only be drawn by Rawls from his Original Position thought experiment by including ideas, open or often tacit, about the basic purposes or interests of the parties. *WHD* clarified the relationship of Nussbaum's views to other theories, too. It gives informed desire theory a subsidiary normative role and shows in detail how closely it and her approach can converge on implications.

Another deepening of the approach, to some eyes and in terms of both argument and tone, comes in Nussbaum's thorough and sympathetic response to the criticism that spiritual and religious aspirations were slighted in her previous accounts of central capabilities. She now highlights religion as a legitimate response to needs for expression, association and affiliation (2001a: 419), while maintaining principled limits to the free exercise of religion; it is not to be free of reason, consistency and humanity.

One further strength is her practice sometimes of the style of 'internal criticism', expounded in a 1989 paper written jointly with Sen. They argued that the range of intellectual sources and resources within a culture provides bases for it to learn and evolve, including in response to influences from outside, rather than by demanding acceptance of 'parachuted-in' external packages of ideas that may lack local resonance, relevance or acceptability. Commentators and critics are likely to have more influence if they build to a great extent on internal sources and resources. Hans Küng's global ethics project offers a good example of how to build from within as well as without (Küng 1997). A parallel claim exists regarding discussion and criticism of intellectual schools and particular authors: that it is generally more effective for critics to take seriously the authors' aspirations, projects and sincerity, and show how the aspirations can be better fulfilled by certain substitutions. Nussbaum's recent books frequently practise this, and seek agreements on conclusions even where there is some disagreement on premises and routes.

Her late 1980s' and early 1990s' pieces on capabilities had relied heavily on an externally specified neo-Aristotelian vision of 'the good life for man' and met extensive resistance in some quarters. Inspired by passion, Nussbaum's replies seemed occasionally distorted by it, further departing from the spirit of internal criticism. *WHD* helpfully proceeded more in that spirit, for example in Chapter 3 on religion, where Nussbaum listens intently within a culture and builds upon its own moral tradition and categories. This is consistent, too, with adoption of a Rawlsian political liberalism, which provides space for various comprehensive ethics rather than trying to enforce any one, and extends her approach's tool-kit and political relevance. At the same time Nussbaum notes the danger that internal discourse in tradition-based ethics can become ethnocentric re-endorsement of discrimination, and incisively shows the need for external critical inputs.

Aspects of Nussbaum's tactics, and occasionally tone, in this difficult balancing act can be questioned. She has sometimes ventured emphatic views on various Indian matters which she might understand insufficiently.

In the course of her overall defence of people's rights to form, have and use opinions, and to be able to do so, she yet declares, 'The nation is in no position to enforce either these laws [that mandate compulsory education] or laws against child labour at this time' (2000a: 231), a statement that can be queried given what has been achieved in Sri Lanka, Kerala and elsewhere.[6] Lack of cross-checking of details on India also significantly affects *The Clash Within*, potentially compromising its important message and ensuring that Nussbaum's opponents will ignore that.[7]

Nussbaum appears sometimes overemphatic in her political judgements about a country of which she still knew relatively little. One respects, however, her project of internal criticism, that involves close reference to debates within India and the concepts and judgements which they presume, and her belief that traditions are more than a set of petrified practices and instead contain sub-traditions of reflection and the potential to evolve. Elsewhere in much of her work she is admirably thorough in letting us see analytical options and what is at stake.

When Nussbaum feels passionately that a particular view is not just mistaken about something important but actually dangerous, her eloquence has turned her prolific pen into a double-edged sword. Convinced of her cause, she sometimes leaves no prisoners; those declared guilty are publicly despatched, even in many published versions. A 1980s' dispute with the Marglins was prominent in a 1992 article, a 1995 book, and still in 1999's *Sex and Social Justice*. A grey-material pamphlet by Veena Das from 1981 is impaled in that same book, and again in 2000 in *Women and Human Development*. In the 'Professor of Parody' case in *New Republic* during 1999, most of Nussbaum's comments as reviewer seem well argued and some of the reactions to them (collected in the issue of April 19) misplaced or overheated, but there is overkill in her tone and some unnecessarily hurtful flourishes. These

---

[6] To mention briefly some other India examples from *WHD* which can affect authorial authority: Gandhianism is presented as the antithesis of the Western, although its founder spent twenty-five formative years in Britain and South Africa to return to India as a dedicated revolutionary (2000a: 67); p. 27 cited 10,000 aborted Indian female fetuses p.a., a vast underestimate, and p. 30 reported just two girls raped a day, in a nation of 1 billion. Similarly, from the 2011 book: school midday meals, on a large scale, were pioneered in Tamil Nadu, not Kerala (p. 38).

[7] Among the disconcerting inaccuracies that could have been avoided through use of a co-author, p. 96 can be read as presenting Vishnu and Rama as different and hostile deities (though Rama is an incarnation of Vishnu); p. 113 states that Gandhi for a while gave support to Japan during the Second World War (rather, he withdrew his initial support for Britain); and p. 179 misidentifies politician George Fernandes as a BJP member. After giving the official data of a steady rise in the Muslim share of India's population, p. 203 declares: 'So the idea that Muslims have been outstripping Hindus in their birthrate has no substance.'

failings recur at points in the appropriately titled *The Clash Within*. For example, an intemperate attack on (the sometimes intemperate) Arun Shourie falls short in both empathy and compassion.[8] Nussbaum needs to maintain within her discursive circle scholars such as Seyla Benhabib and Nancy Fraser, two of those who protested at the 'Parody' paper's manner. Arjo Klamer and Deirdre McCloskey's 'The rhetoric of disagreement' (1989) offers good advice, including a 'Maxim of Presumed Seriousness' in relation to those with whom one disagrees. We should not use the weaker possible formulations of our opponents' views. And just as there are standard reasons for mercy and sympathetic mitigation, well expounded by Nussbaum, there are good reasons, too, for cool understatement in debating disagreements.

Nussbaum's primary audience is North American, explicitly so in *Cultivating Humanity* or *The Clash Within*, implicitly in several other books' lengthy discussions of US law cases and *WHD*'s style of periodic advice to Western feminists, and still so in *Creating Capabilities*.[9] Especially if there are any conventions and imperatives in American public discourse which reward and motivate overstatement, one should remember a danger that some non-American audiences can stereotype 'Americans' as sometimes arrogant, naïve, dominating and overinfluential. American authors seeking a global audience have to counteract this. Most of Nussbaum's work counters the danger with style and grace, but with occasional problem spots such as those mentioned. There is much to be learned from Sen's tactics and style, which contribute to his ability to mobilize collaborators and have influence through diverse research and policy networks (see Gasper 2000b). He takes care to identify common ground, to build and preserve a convincing ethos, to encourage others, and to collaborate and lead in joint work.

Concluding remarks

Martha C. Nussbaum's already impressive contribution has been considerably broadened and deepened by her published work since the late 1990s, including advances in each of the aspects of persuasion – logos, pathos, ethos. Both *Creating Capabilities* and *Women and Human*

[8] Shourie's work on religion did begin in the 1970s, including a 1979 book after his handicapped son was born mid-decade. See Shourie's 1982 biography written when he was awarded a Ramon Magsaysay award for journalism: www.rmaf.org.ph/Awardees/ Biography/BiographyShourieAru.htm.
[9] P. 66 speaks of 'Our Supreme Court', and 'in this country' refers to the USA (2011: 16).

Development, for example, give systematic and rewarding treatments of her capabilities approach, and *Frontiers of Justice* provides major extensions of the approach: for the disabled, across national boundaries, and for non-human life.[10] The books remain a work in progress which leaves various issues requiring further attention. The priority capabilities list, for example, can be upgraded with a framework such as Doyal and Gough's or Alkire's.

Nussbaum's formulations on capabilities must be understood, however, not just as a priority list but as a way of proceeding, a broad *approach* to ethics and human development. This chapter has centred not on fine-tuning a list and details of the approach's theory of the good but on the roles of a list and the approach's other components. We identified and considered major elements other than those which refer directly to capabilities: ideas about audiences and purposes, background concepts and values, including concepts of personhood and emotion, and the approach's sources and methods for obtaining and interpreting materials. We considered how the choices of purpose, audience and stage of work could influence the choices of methods and sources.

Various choices of audience and of the line and timespan of projected influence are legitimate. Nussbaum's focus matches some essential arenas, purposes and audiences. She seeks longer-run influence on constitutional and legal frameworks and on political culture, in order to buttress compassion, cosmopolitan concern and human rights. She aims to influence how people listen, see and act, and thus to change listeners, not only their information set. We saw, for example, that Sen's hypothesis that a democracy will prevent famines relies on a degree of felt political community. If there is little such community, crippling shortage among marginal groups may not receive attention and concern in the national or even regional metropoli, let alone internationally. Given the extent and even growth of selfishness and narrow groupism, both globally and intra-nationally, for example in relation to climate change, Nussbaum's attention to the bases of concern for others is highly relevant in policy ethics, not only in personal ethics. Her time horizon is consciously relatively long term, as reflected in her stress on upgrading of school and college education, not least in rich countries (1997, 2010).

We see, then, the pertinence of her focus on the analysis and education of emotions, especially compassion. Nussbaum connects the worlds of socio-economic and philosophical discussion of human development to

---

[10] On *Frontiers of Justice*, see Gasper (2006).

these more intimate realms. For social and development policy, the emotion of compassion may be central, and Nussbaum provides a rich examination. She points out its vulnerability to narrowly defensive specifications of who is within the universe of moral consideration, of how seriously they are or would be harmed by a situation, and of how far they are themselves to blame for it. However, one can doubt Nussbaum's adoption of the Aristotelian conceptualization of compassion as necessarily or contingently arising only when a misfortune is undeserved. A non-desert criterion is relevant, but to make it essential may be questionable.

We can gratefully endorse Nussbaum's advocacy of intent study of imaginative literature in order to examine and educate compassion and the emotions more generally, though with a proviso that the power of 'Great Books' for many audiences can be exaggerated. Questions remain about the balance between types of literature (fictional, historical, biographical, autobiographical etc.) and about how one might feasibly and effectively promote such study within the confines of education in social sciences and the professions, even in international development studies. We cannot look to Nussbaum for all these answers; it is an area that demands ongoing work (see Lewis *et al.* 2008).

Nussbaum's enormous agenda brings a need for many types of evidence, collaboration and interaction. Perceptions of her own degrees of empathy, compassion, mercy and cosmopolitanism become important, especially given the frequency of reactions elsewhere against Americans from elite settings. In debate with those who differ, and in seeking to attract cooperators and fellow travellers, tact and tactics are vital. Nussbaum's writings overall are impressively empathetic, compassionate, judicious and merciful, but with some possible lapses, of commission (in disputes) and omission (in collaborations). We can learn from how effectively Sen has fostered a major research programme through building collegiality, networks and partnerships and through defusing resistance. He has attracted and kept the support or attention of a wide family of potential collaborators and potential users.

While it was useful to itemize and contrast the contents of Sen's and Nussbaum's approaches, as attempted here, neither approach is fixed and finished. The purpose of the comparison was to better understand what they say, to try to assist each of these sister programmes to improve, and to promote a well-articulated connection and a productive and cooperative working relationship between them. We require a capability/capabilities/post-capabilities approach that transcends and outlives its founders, and that contributes effectively towards human development.

REFERENCES

Adamson, Jane, 1998. Against tidiness: literature and/versus moral philosophy. In Adamson *et al.* (eds.), 84–110.

Adamson, Jane, Freadman, Richard, and Parker, David (eds.), 1998. *Renegotiating Ethics in Literature, Philosophy and Theory.* Cambridge University Press.

Alkire, Sabina, 2002. *Valuing Freedoms.* Oxford University Press.

Becker, Howard, 1998. *Tricks of the Trade.* University of Chicago Press.

Benner, Patricia, 1991. The role of experience, narrative and community in skilled ethical deportment. *Advances in Nursing Science,* 14(2), 1–21.

Booth, Wayne, 1961. *The Rhetoric of Fiction,* University of Chicago Press.

Braybrooke, David, 1987. *Meeting Needs.* Princeton University Press.

Chang, Jung, 1991. *Wild Swans.* London: HarperCollins.

CHS/Commission on Human Security, 2003. *Human Security Now.* New York: UN Secretary-General's Commission on Human Security.

Comte-Sponville, André, 2002. *A Short Treatise on the Great Virtues.* London: Heinemann.

Crocker, David A., 1995. Functioning and capability; the foundations of Sen's and Nussbaum's development ethic, part 2. In Nussbaum and Glover (eds.), 153–98.

2008. *Ethics of Global Development – Agency, Capability and Deliberative Democracy.* Cambridge University Press.

Diamond, Cora, 1998. Martha Nussbaum and the need for novels. In Adamson *et al.* (eds.), 39–64.

Doyal, Len and Gough, Ian, 1991. *A Theory of Need.* London: Macmillan.

Elster, Jon, 1999. *Alchemies of the Mind: Rationality and the Emotions.* Cambridge University Press.

Gasper, Des, 1996. Needs and basic needs – a clarification of foundational concepts for development ethics and policy. Pp. 71–101 in *Questioning Development,* ed. Gabriele Köhler *et al.*, Marburg: Metropolis.

1997. Sen's capability approach and Nussbaum's capabilities ethic. *Journal of International Development,* 9(2), 281–302.

2000a. Anecdotes, situations, histories – varieties and uses of cases in thinking about ethics and development practice. *Development and Change,* 31(5), 1055–83.

2000b. 'Development as freedom': moving economics beyond commodities – the cautious boldness of Amartya Sen. *Journal of International Development,* 12(7), 989–1001.

2002. Is Sen's capability approach an adequate basis for considering human development? *Review of Political Economy,* 14(4), 435–61.

2004. *The Ethics of Development.* Edinburgh University Press.

2006. Cosmopolitan presumptions? On Martha Nussbaum and her commentators. *Development and Change,* 37(6), 1227–46.

2007a. What is the capability approach? Its core, rationale, partners and dangers. *Journal of Socio-Economics,* 36(3), 335–59.

2007b. Adding links, adding people, adding structures – using Sen's frameworks. *Feminist Economics,* 13(1), 67–85.

2008. From 'Hume's Law' to policy analysis for human development – Sen after Dewey, Myrdal, Streeten, Stretton and Haq. *Review of Political Economy*, 20(2), 233–56.

2009. From valued freedoms, to polities and markets – the capability approach in policy practice. *Revue Tiers Monde*, no. 198 (April–June), 285–302.

Gough, Ian, 2000. *Global Capital, Human Needs and Social Policies*. Basingstoke: Palgrave.

2013. Lists and thresholds: comparing the Doyal–Gough theory of human need with Nussbaum's capabilities approach. (In this volume.)

Haines, Simon, 1998. Deepening the self: the language of ethics and the language of literature. In Adamson *et al.* (eds.), 21–38.

Klamer, Arjo and McCloskey, Donald, 1989. The rhetoric of disagreement. *Rethinking Marxism*, 2(3), 140–61.

Küng, Hans, 1997. *A Global Ethic for Global Politics and Economics*. London: SCM Press.

Lewis, David, Rodgers, Dennis and Woolcock, Michael, 2008. The fiction of development: literary representation as a source of authoritative knowledge. *Journal of Development Studies*, 44(2), 198–216.

Liang, Heng and Shapiro, Judith, 1983. *Son of the Revolution*. London: Chatto & Windus.

Nair, D. Radhakrishnan, 2000. Identity, ideology and narrative. Pp. 107–16 in Nair, D. Radhakrishnan and Varghese, Baby M. (eds.), *The Web of Our Life*. Kothamangalam: Cheerothottam Kudumbayogam.

Narayan, Deepa, *et al.*, 2000. *Voices of the Poor: Can Anyone Hear Us?* New York: Oxford University Press.

Nussbaum, Martha C., 1988. Nature, function and capability: Aristotle on political distribution. *Oxford Studies in Ancient Philosophy*, suppl. vol., 145–84.

1992. Human functioning and social justice: in defense of Aristotelian essentialism. *Political Theory*, 20(2), 202–46.

1993. Non-relative virtues: an Aristotelian approach. Pp. 242–69 in Nussbaum and Sen (eds.) *The Quality of Life*. Oxford: Clarendon Press.

1994. Patriotism and cosmopolitanism. www.phil.uga.edu/faculty/wolf/ nussbaum1.htm (consulted 28 August 2002).

1995a. Introduction. Pp. 1–34 in Nussbaum and Glover.

1995b. Human capabilities, female human beings. In Nussbaum and Glover, 61–104.

1995c. *Poetic Justice: The Literary Imagination and Public Life*. Boston: Beacon Press.

1997. *Cultivating Humanity: A Classical Defence of Reform in Liberal Education*. Cambridge, MA: Harvard University Press.

1998. The literary imagination in public life. In Adamson *et al.*, 222–46.

1999a. *Sex and Social Justice*. New York: Oxford University Press.

1999b. Interview by Cogito, www.philosophyarena.com/philosophyarena/ Consulted 28 August 2002. (Also in Pyle, Andrew (ed.), *Key Philosophers in Conversation: The Cogito Interviews*, London: Routledge.)

1999c. The professor of parody. *New Republic*, 22 February.

2000a. *Women and Human Development: The Capabilities Approach*. Cambridge University Press; Delhi: Kali for Women.

2000b. Aristotle, politics and human capabilities: a response to Antony, Arneson, Charlesworth, and Mulgan. *Ethics*, 111 (October), 102–40.

2001a. *Upheavals of Thought – The Intelligence of Emotions*. Cambridge University Press.

2001b. *The Fragility of Goodness – Luck and Ethics in Greek Tragedy and Philosophy* (Revised Edition). Cambridge University Press.

2003. Capabilities as fundamental entitlements: Sen and social justice. *Feminist Economics*, 9(2&3), 33–59.

2006. *Frontiers of Justice*. Cambridge, MA: Harvard University Press.

2007. *The Clash Within: Democracy, Religious Violence, and India's Future*. Cambridge, MA: Harvard University Press.

2010. *Not for Profit: Why Democracy Needs the Humanities*. Princeton University Press.

2011. *Creating Capabilities – The Human Development Approach*. Cambridge, MA: Harvard University Press.

Nussbaum, Martha C. and Glover, Jonathan (eds.), 1995. *Women, Culture, and Development – A Study of Human Capabilities*. Oxford: Clarendon.

Nussbaum, Martha C. and Sen, Amartya, 1989. Internal criticism and Indian rationalist traditions. In Krausz, Michael (ed.), *Relativism*. Notre Dame, IN: University of Notre Dame Press.

(eds.) 1993. *The Quality of Life*. Oxford: Clarendon Press.

Parker, David, 1998. Introduction: The turn to ethics in the 1990s. In Adamson *et al.*, 1–17.

Robertson, Dennis, 1956. What does the economist economize? In Robertson, Dennis, *Economic Commentaries*. London: Staples Press, pp. 147–155.

Sen, Amartya, 1999. *Development as Freedom*. New York: Oxford University Press.

2005. Why exactly is commitment important for rationality? *Economics and Philosophy*, 21(1), 5–14.

2006. *Identity and Violence: The Illusion of Destiny*. London: Penguin.

Spivak, Gayatri, 1999. Letter to *New Republic*, 19 April.

Staveren, Irene van, 2001. *The Values of Economics – An Aristotelian Perspective*. London, Routledge.

Taylor, Charles, 1989. *Sources of the Self*. Cambridge, MA: Harvard University Press.

Wiltshire, John, 1998. The patient writes back – bioethics and the illness narrative. In Adamson *et al.* (eds.), 181–98.

4   Building capabilities: a new paradigm for human development

Flavio Comim

Much of the applied work on the capabilities approach[1] has focused on evaluation.[2] The approach has been used as a foundation for the human development perspective[3] and for evaluating human well-being in a variety of situations. Most notably, in Martha C. Nussbaum's work the approach has been used to put forward minimum requirements of justice, questioning conventional ideas of social cooperation, equality and human rights. But in her work, differently from what has been suggested by many commentators (e.g. Uyan-Semerci, 2007; Anand *et al.*, 2005), we can find more than a list of necessary conditions for a decently just society leading to the elaboration of constitutional principles. Throughout the years Nussbaum has put forward a range of policy proposals for building capabilities that have remained largely unappreciated by the human development literature (in particular by Human Development Reports (HDRs)). And yet, these proposals have the potential to revolutionise the way in which we think about development policies. Within this context, the main objective of this chapter is to delve into, and elaborate further, Nussbaum's ideas on 'building capabilities' (in contrast to using the approach exclusively to evaluate capabilities). The chapter tries to move beyond a mere compilation of Nussbaum's writings and focuses on concrete policy recommendations that can be derived from the characterisation of her proposal for 'building capabilities'.

---

[1] We use interchangeably here the denominations 'capability approach' employed by Professor Amartya Sen and 'capabilities approach' used by Professor Martha C. Nussbaum, but later in the text we adopt the respective terminologies to separate the two versions.

[2] The literature on the capabilities approach has boomed – see, for example, papers in collections such as *Against Injustice: the new economics of Amartya Sen* (2009) edited by Reiko Gotoh and Paul Dumouchel (Cambridge University Press) or *The Capability Approach: concepts, measures and applications* (2008) edited by Flavio Comim, Mozaffar Qizilbash and Sabina Alkire (Cambridge University Press) as good illustrations of the approach being used for evaluation purposes.

[3] See, for instance, UNDP, *Human Development Report: The Real Wealth of Nations: Pathways to Human Development* (2010), Chapter 1.

In general, when capabilities enter into the discourse of what can be called 'traditional human development policies' (e.g. in HDRs), it is to justify broad support for health and education policies as 'capability-expansion policies'. However, this particular use of the approach, namely, as a philosophical justification of implicit normative choices carried out by human development policies, is very narrow given that it does not produce implications that are substantively different from those derived (as they should be) from other approaches, such as the basic needs approach or more instrumental approaches like human capital (for instance, for the formulation of 'capabilities-oriented' educational policies).

Alternatively, in Nussbaum's perspective for 'building capabilities', a different picture emerges. Here, her humanistic conception of ethical (and public) reasoning invites us to consider the cognitive role of emotions and human values in shaping people's deliberations. Her proposal for 'cultivating humanity' comprises a wide range of instigating themes such as children's upbringing, teachers' and parents' roles in moral education, literary understanding, redesign of public spaces, restructuring of workplaces and locations for public policies. Many of these themes feature only marginally in the current human development agenda – that quite often prefers to concentrate on governments' policies as a panacea for development problems. Nussbaum also attaches due importance to the role of governments in promoting development and social justice but at the same time delves into a complex web of ordinary life daily struggles that shape development from a bottom-up perspective. By doing so, Nussbaum gives concrete sense to John Rawls's (transcendental) concept of public reasoning, going beyond a deliberative mechanism of evaluation towards concrete measures of daily practices that seem to unveil the essence of human development. It is this perspective that this chapter aims to explore.

The chapter is divided into three parts and a conclusion. The first part examines key concepts in Nussbaum's writings on 'cultivating humanity' and the capabilities approach and proposes a model for 'building capabilities' inspired by her work. The second part examines some of the specific proposals that she puts forward for building those capabilities. The third part delves into some of these proposals, further developing them into new areas for concrete human development policies.

How do we recognise other human beings?

Although Nussbaum's work on the capabilities approach has been more fully and formally developed in her books *Sex and Social Justice* (1999), *Women and Human Development* (2000), *Frontiers of Justice* (2006) and

Creating Capabilities (2011), her approach to human development issues seems to have been strongly influenced by early works such as *Love's Knowledge* (1990), *Poetic Justice* (1995) and *Cultivating Humanity* (1997). In particular, it is interesting to note that in *Cultivating Humanity* Nussbaum raises a fundamental question that informs much of her subsequent work on capabilities, namely, she discusses the basis for alterity and the necessary conditions for cultivating this capacity in human beings. Her analysis begins with a straightforward question: how do we recognise that other people are worthy of human dignity? Instead of simply delving into explanations of failures and deviations from this condition, she chooses to think prospectively, asking what can be done to develop this moral capacity in human beings. Her methodological choice is not merely refreshing but lays the foundation for a policy agenda for 'creating capabilities'.

For Nussbaum (1997: 14), becoming a human being is a process that can be taught (and learned!). This means that individuals can learn to love and think about other people without class or ethnic or gender or nationality barriers. According to her (1997: 58–9), the fundamental ingredients for humanity are reason, narrative imagination and moral capacity. Reason is essential for building an 'examined life' in which people would voice more than conventions or traditions in their speeches and actions. Within this context, moral education should comprise a view that goes beyond our personal experience towards reasons and arguments that can be discussed and defended to other people. But in order to develop people's capacity for humanity it is also necessary that they are encouraged to be exposed to 'appropriate emotions' because they have the power to show what is morally valuable given particular contexts. According to Nussbaum, three capacities are essential for cultivating one's humanity (1997: 10–11):

1. Capacity to critically examine oneself and one's traditions.
2. Capacity to see ourselves beyond our groups.
3. Capacity to develop our narrative imagination.

The development of people's ability to reflect on their actions and history is part of a broader process in which individuals are able to communicate with fellow human beings, also acknowledging responsibilities that they have in relation to each other. Cultivating narrative imagination is thus a crucial process in understanding the world from the point of view of others; it is part of people's preparation for moral interaction and the development of their humanity (Nussbaum, 2011: 10).

Humanity, or human dignity, is the central intuitive idea used by Nussbaum (2000, 2006) to define a core set of basic capabilities as fundamental entitlements that are necessary for life. It is important to emphasise that for her the capabilities approach is a political doctrine. Her concern with decency and justice materialises in her suggestions for a set of basic capabilities that individuals should be able to enjoy for a dignified and decent life. So, it seems necessary that individuals should be able to develop a moral sense of a life worth living. This is a precondition for the development of decent societies. As she argues (2006: 182), 'the "basic capabilities" of human beings are sources of moral claims wherever we find them'. As such, they anchor not simply her approach to human development but, more importantly, her views on social justice.

In *Frontiers of Justice* (2006) she expands Rawls's conception of social contract by going beyond the core idea of 'mutual advantage' in defining the fundamental principles of social justice. As much in theory as in practice, her argument depends on the existence of human forms of sociability based on moral sentiments such as benevolence, reciprocity and so forth that extend beyond a narrow motivation of individual advantage. Her arguments seem to convey a deep conviction that new forms of sociability can be engendered and that they are foundational for how we think about public reason and public spaces as well. She refers to the notion of a *shared public conception of the person*, in which individuals exhibit a strong commitment to the good of others. She explains the Aristotelian roots of this argument, mentioning that (2006: 158) 'the good of others is not just a constraint on this person's pursuit of her own good; it is part of her good'. Thus, the design of fundamental political principles in society depends on this notion of publicness which in turn depends on how human forms of sociability are shaped by cultures, histories and political ideas. Ultimately, political procedures, such as a constitution or a chosen economic system, depend on the creation of these forms of sociability and shared public conceptions of the person (2011: 96).

The relevance of Nussbaum's argument should not be underestimated. For her, the concepts of human dignity and human forms of sociability are not mere justifications for her capabilities list. Rather, they are anchoring her views about justice on necessarily desirable characteristics of human beings and of their interactions in society. Following Rawls's views about the importance of institutions for the promotion of justice, she emphasises the role of constitutional structures in defining minimum requirements of justice (basic capabilities providing fundamental entitlements for social justice). At the same time, the existence of these constitutional structures and of the basic political entitlements that they generate depends on people's humanity and their ideas of social cooperation.

But is this claim not contrary to her basic Rawlsian perspective, according to which theories of justice should not depend on any comprehensive doctrine? This does not seem to be the case. As she argues (2006: 352):

In the human case, the capabilities approach does not operate with a *fully* comprehensive conception of the good, because of the respect it has for the diverse ways in which people choose to live their lives in a pluralistic society. [emphasis added]

The approach does not require a *fully* comprehensive conception of the good partially because it does not venture into going beyond a small list of basic entitlements defined in terms of capabilities, not functionings. A fully comprehensive conception would imply all values and virtues of an articulated moral system. Alternatively, a partially comprehensive conception would include only a number of values and virtues not necessarily articulated. Respect for people's diversity in a pluralistic society is a core tenet of the capabilities approach. And yet, the approach does convey at a very foundational level a general (or partial) conception of the good[4] in regard to arguments about the meaning of human dignity and human forms of sociability. One way in which this takes place is that the capabilities approach includes benevolent sentiments from the start in analysing people's relation to their good. As Nussbaum explains (2006: 91): 'This is so because its [the capabilities approach] political conception of the person includes the ideas of a fundamental sociability and of people's ends as including shared ends.' So, as much as there is no particular attachment to any particular fully comprehensive doctrine (religious, ideological, etc.), there is at a foundational level a commitment to a notion of good that involves the idea of 'shared ends', expressed by sentiments such as sympathy, benevolence, justice, respect for one another, understanding and compassion [in addition to Rawls's definition of 'moral persons' that includes moral powers of being reasonable (having a sense of justice) and rational (having a capacity for a conception of the good)].

According to Nussbaum, moral sentiments should not be assumed; rather, they can be constructed. For this reason she supports the development of schemes of *public moral education* that would foster the political principles of the capabilities approach based on promotion of human dignity. As she argues (2006: 411), 'many aspects of our emotional life

---

[4] Reeve (1996) explains that conceptions of the good may be more or less comprehensive, encompassing particular or general features of life. In Nussbaum's theory, the notion of human dignity that she brings to the discussion is seen as a pervasive but general feature of human life.

are socially shaped'. The promotion of public moral education is a complex problem within the context of liberal societies where indoctrination is avoided and individual freedoms respected. Nevertheless, Nussbaum's grounding of the capabilities approach on the promotion of human dignity invites us to consider the essential issue about how capabilities are built (not simply as a theoretical necessity for the stability of the partial theory of justice that she defends but also in practice, in daily life). The implications of this reorientation have the potential to redefine human development policies. In what follows we discuss a scheme for building capabilities inspired by her work, in which we try to highlight its added-value for the elaboration of new human development policies.

In order to stress the differences between the features of the human development approach and those arising from the perspective of building capabilities, we use the term 'traditional human development approach' to designate the characteristics of policies as put forward by UNDP's *Human Development Reports* (HDRs).

We can discuss a 'model' for building capabilities, inspired by Nussbaum's work, only in a very general sense of some principles or 'pillars' that embody a different way of thinking about development. These principles represent some attributes that are closer to the elaboration of the capabilities approach as formulated by Nussbaum than to the constitution of the capability approach as defined by Sen.[5] Without entering into unnecessary controversies, we highlight and characterise a new perspective to human development policies that is:

1. *Micro-dimensional*: it focuses on people's attitudes and daily practical choices where shared public conceptions of the person are developed and shaped by different instances in which public moral education is put to the test. In the traditional human development approach great emphasis is given to policies that promote individual rights, such as right to water (2006 HDR), right to environmental safety (2007/2008 HDR) or right to mobility (2009 HDR). Constant attention to the promotion of health, education and inclusive growth policies is given by the use of the Human Development Index. Other composite indexes of the human development family focus on gender and income inequality and on poverty, in addition to a wide range of statistics that explores political and environmental aspects, among others. However, despite the conceptual and empirical emphasis on individual rights in the traditional human development approach, it is

---

[5] The used benchmarks are the features of Sen's capability approach as found in *Development as Freedom* (1999) and *Inequality Re-examined* (1992).

fair to say that most proposed policies tend to address institutional change and are aimed to inform government policies. Nussbaum attaches great importance to government policies but also delves into a micro-dimension of development that acknowledges the fundamental role of citizens in the construction of just societies. Quite often people continue to be seen as 'passive beneficiaries of development policies' and policies are designed *for the people*. Here, it is proposed that policies should be designed and implemented *with the people*.

2. *Intertemporal*: it recognises that human life is constituted by a succession of temporal stages and that, as such, should be understood in their temporal particularities, as it happens during childhood or at old age. This means that policies should be thought up according to their intertemporal effects and sequencing coherence. In the traditional human development approach, not much attention is given to intertemporal aspects of development policies. Policies are not often intertemporally linked and sequenced. Time-frames (e.g. short- vs long-term) are only occasionally considered the essence of the matter (for instance in the 2007/2008 HDR on climate change).

3. *Pro-active*: it proposes that policies should be seen not merely in terms of their impacts but also in terms of the 'antecedent conditions' that produce the issues to be tackled by them. A deeper understanding of the links between social problems and their causes might help policy-makers to focus on antecedent requirements in terms of human forms of sociability and human dignity that could prevent social problems happening in the first place. This perspective (which extrapolates Nussbaum's theoretical requirements to empirical conditions) contributes to 'cultivate humanity' and to foster conditions for people to flourish as human beings. Being pro-active means that policies do not have to wait for the problems to appear but that it is possible to think about desired scenarios in advance, considering intertemporally what needs to be done so that desired outcomes might become more likely. This contrasts with the traditional human development approach that is essentially reactive, dealing with urgent, well-established problems (quite often comprising human rights violations) without a deeper reflection about pro-active solutions.

4. *Motivationally rich*: it is built around a richer view of people's moral sentiments, contrary to some versions of the social contract that begin from egoistic rationality, benefiting from Nussbaum's analytical framework for thinking about emotions as judgements of value (as discussed in her *Upheavals of Thought*, 2001) and from a perspective that (2006: 91) 'can tap into what is fine in actual human beings'. This is an area that the traditional human development perspective has so far avoided, perhaps fearing that discussing people's emotions or

moral sentiments and the role of love and compassion in building capabilities would be a way of smuggling utilitarianism or subjectivism into the human development analysis. However, the capabilities approach seems to suggest that the implementation and efficacy of some policies might depend on how people consider their actions and behaviour morally valuable.

5. *Public/private*: it argues that the divide between the public realm, characterised in contract theories by reciprocity among equals, and the private realm, where families share love and affection, ignores that family is a political institution basic to society. Indeed, as Nussbaum emphasises (2006: 212): 'The capabilities approach rejects the familiar liberal distinction between the public and the private spheres, regarding the family as a social and political institution that forms part of the basic structure of society'. To a certain extent this feature is related to the micro-dimensional aspect of the capabilities approach, but goes further in claiming that issues perceived as uniquely 'private' can prevent important political principles from being applied, such as in the case of the problems of justice internal to family life. This essential issue has barely been the object of consideration by the traditional human development approach that seems to focus on public policies as a realm distinct from the private. Even when it addresses issues of gender inequality, the traditional approach privileges issues regarding educational achievements and labour market discrimination (important though they are) without paying too much attention to how these discriminatory behaviours are shaped by family cultures.

These five pillars do not appear in Nussbaum's work in this analytical format and quite often are part of discussions in which they interact and assume each other's role, for instance when Nussbaum is tackling real cases with a high degree of complexity imposed by actual practical contexts (characterised by diversity and changes that follow a historical path). Nevertheless, they serve to convey a picture of a different way of thinking about human development policies that are micro-dimensional, intertemporal, pro-active, motivationally rich and not limited to a public/private divide. In order to move beyond general principles, we examine below some specific proposals that Nussbaum has put forward for building capabilities, trying to associate them with these principles.

Locations for valuable public policies

When analysing the general problem of care, Nussbaum (2006) suggests that there are 'locations' for public policies. The structure that she offers seems broad enough to account for public policies at large, beyond the particular focus on the care issue. According to her (2006: 212), public policies have three locations: the public sector, the educational system and the workplace.

The public sector is responsible for legislation and for social programmes that have the power to shape political views and attitudes of ordinary citizens. The public sector interferes with family life by passing laws that assume that certain patterns of behaviour will be carried out. It suggests to society what is important or not by acknowledging certain categories of social spending in the annual budgets. The public sector also sponsors policies that influence the achievement of people's basic capabilities, such as health and education. But the educational system, for Nussbaum, is an enterprise that is by no means under the exclusive responsibility of the public sector given that, in its micro-dimensional perspective that goes beyond the public/private divide, it should also be the responsibility of schools and parents. 'Education does not take place only in schools,', as Nussbaum (2010: 8) puts it. The workplace, the cultures and norms that it comprises, should also be considered an important location for public policies.

The public policies advocated by Nussbaum seem to take into account how forms of human sociability are built and how people's shared public conception of the person is formed. These policies are conceived to promote 'educated citizens', that is, individuals capable of moral sentiments. But that would not be enough, according to her. It would also be necessary for these individuals to be able to have an 'examined life' so that their humanity is also an expression of their autonomy and not of mere tradition, fashion or convention (Nussbaum, 1997: 28–9). Four sets of policies are suggested below to represent the perspective of building capabilities, as put forward by Nussbaum's work. They are all about 'humanising policies' that are micro-dimensional, that take into account time as an important factor, that expect people's pro-active behaviour, and that are based on a wide range of motivations not restricted to the role of the public sector in promoting development. Within this context, we now briefly examine Nussbaum's proposals for 1) redesigning public spaces, 2) caring for children's moral education, 3) transforming the workplace and 4) art for human capabilities, all of which will be further analysed below.

The redesign of public spaces

The proposal for redesigning public spaces appears in Nussbaum's work when showing the inadequacies of assessing the capabilities of a person in a wheelchair from a utilitarian perspective. Simply dedicating resources for moving this person around would not amend the fact that the person's dignity should be respected in his or her right to move as he or she pleases. For this reason, as Nussbaum argues (2006: 167): 'The task of integrating people with impairments into public space is a public task, which requires public planning and a public use of resources.' After identifying the public sector as a key location for the issue of public space, she extends her analysis, introducing the categories of public arrangements for 'a decent public culture'.

So, a picture of 'development as publicness' seems to emerge from her acknowledgement that a redesign of public spaces is important for disabled people. It suggests that other redesigns might be valuable for people with a diversity of other features. From an intertemporal perspective, public spaces are important for children and for people in their old age, but not only for them. If public spaces are essential to people's dignity and self-respect, there is an entire field ahead to be explored by the human development approach.

Caring for children's moral education

Attention to children's education for public rationality has been one of the public policy areas in Nussbaum's work for more than fifteen years. Initially, her concern was with a humanistic conception of public reasoning that would welcome emotions and the development of literary imagination as key concepts in shaping children's moral lives, as expressed in *Poetic Justice* (1995). She allowed an important role for teachers and parents in fostering children's human identity. Later, in *Cultivating Humanity* (1997), she delved into policies for building children's capabilities. More recently in *Not for Profit* (2010) she delves into different models of learning that can stimulate children's active participation and cultivate their compassion.

Her view of education was not limited to schooling. For her, no curricular formula can substitute the role played by teachers because their personal attributes (e.g. being perceptive and provocative) are key for stimulating critical reasoning and for promoting an unprejudiced and just understanding of the world – which she would call ' education for world citizenship'. This does not mean that children should be taught to suspend criticism towards other individuals and cultures, but rather that by understanding how humanity can be diverse children might learn about respect and understanding. Similarly, parents should have an active role in fostering the moral sentiments of their children.

Indeed, her micro-dimensional perspective demands that not only the state and teachers but also parents should acknowledge their respective roles. In particular, she argues that actions not normally seen as 'public policies', such as storytelling, should be part of parents' repertoire as soon as children are in a position to understand them. For her (1997: 93), "the basis for civic imagining must be laid in early life", reinforcing the importance of intertemporality in thinking about human development. This is so because narrative imagination, which is essential for moral interaction, should be internalised through habits that are laid out from a very early age. Following this perspective of building capabilities puts parents in the driving seat of their children's education: they do not have to wait for the state and the schooling system to educate their children, but rather, they can be pro-active in acknowledging that they may have an important role to play in influencing educational policies by following simple actions such as storytelling. As Nussbaum puts it (1997: 89):

When a child and a parent begin to tell stories together, the child is acquiring essential moral capacities. Even a simple nursery rhyme such as 'Twinkle, twinkle little star, how I wonder what you are' leads children to feel wonder – a sense of mystery that mingles curiosity with awe. Children wonder about the little star. In so doing they learn to imagine that a mere shape in the heavens has an inner world, in some ways mysterious, in some ways like their own. They learn to attribute life, emotion, and thought to a form whose insides are hidden. As time goes on, they do this in an increasingly sophisticated way, learning to hear and tell stories about animals and humans. These stories interact with their own attempts to explain the world and their own actions in it. A child deprived of stories is deprived, as well, of certain ways of viewing other people. For the insides of people, like the insides of stars, are not open to view. They must be wondered about.

In this passage Nussbaum sums up the rationale behind the promotion of children's narrative imagination, opening up a conception of education different from what usually appears in HDRs. The differences are not merely qualitatively important (moral education vis-à-vis instrumental knowledge – literacy and maths) but also entail a different conception of public policy not limited to government's actions, since people as parents or carers are centre-stage of the development process. Later in life, literary scenarios tend to become more complex, allowing older children to develop moral sentiments such as fairness, dignity, compassion, among others. The proposal of building capabilities has the potential to redefine how children are part of the development discourse in an inter-temporal perspective.

Transforming the workplace

The traditional human development approach has been established to a large extent on a critique of economic growth as a development paradigm

(Haq, 1996). Part of the critique is about how, in the midst of human diversity, resources are imperfect indicators of human well-being given that different people might convert differently their resources into human achievements. Perhaps for this reason, not much attention has been given within the approach to the issue of how incomes are generated, that is, about the workplace. However, within Nussbaum's perspective of building capabilities, beings and doings developed in the workplace are ethically assessed. In the context of corporate structures and organisational cultures, she criticises how the pressure for profit and the workload have limited employees' freedoms to flexibly allocate their time. According to her (2006: 215): 'The capabilities approach suggests that a major aim of public policy ought to be the transformation of the workplace, through new flexibility and new ethical norms.'

Transformations of the workplace are complementary to other types of transformation in society, such as caring for children's moral education as discussed above. When parents are under extreme stress due to their workload, possibilities for paying greater attention to their children are much reduced. Similarly, when career promotion schemes downgrade those who, for instance, enjoy parental leaves, they will subsequently feel less encouraged to take new leaves. Not to mention the insane competition for long hours on the job that is part of many corporate structures, as discussed by Nussbaum. Transforming the workplace means changing organisational cultures and how people envisage the work–life balance in their lives. It is about respecting people's freedom and believing in a motivationally richer structure behind people's desire to have productive lives.

The traditional human development perspective has so far not dedicated much thought to the workplace and how beings and doings (and cultures) shaped by it have a powerful impact on people's human development, and on future generations. Nussbaum's proposals, not only in the context of care, open up an exciting field for a better understanding of how beings and doings are shaped (and therefore, how they can be changed) in several spheres of life, such as the workplace.

Art for human capabilities

The idea of building capabilities conveys an agenda of humanisation of human beings. It is not simply a proposal for the development of particular emotions and moral sentiments that are relevant for more enlightened forms of social contract. Nussbaum's proposal goes beyond that by discussing how fundamental ingredients for humanity can be promoted.

Different forms of art, such as music,[6] dancing or painting, to name just a few, are essential for cultivating capacities of judgement that can further individuals' understanding of the world from the point of view of the other. The cultivation of narrative imagination may advance one's ability for compassionate understanding and for being sensitive about the lives of other human beings. Art can nourish people's moral sentiments and promote, following Nussbaum's arguments, a shared public conception of the person that is essential for human development.

But art can go beyond the advancement of people's sensitiveness to humanity. Art has the power to make people see the world from a different perspective and, as highlighted by Nussbaum (1997: 99), 'a central role of art is to challenge conventional wisdom and values'. This is essential for building capabilities in which people's choices are often constrained by conventional or traditional wisdom. Art can help people to build 'examined lives', questioning and critically thinking about the world. Emotions have an important role to play in allowing people's access to these different realms of human possibilities. The power of art for shaping human development remains a topic that deserves to be fully explored. In the past, the view of culture within the traditional human development paradigm has focused on the 'negative freedom aspects' of cultural liberty (e.g. 2004 HDR) and respect for ethnicity, religion, language and other multicultural features of societies. But it has not seen art as a positive form of unveiling new horizons and opportunities for cultivating humanity and people's moral capacities.

It is difficult to assess Nussbaum's proposals for building capabilities with the lenses provided by the traditional human development approach. Part of this difficulty is because this traditional approach has remained 'macro' throughout the years, focusing its energies on measuring up against economic growth as the most important standard for assessing development.[7] In addition, the traditional approach has been much influenced by UNDP's institutional role in providing support for national governments, downplaying policies that otherwise could be micro-dimensional and addressed to civil society (e.g. on families, teachers, workplace, etc.). Moreover, it could also be argued that most of the problems assessed by HDRs are pressing and for this reason the great majority of the policies there suggested are designed for immediate implementation, missing intertemporal possibilities that could result from pro-active policies that would prospectively look forward to

---

[6] Nussbaum (2001, Chapter 5) offers a very interesting discussion about the links between music and emotion.

[7] Chapter 3 of the 2010 HDR provides a good illustration of this line of argument.

different scenarios to be built. It appears that the traditional human development approach could greatly benefit from Nussbaum's proposals for pro-actively building capabilities. In what follows, we expand on the proposals discussed above in directions that could motivate additional human development policies.

Policies for a new human development approach

The traditional human development approach is grounded on the ambition to replace – or at least to broaden – welfarist policies (based on utilitarian principles) with a freedom perspective informed by the capability approach. However, what Nussbaum's arguments suggest is that a pure freedom perspective on Kantian lines might not be enough for thinking in broader terms about social justice and human development. Her reconstruction of Rawls's conception of social contract, based on richer forms of human sociability, seem to build on her previous arguments put forward in books such as *Poetic Justice*, *Cultivating Humanity* and *Upheavals of Thought*. But her arguments go beyond a reconstruction. By introducing categories of benevolence, compassion, sympathy, understanding, respect, etc. she examines the importance of moral sentiments to human development and how human values and virtues are strategically relevant for understanding the foundations of social justice.

It might be difficult to talk about values, virtues and moral sentiments in a liberal perspective where arguments that might be perceived as curtailing choice are often seen as judgemental. But after seeing some of Nussbaum's policy proposals it is also difficult to conclude that individuals and governments should be neutral on matters of virtue and vice and that just societies do not need to cultivate pro-actively good moral sentiments and attitudes in their citizens. In liberal societies, people are often ambivalent regarding judgements about virtue, ready to make them but reluctant to see them finding their way into the law. As Sandel (2009: 9) puts it: 'This dilemma points to one of the great questions of political philosophy: Does a just society seek to promote the virtue of its citizens? Or should law be neutral toward competing conceptions of virtue, so that citizens can be free to choose for themselves the best way to live?'

Sandel sides with the first alternative and it seems that Nussbaum provides a third way demanding conceptions of virtue as a foundation for her freedom arguments and revision of Rawls's conception of social contract. Moreover, she focuses on virtues as *public values*, conducive to public reason and human development. These are values that facilitate people's respect for one another, compassion, understanding of human diversity and multicultural characteristics, without abandoning her freedom perspective that allows people to make their rational and examined choices. It is within this context that we try to develop Nussbaum's proposal of building capabilities by expanding on some areas of public policy introduced above.

In order to do that, it is useful to consider an important insight from social psychology that sees human values – it does not use the more philosophical language of 'moral sentiments' but characterises some values as such – not as abstract principles but as 'guides to action' (Kluckhohn, 1951; Rokeach, 1973; Schwartz, 1994). This perspective is coherent with the capabilities approach that assesses people's well-being not for the resources that they have or their unexamined subjective views but for their sets of 'beings and doings'. Following this line of reasoning allows us to see human values as principles that guide people's behaviour. Of course, depending on people's different contexts, their attitudes can be different from what would be expected from their values. Similarly, people might decide to behave otherwise due to the influence of norms, customs and traditions. After all, people are in a constant process of confronting their different values with observed behaviours and practices. It is this process and corresponding dynamics that shape people's values. Values are then formed by living experiences, by practices, by different beings and doings rather than merely by speeches.

The redesign of public space

The concept of public space can have a physical and a political dimension. In its physical dimension the public space constitutes the loci where people meet and share different experiences. By doing so they are exposed to different concrete situations and forms of life that provide circumstances for normative exchanges between people. Thus, public spaces offer 'multiple possibilities for interaction' – that people might wish to realise or not – and material conditions for establishing forms of sociability conducive to a shared public conception of the person. Yet, in its political dimension, public space is a precondition for the creation of political consensus among people – 'political' in the sense of allowing dialogues – because values are not idiosyncratic constructions. Whereas some political consensuses last provisionally, others prove to be more robust, for instance when they are translated into constitutional principles or other forms of contracts. In any case, in its political dimension, the existence of public space is important for the creation of social priorities as political objectives.

Investment in public spaces is vital for young children. They could be translated, for instance, into green areas and public parks for stimulating human forms of sociability from very early stages in life. Public spaces are important, in their physical dimension, as spaces for socialisation where children might learn to see 'different' children and think about their commonalities and differences as human beings. In addition, if values are influenced by practices and habits, public parks can provide possibilities for shortening social distances that always increase when physical space is fragmented. At the same time, disregard for public spaces can increase people's insecurity towards their fellow citizens, when people are segregated and isolated because of their race, poverty, etc. Investment in public spaces, starting from spaces for young children, can reduce people's feeling of social isolation and increase their feeling of security towards each other. Moreover, they can contribute to building a shared public conception of the person necessary for the creation of new forms of sociability.

A range of policies, in addition to what has been said about parks and green areas, can be derived from the idea that the promotion of public spaces is part of a society's options for building capabilities, such as *humanisation of housing policies* (with more emphasis on parks, trees, the streets, improvement of accessibility, etc.) where people can physically appropriate public spaces; *humanisation of public transport policies* (not simply for environmental reasons but for facilitating people's circulation in their cities); and *communication campaigns* (that could help building public reason about core normative issues related to their role as citizens), promoting accessibility to certain sorts of knowledge important for people exercising their citizenship rights. The idea that information accessibility is important for the construction of public spaces in the political sense of the concept is not new. It is behind the existence of national television channels such as the BBC in the UK, TV5 in France and TVE in Spain, among others. The redesign of public spaces, both physically and politically, is a vital challenge for democratic societies willing to create living experiences for their citizens that might allow them to flourish as human beings moving beyond shackles of narrow motivations of individual advantage towards human forms of sociability based on moral sentiments. A new range of human development policies might emerge from thinking pro-actively about how different public spaces can allow individuals to build their capabilities themselves.

Caring for children's moral education

Much has been said by the traditional human development approach, as can be seen in several HDRs, about the distinction between 'means' and 'ends' of development. In regard to education, it has consistently been remarked that education is important to human development not only for being instrumentally relevant for the promotion of other freedoms but also for being constitutively significant for human beings. But not much more has been said about the main characteristics of this education, as we find in Nussbaum's work. The lack of depth in the treatment of educational issues from a human development perspective confines its discourse to a direct advocacy of education as we could already find in human capital theories and basic needs arguments. In other words, it can be said that there is not much in HDRs about what types of education would be necessary to cultivate people's humanity and promote human forms of sociability necessary for fairer societies.

It is important to note that education in its broadest sense extrapolates school walls. In fact, from a very early age children start their education paying attention to what people in their surroundings do. The relevance of families for shaping people's humanity has remained a topic largely neglected by the traditional human development perspective. But if we think intertemporally about human development, as Nussbaum invites us to do, we cannot avoid considering issues regarding children's socialisation and the role of their families in cultivating their values and moral sentiments.

By 'family' here we understand a network of care and love, rather than a particular configuration of people. Families are structurally diverse and dynamic and should be respected in their plurality so that their role can be fully appreciated. Families are foundational to the biological, psychological and social development of human beings. They cater for babies' and children's needs, allowing their physical–cognitive development. They provide opportunities for affective interactions throughout one's life, supporting (or not) one's emotional development. They are the first instances where children are exposed to values, cultures and conflicts (Grusec, 2002). This means that parents or carers might have certain influence, at least initially, on the formation of their children's humanity. This early influence, however, comes not necessarily from what parents and carers mean to do or to say but from what they actually do.

Actions speak louder than words. If parents or carers maintain a nice speech about human values but if they harm (physically or psychologically) their children, if they are inconsistent in the norms they propose, if they are negligent, indifferent or simply do not live according to the values they claim, their words are empty (Roest et al., 2009). For this reason, it is crucial to think in terms of actual *doings and beings* in trying to characterise how values and humanity can be intergenerationally transmitted. In fact, evidence from social psychology (Schönpflug, 2001) suggests that there is no process of 'transmission' *per se*, but that it is from diverse family interactions and parents' behaviour that children build their values. Parents, in their daily attitudes and practices, reflect normative priorities that might be unnoticeable but that shape little by little the emotional environment in which their children live during their childhood (Darling and Steinberg, 1993). The parents' influence might dramatically diminish later, during adolescence (Spera, 2005).

The concept of 'parental practices' is at the core of a new vision for human development built around the proposal of building capabilities. It overcomes the public–private divide where children's education is seen only as a school or government problem. For this reason, it is micro-dimensional, demanding a coherent arrangement of the actions of many stakeholders. Because it focuses on the promotion of motivationally rich individuals, a process that takes time to build, it requires an intertemporal perspective for pro-active policies. But how can this happen in practice?

Pro-active policies that involve strong participation of parents and carers should focus on daily attitudes and practices. For instance, a father intending to convey values of tolerance and understanding to his children might choose to lecture them on these principles. But he will probably fail in his intended results if at the same time he behaves in contradiction with what he preaches (Blasi, 1995). So the 'policies' for parents and carers are simple: to put into practice what they say and to translate their values into behaviour (represented by valuable beings and doings). By doing so, they can provide a proper environment for children to develop their moral sentiments.

In very concrete terms, parents can follow 'positive parenting practices' (PPP), which entail:

- positive monitoring of their children, without pressure or exaggerations but fostering communication, showing affection to children when they are under stress;
- parental modelling, by teaching children by example – so, the practice of benevolence, understanding and compassion is key for the creation of an environment in which children can reflect on the consequences of their actions;
- positive communication, fostering dialogue as a practice whenever possible, but in particular during conflicting situations;
- positive feedback, praising children when they behave properly or achieve good results at school – the perception of being 'an achiever' is very important for the development of children's self-esteem and school results (Flouri, 2006);
- adequate discipline, based on a temporal suspension of attention and affection or on calling attention to the impact of one's actions on others (Grusec *et al.*, 2000).

These practices represent a 'thin' conception of the good, based on actions promoting human values that represent very general forms of human sociability that are necessary for a new and broader vision of social contract as argued by Nussbaum (2006).

There is a higher probability of success in implementing PPPs when the chosen parental discipline approach is based not on coercion but on an authoritative style that promotes values of solidarity, compassion and self-determination and at the same time specifies clear limits for what children can do. The proposal of building capabilities puts parents and carers at the centre-stage of educational policies. Human development policies start at home. They can then move to schools where parents' and carers' participation is essential for the promotion of dynamic environments and where students, parents and teachers could work together for the *humanisation of schools*, promoting practices and living experiences based on values (McCowan, 2008; McCowan and Unterhalter, 2010; Starratt, 1994).

Transforming the workplace

Work is a very important part of adult life. It is not simply about earning a living, it is about relationships, values, strategies, communication, behaviours and growing as a human being. Within this context, the workplace can be characterised by a set of limits, times, norms, languages and demands that organises one's life and relationships. Different beings and doings when consolidated in people's daily actions become part of cultures, norms and procedures. The workplace offers a universe of negative and/or positive life experiences that influences people's values and motivations. It shapes human forms of sociability and as such influences people's personal histories and psychic structure (Bond *et al.*, 2010). Negative life experiences in the workplace comprise feelings of fear, dissatisfaction, insecurity, lack of orientation, powerlessness, alienation, vulnerability, frustration, agony, depression, sadness, aggressiveness, physical and emotional distress, guilt, tension, anger, among others. Positive life experiences in the workplace entail feelings of recognition, appreciation, solidarity, pride, realisation, and freedom.

Many companies still ignore the heterogeneity of needs and abilities of their employees and their aspirations to become better human beings through their work. Traditional management practices, based exclusively on productivity targets and control of absenteeism, often ignore the need for managers to listen actively to the problems faced by employees (Golembiewski *et al.*, 1983). Managers, instead of denying the suffering – whether occasional or frequent – that they observe, should try to promote their employees' psychological satisfaction and social recognition in the workplace. When personnel management fails, we can observe fear, pressure, distrust, norms that tend to be too narrow or too broad, strengthening of hierarchical powers, communication without visibility, inadequate assessment systems, internal competition, rivalry among colleagues, etc., with clear disarticulation of collective work, individualism and isolation in the workplace.

Policies for building capabilities in the workplace should foster managerial powers of qualified listening and communication practices among employees improving interpersonal skills. Following the capabilities approach, it is important that companies recognise people's diversity and support not only more flexibility in the workplace but also the promotion of respect and autonomy of their employees. The creation of 'public spaces' in which employees could manifest themselves is essential for the promotion of shared values of tolerance, understanding and public scrutiny. In addition, the introduction of managerial concerns for employees' health and transparency as part of their internal communication strategies is an important element in building capabilities in the workplace.

Traditional human development criticism of economic growth focuses on its insufficiency to guarantee human well-being on the grounds that resources are imperfect indicators of well-being. But economic growth is also an issue because of the practices and living experiences that it may impose on societies. The workplace is a key public space for the proactive construction of new human forms of sociability based on a broader understanding of individual and collective social advantage.

Art for human capabilities

Building capabilities through art is a subject that is much discussed in the fields of aesthetics and art criticism: from foundational critiques of the morality of artistic production and enjoyment (Barrett, 1982) to debates about the best approaches and strategies for teaching arts at school (such as 'discipline-based art education', the 'visual-culture' or the 'choice-based art education': see Prince, 2008). The natural focus of the debate seems to be about how schools can contribute to explore art as a formative element of children's personality (Bloomfield and Childs, 2000), but there are also discussions that involve parents in teaching art to children (Beal and Miller, 2001).

Art is an important source of instrumental knowledge (literacy and numeracy) and moral cognition for children. It is not simply about nurturing their creative self but about stimulating affective modes of learning that are central for cultivating their humanity. It is also about building their self-esteem by validating their unique form of artistic expression. It is about respecting each other's work. Within the school environment, policies for building children's capabilities through art would involve:

- a change in the role and status of the arts in school curriculum, avoiding boxing them into a single discipline;
- a stronger engagement of parents in carrying out art activities at home, thinking about their houses as 'learning environments' for their children.

But access to art should not be a privilege of children. Its importance for society cannot be overestimated. Art is crucial for people not simply because it is a repository of human values or because it has the power to structure social elements. Art matters because it is intrinsically valuable *per se* and its usefulness does not need to be justified. As Belfiore and Bennett (2008: 4) put it when analysing the social impact of art: 'A belief in the power of the arts to transform lives for the better represents something close to orthodoxy amongst advocates of the art around the world.' When we consider art at large, policies for building citizens' capabilities through art would involve a focus of governments' cultural policies on promoting and funding cultural initiatives in their plurality and diversity. A capabilities approach to art would advocate its qualities of promoting more humane individuals and more humanitarian forms of social organisation necessary for social justice.

Conclusion

In the last twenty years, the human development perspective has constructed a strategic development agenda that has tackled many fundamental issues for individuals and societies, such as poverty, inequality, gender and other forms of discrimination, respect for human rights, promotion of health, education and economic growth, institutional development, safer environment, democracy, cultural liberties, among other relevant issues. Nevertheless, it can be argued that much of what has been achieved has evolved within certain limitations imposed by a way of thinking that owes more to its past (i.e. the view that the main challenge of human development was to overcome the growth perspective) than to its future, as argued above. Martha C. Nussbaum's work is difficult to categorise and label and it has the potential to be misinterpreted when applied outside its context. But it provides powerful insights and inspirations for thinking about a new human development approach:

less absorbed in macro comparisons, more focused on micro; less reactive and more pro-active; less static and more dynamic (intertemporal) in
its considerations; less concerned in exclusively supporting government
policies, more concerned in supporting civil society's actions; less dedicated to quantitative targets, more committed to building capabilities
and human dignity.

Nussbaum invites us to think about a different set of human development policies that talks about art, public spaces and the workplace, and
that puts children and their carers centre-stage of development processes. These are development policies to be designed not simply *for*
people but *with* people. This way of thinking about development recognises the role of government in the promotion of decent societies, but
also claims an important responsibility for ordinary citizens. Nussbaum
invites us to consider development as a long-term route towards human
flourishing and suggests that the most sensible way to start building a
house is from its pillars.

Moreover, the policies that are derived from this perspective of building capabilities are based on concrete actions that ordinary people can
understand. For this reason they fulfil the mission of human development of promoting public reasoning and active citizenship. A logical
extension of these policies can be seen in the form of humanisation
strategies for health, education, housing, etc. that add, in a much more
credible sense, the adjective 'human' to human development policies.

REFERENCES

Anand, P., Hunter, G. and Smith, R. (2005) 'Capabilities and well-being:
     evidence based on the Sen–Nussbaum approach to welfare,' *Social Indicators
     Research*, vol. 74, no. 1, 9–55.
Barrett, C. (1982) 'The morality of artistic production,' *The Journal of Aesthetics
     and Art Criticism*, vol. 41, no. 2, 137–44.
Beal, N. and Miller, G. (2001) *The Art of Teaching Art to Children: in school and at
     home*. New York: Farrar, Straus and Giroux.
Belfiore, E. and Bennett, O. (2008) *The Social Impact of the Arts*. London:
     Palgrave Macmillan.
Blasi, A. (1995) 'Moral understanding and the moral personality: the process of
     moral integration.' In: Kurtines, W. and Gewirtz, J. (eds.) *Moral
     Development: an introduction*. London: Allyn & Bacon.
Bloomfield, A. and Childs, J. (2000) *Teaching Integrated Arts in the Primary
     School: dance, drama, music, and the visual arts*. London: David Fulton
     Publishers.
Bond, Stephanie A., Tuckey, Michelle R. and Dollard, Maureen F. (2010)
     'Psychosocial safety climate, workplace bullying, and symptoms of
     posttraumatic stress,' *Organization Development Journal*, vol. 28, no. 1, 37–56.

Cohen, D.A. and Rice, J. (1997) 'Parenting styles, adolescent substance use and academic achievement,' *Journal of Drug Education*, vol. 27, no. 2, 199–211.

Comim, F., Qizilbash, M. and Alkire, S. (eds.) (1998) *The Capability Approach: concepts, measures and applications.* Cambridge University Press.

Darling, N. and Steinberg, L. (1993) 'Parenting style as context: an integrative model,' *Psychological Bulletin*, vol. 113, no. 3, 487–96.

Flouri, E. (2006) 'Parental interest in children's education, children's self-esteem and locus of control, and later educational attainment: Twenty-six year follow-up of the 1970 British Birth Cohort,' *British Journal of Educational Psychology*, vol. 76, no. 1, 41–55.

Golembiewski, R.T., Munzenrider, R. and Carter, D. (1983) 'Phases of progressive burnout and their work sites covariates,' *Journal of Applied Behavioral Science*, vol. 19, 461–81.

Gotoh, R. and Dumouchel, P. (eds.) (2009) *Against Injustice: The new economics of Amartya Sen.* Cambridge University Press.

Grusec, J.E. (2002) 'Parental socialization and children's acquisition of values.' In: Bornstein, M. (ed.) *Handbook of Parenting: Vol. 5 Practical Issues in Parenting.* Mahwah, NJ: Lawrence Erlbaum, pp. 143–68.

Grusec, J.E., Goodnow, J.J. and Kuczynski, L. (2000) 'New directions in analyses of parenting contributions to children's acquisition of values,' *Child Development*, vol. 71, 205–11.

Haq, M. (1996) *Reflections on Human Development.* Oxford University Press.

Kluckhohn, C.K.M. (1951) 'Values and values orientation in the theory of action.' In: Parsons, T. and Shils, E. (1951) *Towards a General Theory of Action.* Cambridge, MA: Harvard University Press.

McCowan, T. (2008) 'Curricular transposition in citizenship education.' *Theory and Research in Education*, vol. 6, no. 2, 153–72.

McCowan, T. and Unterhalter, E. (2010) 'Education for democratic citizenship: a capabilities perspective.' Mimeo, background paper for the Brazilian Human Development Report 2009/2010.

Nussbaum, M.C. (1990) *Love's Knowledge: essays on philosophy and literature.* New York: Oxford University Press.

(1995) *Poetic Justice: the Literary Imagination and Public Life.* Boston, MA: Beacon.

(1997) *Cultivating Humanity: a classical defense of reform in liberal education.* Cambridge, MA: Harvard University Press.

(1999) *Sex and Social Justice.* New York: Oxford University Press.

(2000) *Women and Human Development.* Cambridge University Press.

(2001) *Upheavals of Thought: the intelligence of emotions.* Cambridge University Press.

(2006) *Frontiers of Justice: disability, nationality, species membership.* Cambridge, MA: The Belknap Press.

(2010) *Not for Profit: why democracy needs the humanities.* Princeton University Press.

(2011) *Creating Capabilities.* Cambridge, MA: Harvard University Press.

Prince, E. (2008) *Art Is Fundamental: teaching the elements and principles of art in elementary.* Chicago: School Zephyr Press.

Reeve, A. (1996) 'Impartiality between what? Lifestyles, conceptions of the good, and harm,' *Political Studies*, vol. 44, no. 2, 314–17.

Roest, A.M.C., Dubas, J.S. and Gerris, J.R.M. (2009) 'Value transmissions between parents and children: gender and developmental phase as transmission belts,' *Journal of Adolescence*, vol. 30, no. 1, 1–11.

Rokeach, M. (1973) *The Nature of Human Values*. New York: The Free Press and Macmillan.

Sandel, M. (2009) *Justice: what's the right thing to do?* London: Penguin Books.

Schönpflug, U. (2001) 'Intergenerational transmission of values: the role of transmission belts,' *Journal of Cross-Cultural Psychology*, vol. 32, no. 2, 174–85.

Schwartz, S.H. (1994) 'Are there universal aspects in the structure and contents of human values?' *Journal of Social Issues*, vol. 50, no. 4, 19–45.

Spera, C. (2005) 'A review of the relationship among parenting practices, parenting styles, and adolescent school achievement,' *Educational Psychology Review*, vol. 17, no. 2, June, 125–46.

Starratt, R. (1994) *Building an Ethical School: a practical response to moral crisis in schools*. London: Falmer Press.

UNDP (2010) *Human Development Report: The Real Wealth of Nations – Pathways to Human Development*. New York: Palgrave Macmillan.

Uyan-Semerci, P. (2007) 'A relational account of Nussbaum's list of capabilities,' *Journal of Human Development and Capabilities*, vol. 8, no. 2, 203–21.

5   Capabilities or functionings?
Anatomy of a debate*

Marc Fleurbaey

Introduction

The "equality of what" debate has burgeoned in many directions, but a central issue ever since Rawls (1971, 1982) and Dworkin (1981) argued that individuals should assume some responsibility has been whether individual situations should be evaluated and compared in terms of opportunities or in terms of achievements. The advocates of the former option have been the most vocal, and beyond many subtle differences one can find a basic convergence in the views expressed in Arneson (1989, 1990), Cohen (1989), Nussbaum (1990), Roemer (1993), and Sen (1985, 1992).

Martha C. Nussbaum's approach, interestingly, has developed at the intersection of two lines of thought. One is, along the "equality of what" debate, the emergence of Amartya Sen's concepts of functionings and capabilities (Sen 1985, 1992), which are very comprehensive and therefore appear able to capture all relevant aspects of human well-being. Recall that a functioning is any kind of "doing or being" that an individual life can contain, while a capability set is the set of combinations of functionings that a given individual has access to and can choose if she wishes to. The other line of thought is the exploration of the possibility of a universalist notion of human good, inspired by the Aristotelian tradition (Nussbaum 1988, 1990, 1993). The interplay between these two lines of thought is important for the following reason. One of the difficulties with Sen's capability approach is to finalize the methodology for evaluating individual and social situations. This requires weighting the various dimensions of human good. Although Sen mentioned that this should ideally be performed in a way that takes account of the population's values, he never proposed a precise way to do it. This problem can be at least partly alleviated if it is possible to define a list of basic

* This chapter is based on a talk given at a workshop in Leuven, and has benefited from reactions of the audience and especially M.C. Nussbaum.

capabilities that has *universal* validity, because the problem of the diversity of values and preferences is then less pressing regarding these basic capabilities. Moreover, Nussbaum restricts the prescriptions of justice to the requirement that society should *at least* provide such a basic list of capabilities to each and every member. In this fashion it is not a priority to worry about the complexities that remain attached to the evaluation of more ambitious social policies that go beyond ascertaining that the minimum is attained by every member of society. If all the capabilities from the selected list must be provided to every member, there is no apparent need to weigh one capability against another.

In this context, the focus on capabilities (i.e., opportunities) rather than functionings (i.e., achievements) is also essential because it leaves it possible for populations and individuals to seize or not to seize the opportunities as they see fit according to their particular values. The possible charge of paternalism is assuaged by the fact that there is no obligation for any individual to make use of the capabilities that are provided. Among the key examples listed by Nussbaum are sex, food, and play. It may be important to provide individuals with sufficient opportunities in each of these domains, but this leaves it possible for anyone to embrace a life of monkish celibacy, of frequent fasting, or of hard work.

Richard Arneson's views on this issue come from a different inspiration and have evolved. He initially defended the thesis that justice requires equalizing opportunities for welfare. Taking welfare as the relevant measure of achievement is usually considered an obvious way, if not the only way, of avoiding the charge of paternalism. The focus on opportunities in his theory was motivated by different considerations, namely, the idea that, in fairness, society does not have any duty to compensate disadvantages for which an individual is personally responsible. After having defended an evaluation of well-being exclusively formulated in terms of opportunities, however, he has developed a different conception (see Arneson 1999, 2000a) in which achievements are at the center of attention, although their evaluation ought to be responsibility-sensitive. More precisely, he proposes to modulate the social priority of providing any given individual benefit depending on how responsible for his current situation the individual is, in addition to the usual variables that determine priority in a prioritarian approach, namely, the size of the benefit and the initial well-being level of the individual. An individual who is responsible for his low level of well-being would obtain a lower priority than someone who is at the same level of well-being without being responsible for it.

In 2000, *Ethics* published a symposium on Nussbaum's philosophy in which, among other things, Arneson engaged Nussbaum on the opportunities/achievements issue. The debate between these two authors (Arneson 2000b, Nussbaum 2000a) is an excellent introduction to the underlying questions as well as a nice and entertaining perspective on their theories. In this chapter I would like to analyze this interesting debate between two of the most prominent authors in the field, and to propose my own reflections on certain specific issues for which, it seems to me, new ideas and possibilities are worth considering.

Arneson's critique

In a section entitled "Capability versus functioning," Arneson sets out to examine possible foundations for a focus on opportunities rather than achievements, and distinguishes two basic values which could provide such foundations: responsibility and freedom. Responsibility was indeed the motivation for his own initial theory of equality of opportunity, while freedom is a notion that is, for instance, prominent in Sen's advocacy of the capability approach. Moreover, these two values are not exclusive and can mutually support an opportunity-oriented approach.

Regarding responsibility, Arneson has no objection against the idea that personal responsibility reduces the duty for society to provide help. But he questions the view that this implies an exclusive focus on opportunities. "One might rather hold that the obligations of society toward an individual are limited in extent but are obligations to help the individual achieve functioning not just capability" (p. 60). This alternative view, which is obviously inspired by Arneson's own recent theory, is backed by two examples. The first example concerns "pointless opportunities." Consider an individual who does not care about being provided certain opportunities and is firmly decided not to make use of them. Why insist on evaluating his situation in terms of capabilities? An opportunity metric appears to be blind to what really matters and it therefore seems more reasonable to be concerned with the provision of functionings and of opportunities which are in some relevant sense conducive to functionings. The second example is that of the "capability squanderer" and turns the responsibility argument on its head. If individual responsibility diminishes society's duties, why guarantee a distribution of capabilities independently of how individuals themselves contribute to shaping their own capabilities? If someone repeatedly destroys his capabilities, at some point, Arneson says, society's duty to restore his capabilities is eroded. This second example is perhaps less powerful because it depends on a particular interpretation of capabilities. It assumes that capabilities are possibilities of immediate functionings. If, instead, they are understood as opportunities for functionings over the whole life span, it is possible to

view the capability squanderer as someone who simply chooses a mediocre functioning vector for the whole course of his life, from a capability
set that contained the possibility to enjoy good functionings throughout.
Under such interpretation society provides the whole-life capabilities and
there is no "capability squanderer" because what individuals choose is a
vector of functionings.

Considering freedom as a possible basis for the capability approach,
Arneson considers two possible ways in which an argument can be built.
The first simply invokes the value of freedom. Arneson does not object to
the fact that freedom is an important good. Noting that it may be better
to be left to choose the best option in a large set rather than getting this
same option without any choice, he even admits that freedom has intrinsic, not just instrumental, value. But all the arguments about the importance of freedom only imply that "freedom is one important good among
other goods. So to do the best we can to facilitate people's achieving good
lives we will inter alia have to provide them wide freedom. There is no
consideration here that even suggests an exclusive focus on freedom as in
the view that social justice entirely consists in fair provision of capabilities
or real freedoms" (p. 61).

A second way in which freedom can be invoked to justify an
opportunity-oriented theory of justice has to do with the defense of a
private sphere. Personal sovereignty requires that individuals are left free
to choose and exercise autonomy in their life rather than simply being
granted good conditions of life. This is especially important as a protection against the potentially intrusive aspects of the kind of perfectionism
that is associated with a universalist conception of the good life. But here
again the argument falls short of the objective because guaranteeing a
private sphere for each individual does not require an evaluation of
individual situations in terms of opportunities. If the ultimate objective
is to promote a certain perfectionist ideal while respecting personal
sovereignty, one should assess whether the organization of society is
efficient in this respect. A variant of the objection of "pointless opportunities" can be raised again. As Arneson writes, "an individual under a
capability regime is entitled to pursue, say, a life of trivial pleasures rather
than one of perfectionist achievement. But the individual, rather than be
allotted circumstances that give her a specified level of capabilities, might
well prefer that she be allotted circumstances that would enable her to
gain a higher level of trivial pleasure over the course of her life" (p. 61). In
this example it is a pure waste to provide capabilities.

Finally, Arneson notes that Nussbaum's examples (sex, food, play)
"share the feature that it is very hard to see how a society, particularly by
coarse-grained measures such as law and social policy, could do anything

to promote functioning beyond providing capability" (p. 62). It would be more interesting to look at examples in which policies targeting opportunities and policies targeting achievements would clearly differ. As an example, he suggests contrasting a policy making opera available to everyone and a policy promoting opera events in a more direct way. He submits that "when we imagine a clear case in which it is clear that by providing less capability for flourishing we could get more flourishing fairly distributed, one ought to opt for more flourishing" (p. 63). Note the importance of the proviso of fair distribution. One would indeed hesitate to prefer a policy promoting opera if most of its effects were beneficial only to a social or cultural elite.

For Arneson, more generally, within the general frame of liberal egalitarianism there is no need to worry that perfectionism could be politically ominous and, therefore, no need to seek protection in an opportunity-oriented theory. In this context it is indeed plausible, as J.S. Mill argued, that paternalism is counterproductive in the long run. It is also possible to say that if restrictions of liberty are needed to promote more human good fairly distributed, they are acceptable.[1] In a nutshell, Arneson's view is that the capability approach is not needed as a protection against the intrusiveness of perfectionism, provided that liberal egalitarianism prevails. Moreover, the capability approach is justified neither by reference to responsibility nor by reference to freedom.

Nussbaum's rejoinder

In her reply Nussbaum first rejects the association of her approach with perfectionism that underlies Arneson's paper. "Individuals have and pursue many different reasonable comprehensive conceptions of what has value. Respect for persons therefore entails that we respect those reasons and create, and protect, spaces within which those different conceptions will be chosen. So the capabilities are now envisaged as a core that we promote for political purposes, knowing that citizens will attach them in many different ways to their comprehensive conceptions" (p. 128). As she writes in her book, "the use of the list is facilitative rather than tyrannical; if individuals neglect an item on the list, this is just fine from the point of view of the political purposes of the list, so long as they

---

[1] Surprisingly, Arneson does not envisage the possibility to define the virtues of perfection in a way that incorporates a central concern for autonomy and freedom (as in Raz's theory). Perfectionism then becomes an ally, not an enemy, in the promotion of freedom and the defense of personal autonomy. If certain specific restrictions of liberty appear warranted according to this ideal of perfection, there is no fear that they could extend into a general form of oppression.

don't impede others who wish to pursue it. And if they pursue an item not on the list, that is to be expected, and exactly what the list is meant to make possible. It is in this sense that the list is, emphatically, a partial and not a comprehensive conception of the good" (2000b, p. 96).

It seems clear, at this point, that resorting to the capability metric is essential and in Nussbaum (2000b) the "concerns about paternalism and pluralism" play a key role indeed: "If we were to take functioning itself as the goal of public policy, pushing citizens into functionings in a single determinate manner, the liberal pluralist would rightly judge that we were precluding many choices that citizens may make in accordance with their own conceptions of the good, and perhaps violating their rights" (p. 87). Consistently with this concern, in the symposium debate Nussbaum (2000a) replies to Arneson that "respect for choice" is the best reason for capabilities. It must be understood "not in terms of a comprehensive liberal ideal of autonomy, but in terms of an idea of respect for the diversity of persons and their comprehensive conceptions" (p. 129).

She acknowledges that the fact that "some comprehensive conceptions do not highly value choice" (p. 130) raises a potential problem, and this partly motivates her special interest for family and religious issues addressed in her book (Nussbaum 2000b). But, she argues, "respect for persons as equal citizens demands providing all with all the capabilities, even though we know ahead of time that some will not be used" (p. 130). As an example, she mentions the Amish who refuse to participate in politics but should not be deprived of their political rights for that matter.

Considering Arneson's charge that her examples (sex, food, play) are about domains for which policies and social institutions can only impact capabilities, she proposes examining the issue of whether voting should be made compulsory. In this case it is clearly possible to distinguish between institutions that focus on access (political rights, organization of elections) and policies which are aimed at actual practice. She opposes making voting compulsory, just as she opposes mandatory religious practices, while acknowledging that it is important to take care of the many subtle obstacles to political participation that may affect the disadvantaged groups of society. In Nussbaum (2000b), she even writes: "Compulsory voting would not be ruled out, if we were convinced that requiring functioning is the only way to ensure the presence of a capability" (p. 93).

While insisting that capabilities, not functionings, are the proper focus of social justice, she then lists a number of reasons why a direct concern for functionings is, in some specific cases, justified. This obviously holds as regards children. "Even where adults are concerned, we may feel that some of the capabilities are so crucial to the development or maintenance of all the others that we are sometimes justified in promoting functioning rather than simply capability, within limits set by an appropriate concern for liberty" (2000a, p. 130). Health and safety are the prime examples. In such domains, moreover, some "regulations are justified because of the difficulty of making informed choices in these areas and because of the burden of inquiry such choices would impose on citizens" (p. 130). In particular, "we should be especially concerned with choices citizens may make to surrender permanently the necessary condition of a function" (p. 131), as in sterilization or suicide. Regarding dignity, she does not oppose leaving it possible for people to put themselves in humiliating situations, but suggests that public policies should always treat people in a dignified way. She then raises the issue of practical reason, for which the functioning rather than the capability seems key to a truly human life. She would oppose a repression of practices in which people relinquish their autonomy to follow gurus or fortune tellers, but would consider it appropriate to promote practical reason in general, "as a way of expanding capability, not mandating actual functioning of a specific type" (p. 132).

As she writes in conclusion of this section, "[her] position on capability and functioning is subtle, and [she does] not altogether disagree with Arneson about the importance of functioning in certain cases" (p. 132). Although these two authors have complex and subtle views, it is clear that the central bone of contention is whether respecting choice implies that "capability, not functioning, is the appropriate political goal" (2000b, 87). In the rest of this chapter, I question the role played by choice in Nussbaum's approach, and suggest that a better way of respecting the diversity of individual conceptions of the good life is to seek a metric of well-being that respects individual preferences. I then analyze how this alternative approach bears on the capability/functioning debate.

Should we respect choices?

A key element in Nussbaum's reasoning is the belief that defining the goals of social policy in terms of functionings implies using constraint, forcing individuals to live against their own conception of the good life, or even violating basic rights. If that were true, it would indeed provide a definitive reason for abandoning a functioning approach. There are two parts in this assumption and it is useful to separate them. The first part is that taking functionings as the goal implies that a "single determinate manner" will define how the various functionings should be achieved by individuals. In other words, a uniform metric of achievement will be imposed on all individuals, regardless of their conceptions of the good life. The second part is that if a uniform metric of achievement is used in the formulation of public goals, then constraint and force will necessarily be part of the ensuing policies. Both parts are, actually, questionable.

Let us consider the latter first. There are at least two ways in which force and constraint would be counterproductive in the promotion of a specific measure of individual achievement. First, there are many functionings for which forcing people does not produce good results. It is very hard to use constraint in order to trigger intellectual interest, emotional flourishing and religious devotion. One may impose certain practices such as specific studies, marital status or religious ceremonies, but if the relevant functionings have to do with intrinsic motivation there is a gap between such external practices and the ultimate objective.

Arneson (2000b, p. 45) discusses Mill's conjecture that the sum of utility is maximized by a liberal government rather than by paternalism, and notes that a weakness of this conjecture is that it may be right if the gains of those who benefit from non-paternalism exceed the losses of those who would be better off under paternalism. The problem is that it is likely that the latter section of the population contains the worst off, those who, because of various disadvantages, would be bad choosers under the liberal government. If that is so, an egalitarian would actually prefer the paternalist government. However, if the metric of achievement that is used involves functionings such that, for essentially all individuals, constraint would really hamper the outcome, it appears that a dose of freedom is needed at least for these particular functionings.

The second way in which force and constraint may appear problematic in a functioning-oriented setting is that personal autonomy and the use of practical reason may be enlisted as key functionings. How could one promote such functionings and submit individuals to substantial constraints? Depending on the weights of such "freedom" functionings in the overall metric of achievement, a certain degree of constraint in order to boost the other functionings may be warranted, but the presence of such functionings in the overall metric would guarantee against any serious intrusion in people's lives and especially against any serious contradiction between the content of their lives and their conceptions of the good life. Any such contradiction would indeed be extremely damaging to the achievement of personal autonomy. Nussbaum defends the promotion of practical reason "as a way of expanding capability, not mandating actual functioning," but the mere fact that a functioning expands freedom should dissolve the worry that promoting functionings is illiberal.

Up to this point we have considered arguments to the effect that force may be counterproductive relative to functionings. One can also, less ambitiously, argue that an achievement-centered set of goals can be made *compatible* with a substantial respect for freedom. Indeed, it is possible to erect a protection of individual freedom within a functioning approach simply by defining the social goals with a list of functionings that ignores the functionings pertaining to a certain private sphere. Arneson argues that the protection of a personal sphere of sovereignty does not require an opportunity approach. The simple device of ignoring the corresponding functionings in the evaluation of individual situations shows how to do it.

All that being said, one must admit that even if a uniform metric of achievement need not trigger important violations of personal autonomy and is compatible with a substantial degree of liberalism in institutions and policies, this may not appear sufficient. One would like a definition of social goals which embodies the respect for the diversity of conceptions of life in a more complete way. At this point one must turn to the first part of Nussbaum's view about the connection between functionings and constraint. Recall that this first part says that a functioning approach must involve a unique set of weights for the various dimensions of functioning, thereby ignoring the diversity of individual views. As a matter of fact, this view is unduly pessimistic. It is possible to combine an approach centered on achievements and the respect for individual preferences. The most famous approach claiming to do just this is utilitarianism. More generally, relying on utility indexes that properly represent individual preferences, whether these indexes are added up as in utilitarianism or treated in a more egalitarian (or prioritarian) way, is indeed respectful of the diversity of preferences in the sense that if a single individual is affected by a particular decision, the social criterion will always agree with the individual's view on the matter. Subjective utility, however, has been rejected by many authors, most prominently by Sen (1985) who pointed out that subjective utility adapts too easily to people's conditions of life. Differences in subjective utility are therefore unlikely to reflect the true gaps between the advantaged and the disadvantaged. The flaws of "subjective welfarism" are discussed at length in Nussbaum (2000b, Chapter 2). In the next section, we will see that it is possible to respect the diversity of individual conceptions of the good life without suffering from the flaws of subjective welfarism. One is not obliged to adopt a uniform set of weights in the construction of an index of functionings.

Before that, it is important to emphasize the difference between respecting the diversity of individual preferences and giving individuals "choice." Arguably, the former is more important and more compelling, as a social goal, than the latter. Indeed, providing choice is not always the best way to respect preferences. Even if one sets aside all the limitations to individual rationality that so often induce people to make bad choices, i.e., choices that do not really reflect their true personal goals, it is simply not true that for all conceptions of the good life individuals want to be given the maximum amount of choice. Choosing is a costly activity and there is in general a moderate amount of choice that is optimal in people's eyes, between the two extremes of getting-the-best-option-with-out-choice and getting-to-choose-from-an-overwhelming-menu. A good life is not one spent on choosing, but one that corresponds to what one wants and values, i.e., a life in which the circumstances are favorable and the amount of choice is reasonable and leaves it possible to enjoy the chosen options. While Sen criticized Rawls's theory for suffering from a fetishism of resources, one may detect a certain fetishism of choice in the capability approach.

To some extent, this observation is similar to Arneson's objection involving pointless opportunities, but it extends it. Even when opportunities are not pointless because individuals do give some value to them and do seize them, it may happen that the amount of choice that is implied by the content of the capability sets offered to individuals exceeds what they would ideally like in their lives. One illustration of the fact that people dislike spending too much time and energy in choosing is provided by the anchoring effect that is generally observed when a menu of options has a default option. Many people are then induced to pick that option although they would have picked another one if the default option had been different (see, e.g., Sunstein and Thaler 2008). This phenomenon is sometimes invoked as supporting the view that human behavior departs from the rational choice model with fixed preferences. However, this observed behavior is compatible with a deeper underlying rationality, if one takes on board the fact that studying all the options and making up one's mind is a costly activity. The presence of the default option may be used by choosers as a cost-saving device. Other considerations may of course be relevant, such as, for instance, the fact that the default option may be interpreted as the option that most people choose, inducing the conformist to take it in order to satisfy their preference for being like the others. This additional explanation is also compatible with the rational choice model.

How to respect preferences

Respecting the diversity of individual conceptions of the good life is therefore, more than giving them "choice," a valuable and important goal for just social institutions. Let us hasten to say that there is no contradiction between this assertion and acknowledging that individual preferences are often the result of social customs and entrenched mores. Nussbaum (2000b, Chapter 2) criticizes subjective welfarism for ignoring this fact. She also rightly notes that the adaptation phenomenon, which is central in Sen's criticism of subjective welfarism, is sometimes beneficial (when the little girl who dreamt of becoming an opera singer learns to form more realistic goals) and sometimes harmful (when the tamed housewife learns to like her subdued situation). More controversially, she claims that it is impossible to distinguish between the beneficial and the harmful cases without an external set of values, and therefore that preferences, even when they are checked and filtered through a proper deliberation, cannot be the sole basis of evaluation of lives. This line of argument is not fully convincing, because there is clearly a difference between adaptation to real technical constraints (we must learn to live with our inability to fly like birds, men must live with their inability to bear children, most people must live without any hope of becoming opera stars), and adaptation to unfair social institutions. The psychological process of adaptation is the same in both kinds of contexts, so that Nussbaum is right that there is no *internal* distinction if one has no way to say that certain preferences are good (liking to stay on the ground, to father, to be in the opera audience) and others are bad (liking a slavish life). But an *external* distinction is easy to make, on the basis of the characterization of the conditions to which people adapt. Adaptation to reality is good, adaptation to injustice or inequality is not.

The bottom line is this: preferences are often not respectable in practise, either because they are superficial or because they result from adaptation to problematic social circumstances, but this does not detract from the project of respecting the diversity of individual views about life, it only makes it more complicated to implement in practice. Now, how can one proceed when one is in the presence of an ideal population of individuals who have respectable conceptions of the good life that display a substantial degree of diversity? It is only when one is able to answer this question that one can turn to the more difficult cases in which preferences have to be processed first in order to find the underlying respectable conceptions of the good life.

Recalling that the main criticism against subjective welfarism involved examples of problematic adaptation, one may wonder if subjective welfarism becomes acceptable when the harmful instances of adaptation are absent from the population at hand. The answer is clearly negative, because the adaptation problem is related to a deeper problem than simple cases of adjustment to injustice. The deeper problem has two parts. First, consider two individuals who have the same conception of the good life. They therefore evaluate all possible lives in the same way.

Nevertheless, they may use different standards of evaluation when they make a graded judgment (such as "good," "mediocre," "poor," or giving numbers between 0 and 10, as in the recent World Gallup surveys). For instance, one of them may compare himself to his affluent parents and the other may compare himself to his less affluent neighbors. Therefore, it may happen that they have lives that they deem equally good even though they give different grades to these equally good lives. A subjective welfarist measure might consider that the individual who attributes to such lives a lower grade than the other individual, because of his more demanding standards, is worse off. This evaluation contradicts the individuals' own evaluation that their lives are equally good, and therefore fails to respect their preferences. The received wisdom that subjective welfarism respects preferences only considers the issue of respecting an individual's views about possible lives for herself, but ignores another dimension of the respect for preferences, which is that the ranking of possible lives by an individual also implies interpersonal comparisons. When individuals form the same rankings about possible lives but use different grading scales, subjective welfarism fails to respect their judgments about interpersonal comparisons that directly follow from their preferences about possible lives. In other words, subjective welfarism respects individual preferences only to the extent that they apply to intrapersonal comparisons but not when they are used in interpersonal comparisons.

Now, suppose that the problem of different standards is eliminated for individuals having the same ordinal preferences about lives. In this case, can we use a subjective welfarist measure? Such a measure would then respect individual preferences not only for intrapersonal comparisons, but also for interpersonal comparisons among subgroups of individuals with identical preferences. But what about interpersonal comparisons between individuals with different preferences? The problem is that in these kinds of comparisons, it is hard, if not impossible, to establish a correspondence between standards applying to different rankings. Does it make sense to equate "good" for Socrates' view of the good life with "good" for piggish preferences? Rawls (1982) strongly rejected the possibility of such a correspondence, on the ground that different preferences are incommensurable and that the construction of such a correspondence would be tantamount to constructing a "shared highest-order preference function" (p. 179). It is indeed highly problematic to define a kind of universal standard of appraisal that covers all conceptions of the good life. Even if there were a "best" life and a "worst" life for every sort of preferences, and if one could rightly equate the "best" across all preferences and the "worst" across all of them, it would remain deeply problematic to establish a correspondence for the middle-ranked lives. A popular procedure to this effect consists in relying on cardinal utilities representing preferences over uncertainty, but there is little foundation for this method. It implies the same kind of disrespect of interpersonal comparisons as that described in the previous paragraph. Two individuals with the same preferences and the same life may be given different welfare levels by this method if they have different degrees of risk aversion. The more risk averse would be considered systematically better off than the other at all possible lives that they could jointly have, contradicting their own judgment that their identical lives are (obviously) equally good.

Ironically, although the respect for individual preferences is the standard selling argument of subjective welfarism, it is, as it turns out, precisely because it fails to respect individual preferences beyond intrapersonal comparisons that subjective welfarism must be rejected. Truly enough, this rejection is justified only if one can find an alternative approach that performs better than subjective welfarism in this respect. Clearly, any approach like the capability approach that uses a single system of weights in order to aggregate the various dimensions of life is not an acceptable candidate, as it involves no direct adjustment to the diversity of individual preferences. Even if, as we know, focusing on capabilities is meant to leave room for diverse individual choices, it may happen that an individual would prefer a life to another although the capability measure would judge otherwise. In other words, a capability measure does not even respect preferences in the intrapersonal context.

The equivalence approach

The equivalence approach is a more promising candidate. As shown in Fleurbaey (2007) and in Fleurbaey *et al.* (2009), it is even the only possibility if one wants to respect individual preferences either in the intrapersonal context or in the interpersonal context, and satisfy some weak version of Sen's intersection principle according to which a life that is better in all dimensions than another must be judged better. Before giving a sketch of this argument, let us first explain what the equivalence approach does. What it compares across individuals is not subjective utility, but indifference sets. An indifference set is a set of lives that are deemed equally good by the individual. The equivalence approach proceeds as follows. First, it requires picking a reference set of lives such that every pair of lives in this reference set is such that one life is better than the other in all dimensions. The evaluation of the situation of an individual is then made by looking at the life from the reference set that the individual deems equivalent to his own life. Such a life is, then, at the intersection of the individual's current indifference set (i.e., the indifference that contains his actual life) and the reference set.

A relatively easy, and intuitive, way to implement this approach consists in separating income (or wealth) from the non-monetary dimensions of life, in fixing a reference level for the latter dimensions, and in computing the "equivalent income" (or wealth), i.e., the income (or wealth) level which, combined with the reference level in the non-monetary dimensions, would provide a life that the individual deems equivalent to his actual life. For instance, a life with some health problems and an annual income of $20,000 might be deemed equivalent to a life without these health problems and an income of $17,000. The equivalent income of the individual is then $17,000 when the reference level for health is "having a good health." Another individual who cares less about health would have, in the same objective situation, a higher equivalent income. The advantage of this method is that it renders all individual situations equivalent, in the individuals' own eyes, to another set of situations which are identical in the non-monetary dimensions of life and differ only in terms of (equivalent) incomes.

One can then see how this approach respects individual preferences not only in the intrapersonal but also in the interpersonal context. First, consider the intrapersonal case. If an individual prefers a life to another possible life, the indifference set containing the former is above that containing the latter, and therefore the equivalent situation in the reference set is better for the preferred life. Therefore a preferred life is indeed deemed better by the approach, whatever the individual's preferences. Now consider the interpersonal context. If two individuals have the same preferences, finding their equivalent lives in the reference set is the same exercise as finding the equivalent lives corresponding to their two lives, according to the preferences of any of them. Therefore, when they prefer one's life to the other's (they have to agree because they have, as assumed here, identical preferences), the ranking in terms of equivalent lives agrees with them just as it agrees in the intrapersonal case. Although this seems an immediate extension of the intrapersonal case, it makes a big difference from subjective welfarism, which does respect preferences in the intrapersonal case but not in the interpersonal case.

It turns out that the equivalence approach is salient among the methods that respect individual preferences, because of the characterization argument that was mentioned earlier. Here is a sketch of the argument. An individual situation is the combination of a life and of a preference ordering on all possible lives. It is assumed that preferences are always such that for every dimension of life, more is better. (This is a substantial restriction and the extension to more general kinds of preferences is still an open issue.) We want to rank individual situations, so as to satisfy two requirements. First, for a given preference ordering, a situation involving life A is better than a situation involving life B if and only if life A is preferred to life B for this ordering. This property embodies the respect for individual preferences (intra and interpersonally). The second requirement is that for at least a certain subset of possible lives, if a life A is better than life B in all dimensions, then a situation involving life A is better than a situation involving life B, no matter what preference orderings are associated with them. This second requirement is inspired by Sen's intersection principle (Sen 1985, 1992). It is weaker because it does not require the application of the requirement to all possible lives, and it is an important observation that the full version of the intersection principle is incompatible with the first requirement. As a result, the intersection principle can actually apply only to a subset of lives, which plays the role of the reference set in the definition of the equivalence approach. The characterization result is then that combining the two requirements implies that the ranking of individual situations is based on the equivalence approach, with the intersection principle being applicable only on the reference set of lives.

This is why the application of the equivalence approach requires picking a reference set of lives. This is not an innocuous matter because it may affect the ranking of lives that is obtained. This raises interesting ethical issues, which are still a field of research and cannot fully be addressed here. One indication may, however, help to see a key element of the issue. A unique property of the lives belonging to the reference set is that, with the equivalence approach, they can be compared without relying on individual preferences, because no matter what an individual's preferences are, his equivalent life is identical to his actual life when the latter belongs to the reference set. This is useful when thinking about what kind of lives could belong to the reference set. For instance, if one uses the "equivalent income" approach, the reference level for a non-monetary dimension should be such that it seems acceptable to compare individuals simply in terms of income when they enjoy this level whereas it makes more sense to ask about their preferences when they are not at this level. For instance, in the case of health, it is intuitively acceptable to look simply at incomes when people are healthy, whereas it seems important to ask about their preferences when their health is not good. Therefore a good level of health is the appropriate reference level. These brief considerations fall short of solving the issue, but at least it is important to see that the choice of the reference set is not a matter of arbitrariness.

The equivalence approach is somehow in between the fixed-weights methodology favored by the capability approach and subjective welfarism. Unlike the former (but like the latter), it allows for the diversity of individual conceptions of the good life. Unlike the latter (but like the former), it is immune to the problem of differences in scales and standards across individuals. Let us note, however, that it does not completely eliminate the problem of adaptive preferences. It only avoids the part of this problem which has to do with the adaptation of standards, i.e., the fact that a disadvantaged individual may have lower standards and declare herself satisfied too easily. The equivalence approach does not, by itself, avoid the part of the problem which involves the orientation of ordinal preferences. If women prefer jobs in less paid sectors of the economy, this may be due to entrenched inequalities or a conventional division of labor. The equivalence approach has no built-in device that protects against such biases in preferences. As we explained above, what is needed then is a way to find out what the "true" preferences are. The equivalence approach is worth applying only when one has found preferences that deserve to be respected.

The equivalence approach makes the need for a capability metric of advantage, as opposed to a functioning metric, much less pressing. If one can respect individual conceptions of the good life directly, why bother to provide opportunities from which they can choose? Why not simply try to satisfy their preferences, including their preferences about the degree of choice that they want in their lives? This is definitely less paternalistic than the capability approach. However, the problem is perhaps a little more complicated, as explained in the next section.

A different role for capabilities

Once a method of measuring advantage like the equivalence approach makes it possible to respect individual preferences not only in intrapersonal issues but also in interpersonal comparisons, it is tempting to rely on it to evaluate individual situations for all purposes whenever preferences are respectable. But the proviso about respectable preferences may reduce the scope of the method more than the discussion of the previous section suggests. In order to be respectable, preferences not only must be well informed and formed in certain ways, i.e., without questionable forms of manipulation and conditioning, but in addition they must be compatible with the basic duties of the members of a just society. We are talking here about conceptions of the good life. It is obvious that lifestyles that involve unfair relations between individuals cannot be accepted, and preferences for such lifestyles cannot be deemed worthy of respect. Preferences for domestic assistance in the form of a slave-like servant, for instance, are not respectable.

Moreover, and more relevantly for the present discussion, assuming the role of a member of a just society implies not only duties toward others but also duties toward oneself that derive from duties toward others. A member of a just society must assume some basic autonomy in her life, should not abandon her life to the will or dominion of any other member, and should make reasonable efforts not to put herself in the situation of becoming a burden to others. As a result, there is a place for a requirement of basic capabilities to be enjoyed by every member of society. The rationale is not, as in Nussbaum's approach, the fear of paternalism that would be associated with a functioning metric, but, in a quite opposite way, a perfectionist duty, for every member of society, of complying with the requirements of individual autonomy that go with any plausible conception of a just society. And what is important about capabilities in this perspective is not that the individual may decide not to make use of them, but rather that the individual must retain the ability to do certain things or be in certain states.

Maintaining such capabilities is a joint duty of the society and the individual. When Arneson talked about the "capability squanderer" and criticized the capability approach for failing to limit the duties of society when an individual repeatedly destroys his capabilities, we noted that the capability approach can be formulated in a lifelong perspective that accommodates this concern. However, the capabilities that are part of a duty of autonomy are indeed instantaneous capabilities that must be maintained throughout life. The capability squanderer, when basic capabilities are at stake, creates a responsibility for society to intervene and see how his autonomy can be restored and on what bases he would accept the corresponding duty to preserve it in the future. A preference for being illiterate, or for being physically or mentally disabled,[2] cannot be considered respectable in this context and requires some kind of intervention that preserves the dignity and seeks to restore the autonomy of the person.

Consider the situation of a drug addict who adopts a lifestyle that progressively destroys his mental abilities and his ability to work and relate to others in an autonomous way. Viewed from the perspective of lifelong opportunities, one might judge that his situation is not worse

---

[2] There is a controversy about what should count as a disability. The mere fact of wanting to have a certain disability might make it unsure whether this really is a disability for the person in question. But there certainly are basic capabilities without which an individual is no longer a participating member of society.

than the situation of someone who, endowed with similar initial possibilities, developed a healthy and flourishing life. This evaluation seems rather inappropriate, failing to acknowledge that this person shirks his duty to maintain basic capabilities. He deserves some attention and help for that reason, because the maintenance of basic capabilities is a joint responsibility of the individual and the society.

It is possible that this approach to basic capabilities would imply a different list from the list proposed in Nussbaum (2000b), but this is not sure because the main elements in the list are indeed things that one cannot deprive an individual of without jeopardizing her autonomy in a severe way. The only item in the list[3] that perhaps does not seem to be connected mainly to autonomy as such is the ability to relate to other species and nature in a certain respectful way. One can, however, easily find other perfectionist values that contribute to justifying a concern for this ability.

Beyond what is required by the maintenance of basic capabilities, the evaluation of individual situations by the equivalence approach or any similar approach that respects individual preferences appears acceptable. It makes it possible, in particular, to give choice its proper place in people's lives. Those who, beyond the basic requirements of autonomy described above, are happy with a rather passive life would see their situation evaluated in a way that would take account of the excessive burden imposed on them by the many choices that are typical of modern life, or would not be considered disadvantaged if they adopted a lifestyle that suits them and contains limited capabilities but with the functionings they like. Adopting the capability approach throughout is definitely paternalistic and, as pointed out by Arneson, potentially wasteful in terms of well-being. Adopting the capability approach as Nussbaum suggests, i.e., as a requirement of basic levels, is still paternalistic but, it has been argued here, justifiably so.

Conclusion

In a nutshell, the debate between Arneson and Nussbaum can be summarized as follows. Arneson's main criticism is that certain capabilities may be pointless to some individuals and it may therefore be wasteful to focus on such capabilities rather than on an achievement measure of

---

[3] The full list contains: 1) life, 2) bodily health, 3) bodily integrity, 4) senses, imagination and thought, 5) emotions, 6) practical reason, 7) affiliation, 8) relation to other species, 9) play, 10) control over one's environment. More details about the items can be found in Nussbaum (2000b, pp. 78–80) or at http://en.wikipedia.org/wiki/Capability_approach.

well-being. An exclusive concern for opportunities as a metric of advantage can be grounded neither on the value of responsibility nor on the value of freedom. Nussbaum's main reply is that respecting individual choice is essential to avoid paternalism, which justifies a focus on capabilities rather than functionings, although some degree of paternalism is justified and may imply some concern for certain functionings.

The main point of this chapter is that one need not take an opportunity approach in order to avoid paternalism (as proved by the existence of such metrics of advantage as the equivalence approach). Quite to the contrary, Arneson's critique about pointless opportunities can be reaffirmed in order to argue that an opportunity approach is paternalistic when it implies allocating resources in a way that does not respect individual preferences. But Nussbaum's case for a moderate form of paternalism is convincing. Not only may a moderate form of paternalism recommend a concern for certain functionings, it may also justify a concern for the basic capabilities of Nussbaum's list, grounded on the perfectionist value of autonomy. This suggests a substantial change of perspective on capabilities. While Nussbaum's defense of the approach is, "this is how one avoids paternalism," it has been suggested here that a more convincing defense would say, "this is an acceptable form of paternalism." This is a limited defense in the sense that it only justifies a concern for basic capabilities, not an exclusive concern for them. A full metric of advantage like the equivalence approach is needed in order to obtain a more comprehensive method of evaluation of social states that respects individual preferences beyond what the moderate form of paternalism warrants.

Interestingly, with such a method, whether capabilities or functionings should be the focus is no longer a matter of philosophical quarrelling about a general metric applicable to all individuals. Instead, the issue must be dealt with at the individual level, as a matter of preferences and conception of the good life. In liberal egalitarianism, apart from the issue of delineating an acceptable moderate form of paternalism, the academic debate on "capabilities or functionings" should therefore be terminated.

REFERENCES

Arneson R. 1989, "Equality and equal opportunity for welfare", *Philosophical Studies* 56: 77–93.
  1990, "Liberalism, distributive subjectivism, and equal opportunity for welfare", *Philosophy & Public Affairs* 19: 159–194.
Arneson R. J. 1999, "Equality of opportunity for welfare defended and recanted", *Journal of Political Philosophy* 7: 488–497.
  2000a, "Luck egalitarianism and prioritarianism", *Ethics* 110: 339–349.
  2000b, "Perfectionism and politics", *Ethics* 111: 37–63.

Cohen G. A. 1989, "On the currency of egalitarian justice", *Ethics* 99: 906–944.

Dworkin R. 1981, "What is equality? Part 2: Equality of resources", *Philosophy & Public Affairs* 10: 283–345.

Fleurbaey M. 2007, "Social choice and the indexing dilemma", *Social Choice and Welfare* 29: 633–648.

Fleurbaey M., E. Schokkaert, and K. Decancq 2009, "What good is happiness?", Université catholique de Louvain, Belgium: CORE Discussion Papers.

Nussbaum M.C. 1988, "Nature, function, and capability: Aristotle on political distribution", *Oxford Studies in Ancient Philosophy* suppl. vol.: 145–184.

1990, "Aristotelian social democracy", in R. B. Douglass, G. Mara, and H. Richardson (eds.), *Liberalism and the Good*, New York: Routledge.

1993, "Non-relative virtues: an Aristotelian approach", in M. C. Nussbaum and A. K. Sen (eds.), *The Quality of Life*, Oxford: Clarendon Press.

2000a, "Aristotle, politics, and human capabilities: a response to Antony, Arneson, Charlesworth, and Mulgan", *Ethics* 111: 102–140.

2000b, *Women and Human Development*, New York: Cambridge University Press.

Rawls J. 1971, *A Theory of Justice*, Cambridge, Mass.: Harvard University Press.

1982, "Social unity and primary goods", in A. Sen and B. Williams, *Utilitarianism and Beyond*, Cambridge and Paris: Maison des Sciences de l'Homme and Cambridge University Press .

Roemer J. E. 1993, "A pragmatic theory of responsibility for the egalitarian planner", *Philosophy & Public Affairs* 22: 146–166.

Sen A. K. 1985, *Commodities and Capabilities*, Amsterdam: North-Holland.

1992, *Inequality Reexamined*, Oxford: Clarendon Press.

Sunstein C. R. and R. H. Thaler 2008, *Nudge. Improving Decisions about Health, Wealth, and Happiness*, New Haven, Conn.: Yale University Press.

6   From humans to all of life: Nussbaum's transformation of dignity*

Jeremy Bendik-Keymer

> *We need an expanded notion of dignity since we now need to talk not only about lives in accordance with human dignity but also about lives that are worthy of the dignity of a wide range of sentient creatures. ... The Capability Approach regards each type of animal as having a dignity all its own. ... The species plays a role in giving us a sense of the characteristic form of life that ought to be promoted.*
>
> Martha C. Nussbaum, *Creating Capabilities* (2011, 161)

Some ideas, when they change, show us history in the making. This may be the case with the idea of dignity, historically so important to the rise of human rights, of which the capability approach is a species (Nussbaum, 2006a, 7; 2011, 62). In Martha C. Nussbaum's work, at least, dignity is changing – and with it, the human rights tradition and the relation between dignity and justice.

In this chapter, I will argue that Nussbaum's latest work severs the relation between dignity and justice. Having dignity, for Nussbaum, is no longer sufficient to make one a subject of justice. The reason why is that all forms of life have some kind of dignity, but not all forms of life deserve justice. Rather, to be a subject of justice, one must not only have dignity but also have sentience and motion. These last are needed for being the subject of claims.[1]

An interesting corollary concerns the moral emotions that lead us to apprehend moral worth. Throughout the human rights tradition, empathy – or what Nussbaum calls "compassion" – has been the most basic moral emotion, leading people to discover dignity (Hunt, 2007, 26–34). Yet in her latest work, Nussbaum is committed to thinking that

---

* Regarding this essay, I wish to thank Flavio Comim, Breena Holland, David Keymer, David Schlosberg, and an anonymous reviewer for Cambridge University Press. Thanks also go to Martha C. Nussbaum, who has been a fair, inspiring, and consummately professional teacher.
[1] In her commentary on this chapter, Martha C. Nussbaum agreed that the interpretation of her work summarized in this paragraph is correct. See also Martha C. Nussbaum (2011, 158–9).

wonder, not empathy, leads people to discover dignity. Empathy, rather, has a role in showing us which beings can be subjects of claims.[2]

I will approach my main argument within the context of the corollary, because I think doing so will provide a fuller and more intuitive picture of how Nussbaum's ideas try to shift the human rights tradition to a more *biocentric* view of political responsibility. "Biocentrism" is a technical term from environmental ethics for any view that holds that life as such deserves respect. What Nussbaum has done is to root her capabilities approach in biocentrism. Specifically, she is a *biocentric individualist* – one who holds that individual lives, not species, deserve respect because of their dignity.[3]

By focusing on her outlook, where wonder is the base moral emotion, I hope to display both the main argument of my chapter and the larger claim about how Nussbaum's capability approach seeks to green the human rights tradition by placing it within a biocentric outlook.

Nussbaum's outlook

How does Nussbaum see dignity? In what follows, I am concerned with reconstructing Nussbaum's account, not with justifying it. Throughout this article, I will slowly introduce questions that could, on reflection, call one to revise her account. But that is not my main goal here. I want to explain her account in the best possible terms and point to its limits and *aporias*.

Nussbaum holds that dignity is part of a *concept family* with respect (Nussbaum, 2006b, 2; 2011, 30, "respect is a particularly important relative"). A concept family is a collection of concepts that need to be understood in relation to each other in order to understand any one of them. Nussbaum is claiming that to understand dignity, we should understand respect, and in order to understand respect, we should understand dignity. The unity to this family is provided by the idea of being an end and not a mere means.

---

[2] As I will point out at the right time, Nussbaum disagreed in her commentary with my use of "empathy." She would focus, instead, on compassion. She agreed that wonder must have an important place in her theory of moral sentiments.

[3] Nussbaum agreed with this assessment of her position. On biocentric individualism, see Albert Schweitzer (Meyer and Berquel, 2002), Paul Taylor (1986), and – more recently – Gary Varner (2002). My biocentrism (2006) was influenced by studying with Nussbaum, but is more Deweyan than Aristotelian.

Biocentrism is often contrasted with *eco-centrism* – the view that organic collectives have moral standing or are the proper frame of reference for moral judgment. See Aldo Leopold (1968), J. Baird Callicott (1989), and – in a different vein – Holmes Rolston III (1989).

One good general way of thinking about the intuitive idea of dignity is that it is the idea of being an end rather than a mere means. If something has a dignity, ... it does not merely have a price: it is not merely something to be used for the ends of others, or traded on the market. This idea is closely linked to the idea of *respect* as the proper attitude toward dignity; indeed, rather than thinking of the two concepts as totally independent, so that we would first offer an independent account of dignity and then argue that dignity deserves respect (as independently defined), I believe we should think of the two notions as closely related, forming a concept family to be jointly elucidated. Central to both concepts is the idea of being an end and not a mere means. (Nussbaum, 2006b, 2)

Since respect is the "proper attitude" toward dignity, we can say that dignity is one pole of a relation where the other pole is respect. A moral *subject* ought to have respect for any *object* with dignity, and any *object* with dignity deserves respect in any moral *subject*.

What joins dignity and respect is the idea of being an end and not a mere means. Nussbaum associates this idea with the Kant of the *Groundwork* (Nussbaum, 2006b, 2). There is a fair amount of debate about what Kant meant by being an end, so I will leave the Kant interpretation to the side.[4] What Nussbaum makes of Kant's idea is what is relevant here. She thinks that being an end and not a mere means makes the end more than a *price* and more than an *instrument*.

You might think of the distinction this way. As an end, you are a *pride*[5] and not a *price*. Anything with a price is fungible, but a pride is not. It is non-exchangeable. Similarly, as a pride and not a price, you are not a *tool* – you act as a *rule*.[6] Rather than be under my will, you have an authority over me – at least when it comes to what I'd like to do with you. Your authority sets boundaries on what I may and may not do. If I want to use you to climb to some higher status, as a moral being, I *may* not. You set limits to my actions. *As* a moral being, I am to consider what you want.

Respect and dignity are joined around these ideas of being non-exchangeable and being a limit on use. Having dignity means you are a pride and act as a rule. Correlatively, respecting you involves refusing to price you and treat you like a tool. Pole to pole. Each pole helps explain the other.

When we see dignity, why should it matter to us? Dignity helps articulate the idea of being a pride and not a price, a rule and not a tool. Such distinctions rest deep in our form of life when we raise children.

---

[4] For instance, it seems that David Velleman (2006) would disagree with Nussbaum on her understanding of what an end is in the sense of a person being an end.

[5] As when we say, "he is my pride and joy."

[6] That is, as a determinant of my action – as an authority over what I can and cannot do.

Children learn early that people are not things. You may kick a stone around a playground, but not a person. You may pay money for a ball that you can dispose of as you wish, but not so with a person. Dignity and its family member – respect – constitute the distinction between persons and things. They help us see that people have a special kind of worth.

Why, though, does someone have a special kind of worth? And is Nussbaum speaking only of humans? Here, her answers start to become non-traditional, departing from the human rights tradition. We can see them by considering her *outlook*.

As Nussbaum says, the moral intuitions underlying her theory of justice are part of a way of looking at the world. Nussbaum (2006b, 4–6) describes her outlook as "Aristotelian/Marxist," and in *Frontiers of Justice* (2006a, 346–352), she draws mainly on Aristotle. The outlook really is Aristotelian. Quoting from Aristotle's *Parts of animals* (1995, 1004/645a 17), Nussbaum asserts:

In everything in nature, there is something wonder-inspiring (Nussbaum, 2006a, 348).[7]

That line is the core of Nussbaum's outlook. It forms the central passage for her section on types of dignity in *Frontiers of Justice*. She echoes it often. For instance, she writes later on in the book:

If we feel wonder looking at a complex organism, that wonder at least suggests the idea that it is good for that being to persist and flourish as the kind of thing it is (Nussbaum, 2006a, 349).

Or, finishing the introductory section of the book, she echoes:

[My] approach is animated by the Aristotelian sense that there is something wonderful and worthy of awe in any complex[,] natural organism (Nussbaum, 2006a, 93–94).

Lest there be any doubt about how expansive this outlook is, she emphasizes that it "embrac[es] of all of life" (Nussbaum, 2006a, 447, footnote 25). This emphasis comes when Professor Nussbaum prods *Aristotle* to live up to his own vision! *Each and every* living being has something awesome or wonderful about it. This is biocentric.

Nussbaum is not speaking of only humans, then, when she speaks of dignity and respect. Someone has a special kind of worth because she is a *living* being. As a living being, she has a "beautiful" teleology where we find "absence of haphazard and conduciveness of everything to an end"

---

[7] An alternative translation (Aristotle, 1995, 1004/645a 17) reads: "Every realm of nature is marvelous."

(Aristotle, 1995, 1004/645a 23–25), and that means not only she but every living being has a like special worth. If I may speculate, the *dignity* seen in her being alive comes from her having a special order that "unfolds" toward an end (as Nussbaum clarified in commentary on this chapter; cf. also her 2011, 31: "The idea of dignity is closely related to the idea of active *striving*" [emphasis mine]). The biocentric outlook is doing a lot of moral work.

We can see Nussbaum's outlook as a natural extension of her view in *Women and Human Development* (2000). There, she writes of human dignity:

We react to the spectacle of humanity ... assailed in a way very different from the way we react to a storm blowing grains of sand in the wind. For we see a human being as having worth as an end, a kind of awe-inspiring something that makes it horrible to see the person beaten down by the currents of chance – and wonderful, at the same time, to witness the way in which chance has not completely eclipsed the humanity of the person (Nussbaum, 2000, 72–3).

The awe for human striving has extended to a wonder at any living striving – unlike "grains of sand in the wind."

So dignity is found in a concept family that involves not only respect but a kind of wonder. That wonder sees dignity in any living being and is ultimately the answer as to why we should hold some beings as especially worthy. Their teleological order should make us wonder. It should fill us with awe. It should be beautiful.[8]

"[T]he world contains many distinct varieties of dignity" (Nussbaum, 2006b, 9). Nussbaum sees through the eyes of wonder. If you appreciate life, you should appreciate a living being's special kind of dignity (cf. Nussbaum 2011, 29, "the dignity appropriate to the species in question"). And how could you be moral, if you did not appreciate life?

For Nussbaum, being of a living kind is *sufficient* for you to have dignity. Is it necessary? It would seem so, given Nussbaum's emphasis on Aristotle the biologist. Yet she does imply that God has moral standing (Nussbaum, 2006a, 362). As I understand Jewish theology, God is not a living being, although God is a rational being (subject to bouts of irrationality and temper). Nussbaum implies that God's being rational is sufficient to give Him moral standing. Does moral standing imply having dignity? It would seem so, and the human rights tradition certainly holds so. The usual idea is that only beings with dignity have moral standing.

---

[8] At the chapter's end, I will raise questions about the sources of normativity for these claims.

Nussbaum does not stop with God, though. She leaves open the theoretical possibility of a science fiction being with moral standing. Consider an artificial intelligence like *HAL* from *2001: a Space Odyssey*. It has emotions, and an emotional being has moral standing (Nussbaum, 2006a, 362).

Of course, Nussbaum doesn't think nature operates "like science fiction or theology" but she accepts their consideration for "theoretical purposes" (Nussbaum, 2006a, 362). Accordingly, it would seem that if moral standing implies having dignity, then being of a living kind is sufficient for having dignity, but it is *not* necessary.

Nussbaum would have to accept this view. It seems obvious that the Jewish God has dignity for Jews. And it seems likely that *HAL* is just as wonder-inspiring as "everything in nature." *HAL* is as complex as many things in nature and acts of its own accord. *HAL* has teleology like life-forms do. Finally, there is the fact that, traditionally, moral standing implies dignity, since dignity is a necessary condition for it. As we saw, dignity is respect-worthiness.

We are left, then, with an intriguing conception of dignity. It is part of a concept family with respect and a kind of wonder, and it reflects beings with the teleological organization characteristic of life. Most of these are natural, but some could be supernatural or artificial. Any one has dignity, and so deserves our wonder and respect.

All this biocentrism (and beyond) is interesting, but it is a far cry from the human rights tradition of which the capabilities approach is a species. What has become of that tradition and of justice in Nussbaum's discussion? Isn't Nussbaum's focus justice?

Dignity's relation to justice

If, on the one hand, dignity demands respect, and if – on the other hand – all wonder-inspiring, living or life-like forms have a kind of dignity, then it might appear justice would be due to all forms of life (and to gods, and to artificial intelligences). After all, since at least the eighteenth century, dignity has been both necessary and sufficient for becoming a subject of justice (adapted from Hunt, 2007).

Yet Nussbaum's position is clear. She severs the relation between dignity and justice. There are many kinds of dignity, but not all of them deserve justice. Rather, while dignity appears within the light of wonder, only some kinds of dignity deserve justice. At first, she is not clear which, but eventually claims that only moving, feeling beings deserve justice. Nussbaum makes activity and sentience – or what can also be glossed as "movement" and "feeling" – further conditions on becoming a subject of justice. Nothing unfeeling or unmoving deserves justice. And the question is why.

Let's see how she isolates movement and feeling. As she most commonly puts it, everything seems to hinge on whether the being with dignity is "active" and "sentient." At the beginning of *Frontiers of Justice*, she writes:

Our choices affect the lives of nonhuman species every day, and often cause them enormous suffering. Animals are not simply parts of the world; they are *active* beings trying to live their lives; and we often stand in their way. That looks like a problem of justice. (Nussbaum, 2006a, 22, [my emphasis])

In her bioethics paper, she claims:

[Animals] are complex[,] living and *sentient* beings endowed with capacities for *activity and striving*. (Nussbaum, 2006b, 10 [my emphasis])

This last quote comes in her attempt to figure out whether animals have political entitlements – i.e., whether they are subjects of justice.

So does justice come when, and only when, a being can move and feel? Of course, in *Frontiers of Justice* Nussbaum speaks in terms of the disjunction, moving *or* feeling (Nussbaum, 2006a, 362). But in her more recent bioethics paper, she speaks in terms of a conjunction – she talks about subjects of entitlement moving *and* feeling. When Nussbaum introduces "extending the notion of dignity" for the sake of "animal entitlements," she claims that what she has "said about dignity in humans goes as well for most animals (at least all those who move from place to place *and* have complex forms of sentience...)." Moreover, she is not going to "comment on sponges and other related 'stationary animals'" (Nussbaum, 2006b, 9 [emphasis on "and" is mine]). For now, then, I will accept this later use of a conjunction – moving *and* feeling – because we'll see that it may have an explanation. The question then becomes: why would she think a dignity deserving of justice appears with, and only with, motion and feeling?[9]

---

[9] There is a bit of turbulence in Nussbaum's reflection on the status of sentience, movement, and other capabilities. It becomes steadier, adopting the position I reported, as time goes on. At the beginning, though, it appears contradictory. For instance, Nussbaum claims that:

Sentience is not the only thing that matters for basic justice; but it seems plausible to consider the possession of sentience as a theshold condition for membership in the community of beings who have entitlements based on justice (Nussbaum, 2006a, 361).

But she then goes on to say only a page later:

[W]e should adopt a disjunctive approach: if a creature has *either* the capacity for pleasure and pain *or* the capacity for movement from place to place *or* the capacity for emotion and affiliation *or* the capacity for reasoning, and so forth (we might add play, tool use and others), then that creature has moral standing (Nussbaum, 2006a, 362).

If in the first passage she means by sentience being a "theshold" condition that it is a *necessary* condition, then her first passage contradicts her second. Because her second passage makes it possible for something to be a subject of justice without sentience. And she even says on page 362 that sentience is *not* a necessary condition. Yet by the time of

Her answer is that these kinds of creatures "reach out, as it were, for [their] type[s] of functioning" and "are frustrated or [their efforts] are made vain if the animal is not permitted to develop" (Nussbaum, 2006b, 9). In other words, animals that move can be blocked, and animals that feel can feel they are hurt. What, though, is it about these two possibilities that make their bearers exclusive candidates for justice? Why is it that if and only if I can be thwarted in movement and made to feel pain that I deserve justice? Why does it matter if I move my legs or wings as opposed to if I grow? Why is motion and not *growth* the key notion? Why does it matter if I can feel hurt as opposed to *be damaged?*

Let's take movement first. Movement – like activity – involves intentionality. The plant does not *intend* to grow. It just grows. By contrast, we might say that even if a dog can't explain its intentions, it still has them. Anything with intentions has a stake in realizing the intention. Block it, and it will squirm, swerve, hop, speed, or fight to get where it was going. A plant may bend around an obstacle to find the light, as the tree does in the opening of Rousseau's *Émile*, but there does not seem to be any behavior that shows it cares about getting where it was growing. It simply lives or dies, bends or does not. An intentional being has a stake in its existence.[10]

Now let's take sentience. Sentient beings can in some sense be said to care about the damage done to them. Hurt is hurt *to* them. By contrast, plants can be damaged, but not hurt. The damage is not an issue *to* the plant. When a sentient being is hurt, though, the damage *is* an issue to the being. It panics, becomes aggressive or what have you.[11] Thus, it seems fairly straightforward with sentience to say that a sentient being, too, has a stake in its own existence. The common idea between sentience and movement is having a stake in one's own existence.

Here is, then, my best explanation for why – on Nussbaum's account – only some animals deserve justice when all life has dignity.

her bioethics paper (Nussbaum, 2006b) it appears she thinks both sentience and the capacity for movement are necessary (recall the remark about "stationary animals").

[10] It is possible to push this distinction until either it collapses or one abandons movement as a necessary condition on being a subject of justice. Why in principle does it matter whether a being moves its legs to avoid a problem or bends its stalk to reach around an obstacle? However, one might say the being with movement has some kind of awareness that precedes movement. But then it is sentience – or awareness – that is doing the work. In other words, it is possible to claim that only on sentience can one make the kind of distinction that would preserve Nussbaum's account from inconsistency.

[11] The issue here is pain, though, not movement. If we subtract feeling from the example, it doesn't seem easy to distinguish "panicking" from "growing around the obstacle and toward the light." Take away pain, and the latter is slow-motion aversion.

Having intentions and the capacity to panic or show ire over damage done to you is decisive for justice, because with and only with these do we have a stake in our existences, and when and only when we have a stake in our existences can we be subjects of claims.[12] Respect-worthiness that generates claims is different from respect-worthiness that does not. And we can be subjects of justice if and only if we are the subjects of claims. At least that is what the logic of justice looks like.

Let me explain. I have been led to this point, because I am trying to find a principled reason why Nussbaum claims that:

(a) Beings with dignity deserve respect.
(b) All living beings have dignity.
(c) Yet only some living beings deserve justice.

The key here must be in the idea that not all respect is a matter of justice. My proposal is to look at the traditional logic of justice. On that tradition, which some say stretches back to Aristotle (Thompson, 2004), justice is a matter of duties *to* people.[13] But there can also be duties *regarding* people. They are not matters of justice. In fact, you can't wrong someone if you have only broken a duty regarding her or him. The idea here is in a wrong *to* someone. Wrongs to someone violate *claims*.

If I am right, Nussbaum's account makes most sense as an attempt to stick with this intuition about justice, combined with her expansive Aristotelian sense of dignity. What emerges is a view of those properties that would appear to be needed at the minimum in order to be the kind of being that can be wronged. They are movement and feeling. Without at least those, it seems impossible to account for how a being could have

---

[12] This claim can be revised to read, "if and only if we are the *kind* of beings who have a stake in our own existences, can we be the subjects of claims," if we need to handle the case of the – e.g. – human who no longer cares about life but yet deserves justice. This is consistent with the way Nussbaum uses the species norm to conceptualize the demands of justice – e.g., "The species norm is evaluative" (Nussbaum, 2006a, 347).

I should note that one might press the prior claim that *only* with movement and sentience can we have a stake in our existences. For one, we might claim that *either* one is necessary, but not both. And it could be the case that an immobile, unfeeling being – some form of future, artificial or alien intelligence – has a stake in its own existence. But I am doing my best to reconstruct Nussbaum's account at this point. I think that if we expand sentience to simply mean *awareness*, then it would seem to be necessary and sufficient for our having a stake in our existences.

[13] Thompson, however, requires that subjects of justice be agents capable of explaining their reasons for action. We might avoid this problem when it comes to non-humans – as Thompson would when it comes to marginal human cases (e.g., mental disability) – by considering trustees for beings with interests.

a wrong done *to* it, because it would not seem to have a stake in its own existence. But with those, it does have a stake in its existence, and from there can have a wrong done to it. But once and only once a being can have a wrong done *to* it, can it be the subject of claims – e.g., a claim of justice.[14]

Nussbaum talks this way when she discusses justice. She writes:

When I say that mistreatment of animals is unjust, I mean to say not only that it is wrong *of us* … but also that … it is unfair *to them* (Nussbaum, 2006a, 337).

That's clear. So let me summarize. Movement is intentional, and feeling cares. The common thread with both is the idea of *having a stake in one's own existence*. Whatever – and only whatever – has a stake in its own existence is the kind of thing that can be the subject of a claim. Traditionally, whatever – and only whatever – is the subject of a claim can be a subject of justice. So moving, feeling beings can be subjects of justice – but there are other living beings that cannot be. As Nussbaum has said most recently (2011, 158–9), " [t]he idea of justice is conceptually bound up with the idea of experienced harm or thwarting, or so I believe." My further suggestion to her is to underline that the logic of claims – of wrongs *to* – does the work on the basis of harming or interfering with beings having a stake in their own existences.

What has happened to empathy?

I've just tried to reconstruct Professor Nussbaum's account of dignity so that it is not inconsistent. This is not to say there are not further problems with the notion of dignity, as we have already sensed. Nonetheless, having dignity is necessary for deserving justice, but it is not sufficient. What dignity is sufficient for is deserving some kind of respect – either respect *to*, which involves justice – or respect *regarding*, which involves consideration. In both cases, the being with dignity should not just be used, nor simply priced.[15] But in the case of a moving and feeling being,

---

[14] In notes 10 and 11, I suggested that what really does the work in Nussbaum's account is *awareness*. I do not have room to follow out this idea here.

[15] One gray area is whether Nussbaum's invocation of being an end and not a mere means applies to beings with dignity who are only due regard, not justice. Can a being that cannot be directly wronged be treated as an end?

For the consistency of Nussbaum's account, it would have to be the case that a being that can only be indirectly wronged can nonetheless be treated as an end. I think it can (although I doubt Kant would agree). If what it means to be an end is that you should neither be priced nor tooled, then we can make sense of how – e.g. – a tree could be treated accordingly. A tree could be an end, although it cannot be directly wronged and so cannot be a subject of justice.

the way respect is shown appears to involve a direct connection with the being, taking its perspective into account, the way it has a stake in its existence.[16] The rest of the chapter will try to see if we can get a grip on how we relate to dignity and what dignity is.

Nussbaum works within the modern human rights tradition to this extent: she thinks justice becomes sensible through a variant of what I and historians of human rights (Hunt, 2007) call "empathy." In *Frontiers of Justice*, Nussbaum focuses on "sympathetic imagining." She writes that such "imagining" is used "to extend and refine our moral judgments" concerning the lives of animals (Nussbaum, 2006a, 355). That makes perfect sense within the human rights tradition. Empathy is the great grower of justice. As recent research has shown, empathy discovering dignity discovering justice appears to be an old pattern, dating back to the eighteenth century, and its trace can be felt in the *Universal Declaration of Human Rights*, especially in the Preamble and Article 1 (Hunt, 2007; Bendik-Keymer, 2002). The question is, though: on Nussbaum's account, what does "sympathetic imagining" have to do with dignity?

The answer clues us into what dignity might be and also to how it is related to justice. What I am calling "empathy" is the emotion of claims – of direct connection that allows one to see how another being has a stake in its existence and so how a wrong could be done *to* it. As Nussbaum writes:

[I]magining the lives of animals makes them real to us in a primary way, as potential subjects of justice (Nussbaum, 2006a, 355).

Preceding this quote, she makes much of J. M. Coetzee's line from *The Lives of Animals* (later a chapter in *Elizabeth Costello*), a line said by Elizabeth Costello:

The heart is a seat of a faculty, *sympathy*, that allows us to share at times the being of another (Coetzee, 1999, p. 45; Nussbaum, 2006a, 355).

Nussbaum is after a mode of emotional understanding where we put ourselves in another's place. She uses "sympathy" in *Frontiers of Justice*,

---

What is doing the work on my interpretation of Nussbaum's account of justice is the idea of being able to have a wrong done *to* you. There is an idea of awareness – of feeling and potent intentionality – there. A wrong can be done *to* you. It shows up in your awareness. Of course, it's not clear to me why such a minimal condition should be decisive for justice beyond the logical point that it makes sense of claims. Our whole grammar of norms and virtues seems to become diaphanous in these regions.

[16] A further problem that bothers me is how to fill out the idea of respect *regarding* – not *to* – a being. Besides the difference in deontic logic, is there any *substantive* difference in the kinds of treatment we should actually give the being?

but we can use "empathy" because of the following reasoning. Sympathy is, by definition, "feelings of pity and sorrow for someone else's misfortune" (Oxford, 2005). Empathy, by contrast, is "the ability to understand and share the feelings of another" (Oxford, 2005). What Nussbaum and Coetzee's character Costello are after is the ability to imagine or share another being's perspective. That is empathy, not sympathy. Moreover, Nussbaum and Costello are after justice, not simply pity or sorrow. They are after dignity, not simply misfortune. Hence, empathy.[17]

Empathy is a mode of emotional understanding where we put ourselves in another's place. It is obvious how this is key to justice. What does it take to understand that a being could have a wrong done *to* it? That we see the way it has a stake in its own existence. How do we imagine it has a stake in its own existence? We put ourselves in its place.

Empathy appears to be important, then, to *discovering* justice, to discovering new beings that deserve justice because they (a) have dignity and (b) are the subject of claims. Wonder, on Nussbaum's account, has discovered dignity, but putting ourselves in another's place and seeing it could have a wrong done to it shows us that this being with dignity ought also to be a subject of justice. It is not surprising, then, that Nussbaum's method in *Frontiers of Justice* relies on "sympathy" to "extend" our moral horizons to moving, feeling animals.

At the same time, her account of dignity makes the use of what I am calling "empathy" novel. This point is a subtle one and is interesting. Previously, as I read the human rights tradition, empathy was an emotion that discovered *dignity*. This appears to be the role empathy had at the dawn of modern human rights (Hunt, 2007, 28–34). It is easy to see why. I learn to enter into your world – me, a rich, well-educated novel reader of pre-revolutionary France; you, a poor, window-maker on a side street in Paris, Rue des Verreriers. As I do, I learn that you have a life just as I do. You care about it. It has its form, its duties, its order, its struggles – its *dignity*. There you are, closing the shutters at the end of a long day and lighting the candles. You think about how many more

---

[17] In *Upheavals of Thought* and in her second edition of *The Fragility of Goodness*, Nussbaum emphasizes – as she did in commentary on this chapter – that the relevant emotion for justice is *compassion*, because compassion on her understanding implies acting to redress some wrong, whereas even sympathy does not. Moreover, empathy can be a tool of evil (c.f., a torturer's empathy). I agree with all these points. However, (1) Nussbaum does use "sympathy," not "compassion," in *Frontiers of Justice*, and (2) what she needs is an emotion that articulates the logic of claims, and that is – by definition – empathy, not sympathy.

windows you must make to buy medicine for your daughter. You think
about the way the last patron was dissatisfied and threatened you. That
person had no respect, although you are hard working and a human,
too. As I see these things about you, I see your dignity. Yes, you have
dignity, too, and you deserve justice just as any human does. – That is
the traditional story.

But Nussbaum does something different. Her story goes like this.
When we meet, I know you deserve respect. You deserve respect,
because you made me wonder. Your order itself – beautiful, even
awe-inspiring – convinced me you have a dignity all your own I ought
to treat as a pride, not a price, a rule, not a tool. "In everything in nature,
there is something wonder-inspiring." When I have had time to observe
you, I've noticed that you have a life of your own, feelings, a good and
a bad day, joy, fear, something like playful wit. You move about at the
edge of my world with an intelligence that is unlike mine but is
undeniable.

What kind of respect do you deserve? I approach you in my
imagination and with my feelings. I put myself in your place. I try to
imagine what it must be like to be you. I imagine how it feels when the
shopping mall goes in and you have fewer places to go, how it felt that
time the neighbor's kid cornered you in a fenced-in area and taunted you
with a stick. I can feel how you, with a stake in your own existence, were
at your limit with emotion, straining to break free. You have a claim on
us. And because you do, we directly wronged you.

That is *Nussbaum's* story. Dignity, she suggested, is seen by wonder,
not empathy. Empathy, rather, perceives justice.[18] It imagines others as
subjects of claims, of having a stake in their existences just as I do.
Hence, as beings who can be directly wronged. Thus empathy is no
longer occupying its traditional place – and neither is dignity. Empathy,
now, is important for discovering dignity *under the aspect of* justice. And
dignity, now, is *not* what we recognize in order to see if justice is due.
Rather, it determines a broader respect-worthiness within which some
beings might deserve justice. These are subtle and, I think, interesting
points. Empathy is very important, but not in the way it traditionally has
been, and that reflects the way dignity has proliferated in the eyes of
wonder.

---

[18] These two sentences respond to Nussbaum's worry, raised in her commentary, that my
reconstruction would leave open the door to the empathic torturer. But the door is
closed, precisely because of her biocentrism and the way it gives pride of place to wonder
in discovering what deserves respect. Once a living being deserves respect, one may not
be empathic *and* – e.g. – torture the being.

A politics of wonder

We really need to look at wonder. Empathy is no longer discovering dignity, wonder is. Empathy simply realizes that a being with dignity deserves justice. Does this idea make sense?

It helps to think about how wonder relates to empathy. Empathy would not be possible without wonder. In fact, wonder forms the heart of empathy – at least human empathy.[19] This is because I cannot so much as put myself in your place without wondering what it would be like. All "sympathetic imagining" is based in wonder. What is it like to be you? What do you care about? What forms the burden and relief of your day? What does it feel like for you to be hurt? How do you feel when you have obtained a moment to play? What is it like to eat fallen seeds? What is it like to climb a tree high, so high that no human could go there? What is it like to hear the forest at night cascade like the waves we hear on the shore and then hear a motor, shrill and at a frequency that nothing natural whines? Empathy may bring us justice, but *wonder brings us empathy*.

Wonder, then, is inside empathy. It is a separable moment, yet we think of it as part of empathy, because it quickly gets absorbed in the rush of feelings clustered around this living being quivering with a stake in its own existence. What should we make of this idea, that *the beginning of right is a wondering mind*?

Here we see one area in which Nussbaum's ideas portend a shift in the human rights tradition. A politics of wonder is an as-yet-unconceptualized possibility. It would appear to be a far cry from shouting in the streets as if all that were needed to make people see justice is a loud enough voice. I repeat: Nussbaum is committed to thinking that the beginning of right is a wondering mind. She is also committed to thinking that *global justice begins with a politics of wonder*.

These are beautiful suggestions, sparking ideas throughout education, civic engagement and public arts. But they remain merely beautiful until Nussbaum clarifies wonder. The area that needs to be explored is why wonder should be the key to dignity. It is easy to imagine forms of wonder that do not result in recognizing moral worth or respect-worthiness. Yet Nussbaum's Aristotelian outlook draws on

---

[19] Dogs are empathic. Do they wonder in order to be empathic? Often, they cock their heads to the side and look perplexed. Is that found in empathy? Yet it seems impossible to say a human has fully developed empathic powers without the ability to wonder being part of them. Irene Liu helped me see this point about human empathy.

an emotion which, translated, we call "wonder," and yet which does not survive the translation intact.

In an age like ours where global warming's habitat changes portend massive species loss over the next century, these questions about wonder are not merely academic. They call not merely for people-centered development, but for *bio*-centric development. The great interest in Nussbaum's account of dignity is that she challenges us to respect not just human life, but all forms of life. This is *how* she aims to shift the human rights tradition that has done so much on the basis of dignity. But her biocentrism hinges on a clarification of "wonder."

What kind of wonder is this that should lead us to be biocentric? What makes it clear there is something "wanton" even in killing "mosquitoes" for no good reason (Nussbaum, 2006a, 362)? Perhaps we could know better if we jointly elucidated dignity, since "wonder" appears to be in a concept family with both dignity and respect.

Yet what becomes of dignity in Nussbaum's Aristotelian outlook is almost as hard to understand – and as interesting – as what happens to empathy and wonder. *What* is dignified in a mosquito's life? Where do the sponges and lichens and mulches shine in our moral imaginations? At stake in Aristotle's vision, and still in need of more elucidation, more careful explanation from Nussbaum and others, is the idea of dignity being the only fit response to a *living or life-like, teleological order*. Here is not a dignity the being feels – that is the dignity empathy especially touches, the dignity of a being that has a stake in its existence. Rather, the dignity disclosed by wonder reaches far out into the amazingness of something that changes from within itself and takes on order, that has what biologists call a "teleology."

Yet we can't just point to the properties of changing from within itself, organization and teleology, without explaining why these ought to strike us with wonder when they are conjoined, and then why that "wonder" ought to make us recognize a "dignity" that demands respect. Are these properties part of a general category of living thing, as Michael Thompson would appear to hold (Thompson, 2008)? And do we use that category analogically with gods and artificial intelligences? Why should the category be anything more than descriptive?

We need a vocabulary for this kind of frontier dignity – a dignity beyond the frontiers of justice. The word "dignity" wears thin on it. We do speak of trees having dignity, but it seems odd to say a bacterium does. Maybe we ought to call what we're after, simply, "striving" and realize that living form is not just a *descriptive* category but also implies a moral idea like agency. Maybe living form is inviolate, because it strives.

Then the way we see life would see that respect-worthy order we once called "human dignity" back in the eighteenth century. Now we call it "striving," and we see it wherever we see the living.[20]

REFERENCES

Aristotle (1995) "Parts of Animals," in J. Barnes (Ed.), *The Complete Works of Aristotle, the Revised Oxford Translation*, Princeton University Press.

Bendik-Keymer, J. (2002) "Conscience and Humanity," Dissertation submitted to the University of Chicago Department of Philosophy.

(2006) *The Ecological Life: Discovering Citizenship and a Sense of Humanity*, Rowman & Littlefield, Lanham, MD.

(2007) "Review of James Rachels's The Legacy of Socrates," *Ethics*, 117:4, 780–784.

Callicott, J. B. (1989) *In Defense of the Land Ethic: Essays in Environmental Philosophy*, SUNY Press, Albany, NY.

Coetzee, J. M. (1999) "The Lives of Animals," in Amy Gutmann (Ed.), Princeton University Press.

Hunt, L. (2007) *Inventing Human Rights: a History*, W.W. Norton & Company, Inc., New York.

Leopold, A. (1968) *A Sand County Almanac and Sketches Here and There*, Oxford University Press, New York.

Meyer, M. and Berquel, K. (Eds.) (2002) *Reverence for Life: the Ethics of Albert Schweitzer for the Twenty-First Century*, Syracuse University Press.

[20] In this chapter, I have not addressed at all the most important practical matter for a biocentric position: how much moral weight do different living individuals deserve when their lives come into conflict? When it comes to deserving justice, do humans matter more than dogs, and if so, why? And when it comes to deserving consideration, do sponges deserve more than bacteria, and if so, why?

I have not addressed this issue, because the article concerns what I call "ground status" – whether you are in or out of the moral universe and through what kind of relation you are addressed if you are in. I suspect Nussbaum would have to make an argument for the higher moral worthiness of some capabilities – e.g., practical reason, sentience – in order to resolve the issue of how *much* consideration each kind of being deserves. And when looking at plants, she might have to take up some new kinds of capabilities to create a weighting-scheme for how much respect different kinds of organisms deserve. I also suspect she would have to use the idea of a right to self-defense in many cases.

For myself, I lean toward an approach James Rachels (2006) developed, one that I call "radical moral individualism" (Bendik-Keymer, 2007). According to it, we have to identify morally relevant properties in any entity and see each as a reason to treat – or not treat – the being in a way determined by the property. So, e.g., a rational being should not be deceived, and a sentient being should not be hurt. I believe that by mapping our moral universe through the relations implied by morally worthy properties, we will come closest to envisioning the utopian requirements for a world where humans respect life in the ideal way. We can use the weight of reasons to decide what to do. See also David Schmidtz (1998). How this approach fits inside the sense of humanity – which does not begin by tracking properties per se (Bendik-Keymer, 2006, lecture 4) is a matter for future work.

Nussbaum, M.C. (2000) *Women and Human Development: the Capabilities Approach*, Cambridge University Press, New York.

(2001a) *The Fragility of Goodness, Luck and Ethics in Greek Tragedy and Philosophy*, 2nd Ed., Cambridge University Press, New York.

(2001b) *Upheavals of Thought, the Intelligence of the Emotions*, Cambridge University Press, New York.

(2006a) *Frontiers of Justice: Disability, Nationality, Species Membership*, The Belknap Press of Harvard University Press, Cambridge, MA.

(2006b) "Human Dignity and Political Entitlements," MS, prepared for the President of the United States's Bioethics Committee.

(2011) *Creating Capabilities: the Human Development Approach*, The Belknap Press of Harvard University Press, Cambridge, MA.

"Oxford" (2005) *Oxford American Dictionaries*, Apple Computer, Inc., n. l.

Rachels, J. (2006) "The Legacy of Socrates," in S. Rachels (Ed.), Columbia University Press, New York.

Rolston, H. (1989) *Philosophy Gone Wild: Environmental Ethics*, Prometheus Books, Amherst, NY.

Schdmitz, D. (1998) "Are All Species Equal?" *Journal of Applied Philosophy*, 15, 57–67.

Taylor, P. (1986) *Respect for Nature*, Princeton University Press.

Thompson, M. (2004) "What Is It to Wrong Someone? A puzzle about justice," in R. J. Wallace, P. Pettit, S. Scheffler and M. Smith (Eds.), *Reason and Value, Themes from the Moral Philosophy of Joseph Raz*, Oxford University Press, New York, pp. 333–384.

(2008) "The Representation of Life," in *Life and Action: Elementary Structures of Practice and Practical Thought*, Harvard University Press, Cambridge, MA, Chapters 1–4.

Varner, G. (2002) "Biocentric Individualism" in D. Schmidtz and E. Willot (Eds.), *Environmental Ethics: What Really Matters, What Really Works*, Oxford University Press, New York, pp. 108–120.

Velleman, D. (2006) *Self to Self*, Cambridge University Press, New York.

Part II

Gender

7   Questioning the gender-based division of labour: the contribution of the capabilities approach to feminist economics*

Ulrike Knobloch

> Women suffer injustice not only through discrimination in the public world, but through the ways labor is organized and income is distributed within the family itself.
>
> (Nussbaum 1992b: 2/12)

> An unequal division of labor within the family presents obstacles to women in their lives outside the family; and these inequalities are often supported by social traditions and expectations. [...] since women evidently suffer injustice, a theory of social justice forfeits its claim to our attention if it omits so much of its topic.
>
> (Nussbaum 1992b: 3/12)

One central concern of feminist economics is the gender-based division of labour and the questions of justice connected with it. To render these questions of justice fully visible, an elementary conception of the good is needed, because an elementary conception of the good preconditions the questions of justice. In the following I will discuss three conceptions of the good – the preference-based approach, the primary goods-based approach and the capabilities-based approach – and examine their potential to answer the questions of justice, especially the questions concerning the gender-based division of labour. But first of all I will have a closer look at feminist economics and the subject of gender-based division of labour.

The gender-based division of labour as a question of justice

In the socio-economic literature we find an extensive discussion of the different types of social division of labour which is mainly related to paid work. Well-known is Adam Smith's first chapter of his *Wealth of Nations* (1776). There he argues that all kinds of social division of paid labour will

---

* For helpful comments and suggestions, I thank Maren A. Jochimsen, Flavio Comim, Martha C. Nussbaum and the anonymous reader of Cambridge University Press. I am also grateful for the commentaries of the participants of the session "Gender and Work" at the conference "Promoting Women's Capabilities", 9–10 September 2002 in Cambridge.

lead to an increase of productivity and well-being of the individual and the society as a whole, however omitting unpaid labour and its social division in this book:

The division of labour, however, so far as it can be introduced, occasions, in every art, a proportionable increase of the productive powers of labour. The separation of different trades and employments from one another, seems to have taken place, in consequence of this advantage. [...] It is the great multiplication of the productions of all the different arts, in consequence of the division of labour, which occasions, in a well-governed society, that universal opulence which extends itself to the lowest ranks of the people. (Smith 1976: 15 and 22)

Adam Smith – as most of the classical economists apart from John Stuart Mill and Harriet Taylor Mill (Mill 1986) – was not interested in the gender-based division of labour, which to him probably was innate and nothing to be concerned about.

In his book *De la division du travail social* (1893) sociologist Emile Durkheim takes on the social division of labour. But the gender-based division of labour (which he still calls "sexual division of labour") is mentioned only twice. In his view a gender-based division of labour is necessary for every society whose role "is not simply to embellish or ameliorate existing societies, but to render societies possible which, without it, would not exist" (Durkheim 1933: 60). And he stresses "the particular solidarity which unites the members of a family in accordance with the division of domestic labor. [...] Far from being only an accessory and secondary phenomenon, this division of familial labor, on the contrary, dominates the entire development of the family" (Durkheim 1933: 123).

In contrast to Smith and Durkheim, feminist economics has argued that the gender-based division of labour is neither innate nor a social necessity, but a result of specific forms of socialisation of men and women and very much touches upon problems of justice. Even though traditional economists are seldom aware of it, *gender* has become the structuring element of the social division of labour: "In modern society gender division of labour is not a part of the social division of labour, but the social division of labour is gender-based" (Bennholdt-Thomsen 1992: 204, own translation).

In the German-speaking countries, the questioning of economic structures from a feminist perspective for a very long time was left to disciplines other than economics, e.g. sociology. One important approach in this context is the subsistence approach developed in the 1980s by three German sociologists, Veronika Bennholdt-Thomsen, Maria Mies and Claudia von Werlhof (Bennholdt-Thomsen *et al.* 1992; Mies 1986).

They criticized the economic system for excluding women and subsistence production and argued that "[a] feminist conception of an alternative economy [...] will place the transformation of the existing sexual division of labour (based on the breadwinner-housewife model) *at the centre* of the whole restructuring process" (Mies 1986: 221; original emphasis).

By now feminist economics is, especially in the US, an important part of economics focusing on the economic situation of women, their time use for activities in the market and the non-market economy making the gender-based division of labour visible (e.g. Bergmann 1986; Ferber, Nelson 1993; Folbre 1994; Nelson 1996; Blau *et al.* 1998). Feminist economics starts with the identification of a domain of study. Julie Nelson, for a very good example, has suggested

that our discipline take as its organizational center the down-to-earth subject matter of how humans try to meet their needs for goods and services. Economics should be about how we arrange provision of our sustenance. [...] Economic provisioning and the sustenance of life becomes the center of study, whether it be through market, household, or government action, or whether it be by symmetric exchange, coercion, or gift. (Nelson 1996: 36)

Feminist economists agree that the economy consists of two main parts, the monetary income-generating economy and the household or maintenance economy, and that only both parts together constitute the whole economic system (e.g. Jochimsen and Knobloch 1997; Himmelweit 2002). And they continue to redefine labour: labour is paid *and* unpaid labour, market work for wages *and* maintenance work, so that the criterion of distinguishing labour from non-labour is not income any more. In looking for another criterion to distinguish labour and non-labour, some go back to the *third person criterion* put forward by Margaret Reid (Reid 1934). According to the third-person criterion an activity is considered labour if a third person, e.g. a hired employee, can do it instead of oneself. So, for example, cooking is considered work, eating is not, making the bed is labour, sleeping is not.

Neglecting the maintenance economy with all its time-consuming work means living in an imaginary world, where tables fill themselves, dishes wash themselves, the sick and old care for themselves, children educate themselves and so on. I have called this phenomenon the *wishing-table-fantasy* (Knobloch 2001) after the German fairy tale *Tischlein-deck-dich*. This fantasy easily serves as an illustration for the dominant economic thinking even for the more critical yet non-feminist one. Most economists neglect the whole process of household and other non-market activities, e.g. how food gets on the plate, with the underlying belief they could – as in the fairy tale – come home, say "little table, spread yourself" and meals would be ready.

The feminist perspective reveals that there is no wishing table; furthermore, that the division of labour between the sexes which underlies the wishing-table-fantasy is unjust, especially because the domestic work load is not distributed equally. Women do often have a "double day", which means doing paid work as well as being responsible for the housework and other unpaid work. Much more often than men, women cross the border between market and non-market economy back and forth and have learned to bridge the differences between market and non-market work. Therefore, women may be called the *mediators* between market and non-market economy (Busch-Lüty *et al.* 1994: 7).

Even though we speak of the gender-based division of labour mainly when it occurs *between* the market and the maintenance or home economy, we find it *within* the market economy and *within* the home economy as well. Therefore, it seems helpful to distinguish three kinds of gender-based division of labour:

(a) Gender-based division of labour *between market and maintenance economy*: men do more of the paid market work and women do more of the unpaid non-market work. This traditional distribution of work is still very common. Worldwide men do three quarters of their work paid and only one quarter unpaid, women do two thirds of their work unpaid and only one third paid (UNDP 1995).

(b) Gender-based division of paid work *in the marketplace* with two main lines:

  (1) Many jobs are either predominantly female, such as dietician, nurse, kindergarten teacher, or predominantly male, like engineer, surgeon, architect (Blau *et al.* 1998: 127–8). Jobs done by women are often paid less and have lesser reputation than men's jobs.

  (2) Women in leading positions are still exceptions. There seems to be a glass ceiling, which keeps them off the highest positions.

(c) Gender-based division of unpaid work *in the non-market economy*, e.g. the household: women are held responsible for caring activities around the household even though they are employed outside the home, working twice as much as men in the non-market economy. Men's activities in the domestic economy differ not only in degree but also in kind, e.g. they are more often than women, at least in Germany, occupied with activities such as repair and do-it-yourself; in all other unpaid activities women work longer hours (Blanke *et al.* 1996: 73).

The common task of the different approaches to feminist economics is the inquiry of the distribution of market and domestic work between men and women. Because the gender-based division of labour is not symmetrical, not reciprocal, but hierarchical, patriarchal, asymmetric, the main argument here is that it has to be seen as a question of justice. Taking the gender-based division of labour for granted, therefore, would leave the underlying problems of justice invisible.

The hypothesis of this chapter is that we have to look at the distribution of labour in and between market and maintenance economy and in looking at it we need a method which by its conception of the good helps us to get a clear idea of the injustice due to the gender-based division of labour. The three approaches discussed in the following all start from a different conception of the good. They will be studied according to two questions: (a) Do they take women's life and work into account, that is, is the household or maintenance economy part of their subject matter? (b) Is the method, especially their conception of the good, able to make the injustice due to the gender-based division of labour visible?

The preference-based approach

Around the turn from the nineteenth to the twentieth century, two disciplines were emerging: on the one hand neoclassical economics, which later became mainstream economics, and on the other hand home economics, which for a long time was not regarded as economics at all. I will take a short look at how these two approaches as well as the New Home Economics of the 1960s deal with the gender-based division of labour.

Neoclassical economics defines itself not by subject matter but by specific methodological approach. Central to this approach is the individual as rational, autonomous, self-interested and maximizing his or her personal well-being. In neoclassical economics the gender-based division of labour between market and home stayed invisible. This invisibility is due to two main reasons:

(a) *Exclusion of housework and all other caring activities*: neoclassical economics has concentrated on the individual and its market activities – such as consumption, paid work and production – with a neglect of all non-market activities, especially household production.

(b) *Preference-satisfaction view of well-being*: neoclassical economics is based on a preference conception of the good identifying well-being with the satisfaction of preferences. That means, subjective preferences and desires are the criteria of what is good for the individual and society (Hausman and McPherson 1996: 42–5; 73–81).

Home economics, in contrast, understands housework as productive and discusses the production of the household intensively (Yi 1996).

Home economist Margaret Reid argued that household production consists of those household-produced goods and services that could be substituted for by market-produced goods and services, defining household production by the third-person criterion as "unpaid activities which are carried on, by and for the members, which might be replaced by market goods, or paid services, if circumstances such as income, market conditions, and personal inclinations permit the service being delegated to someone outside the household group" (Reid 1934: 11). Yet, focusing exclusively on household production, home economics is not aware of the problems of justice underlying the gender-based division of paid and unpaid labour.

The New Home Economics which goes back to Gary S. Becker's and Jacob Mincer's research on the family in the 1960s (Becker 1965, 1976, 1991; Mincer 1993) seems to combine both of these disciplines: the method of neoclassical economics with the subject matter of home economics. In New Home Economics not the individual but the family is in the centre, the family understood as "a unit whose adult members make informed and rational decisions that result in maximizing the utility or well-being of the family" (Blau *et al.* 1998: 33). New Home Economics applies the tools of neoclassical economics to the analysis of the division of labour within the family. Its main focus is on the allocation of time between home and market, especially on the intra-household time use. It is seen that most goods are not consumed as they have been bought in the market, but have to be prepared for consumption, e.g. cooking. This preparation needs time which is not market labour time but home labour time. In the household market goods are transformed into commodities:

Commodities are produced by combining the home time of family members with goods and services purchased in the market, using labor market earnings. Virtually all market-purchased goods and services require an infusion of home time to transform them into the commodities from which we may derive utility [...]. Thus, time spent on paid work produces the income necessary to purchase market goods, which in turn are needed together with home time to produce commodities. A crucial question for the family is how time should be allocated between home and market most efficiently in order to maximize satisfaction. (Blau *et al.* 1998: 34)

Therefore, New Home Economics is confronted with the distribution of work inside and outside the home. But instead of analyzing the gender-based division of labour, New Home Economics seems to look for good reasons to explain the traditional breadwinner-housewife model assuming that the family reaches the goal to maximize its utility or satisfaction. On the one hand, New Home Economics claims natural grounds for the existing gender-based division of labour, innate abilities of women and men (Becker 1996: 148–55; Boserup 1989; Grossbard-Shechtman 2001: 108). On the other hand, it is argued that women and men have specialized in different tasks (Becker 1989: 70–1; 1996: 148–55): "[C]ommodity production is carried out most efficiently if one member of the family specializes, at least to some extent, in market production while the other specializes, at least to some extent, in home production" (Blau *et al.* 1998: 34). The result of this specialization is greater efficiency, which usually is gained from specialization of women inside and men outside the house. The specialization and efficiency argument, however, neglects the asymmetry and hierarchy of the gender-based division of paid and unpaid labour.

New Home Economics shifts its view from market activities to non-market activities in the families, holding on to the preference conception of well-being: subjective preferences and desires are the criteria of what is good for the family and for society as a whole. Even in case the preference view of the good is modified, the main point of criticism concerning adaptation and social construction of preferences and desires remains:

Preferences are not exogenous, given independently of economic and social conditions. They are at least in part constructed by those conditions. Women often have no preference for economic independence before they learn about avenues through which women like them might pursue this goal; nor do they think of themselves as citizens with rights that were being ignored, before they learn of their rights and are encouraged to believe in their equal worth. [...] Men's preferences, too, are socially shaped and often misshaped. Men frequently have a strong preference that their wives should do all the child care and all the housework – often in addition to working an eight-hour day. Such preferences, too, are not fixed in the nature of things: they are constructed by social traditions of privilege and subordination. Thus a preference-based approach typically will reinforce inequalities: especially those inequalities that are entrenched enough to have crept into people's very desires. (Nussbaum 2000b: II 2/4)

Holding on to the preference-satisfaction view of well-being and neglecting the underlying power structures and the asymmetry of paid and unpaid work, New Home Economics is not aware of the related questions of justice. Therefore, we have to look for another conception of the good to deal with the problem of gender-based division of labour as a problem of justice.

The primary goods-based approach

Modern political philosophy has been strongly influenced by John Rawls's *A Theory of Justice* (1971). Central to this theory is the concept of the Original Position. In this thought experiment hypothetical people decide on principles of justice behind a veil of ignorance, not knowing which place in society, e.g. status, talents and occupation, they will have in life. Selecting principles of justice behind this veil of ignorance all human beings "have to consider the well-being of everyone, from the best-off to the worst-off, on the hypothesis that they could be any one of them" (Nussbaum 1992b: 4/12). By contrast, whether human beings will be male or female is not a criterion included in the assumptions of the Original Position.

As the liberalism–communitarianism debate has shown (e.g. Honneth 1993), even though the just has priority over the good, we need an elementary conception of the good as precondition for the just (Pauer-Studer 1996). Rawls needs such a conception of the good as a basis of the Original Position and the decision process about principles of justice. The elementary conception of the good, on which Rawls bases his theory of justice, is the conception of social primary goods. Primary goods are "things that every rational man is presumed to want. These goods normally have a use whatever a person's rational plan of life" (Rawls 1973: 62). In *A Theory of Justice* Rawls names these goods which everybody wants to have no matter what else he or she wants throughout the text. Later, for example in his book *Political Liberalism* (1993: 181), he puts the primary goods together in a short list.

List of primary goods (John Rawls)

1. Basic rights and liberties.
2. Freedom of movement and free choice of occupation against a background of diverse opportunities.
3. Powers and prerogatives of offices and positions of responsibility in the political and economic institutions of the basic structure.
4. Income and wealth.
5. The social bases of self-respect.

To get to know more about how the issue of gender division of labour is dealt with in Rawls's theory, a look at his model of the family may be helpful. Rawls sees the family as a decision unit with a head who decides altruistically for all members of the family (e.g. Rawls 1973: 128). And how does the gender-based division of labour between market and domestic work figure in Rawls's theory? It is mentioned nowhere explicitly. Due to this circumstance Rawls is not aware of the problems of justice within the family and the household and does not apply his theory to either of them. But he has to assume that families are just, otherwise he cannot hold on to his theory of moral development which argues that children get their sense of justice in the family (Okin 1989b: 249).

In her book *Justice, Gender and the Family* (1989), Susan Moller Okin takes Rawls's theory of justice to look at the "family of some sort or other" (Okin 1989a: 18). She holds on to Rawls's thought experiment of the Original Position, but she takes into account the category "sex" as an element of which people are not aware when selecting principles of justice (Okin 1989a: 91):

> If those in the original position did not know whether they were to be men or women, they would surely be concerned to establish a thoroughgoing social and economic equality between the sexes that would protect either sex from the need to pander to or servilely provide for the pleasures of the other. They would emphasize the importance of girls' and boys' growing up with an equal sense of respect for themselves and equal expectations of self-definition and development. (Okin 1989a: 104–5)

New to Okin's approach is that she applies Rawls's primary goods-based theory of justice to the family and domestic activities, where inequalities in the primary goods power and income are most relevant. In doing so, Okin looks at "issues such as the distribution of work (paid and unpaid), income, power, opportunity to choose one's occupation, self-respect and esteem, and availability of exit" (Okin 1989a: 150). But she does not discuss these issues, which differ from Rawls's list of primary goods, as elements of a conception of the good.

If a theory of justice is to be persuasive it must to some extent take a stand on the question of what conditions and ways of acting are good ones (Nussbaum 1992b: 8/12), as Rawls does in favour of his short list of primary goods. But Rawls is not aware that the list of primary goods might change, in case the veil of ignorance hides the sex of the people in the Original Position. What about the conception of primary goods in Okin's theory? It seems that Okin, here, is following Rawls, because she does not discuss the conception of primary goods anywhere in her book. However, one might expect the introduction of sex as analytical category to have an impact on the list of primary goods and their distribution: are there more goods to be added to the short list of primary goods? How far would the conception of primary goods have to be extended to be able to overcome injustice due to the gender-based division of labour? Being in the state of the Original Position, what would everybody need to have – not knowing whether they will be male or female, young or old, healthy or sick? An equal sharing of home and paid work as well as forms of institutionalized care for the young, old and sick apart from the nuclear family?

Rawls's list of primary goods has been criticized for containing goods which are not good in themselves, e.g. income and wealth, and his resource-based thin theory of the good for being not sufficient to give direction to public policy and economy (Sen 1999):

such a list fails to demonstrate the very point and importance of those goods, which is to serve as instruments for human functioning. Unless we show how the goods on Rawls's list enable people to choose to live in ways that have value, we have not shown why they have any value at all; [...] What should be clear is that a theory of justice based only on the resources people should have is inadequate when it is not guided by a conception of what people do with these resources (Nussbaum 1992b: 8–9/12).

Among all the discussed additions and revisions to the list of primary goods, Eva Kittay's argumentation for the need of care as an additional primary good (Kittay 1999) seems to be the most important and challenging one to Rawls's theory. But the problem with this and other additions to the list of primary goods lies on a different level. As Nussbaum has shown, it is not possible to add more capability-like primary goods to Rawls's list:

He will be in very great difficulty, in the terms he has set for himself, if he admits this highly heterogeneous list of "primary goods", all of which seem highly relevant to the determination of relevant social positions. A desired simplicity, both in indexing relative social positions and in describing the point of social cooperation, will be jeopardized. (Nussbaum 2006: 142)

Taking these different points of critique seriously, Rawls's primary goods-based political liberalism is not adequate to reduce and avoid injustice due to the gender division of labour.

The capabilities-based approach

As Amartya Sen has argued in his influential article *Equality of What?* (1982), equality of resources differs from basic capability equality. Therefore, we will go on to the capabilities approach and link it to the subject of the gender-based division of labour as a question of justice. There are two different capabilities conceptions on which I shall base my argumentation: Martha C. Nussbaum's capabilities approach and the capabilities conception as part of the integrative approach to ethics and economics by Peter Ulrich.

Martha C. Nussbaum has been developing her capabilities approach since the 1990s, partly together with Amartya Sen (Nussbaum 1990, 1992a; Nussbaum and Sen 1993). Both of them aim at capabilities rather than resources such as income and wealth, defining capabilities as things that people are able to be or to do. The reason is

that individuals have varying needs for resources, in accordance with their social and physical circumstances, the special obstacles they face and so forth. Two people may be given the very same amount of basic resources, and yet end up being unequal in their ability to perform valuable human functions [...] In order to deal with such individual variability, we have to say which functions we care about, and examine the varying needs of individuals in connection with these functions. (Nussbaum 1992b: 8/12)

People should be capable of choosing to function in various desirable ways: "The just society will make sure that people can be well nourished, but will not force-feed them if they choose to fast" (Nussbaum 1992b: 8/12). Drawing a clear distinction between functions and capabilities, Nussbaum emphasizes that "capability, not functioning, is the appropriate political goal" (Nussbaum 2000a: 87) and that "the structure of social and political institutions should be chosen, at least in part, with a view to promoting at least a threshold level of these human capabilities" (Nussbaum 2000a: 75), "the level at which a person's capability becomes [...] *worthy* of a human being" (Nussbaum 2000a: 73).

Nussbaum develops an elementary conception of the good, which is based on a list of universal human capabilities (see the capabilities list, Table 17.1, below). The underlying assumption is that there are "central elements of truly human functioning that can command a broad cross-cultural consensus" (Nussbaum 2000a: 74). Hence, a human life, which lacks one of these elements, is not to be considered a human life.

A just society faces the task to make visible and critically examine its underlying gender order and related asymmetries. Therefore, institutions such as the nuclear family need to be examined and justified. It has to be discussed, for example, what might be the consequences for people's capacities and abilities of being raised, or not raised, in a nuclear family. The patterns of family life limit women's opportunities in many ways: "by assigning them to unpaid work with low prestige; by denying them equal opportunities to outside jobs and education; by insisting they do most or all of the housework and child care even when they are also earning wages" (Nussbaum 1992b: 2/12). Against this background an account of justice and the family is critical of Rawls's approach. Would the parties in Rawls's Original Position design a society with families in it? What would be their arguments for doing so (Nussbaum 1992b: 6/12)? And if public policy determines that the nuclear family is an institution worthy of public support, there is a variety of arrangements by which children may be raised with love and taught standards of justice, because the capacities of children, rather than the institution of the family itself, are what society is committed to supporting (Nussbaum 1992b: 9/12).

But should the standards of basic capabilities differ for men and women? And do women and men have different capabilities? On the one hand, it is argued that men and women have different capabilities by nature (e.g. Bennholdt-Thomsen 1992: 199). But Nussbaum disagrees with this position: "There may be innate differences between the sexes, but so far we are not in a position to know them" (Nussbaum 1999: 52). On the other hand, it is argued that men's and women's capabilities do not differ, because capabilities are not special to some people but basic for all human beings, male and female (Nussbaum 1995). Discussing two possibilities within this position Nussbaum refuses the position of the *same* capabilities in *separate* spheres, that is associated with traditional forms of hierarchy, but claims the position of the *same* capabilities in the *same* spheres as the only just one:

Women in much of the world lack support for the most central human functions, and this denial of support is frequently caused by their being women. But women, unlike rocks and plants and even horses, have the potential to become capable of these human functions, given sufficient nutrition, education, and other support. That is why their unequal failure in capability is a problem of justice. (Nussbaum 1999: 54).

Nussbaum's capabilities approach is a good starting point to discuss the threefold gender-based division of labour, not in distinguishing special women's capabilities but by listing universal human capabilities, which include women's capabilities, not by holding to the usual public versus private distinction but by pointing at the unjust structures of private institutions like the family. It therefore gives feminist economics a solid ground, but we could get still one step further, as I will show below.

Swiss social economist Peter Ulrich has developed a socio-economic approach that aims at integrating ethics and economics. Starting from the communicative or discoursive ethics of the German philosophers Karl-Otto Apel and Jürgen Habermas, and also taking into account the political philosophy from Immanuel Kant to John Rawls, Ulrich criticizes the narrow view of rationality in economics and the monetarizing effects of the global economic system, and starts anew with a reflection upon the normative foundations of economics and the aim of economic activity (Ulrich 1993, 2008):

The decisive criterion of all economic activity should not be the creation of market value but – in spite of all the practical constraints involved – *the service of life*. (Ulrich 2008: 186)

Prior to the efficiency criterion is the service of life (*Lebensdienlichkeit*) of the economy in its two dimensions: the question of meaning (the good life) and the question of legitimation (the just social life). Whereas the question of meaning is oriented to securing the means of human subsistence and the abundance of human life, the question of legitimation focuses on the basic human rights (Ulrich 2008: 185–8).

There are three types of basic rights for every human being to be distinguished: personal rights, political rights and basic socio-economic rights. The socio-economic rights, which are necessary to live a coherent and self-determined life, Ulrich formulates as "economic citizenship rights" (Ulrich 2008: 225–7). The question of legitimation or justice based on these rights is closely linked to the question of meaning, because it is grounded on an elementary conception of the good. The idea behind this conception of the good is that every person should have the right to develop a set of very basic human capabilities and to get the resources needed to lead a self-determined life. To guarantee this right and to advance the basic capabilities of human beings is the best way to secure the existence and the dignity of human life:

It is, therefore, clear that we must couple the empowerment of individuals to satisfy their (self-determined) needs with their entitlement to free disposition over a basic minimum of resources (ultimately purchasing power). We must see this as the central precondition which will enable them to lead a life worthy of a human being in accordance with their culturally determined needs. (Ulrich 2008: 248)

Ulrich's idea of economic citizen rights gets its strength from aiming in two directions. On the one hand, these rights aim at the entitlement and the capability of all human beings to integrate themselves into the market-oriented production and consumption process on a basis of equal opportunities. On the other hand, they aim at the entitlement and capability of all human beings to (partially) emancipate themselves from the compulsory functions of the economic system (Ulrich 2008: 250).

To determine the different economic citizenship rights, Ulrich sketches a conception of capabilities of his own and suggests the following list of socio-economic basic capabilities with their corresponding rights (Ulrich 2008: 251–2).

Socio-economic basic capabilities and rights (Peter Ulrich)

1. Capability to understand the contexts of one's life and to orientate oneself therein
   - right to education
2. Capability to develop one's personality, self-confidence and self-respect
   - right to inviolable identity and appropriate participation in decision-making also in the economic realm
3. Capability to develop social relationships
   - right to social integration
4. Capability to claim one's rights
   - right to legal protection and fair legal procedure

5. Capability to form and maintain a family
   - right to marriage and children and to appropriate social support of families
6. Capability to participate as a full citizen in the social and political discourse of democratic societies
   - right to participation in the public discourse
7. Capability to earn a living wage
   - right to professional training, right to work, fair work conditions and appropriate income as well as self-employment and private property
8. Capability to live one's life in human dignity even in situations of economic need
   - right to existential security and social care

In his integrative approach to ethics and economics Ulrich concentrates on the market economy and the emancipation from it. He distinguishes market participation and employment from leisure time, which should be free of market restraints. But the third sphere which any human being also belongs to and has responsibilities in – namely the non-market, caring or maintenance economy – is not systematically included in this approach. Non-market activities are not looked at as labour but only as leisure time, so that, for example, whether a reduction of market labour increases non-market labour remains open.

Consequently, similarly to Rawls, Ulrich is unable to see the implications of the gender-based division of labour within the family, the household and the whole maintenance economy, let alone discuss the problems of injustice connected with it. Although the family is mentioned in his list of socio-economic basic capabilities, it is not discussed any further in his integrative approach to ethics and economics. Whether family structures and the distribution of non-market work are just, therefore, remains an open question.

But we cannot talk about the gender division of labour without taking into account the market and non-market economy, the paid and unpaid labour. Only together do they give the whole picture of economics and economic life:

Economic life equally depends on unpaid activities carried out within a domestic sector. This sector provides caring services directly to household members as well as to the wider community, and these are vital to individual socialization and to the production and maintenance of human capabilities upon which economic life depends. (Himmelweit 2002: 52)

Is Ulrich's capabilities and rights approach then helpful to make visible the injustice connected with the gender division of labour? Or is it still captured in the wishing-table-fantasy? To show the strength of Ulrich's approach I would like to distinguish two aspects: the principal idea behind his capabilities and rights approach, and his suggested list of capabilities and economic citizen rights.

The principal idea behind Ulrich's list of socio-economic capabilities with their corresponding rights is the right to develop a set of human capabilities and to get the resources needed to lead a self-determined life. Ulrich's universal principle is open to include capabilities and rights, which play an important role for the economic life of men and women, for paid and unpaid labour. This idea of socio-economic rights as economic citizen rights becomes extremely important in times of globalization, with its enormous impact not only on the market economy but also on the households and other parts of the non-market economy.

But his capabilities list needs further discussion and revision – a procedure Nussbaum's list has already undergone (Knobloch 2003). In Ulrich's list, capabilities are to be added or revised so that women, like men, are able to attain full status of an economic citizen. An economic citizen is responsible not only in the paid but also in the unpaid economy for the housework and other unpaid labour. And this would be rather important for the discussion of at least two of the three forms of the gender division of labour. So far, Ulrich's capabilities and rights list seems to be developed much more around a man's than a woman's biography in economic life.

With his linkage of economic citizen rights to the basic human capabilities Ulrich goes beyond Nussbaum's and Sen's capabilities approaches (Ulrich 2004: 14). But whereas the universal idea of an economic citizen with socio-economic capabilities and corresponding rights could be helpful to analyze the threefold gender division of labour as a matter of justice, Ulrich's list of the capabilities and rights of an economic citizen does not support this analysis as long as the capabilities and rights are not formulated in a way to allow for the economic citizen to be either a man or a women.

As the care economy debate has shown (e.g. Folbre 1994; Jochimsen and Knobloch 1997; Himmelweit 2002; Jochimsen 2003), structure and motivation of labour in the non-market economy could be quite different from that in the market economy. Whether care should be integrated into the capabilities and rights list as a capability of its own or a corresponding socio-economic right is open to discussion. Whereas Nussbaum argues a special capability to care is not necessary, because it is included in the other capabilities (Nussbaum

2006), I myself opt for a socio-economic right to be looked after and cared for (Knobloch 2007).

Nussbaum's position in this discussion is

that care is not a single thing, and therefore that it should not be, or at least need not be, introduced as a single separate extra capability in addition to the others. Thinking well about care means thinking about a wide range of capabilities on the side of both the cared-for and the caregiver. [...] In short, given the intimate and foundational role that care plays in the lives of the cared-for, we have to say that it addresses, or should address, the entire range of the central human capabilities. (Nussbaum 2006: 168f.)

Although the right to social care is part of Ulrich's list, the focus there is on the exceptional case in which an independent person needs care, not on the common case, that everybody is dependent on care throughout at least parts of his or her life. But every human being is dependent on care – definitely as a child, shorter or longer terms or even permanently during or at the end of one's life. Therefore, it seems necessary to formulate a socio-economic right to be looked after and cared for as a basic foundation of any just society and economy.

Such a right would make very clear that care is no natural resource but a responsible and time-consuming task, nothing which is innate to women, but often very exhausting and strenuous work – physically and psychically. The further discussion will show whether we should include a basic human capability to care with a corresponding socio-economic right to be cared for. But important at this moment is that we have to include care work systematically to understand the different aspects of gender division of labour as a question of justice.

A gender-aware vision of a modern economy and society necessarily implies that men and women take equal responsibility for the children and the elderly and all other unpaid work to live on equal terms both inside and outside the home. In analogy to Ulrich's two directions concerning the market process, what is also necessary is the emancipation from the maintenance economy on the one hand and appropriate participation in it on the other. A more egalitarian distribution of the workload will be reached only if men participate responsibly and equally in non-market work, that is, if women's current life patterns become the norm for everyone, a vision which goes back to the political philosopher Nancy Fraser:

Women today often combine breadwinning and caregiving, albeit with great difficulties and strain. A postindustrial welfare state must ensure that men do the same, while redesigning institutions so as to eliminate the difficulty and strain. We might call this vision *Universal Caregiver*. (Fraser 1997: 61)

Conclusion

Feminist economists are concerned with the unequal division of tasks between men and women in the paid and unpaid economy. To discuss the gender-based division of labour as a question of justice, we need not only an appropriate theory of justice but also an elementary universal conception of the good. From the discussion in this chapter it should be clear that neither preferences nor primary goods are an adequate foundation to deal with the gender division of labour as a question of justice. The capabilities approach, with its corresponding socio-economic rights, however, is. In focusing on human basic capabilities and the corresponding basic rights we are able to make visible the injustice underlying the gender-based division of labour if capabilities and socio-economic rights which are universal to men's as well as to women's lives are explicitly included. Against this background we get an orientation for our way to a just distribution of work between men and women. A just society focuses on the participation in the income-generating economy as well as on the participation in the maintenance economy, on the distribution of income-generating labour as well as on the distribution of maintenance labour, on the emancipation from the income-generating economy as well as on the emancipation from the maintenance economy. The gender-based division of labour is no efficiency problem and nothing to find good reasons for, but something which is unjust as long as it hinders people from fully developing their basic human capabilities.

REFERENCES

Becker, Gary S. (1996): *Accounting for Tastes*, Cambridge, MA, London: Harvard University Press.
(1991): *A Treatise on the Family*, enlarged edition, Cambridge, MA: Harvard University Press.
(1989): Family, in: John Eatwell, Murray Milgate, Peter Newman (eds.), *Social Economics*, New York, London: W.W. Norton, 64–76.
(1976): *The Economic Approach to Human Behavior*, Chicago University Press.
(1965): A Theory of the Allocation of Time, *The Economic Journal* 75 (299), 493–517.
Bennholdt-Thomsen, Veronika (1992): Zur Bestimmung der geschlechtlichen Arbeitsteilung im Kapitalismus, in: Bennholdt-Thomsen *et al.*, 194–212.
Bennholdt-Thomsen, Veronika, Mies, Maria and von Werlhof, Claudia (1992): *Frauen, die letzte Kolonie. Zur Hausfrauisierung der Arbeit*, 3rd edition, Zürich: Rotpunktverlag.

Bergmann, Barbara R. (1986): *The Economic Emergence of Women*, New York: Basic Books.

Blanke, Karen, Ehling, Manfred and Schwarz, Norbert (1996): *Zeit im Blickfeld. Ergebnisse einer repräsentativen Zeitbudgeterhebung*, Stuttgart, Berlin, Cologne: Kohlhammer.

Blau, Francine D., Ferber, Marianne A. and Winkler, Anne E. (1998): *The Economics of Women, Men, and Work*, 3rd edition, Upper Saddle River, NJ: Prentice Hall.

Boserup, Ester (1989): Inequality between the Sexes, in: John Eatwell, Murray Milgate, Peter Newman (eds.): *Social Economics*, New York, London: W.W. Norton, 165–170.

Busch-Lüty, Christiane, Jochimsen, Maren A., Knobloch, Ulrike and Seidl, Irmi (eds.) (1994): Vorsorgendes Wirtschaften. Frauen auf dem Weg zu einer Ökonomie der Nachhaltigkeit, *Politische Ökologie*, special issue No. 6, Munich: œ.

Durkheim, Emile (1933): *The Division of Labor in Society*, translated by George Simpson, London: Macmillan [Original: 1893].

Ferber, Marianne A. and Nelson, Julie A. (eds.) (1993): *Beyond Economic Man. Feminist Theory and Economics*, Chicago, London: University of Chicago Press.

Folbre, Nancy (1994): *Who Pays for the Kids? Gender and the Structures of Constraint*, New York, London: Routledge.

Fraser, Nancy (1997): *Justice Interruptus. Critical Reflections on the "Postsocialist" Condition*, New York, London: Routledge.

Grossbard-Shechtman, Shoshona (2001): The New Home Economics at Columbia and Chicago, *Feminist Economics*, 7 (3), 103–130.

Hausman, Daniel M. and McPherson, Michael S. (1996): *Economic Analysis and Moral Philosophy*, Cambridge, New York: Cambridge University Press.

Himmelweit, Sue (2002): Making Visible the Hidden Economy: The Case for Gender-Impact-Analysis of Economic Policy, *Feminist Economics*, 8 (1), 49–70.

Honneth, Axel (ed.) (1993): *Kommunitarismus. Eine Debatte über die moralischen Grundlagen moderner Gesellschaften*, Frankfurt a.M., New York: Campus.

Jochimsen, Maren A. (2003): *Careful Economics. Integrating Caring Activities and Economic Science*, Boston, Dordrecht, London: Kluwer Academic Publishers.

Jochimsen, Maren A. and Knobloch, Ulrike (1997): Making the Hidden Visible: The Importance of Caring Activities and Their Principles for Any Economy, *Ecological Economics*, 20 (2), 107–112.

Kittay, Eva (1999): *Love's Labor: Essays on Women, Equality, and Dependency*, New York, London: Routledge.

Knobloch, Ulrike (2007): Begründung und Formulierung sozialökonomischer Grundrechte aus genderbewusster Perspektive, in: Johannes Hirata, Peter Ulrich (eds.), Auf dem Weg zu universalen Wirtschaftsbürgerrechten. Die Chancen einer rechtebasierten Sozialethik für eine interkulturelle Wirtschafts- und Gesellschaftspolitik, *Reports of the Institute for Business Ethics*, 109, St. Gallen: Institute for Business Ethics, 61–67.

Knobloch, Ulrike (2004): Vorstellungen des Guten in der integrativen Wirtschaftsethik – Hinführung und Weiterentwicklung, in: Dietmar Mieth, Olaf J. Schumann, Peter Ulrich (eds.): *Reflexionsfelder integrativer Wirtschaftsethik*, Tübingen, Basel: A. Francke Verlag, 51–68.

(2003): Der Fähigkeitsansatz als Orientierung für eine feministische Wirtschaftsethik, Korreferat zum Beitrag von Martha Nussbaum, *Journal for Business, Economics & Ethics*, 4 (1), 32–37.

(2001): Kooperation in der feministischen Wirtschaftsethik, *Bremen Contributions to Institutional and Social-Economics*, 47, University of Bremen: Institute for Institutional and Social-Economics.

Mies, Maria (1986): *Patriarchy and Accumulation on a World Scale. Women in the International Division of Labour*, London, Atlantic Highlands, NJ: Zed Books.

Mill, John Stuart (1986): *The Subjection of Women*, Buffalo, NY: Prometheus Books [Original: 1861].

Mincer, Jacob (1993): *Studies in Labor Supply: Collected Essays of Jacob Mincer, Vol. 2*, Aldershot: Edward Elgar.

Nelson, Julie A. (1996): *Feminism, Objectivity and Economics*, New York, London: Routledge.

Nussbaum, Martha C. (2006): *Frontiers of Justice. Disability, Nationality, Species Membership*, Cambridge, MA, London: Harvard University Press.

(2000a): *Women and Human Development. The Capabilities Approach*, Cambridge, New York: Cambridge University Press.

(2000b): Women and Work – The Capabilities Approach, *Little Magazine 1*, Issue 1. Available online at www.littlemag.com/2000/martha.htm

(1999): *Sex and Social Justice*, New York, Oxford: Oxford University Press.

(1995): Human Capabilities, Female Human Beings, in: Martha C. Nussbaum, Jonathan Glover (eds.), *Women, Culture, and Development. A Study of Human Capabilities*, Oxford University Press, 61–104.

(1992a): Human Functioning and Social Justice. In Defense of Aristotelian Essentialism, *Political Theory*, 20 (2), 202–246.

(1992b): *Justice for Women!* New York Review of Books. Available online at www.nybooks.com/articles/2802.

(1990): Nature; Function, and Capability: Aristotle on Political Distribution, in: Günther Patzig (ed.), *Aristoteles' "Politik", Akten des XI. Symposium Aristotelicum Friedrichshafen Bodensee*, Göttingen: Vandenhoeck & Ruprecht, 152–186.

Nussbaum, Martha C. and Sen, Amartya (eds.) (1993): *The Quality of Life*, Oxford: Clarendon Press.

Okin, Susan Moller (1989a): *Justice, Gender, and the Family*, New York: Basic Books.

(1989b): Reason and Feeling in Thinking about Justice, *Ethics*, 99 (2), 229–249.

Pauer-Studer, Herlinde (1996): *Das Andere der Gerechtigkeit. Moraltheorie im Kontext der Geschlechterdifferenz*, Berlin: Akademie Verlag.

Rawls, John (1993): *Political Liberalism*, New York: Columbia University Press.

(1973): *A Theory of Justice*, Oxford, New York: Oxford University Press [Original: 1971].

Reid, Margaret G. (1934): *Economics of Household Production*, New York: John Wiley.

Sen, Amartya (1999): *Development as Freedom*, New York: Knopf.

(1982) "Equality of What?" in Amartya Sen, *Choice, Welfare, and Measurement*, Cambridge, MA: Harvard University Press, 353–369.

Smith, Adam (1976): *An Inquiry into the Nature and Causes of the Wealth of Nations*, edited by R.H. Campbell, A.S. Skinner and W.B. Todd, 2 volumes, Indianapolis IN: Liberty Press [Original: 1776].

Ulrich, Peter (2008): *Integrative Economic Ethics. Foundations of a Civilized Market Economy*, Cambridge University Press [Original: Integrative Wirtschaftsethik. Grundlagen einer lebensdienlichen Ökonomie 1997, 4th edition 2008].

(2004): Was ist 'gute' sozioökonomische Entwicklung? Eine wirtschaftsethische Perspektive, *Journal for Business, Economics & Ethics*, 5 (1), 8–22.

(1993): *Transformation der ökonomischen Vernunft. Fortschrittsperspektiven der modernen Industriegesellschaft*, 3rd edition, Bern, Stuttgart, Vienna: Verlag Paul Haupt.

UNDP – United Nations Development Programme (1995): *Human Development Report 1995*, New York: Oxford University Press.

Yi, Yun-Ae (1996): Margaret G. Reid: Life and Achievements, *Feminist Economics*, 2 (3), 17–36.

8 Primary goods, capabilities, and the millennium development target for gender equity in education

Elaine Unterhalter and Harry Brighouse

Introduction

A large proportion of the estimated 835 million people in the world (nearly one sixth of the population) who have had no access to schooling are women and girls. According to official statistics, 53% of the 61 million school-age children out of school in 2010 were girls (UNESCO, 2012, 355); 64% of the estimated 775 million adults who have not been taught to read or write are women (UNESCO, 2012, 32). This injustice has been a focus of attempts at coordinated international policy intervention since the 1970s, but the scale of the problem remains vast and the resources committed to tackling it far too few. Arising from the Millennium Declaration adopted at the UN General Assembly in 2000, two Millennium Development Goals (MDGs) touching education emerged. A target for MDG3 was the elimination of gender disparity in access to primary and secondary education by 2005 and at all levels by 2015. MDG2 envisages that all girls and boys in every country in the world access and complete a full course of primary education by 2015. The Education for All (EFA) goals articulated in the Dakar Framework of Action adopted in 2000 by 164 governments also set out a wider range of actions to be taken to ensure high-quality education provision, including provision for adult literacy, that takes account of gender equality (UNESCO, 2003, 27).

By the mid 1990s a widespread consensus was emerging that the concept of rights provided a fruitful theoretical, political and policy way forward on this issues. Policy documents and declarations took on a language of rights, which supplanted earlier ideas of basic needs and concerns with gender interests. For example, the UNESCO EFA Global Monitoring Report of 2003 developed an argument for gender equality in education partly on the basis of the existing international declarations on human rights and partly on the rates of return to education of girls, contrasting the policy declarations and the framework of rights with a frequent lack of political commitment to make instruments work (UNESCO, 2003, 24–30). The report distinguishes between gender equality rights to education, rights within education and rights through education achieving equality of outcomes. In some UN documents a discussion of rights is linked with accounts of capabilities drawing on work undertaken by Amartya Sen and Martha C. Nussbaum (see, for example, UNESCO, 2002; UNDP, 1995).

Martha C. Nussbaum has discussed the extent of women's lack of education worldwide and the forms of solutions needed (Nussbaum, 2003). She points out how efforts to expand and enhance women's and girls' education are under attack, often directly by recourse to arguments based on the importance of preserving tradition or multiple cultures, and indirectly by neglect in the international development world. She makes a powerful case for the importance of global action in this field, while also highlighting some of the difficult issues entailed.

Building from these concerns the aim of this chapter is to show how policy formulations addressing the gender gap in education in terms of basic needs, rights or capabilities, without a theory of justice, fail to address the key distributional questions which must be settled in order to realise the EFA agenda. Part 1 outlines some dimensions of the exclusion of women and girls from schooling. It also charts some of the international policy initiatives to address this and discusses some of the social theory that has been used to develop this policy. Part 2 discusses two approaches to distributive justice: John Rawls's theory of justice as fairness, and the capabilities approach developed by Sen and Nussbaum. We argue that the two approaches are more similar than their proponents (including Sen and Nussbaum, but also including Thomas Pogge) seem to believe.[1] The capabilities approach has been more influential in the field of development, but we argue that Rawls's theory is clearer in its demand for the redistribution of income and wealth, and this is a virtue that students of development should be aware of. In Part 3 we look at some of the social theories that have engaged with the EFA policy on addressing the gender gap in education. These theories, though generally derived from empirical investigation, have been used as if they were fully normative, that is, as if they can guide action without resort to a further theory of distributive justice. But they are no substitute for fully normative theories, and we argue that the theories of justice developed by Rawls, Sen and Nussbaum are necessary supplements and provide greater clarity than either the weaker catch-all concept of rights or encyclopedic compilations of highly contextualised empirical studies.

---

[1] Both Sen and Nussbaum are explicit about their debt to Rawls and in particular that they have worked out their approaches in dialogue with Rawls's theory. But they both express disagreements that we think (and will show, later) are more apparent than real.

Part 1: Towards gender equity in education by 2005: human capital, social capital, empowerment?

Global inequalities in the distribution of education have been a matter of international concern since at least 1948 and the adoption of the Universal Declaration of Human Rights. In the 1990s governments committed themselves to provide free, basic compulsory education to all children and adults at the World Conference on Education for All, held in Jomtien, Thailand. In the ensuing years some took action, albeit unevenly and with contradictory results. Kevin Watkins, writing for Oxfam in 2000 and reviewing the progress since Jomtien, concluded that the promises made by governments had been

comprehensively broken. No human right is more systematically or extensively violated by governments than the right of their citizens to a basic education. (Watkins, 2000, 1)

Many initially considered that the renewed commitments made by governments and non-government organisations (NGOs) to deliver on EFA at the World Education Forum in Dakar in 2000 would be treated with a similar lack of urgency and that the consequences of this would fall disproportionately on women and girls (Elimu Yetu, 2005; Watkins, 2000, 2). While the 2005 goal for gender parity was missed, one effect of the MDG and EfA focus on expanding access to primary school from 2000 was a drop in the numbers of out of school children and young adults who were illiterate. However, there were still many countries with large proportions of children with little or no schooling. Concerns with quality showed up that often children were enrolled in school but learned little (Perlman Robinson, 2011). Gender inequalities continued to be marked. By 2012, 68 countries had still not achieved gender parity in primary enrolments (UNESCO, 2012, 6). In Africa, which suffered some of the worst effects of high debt, structural adjustment programmes, wars often fuelled by demand for natural resources, and HIV/AIDS, despite some significant expansion of provision, for example in Ethiopia and Senegal, there were countries where gender ratios worsened, such as Angola and Eritrea (UNESCO, 2012, 6), and others where there were stark regional differences in education provision based on socio-economic status, locale, and gender. For example in Nigeria, for the 17-22 age group based on 2012 data, the national mean was that young men had 8.16 years of schooling, while young woman had 4.96 years of schooling. However, amongst those with less than 2 years of schooling, rural women from the North East region, and the poorest socio-economic groups, make up the majority (WIDE, 2013).

218   *Elaine Unterhalter and Harry Brighouse*

Table 8.1 *Primary net enrolment ratio and survival rate to last primary grade by gender 2010*

	Female NER	Male NER	GPI NER
Sub Saharan Africa	74.0	78.0	0.95
Arab states	84.0	89.0	0.94
Central Asia	89.0	91.0	0.98
South and West Asia	87.0	89.0	0.98
East Asia and Pacific	95.0	95.0	1.00
Latin America & Caribbean	94.0	94.0	1.00
North America & Western Europe	97.0	96.0	1.00
Central & Eastern Europe	94.0	94.0	1.00

Source: UNESCO, 2012, 355

While there have been improvements in the gender disparities in enrolments in a number of countries since the 1980s and 1990s, there are still disparities in enrolment, but even more so incompletion, as official data for 2010 collated by the UNESCO Institute for Statistics indicated. Table 8.1 lists the net enrolment ratio (NER), the proportion of all children in the appropriate age range in primary school (generally 6–11) and the gender parity index in NER, that is the ratio of females to males in NER, where 1 would indicate parity between boys and girls, a variation between 0 and 1 a disparity in favour of boys, and a GPI greater than 1 a disparity in favour of girls. It can be seen that fewer girls than boys are in primary school in some regions but these aggregated figures mask differences associated with region and wealth, where gender disparities are particularly marked (WIDE, 2013).

Enrolment ratios provide information only about children who are registered at school. Gender disparities are often higher if attendance or completion at school is measured, although there is considerable variation between countries as to whether it is girls or boys who fail to attend and complete (UNESCO, 2003, 55; UNESCO, 2013). Table 8.2 gives figures for selected countries in East Africa.

On the proportion of the age cohort aged 17-22 in 2011, who had less than 4 years of schooling. It can be seen that in some countries (Burundi, Rwanda and Tanzania), a larger proportion of young women have little education, while in others the proportion of young women and men who have had little or no schooling is roughly similar.

Large numbers of adults have very minimal education. Table 8.3 shows some of the gender dimensions of this. The figures show how in many countries the difficulties governments encounter in delivering on

Table 8.2 *Proportion of age cohort aged 17–22 in 2011 with less than four years of education in selected East African countries*

	Female	Male
Burundi	46	31
Ethiopia	49	35
Kenya	4	4
Rwanda	29	29
Uganda	14	14
Tanzania	20	14

Source: WIDE, 2013

Table 8.3 *Women as a proportion of the projected population of adult illiterates, 2015*

	Female%	Total (000)
Sub Saharan Africa	62	176,170
Arab states	67	49,105
Central Asia	59	253
South and West Asia	65	381,810
East Asia and Pacific	71	83,377
Latin America & Caribbean	55	32,523
North America & Western Europe		
Central & Eastern Europe	65	8,544

Source: UNESCO, 2013, 327

commitments for the provision of education often fall disproportionately on girls and women.

The orthodox move in international development treatments of these failures is to highlight how low levels of women's literacy and high gender gaps in primary education correlate with high levels of infant mortality, maternal mortality and low levels of gross domestic product (GDP) per capita. A key World Bank policy document of the mid 1990s, echoed by a UNESCO commission, made the argument for increasing the access to education for women and girls in terms of the benefits that would flow to their existing and future children's health and to the GDP of their countries. The World Bank education strategy paper stated:

Education, especially basic (primary and lower secondary) education, also contributes to poverty reduction by increasing the productivity of the poor's labour, by reducing fertility and improving health, and by equipping people to participate fully in the economy and society. In addition, education contributes to the strengthening of the institutions of civil society, to national capacity building and to good governance, all of which are increasingly recognised as critical elements in the effective implementation of sound economic and social policies. (World Bank, 1995)

In commenting on women's education it went on to assert:

Mothers with more education provide better nutrition to their children, have healthier children, are less fertile, and are more concerned that their children be educated. Education – in particular female education – is key to reducing poverty and must be considered as much part of a country's health strategy as, say, programs of immunisation and access to health clinics. (World Bank, 1995)

The Bank's justification for educating women and girls, then, lies not in its benefit for those women and girls but in its benefit to their children (actual and prospective) and the society they inhabit. Of course, if it does yield those benefits then, depending on how they are distributed, the women and girls themselves may eventually partake in them. There is also brief mention of the fact that the educated person has an enhanced ability to participate in the labour market. But these powerful policy-making bodies paid little attention to how education might directly contribute to the autonomy of women and girls and to the choices they might make about arrangements within their families, decisions concerning work or forms of social and political organisation they would value. Only one international policy document of the 1990s, the fiercely contested Beijing Declaration on women, articulated aspirations in this direction (Unterhalter, 2000).

Thus, a powerful consensus has developed, drawing mainly on human capital approaches, that the value of education for women and girls lies in the intergenerational transfer of opportunities for health and income and the aggregated benefits for countries that flow from this. A refinement and advance on this position was developed in the World Bank's publication *Engendering Development* (World Bank, 2001). This document does not argue exclusively for a growth-oriented approach to development, where reducing gender gaps in education is claimed to foster economic growth (as was the case in earlier World Bank documents), but for a combination of growth-oriented and rights-based (or institutionally oriented) approaches, both drawing on the benefits of equal access to education. These are seen to be key elements in a long-term strategy to promote gender equality (World Bank, 2001, 21). Here is an example of the way the document knits these two together:

Where per capita income and gender equality in rights are low, increasing either equality in rights or incomes would raise gender equality in education levels. Improving both rights and incomes would yield even greater gain. (World Bank, 2001, 21)

This form of analysis adds institutional development, for which women's representation in parliament is taken to be a proxy indicator, to the non-monetary public benefits of education. The expansion of rights through legal reform is one of the private benefits. Thus World Bank thinking has rejected some of the oversimplifications of work encouraged by the Bank more than a decade ago, grafting some of the writing about barriers to women's legal and political participation onto the earlier approach (we address some of the difficulties with this position in Part 3).

Concrete policy examples of this new form of thinking are to be found in UNGEI (United Nations Girls Education Initiative), launched by Kofi Annan at the Dakar World Education Forum in 2000. UNGEI publicity papers assert:

Girls' education is a fundamental human right, underpinning all other rights and an essential element of sustainable human development. (UNGEI, 2002, 3)

This orientation to education as a foundational right leads to a policy that stresses first and foremost the institutional location of rights. Thus chief among UNGEI's strategic objectives is to 'build political and resource commitments for girls' education' (UNGEI, 2002, 8). A further objective is to 'eliminate gender bias within national educational systems', while another is to 'eliminate social and cultural discrimination that limits the demand for girls' schooling'. UNGEI strategy focuses on governments and partnerships with civil society 'to eliminate institutional and systemic gender disparities and bias' (UNGEI, 2002, 9). It is through changes effected at this level, the argument runs, that an expansion of girls' education will be achieved and will lead to 'protection of their human rights and an improved quality of life'.

To some extent UNGEI and the 2001 World Bank strategy paper take on some of the critiques of human capital approaches that were mounted by feminist writers on gender and development. Challenges to the simple human capital position and its incorporation of notions about rights have tended not to tackle its assumptions head on but instead to affirm one or two supplementary positions. First, a number of writers commented on how women's engagement with formal education, either on their own behalf or on behalf of their children, was enhanced by building and sustaining women's organisations, that is by enlarging social capital. This may or may not yield benefits for individual women, but does enhance the social resources available for governments and NGOs to take forward education and health programmes or to build the institutional conditions for a more equal society – for example, through women's organisations mobilising for land or marriage law reform (Goetz, 1997; Unterhalter and Dutt, 2001; Khandekar, 2001). So arguments using a form of social capital theorising often implicitly endorse some ideas linked to human capital about the transfer of value from individual women to their children or to the social networks in which they participate. But in contrast to human capital approaches, these arguments suggest that schooling creates this value not as a form of inoculation against poverty but as education linked to widening horizons and growing confidence through the mobilisation of a range of social organisations for a wider project.

These feminist writers, linked by a shorthand as gender and development (GAD) theorists, display what Gamarnikow and Green (2000) have termed a version of 'left' social capital theorising. Networks (in this case women's organisations) represent a type of democratic engagement and community involvement that expresses the view of the 'empowered citizen'. Gamarnikow and Green contrast this approach with what they call 'authoritarian' or 'right' social capital theorists who emphasise how community participation enhances social control, a moral regime of sanction around 'decency' and the responsibility of citizens. At this right pole they position mainstream social capital theorists such as James Coleman, Francis Fukuyama and Robert Putnam.

The ambiguity of the concepts of 'rights' and 'voice' means that some of the content of the argument made by 'left' social capital theorists can be appropriated by a body such as UNGEI, urging government partnerships with civil society in linking social development and institutional change with rights and an expansion of girls' education, but saying virtually nothing about the orientation of social development, or links to women's autonomy and issues of distribution, and leaving questions about the content of education outside the frame of analysis. The problem is that implementing rights requires three kinds of measure. First, some sort of constitutional guarantee is needed – something relevant like the US Bill of Rights. But this can, in itself, be worthless, since public pronouncements need not be matched with concrete commitments. So, second, mechanisms of enforcement are needed. But these are much harder to measure and scrutinise than public pronouncements, and it is especially hard to measure how well they are instituted for different groups within a population. Finally, people need resources to make use of their rights. This is because even in societies in which the state makes a strong commitment to rights protections, individuals need to be able to alert authorities to rights violations, and for this they need education, information and alternatives. Consider a workplace in which rights are being violated. The state cannot be everywhere at once and has to rely on the willingness of victims to come forward. So if an individual has good reason to believe that if she complains (whether to the management or to the state) she will be fired, and she has no financial or social resources to fall back on, she will have a strong incentive not to complain. But, like the mechanisms for enforcement, it is difficult to monitor whether people have the relevant resources. The focus on rights, without explicit calls to monitor the distribution of resources, encourages less well-willed governments to make approved public pronouncements, without taking seriously the necessary enforcement mechanisms and implications for resource distribution.

A second challenge to the agenda of inter-government organisations, such as the World Bank, has arisen more explicitly out of a direct critique of human capital approaches. A range of writers in development studies works with the concepts of 'empowerment' and women's interests. The concept of empowerment centres analysis on the interface between generally poor and marginalised women and their capacities to exercise power particularly through self-expression, decision-making and distribution of resources. Rowlands, developing ideas initially formulated by Naila Kabeer, makes two intersecting distinctions (Kabeer, 1994; Rowlands, 1997). First she distinguishes between three different formations of empowerment: power over (the power to control and direct); power to (the power from within to reflect on information or take decisions); and power with (the power to work with others for change). Thus *power over* would entail a teacher having the power to take decisions about what should and should not be included in a curriculum. *Power to* indicates the information she draws on to take these decisions, while *power with* denotes how she works with other teachers, parents, children and the education bureaucracy to implement these decisions. Note that these different levels of describing power rely on a surrounding set of assumptions about gender equity to give notions of empowerment content. There is nothing in this theorisation of empowerment that suggests what empowerment should be about.

Rowlands (1997) also identifies three different arenas in which empowerment occurs – the personal arena, close relationships such as the household, and the collective arena, such as the women's organisation. Kabeer (1999) has pointed to the need for empirically grounded studies of empowerment that look at women's agency, not just the inference of agency from the form of outcome. Implicit in this analysis is the suggestion that a particular outcome, for example a woman becoming literate, might have occurred without any utilisation of agency valued by the woman. Thus a woman might have been compelled to attend a literacy class by village elders in order to meet a quota set down by development officials. For theories of empowerment this example would be problematic because while the woman might have acquired power over the written word, she would not have drawn either on 'power to', that is her sense of agency, or 'power with', that is her aspirations to associate with, say, some kin groups who are illiterate groups rather than members of a class identified through a village development project in which she has no say. But while these distinctions about forms of empowerment are useful, to refocus the analysis on agency, as if this were normative, remains problematic.

A number of writers stress the importance of theorising women's interests and gender interests in assessing development strategies (Rai, 2001). But while these writers once made confident paradigmatic assertions about practical and strategic gender interests (Molyneux, 1989; Moser, 1993), there have been considerable difficulties in putting these into practice. Although Molyneux has continued to work theoretically on understanding aspects of women's interests and needs (Molyneux, 1998), the general trend has been for a focus on situated and grounded studies of particular organisations which work on advancing women's interests (Goetz, 2001; Molyneux, 2001).

Much of the writing about education, empowerment or practical and strategic gender interests looks at non-formal education programmes (Medel Anoueva, 1997; Robinson Pant, 2000). While empowerment theorists are (implicitly or explicitly) critical of human capital and social capital analyses that fail to take seriously the self-realisation of poor women in and for themselves, there are few studies concerning how we should understand empowerment or gender interests in relation to formal education and its consequences (that is schooling, formal qualifications and the nature of their link with the gendered labour market). At the least, paying attention to strategic gender interests would entail women mobilising to change the legal framework of education systems with regard to curriculum, terms and conditions of the appointment of teachers, and articulation with the labour market. In instances where this has been tried, for example by the femocrat authors of the policy paper on gender equity in education in South Africa commissioned by the Minister of Education in 1997, the experience has not been as fruitful as anticipated. In the ensuing six years it was largely ignored, save for the publication of a guidebook on gender equality for teachers and the appointment of some gender officers in education departments (Department of Education, 2003; Unterhalter, 2002; Wolpe *et al.*, 1998). A number of large and wide-ranging government programmes in education that have gender equity in their overarching goals, in practice pay very little attention to gender issues in implementation, beyond supporting the enrolment of girls (Manion, 2012; Unterhalter, 2012). It seems that only when gender equality or women's empowerment is a central concern of a project in the formal education sector (for example, the PROMOTE programme in Bangladesh to train and deploy more women teachers) do strategic gender interests begin to be addressed.

But the idea of strategic gender interests tends to suggest that empowerment is a profit-and-loss endeavour. That is, gains made in one sphere (say the public realm of education and employment rights) offset losses or constraints in another (say the family or religious sanction). Indeed, the notion of 'strategic interests' implies that certain gains, for example at the political level, will bring about changes in, say, the personal or more private realms. The links between education and the labour market, while not simple as implied by human capital theorists, are not straightforward either. Kabeer, in a study of workers in the Bangladesh ready-made garment industry, found that despite low levels of formal education and high levels of exploitation in sweat shop-type factories, women employed in this sector reported power to exercise some control over the wages they earned and family decision-making. This contrasted with women with similar levels of education employed on family farms in Bangladesh or women in villages with higher levels of education not permitted to work outside the household (Kabeer, 2000). But it is not clear how asserting empowerment in one area (the household or schooling) rather than another (the workplace or the family) throws light on what orientation education or labour market policy or family law should take.

The literature on gender and exclusion from formal education falls into two very different categories, each talking to different policy communities and each understanding educational equality and aspirations for social justice in education differently. The analysis most concerned with distribution is produced by the large UN agencies. This analysis works at the level of countries, regions or districts, and governments and international agencies are the major clients for this information. For these analysts, strongly influenced by human capital approaches, education – particularly formal levels of education (e.g. literacy, completion of primary schooling) – is an indicator of other social 'goods' and is linked with these to aspirations for an increase in per capita GDP. By contrast, analyses linked to social capital or empowerment approaches tend to work at the level of the women's organisation, the village or the block, and it is NGOs (or NGO–government partnerships) organising at this level which are often the clients for this information. For these analysts, education is not a formal, regulated space, funded by the state, but rather the forms of social learning that enable poor women to take control of their lives and win recognition for their aspirations. These two different groups of analysts (and actors) have tended to talk past each other, although the strategy articulated by UNGEI with its stress on civil society partnerships seeks to bring them together (Smyth and Rao, 2005). One of the difficulties in realising UNGEI's strategy of partnerships across two very different constituencies is that for the first group the social conditions that make for lack of access to education are difficult and complex to document and that what is desirable is a standard measure of attendance at school or achievement in a certain grade. For the second group there tends not to be a single measure of success because achievements are embedded in the processes of social mobilisation and political and cultural change that are endlessly different. In this chapter we want to look at how in working with complementary theories of justice we can try to map out some of the connections between the two positions, some difficulties and some possible ways forward.

Part Two: Justice as fairness and the capabilities approach

We will now outline two influential normative approaches. We will quickly describe the two theories and then compare them. We shall argue that they are closer than they may at first appear, and shall then draw out some common features which can serve as the basis for evaluating strategic approaches to development.

First is Rawls's theory of justice as fairness, hugely influential in political philosophy and such fields as medical ethics, legal theory and international law, but largely neglected in education and development studies. Rawls's two principles are:

The liberty principle: each person has an equal right to a fully adequate scheme of equal basic liberties which is compatible with a similar scheme of liberties for all, and the political liberties shall have fair value.

The second principle: social and economic inequalities are to be arranged so that they are both

(a) to the greatest benefit of the least advantaged, and
(b) attached to offices and positions open to all under conditions of fair equality of opportunity.

The liberty principle, for Rawls, has what he calls lexical priority over the second principle, and the fair equality of opportunity proviso (b) of the second principle has lexical priority over the maximin provision (a) (or difference principle). Lexical priority is a very strong form of priority: it means that whenever there are conflicts between the two principles, the prior principle wins out. So, for example, if some measure needed to improve fair equality of opportunity violated the right to freedom of conscience, it would automatically be disallowed. We shall not comment on the argument for lexical priority, but it is worth noting that the priority rules Rawls stipulates do not have the inegalitarian consequences some people think (see Callinicos, 2000, 48, for example).

Priority for the liberty principle does not represent a preference for liberty over equality, for two reasons. First, the liberty principle does not distribute liberty, it distributes liberties, and does so equally. There is a strand of classical liberal and libertarian thinking that talks of liberty as if there is a single metric (typically, 'the absence of coercive interference by one's fellow man') which must be maximised. This is objectionable for two reasons. The command to maximise any good, be it liberty, income or whatever, without regard to who gets how much of it violates the principle of the separateness of persons, the idea that each individual counts as much as any other, and losses to some of a good cannot be justified by appeal to the benefits some others get. Rawls uses the principle of the separateness of persons to reject classical utilitarianism, but it counts equally against libertarian views which call for the maximisation of liberty, without regard to how liberty is redistributed. The second reason that the command to maximise (or equalise, or distribute in any other way) liberty is rejected is that it fails to take account of the fact that different liberties matter more or less independently of the contribution to liberty (which cannot, anyway, be measured). Most of us do not exercise the liberty to stand for office in free and fair elections (and have no desire to do so), and so our liberty would be much less restricted by prohibitions on us standing for office than it is by the frequent diversions caused by roadworks (which coercively prevent us from taking our preferred route to work). But the liberty to stand for office in free and fair elections matters more, and in specifiable ways, than the freedom to use one's preferred route to work.

The second reason that the priority of the first principle does not represent a preference for liberty over equality concerns the nature of the second principle: it does not demand equality but licenses inequality. So the priority of the liberty principle says that inequalities that might be to the material benefit of the least advantaged are ruled out if they threaten the security of a scheme which provides equal basic liberties for all. Suppose, for example, that the trickle-down story were true. Then vast inequalities of income and wealth, of the kind that we see in the US and (to a lesser extent) in the UK, might be permissible according to the second principle. In that case, the difference principle would permit vast inequalities. But vast inequalities of wealth threaten the liberty principle, which says that the basic liberties must be granted equally to all. (For interesting critiques of the priority Rawls gives to fair equality of opportunity over the difference principle, see Arneson 1999, Clayton 2000.)

This is especially clear because Rawls includes the stipulation that the political liberties must be granted fair (by which he clearly means equal) value, which constitutes a particularly strong theory of political equality, as part of the liberty principle. It is unimaginable that in a society with the inequalities of income and wealth that characterise the US, fair value could be guaranteed to the political liberties. So the priority of the liberty principle represents a limit on, rather than a licence for, inequality. Similarly, the priority of fair equality of opportunity means that inequalities that might otherwise benefit the least advantaged are ruled out if they cause (as substantial inequalities are bound to) the next generation to face unequal opportunities for the unequally distributed benefits of social cooperation (Brighouse 1997, 2001).

Rawls's principles specify the rules for distributing what Rawls calls social primary goods – liberties such as freedom of association, freedom of conscience, freedom of religion and the political liberties; opportunities and the powers and prerogatives of office; income and wealth; and what he calls 'the social bases of self-respect'. He arrives at the index of social primary goods by looking at what conditions are necessary for the exercise and development of the two moral powers – the capacities for a sense of justice and a conception of the good – of persons conceived of as free and equal. The capacity for a sense of justice is the ability to understand what justice requires, and to contribute one's fair share to maintaining a just scheme. The capacity for a conception of the good is the ability to have a view of what is valuable in life, and to both reflect rationally on, and act on, that view. These, for Rawls, are the centrally important moral powers of persons, and his index of primary goods reflects this (Rawls 2001, 18–24). (See also the essays in Freeman 2003.)

However, in addition, his theory of primary goods is designed to evade certain disagreements about the nature of the good that he thinks reasonable people are bound to have. A free society is afflicted by what he terms 'the burdens of judgement'. These burdens mean that there will never be unanimous agreement about what he calls 'comprehensive conceptions of the good'. Pluralism about religious matters and deep philosophical questions about the nature of morality are inevitable in a free society because free human reason is not sufficiently acute to divine a single truth about these matters. But Rawls endorses the following principle of legitimacy:

Our exercise of political power is fully proper only when it is exercised in accordance with a constitution the essentials of which all citizens as free and equal may reasonably be expected to be able to endorse in the light of the principle and ideas acceptable to their common human reason. (Rawls 1993, 137)

So a theory of justice, if it is to be implemented legitimately, must appeal only to moral ideas that can be shared beyond the confines of sectarian and 'comprehensive' theories of the human good. Protestant versions of Christianity, liberal versions of Islam, Kantianism, Utilitarianism, the Marx of the Paris manuscripts, the Kantian feminism of Andrea Dworkin and Catherine MacKinnon – none of these can serve as the basis for a liberal theory of justice because all bring in assumptions about the good that are open to contest by reasonable people. Justice as fairness is not a compromise between these many views, nor does it aspire to neutrality between them. Instead it finds its justification in partial ideas about the good which can come to be shared by people who nevertheless disagree about the good more comprehensively conceived. Rawls does not even believe that there is agreement among these different 'comprehensive conceptions' on the moral foundations of justice as fairness. He claims only to have identified moral ideas on which agreement can be forged, so that it is at least possible for the theory to be implemented legitimately (Rawls 1993, 173).

Now we shall describe an alternative to Rawls's theory of justice which its proponents call the capabilities approach. This has been developed by Amartya Sen and, more recently, by Martha C. Nussbaum. Sen and Nussbaum emphasise different features of the capabilities approach. Sen eschews the task of developing a normative index of capabilities, whereas Nussbaum attempts that task, at least for the purpose of guiding constitution formation. This difference reflects what we suspect is a more fundamental disagreement over the possibility of specifying a public conception of the good for the purposes of justice. But we shall put aside their differences because we are focused on the differences and similarities between their shared general approach and Rawls's theory of justice as fairness.

Sen objects to using primary goods as a metric because, he says, the index is too inflexible to deal with some inequalities between people in their ability to convert resources into welfare: the most obvious case being the person with a disability who, with the same holding of primary goods as the ordinarily abled person, will be able to achieve less value. Instead, he thinks, a theory of justice should be concerned with 'the actual living that people manage to achieve (or, going beyond that, on the freedom to achieve actual livings that one can have a reason to value)' (Sen 1999, 73) or 'substantive freedoms – the capabilities – to choose a life one has reason to value' (Sen, 1999, 74). So, he says, justice consists in distributing fairly not primary goods but capabilities,. He distinguishes between functionings, which are actual achievements, and capabilities, which are the freedoms to achieve, and focuses attention on capabilities rather than functionings out of concern for agency or freedom. We need to distinguish, he says, between the circumstances of someone who is starving and someone who is fasting: unlike the starving person, the fasting person has the capability to eat but chooses not to exercise it. In this way Sen builds the idea of freedom into the fabric of the good to be distributed.

Whereas Rawls defends a precise set of distributive rules for the different goods that he thinks constitute the currency of justice (primary goods), Sen specifies equality as the distributive rule for capabilities: we are bound, he thinks, to distribute equally whatever we have found to be the currency of justice (Sen, 1997). Thus, he even interprets Robert Nozick's libertarian theory as an egalitarian theory, since it takes basic rights (interpreted as 'side constraints') as the currency of justice and requires that they be respected equally for all. Sen develops the theory of capabilities in dialogue with Rawls on the one hand, and neo-classical economists committed to a preference-satisfaction metric on the other. But his main use of the capabilities metric is not for the purposes of entering debates among political philosophers about what should be distributed but to engage in a debate among political economists concerning what constitutes the best metric for making comparisons between different countries' standards of living, to displace real income and utility.

Martha C. Nussbaum, in her development of the capabilities approach, emphasises that the capabilities approach is, like justice as fairness, a version of political liberalism: it seeks to be justifiable to, and in terms of, a wide range of reasonable conceptions of the good. Whereas Sen does not develop a list of capabilities, Nussbaum offers ten capabilities which she thinks are essential to enabling someone to have a flourishing life. In her most extensive recent presentation of the view she restricts herself to the case of developing countries, and asserts that justice requires that everyone must have at least some threshold of each of these capabilities. Her list is as follows: Life, Bodily Health, Bodily Integrity, Senses Imagination and Thought, Emotions, Practical Reason, Affiliation, Other Species, Play, and Control over one's own environment (Nussbaum, 2000). Nussbaum does not defend her list against alternatives, but she does give a good account of why each item plausibly belongs on the list.

Both Sen and Nussbaum treat capabilities as an alternative to Rawls's primary goods. Sen accuses the primary goods metric of being 'too inflexible' to account for the great variations in personal qualities and circumstances between people. A focus on primary goods, which are defined without reference to people's abilities to make good use of them, will get things wrong because it neglects what people can do with the primary goods. Nussbaum treats Rawls with more sympathy, but still poses capabilities as an alternative to primary goods. She says:

The capabilities approach, as I have articulated it, is very close to Rawls's approach using the notion of primary goods. We can see the list of capabilities as like a long list of opportunities for functioning, such that it is always rational to want them whatever else one wants. (Nussbaum 2000, 88–89)

She goes on to criticise Rawls for refraining from including imagination and health in his list of social primary goods:

Rawls's evident concern is that no society can guarantee health to its individuals – in that sense saying that the goal is full external capability may appear unreasonably idealistic. Some of the capabilities... can be fully guaranteed by society but many others involve an element of chance and cannot be so guaranteed. My response to this is that, with these items as with self-respect, society can hope to guarantee the social basis of these natural goods, and that putting them on the list as a set of political goals should therefore be useful as a benchmark for aspiration and comparison. (Nussbaum 2000, 89)

We are not going to defend Rawls's reluctance explicitly to place the social bases for health on the list, although we believe that at least many of the social bases for health are on the list. We agree with Nussbaum that if primary goods and capabilities were clear alternatives, then capabilities would be the superior metric. The fundamental problem with the primary goods approach is that it fails, as stated, to make sense of the intuition that people who suffer disabilities are in that respect worse off than people who do not, and that the distribution of resources (and primary goods) should take account of that. Rawls understands this, and in fact develops the theory of justice as fairness on the assumption that 'everyone has sufficient intellectual powers to play a normal part in society and no-one suffers from unusual needs that are especially difficult to fulfill, for example, unusual and costly medical requirements' (Rawls, 1980, 545). The idea is that, if his theory does not work for this case, then it is not worth trying to extend it to the more complicated case covering disability. It is hard to see, though, how the theory could be extended without mimicking some of the language of the capabilities approach, and Nussbaum's list uses the relevant language (Brighouse 2001 and Daniels 2003 both suggest arguments to this effect).

However, we think that Nussbaum and Sen have mistaken the level of abstraction at which they disagree with Rawls. Rawls's list of primary goods is supposed to describe the conditions that are necessary for the exercise and development of what he calls 'the two moral powers': the capacities for a sense of justice and for a conception of the good (Rawls

2001, 18–24). These capacities lie at the foundation of Rawls's theory; primary goods are what social institutions distribute in order to support their development and exercise. Similarly, capabilities are not distributed directly. Social institutions distribute liberties, resources, opportunities, etc: Nussbaum and Sen must think that these should be distributed to support the development of capabilities. So if there is a dispute between the capabilities approach and justice as fairness, it is that there is some difference between Nussbaum and Sen's capabilities and Rawls's capacities.

We do not want to go into too much detail about this dispute because we believe that it is the commonalities rather than the differences between the views that are interesting for our larger purpose. But we do want to raise a difficulty in adjudicating it. Capabilities as Sen and especially Nussbaum describe them appear on the face of it to be more extensive and potentially demanding than Rawls's capacities. However, recent work on Rawls suggests that the interest in being able to develop and exercise our capacities for a conception of the good and a sense of justice are more demanding than they might appear on the surface (see, for example, Callan, 1997; Moellendorf, 2002). Furthermore, Rawls, in his own final restatement of his theory (Rawls, 2001, 168–175), emphasises the flexibility of the primary goods index, in the light of the fact that it is constructed to serve the exercise and development of the two moral powers.

Both Rawls and Nussbaum, at least, claim that their theories are political in a very specific sense – theories that can be justified to people who hold a diverse range of conceptions of the good (Nussbaum, 2000, 74–75; Rawls, 2001, 40–41). This limits how capaciously they can interpret capabilities and capacities, because the more capaciously they are understood, the less likely it is that they will be the object of an overlapping consensus among reasonable people. But both theorists need their theories to be robust: to make serious demands on the structure of social institutions. Whereas defenders of the capabilities approach may appeal to the fact that they appear to be more demanding, the political aspiration places sharp limits on how demanding the approach can be: the more demanding, the less plausible it is that it will command the widespread acceptance which Nussbaum seeks for it.

None of this proves that the two approaches are identical, or even that there are not important differences between them. But it does suggest that it is worth looking at the features they have in common. We shall enumerate five. First, they share a specific version of individualism. The first object of moral evaluation is the individual. Social institutions, and government policies, are justified and evaluated first in terms of their benefits for individual persons, and no individual counts more than any other in this moral accounting.

Second, and relatedly, they share a commitment to the development of someone's productive capacity primarily for their own sake. A just society is obliged to ensure that individuals can be productive, not so that the economy will grow and the society will be rich but so that the individual herself has more command of her own circumstances.

Third, they share a commitment to the value of personal autonomy. Neither of them uses this phrase; indeed, both take care to avoid it. This is because in the specifically philosophical literature the concept of personal autonomy tends to be associated with strong deliberative requirements and, in particular, with Kant's moral theory. Nussbaum uses the less loaded term 'practical reason', and Rawls asserts our interest in being able 'rationally to revise our conception of the good', but both theories emphasise the value of emotional and rational self-governance – autonomy, in ordinary parlance. In justice as fairness this is a foundational value – the capacity for a conception of the good, which informs the whole architecture of the theory – and in the emphasis given to the liberties which govern rational reflection – freedom of expression, freedom of religion and freedom of conscience. In the capabilities approach it is reflected (jointly with a concern with freedom) in the preference for capabilities over functionings. The theories do not command of people that they pursue particular goods, but they require that they are equipped to make judgements about what is good for them and to act on those judgements.

Fourth, they share a concern with freedom – a different notion – having the external conditions necessary to act on one's reflective evaluations. This is reflected in Rawls's commitment to the liberty principle and its lexical priority. Sen and Nussbaum prefer capabilities to functionings as the basis for comparisons precisely to reflect the importance of individual autonomy. Nussbaum distinguishes between internal capabilities (developed states that are sufficient conditions for the exercise of requisite functions) and combined capabilities (internal capabilities combined with suitable external conditions for the exercise of the function). If individual autonomy is as important as Sen and Nussbaum think, then among the external conditions necessary for the exercise of many combined capabilities will be the liberties to act on those capabilities.

Finally, at least Nussbaum shares with Rawls a concern with legitimacy (reflected in the idea of a political liberalism). The idea is that to be fully legitimate, political power must be exercised in accordance with constitutional essentials which are informed by principles that citizens can be expected to endorse in the light of their freely exercised reason (for a discussion of legitimacy that postdates our work on this chapter, see Nussbaum (2004).

Both the capabilities approach and justice as fairness have been widely criticised, and there is no space here to consider all criticisms (see Arneson, 1989, 1990; Arrow, 1973; Gauthier, 1974; Harsanyi, 1975; Pogge, 2002). But we do want to flag some possible difficulties. First, the capabilities approach is frequently criticised for the indexing problem – if we want to distribute capabilities equally (or according to the maximin criterion) we have to be able to compare different functionings according to some single scale, since it is implausible, and not even desirable, that everyone will have the same level of capability of every functioning. So we have to compare the rewards of child rearing with those of work, the rewards of playing sports with those of formal education, and so on. This could be a serious problem in implementing the theory fully, especially given the aspiration that the theory be political, in the special sense Rawls has developed (on which more in the next paragraph). However, Nussbaum's list of ten capabilities listed above is an attempt to offer a partial solution to the indexing problem for practical purposes. It is entirely plausible if we are trying to specify a threshold of capabilities to which all must be entitled, rather than a way of achieving an equal distribution of capabilities.

Second, there may be concerns with the rather strict principle of legitimacy that Rawls specifies and to which Nussbaum implicitly commits herself. Some critics take the principle of legitimacy to imply a commitment to neutrality and complicity with the arrangements in already existing states. We disagree, though for reasons that take us beyond the scope of this chapter (however, see Brighouse, 1996). But it does restrict the grounds on which we can justify a theory of justice to those that can be expected to win widespread acceptance by reasonable people. This is particularly difficult for the capabilities approach when it tries to solve the indexing problem. It seems as if any detailed specification of the relative importance of different capabilities will be open to dispute among reasonable people, so that it will be hard to meet the requirements imposed by legitimacy. We do not have an easy response to this problem, but we do think that in any theory there are going to be tensions between the requirements of legitimacy and those of justice in practice. They are separate moral requirements, and we think they both describe moral conditions that matter a great deal. But they are also, both, matters of degree – a society can be more or less legitimate and more or less just. In non-ideal circumstances, making an unjust society more just may sometimes require means that make it less legitimate, and vice versa. So when there are tensions in practice, we need an account of how to trade them off against each other.

Finally, we should preempt the objection that the theories are individualistic. In the next section we shall show how this is, in fact, an advantage of the theory over some rivals, in that it allows us to make the right kinds of criticisms of human capital and social capital theory. But because liberalism is so widely criticised for being individualistic, it is important to deflect the criticism directly (for more detail see Brighouse and Swift, 2003). Liberalism does not make objectionable assumptions about the motivation of individuals, or about their formation. It recognises that individuals are socially formed and that they are variably motivated and, furthermore, that justice is a constraint on their motivation – they must, according to liberal theory, develop their sense of justice sufficiently that they can recognise and act on the demands of justice. So the liberal individual cannot pursue her own interests independently of responsibility to others. However, the liberal individual does see her own interests as legitimate and as sources of claims on society. Her interest in living a life that is good according to her best judgement is sufficiently important that social institutions must provide her with the access to resources, and the protections from interference, necessary for her to pursue that interest. But it is no more important than anyone else's similar interest.

Part 3: Human capital, social capital, empowerment and justice

Now we shall evaluate the three approaches to gender equity in education – the human capital approach, the social capital approach and the empowerment approach – we outlined in the first section, in the light of the approaches to justice surveyed in the second section. We should emphasise that these three approaches particularly inform development actors and agencies in their decisions about educational infrastructure in the developing world. While the human and social capital approaches have been particularly utilised by multilateral and bilateral donors in their negotiations with governments, social capital and empowerment approaches have been used by NGOs in their mobilisation, advocacy and service delivery work.

First the human capital approach. To reiterate, this approach emphasises the importance of developing human capital – economically productive capacities. It argues that when people are poor and have low levels of education, they are less productive than when they are better educated. So, in poor countries and in countries with large numbers of poor women and high levels of gender inequality, it may seem that the human capital approach will support better education and ultimately enhanced capabilities of and more resources for the least advantaged.

So it may seem to fit well with the theories of justice we have surveyed. However, the approach has no principled concern with distributive issues or, crucially, with the maintenance of basic liberties. Nor, obviously, is it concerned with distributive issues across generations. So the implementation does not look at who benefits, and how much, from the development of human capital, just at how to develop and transmit it. Two examples of situations where the approach ('maximise human capital') conflicts with liberal justice stand out. First are the examples of Taiwan and South Korea, where a huge push to develop human capital has generated considerable growth, and seems even to have promoted equality of opportunity. But it was achieved by dramatically increasing female participation in the workforce, at the least rewarded end, and without a change in culture that diminished their participation in 'domestic' labour. In Taiwan, women were exhorted to turn their living rooms into factories, and benefits to the next generation were achieved through imposing great costs on women in the parental generation. The other striking example is China, about which a story is frequently, and plausibly, told that its continued stable economic growth depends on the ability of the Communist Party to hold the lid on political dissent, including dissent about persistent gender inequality. Rapid development, it is sometimes said, takes strong government, which is usually a code for undemocratic and illiberal government.

Maybe this is false. If so, the human capital approach is consistent with justice. In some circumstances, though, it is entirely plausible that restricting basic liberties, or unequally distributing opportunities, will better serve the development of human capital (understood as productive capacity) than a liberal and meritocratic regime. Sen makes this point with particular reference to Singapore, which has enjoyed high levels of growth simultaneously with the suppression of basic liberties. Sen (1999) worries about the effect on capabilities, which in public parlance are most naturally expressed as rights, but the point applies more generally. Not only basic liberties, but equality of opportunity, and redistribution to the benefit of the least advantaged, can impede the maximal development of human capital. For example, the limits on parental pursuit of competitive advantage on behalf of their children required by equality of opportunity can inhibit human capital development; so can the operation of an effective tax-transfer system. In such cases it is not that we can 'have it all' – maximal development of human capital as well as justice. Liberal justice alerts us to this possibility, and insists that justice takes precedence: that, if you like, human capital be developed only insofar as it can be consistent with justice, not that it be maximised.

Now let's look at the social capital approach. As used by gender and development theorists, this approach emphasises the mobilisation and participation of women to articulate demands concerning education for themselves or their children. Aspirations for education reform are often bundled together with other economic and political reforms. However, the utilisation of arguments grounded in social capital theory, in both its left and right forms, pays no attention to the constraints of justice.

Analysis that stresses the importance of building social capital as a means to foster the participation of girls in school need pay no attention to the form or content the establishment of the networks that generate social capital take. These social networks may be concerned with basic liberties and issues of distribution, but there is nothing in policy based on social capital theory that says they have to be. In fact, there are particular reasons for thinking that in some circumstances restrictions on some basic liberties will enhance social capital and also that the development of social capital will benefit the already privileged over others.

The most obvious case is the conflict between geographical mobility and the maintenance of social capital. If people move frequently, social capital usually suffers, because the start-up costs to individuals of developing relationships in a locale are much higher than the costs of maintaining equally good relationships. In regions with low social capital, one strategy for increasing it is to restrict mobility of members of the community. The costs of making satisfactory relationships with people who have similar backgrounds are also lower than the costs of making relationships with people who are significantly different. So geographic mobility and ethnic diversity threaten social capital. Thus, for example, some indigenous Canadian communities claim the right to say that families can move into their jurisdiction only if one member of the family has at least one full-blood member of the tribe as a parent. This measure helps to preserve ethnic homogeneity, and to restrict mobility, and thus helps maintain social capital within that community. But freedom of association and the opportunity to change occupations and locations is, on any reasonable account, a basic liberty. Furthermore, these measures have a greater impact on the least advantaged than on the most advantaged. They artificially depress house prices (by artificially restricting demand), that for the least advantaged may mean the difference between being able to leave and not being able to. For the more advantaged it does, of course, make moving out less attractive, but it is less likely to make it impossible.

Think of another example. The spectacular increase in girls' enrolment in school in Iran after the Islamic Revolution of 1979 is often linked to the mobilisation of women active in mosques and other Shi'a religious formations to send their daughters to school and keep them there. However, this form of mobilisation of women with high levels of 'legitimate' social capital who were Shi'a Muslims excluded outsiders to this community, such as members of ethnic minorities. It was in these communities that girls' participation in schooling remained at low levels, as their opportunities for schooling were limited due to the absence of suitable schools and teachers (Mehran, 2003, 23–24). Thus, mobilising social capital for some, without paying attention to the distributional issues for all, does not accord well with justice. But without a theory of justice it is difficult to see this.

In addition, basing policy on mobilising high levels of social capital might not be consistent with a respect for basic liberties in practice. The South African mass democratic movement in the 1980s mobilised extensive networks and diverse forms of social organisation, including a national women's organisation, in pursuit of the demand for a democratic government. This campaign was successful and an extremely democratic constitution passed into law in 1996. However, ingraining respect for democracy and the basic liberties into the fabric of everyday culture has not been an easy task. Insiders in the political movements that made the new South Africa continue to report high levels of gender violence within organisations, as well as public institutions such as schools and universities. Since the institution of democratic government in 1994 there have been expressions of xenophobia against refugees from other African countries. Thus successful mobilisation of social capital and the achievement of a democratic constitution do not in and of themselves indicate respect for basic liberties. Policies that advocate building social capital to address the problem of the gender gap in schooling and to supplement the analysis put forward by human capital may or may not be consistent with a theory of justice. Deploying social capital theory to supplement human capital theory without a theory of justice might lead to the fostering of social networks, but this does not tell you how you can judge whether these are good or bad.

What, finally, of the empowerment and gender interests theorists? They, like the social capital theorists, see the need to attend to women's voice and they distinguish between different areas in which this is articulated, that is between collective action oriented towards strategic and ameliorative change. But the assumption that strategic change provides the conditions for more localised or 'practical' change is highly problematic. Without a theory of justice we cannot understand the links between the two arenas or the tradeoffs that might need to be accommodated, and the reasons that underpin this. It is consistent with a theory of justice that all men and women should have voice, and should participate. But empowerment theorists, just like the social capital theorists, beg the question regarding what the content of women's power is and what is being said when we attend to women's voice. Without a theory of justice, we (governments, policymakers, NGOs, external agents) seem forced to the position that we must attend to everything poor women say, because it expresses empowerment. Of course we must attend to everything poor women say because we must attend to everything that everyone says; and we must be particularly sensitive to what poor women say because their voices have been denied and ridiculed for so long. But sometimes poor women talk and ventriloquise the wishes of powerful other groups. For example, in India and Pakistan the reservation of seats for women in panchayats or local councils has enormously increased their representation, but has also led to powerful male political fixers trying to use the women's reserved seats to put forward 'their' candidates. The requirement that women participate either as chair or vice-chair of Village Education Committees in many districts in India, while possibly advancing women's empowerment, does not of itself ensure any commitment to engaging with issues concerning gender equity in education or the distributional problems we have outlined above. Once again, empowerment presents itself as a normative theory while failing to engage with some of the issues concerning individuals, liberties and distribution.

What does all this have to do with our starting point, the inequalities of schooling between boys and girls? To put it simply, these inequalities are not wrong because they inhibit the development of human capital; nor because they erode social capital; nor because they silence women's voice in the public realm. What is wrong with them is that they leave a vast number of women less equipped to lead flourishing lives than they would otherwise be, and less equipped than men are. The fundamental wrong is a wrong to the women who are undereducated, not a harm to the societies they inhabit. None of the approaches we have surveyed explains this fully, not even the empowerment approach. To properly explain it, and address it, requires an individualistic theory of justice along the lines of the capabilities or justice as fairness approach.

The justice approaches have implications for the content of girls' education that may be at odds with the social capital and human capital approaches. Justice as fairness requires that girls be educated at least as well as boys and have equal access to labour markets. But this might have real costs in terms of social capital development, at least until men compensate for the unpaid social capital-building tasks women undertake. Similarly, it seems possible in some circumstances that if women became full participants in labour markets there would be a loss in human capital development, given the work that mothers typically put in to developing the human capital of their children. Rawls's emphasis on the development of the capacities for a conception of the good and a sense of justice has potentially quite disruptive effects on both human and social capital development in the short term. Educated women may find it harder to adapt their ambitions to the social norms that expect them to live entirely for others.

If we take Nussbaum at her word that the capabilities approach requires just a threshold of capabilities, this may be consistent with unequal educational opportunities between boys and girls. But, again, the approach will emphasise the flourishing that the girls themselves will get from the education offered over the benefit that others will get from them being educated. And, in particular, Nussbaum's unusual (but entirely proper) inclusion of the importance of play and playfulness in her list may imply curricular requirements that do not simply optimise human capital development.

Conclusion

We would like to conclude by making two points. The first is simple. Like Rawls, Sen and Nussbaum, we think of justice as the first virtue of social institutions. As such, it is the guiding, and constraining, force for public policy and, in particular, for development policy. Any proposal must take a theory of justice as its starting point. Whether, and to what extent, the policy develops gross human capital or social capital, and the extent to which it is informed by the voices of the dispossessed, must itself be consistent with the demands of justice. We have recommended two, closely related, theories of justice to play this guiding role. To take human capital theory, social capital theory or empowerment as the starting point is simply a mistake. To take our particular case, it takes a theory of justice to explain what is wrong with gender inequity in education, and without attention to a theory of justice we doubt that the right strategies can be developed to correct the injustice.

The second point is a conjectural worry. The language of justice is often absent from public discussions of development. When it is present the issue of justice highlighted is often that between developed and developing countries rather than that within developing countries. The declarations from Beijing, Jomtien and Dakar described above have all tried to correct this. But we suspect that the terminology they have used – freedoms, rights, entitlements, even capabilities – lends itself to misuse. By emphasising the stuff of justice rather than how that stuff should be distributed, the declarations have allowed politicians and policymakers to couch policies in terms of promoting a loose notion of rights, without forcing them to address how the policies will benefit the least advantaged, and how they will improve their condition relative to the more advantaged. A net per-person increase in rights or capabilities does not necessarily benefit the least advantaged, any more than a net per-person increase in GDP does. Mechanisms guaranteeing that the least advantaged benefit at least somewhat from the net increase are essential. Net improvements in capabilities will show up as overall improvements, but to know whether they are real improvements from the perspective of justice or, as is equally possible, deteriorations, we need to monitor the mechanisms of distribution. The declarations provide no reason for governments to do this. A full theory of justice which emphasised the distributive rules would provide more pressure to do this.

While the millennium development target of gender parity in education by 2005 was missed, it does not mean that the aspirations which underpin it should be ignored. Beyond 2005 two paths appear to be opening up: either the articulation of a weak notion of rights, as in UNGEI documents, or the concern to backward map policy from a thousand contextualised studies of the conditions in which it might be implemented, as a number of writers suggest. We have argued that neither of these is satisfactory and a more fruitful way forward in strategising for gender equality in education is to attend to the common ground represented by theoretical demands of justice as fairness and the capabilities approach, which focus on addressing individuals, liberties and questions of distribution.

REFERENCES

Arneson, R, 1999, 'Against Rawlsian equality of opportunity,' *Philosophical Studies* 93, 1, 77–112.
1990, 'Primary goods reconsidered,' *Nous* 29, 3, 429–454.
1989, 'Equality and equal opportunity for welfare,' *Philosophical Studies* 56, 1, 77–93.
Arrow, K, 1973, 'Some ordinalist-utilitarian notes on Rawls's Theory of Justice,' *Journal of Philosophy* 70, 9, 245–263.
Brighouse, H, 2001, 'Democracy and inequality,' in April Carter and Geoff Stokes, eds., *Democratic Theory Today*, Polity Press, pp. 52–72.
1997, 'Political equality in justice as fairness,' *Philosophical Studies* 86, 2, 155–184.
1996, 'Is there a neutral justification for liberalism?,' *Pacific Philosophical Quarterly* 77, 3, 193–215.
Brighouse, H and Swift, A, 2003, 'Defending liberalism in education theory,' *Journal of Education Policy* 18, 3, 377–395.
Callan, E, 1997, *Creating Citizens*, Oxford University Press.

Callinicos, A, 2000, *Equality*, Cambridge: Polity Press.

Clayton, M, 2000, 'Rawls and natural aristocracy,' *Croatian Journal of Philosophy* 1, 3, 239–259.

Daniels, N, 2003, 'Rawls's complex egalitarianism,' in Freeman 2003.

Department of Education, 2003, 'Gender equality in education,' Pretoria: Department of Education on line at http://education.pwv.gov.za/index.asp? src=dvie&xsrc=64 (accessed March 2004)

Elimu Yetu, 2005, 'The challenge of educating girls in Kenya', in Aikman, S and Unterhalter, J, eds., *Beyond Access*, Oxford: Oxfam.

Freeman, S. ed. 2003, *The Cambridge Companion to Rawls*, Cambridge University Press.

Gamarnikow, E and Green, A, 2000, 'Social capital and the educated citizen,' *The School Field* X, 3 and 4.

Gauthier, D, 1974, 'Justice and natural endowment: toward a critique of Rawls's ideological framework', *Social Theory and Practice* 3, 1, 3–26.

Goetz, A, 2001, *Women Development Workers: Implementing rural credit programmes in Bangladesh*, New Delhi: Sage.

Goetz, A. ed. 1997, *Getting Institutions Right for Women in Development*, London: Zed.

Harsanyi, J, 1975, 'Can the Maximin Principle serve as the basis for morality? A critique of John Rawls's theory,' *American Political Science Review* 69, 4, 594–606.

Kabeer, N, 2000, *The Power to Choose. Bangladeshi women and labour market decisions in London and Dhaka*, London: Verso.

1999, 'Resources, agency, achievements: reflections on the measurement of women's empowerment,' *Development and Change* 30, 435–464.

1994, *Reversed Realities*, London: Verso.

Khandekar, S, 2001, 'Women's movement emerging out of a literacy campaign in a Mumbai slum: analysis of activities and reactions,' Unpublished Masters dissertation in Education, Gender and International Development, Institute of Education, University of London.

Medel Anoueva, C, 1997, *Negotiating and Creating Spaces of Power: women's educational practices amidst crisis*, Hamburg: UNESCO Institute for Education.

Mehran, G, 2003, 'Gender and education in Iran,' Background paper prepared for UNESCO Global Monitoring Report 2003/4.

Moellendorf, D, 2002, *Cosmopolitan Justice*, Boulder, CO: Westview.

Molyneux, M, 1998, in Jackson, C and Pearson, R, eds., *Feminist Visions of Development: Gender, analysis and policy*, London: Routledge.

1985, 'Mobilization without emancipation? Women's interests, state and revolution in Nicaragua,' *Feminist Studies* 11, 2, 227–254.

Molyneux, M and Razavi, S, 2001, 'Introduction,' in Molyneux, M and Razavi, S, eds., *Gender Justice, Development and Rights*, Oxford University Press.

Moser, C, 1993, *Gender, Planning and Development. Theory, practice and training*, London: Routledge.

Nussbaum, MC, 2004, *Hiding from Humanity: Disgust, Shame, and the Law*, Princeton, NJ: Princeton University Press.

2003, 'Women's education: a global challenge,' *Signs: Journal of Women in Culture and Society* 29, 2, 325–355.

2000, *Women and Human Development*, Cambridge University Press.

Perlman-Robinson, J, 2011, 'A global compact on learning: Taking action on education in developing countries', *Washington, DC: Center for Universal Education at Brookings*.

Pogge, T, 2002, 'Can the Capability Approach be justified?' *Philosophical Topics* 30, 2, 167–228.

Rai, SM, 2002, *Gender and the Political Economy of Development*, Cambridge: Polity.

Rawls, J, 2001, *Justice as Fairness: A Restatement*, Cambridge, MA: Harvard University Press.

1993, *Political Liberalism*, Columbia University Press.

1980, 'Kantian constructivism in moral theory,' *Journal of Philosophy* 77, 9, 515–572.

1971, *A Theory of Justice*, Cambridge, MA: Harvard University Press.

Robinson Pant, A, 2000, '*Why eat green cucumbers at time of dying?' Women's literacy and development in Nepal*, Hamburg: UNESCO Institute for Development.

Rowlands, J, 1999, *Questioning Empowerment*, Oxford: Oxfam.

Sen, A, 1999, *Development as Freedom*, Oxford University Press.

1997, *Inequality Re-examined*, Cambridge, MA: Harvard University Press.

Smyth, I and Rao, N, 2004, eds., *Partnerships for Girls' Education*, Oxford: Oxfam.

UNESCO, 2003, *Gender and Education for All. The leap to equality*, Paris: UNESCO.

2002, *EFA Global Monitoring Report 2002. Education for All: is the World on track?* Paris: UNESCO.

1997, *Adult Education in a Polarising World*, Paris: UNESCO.

UNGEI, 2002, *A New Global Partnership Meets an Old Global Challenge*, Paris: United Nations Girls' Education Initiative.

Unterhalter, E, 2002, 'Gender justice and the transformation of apartheid education,' in Marks, S, ed., *Siyafunda. Partners in Learning. Education in South Africa – 1994 and Beyond*, London: Kogan Page, 75–84.

2000, 'Transnational visions of the 1990s: contrasting views of women, education and citizenship,' in Arnot, M and Dillabough, J, eds., *Challenging Democracy*, London: Routledge.

Unterhalter, E and Dutt, S, 2001, 'Gender, education and women's power: Indian state and civil society intersections in DPEP (District Primary Education Programme) and Mahila Samakhya,' *Compare* 31, 1, 57–73.

Watkins, K, 2000, *The Oxfam Education Report*, Oxford: Oxfam.

WIDE, 2013, *World Inequality Database on Education*, Paris: EfA Global Monitoring Report (online at www.education-inequalities.org/countries/nigeria#?dimension=all&group=all&year=2008, accessed July 2013).

World Bank, 2001, *Engendering Development through Gender Equality in Rights, Resources and Voice*, New York: Oxford University Press.

1995, *World Development Report*, New York: World Bank and Oxford University Press.

Wolpe, A, Quinlan, O and Martinez, L, 1998, *Report of the Gender Equity Task Team*, Pretoria: Department of Education.

9   The weight of institutions on women's capabilities: how far can microfinance help?

Muriel Gilardone, Isabelle Guérin and Jane Palier

Introduction

Cultural features of a society are generally unfavourable to women. Even when women *formally* have the same rights and liberty as men (which is still not the case everywhere), mentalities are strongly rooted in traditions and existing social norms continue to oppress women. As legal opportunities are essential, but are not themselves sufficient, it seems indispensable to act on *informal* institutions[1] to reinforce women's capabilities. The aim here is to point out that laws are only "the visible part of the iceberg".

There are many theoretical approaches to the assessment of the quality of women's lives. For a long time, welfare economics or development economics rested on a utilitarianism concerned with the social maximization of utility, construed as the satisfaction of preference or desire. The limits of this approach have largely been demonstrated, particularly its indifference to welfare distribution and the fact that preferences and tastes are endogenously shaped by laws, traditions and institutions, tending to reproduce inequalities.[2] For this reason, the chapter will focus on Nussbaum's work, even if *a priori* her universal list of capabilities seems to ignore the important role played by institutions. One can indeed wonder whether her search for ethical objectivity is not as inadequate as the universal calculus generality of utilitarianists, which she criticizes for its lack of consideration for particular contexts and histories. Is it not meaningless to discuss individual lives outside the institutional context? Indeed, institutions without being capabilities *per se* (i.e. ends) are crucial means to develop or restrict capabilities.

In fact, it is clear that Nussbaum (1999a: 5) is aware of the links between women's capabilities and existing (reinforcing or weakening)

---

[1] By "informal institutions" we mean the set of rules of conduct, norms, routines, traditions deeply ensconced in every society and which implicitly commands its organization. One could also call these rules "social institutions".
[2] For example, see Sen 1999, Chapter 3.

244

norms. And that is the reason why she refuses desire-based approaches and relativist views, which use the local criteria of goodness – often unjust to women – to assess their well-being. As preferences are "adaptive", it seems necessary to base studies of women's capabilities on "transcultural norms, justifiable by reference to reasons of universal human validity, by reference to which we may appropriately criticise different local conceptions of the good" (Nussbaum and Sen 1993: 243). And her universal list of capabilities – a kind of objective basis derived from "Aristotelian Essentialism" (Nussbaum 1992) – allows us to put women's lack of liberty to the fore. Why would women have fewer requirements than men in terms of liberty?

The first step in our argument about the improvement of the quality of women's lives, therefore, is to point out the central capabilities to which they have hardly any access. Then, it is crucial to understand what institutions – formal and more especially informal – are incompatible with women's prosperity in order to take appropriate measures. Their freedom of agency is inescapably qualified and constrained by the social, political and economic opportunities that are available to them. Obviously, opportunities for the economic participation of women may help them greatly to foster their own initiatives in overcoming their deprivations; however, this condition cannot be regarded as sufficient. To be content with promoting their economic freedom does not guarantee them an access to *real* freedom. One has to recognize the importance of both individual agency and social arrangements. We have chosen to illustrate and highlight this argument through the example of microfinance. The objective of this chapter would indeed be to assess the links between institutions and quality of life, within a capability framework approach, exploring a relevant empirical issue: microfinance.

Microfinance appears more and more as a tool for women's empowerment. The objectives in view are multiple: to increase their incomes and facilitate their financial independence, to stabilize and professionalize their entrepreneurial activity, but also, and above all, to increase their self-esteem and to promote their self-organizing capacities and thereby their abilities to express themselves and their demands. In theory, microfinance may well initiate a "virtuous spiral" of economic, social and even political empowerment and, consequently, may appear as a means to increase women's capabilities. How do matters stand in practice? Available results of impact studies call for circumspection; microfinance can free women from certain links of dependence. For instance, Nussbaum (1999a: 296–297) has shown how the Self-Employed Women's

Association (SEWA)[3] is likely to free women from prostitution. But microfinance can also forge new kinds of dependence and subordination, thereby strengthening the disparities between men and women, but also among women themselves (Mayoux 1999). Consequently, it is crucial to link microfinance programmes with institutional transformations. This part of the chapter is based on fieldwork and research by the authors in West Africa, Bangladesh and India, and on secondary sources.[4]

Economic freedom: a first step for women's empowerment

Our opportunities and prospects depend crucially on the existing institutions and how they function. At the core of the capability approach are the ideas of equal human worth and dignity, which are closely connected to the idea of liberty. It is clearly opposed to many existing value systems which are highly paternalistic, particularly towards women. Indeed, many value systems treat women as unequal under the law and as lacking full civil capacity; they do not have the property rights, associative liberties or employment rights of males. This distinct sex bias against the females all over the world is much sharper and more widespread in the poorer Third World economies.[5]

Women have to face gender-related problems which, depending on the political and economic circumstances, are very different from one society to another. But all over the world they are more or less concerned with such questions as rape, sexual harassment, hunger, sex-selective infanticide and abortion, denial of the right to work, sex discrimination in family laws, especially in the distribution of food, education and health care.[6] The economic situation of women is certainly not alone in having a dismal record, but it seems to need urgent attention, for the ability of women to work outside often determines their whole life.

---

[3] The SEWA acts both as a microfinance organization (providing loans and skills training) and a labour organization in direction of women working in the informal sector (helping women to bargain for better working conditions and providing more generally a space for collective discussion).

[4] Since this chapter was written, several different studies and research projects have focused on microcredit, but they have not been mentioned. It seems, nevertheless, that the promotion leaflet and proposed conclusions in the article are still the same.

[5] For example, the Government of India amended the Hindu Personal Law Code in the 1950s in order to ban bigamy, facilitate divorce, counter child marriage, etc. Under the law, girls and boys can now inherit equally but only if there is no will, so that in practice cultural traditions of male inheritance are maintained (Das Gupta *et al.* 2000).

[6] See, for example, International Center for Research on Women 1999.

Why reinforce women's economic freedom?

As Nussbaum (1999a: 8) notes, "any living culture [...] contains relatively powerful voices, relatively silent voices, and voices that cannot speak at all in the public space". Women are often in the second category, indeed even in the third, simply because they are women.

Although some women try to improve their relatively bad situation, the way most of them are brought up makes them feel dependent and lacking in self-respect, which prevents them from being aware of their subordination. For this reason, desire-based approaches are unable to analyze sex inequalities, "since it is difficult to desire what one cannot imagine as a possibility" (Nussbaum, Sen 1993: 5). John Kenneth Galbraith, in his analysis of poverty, has already observed that one of the most important causes of the persistence of poverty is "accommodation", that is to say the absence of effort to escape poverty.[7] And he criticizes economists who generally think that the search for material progress is natural. On the contrary, he demonstrates that the trend to prefer resignation to frustrated hope is not only understandable but is rational (Galbraith 1979). Although the standard utilitarian approach makes this assumption, preferences are not always reliable indicators of the quality of life.

What does the capability approach say? Rather than looking only at women's stated satisfactions and preferences, which may be deformed by intimidation, lack of information and habit, Nussbaum urges us to look at their actual "functioning". More exactly, she is interested in the space of functionings, the various things a person may value doing (or being), e.g. the "capability" of a person.

The capability approach to the assessment of the quality of life has been pioneered in economics by Sen. Judging individual well-being, neither in terms of commodities consumed nor in terms of the central metric of utilities, it focuses either on the realized functionings or on the set of alternatives a person has. It is a "perspective of freedom in a positive sense: who can do what" (Sen 1984: 376).

By providing a philosophical justification for supporting the use of wider informational spaces in assessing quality of life, the capability approach can also lead to define basic constitutional principles to promote liberty for each individual. By establishing a list of "central human functional capabilities", Nussbaum indeed goes further than Sen in the

---

[7] According to Galbraith, recognizing the reality of accommodation is very different from accepting poverty as an inescapable phenomenon. It is, above all, the means to understand why many efforts apparently promising to relieve poverty have failed.

will to describe "a life in which the dignity of the human being is not violated by hunger or fear or the absence of opportunities" (Nussbaum 1999a: 41–42). This list is an attempt to answer the question, "What are the functions without which we would regard a life as not, or not fully, human?" (Nussbaum 1999a: 39) and proposes a set of interrelated and indivisible capabilities, conceived as human rights.

According to Nussbaum, raising all citizens above a basic threshold of capability should be taken as a central social goal. We note that, even if functioning is the effective way of living, capability, and not functioning, is the political goal.[8] Respect for choice is crucial to her, but depends on many factors, such as access to a minimal subsistence, level of education, health and also employment, seen as a source of opportunity and empowerment. Indeed, "people who have to fight for the most basic things are precluded by that struggle from exercising their agency in other more fulfilling and socially fruitful ways" (Nussbaum 1999a: 19).

Women's agency and access to minimal subsistence is conditioned by their economic opportunities. And that is why Nussbaum concludes her list of central human functional capabilities with the following item:

Control over one's environment. (a) Political: [. . .] (b) Material: being able to hold property (both land and movable goods); having the right to seek employment on an equal basis with others, having the freedom from unwarranted search and seizure. In work, being able to work as a human being, exercising practical reason and entering into meaningful relationships of mutual recognition with other workers. (Nussbaum 1999a: 42)

On this point, there are poor records for women all over the world. But it is all the more obvious in the developing countries, where women's employment participation rates are very low – not to speak of property holding. On average, the employment rates for women are only 50 per cent those for men (in South Asia 29 per cent and only 16 per cent in the Arab states) (Nussbaum 1999a: 31). This point is not least important, although it is the last item on Nussbaum's list. She insists on the fact that each item on the list is related to the others in many complex ways. For example, employment rights support health and also freedom from domestic violence, by giving women a better bargaining position within the family considered in the capability approach as an "allocative institution". Thus it seems indispensable to study the weight of that fundamental institution on women's capabilities.

---

[8] In conformity with a form of liberal philosophy (inspired by Kant, Mill and Aristotle), Martha C. Nussbaum considers that, in virtue of the basic human capacities for choice and reasoning, citizens must be left free to determine their course thereafter.

Bargaining power within the family For Nussbaum (1999a: 21), "the family is part of the basic structure of political society". Therefore, legal reform of the family should be a part of political justice. While economic and political liberalism tend to remove women from male domination, few things are known and said about family laws. John Stuart Mill was perhaps one of the first philosophers to understand the importance of justice within the family, considering in particular that family shapes children's citizenship powerfully, for good or for ill.[9]

The leading economic approach to the family today, however, is that of Gary Becker, an approach which poses certain problems. Indeed, Becker assumes that the family's goal is the maximization of its whole utility (as if the family were one individual), ignoring the fact that this supposed organic unit often constructs unequal capabilities for various types of functioning.[10]

However, as "the family is often the decision-making unit for work and consumption" (Sen 1984: 360), the existence of substantial intra-family disparities has serious implications on what we are concerned with, i.e. women's capabilities. According to Sen, in order to understand the distribution of "entitlements" within the family, there has to be a clearer analysis of the existence of both cooperative and conflicting elements in family relations. He relates this problem to what Nash calls "the bargaining problem":

The essence of the problem is that there are many cooperative outcomes – beneficial to all the parties compared with non-cooperation – but the different parties have strictly conflicting interests in the choice among the set of efficient cooperative arrangements. [...]
Second, the bargaining problem of finding a particular cooperative solution, yielding a particular distribution of benefits, will be sensitive to various parameters, including the respective powers of the different members of the family, given, for example, by the nature of the "fall-back" positions if there should be a breakdown. (Sen 1984: 375)

How is bargaining power established within the family? This question can be best approached via three somewhat more concrete questions. Who does what? Who is allowed to consume what? Who decides what? And it is likely that men typically have better bargaining power, related to

---

[9] Mill also developed an in-depth analysis of the "artificial" dimension of women's character and can be considered as a pioneer of adaptive preferences (it is also worthwhile noting that he was greatly influenced by his wife, Hariett Taylor). Mill, 1869 (1975).

[10] Our criticism of Becker's theory is obviously too brief and thus overly simplistic. To provide a full criticism of Becker's analysis goes far beyond the aim of this chapter. See, for example, Folbre 1996.

better outside job opportunities, which leads to a correspondingly more favourable cooperative outcome for the men. Economic independence definitely seems to be more powerful than a contribution which is vital for the family, but not remunerated.

Indeed, a woman's perceived contribution to the well-being of the family unit is often determined by her ability to work outside, e.g. her wage, and this determines, in turn, her bargaining position within the family unit. As Nussbaum (1999a: 88) observes, "the wage labour outside the home is highly correlated with a woman's ability to command food and other goods within it". Sometimes the connection is direct, for example in the case of Indian widows starving because of norms that prevent them from earning money. Sometimes the connection is more indirect, through a perception of a woman's importance to the future of the family. In any case, cash wages are usually perceived as making a great contribution to the family's well-being, whereas housework is not.

Thus, since they work outside, women's participation becomes more visible. And because their independence increases, their voices become more audible. Finally, outside work helps them to stop being only supporters of the ends of others and subordinating their interests to the larger goal of the family unit. Finally the evolution of their status modifies the generally accepted ideas about their role of reproducers and care-givers.

This idea does not mean that individual welfare is independent of the welfare of the rest of the family. There is a fundamental difference between the concepts of separateness[11] and independence concerning individual welfare (Sen 1984: 362). In fact, individual welfares may be interdependent, but distinct. The problem concerning women comes from their common propensity to subordinate themselves to others and to sacrifice their well-being for that of their family. This trend is obviously the consequence of long habits of domination and subordination. Nussbaum (2000: 3) links it to Marx's concept of exploitation: "Marx, like his bourgeois forebears, holds that it is profoundly wrong to subordinate the ends of some individuals to those of others. That is at the core of what exploitation is, to treat a person as a mere object for the use of others."

Thus, as the capability approach promotes a society in which all individuals are treated as worthy of regard, it has to take account of what is valuable in a given society. Today, employment is a central value in

---

[11] In accordance with a liberal political conception, it is crucial to insist on the concept of separateness. This means that one must distinguish one's life from that of another, and recognize "the equal importance of each life, seen on its own terms rather than part of a larger organic or corporate whole" (Nussbaum 1999a: 10).

people's existence.[12] It not only gives an income to the employed, it also gives him or her "the recognition of being engaged in something worth his while" (Sen 1984: 242). This has not always been the case, but is historically and culturally dated. For example, "in ancient Greece, there was a common aristocratic prejudice against earning wages. The ancient Greek gentleman was characterized by 'leisure' – meaning that he did not have to work for a living" (Nussbaum 1999a: 278). For Aristotle, the idea of freedom, and dignity, is closely connected to the capacity of not being preoccupied with the baser things in life. At that time, one could be a citizen only if not constrained by economic problems, leaving work to slaves and home management to women. Politics was the central value and economics was seen as a contemptible domain.[13] And one again notes that women were confined to a devalued sphere.

In short, "it is likely that women's subordination will not be adequately addressed as long as women are confined to a sphere traditionally devaluated, linked with a low 'perceived well-being contribution'" (Nussbaum 1999a: 52). That is why their ability, or even their inclination, to accept outside employment is crucial for their empowerment. And it explains why we chose to focus on economic freedom: it is not one freedom among others but is perhaps one of the most important for our societies.

It is clear that the propensity of women to be confined to the family sphere is reinforced by institutions. "Such dispositions have been formed, often, in unjust conditions and may simply reflect the low worth society itself has placed on women's well-being" (Nussbaum 1999a: 8). Many constraints prevent women from developing income-generating activities, among the first of which are the absence of financial assets and a very limited access to credit. For this reason, microfinance has an important role to play in order to enhance their capability by offering an economic opportunity and is increasingly promoted by international cooperation.

Why use microfinance?

Credit "for the poor" already has a history and much experience has been accumulated over the last two centuries in different regions of the world.

---

[12] See Gilardone 2003.

[13] This idea has largely been developed by Hannah Arendt in her book *The Human Condition* (1958). One of her fears was to observe how modern society brutally became a "society of workers", while technical progress made it possible to work less. For her, the relatively new ideology that glorifies work is due to economists such as Adam Smith or even Karl Marx. She notes that, in their writings, work is seen either as the cause of wealth or as a central value.

What is rather new, however, is that women are targeted. While they were deliberately excluded from the first experiments which took place during the twentieth century (Fournier and Ouédraogo 1996), today they represent an important part of the clientele. According to the statistics of the International Food Policy Research Institute (IFPRI) concerning Africa, Asia and Latin America, women represent 45 per cent of the clientele (Lapenu and Zeller 2001). The last database built by the International Labour Office gives similar results (44 per cent) for western Africa, and of 174 inventoried microfinance intermediaries, 46 (that is, 26 per cent) are exclusively intended for women (BIT/BCEAO 1999a).

Let us begin with a first observation: in addition to our own fieldwork – an impact study carried out in Senegal on a women's programme set up by the Crédit Mutuel[14] – various studies have shown the positive effects of microfinance, even if they are contrasting. This contrast holds as much in the variety of the socio-economic context, in the profile of the borrowers, as in the offer of credit, and probably as well in the methods of data collection.

In particular, there is no universal definition of empowerment, even if everyone recognizes that this concept is about change, choice and power. Evaluating the impact of microcredit programmes on empowerment implies choosing accurate indicators that vary from culture to culture. For example, Naila Kabeer's main conclusion about conflicting findings in impact assessment of microcredit programmes in Bangladesh is that differences lie in the understanding of intra-household power relations (Kabeer 2001). Results of empowerment evaluation depend on the priority which is given. Positive views focus more on outcomes, whereas a negative verdict is based more on processes of change. Moreover, implicit preconceptions presume results, i.e. negative studies give more priority to conflict in households than to cooperation, and insist more on individualized behaviours.

The reduction of economic vulnerability The first and most frequently used indicator to assess the impact of microfinance on poverty alleviation is the improvement of household income, which is considered as a means to evaluate economic empowerment. Paul Mosley and David Hulme (1996) have estimated the impact of thirteen microfinance

---

[14] The research uses both qualitative and quantitative data from a case study in Thiès District, both in rural and urban areas. The qualitative analysis is based upon focus group discussions with fifty women's groups and in-depth interviews ("life stories") with twelve women. The quantitative analysis is based on one structured survey administrated to 100 women who represented a broad cross-section of the target population of the microfinance programme. Data were collected in 1996–1997 (Guérin 2003).

intermediaries in seven Asian countries. Their work shows a net correlation between the levels of initial incomes of the borrowers and the increase in income induced by the credit: the farther they are situated below the poverty line, the weaker are the benefits induced by credit. It can even be worse when borrowers have been forced to get into debt to make repayments (i.e. benefits are negative). Consequently, researchers are rather sceptical about a massive generalization of microfinance which would not take into account the financial instability of the most deprived. They suggest an adaptation of microfinance services, by combining credit, savings and insurance; this combination may allow borrowers to be less exposed to risks.[15] Our observations in Senegal point in the same direction. The poorest women are over-represented in the cases of loss, i.e. when the profits of the activity are not enough to repay loans. Conversely, it is for the richest that the margins are the largest. The result is nevertheless not dramatic since the women belong, in a formal way or not, to a system of insurance. In this particular case in Senegal, the programme, probably wrongly, foresaw no such thing, but the women insured themselves mutually, using informal financial systems such as rotating savings and credit associations (ROSCAs).

Besides, if one argues in terms of well-being and the feeling of independence and not strictly in terms of incomes, the impact is really significant and becomes completely convincing for the most vulnerable. In India and in Sri Lanka, the SEWA Bank (the bank of the Self-Employed Women's Association) allows the most deprived women, belonging to the lowest castes, to settle former debts, thus terminating a relation of quasi-exploitation (Schrieder and Sharma 1999). For the customers of the Grameen Bank in Bangladesh, those of the "Caisses villageoises" (village banks) in Dogon country and Kafo Jiginew in Mali, or again for the customers of various microfinance organizations in the Plain of Rushes in Vietnam, microcredit allows them above all to avoid capital reduction or expensive credit such as usury (Doligez and Le Bissonnais 1996). We had similar findings in Senegal. The women feel "more comfortable", "less bound". They also say that they "manage" better, and that they have "to beg" less, and a woman who "does not beg" is more respected. Before microcredit, either the commercial activity did not exist, or it was financed by a very expensive credit or by the sale of

---

[15] Two recent desk reviews confirm the pioneer work of Hulme and Mosley: the fact that most microfinance programmes do not reach large numbers of the "poorest of the poor" does not mean that they cannot reach them, or that very poor people cannot benefit from them, but it does mean that the majority of microfinancial products are not designed to respond to the needs of the poorest. Morduch, Haley 2002; Simanovitz, Walter 2002.

farm products normally intended for domestic consumption; very often, profits are partially dedicated to the repayment of certain debts. Micro-savings may play a great part in helping women to manage their finances better and to feel less dependent, especially when they are accustomed to living entirely on credit. This is especially the case in India, where the least income is used to pay back previous debts. The women's satisfac-tion derives from the feeling of security that microcredit produces.[16]

Still in Senegal, the most important effect concerns the stabilization of the commercial activity of those who, up to then, were regularly obliged to stop their commercial activity. This result is contrary to many impact studies which have concluded that microfinance has no effect in terms of accumulation. Not only do consumption needs absorb a good part of the profits, but borrowers often prefer diversification rather than risk economies of scale by venturing on a single activity. One understands easily that in a context of strong uncertainty, it is more reassuring to opt for a distribution of risks. For others, if there is no accumulation, it is because they simply have no ambition to enlarge their business, or even to stabilize it. For example, in Senegal, commercial activity remains for some women a punctual and temporary answer to a clearly determined need (a ceremony, the re-opening of school, etc.). All the same, it is possible to observe certain forms of accumulation by capitalization of the commercial working capitals, or at least a stabilization of the activity. This process is possible in particular when borrowers have a repeated access to a short-term credit (Doligez 2002) and provided that it is not transformed into a relation of dependence towards the microfinance intermediary (Diarra Doka 1998). When the credit is provided to groups of borrowers, it sometimes happens that the group uses microcredit to develop a regular credit activity for its members. This is what we observed in Senegal.

The improvement of women's autonomy and family's quality of life
Empowerment is not only economic upgradation but can be also evalu-ated by the improvement in the family's quality of life. Targeting women in microfinance programmes is both effective (women are more serious borrowers who assimilate repayment as a moral duty) and useful to the well-being of the household because women often spend more of their income on their families, whereas men are viewed as wasteful.[17] For

---

[16] For example, in Andra Pradesh (India), one woman told us that for the first time in her life she had the feeling of holding in her hand bank notes which actually belonged to her. Braham, Guérin 2003.

[17] Such situations have been documented in numerous studies. For a review, see Guérin 2003.

example, one of the reasons given by Indian microfinance organizations for targeting women rather than men is that the latter use credit for drinking or gambling. Assisting women generates a multiplier effect that enlarges the impact of the microcredit programmes.

A large part of the profits[18] generated by microcredit – about 50 per cent on average – and often a part of the credit, is allocated to expenditures which improve appreciably daily life, even if they can be viewed as "unproductive". This observation illustrates the priorities of the borrowers. For example, among borrowers in Senegal, the poorest are more worried by expenditures for food, clothing, health, schooling and ceremonies, whereas the wealthiest invest in order to develop their commercial activity, to build their house or to send their children abroad.

Several longitudinal studies show that the effects are sometimes long term. This kind of effect has been observed in several fields: food security in Ghana, education in Cameroon (Schrieder and Sharma 1999), health, clothing and construction in Bangladesh (Doligez and Le Bissonnais 1996)and in Guinea (Doligez 2002). In Niger, women invest first and foremost in the dowry of their daughters. This, normally, assures them a more respectable marriage and thus a better future [(Schrieder and Sharma 1999). One also observes that the effects sometimes exceed the domestic scale and involve local and regional markets. In Guinea, for example, 30 per cent of the incomes induced by the credit are assigned to the improvement of housing, which greatly revitalizes the local construction market (Doligez 2002). In Senegal, the credit allows women to master some distribution channels more advantageously by bypassing one or several intermediaries (for example, in the fish or textile markets, etc.).

As we mentioned earlier, one indirect link is that women, by using credit for the education of their daughters, contribute to a better future for them and therefore to their empowerment. Thus, wagering on women is seen as a good instrument for changing informal institutions and mentalities. For example, according to a NABARD report[19] on the impact evaluation of the Self-Help Group-Banks-Linkage programme, 55 per cent of the Self-Help Group[20] members protested against the abuse of women in films during the pre-group situation, whereas 82 per cent of them protest now. Similarly, about 95 per cent of them strongly protested against husbands beating their wives, as compared with 71 per cent

---

[18] We noticed that microcredit generates profits which can be important. The rate of profitability is on average between 50 and 100 per cent. Guérin 2002.

[19] The NABARD is the National Bank for Agriculture and Rural Development, an apex financial institution in India.

[20] A self-help group is formed by a maximum of twenty members who contribute regularly to a fund that is lent to members to meet their emergency or productive needs.

of them having done so in the pre-group situation. The protests against gambling and drinking also involved a higher proportion of the members in the post-group situation than in the pre-group situation (Puhazhendhi and Satyasai 2000).

This can be linked to Nussbaum's statement (1999a: 12) that, "if men are possessive and tyrannical, it may be less because of unchanging male aggression than because society gives permission to males to form and to express such attitudes". Indeed, empowerment is also a process of raising awareness on women's issues.

Access to resources does not automatically translate into empowerment, but microfinance may improve women's autonomy, i.e. their self-confidence, their mobility and access to networks, and their role in household decision-making. Several studies have tried to assess the impact of microfinance on women's empowerment, although choosing an appropriate methodology and isolating the impact of microcredit is a very difficult task.

Let us report the findings of one impact study conducted in two Bangladeshi microfinance organizations, (Grameen Bank and BRAC). S.M. Hashemi *et al.* (1996) used a composite index to assess women's empowerment, which included mobility, economic security, ability to make small and larger purchases, involvement in major decisions, relative freedom from domination by the family, political and legal awareness, and participation in public protests and political campaigning. Their main conclusion is that microfinance does empower women because the programmes of both organizations have significant effects on each dimension of empowerment. Another case study carried out in the Philippines concludes that the women's involvement in two microcredit programmes has increased their self-confidence as a result of their interaction with various individuals and groups and has given them the opportunity to expand their activities outside their homes, thus increasing their mobility and sphere of participation (Anolin 2002).

We wish to conclude with one major aspect of women's empowerment, their ability to influence or make decisions that affect their lives and their families, i.e. their bargaining power. For example, one microfinance organization in Nepal showed an average of 68 per cent of women who experienced an increase in their decision-making roles in the areas of family planning, children's marriage, buying and selling property and sending their daughters to school (Cheston, Kuhn 2002).

Thus, while microfinance offers women economic opportunities, it also illustrates the complex link that exists between economic freedom and real freedom. It is clear that microfinance appears as a means to improve their economic freedom but, as we will see in the following part of this chapter, if other institutional changes do not take place at the same time, this economic freedom does not necessarily promote their autonomy and their real freedom.

Economic freedom does not necessarily lead to real freedom

"Sometimes, the traditions have become so deeply internalized that they seem to record what is right and 'natural', and women themselves endorse their own second-class status" (Nussbaum 1999a: 29). It would be irrelevant to consider the economic situation as disconnected from the other spheres of existence, as is often done in economic analysis. Offering women opportunities and legal reforms to improve their economic situation is often not sufficient, and can even lead to perverse effects by reinforcing their constraints.

In this second part, we will first highlight the danger of placing too much confidence in economic opportunities in the empowerment women. Second, we will assume that a political anchoring of microfinance activities is a good way to promote women's real freedom.

How microfinance can generate perverse effects

The weight of informal institutions A relationship of reciprocity exists between prejudices and social status. The traditional division of labour according to gender – male breadwinner, female homecare – leads to a belief that, on the one hand, males are naturally "autonomous", capable of practical reasoning, independent and self-sufficient, allegedly good at political deliberation. On the other hand, females are considered to be naturally focused on pleasing others and good at caring for others, but dependent on males because of their incapacity for practical reasoning.[21]

As a consequence of the inequalities in education, or of sexist discrimination in the job market, the traditional arrangement that often emerges is of women doing housework and taking up outside work only if it is supplemental. Even when women are employed, it is not only often in addition to long hours of unpaid household labour but is generally restricted to a range of jobs offering low pay and low respect. As Nussbaum (1999a: 51) underscores, "the very perpetuation of separate spheres of responsibility might reinforce subordination".

---

[21] See Nussbaum 1999a, pp. 52–54 in particular.

Furthermore, Sen explains that the traditional division labour by gender corresponds to what he calls "the social technology".[22] Generally, "work" is considered to be a production in compensation for which a wage is given. Does this mean that unpaid work is unproductive? Although it is often perceived as such, unpaid work is nevertheless necessary for the social organization and to allow what is seen as "real production". While it is obvious that workers have to take sustenance, to survive and to reproduce when they are at home, the activities that allow the satisfaction of these vital needs are rarely considered to contribute to the production.

This point has been largely developed by Marilyn Waring, who demonstrates how these invisibilities have been institutionalized. She also describes how economic orthodoxies exclude most of women's productive and reproductive work, arguing that this unpaid work has few or no effect on microeconomic activity and, *a fortiori*, on macroeconomic activity. According to her, women's work – that is to say, half of the world's population's work – fuels the economies of every country in the world, but traditional economics is inaccurate to take it into account because of an unbelievable lack of imagination. The assumptions of this "one-eyes economics" perpetuate "the power dynamics of who chooses, who judges, who defines, who rules, who imposes" (Waring 1993). Thus, Waring urges us to rethink basic economic concepts such as gross domestic product. Indeed, all women's subsistence agriculture, and activities such as carrying water and collecting fuel wood, should now be counted in the main production accounts.[23] Women's inventiveness and work are an economic contribution far from being negligible, but as they do not pass by the market, their value is ignored.[24]

Moreover, since women work outside their home, there is a kind of imbalance in the "social technology" because they have less time for their traditional activities. As mentalities change slowly, the "division of labour" is strongly rooted in traditions and often becomes an "accumulation of labour" for women. The evolution is long until a more appropriate "social technology" emerges to ensure real opportunities of choice for women between care work and paid employment. And this

[22] See Sen 1991, p. 237 in the French translation of 1993, Presses Universitaires de France.

[23] According to Waring, time-use surveys are more able than traditional economics based on money or market transactions to pull public policy into women's real world. "Time is the one commodity we all have. We might not all have as much discretion as we'd like about what we do with it, but you can't make more time, and you can't take it away" (Waring 1993).

[24] This point raises the fundamental question to know what economics values and how it values it. Usually, if one asks people, they would say my children, my partner, my health, my religion. All this cannot be bought; it is not a market commodity or a service.

evolution is enormously influenced by social arrangements for education, health care and other public policies.

For example, the way a society organizes childcare and work at home is a key issue in terms of the position of women, and men, on the labour market. The model differs radically from country to country. The integration of mothers of small children in the labour market can be facilitated by the welfare state, particularly by the well-developed childcare systems, nursery schools or crèches. This is especially the case in the Scandinavian countries or in France. But German society does still support the "Hausfrau" model. And although the German state offers joint-family income taxation and women's pensions are calculated on the basis of their husband's income, many young German women choose paid employment despite the fact that childcare costs swallow almost their entire salary. This last case shows clearly that the wage is not the only thing at stake in employment.[25]

One thing is clear: cultures are changing, in the North but also in the South. As usual, they all contain plurality and conflict, tradition and subversion. Against reactionary political forces, Nussbaum (1999a: 36) assumes that "cultures are not museum pieces, to be preserved intact at all costs". On the contrary, she thinks that it would be condescending to preserve for contemplation a way of life that causes real pain to real people.[26]

Nussbaum views the capability approach as urging us to "see common needs, problems, and capacities", but also as reminding us that "each person and group faces problems in a highly concrete context" (Nussbaum 1999a: 47). Its universalism is to arise from history and from human experience, which means that the procedure for reinforcing women's capabilities should be neither ahistorical nor *a priori*. We will illustrate this last idea in the following part by our studies on microfinance.

Increasing the burden of obligations As we have seen above, microfinance is a potentially powerful instrument to reduce vulnerability and stabilize commercial activities; to improve the quality of life of the whole family and the bargaining power of women. But it can also lead to an increase in the weight of obligations. First of all, the question of

[25] Nussbaum (1999a: 297) clearly argues that the SEWA, by forming groups, allows "to diminish the isolation and enhance the self-respect of working women in low-paying jobs" and so "to avoid prostitution for themselves or their daughters" even when it is better paid.

[26] We can here refer again to Marilyn Waring's work. Indeed, she considers that women's unpaid household work could be defined as servitude. Then all the countries noted for human rights would be in breach of their fundamental human rights obligations (Waring 1993).

"who controls the credit" is crucial. In the case of women, their husbands or other male members of the family can appropriate the credit. For example, according to research carried out in Bangladesh (four microfinance programmes were studied), 10 per cent of the borrowers from the Grameen Bank have little, even no, control over the use of their credit. This proportion ranges from 40 per cent to 60 per cent for the three other programmes (Goetz and Gupta 1996). Other field studies reveal the determining influence of the husband on the customers of the Grameen Bank and the way they decided to apply for microcredit. This influence is probably valuable when it prompts the women to challenge tradition, but sometimes it is similar to veritable manipulation; the woman is ultimately only a "way" to obtain a loan without being involved in the reimbursement (Rahman 1999). The difficulties met by the "Petit projet de crédit rural" (small rural credit project) in Burkina Faso illustrate another implication of the targeting of women. In a Sahelian context, where the opportunities of commercial activities are limited for women as well as for men, the emergence of a female competition with male entrepreneurship collided with male resistance, and one can wonder whether targeting women was really relevant. In other contexts, where male patriarchy is very strong, and where women are not allowed to enter public spaces and have to stay at home, for example in certain regions of Niger, several microfinance experiences which excluded men led to bad results. The absence of dialogue with the men indeed provoked a strong destabilization of local social relationships (Schrieder and Sharma 1999].[27] Finally, a last risk should be mentioned: microcredit may lead to a greater burden on women's responsibilities when men put this "feminine privilege" forward to disengage themselves from their own obligations.

Ambivalence of the collective approach Women are having access to credit in increasing numbers in the developing world, on condition that they join groups and mutually stand surety. IFPRI statistics show that collective loans with joint liability are mainly adapted for women borrowers, who represent 80 per cent of the clientele, while they represent less than a third of the clientele for individual loans (Lapenu and Zeller 2001). It is a question of efficiency: through cost reductions, collective loans are supposed to ensure efficiency and even viability.[28] It is also a

---

[27] In such situations, a first stage would have consisted in convincing men to allow their wives to join the groups.

[28] They are different rationales offered for placing priority on targeting only women in microfinance programmes and the feminist justification is only one among others. See Cheston 2002 and Palier 2003.

question of mobilization of the female civil society; through the collective management of credit, one hopes to strengthen their self-organization capacities.

Certainly, a collective approach has many advantages. In rural Bangladesh, the custom of *purdah* isolates women from men and from markets.[29] This custom is more or less pronounced from one village to another; there are some 'pockets' of clear conservatism where women's mobility is no more than a few hundred metres, and where women's collective action, or at least women's collective discussions, do not exist. Bearing in mind such a situation, one can imagine to what extent the simple fact of meeting in a group is a considerable progress. The attendance of meetings in order to save and benefit from credit provides a socially accepted excuse to gather and to talk.

While in some places (mostly South Asia, North Africa and the Middle East) women are neither accustomed to meetings nor allowed to enter public spaces, in others (especially West Africa) there is a long tradition of local women's groups. They are accustomed to joining for religious, social and agricultural purposes and, more and more, for income-generating activities. Their dynamism and their self-organization capacities are absolutely fascinating.

However, Nussbaum (1999a: 49) seems to have developed a perhaps overly positive point of view regarding women's groups, as she writes:

In women's groups I have visited in India and China, the first benefit that is typically mentioned is that of affiliation and friendship with other women in pursuit of common goals. [...] Universal values build their own communities, communities of resourcefulness, friendship, and agency, embedded in the local scene but linked in complex ways to groups of women in other parts of the world. For these women the new community was a lot better than the one they have inhabited before.

One has to be aware that a collective loan can favour individual autonomy but can also deny it by consolidating existing links of dependence, or even by forging new kinds of dependence. It may strengthen social networks, but may also destabilize them. It can support collective capabilities of organization and management, but can also foster and encourage the creation of fictitious or monopolistic groups. Thus, a romantic and functionalist approach to collective action is not sufficient.

[29] Such prohibitions are strongly rooted in traditional practices and norms. For example in Bangladesh (Tangail District), when we asked them, naively, "Don't you think it would be worthwhile going to the village to sell eggs instead of using an intermediary?", at first they did not understand the question and then the question seemed completely incongruous to them ("That is not our culture") (Braham, Guérin, 2003).

The heterogeneousness of female groups forbids any generalization. In Senegal, for example, some groups are very small, with only a dozen members, whereas others have several hundreds, mainly in rural areas. This variety depends also on what activities are conducted: local business, but also import–export, education, organization of religious or political events by way of "talks", moments of exchanges and discussions about extremely varied subjects. Of this variety ensue various degrees of intellectual and financial autonomy, social cohesion and economic dynamism. If some groups are based on traditional social mutual-aid networks, others were formed only to get financing or to establish an individual's political authority. To this first risk, one can add that of a strong hierarchy. Nobody will go to exert pressure on the president of a group who uses the credit to finance her daughter's marriage. For that reason, many women prefer individual loans. Conversely, women can be urged to belong to a group and to get a loan even when they do not need it. As for the choice of activity financed by the credit, they imitate those who are successful, but without enjoying the same advantages (free transport, a well-established clientele, etc.).

Microfinance: not only an economic instrument but a political one

Microfinance should not imply a state disengagement The contrasting results we have just pointed out must not lead to relinquish the idea of providing microfinance services specifically for women; they just call for vigilance regarding the different possible dangers and risks.

First, bottom-up development has limits: when a group is well balanced between its own activities and its external relations, access to credit can become a useful tool to improve women's autonomy. But the delegation of responsibilities to groups must not cause one to consider only groups as a whole without taking into account intra-group relations. Once again, socio-cultural norms and power relations must not be ignored. When collective interest is more powerful than the individual interest of the members, it can become coercive for them and lead to negative outcomes: applying for a loan without need, launching unviable business enterprises, becoming indebted to moneylenders to make repayments at all costs, etc.

Second, if microfinance can have a positive impact on women's capabilities, it has to be understood that its scope can be seriously limited in a context of state disengagement. Indeed, the recognition of the role played by grass-roots organizations such as women's groups must not lead one to underestimate the responsibility of the national state and international organizations, such as the International Monetary Fund or the World Bank. Supporting and strengthening people-based initiatives is legitimate and justified. But the goal of NGOs (or other grass-roots institutions) is neither to compensate for state disengagement nor to compensate for the costs of structural adjustment policies. The risk of microfinance, already pointed out by some authors, would be that public authorities take advantage of it to increasingly disengage themselves, giving priority to the integration of the poor in market mechanisms – and this at the expense of their access to economic and basic social rights – while taking a chance with the capacity of NGOs and the self-organization of local populations to face the problems of poverty.

Feminist movements were the first to denounce the dangers of this approach. They do not question the legitimacy of microfinance, but plead in favour of its political anchoring. According to these movements, microfinance projects are justified only if strategic links are established with other forces of change, among which are networks and women's movements, as well as defence organizations and lobbies for women (Mayoux 1999; Hoffman and Marius-Gnanou 2001). The Social Finance Unit of the International Labour Office adopted the same position by recognizing that microfinance has no vocation to eliminate poverty problems, especially female poverty, and that it is justifiable only if it is integrated into a more global reflection on the valuation of funda-mental rights, in particular of women (BIT 1999).

For a political anchoring of microfinance To advocate political anchoring is all the more relevant as microfinance can facilitate women's mobilization through collective discussion, debate and action. Thus women can accede to public space and acquire a public voice, which can be favourable to the real freedom of women. Laws cannot impose all the gender-related issues. Whatever the context, even when state inter-ventions can influence the level of gender equity achieved by legal means or public schemes, only "social dialogue" or public debate can deeply transform mentalities and traditions or cultural norms (Sen 2000a, 2000b). As we observed above, women are not only often deprived of the same rights as men, but most of the time they are also not aware of their subordination and deprivation. Once again, only "social dialogue" can allow them to make personal choices and can enable needs to be expressed or to emerge. That is why, whatever policy is set up to fight inequalities, it must associate economic freedom and political freedom.

How evocative is this "social dialogue"? To rely on the mass mobiliza-tion of people in traditional forms of commitment such as trade unions or political parties is no longer the only solution. People, and more specif-ically women, need to be involved in shorter commitments in order to resolve concrete problems. This is why local spaces of discussion, where everybody can express an opinion and discuss with others the preoccupations of daily life, can be a means for this "social dialogue".[30] But this is not sufficient. It is also necessary that women want to promote institutional change and do not limit themselves to the resolution of daily and practical problems. At a local level, women's groups are able to influence public policies and can contribute to local development. But going beyond the local level is one of the most delicate aspects of this issue. If we consider Nussbaum's list of capabilities as a basis for constitutional principles, "we should use the list to criticize injustice, but we should not say anything at all without rich and full information" (Nussbaum, 1999a: 47). Her list which focuses on universal capabilities must be specified according to the concrete context and "the best specification will most reasonably be done by a public dialogue" (Ibid.). One can imagine that local discussions could feed the general debate on the way to apply this list in a specific context.

The difficulty in enforcing laws – which aim to improve women's participation in the public space – even at the local level, can be illustrated by a constitutional change which occurred in India in 1992.[31] This initiative set up a three-tier system of decentralized governance for spreading local democracy in the country through elective bodies. But it also represents a powerful strategy to increase women's participation in the political process because the legislation reserves one third of all seats in the local bodies for women.[32] This new system, which ensures the political representation of women, is no longer a contested issue; in Karnataka state, for example, elected women exceed the 33.3 per cent quota (Sekher 2001). As with all innovations, this must be treated with care. First, powerful and deep-rooted patriarchal norms in Indian society prevent women from a truly equitable sharing of powers; reservation of seats is not yet a qualitative change, but is above all a quantitative one. Second, the vast majority of elected women come from the "elite", which goes together with a high level of education. They belong to families with privileged economic and socio-cultural status or where men already have

---

[30] See Eme, Laville (1994) about the concept of "espaces publics de proximité".

[31] The 73rd Constitutional Amendment Act for Panchayati Raj (rural) and the 74th Constitutional Amendment Act for Municipal (urban) governance in 1992. Additional information is available on the website of the Urban Development Ministry at http://moud.gov.in and the Plan Commission at www.nic.in/ninthplan/vol1/v1c6-2.htm

[32] According to a World Bank report, there are, spread among 25 states (28 since 2000) and 7 union territories, 3,586 urban local bodies and 234,078 rural local bodies (Banque mondiale 2000, Le développement au seuil du XXIe siècle: rapport sur le développement dans le monde 1999–2000, Paris, Eska, 329p.).

political positions. One can note that a quota of seats is also reserved to depressed castes, but candidacy selection is often confined to the "elite". This pessimistic point of view must be counterbalanced by the fact that women have now a "voice" in the local political arena and a role in decision-making; they can acquire useful political and administrative skills, which is one step towards empowerment or improved capabilities. The challenge is to transform the presence of women in the local bodies into effective participation in the process of governance. Besides, efforts to extend seat reservation to the federal parliament and state legislatures have not yet fructified due to the reluctance within the male-dominated political system to share power with women (Sekher 2001).

Political anchoring of microfinance: the case of India[33] One of the most significant examples of political anchoring seems to be that of Indian microfinance organizations. By and large, their main goal is multidimensional development of their members; the provision of financial services is only one tool among others to alleviate poverty and to empower women so they also implement programmes to improve education, health, housing, etc. For example, the two essential elements in the strategy of the Baroda Citizen Council (BCC)[34] are community participation in efforts to improve its standard of living, with as much reliance as possible on its own initiatives, and the provision of technical, managerial and other services in order to encourage self-help initiatives. The BCC shares "the belief that social improvement does not come until the people involved believe that improvement is possible" (World Sanitation Program 1999a). Similarly, "the main philosophy guiding the promoters of SPMS (Sri Padmavathy Mahila Abyudaya Sangam, a federation of women's Self-Help Groups in Tirupati, Andhra Pradesh) is that poor women should be organized and helped in capacity-building, so that they can solve their own problems" (World Sanitation Program 1999c). The structure of governance of these Indian microfinance organizations (such as Working Women's Forum (WWF), an NGO in

---

[33] Since independence in 1947, Indian associations which champion women's cause have been trying to change existing laws: laws banning widow-immolation or *sati* (1829), enabling Hindu widows to remarry (1856), banning female infanticide (1870) and against child marriage (1891, 1929), and to fight against murdered daughters-in-law (because of inadequate dowry), rape, child labour, girls' prostitution, etc. They recognize favourable Indian legislation but regret its weak application. Besides, as noted above, because of deep-rooted cultural norms, women "prefer" staying married, even if they are beaten, rather than divorcing, which implies being rejected by their family and community (joint family and status of rural Indian women are discussed in Marius-Gnanou 1998).

[34] An NGO in Vadadora (Gujarat), formerly known as Baroda.

Chennai, Tamil Nadu) reflects the philosophy guiding their action. They are classified as "people's organizations" in which full ownership rests with its members. The WWF and the SPMS explicitly claim to be women's organizations created for and by women. Recurring key terms used by Indian microfinance organizations to describe their philosophy are women's empowerment and self-reliance by capacity-building and self-help.

Since the 1970s, the Self Employment Women's Association[35] has been fighting to "serve" the condition of the female workers from the informal sector (small shopkeepers, peddlers, home-workers, etc.[36]) as a labour union registered in 1972. These unsalaried home- or street-workers are "invisible" because their labour and income are ignored by statistics (economical disempowerment). Besides, they do not have their own social status, but are "wife of" or "daughter of" (social disempo-werment). SEWA's main goal is to organize women for full employment (employment providing work security, income security, food security and social security), at the household level and for self-reliance. To achieve these goals, SEWA has chosen an integrated and holistic approach which attempts to strengthen them, to cover the risks they face and to reduce their vulnerability. SEWA has considerably extended its activities, while pursuing the same objective – to improve women's autonomy – and with the same method, widely inspired by Gandhian philosophy. It acts simultaneously on the political, economic, social and cultural planes by articulating local action and institutional change (Hoffman and Marius-Gnanou 2001; Palier 2001). SEWA's strategy involves struggles (against the many injustices women face, for visibility and recognition, for political and economic leadership) and constructive activities by creating employment (production cooperatives), developing financial services (the SEWA Bank was recognized by the Indian banking authorities in 1974), capacity-building training, health and childcare, housing services, insurance, etc. One of these activities concerns educational activities with the SEWA Academy. Its explicit objective is to strengthen women's capacities in collective management and in political action. Political strategy is oriented towards collaboration with public or private institutions, either in specific projects and events (slum upgradation by building drainage and sanitary connections, drought in 1995, etc.)

---

[35] There are many published reports and other types of documentation about SEWA, some of which are included in our references.

[36] See Prügl, Tinker (1997) for a presentation of SEWA as an example of a successful organization which supports home-based workers by combining microentreprise development and union organization.

or in forming partnerships to change existing structures over the long term. At the international level, this association works with the International Labour Organization (ILO); one of its main achievements was the adoption of an ILO convention on home-workers (Krauss and Osner 1999).

Conclusion

Women who "can" have economic independence, in the sense that no law prevents them, may be prevented simply by lacking assets or access to financial services. As Nussbaum (2001: 1) writes, "liberty is not just a matter of having rights on paper, it requires being in a material position to exercise those rights". For this reason, microfinance organizations have an important role to play in the improvement of women's capabilities by offering them real opportunities. Besides, the strong resistance which still exists against women's participation in the market economy is not only unjust but also inefficient. Eliminating this discrimination is indeed not only a question of justice, promoting equality between the sexes, it is also a way to increase national income. There is now overwhelming evidence that women's empowerment, through schooling and employment opportunities among other things, carries a financial and social benefit for all – men, women and children. It has an immediate effect on children's nutritional status, health and development, on the mother's health and on the size of the family. Thus, it is more influential than economic growth in moderating fertility rates and reducing child mortality. For this reason, it cannot be assumed that women's work outside the home would have perverse effects on the well-being of children. On the contrary, as their bargaining power increases within the family, women are more able to plan the family's future and to invest in child health and education. As Nussbaum (1999a: 51) writes, "the disability imposed by childbearing on a member of the labor force is to a large extent socially constructed, above all by the absence of support for childcare, from the public sphere, from employers, and from male partners".

Legal guarantees established by the state, as well as opportunities created by non-governmental organizations, help women to have a real access to certain functionings and do not erode agency. They create "a framework within which people can develop and exercise agency" (Nussbaum 1999a: 19). But the state that proposes to guarantee people's rights effectively has to recognize norms beyond the small menu of basic rights. As Sen (1999) underscores, beyond the rights concerning their well-being, it is crucial to confer on women a role as agents in change.

In order to effectively improve their condition, they should not be passive addressees of reforms pertaining to their status but dynamic initiators of social transformations affecting their existence as well as that of men.

At the same time, local traditions and practices are often complex and interconnected. Changing one rule of conduct inexorably affects the way other institutions work. That is why imposing cultural changes through legislation alone can be very perverse. When inertia and tradition are opposed to social change, the only solution consists in discussion in the public sphere. We agree with Sen when he says that economic and political freedoms are inseparable because the two processes foster one another.

Let us come back to our initial question: given the weight of institutions, usually unfavourable to women's freedom, how far can microfinance help? As we have attempted to show in this chapter, under certain conditions, microfinance may serve as a vehicle for economic and social change. Through its ability to combine economic, social and political opportunities, microfinance may help the access to real freedom. Through its ability to promote local spheres of discussion, microfinance allows the expression and formulation of economic and social needs, their assertion and sometimes their resolution. And these local spheres may contribute to institutional changes more favourable to women, a contribution that consists as much in their participation in the elaboration of public policies as in their ability to introduce change to the collective perception.

However, such a virtuous circle is far from being spontaneous. The political anchoring of microfinance organizations must be explicitly part of the objectives. Microfinance organisations should not only provide financial services but also engage in awareness-raising and encourage links with collective and political actions. New laws and new opportunities for women have to be understood and admitted by them, and perhaps above all by men, to be applied in a way that is not too removed from the initial intention. Microfinance is not blessed with the ability to right the power imbalances which result from inequalities in the way society treats men and women. It may be able to make such a contribution, but it requires a clear commitment and a strategic approach.

REFERENCES

Anolin A.L.C., 2002, *Women and Micro-Finance Programs*, Brighton, Sussex: IDS.

Arendt H., 1958, *The Human Condition*, French translation: *Condition de l'Homme Moderne*, 1961, Paris: Calmann-Lévy.

Balkenhol B., 2001, "L'action du Bureau international en matière de microfinance," in: J-M Servet, D. Vallat (eds), pp. 201–215.

1991, "L'épargne, le crédit et les pauvres: quel rôle pour l'organisation internationale du travail dans le secteur financier?" *Revue Internationale du Travail*, 130, 5–6, pp. 726–740.

Banque Mondiale, 2000, "Gestion du risque social. Cadre théorique de la protection sociale," Document de travail no. 0006 (sur la protection sociale), February, Washington: Banque mondiale.

Baumann E., 2001, "Burkina Faso: heurts et quelques malheurs de la microfinance," in: J-M Servet, D. Vallat (eds), pp. 185–198.

1999, "Société civile et microfinance. Réflexions à partir d'exemples ouest-africains," in: J-M Servet *et al.* (eds), pp. 291–304.

Bayart J.-F., 1989, *L'État en Afrique: la politique du ventre*, Paris: Fayard.

Bennett L. and Cuevas C., 1996, "Sustainable banking with the poor," *Journal of International Development*, 8, 2, pp. 145–152.

Bisilliat J. and Verschuur C. (eds), 2001, *Genre et économie: un premier éclairage*, Paris: l'Harmattan (coll. "Cahiers Genre et développement," AFED – EFI, n°2).

BIT (Bureau International du Travail), BCEAO (Banque centrale des États d'Afrique de l'Ouest), 1999a, "Banque de données sur les systèmes financiers décentralisés 1997–1998," UEMOA, Dakar: OIT.

BIT (Bureau International du Travail), 1999b, "Gender and the access to financial services," International Labour Organization.

Bloy E. and Mayoukou C., 1994, "Analyse du risque et intermédiation de l'épargne en Afrique sub-saharienne," *African Review of Money, Finance and Banking*, 1, 73–95.

Braham M. and Guérin I., 2003, "Microfinance and Bonded Labour. An ILO Project in South-Asia (Bangladesh, India, Nepal, Pakistan)," Report for the ILO (Mid-Term Evaluation of Family Indebtedness with Microfinance Schemes & Related Services (Ras/99/Mo1/Net), January.

Chen M.A. and Snodgrass D., 1999, "An assessment of the impact of SEWA Bank in India: baseline findings," Assessing the Impact of Microenterprise Services, Washington DC: USAID.

Cheston S. and Kuhn L., 2002, *Empowering Women through Microfinance*, Illinois: International Opportunity.

Das Gupta M., Lee S., Uberoi P., Wang D., Wang L. and Zhang X., 2000, "State policies and women's autonomy in China, India and the Republic of Korea," Policy Research Working Paper No. 2497, Washington DC: World Bank, November.

Diarra Doka M., 1998, "Femmes et micro-économie au Niger: le petit crédit," in: Y. Preiswerk (ed), pp. 195–206.

Doligez F., 2002, "Dix ans d'études de l'impact de la microfinance: synthèse de quelques observations de terrain," in: J-M Servet and I. Guérin (eds), pp. 88–112.

Doligez F. and Gentil D., 2001, "Les approches du financement local: une perspective historique," in: J-M Servet and D. Vallat (eds), pp. 185–198.

Doligez F. and Le Bissonnais A., 1996, "Étude bibliographique, Programme régional d'appui aux opérations de crédit décentralisé," *Étude financement et développement*, Paris: Ministère de la Coopération, IRAM, June.

270   *Muriel Gilardone, Isabelle Guérin and Jane Palier*

Eme B. and Laville J.-L. (eds), 1994, *Cohésion sociale et emploi*, Paris: Desclée de Brouwer (coll. "Sociologie économique").

Favreau L. and Fréchette L., 2000, "Économie sociale, coopération Nord/Sud et développement," Cahiers du CRISES, No. 0002.

1999, "Développement communautaire et économie sociale: l'expérience péruvienne de Villa el Salvador," Cahiers du CRISES, No. 9908.

Favreau L. and Tremblay D., 2001, "Conjoncture internationale, société civile, économie sociale et solidaire dans une perspective Nord/Sud," Cahiers du CRISES, No. 0114.

Folbre N., 1986, "Hearts and spades: paradigms of household economics," World Development, 14, 2, 245–255.

Fournier Y. and Ouédraogo L., 1996, "Les coopératives d'épargne et de crédit en Afrique," *Revue Tiers Monde*, XXXVII, 145, January–March, 67–83.

Galbraith J. K., 1979, *The Nature of Mass Poverty*, Cambridge MA: Harvard University Press.

Gentil D., 2002, "Au bord du gouffre," in: J-M Servet, I. Guérin (eds), pp. 40–48.

Geshiere P., 1995, *Sorcellerie et politique: la viande des autres*, Paris: Karthala.

Gilardone M., 2001, "Amartya Sen: le retour à l'esprit éthique de l'économie politique," Mémoire de DEA en sciences économiques, Université Lumière Lyon 2.

2003, "La pensée économique d'Amartya Sen sur le travail," Des économistes et les tâches du présent. Analyse du travail et dialogue des savoirs. Sous la direction de Renato Di Ruzza et Patrick Gianfaldoni. Toulouse: Editions Octarès.

Goetz A.-M. and Gupta R. S., 1996, "Who takes the credit? Gender, power and control over loans use in rural credit programs in Bangladesh," *World Development*, 24, 1, 45–63.

Guérin I., 2003, *Femmes et économie solidaire*, Paris: La Découverte.

2002, "Autonomie féminine et microfinance," Bureau International du Travail, Unité Finance et Solidarité, Document de travail No. 32, September.

Hashemi S., Schuler S. R. and Riley A. P., 1996, "Rural credit programs and women's empowerment in Bangladesh," *World Development*, 24, 1, 635–653.

Hoffman E. and Marius-Gnanou K., 2001, "L'approche genre dans la lutte contre la pauvreté: l'exemple de la microfinance," Communication au Colloque Pauvreté et développement durable, November, Chaire Unesco de l'Université Bordeaux IV.

Innovation et Réseaux pour le développement, 1999, "SEWA," Peuples et Pouvoir. Organisations populaires en marche. Afrique – Amériques – Asie, IRED, Paris: L'Harmattan, pp. 53–111.

International Center for Research on Women, 1999, "Domestic violence in India. A summary report of three studies," Washington DC: ICRW, September.

Kabeer N., 2001, "Conflicts over credit: re-evaluating the empowerment potential of loans to women in rural Bangladesh," *World Development*, 29, 1, 63–84.

Krauss A. and Osner K., 1999, "SEWA – Inde. L'accès au pouvoir et l'expérience de la SEWA," in: IRED, Peuples et pouvoirs. Organisations populaires en marche. Afrique – Amériques – Asie. Paris: L'Harmattan, pp. 49–112.

Labie M., 2002, "De Finansol à Finamerica: quelques leçons d'une crise majeure dans le monde de la microfinance latino-américain," in: J-M Servet, I. Guérin (eds), pp. 49–55.

Lapenu C., 1999, "Le système financier rural indonésien: des liens financiers au service du développement rural," in: J-M Servet *et al.* (eds), pp. 119–129.

Lapenu C. and Zeller M., 2001, "Distribution, growth and performance of microfinance institutions in Africa, Asia and Latin America," FCND Discussion Paper, No. 114, Washington DC: International Food Policy Research Institute, June.

Lecarme M., 1993, "Marchandes à Dakar. Négoce, négociation sociale et rapports sociaux de sexe en milieu urbain précaire," Thèse de doctorat en anthropologie urbaine. École des hautes études en sciences sociales, Paris.

Lecour Grandmaison C., 1970, *Femmes dakaroises*. Paris: Éditions du CNRS.

McGuire P. and Conroy J.-D., 1997, "Partenariats banques – ONG et coût du crédit collectif aux populations pauvres: exemples de l'Inde et des Philippines," in: H. Schneider (ed), *Microfinance pour les pauvres*, Paris: FIDA/OCDE, pp. 79–94.

Marie A., 1995 (ed), *L'Afrique des individus*, Paris: Karthala.

Marius-Gnanou K., 1998, "L'impact des programmes de développement économique sur les femmes en milieu rural – Le cas de l'Inde," in: Y. Preiswerk (ed), pp. 73–97.

Mayoux L., 1999, "Microfinance and the empowerment of women. A review of the key issue," Working Paper No. 22, International Labour Organisation.

Mill J. S., 1975, *L'asservissement des femmes* [*Subordination of Women*, 1869], trad. et préface M.-F. Cachin, Paris: Petite Bibliothèque Payot.

Morduch J., 1999, "The microfinance promise," *Journal of Economic Literature*, XXXVII, December, 1569–1614.

Morduch J. and Haley B., 2002, "Analysis of the effects of microfinance on poverty reduction", NYU Wagner Working Paper No. 1014.

Mosley P. and Hulme D., 1996, *Finance Against Poverty. Volume 1*, London and New York: Routledge.

National Institute for Working Life, 2000, "Child care, domestic services, employment and gender inequality" (www.niwl.se/wl2000/workshop23/article_en.asp).

Nussbaum M. C., 2001, *Women and Human Development. The Capabilities Approach*, rev. edn., Cambridge University Press.

2000, "Women and work – the capability approach," *The Little Magazine* (www.Littlemag.com/2000/Martha2.htm).

1999a, *Sex and Social Justice*, Oxford University Press.

1999b, "Special issue: women, gender and work," *International Labour Review*, 138, 3.

1992, "Human functioning and social justice: in defense of Aristotelian essentialism," *Political Theory*, 20, 2, 202–246.

Nussbaum M. C. and Sen A. K. (eds), 1993, *The Quality of Life*, Oxford: Clarendon Press.

Olivier de Sardan J.-P., 1995, "Anthropologie et développement," Essai en socio-anthropologie du changement social, Paris/Marseille: Karthala/APAD.

Palier J., 2003, "Définition et mesure de l'empowerment appliquées au champ de la microfinance en Inde," in: I. Guérin and J.-M. Servet (eds), pp. 513–534.

Palier J., 2002, "La microfinance en Inde: des pratiques d'économie solidaire," in: J.-M. Servet and I. Guérin (eds), pp. 67–87.

Palier J., 2001, "Les pratiques urbaines de microfinance indienne: de l'efficacité à la pérennité," Mémoire de DEA de sciences économiques, Université Lumière Lyon 2.

Preiswerk Y. (ed), 1998, *Les silences pudiques de l'économie*, Geneva: IUED/ UNESCO.

Prügl E. and Tinker I., 1997, "Microentrepreneurs and homeworkers: convergent categories," *World Development*, 25, 9, 1471–1482.

Puhazhendhi V. and Satyasai K. J. S., 2000, "Micro finance for rural people. An impact evaluation," National Bank of Agriculture and Rural Development.

Rahman A., 1999, "Microcredit initiatives for equitable and sustainable development: who pays?" *World Development*, 27, 1, 67–82.

Reveyrand-Coulon O., 1993, "Les énoncés féminins de l'Islam," in: J.-F. Bayart (ed), *La réinvention du capitalisme*, Paris: Karthala, pp. 62–100.

Ryckmas H., 2001, "Les associations féminines en Afrique: une décennie d'ajustement après la décennie de la femme," in: J. Bisilliat and C. Verschuur (eds), pp. 195–221.

Sarr F., 1998, *L'entrepreneuriat féminin au Sénégal. La transformation des rapports de pouvoirs*, Paris: L'Harmattan.

Schrieder G. and Sharma M., 1999, "Impact of poverty reduction," *Savings and Development*, 1, XXIII, 67–93.

Sekher M., 2001, "Public space for women in governance: the experience of India," *Newsletter of the Center for Research on Women and Politics*, 1, 2, 3 (www.crfp-rcwp.uottawa.ca/bulletine.htm).

Self-Employed Women's Association, 2000, *Annual Report*, Ahmedabad: SEWA.

Sen A. K., 2000a, *Repenser l'inégalité* [*Inequality Reexamined*, 1992], trad. P. Chelma, Paris: Seuil.

2000b, *Un nouveau modèle économique. Développement, justice, liberté* [*Development as Freedom*, 1999], trad. M. Bessières, Paris: Odile Jacob.

1999, *L'économie est une science morale*, textes choisis et trad. M. Saint Upéry. Paris: La Découverte (coll. "Cahiers libres").

1993, *Éthique et économie* [*On Ethics and Economics*, 1987], trad. S. Marnat. Paris: PUF (coll. "Philosophie morale").

1991, *On Ethics and Economics*, Oxford: Blackwell Publishers.

1984, *Resources, Values and Development*, Cambridge, MA: Harvard University Press.

1973, *On Economic Inequality*, Oxford University Press.

Servet J.-M., 1997, "Les limites du partenariat dans la mise en place et le développement de systèmes financiers décentralisés au Sud – Modèle démocratique du marché versus hiérarchie," in: *Rapport moral sur l'argent dans le Monde 1997*, Paris: AEF/Montchrestien, pp. 399–416.

Servet J.-M. and Guérin I. (eds), 2002, *Rapport du Centre Walras 2002. Exclusion et liens financiers*, Paris: Economica.

Servet J.-M. and Vallat D., (eds), 2001, *Rapport du Centre Walras 2001. Exclusion et liens financiers*, Paris: Economica.

(eds), 1998, *Rapport du Centre Walras 1997. Exclusion et liens financiers*, Paris: AEF/Monchrestien.

Servet J.-M., Blanc J., Guérin I. and Vallat D. (eds), 1999, *Rapport exclusion et liens financiers 1998–1999*, Paris: Economica.

Simanovitz A. and Walter A., 2002, "Reaching the poorest while building financially self-sufficient institutions, and showing improvement in the lives of the poorest women and their families," in: S. Daley-Harris (ed), *Pathways Out of Poverty: Innovations in Microfinance for the Poorest Families*, Bloomfield, CT: Kumarian Press, pp. 1–74.

Stiglitz J. E., 1990, "Peer monitoring and credit market," *World Bank Economic Review*, 4, 351–366.

Vallat D., 1999, "Exclusion et liens financiers de proximité (financement de micro-activités)," Thèse de doctorat en sciences économiques, Université Lumière Lyon 2.

Waring M., 1993, *Counting For Nothing, What Men Value and What Women are Worth*, Wellington: Bridget Williams Books.

World Sanitation Program, 1999a, Baroda Citizens Council, Water and Sanitation Program of the UNDP and World Bank – South Asia Region.

1999b, SEWA Bank, Water and Sanitation Program of the UNDP and World Bank – South Asia Region.

1999c, Sri Padmavathy Mahila Abyudaya Sangam, Water and Sanitation Program of the UNDP and World Bank – South Asia Region.

Zeller M. and Sharma M., 1998, *Rural Finance and Poverty Alleviation*, Washington DC: International Food Policy Research Institute.

10 The capabilities of women: towards an alternative framework for development*

Santosh Mehrotra

One of the principal reasons why the capabilities approach has gained ground in recent years, at least among some development economists, is that the approach has tended to place human beings and their well-being at the centre of its concerns. A related reason for the attraction of the capability approach to development theorists should be that it places the capabilities of women up-front and centre, for their intrinsic as well as instrumental value.

Amartya Sen's and Martha C. Nussbaum's work has been critical to the latter phenomena. Nussbaum's main project is to work out the grounding for basic political principles to which their citizens should hold all nations. Her project leads her to identify *central human capabilities*.[1] She adopts the principle of each person as an end, and the principle of each person's capability. Since women have normally been treated as the supporters of the ends of others, rather than as ends in their own right, this principle has particular force in regard to women's lives.

Like Nussbaum's own approach, this chapter also uses a normative framework that is universal. Like her objective, the goal of this chapter is also to influence public policy; although, unlike her, the goal is to specifically recommend an approach to an alternative development strategy for developing countries, the cornerstone of which is gender equality. The chapter attempts to answer one main question: why should good development give priority to the well-being and agency of women, and one subsidiary question, what does Nussbaum (in contrast to mainstream economics) provide (and not provide) to help answer that question? While our answer to the subsidiary question emerges later in the chapter, our answers to the main question are essentially two. The first

---

* This chapter was a paper presented at a conference of the Capability Network, at St Edmund's College, University of Cambridge, 9–12 September 2002. Thanks are due to Flavio Comim, Martha C. Nussbaum, Tanni Mukhopadhyay, Enrique Delamonica and two anonymous referees for very useful comments.
[1] See Nussbaum, 2001, pp. 78–80 for her list of central human capabilities.

argument is that without targeting gender equality, any development strategy is bound to fail – in a way that was not necessary at a comparable stage of development in the now industrialised countries. In other words, gender inequality could continue to persist, as it does today, in the now industrialised countries through the entire period of the structural transformation in Western Europe. It argues, however, that there could be no similar transformation without a direct attack on most forms of gender discrimination and inequality in developing countries.

The second answer is that a capability-driven theoretical framework – which explicitly recognises the centrality of women's agency – must inform the policy framework in order to trigger the synergies between economic growth, income-poverty reduction and health/education improvements that presumably are the goal of development theorists and practitioners of *all* persuasions. This alternative theoretical framework also tries to establish why the capabilities and agency of women – and their determinants – are far more central to this transformation than mainstream economists care to recognise, partly because of mainstream economics' inability to recognise the gender dimensions of intra-household dynamics.

Why is gender equality central to the structural transformation in developing countries?

This section of the chapter explores why women's autonomy is so central to the structural transformation of developing countries – or at least a hastening of the transformation in a way that was less fundamental to an earlier transformation in the West. The rationale derives primarily from the dire need to hasten the demographic transition in the developing world.

It is first important to establish why this is necessary by comparing the population increase in Europe and North America over the first century (1800–1900) of the industrial revolution with that in developing countries as they attempted a similar revolution in the twentieth century. In 1800 the world's population was 906 million; by 1900 it had not even doubled, to 1608 million. Similarly, in Europe, where the industrial revolution began in the first quarter of the nineteenth century, the population was 185 million in 1800, and had only doubled to 400 million in 1900, over the first century of the industrial revolution. However, over the next century, when developing countries were attempting their own industrial revolution, populations multiplied several-fold: from 62 million in 1900 in Latin America to 480 million in 1995; from 118 million in Africa to 732 million; and from 937 million in Asia to 3458 million. Thus there is a considerable difference here between what the North experienced during its industrial revolution and what the South has faced, in terms of a population explosion in comparable periods in their development. The relatively slow growth of population in Europe (and North America) over the first century of the industrial revolution enabled per capita income to rise in a secular manner. However, that was not universally the experience of the developing regions, or most countries in most developing regions in the twentieth century. Hence, without women being able to control their reproductive life, which would bring down population growth rates, the likelihood of the structural transformation occurring in developing countries within the next half-century looks bleak.

By the structural transformation we do not imply here that the South should replicate the exact pattern and level of development that the North experienced in the twentieth century. That, in any case, is inconceivable for at least one very important reason (among many others). The richest one-fifth of mankind – including wealthy minorities in poor countries – consumes energy and resources at such a high rate that providing a comparable lifestyle to the rest of the world's population would require the resources of four planets the size of earth. However, with structural transformation, first, significant growth in industrial and corresponding service sector output is necessary (and with it an alteration in the structure of employment between primary, secondary and tertiary activities). Its second connotation – per capita income growth – should occur simultaneously, driven by more productive (relative to agriculture) sectors within industry/services, but that is stemmed by high fertility and women's lack of control over their reproductive rights.

Yet it was per capita economic growth that stalled over the last two decades of the twentieth century for a large group of countries, after the Golden Age of income growth between 1950 and 1973 during which both developed and developing country economic growth was rapid by historical standards. Except for a minority of countries in East, South and South East Asia, the majority of developing countries are further away from their expected structural transformation than a quarter of a century ago. Underlying phenomena behind slow per capita income growth – which could be explained by domestic and international policy failures – are beyond the scope of this chapter, but the development paradigm influenced by mainstream economics is certainly part of the explanation (as we discuss in the following section).

The reproductive rights of women are central to the other side of the coin of *per capita* income growth. Lower fertility in most households, especially the poorest ones, is a necessary condition of the transformation. In the now industrialised countries, the demographic transition occurred without any dramatic changes in the position of women in society (though there were indeed some changes).[2]

In fact, it is remarkable that the demographic transition in Western Europe occurred despite the absence of modern methods of contraception, which is one important source of freedom for women in patriarchal societies where decisions about women's reproductive rights usually are taken by men. But the existence of modern contraception cannot be translated into women's freedom without broader societal changes. There is evidence from history that gender inequality may persist despite the occurrence of a demographic transition. Thus the transition in Western Europe occurred despite ineffective contraception methods, high maternal mortality, continuing domestic drudgery for women and their limited access to income.

Modern methods of contraception may have created the conditions for hastening and facilitating the demographic transition in developing countries. However, the existence of the means of contraception does not necessarily translate into control over reproductive rights of women. Establishing gender equality is essential to the behavioural change necessary to lowering birth rates and hastening the demographic transition in developing countries.

The growth rate of populations is determined by two kinds of trends, one at the macro-level (the overall population) and another at a micro-level (within the household) (Ray, 2000). At the macro-level, developing countries in particular have large youthful populations. As the share of the young in total population is large, as the young enter reproductive age they will keep birth rates high, even with the most effective family planning programme in place. This puts the phenomenon of birth control somewhat outside the pale of policy-makers. However, there is another inertia at the household level, which is subject to policy manipulation. Poor households tend to have more children, as children are a substitute for the absence of institutions such as old-age pension and social security. The 'children for old-age security' argument, in a situation where the probability of children dying in infancy or under the age of five is high, leads to parents over-compensating by having more children than they really 'need'. Another reason that keeps birth rates high is son-preference, since social norms imply that the son looks after the parents in old age. At low levels of income, the prospect for

---

[2] Thus, women gained the right to vote, as the franchise expanded in Western Europe and North America. Voting rights in the earlier years were based on property, and were confined to those with certain levels of income, and also to male adults.

governments providing old-age security to offset the incentives that lead to high fertility is limited. This underlines the need for behavioural change. In this context, the tendency of mainstream microeconomics to treat the household as a homogeneous entity (with no difference between sexes in intra-household power relations) is particularly misplaced since behavioural change, which reduces fertility, implies improvement in the bargaining position of the women in the household, and also a decline in son-preference.

We have already suggested that populations grew much more slowly in Europe than in developing countries during comparable periods of their development. Why was this the case? Let us take a moment to digress into the divergent nature of the demographic transition in developed and developing countries, which would highlight our argument that achieving gender equality *now* is central to the enterprise of the structural transformation of developing countries in the future.

The first phase of the demographic transition everywhere, with very slow population growth from the beginning of settled agriculture, was characterised by high death and birth rates. The advent of settled agriculture enabled the carrying capacity of the earth to rise, and population to grow, but as Malthus (1798) wrote, population growth was checked by plague, pestilence, war and famine. Hence population grew only slowly in this first phase.

Soon after Malthus wrote, with the advent of sanitation, the increase in agricultural productivity and the rise in industrial productivity, Europe's population increased gradually. As death rates declined, birth rates rose during this second phase. However, this second phase was quite extended in Europe (unlike in developing countries). The fall in the death rate in Europe was relatively gradual, driven by the heuristic processes of innovation.[3] The improved production of food, the institution of sanitation methods, and the understanding of and control over disease produced by medical advances all had to be discovered and invented. There was no pre-existing stock of knowledge to be transferred, as there was in the case of developing countries (which sent death rates plummeting and population growth soaring).

Also, during this second phase, birth rates in Europe never reached levels that we see in developing countries for several reasons, including

---

[3] Szreter (1996) rightly notes that awareness among the elites was important to improvements in sanitation and housing by the end of the nineteenth century. It was not an automatic process driven simply by processes of innovation. There was a strong human element with the creation of schools and hospitals. Reasons of space preclude further discussion here.

norms of late marriage in many European countries and the provision of social security (which 'compensated' for children as a means of security). The late marriages might have been induced by the expansion of schooling rapidly through the latter half of the nineteenth century (as literacy reached 90 per cent around 1900 and elementary schooling was universalised). The fall in birth rates may have resulted also as women increasingly entered the labour force starting the last quarter of the nineteenth century in Europe.[4] Further, the introduction of social security from the middle of the nineteenth century onwards in Europe induced a behavioural change that led to fertility decline.[5] Cigno and Rosati (1996) find a close relationship between the introduction of social security and the fertility decline in Germany, the UK and the US.[6]

In the third phase of the transition, birth rates fell slowly, in part due to a greater carrying capacity made possible by technical progress. In other words, the decline in both death rates and birth rates was slow in Europe.

Thus the single most important fact of the demographic transition in Europe and North America was its protracted nature, and the time span of centuries compensated for the relatively low net growth rate. In fact, developing countries experienced a decline in death rates that was widespread and sudden in the first few decades after independence from colonial rule in Asia and Africa. Meanwhile, birth rates grew rapidly, in the absence of formal old-age pension, a lack of widespread education for girls, and continuing early marriage. As a result, population grew rapidly during the second phase of the demographic transition.

Most developing countries have entered the third phase of a declining death and birth rate, but there is little doubt that the carrying capacity of the earth is being stretched to the limit.[7] There is a vicious cycle of

[4] Women's entry into the labour force replaced children in the labour force in the latter half of the nineteenth century. However, until then, data for England 1790–1865 show that children's contributions to the family budget were always greater than those of mothers; the findings are similar for the US and four European countries (Belgium, France, Germany, Switzerland) (Cunningham and Viazzo, 1996).

[5] One could argue that providing social security and old-age pensions in contemporary developing countries of South Asia, Africa and Latin America would lower fertility and thus substitute for gender equality. But social security has immediate fiscal costs that are not inconsiderable when most employment is in the informal sector, and hence governments are unwilling to bear such fiscal costs. Hence there is an added need to focus on gender equality as a means of hastening the demographic transition.

[6] Cigno and Rosati (1992) similarly found that three-quarters of the fertility decline in Italy – which was a late industrialiser in Europe – between 1930 and 1985 can be attributed to the extension of pension coverage.

[7] For example, the amount of fresh water available to each person in 1950 was 17000 cubic metres. In 1995, this had declined to 7000 cubic metres, and it is now going down so fast that up to 1 billion people will experience 'high water stress' by 2020, and water could replace oil as the world's leading source of conflict.

population growth, poverty and environmental degradation (PPE) that has been in place for several decades in most developing countries (Cleaver and Schreiber, 1994). Nussbaum's excellent work on women's capabilities does not take into account these historical differences between the demographic transitions of the now-industrialised and still developing countries. However, these differences are critical for underlining the importance of gender equality to the policy project of hastening the demographic transition and the economic transformation of most developing countries (outside of East Asia). Meanwhile, the vicious cycle continues.

If the vicious PPE cycle is to be broken, and a virtuous cycle is to be triggered, two sets of synergies need to be set in motion – and gender equality is central to those synergies. It is to these two synergies that we turn our attention later. However, mainstream economics suffers from too many conceptual weaknesses for it to be the basis of our dual synergy model. These weaknesses are discussed in the following section and in discussing these we essentially follow Nussbaum and Sen, but also others who have been critical of the mainstream economics understanding of intra-household dynamics.

Mainstream economics, utilitarianism and gender

'We have to grapple with the sad fact that contemporary economics has not yet put itself onto the map of conceptually respectable theories of human action' (Nussbaum, 2001, p. 122). It takes a philosopher to remind economists at the beginning of a new millennium that a profession that has existed for over two centuries still lacks theories of human action that are credible. This section examines only one critique of mainstream economics: its notion of the family.

With Milton Friedman (1953) one would agree that positive economics can and should, like other social sciences, be simple and that its assumptions should not in all respects correspond to the complex phenomenology of human action in real life. However, Nussbaum (2000) rightly questions whether the assumptions of positive economics are 'too crude, so over simple' that they fail to pick out those elements of the real world that are most important for predictive purposes.

Sen (1974) subjected the utilitarian treatment of people as self-interested maximisers of utility to several criticisms. Among the many, a salient one was that between the claims of oneself and the claims of all lay the claims of many groups – families, friends, communities, peer groups, and economic and social classes. Such groups provide the focus of many individual actions involving commitment. For women, for example, a most important such group is the family. In fact, it is surprising that Nussbaum does not make intellectual capital of the multiple commitments of women, particularly in their relations with the family. Nussbaum is right in cogently arguing that women's care giving, their love and care, is socially constructed – in the sense that it is shaped by history, custom and law – and that women's propensity to give love and care is not 'by nature'. She is also right in arguing that while love and care do exist in families, so too do domestic violence, marital rape, undernutrition of girls, unequal health care, unequal educational opportunities, and so on.

However, women's care giving is a powerful basis for placing the centre of gravity of public policy around precisely this dimension of the family. As argued in the final section, in poor households, when resources are scarce, this commitment of the mother is a powerful force working in favour of the well-being of all. In fact, women's care giving is an essential ingredient in our argument for placing women at the centre of an alternative framework for development strategy.

The cause of gender equality in development economics has not been fostered by the fact that traditional micro-economics tends to treat the household as a homogeneous entity, without regard to, or recognition of, the often unequal allocation of resources within the household that occurs – especially, but not only, in developing countries. Hence there is a need in development theory and practice to further recognise the dynamics of intra-household resource allocation and power.

Thus Nussbaum rightly takes to task a variant on the utilitarian approach to quality of life assessment – Gary Becker's model of the family. Becker not only thinks of the goal of the family as a unit of maximisation of utility but also that utility (or satisfaction of preference or desire) is a relevant unit to compare families' well-being. More importantly, he believes the family is being held together by motives of altruism. The model has been highly influential. Nussbaum notes that the model is an inadequate basis for normative thinking as it is not individualistic enough; it does not examine people as individuals, and how each one may be doing. To the extent that women adapt their preferences to that required by the head of the household, it underlines that preferences are totally unreliable as a guide to social choice and especially justice.

There is no doubt that new bargaining models of the family do attempt to reflect reality better.[8] Dasgupta (1993), Deaton (1997), Elson (1995)

---

[8] Although Nussbaum cites Dasgupta (1993) as a good example of such a bargaining model of the household, it is still interesting that the latter's study relies consistently on the notion of utility as well as Pareto-optimal solutions in the bargaining process.

and Ghosh and Kanbur (2008) are good examples.[9] Or, for instance, Kanbur and Haddad (1994) investigate the implications of intra-household bargaining models for the behaviour of intra-household inequality as a function of total household resources. They find theoretical support for Kuznets effects, i.e. a systematic pattern of inequality change as the total household resources increase. Discussing some policy implications of this relationship, in particular, the authors find that bargaining models tend to lead to a greater emphasis on targeting to disadvantaged members of a household.

Bargaining models that treat persons as the target of concern, rather than households, are clearly the way forward if equality between the sexes within the household is to become the object of public policy. Traditional economics has indeed made much progress in this area. The question may be: why has more progress not been made? Perhaps because mainstream work is based on utilitarian foundations (with all their limitations), we need to use the capabilities approach to further our understanding of the centrality of gender equality within the family, and in general for the promotion of development.

The two synergies – an alternative conceptual approach to development strategy

As we suggested earlier, mainstream economics is insufficient as a heuristic device to allow us to understand the main intricacies and complexities concerning gender as part of development strategy. Mainstream economics, with its theoretical foundations in utilitarianism, and its limited success so far in unbundling the family and examining intra-household allocation of resources, has been the basis for much of public policy in both macro-economic and social areas. The application of such policies has demonstrably contributed to slower economic growth in the last two decades in developing countries, and to worsening inequality in income distribution in a majority of countries (Cornia, 2004). Therefore

---

[9] Ghosh and Kanbur (2008) show how an apparently welfare-improving phenomenon like an increase in the wage of the male member of a family can result in a seemingly paradoxical result where the entire family is worse off. There is male and female specialisation in activities such that the female member is involved in a community-level public good. A rise in the male wage leads to adjustment of household time allocation, with the male working more in the market and less on household activities. In turn, the female works more on household activities and less on the community public good, failing to internalise the negative externality imposed on other members of the community. Under quite general conditions the implied negative effect can more than offset the positive effect of the male wage raise, and the entire family is worse off. The theoretical results are consistent with empirical findings in the literature.

there is need for an alternative framework for development, which is founded on human development and the capability approach.[10]

The work of Amartya Sen, Martha C. Nussbaum and others on human capability (Nussbaum, 2001; Sen, 1985, 1995) resulted in the gradual emergence of a human development paradigm – partly manifested in the Human Development Reports (of UNDP) and the much used composite index of ranking countries, the Human Development Index (HDI). In fact, 'human development' became an overly popular term after 1990 – popular even with the IFIs, which reorganised departments and now called some of them human development networks. However, the consensus within which the term 'human development' was used was a neo-liberal, Washington-based Consensus. For the adherents of the Consensus, the term human development (HD) was used, but the theory underlying it was human capital (HC) theory,[11] not the capability approach that gave birth to the term. The critique of economic growth as a measure of development success predates the emergence of the HD paradigm by at least three decades;[12] the IFIs did not subscribe to that critique. Yet the term 'human development' has been appropriated by all and sundry.

An alternative framework for policies is necessary as the theoretical basis of the Washington Consensus is weak, and as the philosophical foundation of the theory on which it is based is even weaker. Moreover, the result of Consensus-based policies has been that growth did not improve after liberalisation and the rate of progress in social indicators declined. The rest of this chapter is devoted to spelling out that alternative framework.

In this alternative framework, we posit that two kinds of synergies exist. One exists between interventions in health, nutrition, family planning, water and sanitation and basic education. The other is between interventions that are the basis of income growth, the reduction of income-poverty and improved health and educational status. The first synergy is actually a sub-set of the second. With these two synergies as

---

[10] The post-Washington Consensus that has emerged in the wake of Stiglitz's critique of IMF–World Bank policies is not, we believe, an alternative framework. That discussion is, however, outside the scope of this chapter. For a discussion, see Fine et al. (2001), Mehrotra and Delamonica (2007) and Standing (2001) for a critique of the post-Washington Consensus.

[11] The work of Gary Becker was particularly influential in the evolution of human capital theory. For a statement of the adherence of the IFIs to human capital theory, see World Bank (1986, 1999). For a critique of human capital theory, see Fine et al. (2001), Mehrotra (2005).

[12] The reference here is to the literature associated with the basic needs approach, espoused by the ILO, and supported by a body of academic literature.

foundations, we propose an alternative approach to integrate economic and social policies. As a theoretical construct the notion of dual synergies is a conceptual framework for understanding a given situation in terms of human development outcomes (as we shall see below); it is, at the same time, a framework for drawing policy implications.[13] And women's well-being and their agency are the cornerstones of our alternative framework. They are central to both synergies that constitute this alternative theoretical framework.

In any economic analysis it is important to distinguish the means from the ends. We suggest that the state has a critical role to play in ensuring all three desirable *ends* or outcomes for its citizens: economic growth, income-poverty reduction and improved health and education outcomes. The *means* for achieving these ends – the policies – are not discussed here for reasons of space. The policies that derive from this dual synergy theoretical construct are quite distinct from the policies proposed by the Washington Consensus (and are discussed at length in Mehrotra and Delamonica, 2007).

The discussion in the rest of this section proceeds at a macro-economic level rather than at the level of the individual. It is important that this is clear from the beginning, because at the level of the individual, economic growth (defined as increases in per capita income) is a means to an end: human capability. In our model, human capability of the individual is the ultimate end, but in terms of the dynamic of the model, the processes that lead to enhanced human capabilities are the result of larger macro-economic processes – over which the state and its agents have dominant control.

The synergy among social services and the centrality of gender equality

Interventions in health, nutrition, water and sanitation, fertility control, education and income complement each other, and thus increase the impact of any one from investments in any other – this is the first synergy that policy-makers must trigger. For instance, control of diarrhoea and measles is very important not only for health outcomes but also in reducing malnutrition (by improving the capacity to absorb and retain caloric intake). This means that improved water and sanitation also contribute substantially to achieving desirable health and nutritional outcomes. Similarly, fertility control, by providing easy access to contraceptive means, enables the mother to space births, thus lowering the health risk to herself and the child, thus reducing infant and maternal

---

[13] For a discussion of the dual synergies as a framework of analysis, see Taylor *et al.* 1997.

Social services inputs/ processes	Human development outcomes/outputs				
	Knowledge	Family size	Health status	Nutritional status	Healthy living conditions
Education		↵	↵	↵	↵
Family Planning	↵				
Health	↵	↵		↵	↵
Nutrition	↵	↵	↵		
Water & Sanitation					

Figure 10.1 Education and health feedback effects
Source: Mehrotra and Delamonica (2007)

mortality, and improving not merely survival chances but the development prospects of the child.

In positive economics these interactions are merely referred to as externalities. However, the notion of externalities does not capture the feedback loops that are implied in the notion of synergies. The feedback loops are particularly significant when they enhance the capabilities of the principal care givers, women, in the household, since those affect the capabilities of the entire household, particularly children.

Figure 10.1 represents this notion of the first synergy, i.e. within basic service interventions. On the horizontal rows the various social services are represented as inputs or interventions – education, family planning, health, nutrition and water and sanitation. The vertical columns represent the human development outcomes or outputs – knowledge, family size, health status, nutrition status, and healthy living conditions. The shaded cells are the ones where there is a relationship between a certain intervention and an outcome, e.g. the use of contraception, by helping the spacing of children, benefits the health status of both the mother and the child. The arrows represent feedback effects from human development outcomes to the inputs/processes. For example, the improved health status of a child improves her ability to learn, just as improved nutritional status does. Similarly, reduced family size improves the chances that a poor family will be able to afford education for all the children rather than merely the boy(s) in the family, and so on.

Note that educational inputs have an impact on all types of human development outcomes. Basic education facilitates the rapid adoption of improved hygienic behaviour (Cochrane 1979, 1988; World Bank, 1996). In turn, safe water and adequate sanitation play a fundamental role in determining health outcomes. By reducing morbidity from infectious diseases, especially diarrhoea, safe water and sanitation improve the nutritional status of children and their learning abilities (Behrman and Deolalikar, 1995). Another effect of better access to water takes place through the reduced effort in carrying water, which is usually unduly borne by women and girls – making more time available for infant and child care, attending school and productive activities.

Another important complementary outcome of intervention in health, education, water/sanitation and family planning is the rapid demographic transition. As children survive, families voluntarily curtail the numbers of children. This is not the place to enter the debate on the relative impact of supply of contraceptives versus desired family size in family planning (Bongaarts, 1994; Cassen, 1994; Pritchett, 1994). However, it is clear that lower infant and child mortality plays a major role in reducing fertility rates (Caldwell, 1992). So do education and the availability of information on and access to reproductive health care.

Figure 10.2 also illustrates this synergy between interventions within the social sectors by presenting the feedback loop in the form of a life cycle of an educated girl, with an inter-generational impact represented by the boxes at the bottom of the diagram. An educated girl is likely to marry later than a girl who remains without any education – this is especially true if the girl's education extends to at least junior secondary level and she engages in economic activity outside the home.[14] Also, an educated girl will have fewer children, will seek medical attention sooner for herself and her children, and is likely to provide better care and nutrition for herself and her children (Carnoy, 1992). This would reduce the probability of morbidity through disease and hence improve the survival chances of her children beyond the age of five. At this point, the effects pass from having significance only mainly at the household level to a societal level. Over time, the survival of the educated girl's children will change the behavioural pattern of the family in respect of fertility and contraception, thus lowering the overall fertility rate. Smaller household size improves the care of children, and lower fertility reduces the size of the school-age population – demonstrating how the dynamic plays out at the individual or household level, with macro-social

---

[14] For evidence, see data in India's National Family and Health Survey II, 1998–99 (IIPS, 2000).

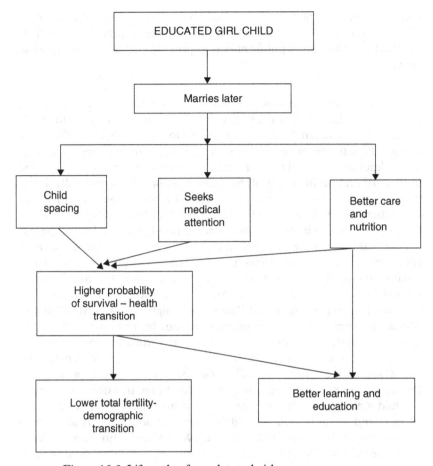

Figure 10.2 Life cycle of an educated girl

impacts. These benefits of girls' education accrue from generation to generation. In other words, in order to maximise the complementarities among basic social services, it is crucial to focus on universal primary education early on, particularly for girls – but it also assumes that health/family planning/water and sanitation services are available (UNICEF, 2000).

In summary, each intervention has ramifications that lie outside its 'sector' and this adds up to a virtuous circle of social and economic development. Markets alone would not ensure universal access – hence the need for the public sector to step in. However, there is widespread government failure in the provision of the financing and provision of basic services.[15] In fact, without collective voice and collective action by the community to put pressure on local governments, there is little prospect of coordinated public action to provide effective access to basic services.[16]

The organic link in the nutritional status of women and children We have suggested above that the well-being of women is critical to the well-being of the entire family, and by extension to the well-being of the entire nation. This is particularly true in developing countries, where gender inequalities in every indicator of human development are rampant.[17] The nutritional and health status of the entire population is organically determined by the nutritional status of women qua women, not just in their role as mothers. There could be no better way of understanding the importance of synergies of interventions (or correspondingly, the lack of them).

Half of the world's malnourished children are to be found in just three countries – Bangladesh, India and Pakistan. Of the seven declared nuclear states in the world, the latter two account for more under-nourished children than any other country in the world. In fact, the child malnutrition rates in India and Pakistan are higher than in Sub-Saharan Africa on average. Child malnutrition cannot be reversed as the child grows into adolescence and adulthood; in other words, lay policy-makers should think twice before dismissing the phenomenon of child malnutrition as something confined to childhood: malnutrition is both a symptom and a cause of poverty – and the inter-generational transfer of poverty.[18]

Child malnutrition has life-long implications. Malnutrition often starts *in utero* and extends well into adolescent and adult life. It also spans generations. First, low-birthweight (LBW) infants who have suffered intra-uterine growth retardation as foetuses are born under-nourished. They are at a far higher risk of dying in the neonatal period or later infancy. If they survive, they are unlikely to catch up on this lost growth and have a higher probability of suffering a variety of developmental deficits. Second, during infancy and early childhood, infections and

---

[15] For a detailed analysis of government failure in the financing and provision of basic services, and successful policy responses, see Mehrotra and Delamonica (2007), Chapter 6.

[16] For a discussion of why mere democracy is not sufficient, and an extension of Sen's ideas on democracy and capabilities, see Mehrotra (2008).

[17] For evidence on these gender inequalities, see Human Development Report 1995 and UNIFEM (2000).

[18] Moreover, poverty incidence can in fact be lower than child malnutrition incidence (as, for example, in India, where child malnutrition runs at 46 per cent of the child population (2006), while the Government of India's Planning Commission estimates poverty incidence at only 26 per cent (2005)).

insufficient intake of nutrients exacerbate the effects of foetal growth retardation. Most growth faltering, resulting in underweight and stunting, occurs from before birth until about two years of age – the effects of which continue. Underweight children tend to have more severe illnesses, including diarrhoea and pneumonia.

Third, in adolescence a second period of rapid growth may serve as a window of opportunity for compensating for early childhood growth failure. However, the potential for significant catch-up at this time is limited. Also, even if the adolescent catches up on some lost growth, the effects of early childhood malnutrition on cognitive development and behaviour may not be fully corrected. 'A stunted girl is thus most likely to become a stunted adolescent and later a stunted woman. Apart from direct effects on health and productivity, adult stunting and underweight increase the chance that her children will be born with low birth weight. And so the cycle continues' (UN ACC/SCN, 2000).

If malnutrition begins *in utero*, then one evidence we get is from the birthweight of the infant. The first cause of the high malnutrition rates in South Asia is the high proportion of infants who are born with low birthweight. South Asia has the world's worst child malnutrition rates, far worse than in Africa (see Figure 10.3). At the same time, as Figure 10.4 shows, the incidence of low birthweight is highest in South Asia, compared with any other region in the world. Nearly a third of Bangladeshi and Indian children and a quarter of Pakistani children are born with low birthweight.

Why is the incidence of low birthweight so high for babies born in South Asia? Low birthweight of babies is essentially an indicator of the nutritional status of mothers. Simply put, small mothers give birth to small babies.[19] In addition, the weight that mothers are supposed to put on during pregnancy in South Asia is lower than what is required for the healthy growth of the child. Thus, during pregnancy, the average woman should gain about 10 kilos in weight. While most women in Africa gain nearly that much weight, most women in South Asia gain around 5 kilos only (WHO, 1995) – a fundamental reason why, despite having higher child mortality, Africa has lower child malnutrition rates. In other words, the baby's nutritional status at birth is a direct outcome of the woman's nutritional status.

---

[19] The fact that Japanese women of the pre-1960s generation were, like Indian women, quite small had inter-generational effects. However, since Japan eliminated malnutrition in the first few decades after the Second World War, the inter-generational handicap has disappeared, with the average height of Japanese men and women having increased tremendously.

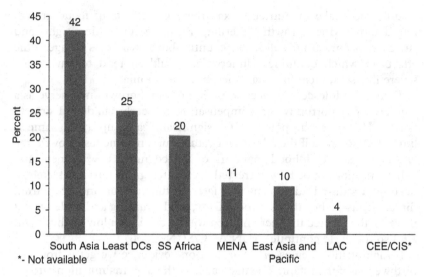

Figure 10.3 Malnutrition rates by regions – under-fives suffering from underweight (Mod+ Severe), 2006–2010
Source: UNICEF, State of the World's Children 2012

The National Family Health Survey – 3 (2005/6) gives us an insight into the nutritional status of women in India. The body mass index (BMI), relating a woman's weight to her height, is used to evaluate thinness (and obesity). Chronic energy deficiency is indicated by a BMI of less than 18.5. As much as 36 per cent of Indian women had BMI below 18.5 in 1998/9 (National Family Health Survey 2). Nutritional problems are especially pronounced for rural women (41 per cent), illiterate women (43 per cent) and scheduled caste and scheduled tribe women (nearly 20 per cent). By 2005/6 the share of adult women suffering from chronic energy deficiency had barely dropped, to 33 per cent (a similar share of adult men had a BMI of less than 18.5).

Another indicator of the nutritional status of women is the prevalence of anaemia. Anaemia is the status of having a low haemoglobin level in the blood.[20] Anaemia may become an underlying cause of maternal mortality and perinatal mortality. In addition it results in an increased risk of premature delivery and low birthweight. While 40 per cent of

---

[20] Haemoglobin is essential for transporting oxygen from the lungs to other tissues and organs of the body. Anaemia results from a deficiency of iron, folate, vitamin B12, or some other nutrients.

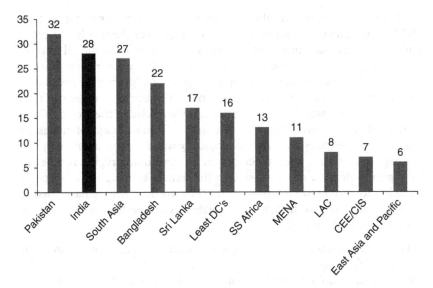

Figure 10.4 Small women create low-birth-weight babies – percentage
of infants with lbw by region
Source: UNICEF, State of the World's Children 2012

women in Sub-Saharan Africa suffer from anaemia, 60 per cent of
women in South Asia do (Ramalingaswami *et al.*, 1996).[21]

Precisely half of pregnant women in India suffer from some form of
anaemia. Those with a height below 145 cm are more likely to suffer
anaemia than those who are taller. Those with a BMI of less than 18.5 are
also more likely to suffer from anaemia than those with a higher BMI.
Anaemia is higher for rural women than for urban women. It decreases
steadily with increases in the level of education, from 56 per cent among
illiterate women to 40 per cent among women who have completed at
least high school.

What is interesting is that women in South Asia have the worst educational indicators relative to men compared with all other regions. Gender
discrimination in respect of education (as manifested in most educational
outcome indicators) exists in all regions of the world. However, the adult
literacy rates for women as a percentage of men are the lowest in South
Asia – 63 per cent compared with 71 per cent in the Middle East and
North Africa (72 per cent in SSA). Primary enrolment rates were also the
lowest, secondary enrolment rates still are.

---

[21] According to National Family Health Survey 3, 56 per cent of pregnant Indian women
suffered from anaemia, and 76 per cent of under-six year olds were anaemic.

This evidence reinforces the argument that the nutritional status of the child is an outcome of a process that goes on over the whole life-cycle, and without the right interventions leads to an inter-generational transfer of ill-being for women (and thus for children). By far the most important evidence of *systematic* gender discrimination over a lifetime is provided by the fact that the life expectancy of women in South Asia is greater than that of men by a smaller margin than anywhere else in the world. Thus, Figure 10.5 (life expectancy of females as a percentage of males by region) demonstrates that while biologically women should have a higher life expectancy, their life expectancy in no developing region reaches its biological potential, as manifested in the female-to-male life expectancy ratio in industrialised countries.[22] In other words, what we have tried to demonstrate here is that while gender discrimination is widespread everywhere in the world:

(i) it takes forms in *all* developing countries which have systematic biological outcomes,
(ii) that these biological outcomes are the worst in South Asia compared with any other region in the world, and
(iii) these outcomes have a life-cycle impact, and affect the well-being of all citizens through an inter-generational transfer of ill-being.

Points (ii) and (iii) above are underlined by Figure 10.6, which shows that in South Asia gender discrimination over the life-cycle is the worst in the world, as only such discrimination can explain the sex ratio prevailing in South Asia (except Sri Lanka), which is far worse than the sex ratio in Sub-Saharan Africa, a similarly poor region but not characterised by such high levels of gender discrimination.

To re-emphasise a point about synergies: the nutritional outcome for a child and her mother is the result not merely of the capability to avoid under-nourishment but also a number of related elementary capabilities: avoiding morbidity and mortality and having some minimal education. For the purposes of our model, the functionings that matter most are the simple ones: being able to read and write, being free from disease, being able to avoid under-nourishment. All these are measurable functionings. But as stated here they are a part of a set of minimum capabilities, i.e. having secondary education goes beyond being able to read and write; being well nourished is far superior to merely avoiding starvation; and being positively healthy is a more robust state of health than merely

---

[22] Although the life expectancy ratio of women to men is higher in CEE/CIS countries compared with industrialised countries, the former cannot be treated as a standard since male mortality has declined in the former after the transition to a free-market economy.

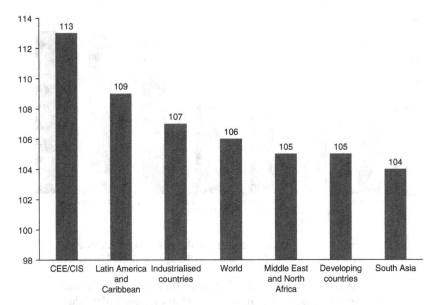

Figure 10.5 Discrimination against women – life expectancy of females
as a percentage of males – by region, 2010
Source: UNICEF, State of the World's Children 2012
Notes :
1. CEE/CIS: Albania; Armenia; Azerbaijan; Belarus; Bosnia and
    Herzegovina; Bulgaria; Croatia; Georgia; Kazakhstan; Kyrgyzstan;
    Montenegro; Republic of Moldova; Romania; Russian Federation;
    Serbia; Tajikistan; The former Yugoslav Republic of Macedonia;
    Turkey; Turkmenistan; Ukraine; Uzbekistan.
2. LAC: Antigua and Barbuda; Argentina; Bahamas; Barbados; Belize;
    Bolivia (Plurinational State of); Brazil; Chile; Colombia; Costa Rica;
    Cuba; Dominica; Dominican Republic; Ecuador; El Salvador;
    Grenada; Guatemala; Guyana; Haiti; Honduras; Jamaica; Mexico;
    Nicaragua; Panama; Paraguay; Peru; Saint Kitts and Nevis; Saint
    Lucia; Saint Vincent and the Grenadines; Suriname; Trinidad and
    Tobago; Uruguay; Venezuela (Bolivarian Republic of).
3. Industrialised countries: defined as those not included in the
    UNICEF Regional Classification, i.e. Andorra; Australia; Austria;
    Belgium; Canada; Cyprus; Czech Republic; Denmark; Estonia;
    Finland; France; Germany; Greece; Holy See; Hungary; Iceland;
    Ireland; Israel; Italy; Japan; Latvia; Liechtenstein; Lithuania;
    Luxembourg; Malta; Monaco; Netherlands; New Zealand; Norway;
    Poland; Portugal; San Marino; Slovakia; Slovenia; Spain; Sweden;
    Switzerland; United Kingdom; United States.
4. Middle East and North Africa: Algeria; Bahrain; Djibouti; Egypt; Iran
    (Islamic Republic of); Iraq; Jordan; Kuwait; Lebanon; Libya;
    Morocco; Occupied Palestinian Territory; Oman; Qatar; Saudi

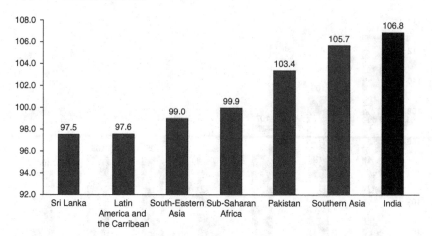

Figure 10.6: Sex ratio by region (males per 100 females), 2010
Source: Department of Economic and Social Affairs, United Nations
Notes:
1. LAC: Caribbean, Aruba, Bahamas, Barbados, Cuba, Dominican Republic, Grenada, Guadeloupe, Haiti, Jamaica, Martinique, Netherlands Antilles, Puerto Rico, Saint Lucia, Saint Vincent and the Grenadines, Trinidad and Tobago and United States Virgin Islands.
2. South Eastern Asia: Brunei Darussalam, Cambodia, Indonesia, Lao People's Democratic Republic, Malaysia, Myanmar, Philippines, Singapore, Thailand, Timor-Leste and Vietnam.
3. Sub Saharan Africa: Africa except northern Africa, with Sudan included in sub Saharan Africa.
4. Southern Asia: Afghanistan, Bangladesh, Bhutan, India, Iran (Islamic republic of), Maldives, Nepal, Pakistan, Sri Lanka.

avoiding disease. The healthier, the better nourished, the more educated an individual, the more likely it is that she will be able to command resources to increase her income and thus avoid poverty. However, at the macro-economic level, what will matter for economic growth and

---

Figure 10.5 (cont.)
Arabia; Sudan; Syrian Arab Republic; Tunisia; United Arab Emirates; Yemen.
5. Developing countries: classified as such for purposes of statistical analysis only. There is no established convention for the designation of 'developed' and 'developing' countries or areas in the United Nations system.
6. South Asia: Afghanistan; Bangladesh; Bhutan; India; Maldives; Nepal; Pakistan; Sri Lanka.

poverty reduction is the overall level of functionings that individuals – aggregated at the societal level – are able to achieve, and the quality of those functionings achieved.

The synergy among basic services, income-poverty and economic growth

The first synergy, discussed above, is itself a sub-set of another synergy in the development process. This second synergy arises from interventions that contribute to human capability expansion (here restricted to the bundles of simple functionings, themselves the result of interventions within basic services), income-poverty reduction and economic growth. What we have in mind can be expressed algebraically:

GNP per capita growth = f_1 (macro-economic policies and technical/structural change, quality of human functionings, income-poverty reduction)   (1)

Income-poverty reduction = f_2 (GNP per capita growth, quality of human functionings, asset distribution)   (2)

Human capabilities expansion = f_3 (GNP per capita growth, income-poverty reduction, social policy)   (3)

In terms of the conceptual framework of Sen and Nussbaum, as well as in our view, equation (3) is of primary importance, but only in the sense that human capability expansion is our common goal and should be the goal of public policy. However, human capability expansion is itself dependent upon equations (1) and (2). As we discuss below, per capita income growth at the aggregate level can be a means to the end of income-poverty reduction, and vice versa, while both would contribute to human capability expansion.

Contrary to what many traditional economists think, the engine of growth (its main determinant) is not macro-economic policy but technological change. Of course, stable prices and low interest rates contribute to a favourable context in which firms would want to work and invest. However, this does not mean that macro-economic stability per se results in economic growth, as evidenced by the standard error of the regressions that try, but fail, to establish this point. For sustained and regular economic growth, both technological change and appropriate macro-economic policies are needed, and the two tend to reinforce each other.

Similarly, balanced macro-economic policies and improvement in human functionings through social policy work together. A macro-economic structural adjustment that increases unemployment and reduces wages or increases gender differentials in wages does not induce

Table 10.1 *Economic growth by level of income-poverty and human development (Average annual growth rate of per capita income, 1990–2000)*

Income-poverty	U5MR		
	High	Medium	Low
High	−1.6	−0.5	0.5
Medium	−2.6	0.9	1.9
Low		0.6	2.7

Source: Computed from Tabatabai (ILO), State of the World's Children (UNICEF), World Development Report various issues (UNESCO)

synergies.[23] On the contrary, it tends to reduce welfare and human capabilities, undermining the feedback loop. Compensatory policies with public funds (e.g. of the Social Fund variety), adopted to soften the adverse human impact of neo-liberal macro-economic policies, merely tend to divert resources; hence the need to integrate macro-economic and social policies at conception. Policies to distribute assets and income are fundamental for poverty reduction and economic growth. It can be perceived intuitively, then, that a series of strategic, small interventions can unleash a powerful virtuous circle.

An empirical exercise can help to underscore the interactions discussed above.[24] Data on changes in income-poverty are limited, but nevertheless, there are close to fifty countries for which data are available on the incidence of income-poverty in the 1980s. For these countries, the under-five mortality rate (U5MR) in 1980 was used as a proxy for the quality of human functionings. Also, the average annual growth rate for the period between 1990 and 2000 is available. The countries were classified according to their initial level of income-poverty and U5MR.[25] Then the average rate of economic growth per capita was calculated for each of the nine groups of countries. Unlike conventional analysis where growth is considered as the explanatory variable for social outcomes, this analysis aims to demonstrate that the argument can also be made in the other direction. Table 10.1 suggests that the rate of economic growth can be explained by the initial

---

[23] For an analysis of the gender insensitivity of adjustment policies, see Elson and Cagatay (2000).

[24] I am grateful to Enrique Delamonica for these estimates. This section draws heavily from our book, Mehrotra and Delamonica (2007).

[25] For income poverty, the categories were high (more than 50 per cent), medium (between 50 per cent and 30 per cent) and low (less than 30 per cent). Also, they were grouped in terms of their levels of U5MR: high (over 170 per 1000 live births), medium (between 170 and 70) and low (less than 70).

conditions concerning income-poverty and the quality of human function-ings (the latter proxied by U5MR).[26]

Low U5MR and high income-poverty did not co-exist in any of the selected countries, nor did high U5MR and low income-poverty. There are only seven groups (not nine) because there are no countries where U5MR is low and income-poverty is high, nor any countries that have a high U5MR and a low level of income-poverty; this is itself revealing.

An interesting pattern emerges when the growth rates of per capita income are compared among the remaining seven groups. Countries with a high initial U5MR experienced negative growth in per capita income. Further, the rates of income growth were positive and were higher for countries with medium or low initial levels of U5MR; in fact, the lower the initial U5MR, the higher the income growth rates. More-over, for all levels of initial U5MR, the rates of income growth were highest when the initial level of income-poverty was lowest. In other words, countries with high levels of human development (low U5MR) and low income-poverty experienced faster growth than countries with high human development and medium levels of income-poverty.

Although these figures show only correlation and not necessarily caus-ality, they strongly suggest that basic social services are of fundamental importance in triggering the virtuous circle between economic growth, income-poverty and human capabilities. Policies that focus on health and educational status, but ignore growth and income-poverty reduction, will lead to human development outcomes that may not be sustainable. Policies that focus on income-poverty reduction and health/educational improvement, without regard for macro-economic imbalances or struc-tural constraints which limit growth, run the risk of reversal in situations of external shock. Policies that focus largely on economic growth without much regard for income-poverty reduction or health/educational status are doomed to unequal income distribution or lower levels of human development (than otherwise possible) that will dampen economic growth prospects in the long run.

This is one of the major respects in which our argument differs from that of the Washington Consensus and post-Washington Consensus. The Consensus suggests that 'economic growth typically does promote human development, and a strong positive relationship is evident from the line of best fit (the "regression")' (Ravallion, 1997). When growth

---

[26] We fully appreciate that the under-five mortality rate is merely an indicator expressing the functioning – the ability to live beyond age five – which underlies the prospect of normal longevity. It is not a capability per se; however, we use the language of capability in order to maintain simplicity and clarity of argument.

and poverty or growth and human development indicators are modelled, it is usually argued that it is growth that affects health indicators or poverty, and not the other way around. 'Economic growth typically promotes human development' is usually the hypothesis, which is proven by the use of regressions, where the regression line is (by its construction) the expected effect of growth on a human development indicator or on poverty. Where growth failed to deliver income gains to the poor, or promote non-income dimensions of welfare (e.g. access to schooling and health care), such cases are called 'quite untypical' (Dollar and Kraay, 2001; Ravallion, 1997).[27] They also argue that the human development approach, which we espouse, devotes 'more attention to residuals' and 'the regression line is ignored'. Indeed, the policy analysis inspired by the Washington Consensus has traditionally placed faith in the outcomes of cross-country (or inter-temporal) regression analysis, rather than explaining the reasons why some countries divert from these average trends and are 'outliers'. To us, the outliers demonstrate that it is possible for countries to relieve the non-income dimensions of poverty and achieve social indicators comparable to those of industrialised countries regardless of the level of income (Mehrotra and Jolly, 2000).

We do not downplay economic growth, but as economic growth is such a predominant part of the Washington strategy, the pace at which social outcomes improve appears to be at a discount. A synergy exists between poverty-reduction, education/health development and economic growth, which does not put increasing the growth rate on a pedestal higher than the other two variables (i.e. improvements in simple human functionings and direct poverty reduction). Instead, it calls for the integration of social and economic policy.

This is not the only way this framework differs from the approach of the mainstream thinking in development. A second difference is that it is not merely an aid to policy-making; in other words, it is not just a framework for a development strategy. It is also a framework for analysis, to understand the economic and social outcomes of different countries. It is a basis for explaining failure in human development outcomes, and also for explaining success.

Thus, we have used this framework to analyse the determinants of success in the so-called high-achieving countries – countries with significant improvements in their social indicators relative to their level of per

---

[27] It is rarely stated that correlation never proves causation. It is acknowledged that 'there are deviations (the "residuals") around this line; these are cases with unusually low, or unusually high, performance in human development at a given level of income or a given rate of economic growth' (Ravallion, 1997).

capita GDP over the preceding three to four decades (Mehrotra and Jolly, 1997).[28] To give just one example of such analysis,[29] the experience of the high-achievers demonstrates that it is important to shift the focus in development strategy from 'welfarist' approaches that treat people as objects of development to approaches that see them as active agents of change (Sen, 1995). This was particularly true for women. Sen (1995, 1999b) argues that where women have certain freedoms they not only become agents of their own well-being but of the whole society: freedom to work outside the home, freedom to earn an independent income, freedom to have ownership rights, and freedom to receive education.

Thus, in respect of education, we found that in the high-achieving countries girls' enrolment has been very high, and on par with that of boys, for several decades – unlike the majority of developing countries. Women's participation in economic life can be measured in different ways: by the freedom to earn an income outside the household and lack of restrictions on owning productive assets. Unfortunately, data on the latter are very limited. However, female participation in the non-agricultural workforce in high-achieving countries is higher than in countries that have achieved less social progress. Similarly, in professional and technical employment women's participation in the labour force is high in the high-achieving countries (Mehrotra, 1997).

A third respect in which our alternative framework differs is the degree to which it places emphasis on gender equality, as the cornerstone of development strategy and policy, and as a guide for evaluating 'good' government. The issue of gender equality is not merely one additional variable to take into account in our alternative framework; it is the most critical variable, unlike in the growing post-Washington Consensus.

The family has a particular claim to be regarded as what John Rawls called the 'basic structure of society', an institution to which principles of justice especially ought to apply, if the goal is to promote justice for all citizens. In a similar way, Nussbaum suggests that public policy should devote special attention to any institution like the family whose influence on the formation of capabilities is profound. But she goes on: 'When we look at the family, whose capabilities do we look at? ... Here ... a

[28] The high-achievers that are analysed there are: in East Asia, the Republic of Korea and Malaysia; in South Asia, Sri Lanka and the state of Kerala (India); in Africa, Botswana, Zimbabwe (their experience until the early 1990s) and Mauritius; and in Latin America and the Caribbean, Costa Rica, Cuba and Barbados.

[29] For further examples of the use of this dual synergy framework to understand varying country experiences in social achievement and economic growth (or lack thereof), see Taylor et al. (1997) and Mehrotra and Delamonica (2007).

principle of each person's capability should guide us ... the family as such has no moral standing within the core of the political conception. It is persons who have moral standing' (pp. 250–1). A focus on 'each person's capability' points the direction of public policy towards gender equality.

Why gender equality is a necessary condition for the second synergy
While we were emphatic in pointing out the central role of gender equality in achieving the first set of synergies (i.e. within interventions that promote simple human functionings), we have said nothing explicitly on how important gender equality is to triggering the second set of synergies (i.e. that between economic growth, income-poverty reduction and the quality of human functionings). The first set of synergies is an integral part of the second set of synergies – hence the centrality of gender equality to the entire process does not have to be repeated. However, is gender equality (in areas unrelated to health and educational outcomes) relevant to the success of triggering the second set of synergies? The answer is an emphatic 'yes'.

The centrality of gender equality for triggering the second set of synergies (in a positive direction) is that in most developing regions women are increasingly joining the labour force. In other words, their economic participation rate has been growing consistently over the past few decades. Hence there has been growing feminisation of the labour force in a majority of countries.[30] There is yet another aspect to this change in the composition of the labour force in developing countries. Most new women entrants into the labour force in developing countries are engaging in activities in the informal sector of the economy. The informal economy has grown in developing countries driven by a number of factors on the supply side: the low elasticity of employment growth to industrial output growth, inappropriate choice of technique and/or pattern of production, and thus poor labour absorption in formal industry; the pressure of population growth on rural land, and hence growing rural-urban migration; and so on. On the demand side, women's higher than proportionate share in the informal labour force is driven partly by the fact that they have poorer educational qualifications and are entering the labour market with limited or no skills. Partly this is because informal sector work enables women to earn an income while giving them reasonably flexible working hours, which fits well into their care-giving responsibilities. Many of them work out of the home, and are engaged in

---

[30] See Charmes (2001) for evidence on both trends.

manufacturing activities undertaken as part of a sub-contracting or putting-out system, where the home-based worker is one end of a value-chain where the other end of the chain may be located in an advanced industrialised country or developing country capital. This makes such employees one of the most vulnerable parts of the developing country labour force. Yet, outside of agriculture (which has traditionally been characterised by large-scale participation of women on the family farm), this kind of informal economic activity is among the biggest sources of income and employment for women around the developing world, especially but not only in urban areas. It is also a growing activity, just as home-based work was a growing activity in the latter half of the nineteenth century with the spread of the industrial revolution in Europe and North America. (It is precisely the kind of economic activity that Nussbaum says engaged Jayamma and Vasanti in *Women and Human Development*.)[31]

The implication of this growing informalisation of the labour force and its concomitant feminisation is that strategies for poverty-reduction and growth-related policies cannot overlook this extremely important source of employment and income for women. The state has again a critical role for putting in place policies which, on the one hand, provide social protection (i.e. social insurance) and, on the other, promote and support the training, marketing and credit needs[32] of such women, in order that informal activities begin to acquire increasingly the character of formal activities. Support for micro-enterprises can be an important source of improved piece-rates for such women workers and thus higher incomes, giving women a stronger hand in bargaining for a better deal within the household. Such higher incomes can translate into decreasing the likelihood of their children working, rather than going to school.

What role for public policy?

The political environment for women's rights became more favourable during the 1990s. In 1990, 10 per cent of the world's countries had ratified all six major human rights instruments.[33] But by February 2000

---

[31] For a detailed analysis of this phenomenon in Asia, see Mehrotra and Biggeri (2007).

[32] In study after study, women have demonstrated themselves as more credit-worthy than men, with repayment rates for loans that normally exceed 95 per cent. In addition, several studies show that borrowing by women is used to improve family well-being, rather than merely for consumption purposes.

[33] International Convention on the Elimination of All Forms of Racial Discrimination, 1965; International Covenant on Civil and Political Rights, 1966; International Covenant on Economic, Social and Cultural Rights, 1966; Convention on the Elimination of All Forms of Discrimination Against Women, 1979; Convention

140 or more countries had ratified all but one of the six. Further, and even more relevant for our purposes, more than three-quarters of the world's countries have ratified the Convention on the Elimination of All Forms of Discrimination Against Women.

So how should public policy now advance gender equality? Within a bargaining framework, Nussbaum advances certain general principles that should guide public action to advance women's capabilities. First, she notes the importance of options for women. She rightly argues that increasing women's economic options is an extremely powerful way of promoting their well-being within the family, and more generally. Since women have very poor exit options from marriage, their breakdown position in the cooperative bargaining unit of the family is much weaker. We agree that access to employment (outside the home, as Sen (1995) emphasises) and credit, land rights and literacy are important for women's capabilities in general. In fact, we have tried to present empirical evidence that in the high-achieving countries, women's literacy and their employment status was far ahead of other countries in their region; and these aspects of the agency of women contributed to the transformation of these countries (Mehrotra, 1997).

The second principle she underlines is the *importance of perceived contribution* within the family. The perceived contribution may or may not be the same as women's actual material and emotional contribution. When women do not work outside the home, the disparity between perceived and actual contribution might be greater, she admits.

The third principle of public policy to promote gender equality is the importance of a sense of one's own worth for women. Both Nussbaum and Sen rightly argue that if the woman in the family thinks others have more worthwhile goals than her own, she will bargain weakly. This is indeed the greatest challenge – the need for challenging the adaptive preference of the vast majority of poor women themselves. As Nussbaum puts it, these women have to undergo a two-stage process of awareness: coming to see themselves in a bad situation, and then coming to see themselves as citizens who have a right to a better situation. We strongly endorse the idea that a most effective way for government to promote women's sense of their worth and their entitlements is to promote women's collectives.[34] However, women's collectives are more likely to

---

Against Torture and Other Cruel, Inhuman or Degrading Treatment or Punishment, 1984; and Convention on the Rights of the Child, 1989.

[34] In studies of manufacturing work sub-contracted to home-based women workers in five Asian countries, Mehrotra and Biggeri (2007) demonstrate the beneficial impact of organised informal-sector workers in improving their children's well-being, especially

be formed among women who have employment outside the home or at least work to bring in an income.

An additional point is that for these reasons, principles one and three should have priority over principle two, since perceived contribution is likely to be significantly affected by the importance of options and also the sense of one's own worth that women have.

Yet another critical means for improving women's self-worth (missed by Nussbaum) is for the state to promote the political participation of women (which goes beyond collectives). Women are half the world's population, but there are only seven countries in the world in which women parliamentarians constitute more than 30 per cent of the members. In the majority of countries, regardless of the region, women occupy less than 10 per cent of the seats in national parliament. Evidence suggests that women are more likely to raise issues of relevance to the well-being of the family than men. A World Bank study on corruption and women in government concluded that higher rates of female partici- pation in government are associated with lower levels of corruption, implying that women may be more concerned with the common good.[35] Countries where there are clear quotas for women in parliament are countries where women's representation is highest. As of March 2000, legal or constitutional quotas for seats in national or local assemblies (typically for 25–30 per cent of seats) had been adopted in only about twenty-five countries; in other words, in the vast majority of countries where the poorest women live, women suffer from extremely poor political representation. Worse still, where quotas were eliminated in the 1990s – in the East European transition economies – there has been a sharp fall in women's representation.[36]

While representation in national parliaments might be important (and such representation increased in the majority of countries in the 1990s, albeit from very low levels), the power to make economic policy-related decisions has moved away from parliaments to corporations, finance ministries and central banks.[37] Since most investment decisions related to the first synergy (within social services) are taken at the local level, it is important for women urgently to be given representation in local assem- blies, so that women are directly involved in decisions in regard to maternal and child health care, schooling, and water and sanitation.

---

through increasing the likelihood that the children do not only work but either go to school and work, or only go to school.

[35] See Dollar et al. (1999) for an assessment of the evidence.

[36] For an excellent discussion of this issue, see UNIFEM (2000).

[37] For a discussion of this phenomenon, see Sen (1999).

Concluding remarks

In this chapter we have tried to establish that gender equality is far more central to the structural transformation of developing countries than it was to that of the now industrialised countries at a comparable period of development. This is primarily because the obstacles to hastening the demographic transition are crucially tied up with gender inequality. While both Sen and Nussbaum have made major contributions to the recognition of gender equality as an instrument of social and economic change, neither explicitly recognises its centrality – as a *sine qua non* of rapid economic growth for contemporary developing countries in a way that it was not for the now-industrialised countries at a comparable historical stage of development.

We have also suggested that mainstream economics has provided a too narrow philosophical and theoretical basis for policies to engineer this structural transformation. An alternative framework is necessary – which Sen and Nussbaum have provided. However, what Sen and Nussbaum do not provide is the link between this alternative conceptual framework (and its concomitant focus on human development) on the one hand, and actual development strategy (and policies[38]) on the other. The alternative framework demands the use of the capability approach, with human capabilities and human rights as the goal of public policy. However, we go further and suggest that public policy should recognise the existence of, and capitalise on, two kinds of synergies between interventions and resulting processes – one within basic services, and another between improving educational/health status, the reduction of the numbers of the income-poor and the depth of poverty, and economic growth – and gender equality is central to both synergies. At the current stage of the demographic transition in many developing countries, public policy that fails to recognise the centrality of women's capabilities and agency to triggering and sustaining both these synergies is inviting failure.

REFERENCES

Arrow, K., Sen, A. and Suzumura, K. (eds) (2002), *Handbook of Social Choice and Welfare*, Amsterdam: Elsevier North-Holland.
Behrman, J.R. and Deolalikar, A.B. (1995), 'Health and Nutrition', in J.R. Behrman and T.N. Srinivasan (eds), *Handbook of Development Economics*, Amsterdam: North-Holland.

---

[38] Policies flowing from this development strategy were not discussed in this chapter for reasons of space. They are elaborated in Mehrotra and Delamonica (2007) and Mehrotra (forthcoming).

Birdsall, N. and Londono, J.L. (1997), 'Asset Inequality Matters: An Assessment of the World Bank's Approach to Poverty Reduction', *American Economic Review*, 87 (2), 32–37.

Bongaarts, J. (1994), 'The Impact of Population Policies: Comment', *Population and Development Review*, 20 (3), 616–620.

Caldwell, J.C. (1991), *The Soft Underbelly of Development: Demographic Transition in Conditions of Limited Economic Change*, Proceedings of the World Bank Annual Conference on Development Economics 1990–1991, Washington D.C.: World Bank, pp. 207–253.

Carnoy, M. (1992), *The Case for Investing in Basic Education*, New York: UNICEF.

Cassen, R. (1994), *Does Aid Work? Report to an Intergovernmental Task Force*, Second edition, Oxford: Clarendon Press, Oxford University Press.

Charmes, J. (2001), 'Informal Sector, Poverty and Gender. A Review of Empirical Evidence', Background Paper for the World Development Report 2001, University of Versailles St-Quentin-en-Yvelines.

Cigno, A. and Rosati, F. (1992), 'The Effects of Financial Markets and Social Security on Saving and Fertility Behaviour in Italy', *Journal of Population Economics*, 5 (3), 319–341.

  (1996), 'Jointly Determined Saving and Fertility Behaviour: Theory, and Estimates for Germany, Italy, UK, and USA', *European Economic Review*, 40 (8), 1561–1589.

Cleaver, K. and Schreiber G.A. (1994), *Reversing the Spiral: The Population, Agriculture, and Environment Nexus in Sub-Saharan Africa*, Washington, D.C.: World Bank.

Cochrane, S. (1979), *Fertility and Education. What Do We Really Know?* Baltimore, MD: Johns Hopkins University Press.

  (1988), 'The Effects of Education, Health and Social Security on Fertility in Developing Countries', Working Paper WPS 93, Population and Health Resources Department, Washington, DC: World Bank.

Cornia, G.A. (ed.) (2004), *Inequality, Poverty and Growth in an Era of Globalization and Liberalization*, Oxford: Clarendon Press.

Cornia, G.A. and Kiiski, S. (2001), 'Trends in Income Distribution in the Post-World War II Period: Evidence and Interpretation', WIDER Discussion Paper 2001/89, Helsinki: UNU WIDER.

Cunningham, H. and Viazzo, P.P. (1996), 'Some Issues in the Historical Study of Child Labour', in H. Cunningham and P.P. Viazzo (eds), *Child Labour in Historical Perspective 1800–1985*, Florence: UNICEF International Child Development Centre.

Dasgupta, P. (1993), *An Inquiry into Well-being and Destitution*, Oxford: Clarendon Press.

Deaton, A. (1997), *The Analysis of Household Surveys. A Micro-econometric Approach to Development Policy*, Baltimore, MD: Johns Hopkins University Press.

Dollar, D., Fisman, R. and Gatti, R. (1999), 'Are Women Really the "Fairer" Sex? Corruption and Women in Government', Policy Research Report on Gender and Development, Working Paper Series No. 1, Washington, DC: World Bank.

Dollar, D. and Kraay, A. (2001), 'Growth is Good for the Poor', Development Research Group, Washington DC: World Bank.

Elson, D. (ed.) (1995), *Male Bias in the Development Process*, Second edition, Manchester University Press.

Elson, D. and Cagatay, N. (2000), 'The Social Content of Macro-economic Policies', *World Development*, 28 (7).

Fine, B. and Rose, P. (2001), 'Education and the post-Washington Consensus', in B. Fine, C. Lapavitsas and J. Pincus (eds), *Development Policy in the Twenty-first Century. Beyond the Post-Washington Consensus*, London: Routledge.

Friedman, M. (1953), *Essays in Positive Economics*, University of Chicago Press.

Ghosh, S. and Kanbur, R. (2008), 'Male Wages and Female Welfare: Private Markets, Public Goods, and Intrahousehold Inequality', *Oxford Economic Papers*, 60 (1), 46–58.

IIPS (International Institute for Population Sciences) (2000), *India – National Family Health Survey (NFHS-2) 1988–1999*, Mumbai, India: IIPS.

Kanbur, R. and Haddad, L. (1994), 'Are Better Off Households More Unequal or Less Unequal?' *Oxford Economic Papers*, 46 (3), 445–458.

Malthus, R.T. (1798), *An Essay on the Principle of Population*, London: Macmillan Press.

Mehrotra, S. (2005), 'Human Capital or Human Development? In Search of a knowledge paradigm for education and development', *Economic and Political Weekly*, 40 (4), 300–310.

(2008), 'Democracy, Decentralisation and Access to Basic Services: An Elaboration on Sen's Capability Approach', in S. Alkire and M. Qizilbash (eds), *Examining Sen's Capability Approach*, Cambridge University Press.

(forthcoming), *Seizing the Demographic Dividend: Policies to Achieve Inclusive Growth in India*, Cambridge University Press.

Mehrotra, S. and Biggeri, M. (2007), *Asian Informal Workers. Global Risks, Local Protection*, London: Routledge.

Mehrotra, S. and Delamonica, E. (2007), *Eliminating Human Poverty. Macro-economic and Social Policies for Equitable Growth*, London: Zed Press.

Mehrotra, S. and Jolly, R. (1997), *Development with a Human Face. Experiences in Social Achievement and Economic Growth*, Oxford: Clarendon Press.

Nussbaum, M.C. (1997), 'Flawed Foundations: The Philosophical Critique of (a Particular Type of) Economics', *University of Chicago Law Review*, 64 (4), 1197–1214.

(2001), *Women and Human Development. The Capabilities Approach*, rev. edn., Cambridge University Press.

Pritchett, L. (1994), 'Desired Fertility and the Impact of Population Policies', *Population and Development Review*, 20 (1), 1–55.

Ramalingaswami, V., Jonsson, U. and Rohde, J. (1996), 'The Asian Enigma', in *The Progress of Nations*, UNICEF.

Ravallion, M. (1997), 'Good and Bad Growth: The Human Development Reports', *World Development*, 25 (5), 631–638.

Sen, A. (1977), 'Rational Fools: A Critique of the Behavioral Foundations of Economic Theory', *Philosophy and Public Affairs*, 6 (4), 317–344.

(1985), *Commodities and Capabilities*, Oxford University Press.

(1987), *On Ethics and Economics*, Oxford University Press.

(1995), 'Agency and Well-being: The Development Agenda' in N. Heyzer with S. Kapoor and J. Sandler, *A Commitment to the World's Women – Perspectives for Development for Beijing and Beyond*, New York: UNIFEM.

(1999a), 'Investing in Health', General Keynote Speech at 52nd World Health Assembly, Geneva, May.

(1999b), *Development as Freedom*, Oxford University Press.

Standing, G. (2001), 'Brave New Worlds? A Critique of Stiglitz's World Bank Rethink', *Development and Change*, 31 (4), September, 737–763.

Stiglitz, J. (2000) 'What I Learned at the World Economic Crisis, The Insider', mimeo, April.

Szreter, S. (1996), *Fertility, Class and Gender in Britain 1860–1940*, Cambridge University Press.

Taylor, L., Mehrotra, S. and Delamonica, E. (1997), 'The Links Between Economic Growth, Poverty Reduction and Social Development: Theory and Policy', in S. Mehrotra and R. Jolly (eds) *Development with a Human Face. Experiences in Social Achievement and Economic Growth*, Oxford: Clarendon Press.

WHO (1995), 'Maternal Anthropometry and Pregnancy Outcomes', *Bulletin of the World Health Organization*, 73, 1–98.

World Bank (1986), *Financing Education in Developing Countries, An Exploration of Policy Options*, Washington, DC: World Bank.

(1996), *World Development Report*, Washington, DC: World Bank.

(1999), 'Knowledge for Development', *World Development Report*, Washington, DC: World Bank.

UN ACC/SCN (United Nations Administrative Committee on Coordination/ Sub-Committee on Nutrition) (2000), *Fourth Report on the World Nutrition Situation*, Geneva: *UN ACC/SCN* in collaboration with IFPRI.

UNDP (1995), *The 1995 Human Development Report*, Oxford, New York: Oxford University Press.

UNIFEM (2000), *Progress of the World's Women 2000*, New York: UNIFEM.

11 Applying the capabilities approach to disability, poverty, and gender

Patricia Welch Saleeby

Introduction and context of disability, poverty, and gender inequality

Despite numerous disability definitions, disability is generally considered a limitation in the completion of activities due to a health problem, or a physical or mental condition. Various factors contribute to disability, such as accidents, aging, chronic disorders, disease, environment, land mines, malnutrition, physical abuse, sexually transmitted diseases, violence, and war.[1] Although disability rates vary among countries, it is estimated that approximately 7–10 percent of the world's population has some type of disability with economic, educational, and/or social consequences.[2] Estimates of the global disability population range from 235 million to 549 million individuals.[3] Consequently, disability has expanded well beyond a medical issue to that of a complex public health and social problem.[4]

Similarly, poverty rates vary between different countries, but it is estimated that approximately 1.4 billion individuals of the world's population experience poverty.[5] Poverty is commonly defined as the inability to achieve a minimal standard of living, or what is necessary to meet one's basic human needs. Not surprisingly, the majority of the world's poor live in developing countries, which are also characterized by high rates of disability.[6] Poverty functions as a proxy for variables that increase

---

[1] Abberley (1987: 5–20); Seelman and Sweeney (1995: 2–13).

[2] See Brundtland (1999) as cited in the Director-General speech given at the Interagency Consultation on Disability, 15–16 June 1999.

[3] As calculated by Metts (2000: 5) by applying UNDP estimates of the proportions of individuals with disabilities in High, Medium, and Low Human Development countries to United Nations population estimates (9.9 percent, 3.7 percent, and 1.0 percent respectively) for those corresponding countries.

[4] Pope and Tarlov (1991: 1).

[5] As calculated by those living on less than $1.25 per day in 2005, the revised World Bank poverty line (Chen and Ravallion, 2008).

[6] See Barnes and Mercer (1995: 37).

the risk of disability, including unsafe living and working conditions, poor health and nutrition, and low educational attainment.[7]

Disability and poverty are related inextricably in every society.[8] Although anecdotal evidence on poverty and disability is abundant, comprehensive studies on these linkages and their relationships are lacking.[9] It is generally concluded that disability is both a cause and consequence of poverty, and disabled people[10] are among the poorest of the poor. However, the strength and extent of each path (from disability to poverty and from poverty to disability) remain largely unknown and unsubstantiated.

Poverty and disability reinforce each other, contributing to increased exclusion and vulnerability.[11] Both poverty and disability affect an individual's capabilities, impacting their full participation in society. Individuals with disabilities and the poor have been denied rights and have faced discrimination. Likewise, parallels can be established between the inequality experienced by the poor and disabled people and that encountered by women in the majority of the world. Although disability and poverty affect men and women worldwide, these issues further compound the subordinate status and situation of many women.

Poverty is related to the gender in several ways. In most countries women hold a lower position than men. Consequently, women have less access to education and training, and they have lower participation in the labor force. These limitations result in lower incomes and the greater likelihood of experiencing poverty, especially if they are the single income-earner in the household (due to death of their husband, a sick or disabled husband, or divorce).

Similarly, disability has a gender dimension. Gender is correlated with specific types of mental and physical disorders (impairments and chronic conditions that often lead to disabilities) as well as with the time (number of years) lived with the disability.[12] Women have an increased risk of malnutrition and of consuming overall less food than their male counterparts in many countries. This is true in countries where food is scarce and by tradition the females eat whatever is left after the males have

---

[7] Seelman and Sweeney (1995: 3).

[8] For an overview of the links between poverty and disability, see Peat (1998: 45).

[9] Elwan (1999) states linkages between poverty and disability have been noted but not systematically examined.

[10] The terms "disabled people" and "individuals with disabilities" will be used in this chapter. Different individuals and groups in the disability community alternatively prefer these terms.

[11] Asian Development Bank (2000: 1).   [12] Kennedy et al. (1997: 131–132).

eaten.[13] However, men have an increased risk of developing disabling injuries or impairments associated with war and conflict.

Contributing to the correlation is the lack of resources, limited access and use of health services, and inadequate treatment for women. In many countries women are not permitted to leave the home for any significant amount of time, even for medical care, since they are responsible for taking care of the home and family. And it is often improper for women to travel unattended or to live away from male relatives (husband, father), making long-term health care and treatment less likely for them.[14] Unlike men in certain countries who receive more governmental assistance for war-based disabilities, women frequently lack assistance and control over monetary resources to pay for their medical care and treatment.

Disability, poverty, and gender inequality have common elements, and individuals with disabilities, those who are poor, and/or women share similar life experiences. Despite these similarities, these situations (namely, disability, poverty, and gender inequality) are measured frequently by different mechanisms. Although the capabilities approach has been applied extensively to poverty and gender inequality, it has only recently been used to examine disability issues.[15] However, the capabilities approach can contribute greatly to the understanding of disability and thereby provide a common strategy to address the relationships between disability, poverty, and gender issues.[16]

Sen's work and understanding disability

According to Amartya Sen, an individual's well-being should be assessed in terms of capabilities, which are the ability or potential to achieve certain functionings.[17] Functionings (achievements) range from elementary (such as being adequately healthy) to complex (such as being socially integrated). The capabilities of an individual reflect the different combination of functionings that person is able to achieve dependent on their particular circumstances. Since functionings may result from constrained choice or reflect a limitation in choices, it is important to evaluate what an individual can do or is able to do, and not just assess

---

[13] Pacey and Payne (1985) as cited in Groce (1997: 181).

[14] Groce (1997: 182) explores these issues for women.

[15] Nussbaum has addressed disability in her book *Frontiers of Justice* (2006); likewise, Saleeby has addressed disability in her work (2003; 2004; 2005; 2007), also published under her maiden name Welch (2002); see also articles written by Baylies (2002) and Mitra (2006).

[16] See initial paper by Welch (2002) emphasizing the use of the capabilities approach in understanding the similarities and relationships between disability, poverty, and gender.

[17] Sen (1980; 1993).

what they actually do. Comparing data on both capabilities (ability to achieve) and functionings (achievement) is important for understanding the individual's situation and for developing useful interventions to promote capabilities development.

Sen argues in support of a capabilities approach to poverty.[18] This is a non-welfarist approach, which uses basic achievements (such as the ability to meet basic needs by converting goods) rather than actual goods or utilities as the means for comparing well-being.[19] To focus upon an individual's opportunity to pursue his/her objectives, one must consider not only those primary goods possessed by that individual but also the relevant personal characteristics governing the conversion of primary goods into the individual's ability to promote his/her ends.[20]

Building on this perspective, the capabilities approach provides an appropriate framework for understanding disability.[21] Many disability definitions, such as the medical model, have emphasized only the body and/or mind impairments and the functional limitations resulting from these impairments. Alternatively, the social model has considered disability a social construct resulting entirely from the environment (society). However, disability has become increasingly recognized as the interaction of the individual in his/her environment.

The advantages of the capabilities approach include its embracing of both individual and environment factors, and its emphasis on their respective contributions in achieving functionings. Disability is considered "the expression of a physical or mental limitation in a social context – the gap between a person's capabilities and the demands of the environment."[22] As illustrated by Sen:

A person who has a disability may have a larger basket of primary goods and yet have less chance to lead a normal life (or to pursue her objectives) than an able-bodied person with a smaller basket of primary goods. Similarly, an older person or a person more prone to illness can be more disadvantaged in a generally accepted sense even with a larger bundle of primary goods.[23]

Therefore, the importance of diversity is recognized within the capabilities framework, a strength that has led to its favor over alternative approaches.

Poverty is considered a deprivation of capabilities. Likewise, disability can be considered a state of capabilities deprivation because the disability experience, considered the outcome of the individual and his/her

---

[18] Sen (1999: 87–88).   [19] Ravallion (1994: 4–5).   [20] Sen (1999: 74).
[21] Mitra (2006).Welch (2002); Saleeby (2003; 2004; 2005; 2007).
[22] Pope and Tarlov (1991: 1).   [23] Sen (1999: 74).

environment, negatively affects individual capabilities and functionings. In this manner, the capabilities approach provides a framework to support the interactive "biopsychosocial" model of disability. Hence, individuals with impairments (physical, mental, sensory, etc.) may certainly have the potential of achieving a number of functionings, or have a large set of capabilities. Yet, these individuals may not be able to develop certain capabilities or actualize their potential (converting capabilities into achieved functionings) as a result of personal constraints and environmental barriers experienced at different stages of the conversion process (commodities to capabilities to functionings). As stated by Sen, "attainment equality" or equal achievement of capabilities may be difficult, or even impossible, in the case of individuals with disabilities.[24]

Nussbaum's contribution to addressing disability

The capabilities approach is concerned with evaluating individual advantage in terms of "actual ability to achieve various valuable functionings as a part of living."[25] Nussbaum, like Sen, uses capabilities to indicate an evaluative space from which comparisons of well-being can be determined, especially due to the effect of diverse characteristics or factors on the conversion process. Contrary to many other approaches, the capabilities framework emphasizes both opportunities and distribution of resources among all individuals as it "asks how all the groups in the population are doing, and insists on comparing the functioning of one group to that of another."[26] Hence, it facilitates a better comparative means to determine equality and inequality among at-risk population groups, such as individuals with disabilities.

Consider the case of a woman with a disability who may possess less income but requires a greater amount to accomplish the same functionings as another woman without a disability (or to meet the same needs aside from the care of the disability). She may be a quadriplegic who earns a smaller salary than a woman without a disability or a woman with a less severe type of disability. However, a large percentage of her income must pay for costs associated with that particular type of disability (high medical bills, wheelchair maintenance costs, an accessible van with a lift, and personal assistance fees), leaving an even smaller percentage to be allocated for other basic living expenses. Even if the context differs between developing and developed countries (for instance, the use of basic adaptive equipment in a developing country versus more expensive

---

[24] Sen (1992: 91).   [25] Nussbaum and Sen (1993: 30).
[26] Nussbaum and Glover (1995: 5).

types of equipment available in a developed country), the conceptual framework remains relevant. There are still greater additional costs generally associated with a disability, which leaves a smaller percentage of discretionary or net disposal income for that individual or family to meet other needs.

As Nussbaum states, "international political and economic thought should be feminist, attentive (among other things) to the special problems women face because of sex in more or less every nation in the world, problems without an understanding of which general issues of poverty and development cannot be well confronted."[27] Similarly, the unique issues experienced by individuals with disabilities, a growing segment of the world's population, must be addressed. "Just as it is sex discrimination not to provide women with pregnancy leave, even though it is a biological fact that only women get pregnant, so, too, it is discrimination against people with impairments not to provide such supports for their productivity, even though it is a biological fact that only they will need them."[28]

Uniquely, Nussbaum identifies a list of central human capabilities and discusses how a threshold level of capabilities provides a basis for fundamental constitutional principles that individuals are entitled to demand from their governments. "In certain core areas of human functioning, a necessary condition of justice for a public political arrangement is that it deliver to citizens a certain basic level of capabilities. If people are systematically falling below the threshold in any of these core areas this should be seen as a situation both unjust and tragic, in need of urgent attention."[29] This is especially applicable to oppressed groups, such as people with disabilities who often lack a voice and the power to address their needs.

By evaluating the capabilities of these marginalized individuals (or groups) and comparing them against an actual threshold, discrepancies are determined which provide justification for advocating social policy changes and strategy recommendations. Consequently, mechanisms promoting capabilities development should be implemented for all individuals, especially marginalized population groups (disabled people, women, and the poor). This fits nicely with the notion of disability being a social construct – namely, that disability is not the direct result of impairment but rather the failure of society to address the needs created by the impairment. Just as important is "affirmation of a political duty of states to ensure that, so far as possible, impairments do not disable."[30]

[27] Nussbaum (2000: 4).   [28] Nussbaum (2007: 113).   [29] Nussbaum (2000: 71).
[30] Baylies (2002: 728).

In cases of individuals with certain types of impairments it may not be possible to achieve certain capabilities or a specific threshold of capabilities – no matter what type of assistance, support, accommodation, treatment, or policy is implemented. Nussbaum's previous argument that all the central human capabilities from her list are implicit in a life worthy of human dignity would be therefore problematic in the ongoing discussion of impairment and disability. Fortunately, Nussbaum has shifted from earlier discussions on basic capabilities stating that "capabilities are not understood as instrumental to a life with human dignity: they are understood, instead, as ways of realizing a life with human dignity in the different areas of life with which human beings typically engage."[31] As emphasized by Nussbaum herself, altering the list of capabilities or changing the threshold of capability for individuals with impairments is "practically dangerous" since it assumes "from the start that we cannot or should not meet a goal that would be difficult or expensive to meet."[32]

It is important to note that Nussbaum's approach to disability, like her approach to gender inequality, is a form of political liberalism, and consequently, her list of central human capabilities is set within this context, rendering them specifically as political goals. Certainly there are other significant issues associated with disability that political principles do not and cannot address (for example, ethical debates over the decision to get cochlear implants in deaf children by their parents to improve their hearing functioning), but these are not the primary focus at this time. Overall, the capabilities approach is particularly useful since it "allows us to examine both personal and environmental factors that affect converting commodities into functionings and that influence developing one's capability set."[33]

Bridging the capabilities approach with the ICF

According to Sen, well-being involves life with basic freedoms, such as the freedom to live a healthy life by having access to adequate medical care and treatment. Development involves expanding the freedoms enjoyed by individuals and removing the obstacles or the sources of unfreedoms, such as poverty and poor economic opportunities.[34] Similarly, disability may be seen as a source of unfreedoms due to its restrictive nature on individuals with impairments. If so, then development in this context involves alleviating or removing disability while promoting capabilities. To build capabilities means to either enhance

[31] Nussbaum (2006: 161).   [32] Nussbaum (2006: 190).   [33] Saleeby (2007: 224).
[34] Sen (1999: 3).

the positive elements (capabilities and functionings) and/or to eliminate the negative aspects (poverty and disability).

This can be accomplished with different interventions based on the conceptual framework embodied in the International Classification of Functioning, Disability, and Health (ICF).[35] Developed by the World Health Organization, the ICF provides a standard framework for describing health and health-related states. The ICF organizes its information into several domains, including body functions and structures as well as activities (execution of a task or activity by an individual) and participation (involvement in a life situation).

These ICF domains are expressed along a continuum of functioning to disability. Functioning is the umbrella term for all body functions and structures, activities, and participation. Disability is the umbrella term for impairments (loss or abnormality of body function or structure), activity limitations (difficulties individuals may have in executing activities), and participation restrictions (problems individuals may experience in involvement in life situations).[36] In comparison, there is compatibility with the ICF terms and those in the capabilities approach. Essentially, functioning(s) represents a set of doings and beings whereas disability is a lack of functioning(s) or capabilities.

As indicated, the capabilities approach emphasizes the need to move beyond functionings to assessing the fundamental capabilities of persons, what persons are really able to be or do, and moreover what environmental factors affect their capabilities. Capabilities represent the life potential or opportunities that exist for any person. In this sense, capabilities are more comparable to the ICF concept of participation since both terms describe a person's involvement in a life situation or their lived experience. Examining both capabilities and functionings together results in an improved understanding of the person's situation.

Using the ICF classification's detailed list of activities and participation allows us to identify a person's list of actual and potential functionings. Additionally, the ICF qualifiers facilitate the assessment of a person's capacity and performance, which would provide extra information on how a person's functioning changes in his/her environment. Finally, the ICF section on the environment provides helpful information on a range of environmental factors that may influence a person's potential and achieved functionings.

[35] The ICF was completed and distributed in 2001. For more information regarding the ICF, see the WHO website.
[36] Disability in the WHO ICF context differs from the traditional view of the term disability as used in the introduction to this chapter.

316   *Patricia Welch Saleeby*

Following the ICF domains, different interventions may be identified to develop the capabilities of individuals and/or to remove the disability. At the impairment (body) level, appropriate interventions are medical or rehabilitative, such as preventative measures or health-promotion activities. The domain of activity limitation involves rehabilitation, including community-based rehabilitation services that attempt to correct or extend the range of individual capacities. Or it can be addressed by the use of assistive technology[37] that compensates for activity limitations. Finally, the participation restriction domain involves interventions that change the environment (remove barriers and/or establish facilitators) as well as those social and political elements necessary to facilitate modification in the environment (research, lobbying, policies, programs, etc.). As indicated by Nussbaum:

Although in some species impairments such as blindness, deafness, paralysis, and severe cognitive impairment will probably doom the creature to a short and miserable life, with the human species this is not so, or at least need not be so. One dividend of our species' considerable control over its environment is the ability to structure environments that enable such species members to participate in social life.[38]

Compatibility of terms and the usefulness of the two frameworks in approaching the construct of disability will facilitate not only an improved understanding of disability but also the use of both approaches among individuals with disabilities and professionals working with disabled people. Like the long-term development of the capabilities approach, the ICF represents a long-term international effort. Therefore, bridging the capabilities approach with the ICF framework is important in promoting both frameworks.[39]

Overlapping issues between disability, poverty, and gender inequality

Poor people, people with disabilities, and women are treated frequently as subordinate groups in society. Individually and collectively, these individuals have been denied rights and have faced discrimination, exclusion, and isolation. All these groups have been deprived of their full

[37] Any item, piece of equipment, or product system, whether acquired commercially off the shelf, modified, or customized, that is used to increase, maintain, or improve the functional capabilities of individuals with disabilities as defined in the US Technology-Related Assistance for Individuals with Disabilities Act of 1988.
[38] Nussbaum (2006: 88).
[39] For further information on the parallels between the capabilities approach and the ICF, see Saleeby (2007).

participation in society as they continue to be marginalized socially, economically, and politically across the world.[40] Such treatment and experiences have placed these individuals at a significant disadvantage in their communities worldwide.

Martha C. Nussbaum has written much about women's experiences dealing with obstacles based on their gender, including intimidation and discrimination.[41] Similarly, disabled people continue to experience barriers based on their disability. As indicated by Nussbaum, "unequal social and political circumstances give women unequal human capabilities."[42] The same perspective applies to individuals with disabilities, and certainly the poor.

Generally, women and poor people and disabled people face unequal distribution within society or a community. If a woman has a disability, she is most likely at a greater disadvantage than either a woman without a disability or a man with a similar disability. Inequities within the household are commonly characteristic with these groups. Differences in intra-household distributions based on gender or disability are present among both poor and non-poor households occupied by women and disabled members.

Poverty analysis determines "what those capabilities are in specific societies, and who fails to reach them."[43] This same objective has application to disability analysis and gender analysis. Comparing aspects of human development (specific functionings and capabilities) between individuals with and without disabilities can provide additional insight into the life situations of disabled people. The same is true for assessments between women and men.

Furthermore, comparisons across variables (with and without disability, poor and non-poor, female or male) facilitate greater understanding of the effects of these variables on the lives of individuals. Using the capabilities approach not only to identify problems associated with poverty, disability, and gender inequality but also to develop appropriate mechanisms to address these problems is necessary. In the case of health domains, the ICF may be useful in conjunction with the capabilities approach to examine any individual's functioning and/or disability.

Overall there is much overlap between these groups that warrants exploration. When poverty is combined with inequality, regardless of whether it is based on gender, disability, or socio-economic status, the result is a

---

[40] For discussion of the oppression and marginalization of individuals with disabilities, see Oliver (1996: 23–29); Coleridge (1993: 4).
[41] See Nussbaum (2000; 1995).   [42] See Nussbaum (2000: 1).
[43] Ravallion (1994: 6) suggests Desai (1990) for capabilities-based poverty measures.

severe failure of capabilities. Interestingly, poor and disabled people as well as women and girls traditionally lack opportunities, resources, and support to develop and promote their capabilities. Thus, the application of a capabilities approach in addressing these areas seems appropriate and a necessary mechanism of intervention for the development of these groups.

Capabilities and human development among the poor, disabled people, and women

Emphasizing human capabilities is the objective of human development. By expanding both choices and opportunities, human development enables and empowers individuals to lead valued and respectful lives, and hence is an appropriate framework for examining marginalized populations such as disabled people, poor people, and women. Furthermore, development involves areas of choice highly valued by all individuals, including "participation, security, sustainability, guaranteed human rights – all needed for being creative and productive and for enjoying self-respect, empowerment and a sense of belonging to a community."[44] Since these same areas parallel those emphasized by the disability rights and independent living movements, it seems fitting to utilize a capabilities approach in addressing disability.

It is especially instrumental in developing countries, which have the majority of the poor and disabled people but currently have limited resources and opportunities for developing capabilities. In many developing countries, disability is not considered a critical issue. While human development can enhance capabilities via appropriate cultural, economic, political, and social re-orientations, some groups remain "structurally excluded from using and enhancing their capabilities."[45]

Disabled and poor individuals, along with women (and girls), have been denied access to capabilities-enabling opportunities, such as education. Individuals with disabilities "lack access to vocational training and are often trained into trades for which there is no demand or that do not provide decent livelihoods."[46] Moreover, rehabilitative services and assistive technology are not available or not affordable, especially in developing countries. Therefore, it is fundamentally important to promote capabilities development among these groups.

[44] UNDP Human Development Report 2000 (2000: 17).
[45] As discussed in the Nepal human development report published by the United Nations Development Programme (1998: 1).
[46] See Asian Development Bank, Report of the workshop on disability and development (1999: 13–14).

Conclusion

Poverty, disability, and gender affect an individual's capabilities, impacting their full participation in society. Not only can the concept of capabilities be used to examine poverty, it is also useful in assessing the dynamics of disability. Similar to poverty, disability may be considered a capabilities-deprived state where individuals with disabilities may be seen as less capable than individuals without disabilities.[47] The same can be viewed in regard to women and their traditional gender roles and their lowered status in most societies.

Furthering the understanding of the unique circumstances of individuals, including women, experiencing disability and poverty is crucial for development efforts. A dearth of policies currently exists to assist individuals with disabilities who face poverty. This situation is even more relevant to women since they are at an increased risk of becoming disabled throughout their lifetime and once disabled they are at an increased risk of being sicker, poorer, and more socially isolated than either men with disabilities or women without disabilities.[48] Utilizing the capabilities approach, including both Sen's and Nussbaum's approaches, will contribute to the knowledge base regarding disability, poverty, and gender.

For a capabilities approach to be adopted in addressing disability and poverty, we need to identify the unique needs of people with disabilities in both developed and developing countries, and understand how to meet their needs in the context of limited resources and support. The implications for the additional burden of disabilities and the traditional female role require thoughtful consideration and enlightened policies.[49] For this reason, we need to highlight the unique circumstances of those who are poor with disabilities as well as women with disabilities, who experience additional disadvantage.

REFERENCES

Abberley, P. (1987). The concept of oppression and the development of a social theory of disability. *Disability, Handicap and Society*, 2(1), 5–20.
Asian Development Bank (2000). *Technical assistance for identifying disability issues related to poverty reduction*. Manila: ADB.
(1999). *Report of the workshop on disability and development*. Manila: ADB.

[47] Goffman (1965).
[48] International Labor Organization (1989) and McPherson (1989), as cited in Groce (1997: 180).
[49] Kennedy *et al.* (1997: 152).

Barnes, C. and Mercer, G. (1995). Disabled people and community participation. In G. Craig and M. Mayo (Eds.), *Community and empowerment: A reader in participation and development* (pp. 33–45). London: Zed Books.

Baylies, C. (2002). Disability and the notion of human development: Questions of rights and capabilities. *Disability & Society*, 17(7), 725–739.

Brundtland, G.H. (1999). Speech presented at the Interagency Consultation on Disability, WHO. Retrieved August 24, 2000, from: www.who.int/ directorgeneral/speeches/1999/english/19990615_interagency-consultation. html

Chen, S. and Ravallion, M. (2008). The developing world is poorer than we thought, but no less successful in the fight against poverty, Policy Research Working Paper No. 4703. Washington, DC: World Bank.

Coleridge, P. (1993). *Disability, liberation and development.* Oxford: Oxfam.

Elwan, A. (1999). Poverty and disability: A survey of the literature, Social Protection Discussion Paper No. 9932. Washington, DC: World Bank.

Goffman, E. (1965). *Stigma: Notes on the management of a spoiled identity.* Englewood Cliffs, NJ: Prentice Hall.

Groce, N.E. (1997). Women with disabilities in the developing world: Arenas for policy revision and programmatic change. *Journal of Disability Policy Studies*, 8(1&2), 178–193.

Kennedy, C., Carlson, D., Ustun, T.B., Regier, D.A., Norquist, G. and Sirovatka, P. (1997). Mental health, disabilities, and women. *Journal of Disability Policy Studies*, 8(1&2), 129–156.

LaPlante, M. (1991). The demographics of disability. In J. West (Ed.), *The Americans with Disabilities Act: From policy to practice* (pp. 55–77). New York: Milbank Memorial Fund.

Metts, R. (2000). *Disability issues, trends and recommendations for the World Bank.* Washington, DC: World Bank.

Mitra, S. (2006). The capability approach and disability. *Journal of Disability Policy Studies*, 16(4), 236–247.

Nussbaum, M.C. (2000). *Women and human development: The capabilities approach.* Cambridge University Press.

   (1995). Human capabilities, female human beings. In M.C. Nussbaum and J. Glover (Eds.), *Women, culture and development* (pp. 61–104). Oxford: Clarendon Press.

Nussbaum, M.C. and Sen, A. (1993). *The quality of life.* Oxford: Clarendon Press.

Oliver, M. (1996). *Understanding disability: From theory to practice.* London: Macmillan.

Peat, M. (1998). Disability in the developing world. In M.A. McColl and J.E. Bickenbach (Eds.), *Introduction to disability and handicap* (pp. 43–53). Canada: W.B. Saunders.

Pope, A.M. and Tarlov, A.V. (1991). *Disability in America: Toward a national agenda for prevention.* Washington, DC: National Academy of Press, Institute of America, National Academy of Sciences.

Ravallion, M. (1994). Poverty comparisons. *Fundamentals of Pure and Applied Economics Series.* Switzerland: Harwood Academic Publishers.

Saleeby, P.W. (2007). Applications of a capability approach to disability and the international classification of functioning, disability and health (ICF) in social work practice. *Journal of Social Work in Disability & Rehabilitation*, 6(1&2), 217–232.

(2005). Exploring disability and poverty in Nepal: An application of the capability approach. Ph.D. dissertation, Washington University in St. Louis. Dissertations and Theses: A&I (Publication No. AAT 3207234).

(2004). ICF and the capability approach. *World Health Organization Family of International Classifications Newsletter*, 2(1), 9–10.

(2003). Disability, poverty, and development: An application of the capability approach in Nepal. Conference proceedings, From sustainable development to sustainable freedom. Pavia, Italy.

Seelman, K.D. (2001). Science and technology policy: Is disability a missing factor? In G.L. Albrecht, K.D. Seelman and M. Bury (Eds.), *Handbook of disability studies* (pp. 663–693). Thousand Oaks, CA: Sage Publications.

Sen, A.K. (1999). *Development as freedom*. New York: Alfred A. Knopf, Inc.

(1992). *Inequality re-examined*. Oxford: Clarendon Press.

(1980). Equality of what? In S.M. McMurrin (Ed.), *Tanner lectures in human values, Vol. 1*. Cambridge University Press.

United Nations Development Programme (2000). *Poverty Report 2000*. New York: Oxford University Press.

(1998). Nepal human development report. Retrieved from: www.undp.org.np/keydoc/nhdr98/summary.html

Welch, P. (2002). Applying the capabilities approach in examining disability, poverty and gender. Conference proceedings, Promoting women's capabilities: Examining Nussbaum's capabilities approach. Cambridge.

World Health Organization (2001). *International classification of functioning, disability and health*. Geneva: WHO.

12 Educational transformation, gender justice and Nussbaum's capabilities*

Melanie Walker

Women's education is both crucial and contested.

Martha C. Nussbaum

This chapter explores Nussbaum's capabilities because her ideas have considerable relevance to curriculum, pedagogy and educational transformation in diverse international contexts, and in particular for gender justice in and through education. Capabilities argues that human development involves expanding and widening the capability each person has to choose and enjoy 'valuable beings and doings'. These beings and doings are 'functionings' and they are constitutive of our well-being. Gender justice is understood here to mean 'a life of equality and dignity for all women and men' (Majumdar, 2000, p.1), although the focus and examples in this chapter foreground the lives of girls and women. Because gender in/justice in this chapter is seen as not only a problem of poverty nor only of developing countries but as a complex, subtle and pervasive inequality in all countries, the chapter draws on examples from schooling in South Africa and Malawi on the one hand, and higher education in England and the USA on the other. The chapter thus considers the specific relationship between capabilities and education, raising the question of which 'education capabilities' are non-negotiable for girls' and women, and how capabilities contribute substantially to gender justice theoretically and practically in education.

Nussbaum's work might be thought of as a theory of education[1], insofar as she speculates about what education ought to do, and offers descriptions and guidance for quality in education practice. Above all, she provides a philosophical justification for the formation of persons, of girls and women,

---

* The idea that Nussbaum's work could be considered as theory of education was raised but not elaborated by Holger Ziegler at the University of Bielefeld. I found the idea intriguing and have sought to develop it in this chapter. This chapter is reprinted from my Nussbaum's Capabilities, Gender Justice and Educational Transformations; in H.-U. Otto, and H. Ziegler (eds) *Enhancing Capabilities: The Role of Social Institutions*, Leverkusen: Barbara Budrich, 2013, pp.149-170.

and their values – persons with dignity, who are both autonomous and vulnerable, who care for and are cared for by others, and who understand ties of mutual obligation – a process fundamentally educational. Nonetheless, the chapter closes by considering whether her approach is sufficient for full gender justice in education, and a complete education theory.

The chapter assumes that education is not separate from gender structures in society. Education systems help produce culture, society and personal identity, and where a society contains gender inequalities these will be reproduced inside and through education, but can also be changed, albeit more rarely. Core to my concerns, therefore, is that education provided in the institutional settings of schools and universities builds over time into inter-subjective patterns, shaping what kind of girls and women we recognise ourselves to be and what we believe ourselves able to do. For example, in apartheid South Africa, all children schooled under the grossly unequal system of 'bantu education' were taught to see themselves only as unskilled labourers and domestic servants, and for a very few girls, perhaps as teachers, nurses or factory workers. Across the world there are gender gaps in girls' access to schooling and literacy education (Unterhalter, 2007) and to higher education (Morley et al., 2005), and nowhere is formal education an uncomplicated 'good' (Unterhalter, 2007). Education produces both justice and injustice, equity and inequity, advantage and disadvantage for girls and women, and we need to be able to evaluate why, when, how and for which girls and women capabilities are 'created' (Nussbaum, 2011) and how, when and for whom disadvantage is reproduced. I propose that Nussbaum's work is generative theoretically and empirically for this development and evaluative task.

Gender in/justice and education

It is a sunny late autumn day in 2003 in Cape Town, South Africa, almost a decade after the elections of 1994, which had ushered in new democratic times. I am conducting empirical research (Walker, 2006a), using the capability approach, into the lives and aspirations of black and white girls at four high schools in Cape Town. One of the four schools has an entirely black African intake of boys and girls from poor homes in the nearby townships. A group of sixteen-year-old girls, in their tenth year of school, has met with me over a lunch break to talk about themselves, their hopes and education. In the course of our conversation, they explain why having educational opportunities matters in their lives. Thandi tells me: 'In the old days, if you were a girl, then boys they can make you their wife and you will have no more education. So now we are living a new life, we feel no one will tell us what to do, except yourself.

In the old days our mothers were forced not to go to school, but to be a wife.' Tozi then adds: 'I'd like to say in these days there are opportunities to do what you really like because in the past our mothers were domestic workers, there was no other kind of work they were doing. They couldn't go further at school because of money, they were poor. But in this case we have opportunities to go further; our parents try to educate us.' Nombulelo explains to me: 'If you know how to talk for yourself, you can change things for yourself ... black people struggled for freedom, for their own voice to be heard by everybody.'

School also provides them with social opportunities to develop as persons, forming good friendships so that the quality of being 'warm-hearted' is seen to be important. 'Everything we share, everything,' Lumka says. 'She's doing everything for me when I need help and I do everything for her when she needs help,' adds Kholiswa. 'I'm very shy and they are the opposite of me and I like that because they bring out that part of me, when I'm around them I also talk and become lively,' comments Lillian, who adds: 'Every time I am in trouble she seems always to have the answers and every time she is in trouble, I have the answers.'

But there is also a dark side to their stories – that of harassment by male peers and teachers. However, these girls reject being dealt with in this way. As Sibongile says: 'A boy must talk to a girl nicely and treat her as a human being.' All the girls imagined better lives for themselves than had been possible for their parents. Without the opportunities to go to school, and to complete twelve years at a decent school, these girls would find it difficult to imagine alternative futures to those of their mothers, and harder still to realise those futures in a country in which femaleness is still less valued than maleness, notwithstanding the gender-progressive constitution.

The point of rehearsing the voices of girls above is to underline the key point in this chapter on capabilities and education: the impact of educational arrangements and educational outcomes on the lives, life chances and well-being of girls and women as a matter of justice. This role and value of education is recognised in the capability approach; indeed, education is presented as fundamental to having a range of opportunity freedoms. Thus, Sen (1992, p.44) identifies education as one of 'a relatively small number of centrally important beings and doings that are crucial to [women's] well being', crucial for the expansion of freedom, and hence crucial for gender equality. For Sen, education is personal, interpersonal, social and political, and has redistributive potential. Nussbaum asserts that education is the key to women's empowerment and to women 'making progress on other problems in their lives' (2004a, pp. 319–320). Robeyns (2005, p.74) has also developed a list of fourteen gender-equality capabilities, including 'education and knowledge: being able to be educated and to use and produce knowledge'. Thus, having the opportunity for education and the development of an education capability expands a girl's or a woman's freedoms to choose a life which is good for her. Following the capability approach we would use capability as our measure of how well girls and women are doing in education – do they have genuine and equal opportunity to convert resources into valued functionings? Do they have equality in opportunities to choose education, or more education?

Let's take an example of 'choosing' from a rich, developed country, England, where gender and social class are still persistent determinants of social identities and influence actions and attitudes across society. Thus, even bright working-class girls might find that their schools are less than supportive, and peer cultures reinforce low teacher expectations. In a project (Walker, 2006b) researching the experiences of widening participation in higher education for working-class students, also using the capability approach, Janet explained that at her state school in the north of England, 'We were laughed at at school because it was like, "What are you doing that for, you don't want to do any work, you just want to get a job once you've finished." We had careers advisers but they weren't much help. On the one hand it was, "You've got to do as well as you can" but on the other it was, "Just do your GCSEs and then get a job"' (ibid., p.6). Thus, a working-class girl who is told by her teachers to concentrate on passing her school leaving exams at age sixteen and to find a job because 'university is not for her' may revise her expectations of what she might become and do. If she then does not 'choose' university it is because school and teachers have encouraged her to lower her aspirations and 'adapt' her preferences (Nussbaum, 2000).

To take another example of experiences in education from a recent project (Kamwendo, 2008), Malawian girls said: 'Boys are selfish, they do not even want to sit next to us because they say we will lead them into temptation. They always sit at the back and when we girls dare to sit at the back they chase us and abuse us verbally.' Or the girl who said of her teachers: 'When we ask our teachers questions, they tell us that we will understand some time in future or that they do not have time to explain things. Sometimes they make fun of us and ask us if our grandparents were intelligent and argue that this is why we fail to understand what they teach' (ibid., p.157). These adolescent girls explain their low achievement in schools as 'natural' because 'Girls think that when they get married after finishing school their husbands might not allow them to work outside the home. So they see no point in working hard in school.' And 'When girls try to work hard, they fail to concentrate because they think that they will get married and that their husbands will take care of them and that their job will be to take care of the children' (ibid., p.152). If girls in Malawi in Africa are systematically underachieving relative to boys in all subject areas and failing their school leaving examination, then we have injustice for girls. If Malawian girls are being taught by home, school and society that their only acceptable future is marriage at a young age and children, or that girls must do all the household chores, taking time away from their studies, or if most teachers have lower expectations of girls, and if girls themselves lower their hopes as a result, as Kamwendo's research shows, then there are significant barriers to girls' educational achievements.

Through institutional practices, gender disadvantage becomes normalised in and through curricula, pedagogies and school and college cultures. Iris Marion Young explains how normalisation works:

Unfair normalization occurs when institutions and practices expect individuals to exhibit certain kinds of attributes and/or behaviours that are assumed as the norm, but which some individuals are unable to exhibit, or can only exhibit at an unfair cost to themselves, because they are different. (2006, p.96)

Educational institutions embed such normalisation processes over time in the assumptions about how they operate, making change slow and difficult. This is beautifully captured in Tagore's poem (in Alam and Chakravarty, 2011) 'The Two Birds', which recounts the story of a caged bird which has come to accept its confinement, has lost the strength to fly, and a bird flying free, wild and unfettered in the forest.

But as well as playing an essential role in the process of reproducing gender structures – what girls can be and do – formal education is potentially a source of social transformation, as the capability approach recognises. Education can provide girls and women with the critical and reflective participatory capabilities and forms of consciousness and understanding that will enable them to participate in the creation of more equal and more democratic forms of social life (Nussbaum, 2006a). Education can then contribute to individual well-being – what makes a life go well for each of us now and in the future – and not only or always to ill-being. Returning to Janet's story, she had a different experience at her middle-class post-sixteen sixth-form college, which expected its students to go on to university, to work hard to this end and encouraged her to apply to university. Teachers in turn supported her in achieving the required entry grades, as she explains: 'Even though I struggled a bit ... my English teacher said just work hard, you're fine, you're doing well, and gave me some more support' (Walker, 2006b, p.6).

We can find other examples of moments of equity and transformation in and through education, even where gender structures remain in place in society. Deprez and Butler (2007) apply capabilities to evaluating the educational opportunities of low-income women parents in Maine, USA. They argue that their data 'provide new evidence of the importance of education for greatly expanding the opportunities for and enriching the lives of recipients of welfare' (ibid., p.224). Their rich evidence points to changes in women's self-concept, for example one twenty-seven-year-old single mother who said: 'I have gained so much confidence in myself through this experience. Before I began school I felt absolutely worthless, as if I was a total waste of life ... I cannot imagine how life would have been if I had not entered this institution' (ibid., p.225). Deprez and Butler explore the impact on lives, better employment opportunities, role modelling for children, making a contribution to communities, relationships and a sense of security about the future. They paint a hopeful, evidence-informed picture of women's empowerment through educational opportunities and their capability formation, summed up by the woman who said: 'I will always be grateful to have had the opportunity to complete my education. That is the one factor that can help me from sliding into hopeless poverty' (ibid., p.231).

This transformative potential of education is further captured in recent moves to establish a new women's university in Bangladesh, as described by Nussbaum (2004b). A liberal arts curriculum is being developed because 'nothing else can produce the sort of resourceful critical world citizens that these [developing] nations need if they are to solve their problems' (ibid., 2004b, p.5). Pedagogically, there is an emphasis on women students being active and participatory rather than docile and quiet. Knowledge, pedagogy and identity formation will intersect to produce valued and valuable outcomes and enhanced freedom for women graduates, as critical and challenging thinkers, and as intelligent, imaginative and active participants in learning.

Central (education) capabilities

In my view, Nussbaum's central human capabilities can be generative for thinking about and transforming education so that we maximise the moments of equity and minimise the moments of inequity for girls and women. While in some way all her capabilities bear directly or indirectly on education, there are some which are especially relevant. I would argue that if these were not found in educational provision, experiences and achievements, then there would be gaps in the quality of education on offer, and most likely gaps in what was possible for girls and women. Nussbaum herself points to two capabilities out of her list of ten which she argues are of special importance – 'practical reason' and 'affiliation'. The former capability involves 'being able to form a conception of the good and to engage in critical reflection about the planning of one's life' (2000, p.79). The affiliation capability concerns 'being able to live with and toward others, to recognise and show concern for other human beings, to engage in various forms of social interactions; to be able to imagine the situation of another and to have compassion for that situation; to have the capability for both justice and friendship ... having the social bases of self-respect and non-humiliation; being able to be treated as a dignified being whose worth is equal to that of others' (2000, pp.79–80). As Nussbaum explains further:

Among the capabilities, two, practical reason and affiliation stand out as of special importance, since they both organise and suffuse all the others, making their pursuit truly human. To use one's senses in a way not infused by the characteristically human use of thought and planning is to use them in an incompletely human manner. To plan for one's own life without being able to do so in complex forms of discourse, concern and reciprocity with other human beings is, again to behave in an incompletely human way. (ibid., p.82)

She asserts that 'human powers of practical reason and sociability' (ibid., p.72) are so important that they count as part of who we are, of our humanity, and they count universally. They must, then, be present in education as practices, and present in how we theorise about education.

In addition, we can add her distinctive education capability from her list of 'senses, imagination and thought':

Being able to use the senses to imagine, think and reason – and to do these things in a 'truly human way', a way informed and cultivated by an adequate education, including but by no means limited to literacy and basic mathematical and scientific training. Being able to use imagination and thought in connection with experiencing and producing self-expressing works and events of one's own choice, religious, literary, musical and so forth. Being able to use one's mind in ways protected by guarantees of freedom of expression with respect to both political and artistic speech, and freedom of religious exercise. Being able to search for the ultimate meaning of life in one's own way. Being able to have pleasurable experiences and to avoid non-necessary pain. (ibid., pp.78–79)

Fourth, there is her capability for 'emotions' which is also central to educational practice – when girls feel resentful, upset, frightened, hostile, nervous, humiliated, alienated, they do not learn well. When girls are confident, secure and cared for, they are more likely to learn.

In her writing specifically on education Nussbaum (1997, 2006a) further identifies three capabilities which she sees as fundamental. In her account of liberal education in the USA she advocates three core capabilities for the 'cultivation of humanity': critical self-examination, the ideal of the world citizen, and the development of the narrative imagination. Recently she has written more explicitly about education and democratic citizenship (2006b) and linked capabilities and gender quality in education (2006a). Her three-part model to develop young people's (especially girls' and young women's) capabilities through education is substantially similar to that outlined in *Cultivating Humanity*: critical thinking, world citizenship and imaginative understanding.

As these can be seen as constitutive elements of capabilities on her list (especially practical reason and affiliation, but also emotions and imagination) they flesh out the specificity of her list for educational applications. While not strictly (or narrowly) educational, gender justice education would also have to take into account Nussbaum's capability of 'bodily integrity'; girls in schools tell us that this matters greatly to them (Walker, 2006a). Pedagogical or institutional encounters which are suffused with any kind of threat of harassment or gendered disrespect are not situations for effective or confident exercise of agency. Education policies and systems would need to act to ensure 'bodily health' (learning while ill or undernourished is hard). That not all of the capabilities on Nussbaum's list are non-negotiable in the space of education should not be a problem, given that Nussbaum details a list that includes but goes well beyond education to provide the basis for a decent social and political (not just educational) minimum. We might describe these various capabilities and their exercise as 'fertile functionings' (Wolff and De-Shalit, 2007, p.10) in that having these education capabilities is likely to secure further functionings in the future. Not to have this kind of capability generates 'corrosive disadvantage' (ibid., p.10) in that further disadvantage might follow.

Nussbaum's vision, then, is of education which creates capabilities for critical practical reason and associational life, which must then be equally open to girls and women. Furthermore, Nussbaum's capabilities need not be seen as unduly prescriptive, as I think Unterhalter (2007) suggests, for the form and content of education. They might rather be seen to provide a kind of multidimensional framework for gender-just education which can be tested and adjusted empirically. Her list, particularly the selections which I have noted above as 'education capabilities', enables us to ask evaluative questions about which capabilities are present for education as opportunities for access, participation and success, which are available in education through curriculum, pedagogy and assessment, and which are missing and for whom. The importance here is to construct a lens in which the question 'equality of what?' is not simply answered in terms of resources and preferences; rather, the picture shifts to ask what kind of life girls and women value and are able to choose on the basis of reasoned reflection appropriately nurtured in educational settings.

But Nussbaum is also deeply concerned with the ties that hold human beings together and how education 'can do a great deal to make these ties deeper, more pervasive and more evenhanded' (Nussbaum, 2006c, p.157), producing both capabilities and the valuing of capabilities over time, or put another way what kind of human beings we might become through education. While Sen (1999) might emphasise public reasoning and embed his capability approach in deliberative processes and social choice, Nussbaum, from a philosophical direction, emphasises a public conception of the person which 'cannot imagine living well without shared ends and shared life' (2006b, p.158). It matters what kind of girls and women we become, able to evaluate some ethical values or ideals or goods to be more important than others. To develop girls' and women's capability as 'strong evaluators' (Taylor, 1985) is to develop them as subjects able to reflect on and to be able to re-examine their valued ends, when challenged to do so. They reflect on what is of more or less ethical significance in the narrative interpretation of their lives; these self under-standings constitute who they are.

Being free to choose to do and to be

However, it needs to be said that what Nussbaum has in mind in outlin-ing her approach is capability – not functioning (the beings and doings you choose to enact). Through education students should be enabled to develop their capabilities, especially those of practical reason and affili-ation. But what they choose to do with their lives cannot be pre-determined. Nussbaum is clear on this. 'It is appropriate,' she writes, 'that we shoot for capabilities, and those alone. Citizens must be left free to determine their own course after that' (2000, p.87). Individuals are allowed to pursue their different life paths, and no particular conception of the good life is prescribed.

This refusal to specify in any detail is important in two ways. The first is that it acknowledges the central importance of practical reason. We cannot claim to want to foster this capability and then say what kind of life pupils and students must choose. But she qualifies this position in two key ways for education. The first is to argue that in the area of self respect and dignity, 'the actual functioning is the appropriate aim of public policy' (2006c, p.172). Thus, in schools and colleges it would not be enough to foster capabilities for equal recognition and equal valuing and then allow children and students to act as they pleased towards each other. Nussbaum writes that such an approach would be both 'bizarre and unfortunate' for we want 'political [educational] prin-ciples that offer respect to all citizens and, in this one instance, the principles should give them no choice in the matter' (ibid.). The point is that if we jettison functioning in areas which are crucial to educational development, we turn away from the matter of how girls and women experience their lives in schools and colleges and the actual achievements towards progress in their capabilities and gender equality in education and society. Rather, gender justice ought to unequivocally rule out any condoning of the sexual harassment of girls by their peers or by teachers, or mocking girls for their ambitions or achievements.

Her second qualification is in the case of children and she argues that if we take a mature capability to be 'so important, so crucial to the development or maintenance of all the others' (2000, p.91) then we ought to promote functioning that feeds this capability, whether or not girls say they value it. Nussbaum (2003) would agree on the importance of children learning critical thinking and the skills of critical reflection, whether or not they choose to use or reject these as mature functionings in adult life. Children, she argues, ought not to be 'held hostage to a single conception' (ibid., p.42) of a good life. While she is future focused in relation to children learning about possibilities of good lives other than their own, there is the argument, too, that this is important also in children's present lives as choosers. In general, however, functioning would involve girls and women choosing for themselves how to be active in the world, and this cannot be predicted or prescribed by education; people may still make bad choices. What we can do is foster values in education which assist the exercise of ethical judgements so that girls and women (and all students) might at least learn that freedom ought to be well rather than badly used. 'We want,' Saito (2003, p.29) argues, 'to develop the judgment of the person to be able to value in which way it is appropriate to use capabilities through education.' For example, Saito writes, we may want a student to become a mathematician or an artist but not a drug addict or a murderer. Through education we would try to teach values that make the former choices more valued than the latter, developing both autonomy and judgement about how to exercise autonomy as democratic citizens.

Helpfully, then, Nussbaum (2006a) develops her ideas by linking her three education capabilities explicitly to the formation of democratic citizens and the capabilities required for the political effectiveness of girls and women. She (2006b) reminds us of the importance of education for democracy, drawing on Dewey and Tagore. Dewey's concern is also for democracy as education as much as education for democracy, so that democracy for Dewey 'is primarily a mode of associated living, of conjoint and communicated experience' (quoted in Nussbaum, 2006b, p.5). Children are educated about democracy by doing democracy as a kind of 'cooperative inquiry' in their own classrooms; they learn democracy by being members of a group that acts democratically. Education as democracy creates public spaces and webs of relations, where people respect each other and, through communicating with each other, help to develop the kind of people they will become (Griffiths, 2003, p.126). We build shared agreements to bring about improvements in justice; fostering capabilities in educational settings would contribute to such democratic ends.

Furthermore, although not limited by any means to the education of girls and women, Nussbaum (2006b) is a passionate advocate of the importance of the arts in education and the importance of these to healthy democracies. She has employed the ideas of Dewey and Tagore to mount a counter critique to the current emphasis on the profit motive and the education policy concern with science and technology as crucial to economic competitiveness. Thus, she writes:

If we do not insist on the crucial importance of the humanities and the arts, they will drop away, because they don't make money. They only do what is much more precious than that, make a world that is worth living in, and democracies that are able to overcome fear and suspicion and to generate vital spaces for sympathetic and reasoned debate. (ibid., p.15)

While she has no objection to good scientific and technical education, her concern is the neglect of 'other abilities, equally crucial to the health of any democracy internally, and to the creation of a decent world culture' (ibid., p.2). She associates these abilities with the humanities and the arts and developed them in her earlier work on liberal arts education in universities (1997) and the education of girls (2006a). The arts, Nussbaum argues (2006b, p.8), 'are great sources of joy for children, and indeed for adults as well. Participating in plays, songs, and dances fills children with joy, and this joy carries over into the rest of their education'. Linking the arts, education and gender equality, she explains further:

Entertainment is crucial to the ability of the arts to offer perception and hope. It's not just the experience of the performer, then, that is so important for democracy, it's the way in which performance offers a venue for exploring difficult issues without crippling anxiety. Tagore's notorious performance in which Amita Sen danced the role of the "Green Fairy," and his even more notorious performance in which she danced the Queen and the accompanying text used the word "breast" (until it was changed to "heart") were the milestones for women that they were because they were artistically great and extremely enjoyable. In the end, the audience could not sustain habits of shock and anger, against the gentle assault of beautiful music and movement. (ibid., p.10)

Through these aesthetic experiences we foster rich human being-ness.

Nussbaum: a theory of education

There are several ways in which Nussbaum's capabilities resonate with and are important for educational transformation in general and gender justice in particular, and can be argued to be the principles for a theory of education and social justice. Here I extrapolate a multi-dimensional framework of aims and practices based on her ideas.

The aims of education

(i) *The formation of human beings.* I think Nussbaum has a view about what a 'good' education for girls and women ought to include, and what the aims of education ought to be. The guiding idea behind her list of human capabilities is to ask the question, specifically here in the arena of education, 'what would be a way of being able to live and act that is minimally compatible with human dignity?' (2006c, p.162). This would constitute the key aim for education. Nussbaum takes a stand on which capabilities matter for a life of dignity that is 'truly human'. Conditions that harm this dignity then need attention, and we might include here not only access to education but also participation and success in education. Her stand on human dignity directs us also to pay attention to the lives of the vulnerable and disabled as well as the strong (ibid.), and to the educational opportunities of all.

(ii) *Education forms democratic citizens.* Thus the education capabilities she identifies are 'abilities crucial to the health of any democracy internally, and to the creation of a decent world culture' (2006b, p.4). As noted earlier, the arts and humanities have a distinctive role to play in 'making a world worth living in', as well as being intrinsically enormously worthwhile. Thus Nussbaum's capabilities-based theory of education seeks to foster what is required for each person – not just girls and women, although paying special attention to their inclusion – to function as a full and participating member of a democratic society.

(iii) *Education is intrinsically as well as instrumentally beneficial.* Capabilities and human dignity offer a view of education as more than education for economic development and human capital (see Walker, 2012), incorporating a view of education as an intrinsic good for individuals and society. Nussbaum is especially robust in her critique of 'impoverished norms of market exchange' (2006b, p.5) applied to education (also see Nussbaum, 2010), so that 'the abilities of citizenship are doing very poorly, in every nation, in the most crucial years of children's lives, the years known as K through 12' (ibid., p.12). 'What will we have, if these trends continue?' Nussbaum (ibid., p.15) asks. 'Nations of technically trained people who don't know how to criticize authority, useful profit-makers with obtuse imaginations. What could be more frightening than that?' This is not to say that education is not important for expanding economic opportunities for girls and women; of course it is because these in turn enable girls and women to have a wider capability set for work and life choices. Rather, capabilities captures both the economic and non-economic value of education (Sen 2003; Nussbaum, 2004; Robeyns, 2006) and the intrinsic pleasure in the challenges of learning, understanding and acquiring knowledge. Capabilities thus recognizes that while girls' and women's education can be for something else, such as economic opportunities, or better maternal and child health, they must also be intrinsically good for girls and women, regardless of what else education does.

(iv) *Education transforms constraining adapted preferences.* Nussbaum's capabilities direct us to recognise, understand and work to change the adapted preferences of girls and women where such preferences might not be in the best interests of the chooser. For example, our preferences to have a job or go to university are not 'natural' but shaped by what girls and women think about themselves, their self-confidence and what the society tells them about the opportunities that are likely to be open to them. Unequal social and political circumstances lead to unequal chances and unequal capabilities to choose. These external (material as well as cultural) circumstances 'affect the inner lives of people: what they hope for, what they love, what they fear, as well as what they are able to do' (Nussbaum, 2000, p.31).

(v) *Certain education capabilities are non-negotiable and frame development and evaluation for equality and democracy.* Nussbaum's stand on human dignity directs us to think about some capabilities as irreducibly educational; if they are not being developed, we could not reasonably claim that a process of education was under way. For education, therefore, I suggest that we need to specify what the most valuable capabilities are –through reasoned, inclusive public discussion as Sen advocates (1992), but also through extrapolating core capabilities as Nussbaum (2000) does. Certainly one might argue that without specifying some core capabilities as the aim of gender justice in education, capabilities alone might be 'domesticated' and not take education policy and practice far enough, for example if girls were not allowed to attend school because the equal distribution of education opportunity was not culturally sanctioned, this would not emerge as a priority for public debate. In my view, Nussbaum is of considerable help in this matter in her clarity that in arguing for justice we need to give content to our ideas.

Educational practices

(i) *Curriculum.* Nussbaum does not neglect curriculum, which is crucial for a rounded theory of education. She writes about it in relation to the women's university project in Bangladesh, arguing for a curriculum in which knowledge and critical reflection on the social construction of gender and critical tools to imagine and act for change are essential, specifying knowledge as a central capability, and advocating public education which provides women with information about rights and opportunities as well as images of worth and possibility (2004a). She has written about the contribution of the realist social novel in education (1990, p.84), to equip us with insight and practical wisdom, able to evolve our own view of the good or complete human life, and also able to use these insights to benefit others. She (1997) has also written at length about liberal education and the distinctive role of philosophy in the curriculum. She has further made it clear that publicly funded education contributes significantly to the health of democratic societies (2006a). In general, then, this curriculum guidance points in the direction not always directly at gender justice but at the kind of human beings we might want girls and women to become as we strive for greater equality. Gender justice then articulates with and is integral to wider aspirations for justice in society.

(ii) *Pedagogies.* There is much indirect pedagogical guidance offered by Nussbaum's theory of education. We know that pedagogies need to be developed which foster critical thinking, narrative imagination, and world citizenship. We know that particular forms of associational life matter and should be captured in pedagogical processes which are democratic, inclusive and respectful, and value and recognise all identities. Thus non-recognition, misrecognition, indifference and disrespect in schools and colleges reduce human dignity, rather than expanding capabilities. Equal recognition and valuing from others are essential to the development of a successful and powerful learning identity, to self-confidence, self-esteem and self-respect; experiencing these associational practices is crucial for the positive individual and collective lifelong educational development of girls and women who struggle against already-gendered identities. Nussbaum's (2006b) mobilisation of Dewey and Tagore described earlier further suggests which pedagogical practices she finds educationally

valuable. Dewey, Nussbaum notes, argued that democratic processes experienced in school form democratic citizens, because democracy 'is more than a form of government; it is primarily a mode of
associated living, of conjoint communicated experience' (quoted in
Nussbaum, 2006c, p.5). He argued that education and learning are
social and interactive processes, all students should have the opportunity to participate actively in their own learning; education is then
not only a place to gain knowledge and skills but also a place to learn
how to live. Tagore not only advocated the arts but also followed a
pedagogical approach which was based on reasoning, common
fellowship and dialogic. For both, education can be instrumental in
creating social change – by changing people, by expanding their
capabilities to choose worthwhile lives, reform is possible. Thus,
we have a view of valuable pedagogical practices which are participatory, dialogic, inclusive, empowering, social and confidence-building
for all.

Some reservations

There are gaps in Nussbaum's theory if taken to be a theory of education –
but this is true of most theorists of education. I address two that I see:
whether thresholds is an adequate concept for education and relations of
power and struggles for change.

Nussbaum, in her full theory of capabilities (that is, beyond just attention to education), frames a threshold level in her central capabilities as a
necessary condition of justice. If certain individuals or groups (girls and
women in education) are 'systematically falling below the threshold in any
of these core areas, this should be seen as a situation both unjust and
tragic; in need or urgent attention – even if in other respects things are
going well' (2000, p.71). But there may be a problem of how one deals
with capability 'thresholds' (Nussbaum, 2000) in the space of education,
as opposed to more generally. Should we argue only for basic education
for poor girls and women and leave it there? What might we mean by
'threshold' in education where basic needs can be assumed to have already
been met but where few women in developing counties progress to higher
education? Do we risk limiting our equality expectations by applying
thresholds in evaluating girls' and women's education? Ought not education to be informed by commitments to full flourishing? While basic
education might be all that is achievable in any one country at a particular
historical point, we need to ask whether at that point we have satisfied the
philosophical vision that informs Nussbaum's capabilities such that
struggles for further opportunities ought to continue. Unterhalter (2007)

suggests that there is a more expansive framing of gender equality in education available, challenging unjust forms of power, the denial of rights and capabilities, the inequitable distribution of resources, and restrictions on participation in and empowerment through education. Moreover, we might not want to absolve richer countries of their obligations to support poorer nations in struggling for gender equality in education as a matter of global justice (ibid.). Arguably the logic of Nussbaum's theorisation of capabilities is to take us in this direction, and in her own recent work (2006c) she argues for the importance of globalising justice and for a 'decent global society' (p.324) by 'extending justice to all those in the world who ought to be treated justly' (p.92). From this perspective we would need to hold an expansive view of thresholds in which each girl's and woman's full potential to be educated was kept on the table, however ambitious this project might appear where resources are scarce. We should pragmatically pursue feasible justice, while not losing sight of the need to struggle for full equality and dignity.

Second, a theory of education needs to include relations of power and the links between power, curriculum and pedagogical action if we are to understand how resources are converted into educational functionings and into educational and social change. We are differently positioned in pedagogical encounters through relations of power and 'capital' (Bourdieu, 1986); the voices of girls and women may be weak or silenced in processes of dialogue and agreement making. The focus of capabilities on the development of individuals has limits when we come to address the choices people make, even girls and women who are well educated, or how power influences conversion of resources in education, as well as institutional and systemic exclusions in education through gender injustice. We need therefore to consider both the internal resources women and girls are able to develop through having a good education, and external social arrangements such as public policy for gender equality. Nussbaum (2000) might argue that her notion of combined capabilities does precisely this by distinguishing between internal capabilities and combined capabilities where the latter are defined as internal capabilities plus the external conditions (material and institutional) that make the exercise of a function a possibility. But this is still to emphasise individual capability formation and to neglect the structures that determine what opportunities women and girls have. Wolff and De-Shalit (2007) explain:

Your resources are what you have to play with; the structure provides the rules of the game. Understood this way, aspects of the social structure are just as important in determining your genuine opportunities for secure functionings as your internal and external resources. (2007, p.173)

They suggest that we need to address three dimensions of opportunity: internal resources, external resources and structures. It is not entirely clear that Nussbaum's capabilities address these dimensions fully, or the institutional and cultural barriers to change or even how change can be operationalised.

Moreover, under conditions of structural inequality (national and global), particularly for poor women and girls, individual capabilities are always in process, not fixed achievements. The point is what can be done if individual capabilities have been enabled but cannot be practised structurally. It is even conceivable that capabilities might disadvantage individuals and communities once claims are made (or even exaggerated, as in the UK discourse about 'failing boys') for what girls and women are able to do, as if they are no longer vulnerable, say, to the exigencies of national or global markets, or as if they no longer have a claim on special assistance to enable their functioning. In short, as if broader social and economic arrangements are not at stake, or as if structures of gendered (or raced or classed) power are easily dissolved through capability forma-tion, even though embodying justice in individual girls' and women's capabilities might move us in the direction of broader justice, especially in oppressive societies where acts of solidarity by individuals might still have cumulative effects, 'the power of the powerless even in hard times' (O'Neill, 1996, p.201).

But for Nussbaum's theory of education to be able to account for individual resources and external resources and structures, and above all change in education and through education, it would need to be fleshed out in relation to a finer, more complex examination of the relationship between individual agents and structures, and processes of struggle (a participatory political process) in and through education for transformation. Additional theoretical resources may need to be deployed to do this. Nussbaum recognises that women's education is contested – how, then, does this translate into strategies and implemen-tation, and does her work, understood as a theory of education, need to account for this?

Conclusion

Thinking about Nussbaum's work as a theory of education (with explanatory limits as any theory of education would have) seems a generative way forward for research on education and gender/justice.

Consistent with what I have identified as specifically education(al) capabilities, Nussbaum's capabilities are an invitation to a challenging dialogue, 'a proposal put forward in a Socratic fashion, to be tested against the more secure of our intuitions as we attempt to arrive at a type of reflective equilibrium for political purposes' (Nussbaum, 2000, p.77). The pragmatism of capabilities has appeal for education as a social practice in its emphasis on what 'people are actually able to do and to be' (ibid., p.5). We cannot make good judgements about how well we are doing in reaching for gender justice in education without considering what girls and women actually can do and can become through the curriculum and pedagogical interactions and relationships of teachers and students. Applications would need to be demonstrated empirically through thick description if they are to convince. Abstractions are important, but it is considered attention, especially to particularity and complexities, that accounts for enlarged thought, and which anchors our theoretical justifications in practical implementations.

REFERENCES

Alam, F. and Chakravarty, R. (eds) (2011) *The Essential Tagore* (Cambridge, MA: The Belknap Press)

Bourdieu, P. (1986) Forms of capital: in J.G. Richardson (ed) *Handbook of Theory and Research for the Sociology of Education* (Westport, CT: Greenwood Press)

Deprez, L. and Butler, S. (2007) The Capability Approach and women's economic security: access to higher education under welfare reform: in M. Walker and E. Unterhalter (eds) *Amartya Sen's Capability Approach and Social Justice in Education* (New York: Palgrave)

Griffiths, M. (2003) *Action for Social Justice in Education* (Maidenhead: Open University Press)

Kamwendo, M. (2008) *Gendered Identities and Girls' Achievement in Malawian Secondary Schools. Unpublished doctoral dissertation,* School of Education, University of Sheffield

Majumdar, M. (2000) *Human Development through the 'Prism of Gender'* (Madras Institute of Development Studies)

Morley, L., Sorhaindo, A. and Burke, P.J. (2005) *Researching Women. An annotated bibliography on gender equity in Commonwealth higher education* (London: Institute of Education/Association of Commonwealth Universities)

Nussbaum, M.C. (1990) *Love's Knowledge. Essays on Philosophy and Literature* (Oxford University Press)

(1997) *Cultivating Humanity. A Classical Defence of Reform in Liberal Education* (Cambridge, MA: Harvard University Press)

(2000) *Women and Human Development. The Capabilities Approach* (Cambridge University Press)

(2003) Political liberalism and respect: a response to Linda Barclay, *Nordic Journal of Philosophy*, 4/2, 25–44

(2004a) Women's education: a global challenge, *Signs*, 29/2, 325–355

(2004b) Liberal education and global community, *Liberal Education, Winter*, 90/1, 42–47

(2006a) Education and democratic citizenship: capabilities and quality education, *Journal of Human Development*, 7/3, 385–395

(2006b) Tagore, Dewey, and the Imminent Demise of Liberal Education. Paper presented at the conference on Tagore's Philosophy of Education, Kolkata, March 29–30

(2006c) *Frontiers of Justice* (Cambridge, MA: Belknap Press)

(2010) *Not for Profit* (Princeton University Press)

(2011) *Creating Capabilities. The Human Development Approach* (Cambridge, MA: The Belknap Press)

O'Neill, O. (1996) *Towards Justice and Virtue* (Cambridge University Press)

Robeyns, I. (2005) Sen's Capability Approach and gender inequality: in B. Agarwal, J. Humphries and I. Robeyns (eds) *Amartya Sen's Work and Ideas* (London and New York: Routledge).

Saito, M. (2003) Amartya Sen's Capability Approach to education: a critical exploration, *Journal of Philosophy of Education*, 37/1, 17–33

Sen, A. (1992) *Inequality Re-examined* (Oxford University Press)

(1999) *Development as Freedom* (New York: Alfred A. Knopf)

(2003) Human capital and human capability: in S. Fukudo-Parr and A.K. Kumar (eds) *Readings in Human Development* (New Delhi, Oxford and New York: Oxford University Press)

Taylor, C. (1985) *Human Agency and Language. Philosophical Papers 1* (Cambridge University Press)

Walker, M. (2006a) Towards a capability-based theory of social justice in education, *Journal of Education Policy*, 21/2, 163–185

(2006b) *Social Class Narratives and Constructions of Identity in Higher Education.* Unpublished paper, School of Education, University of Sheffield

(2012) A capital or capabilities education policy narrative in a world of staggering inequalities?, *International Journal of Educational Development*, 32/3, 384–393

Unterhalter, E. (2003) The capabilities approach and gendered education, *Theory and Research in Education*, 1/1, 7–22

(2007) *Gender, Schooling and Global Social Justice* (London: Routledge)

Wolff, J. and De-Shalit, A. (2007) *Disadvantage* (Oxford University Press)

Young, I.M. (2006) Education in the context of structural injustice: a symposium response, *Educational Philosophy and Theory*, 38/1, 93–103

13   The social contract, unpaid child care and women's income capability*

Hilde Bojer

Introduction

In *Women and Human Development*, Martha C. Nussbaum describes her list of capabilities as a 'freestanding moral idea'. Her list also represents minimum or threshold capabilities, such that falling short of any one of them is truly tragic, and she writes: 'Where women are concerned, almost all the world societies are very far from providing the basic minimum of truly human functioning ... I therefore leave the debate about levels of equality for a later stage, when the differences become meaningful in practice' (2000: 86).

The present chapter goes a step further and concerns equality of capabilities between women and men. I argue, first, that the Rawlsian social contract can be extended to include the rights of women as well as the rights of children. Further, I argue that concern for capabilities follows more plausibly from the original position than concern for what Rawls calls primary goods. Since the just social contract must provide for the right of every child to care, nurture and education, the equality of women and men cannot in justice be obtained at the expense of children's well-being. These arguments do not depend on the validity of the difference principle.

I then discuss the connection between women's income capability and the way society organises child care. Child care is an unavoidable social duty if humankind is to survive. No society can afford to be so liberal that children are neglected. But child care is also an activity that reduces income capability. Therefore, I argue, social and economic equality between men and women demands equal sharing of child care.[1]

Susan Moller Okin (1989, especially Chapter 7) convincingly explains how the burden of unpaid housework makes women economically

---

* Comments from the two editors are gratefully acknowledged.
[1] Unpaid care for elderly and sick members of the family also falls mainly on women. In the present chapter, I concentrate on children, since an argument for sharing the other forms of unpaid care would have to be framed differently from the case of children.

vulnerable. Let me supply and update her arguments with some facts about my own country, Norway. The Scandinavian countries are considered, and I believe rightly considered, to be the foremost in the world as regards equality between women and men. In particular, the labour force participation rates of Norwegian women and men are almost the same. And yet in 2009 the average income before tax of women was only 60 per cent of that of men. There are two reasons for this large difference. First, about half of the women in paid work are part timers. Second, the earnings of women in full-time work are about 80 per cent of men's wages. This last difference is probably mainly due to occupational segregation in the Norwegian labour market, with women strongly concentrated in low-paid, mostly caring, professions.[2]

These figures show that full formal and legal equality between the sexes is very far from sufficient to obtain economic equality. Further on, I shall argue that both part-time work and women's low wages are unavoidable consequences of women's burden of unpaid care work.

Extending the social contract

Discussing Rawls and feminism, Nussbaum writes: 'John Rawls's work offers many insights for feminists thinking about justice. In many respects, his theory can be adapted to meet the most serious criticisms feminists have made against it' (2003: 514).

Extending the Rawlsian theory to include women and children is straightforward if we accept his specification of the original position but reject his demand that the parties restrict themselves to treating the situation of adult citizens. The difficulties in Rawlsian theory from a gender point of view stem from the limited scope he gives his social contract, insisting as he does both in *A Theory of Justice* and in several papers that the social contract is a contract about the rights and duties of human beings as citizens in the public sphere. He also insists (1997) that the family, and specifically the division of labour within the family, is outside the public sphere.

But consider the original position in itself, as Rawls describes it. Free and equal persons meet to decide together and unanimously on the basic structure of society. The decision is made from behind a thick veil of ignorance: they do not know their sex, colour, social position or even their

---

[2] These and later statistics are the author's own computations on the Surveys of Income and Wealth produced by Statistics, Norway and supplied to me by the Norwegian Social Science Data Service (NSD). Neither Statistics Norway nor NSD is responsible for my use of the data. Some further results are presented in Bojer 2005.

tastes and opinions. Yet we must imagine them as knowing everything else there is to know about human nature and society relevant to their decision.

The situation can be interpreted as one of choice under uncertainty, but the standard economic theory of such choice is not applicable, since the preferences of the parties are unknown. Rawls also maintains that the probabilities are unknown, but here he is not altogether correct. One probability and one certainty must be known to the parties. Biologically, the probability of being conceived and born as a woman is approximately 50 per cent. And every human being starts life as a helpless baby, born from the womb of a woman. There is no uncertainty at all about this fact of life. It is therefore clearly rational for the parties to agree on equal political, social and economic rights for women and men. It is also rational for them to agree on a social contract that protects the rights of children, including the rights to nurture and education.[3]

It follows that the social contract must deal with the economic provision for children and their mothers: matters considered by many to be within the province of the family. But it does not follow that other family matters should be the concern of the social contract or the state. Sexual arrangements, in particular, need not be regulated, or the ways in which adults choose or do not choose to live together. The extended social contract still defines a liberal society, but a liberal society which draws the line between private and public spheres differently from traditional liberalism.

Income as a primary good

Rawls rejects individual welfare as the good to be justly distributed by society. 'It has always been recognised that the social system shapes the desires and aspirations of its members; it determines in large part the kind of persons they want to be as well as the kind of persons they are. Thus an economic system is not only an institutional device for satisfying existing wants and desires but a way of fashioning wants and desires in the future' (1975 and 1999b: 257).

Feminists, of course, have long argued that character traits and preferences that are supposed to be typically feminine or typically masculine are shaped by the gendered society both women and men grow up in. As Simone de Beauvoir famously put it: 'You are not born a woman, you become one'[4] (1949: 13). It is clear to us that a society that is fair to women will shape the preferences of both men and women differently from one that is unfair.

---

[3] More detailed arguments are found in Bojer 2000 and Bojer 2002.
[4] On ne naît pas femme, on le devient.

The fact that society contributes to forming our preferences is a powerful argument for Rawls's specification of a thick veil of ignorance that hides their very preferences from the parties in the original position. Choosing the basic institutions of society implies choosing preferences to at least some extent.

The parties therefore have to decide on a good or goods to be distributed that do not depend on preferences. Rawls proposes that the parties decide on what he calls 'primary goods', defined as goods that 'normally have a use whatever a person's rational plan of life' (1999a: 54). It is, on the face of it, difficult to understand why these primary goods should not be capabilities. As Nussbaum writes: 'The capabilities approach, as I have articulated it, is very close to Rawls's approach using the notion of primary goods. We can see the list of capabilities as like a long list of opportunities for functioning, such that it is always rational to want them whatever else one wants' (2000: 88).

On Rawls's list of primary goods are 'rights, liberties, opportunities, the social bases for self-respect' (1982: 162). These goods are more or less the same as capabilities, or are necessary for securing valuable capabilities, although one could wish to see them further specified. The crucial incompatibility between Rawls's concept of primary goods and the concept of capabilities seems to be Rawls's inclusion of income and wealth on his list of primary goods.[5]

I shall argue that this is not a good choice, given his definition of primary goods and what he wants to obtain by the social contract.[6] First, Rawls argues that the goods to be justly distributed in society should constitute 'a practical and limited list of things (primary goods) which free and equal moral persons ... can accept as what they in general need as citizens in a just society' (1982: 183). This argument seems to me to be decisive for Rawls's including income and wealth among primary goods, as well as for his rejection of capabilities as suitable distribuenda. But he does not seem to be aware that the term 'income' has several meanings, with different and irreconcilable implications for distributive justice. It is not, therefore, a practical concept, easy to measure and to agree on.

---

[5] The position that income is the distribuendum of distributional justice is sometimes called resourcist, which is an ambiguous term. In economics, resources are thought of as inputs in production. In other words: resources create income. When Ronald Dworkin advocates equality of resources (Dworkin 1981), he uses the term resources in this last sense. If Dworkin is a resourcist (and what else could he be called?), the term resourcist is used to denote two very different positions.

[6] The same arguments apply to wealth as to income. For brevity's sake, and to avoid tiresome technicalities, I shall disregard wealth and concentrate on income. For definitions of income and wealth, see Bojer 2003.

Income can be household income or individual income. When household income is the target for distributional policy, it does not matter which member of the household receives the income in the first place. In the vast majority of married (or cohabiting) couples, all over the world, the husband's income is the larger.[7] Targeting household income is tantamount to saying that the wife's income is of no importance: such a policy ignores women's right to economic independence. Yet if individual income is seen as the target, equality of household income is impossible to achieve as long as people are free to form households or not as they choose.

There are many examples of political disagreement centring on this issue. In Norway more than 40 years ago, married women, after many years of struggle, obtained the right to independent taxation of their income. In many countries this right still does not exist. To continue with the example of Norway, child benefit is universal and paid in cash to the parent chiefly responsible for the care of the child, in most cases to the mother. But there is a continuous debate both about the universality of the benefit and the method of payment. Many people argue that the benefit should be means tested against household income. The implications would be that wives with well-to-do (not necessarily rich) husbands have no right to child benefit for their children. A final example: households with low incomes pay lower fees in daycare centres. But since household income is the criterion, a mother who wants to earn her own income must pay the high charges if her husband earns well, however low her own wages are. So, in spite of the taxation rules, married women's economic independence is far from being accepted by all 'free and equal moral persons' in Norway.

In the United Kingdom, students from poor backgrounds pay lower tuition fees at universities. But students with well-to-do parents who refuse to pay tuition fees receive no public assistance. I suspect that not all middle-class parents are willing to pay for their children, particularly their daughters, to attend university. The British government's argument for increasing tuition fees was that low fees meant subsidising the rich. No attempt was made to distinguish between parents and children.

There are many other examples of the critical significance of distinguishing between household income and individual income in distributional policy. The point I am making should already be clear: choosing one or the other definition implies choosing a principle of distributive justice. For a liberal egalitarian adhering to ethical individualism, the

---

[7] In Norway in the year 2002, the husband was the main income earner in 72 per cent of households consisting of a couple with one or more children.

choice should not be difficult: for adults, the primary good must be individual income. But I am not at all convinced that this is what Rawls himself had in mind.

Second, income in the sense of monetary or cash income is not a good everyone always wants more of, whatever her preferences. Even that insatiable creature, economic man, prefers leisure to more income once his cash income has reached a certain level; this level will, moreover, vary according to preferences. For wage earners, there is a trade-off between cash income and leisure. There is not always freedom to make this trade-off in the best possible way, but the great majority have some leeway in choosing between work and leisure in a normal market economy.[8] As part-time work is growing steadily more common, the amount of time spent in paid work is an increasingly important factor explaining inequality both in household income and individual cash income.[9]

The choice between paid work and other activities is an important one; it is a choice of lifestyle, and depends not only on preferences in a superficial sense but on what is regarded as the good life. The possibility of free choice here must surely be regarded as an important freedom in the Rawlsian society of liberal egalitarianism. Therefore, in a just society, the important good is not cash income but the range of choices available between cash income and leisure. This range of choices is what economists call full income. Full income is, roughly, the largest cash income obtainable by a person who does nothing but work and sleep. If it is possible to choose a shorter working day than, say, sixteen hours a day seven days a week, then full income represents potential cash income but not necessarily actual cash income. In capability terms, cash income is a functioning while full income represents a capability.

Now, Rawls has agreed that full income might be nearer to what he is aiming at than realised cash income (Rawls 1974). But if the primary good logically implied by the Rawlsian social contract is individual full income, then this primary good is, in fact, a capability: the capability of earning an income. I prefer to call it income capability, and shall discuss the concept further in the next section.

Capabilities and income

The capability approach posits human capabilities as the targets of distributive justice. But capabilities are not transferable: they cannot be

---

[8] A referee pointed out that the unemployed do not have a choice. True, but even with an unemployment rate as high as, say, 15 per cent, a majority of 85 per cent are in paid work.
[9] See e.g. Rubery et al. 1999.

handed out to the individual by the government or any other institution. In this respect, capabilities are akin to welfare. And, like welfare, capabilities are affected by income. As Sen writes: 'Income – properly defined – has an enormous influence on what we can or cannot do' (1999: 72).[10] Adherents of the capability approach therefore need to work out in more detail their views on how to define income, what income as an instrument can and cannot do in promoting capabilities, and how it should be distributed.

The relationship between capabilities and income does not seem straightforward. Sen clearly thinks of commodities – and hence also income, which buys commodities – as inputs into capabilities, as seen by his often used example of pregnant women needing more food. Nussbaum, meanwhile, has the right to own property and to engage in paid work on her list of minimum or threshold capabilities. This right seems to correspond to a capability of earning an income.

While commodities create capabilities, there also exists a capability to acquire commodities. There is no paradox or contradiction here: one capability may well be an input into another capability. Sen writes: 'And since enhanced capabilities in leading a life would tend, typically, to expand a person's ability to be more productive and gain a higher income, we would also expect a connection going from capability to greater earning power, and not only the other way around' (1999: 90). What Sen calls earning power is one part of what I call income capability.

In *Development as Freedom*, Sen lists five distinct sources of 'variations between our real incomes and the advantages – or well-being and freedom – we derive from them' (p 70). He calls them 'personal heterogeneities, environmental diversities, variations in social climate, differences in relational perspectives and distribution within the family' (1999: 73). Now income, however defined in other respects, measures the access to market commodities. As a measure of advantage, it will always have to be supplemented *inter alia* by non-market goods. Sen's list consists partly of factors modifying the usefulness of income as measure of access to market goods, partly of non-market goods. Environmental diversities and variations in social climate represent non-market goods and imply that indicators and targets in addition to income are needed. Distribution within the family implies that as regards adults, individual income and not family income is the relevant target.[11] Children are another matter; their well-being must be measured separately from that of their parents,

---

[10] He does not, however, go on to state how to define income properly.
[11] From the context, it is clear that Sen takes it as a matter of course that income is household income.

and individual income is not a relevant measure for them. But this still only implies that indicators and targets in addition to income are needed.

The two other sources more directly affect the question of whether income is a useful distributional target. By 'differences in relational perspectives', Sen means that certain valuable capabilities depend not on our economic position in absolute terms but on our economic position relative to that of others. An example is social participation. Another is Adam Smith's famous example of being able to appear in public without shame. The fact that valuable capabilities depend on relative economic status implies that after a certain level of affluence is achieved in a society, distribution is more important than economic growth for securing capabilities. This is one of the most important insights gained by the capability approach. It is outside the scope of this chapter to pursue this perspective. It is not, however, in opposition to the rest of my argument, which will concern women's income capability relative to that of men.

By 'personal heterogeneities', Sen means that people have different needs, and therefore need different amounts of commodities in order to achieve equal capabilities. Needs must here be understood as more basic than preferences; they are objective needs beyond the individual's immediate control. Examples are the handicapped and the chronically ill who need medication or special equipment in order to be capable of functionings such as mobility or hearing – or working. I do not see this as a serious objection against income as one of several targets. It is not all that difficult to tailor the definition of income to differences in needs. Such tailoring is in fact done by welfare states that distribute either physical equipment and medication or cash benefits or both according to need. Child benefits are a case in point, as are tax reliefs for large families, old-age pensioners or other cases of special needs. There are a limited number of different cases to be handled, and they are in fact handled by distributional systems of existing welfare states.

In the above discussion of the connection between capabilities and income as a source of commodities Sen disregards, as Nussbaum does not, the importance of the way we acquire commodities. We acquire commodities in various ways. They can be received in kind, as when food and other consumption goods are shared in a family, or as handouts of rations in famine relief. We can produce them ourselves, as in subsistence farming or unpaid housework. But the most widespread way of acquiring commodities in the modern economy is by earning an income and using the income to buy commodities; this is in any case true for adult men.

These ways of acquiring commodities are not of equal worth. Women's struggle for economic emancipation from their husbands, or brothers, or fathers is not – at least, not only – a struggle to obtain more consumer goods. It is a struggle for economic independence and power, for economic autonomy. Being able to earn your own living by means of a socially acknowledged contribution to society is also an important part of what John Rawls calls 'the social bases for self-respect', a primary good. This is why we need the concept of income capability, or the capability of independently earning an income.

Income capability must measure economic options, a set of feasible choices, not outcomes of choice. The capability is made of legally enforceable rights. It must, as Nussbaum stresses, be individual: 'The ultimate political goal is always the promotion of the capabilities of *each person*' (2000: 74).

The closest approximation I can find to income capability is a modified version of individual full income, determined by available time, the wage rate and by non-labour income. The non-labour income part consists of capital income and government or private transfers guaranteed by law. Non-labour income must be a part of income capability because not everyone is able to work. But if an unemployed, disabled or old person has secure rights to an unemployment benefit, or a disability or old-age pension, she still has an income capability equal to that benefit or pension. It is natural for a Norwegian to think of such income as government transfers, but they could also come from private insurance or savings. The important thing is to distinguish such legally enforceable benefits and pensions from charitable handouts.

To obtain a good measure of income capability, full income must be adjusted for differences in needs by subtracting the cost of compensating for them.[12]

Income capability is partly determined by social and economic features of society: the rate of unemployment and, especially for women, the presence or absence of legal and social pressures hindering paid work. Given the legal and social possibilities of employment, it is determined by the wage commanded in paid work. There exists one more restraint on income capability, namely time available for engaging in paid work. Such time is constrained by unpaid work, in particular child care.

Child care and income capability

Unpaid work in the care and nurture of children reduces women's income capability relative to that of men in two ways: directly by limiting available time in the short term, and indirectly by reducing women's wage rates in the long term. That it limits time available for paid work in

---

[12] A more detailed discussion of income capability is found in Bojer 2006.

the short run is obvious. The long-run effect arises because long absences from paid work erode the necessary skills and therefore weaken one's position in the labour market. So does part-time paid work.

Discussing the conflict between respect for privacy and protection against tyranny within the family in her commentary on Rawls and feminism, Nussbaum writes: 'I therefore believe that the solution to this problem, if there is one, lies not in the rejection of Rawlsian liberalism, but in a deeper and more extensive reflection about alternative liberal principles for its solution. This search would do well to begin by imaging and studying the many ways in which groups of people of many different types have managed, in different places at different times, to raise children with both love and justice' (2003: 515).

Here, she frames the problem with beautiful precision: both love and justice are needed. Too often, when women (and men) do their work with love, the economic result is unjust. Yet I do not believe that many times and places can be found where women's raising of children has received a just economic reward. And I certainly do not see how justice in this respect can be achieved without state intervention of some kind.

Nussbaum also writes: 'For me, as for Rawls, it is wrong for the state to mandate the equal division of domestic labor or equal decision making in the household' (Ibid.: 279). Her reason is: 'It just seems an intolerable infringement of liberty for the state to get involved in dictating how people do their dishes' (Ibid.: 280). But her example misses the mark. Doing the dishes is a trivial and unnecessary chore compared with caring for children.

Child care is radically different from ordinary household chores. Unlike much other unpaid work, child care cannot be regarded as a hobby, voluntarily chosen. It is a duty. Unpleasant household chores can be mechanised, put off or, at a pinch, left undone. If the husband refuses to do his share of the laundry, the wife can retaliate by refusing to wash his dirty underwear. But if he refuses to change the baby's nappies, she has no choice but to do it herself. Children rely absolutely on provision and care from others. And society cannot survive without children. Therefore, there must be adults in society who give their time and effort to children. And therefore no society can afford to become so liberal that child care is chosen away. And therefore, finally, demanding equal shares of child care is different from demanding equal shares in household work generally.

It is obvious that if mothers and fathers (biological or social) were to take equal shares of caring for children, the main hindrance for economic equality between the sexes would be removed. But is equal sharing also a necessary condition for such economic equality? I believe it is.

Love: children must be raised with love. The implication is that child care should not be wholly professionalised, nor should it be taken over wholly by the state. Private or government-run crèches and day-care centres have their place in child care, but not twenty-four hours a day. Full-time nannies are feasible only if their wages are very low relative to the mothers who hire them. If these nannies wish to become mothers, they will certainly not be able to afford nannies themselves. Some part of child care must take place outside the market and for love, not money.

Justice: one possibility of achieving economic justice might be economic compensation of some kind to mothers (and fathers) for the loss of income due to caring for children. Such compensation is given in the Scandinavian countries in the form of paid leave in connection with the birth of a child; in Norway, nearly a year (forty-nine weeks). The cost is carried by the public social insurance system. Private insurance against becoming pregnant is, of course, not feasible. It is also not feasible to let employers cover the costs: hiring women employees would become too expensive.

Children need care and time from their parents for longer than this paid leave. But paying women the full cost of staying at home for longer than the first year would be very costly. They would have to be compensated not only for the time actually spent at home but also for the loss of future earnings due to long-time absence from the labour market. Also, the taxpayers should consider what they are paying for. Looking after one or two children takes time, but is not a full-time job as they approach school age. Some of the time paid for by the public would be spent on hobbies and on services to healthy adult men. Finally, is it desirable to spend public money on keeping mothers isolated in the home? In modern economies, the work place is important for social interaction and personal development as well as for earning money. In short, I do not believe that compensation in the form of 'housewife salary' is either politically or economically feasible.

But it is also exhausting to combine family responsibilities with a full-time job. As long as women carry the main responsibilities for children and family, they will either have to stay away from paid work for several years or work part time, as many do. In both cases they become second-class employees, commanding lower wages than their men.[13] It is standard theory of labour economics that both seniority and on-the-job training are of importance for wages. However, people become less productive and more difficult to employ the longer they are absent from the labour market. This holds true for both men and women.[14]

---

[13] On this, see also Okin 1989.   [14] See e.g. Manning 2003.

The only feasible way of achieving just equality between women and men is by equalising their shares of unpaid child care. Much can be done towards achieving such equality without coercive intrusion into the family. To give one more example from my own country: some years ago, paternity leave was introduced. This is a paid child care leave that takes effect only if it is taken up by the father while the mother is in paid work. It is not, however, compulsory. This arrangement has been a resounding success: 90 per cent of fathers use the opportunity. Young men wheeling prams and comforting crying babies have become a common sight on the streets of Oslo.

It is possible to make paternity leaves compulsory. It is also possible to legislate for shorter working hours and limitation of overtime, thus allowing fathers the physical possibility of giving time to their children. No society can, of course, by legislation force fathers (or mothers) to feel love and a sense of duty towards their children. But the arrangements outlined will make it easier for those fathers who wish to do their part, as well as strengthen the hands of mothers with reluctant partners.

Will further coercion of unwilling fathers be out of place in a liberal society? The liberalism Nussbaum defends, as I understand it, demands freedom for all except insofar as other people's freedom is not thereby hindered. But choosing life styles that cannot be combined with care and nurture of children is free-riding on the efforts of others. Fathers, in particular, can only neglect their children at the cost of mothers' lack of freedom – and, I believe, at the cost of children developing their capabilities.

Rawls writes that gendered division of labour 'is connected with basic liberties, including freedom of religion'. Now, it is difficult to see how shirking the duty to care for one's children can be a basic liberty. Yet freedom of religion is of course a basic liberty. I do not know to which extent the gendered division of labour in child care is fundamental to some of the world's religions. But even if it were, I can only endorse Nussbaum's statement that 'the state and its agents may impose a substantial burden on religion only when it can show a compelling interest. But, second, protection of the central capabilities of citizens should always be understood to ground a compelling state interest' (2000: 202).

REFERENCES

Bojer, H. (2000), 'Children and Theories of Distributional Justice', *Feminist Economics*, 6 (2): 23–29.

(2002), 'Women and the Rawlsian Social Contract', *Social Justice Research*, 15 (4): 393–407.

(2003), *Distributional Justice: Theory and Measurement*, Routledge, London.

(2005), 'Income Inequality and the Economic Position of Women in Norway 1970–2002', Memorandum No. 07/2005 from the Department of Economics.

(2006), 'Income Capability and Child Care', Memorandum No. 14/2006 from the Department of Economics.

de Beauvoir, S. (1949), *Le deuxième sexe, II*, Gallimard (Folio), Paris.

Dworkin, R. (1981), 'What is Equality? Part 2: Equality of Resources', *Philosophy and Public Affairs*, 10 (4): 283–345.

Manning, A. (2003), *Monopsony in Motion. Imperfect Competition in Labor Markets*, Princeton University Press.

Nussbaum, M. C. (1999), *Sex and Social Justice*, Oxford University Press.

(2000), *Women and Human Development. The Capabilities Approach*, Cambridge University Press.

(2003), 'Rawls and Feminism' in S. Freeman (ed.) *The Cambridge Companion to Rawls*, Cambridge University Press.

Okin, S. M. (1989), *Justice, Gender and the Family*, Basic Books.

Rawls, J. (1971, 1999a), *A Theory of Justice*, Harvard University Press, Cambridge, Mass.

(1974), 'Reply to Alexander and Musgrave', *Quarterly Journal of Economics*, 88: 633–655, also in Rawls (1999): 232–253.

(1975), 'A Kantian Conception of Equality', *Cambridge Review*, 96, reprinted in Rawls (1999): 254–266.

(1982), 'Social Unity and Primary Goods' in A. K. Sen and B. Williams (eds) *Utilitarianism and Beyond*, Cambridge University Press: 159–186, reprinted in Rawls (1999): 359–387.

(1997), 'The Idea of Public Reason Revisited', *University of Chicago Law Review*, 64 (3): 765–807, reprinted in Rawls (1999): 573–615.

(1999), *Collected Papers*, Harvard University Press, Cambridge, Mass.

Rubery, J., M. Smith and C. Fagan (1999), *Women's Employment in Europe. Trends and prospects*, Routledge, London.

Sen, A. K. (1999), *Development as Freedom*, Oxford University Press.

Part III

Equality

14   Lists and thresholds: comparing the Doyal–Gough theory of human need with Nussbaum's capabilities approach*

Ian Gough

Introduction

Martha C. Nussbaum's *Women and Human Development: The Capabilities Approach* (2000, hereafter *WHD*) remains an eloquent, rigorous and passionate statement of her views on human capabilities. It goes further than her earlier work in relating these to the ethics and politics of development. It applies the approach directly and with insight to the predicament faced by women across the developing world, notably in two chapters on religion and care.

This chapter critically discusses Nussbaum's capabilities approach and compares it with the needs perspective developed in the earlier book by Len Doyal and myself, *A Theory of Human Need* (1991, hereafter *THN*). Though there are remarkable similarities between the two, both were written independently. When completing our book, published in 1991, we were unaware of Nussbaum's earliest article on this theme, *Nature, function and capability: Aristotle on political distribution*, published in 1988, while her subsequent work was written in ignorance of our own contribution.

The publication of *WHD* provides an opportunity to compare and evaluate our theory of human need with her first fully developed perspective on human capabilities. However, this chapter limits itself to the very specific issue of 'lists' and 'thresholds'. Unlike Sen, Nussbaum explicitly provides a comprehensive list of 'central human functional capabilities' which we can compare with our hierarchical model of human needs. Many other important issues related to her self-proclaimed neo-Aristotelian approach are ignored, and even within this remit much must be omitted.

* This chapter was first presented at the Conference on *Promoting Women's Capabilities: Examining Nussbaum's Capabilities Approach*, St Edmund's College, Cambridge, 9–10 September 2002. Thanks to David Clark, Flavio Comim, Dan Jones, Toru Yamamori, the seminar participants and an anonymous referee for helpful comments. Apart from the odd sentence and reference, this version is identical to the original.

Throughout I use *WHD* as the core text to illustrate Nussbaum's latest and most developed thinking on this topic. This work developed out of the 1998 Seeley lectures at the University of Cambridge and marks a clear advance on her earlier work on capabilities (Nussbaum 1992, 1993, 1995a, 1995b). According to Gasper (2001) it reflects, among other things, her move to the Chair of Law and Ethics at Chicago and two research visits to India in 1997 and 1998. This focus means that I ignore her important later work, such as *Frontiers of Justice* (2006).

In the first part of this chapter I identify the common project which underlies both Nussbaum's and our own work: to clarify and defend those universal human interests which alone can underpin an emancipatory and effective political programme for all women and men. The next two sections then set out in some detail our different taxonomies of capabilities and needs, and the thinking behind them. Then, in the next section, the two approaches are compared in terms of their components, derivation and thresholds. On the basis of this three-way comparison, I conclude that our theory and operationalisation of human need is in certain respects theoretically more robust and empirically more realistic than Nussbaum's better-known approach.

Arguments for universals

Though Nussbaum uses different terms from us – 'capabilities' versus 'needs' – we have much in common, notably the goal of developing a genuinely universal argument for human emancipation. Though her book explicitly focuses on women's capabilities and options, and engages with the specific obstacles faced by most women and girls on the planet, this is at all times embedded in a theory which applies equally to men and boys. In particular, the two books argue the following three positions.

A 'fully universal' conception of capabilities/needs

Taking for granted a world where many women lack support for fundamental functions of a human life, and where most women have fewer capabilities than men, her goal is to develop a 'universalist feminism' (*WHD* 7), based on 'the principle of each person as an end' (*WHD* 56). The philosophical underpinning for this universalism is the idea of human *functionings*, one respect among several where her work inter-relates with that of Amartya Sen. Sen defines a functioning as 'an achievement of a person: what she or he manages to do or to be' (1985: 12). Elsewhere he writes that functionings 'constitute a person's being'. Since some (not all) of these functionings are 'intrinsically valuable' they amount to states of *well*-being (Sen 1992: 4–7). *Capabilities* then refer to the set of function-ings that is feasible to that person – that she could choose.

However, Nussbaum, whose work in this area began independently of Sen, is more direct in addressing the issues of cross-cultural comparison and evaluation which this entails:

An international feminism that is going to have any bite quickly gets involved in making normative recommendations that cross boundaries of culture, nation, religion, race and class. It will therefore need to find descriptive and normative concepts adequate to that task. I shall argue that certain universal norms of human capability should be central for political purposes in thinking about basic political principles that can provide the underpinning for a set of constitutional guarantees in all nations. I shall also argue that these norms are legitimately used in making comparisons across nations, asking how well they are doing relative to one another in promoting human quality of life. (*WHD* 34–35)

'The account we search for should preserve liberties and opportunities for each and every person, taken one by one, respecting each of them as an end, rather than simply as the agent or supporter of the ends of others' (*WHD* 55). This 'focus on the individual person as such requires no particular metaphysical tradition ... It arises naturally from the recognition that each person has just one life to live' (*WHD* 56).[1]

This compares with our own argument:

Health and autonomy are basic needs which [all] humans must satisfy in order to avoid the serious harm of fundamentally impaired participation in their form of life ... It is possible in principle to compare levels of basic need-satisfaction in these terms not only within but also between cultures. (*THN* 73–74)

To quote Soper (1993b 74): 'What [Doyal and Gough's] work shows, they would argue, is that you can chart basic need satisfaction for "objective" welfare without either embracing relativism or operating at such a level of generality that the pertinence of the theory for specific problems concerning social policy is sacrificed.'

A critique of cultural relativism

Nussbaum develops an explicit critique of relativism[2] by addressing three 'apparently respectable' arguments against universalism: the argument from culture, the argument from the good of diversity, and the argument from paternalism (*WHD* 41–50). We can drastically summarise her three

---

[1] She notes that of the major world religions only Buddhism seriously challenges this sort of emphasis on the individual.
[2] This is one of the contrasts she draws between her work and that of Amartya Sen.

counter-arguments as follows. First, real cultures are always dynamic and evolving: 'People are resourceful borrowers of ideas' (*WHD* 48). She attacks a common critique of universal values based on the dichotomy between 'western' and 'non-western' values. This polarisation she argues simplifies the notion of tradition and underplays ongoing conflicts within cultural systems. Second, the 'argument for the good of diversity' is fine so long as cultural practices do not harm people. But since some practices clearly do, this 'objection does not undermine the search for universal values, it requires it' (*WHD* 50). Not all diversities are worth preserving and only diversities compatible with human dignity and other basic values should be respected. Third, relativist critiques of the 'paternalism' endorsed at some level by universal approaches is a double-edged sword. Many traditional value systems are paternalist in the strict sense of the word. More fundamentally, a commitment to respecting people's choices endorses at least one universal value, that of having the opportunity to think and choose for oneself (*WHD* 51). To preserve these fundamental capabilities may require a public authority to override immediate interests and preferences.

We develop an explicit but different critique of cultural relativism. First, we argue that all contemporary forms of relativism are internally inconsistent. Variants of relativism can be found in exponents of orthodox economics, liberalism, Marxism, critics of cultural imperialism, theories of radical democracy and phenomenological sociology; but 'all have attempted to denounce universal standards of evaluation with one hand only to employ them to endorse some favoured view of the world with the other' (*THN* 33). Second, we address and rebut specific claims that conceptions of health (one of our basic needs) are internal to cultural systems of thought, thus denying any rational choice between them. We tackle this by considering persons from different cultures suffering from (what the biomedical model terms) TB, and then go on to the more difficult case of severe depression (*THN* 57–59, 63–64, 180–181). Even in the case of depression, sufferers exhibit common symptoms across widely different cultures, such as hopelessness, breathlessness, lack of energy and feelings of inadequacy. These common symptoms lead to the same kinds of disability across cultures, notwithstanding divergent and indeed incompatible ways of interpreting them.

An argument that the existence of needs/capabilities entails strong moral claims to meet needs/develop capabilities

Nussbaum's aim is 'to provide the philosophical underpinning for an account of basic constitutional principles that should be respected and implemented by the governments of all nations, as a bare minimum of what respect for human dignity requires' (*WHD* 5).

In certain core areas of human functioning a necessary condition of justice for a public political arrangement is that it delivers to citizens a certain basic level of capability. If people are systematically falling below the threshold in any of these core areas, this should be seen as a situation both unjust and tragic. (*WHD* 71)

The language of rights permits us to draw strong normative conclusions from the fact of basic capabilities (*WHD* 100). In so doing, Nussbaum differs from Sen in regarding all capabilities as equally fundamental and rejecting Rawls's argument for the priority of liberty (*WHD* 12).

This is similar to our statement at the start of THN (2): 'It is difficult to see how political movements which espouse the improvement of human welfare can fail to endorse the following related beliefs:

1. Humans can be *seriously harmed* by alterable social circumstances, which can give rise to *profound suffering*.
2. Social *justice* exists in inverse proportion to serious harm and suffering.'

However, we go further than Nussbaum in relating such rights to corresponding duties. Our argument in brief is as follows (see *THN* Chapter 6 for the full argument):

1. The membership of any social group implies obligations or duties.
2. To ascribe duties to someone presupposes that they are in fact able to perform these duties.
3. The ascription of a duty thus logically entails that the bearer of the duty is entitled to the need satisfaction necessary to enable her or him to undertake that duty. It is inconsistent for a social group to lay responsibilities on some person without ensuring she has the wherewithal to discharge those responsibilities.
4. Where the social group is large, this entails similar obligations to strangers, whose needs we do not directly witness and can do nothing individually to satisfy. This will require support for agencies that guarantee to meet the needs of strangers. This is a plausible definition of a 'welfare state': public rights or entitlements to the means to human welfare in general and to minimum standards of well-being in particular, independent of rights based on property or income. Only the state can guarantee strong entitlements to people of this sort, though this does not require that it directly provides the satisfiers. It is at this stage that we also argue for the equal prioritisation of rights to basic need satisfaction and reject Rawls' lexical ordering (*THN* 132–134).[3]

---

[3] However, we go one step beyond the traditional confines of social policy. This commitment to meet the needs of strangers and to support the necessary welfare

It is clear that the philosophical and political agenda underlying our two approaches is to clarify and defend those universal human interests which underpin an emancipatory and effective political programme for all women and men. The differences that we now go on to outline should be seen as contrasting approaches to pursue a broadly common agenda.

Nussbaum on central human functional capabilities

A critical difference with Sen, claims Nussbaum, is that he has 'never made a list of the central capabilities' (*WHD* 13).[4] Nussbaum tackles this head-on and presents her own 'current list' of ten 'central human functional capabilities' (CHFCs), reproduced as Table 17.1, below. This difference reflects a more fundamental disagreement about the possibility of arguing rationally about the nature of the good. Sen focuses on processes, procedures and deliberative democracy whereas Nussbaum emphasises the role of her list as an evaluative metric or heuristic device to describe the mechanisms for settling central capabilities.[5]

Of her list of CHFCs, Nussbaum identifies two, practical reason and affiliation, as 'architectonic' because 'they both organize and suffuse all the others, making their pursuit truly human' (*WHD* 82). Elsewhere she recognises bodily integrity as of special importance (*WHD* 95). While the ten general categories are constant over time, the specific descriptions of them will change with historical circumstances; thus 'literacy is a concrete specification for the modern world of a more general capability'. Put more strongly, 'part of the idea of the list is its multiple realisability: its members can be more concretely specified in accordance with local

structures cannot stop at the borders of any particular state. The idea of universal human needs leads remorselessly to the global guarantee of their satisfaction. It lends powerful support to contemporary ideas of cosmopolitanism, which sees the entire world as a potential political community – however difficult are the obstacles and however utopian this sounds to our ears today.

[4] This criticism of Sen echoes our own (*THN* 156). Of course, Sen provides examples of functionings but in an unsystematic way. Elsewhere I argue: 'Sen's examples [of functionings] include being happy, being able to choose, having good health, being adequately fed and sheltered, having self-respect, being able to appear in public without shame, and taking part in the life of the community. Though we may well value all these things, it is a rather strange list. It embraces subjective states (being happy) and objective states (being adequately fed), and culturally generalisable conditions (having good health) alongside specifically liberal values (being able to choose). It is not self-evident that all these are "intrinsically" significant in defining the social good' (Gough 2000: 6–7).

[5] This difference was emphasised during the debate between Sen and Nussbaum at the Cambridge conference. I am grateful to Flavio Comim for reminding me of its relevance here.

beliefs and circumstances' (*WHD* 77). Furthermore, it 'is, emphatically, a list of separate components. We cannot satisfy the need for one of them by giving a larger amount of another one. All are of central importance and all are distinct in quality' (*WHD* 81).

Nussbaum first derived this list using a self-proclaimed 'neo-Aristotelian' approach. Following the method in *Nicomachean Ethics* she identified 'spheres of human experience that figure in more or less any human life, and in which more or less any human being will have to make *some* choices rather than others' and to each of which there is a corresponding virtue (Nussbaum 1993: 245). This generated a slightly varying list of ten to eleven spheres of experience. The approach identified 'a *core idea* [my italics] of the human being as a dignified free being who shapes his or her own life in cooperation and reciprocity with others ... A life that is really human is one that is shaped throughout by these human powers of practical reason and sociability' (*WHD* 72). This distinctive perspective generated a 'thick', richer conception of well-being compared with Sen's approach.

Following her adoption of political liberalism in the 1990s she developed a more normative or Rawlsian procedure in *WHD* (reiterated in her new work, Nussbaum 2006, Chapter1). The central capabilities are first identified in an approach informed by an intuitive idea of a life that is worthy of human dignity. These are then presented as the source of political principles for a liberal, pluralistic society, free of any metaphysical grounding. As a result the central capabilities can become the object of an overlapping consensus among people who may otherwise have very different conceptions of the good. In *WHD*, 'the methodology that has been used to modify the list [draws] both on the results of cross-cultural academic discussion and on discussions in women's groups themselves' (*WHD* 151). 'Thus it already represents what it proposes: a type of *overlapping consensus*' (*WHD* 76).[6] The above list is notably the result of discussions in India and elsewhere. 'In this sense the list remains open-ended and humble' (*WHD* 77). The argument from principle at stage one is 'envisaged as a first step in the process of reaching toward such *a reflective equilibrium*' (*WHD* 151, our italics). This liberal reformulation is attractive in principle, but gives rise to some problems and tensions in practice, discussed below.

---

[6] She continues: 'By "overlapping consensus" I mean what John Rawls means: that people may sign on to this conception as the freestanding moral core of a political conception, without accepting any particular metaphysical view of the world, any particular comprehensive ethical or religious view, or even any particular view of the person or of human nature.'

Doyal and Gough: a theory of human need

We develop a list of needs with many points of convergence with the above. However, it is constructed in a very different way. Our approach is hierarchical, moving from universal goals, through basic needs to inter-mediate needs, as summarised in Figure 1 of *THN*.[7] The following summarises our argument in *THN*, predominantly Chapters 4 and 8.

Step 1. Normative/ethical reasoning: identifying universal goals

'Need' refers to a particular category of goals which is believed to be universalisable. The contrast with wants, goals which derive from an individual's particular preferences and cultural environment, is central to our argument. The universality of need rests upon the belief that if needs are not satisfied then serious harm of some objective kind will result. We define serious harm as fundamental disablement in the pursuit of one's vision of the good. It is not the same as subjective feelings such as anxiety or unhappiness. Another way of describing such harm is as an impediment to successful social participation. Whatever the time, place and cultural group we grow up and live in, we act in it to some extent. We argue that we build a self-conception of our own capabilities through interacting with and learning from others. This is an essential feature of our human nature. It follows that participation in some form of life without serious arbitrary limitations is 'our most basic human interest' (*THN* 55).

Step 2. Basic needs: health and autonomy

THN (52–54) develops a neo-Kantian argument in determining univer-sal goals and basic needs:

Although [Kant] was not directly concerned with the character of human need, he did articulate many concepts and arguments relevant to its theorisation. Kant showed that for individuals to act and to be responsible they must have both the physical and mental capacity to do so: at the very least a body which is alive and which is governed by all of the relevant causal processes and the mental competence to deliberate and to choose. Let us identify this latter capacity for choice with the existence of the most basic level of personal 'autonomy' ... To be autonomous in this minimal sense is to have the ability to make informed choices about what should be done and how to go about doing it. This entails being able to formulate aims, and beliefs about how to achieve them, along with the ability to

---

[7] However, it must be stressed that this has nothing in common with Maslow's hierarchical theory of needs as motivations (see *THN* Chapter 3).

evaluate the success of beliefs in the light of empirical evidence... It makes sense, therefore, to claim that *since physical survival and personal autonomy are the conditions for any individual action in any culture, they constitute the most basic human needs – those which must be satisfied to some degree before actors can participate in their form of life to achieve any other valued goals.*[8]

Three key variables, we argue, affect levels of individual autonomy of agency (*THN* 59–59). First, *cognitive and emotional capacity* is a necessary pre-requisite for a person to initiate an action. Since all actions have to embody a modicum of reason to be classed as actions at all, it is difficult to give a precise definition of the *minimum* levels of rationality and responsibility present in the autonomous individual. Generally speaking, the existence of even minimal levels of autonomy will entail the following:

(a) that actors have the intellectual capacity to formulate aims and beliefs common to their form of life;
(b) that actors have enough confidence to want to act and thus to participate in some form of social life;
(c) that actors sometimes actually do so through consistently formulating aims and beliefs and communicating with others about them;
(d) that actors perceive their actions as having been done by them and not by someone else;
(e) that actors are able to understand the empirical constraints on the success of their actions;
(f) that actors are capable of taking responsibility for what they do.

We go on to argue that this aspect of autonomy should at its most basic level be understood negatively – with reference to the serious objective disablement which results when one or more of these characteristics is absent. Mental health is, then, the obverse of this – 'practical rationality and responsibility' (*THN* 62). We address, though by no means systematically, some of the difficult issues of measurement this poses, citing evidence on the experiences and symptoms of mental illness across cultures. We conclude that, despite cultural variations in some features of, say, depression, there is a common core of disabling symptoms found in all cultures, including hopelessness, indecisiveness, a sense of futility and lack of energy (*THN* 180).

---

[8] The term 'need' has been used by some to denote the commodity pre-requisites for a full life (see Sen 1985: 513), but that is not the way we use it. It pertains to a space independent of commodities and utilities, and is thus comparable to Sen and Nussbaum's couplet of functionings and capabilities. That is why I sometimes refer in what follows to 'needs/capabilities'.

The second determinant of individual levels of autonomy is the level of *cultural understanding* a person has about herself, her culture and what is expected of her as an individual within it. This requires teachers and a form of teaching that is conducive to enquiry and further learning. Third and last, autonomy of agency requires a range of *opportunities* to undertake socially significant activities. Again, there is a problem in determining minimum opportunity sets, given that even the most oppressed of people can and will exercise choices. Nevertheless, some minimum freedom of agency is an essential component of autonomy of agency in all cultures.

Lastly, we go on to recognise a higher-order level of autonomy, which we label *critical autonomy*. 'Critical autonomy entails the capacity to compare cultural rules, to reflect upon the rules of one's own culture, to work with others to change them and, *in extremis*, to move to another culture' (*THN* 187). This requires, beyond freedom of agency, some measure of political freedom. This is not to deny that oppressed people exercise extremely high levels of creative and critical deliberation throughout their lives. It is for this reason that we favour defining critical autonomy as the possession of freedom of agency and political freedom (*THN* 68).[9]

Step 3. Satisfiers and 'intermediate needs': the role of codified knowledge

While the basic individual needs for physical health and autonomy are universal, most goods and services required to satisfy these needs are culturally variable. For example, the needs for food and shelter apply to all peoples, but there is a large variety of cuisines and forms of dwelling which can meet any given specification of nutrition and protection from the elements. Following Max-Neef (1989: 19), we call all objects, activities and relationships which satisfy our basic needs 'satisfiers'. Basic needs, then, are always universal but their satisfiers are often relative.[10] However, if this were all we could say, it would have little purchase on the

[9] *Contra* Dworkin (1988: 20), who distinguishes (second-order) autonomy as the capacity of persons to reflect on their first-order preferences, desires and wishes. For us this is a component of autonomy of agency everywhere, not just in political democracies.
[10] Following Sen's similar point in his analysis of poverty: 'Poverty is an absolute notion in the space of capabilities but very often it will take a relative form in the space of commodities or characteristics' [1983: 161]. Like Nussbaum, we stress that needs are plural and non-additive. 'One domain of intermediate need-satisfaction cannot be traded off against another' (*THN* 166). However, we do recognise some limited areas where universal satisfiers are substitutes for one another. For example, a colder environment or heavy labour will increase the food requirements of humans.

issues of rights, morality and development that Nussbaum and we wish to address. Can a conceptual bridge be built to link basic needs and specific satisfiers? We contend that the notion of 'universal satisfier characteristics' can fulfil that role.

This draws on Sen's (1985) analysis, following Lancaster, between commodities, characteristics and functionings. We define 'satisfier characteristics' as that set of all characteristics that has the property of contributing to the satisfaction of our basic needs in one or any cultural setting. We then distinguish within this set a subset of universal satisfier characteristics: those characteristics of satisfiers which apply to all cultures. Universal satisfier characteristics are thus those properties of goods, services, activities and relationships which enhance physical health and human autonomy in all cultures. For example, calories a day for a specified group of people constitutes a characteristic of (most) foodstuffs, which has transcultural relevance. Similarly 'shelter from the elements' and 'protection from disease-carrying vectors' are two of the characteristics which all dwellings have in common (though to greatly varying degrees). The category of universal satisfier characteristics, or 'intermediate needs' for short, thus provides the crucial bridge between universal basic needs and socially relative satisfiers. They provide a foundation on which to erect a list of derived or second-order goals which must be achieved if the first-order goals of health and autonomy are to be attained (*THN* 155–159).

We group these intermediate needs in the following eleven categories:

> Nutritional food and clean water
> Protective housing
> A non-hazardous work environment
> A non-hazardous physical environment
> Safe birth control and child-bearing
> Appropriate health care
> A secure childhood
> Significant primary relationships
> Physical security
> Economic security
> Appropriate education

Roughly speaking, the first six contribute to physical health and the last five to autonomy. The only criterion for inclusion in this list is whether or not any set of satisfier characteristics universally and positively contributes to physical health and autonomy. If it does, then it is classified as an intermediate need. If something is not universally necessary for enhanced basic need satisfaction, then it is not so classified, however widespread the commodity/activity/relationship may be. For example, 'sexual relationships' is not included in our list because some people live healthy and autonomous lives without inter-personal sex.

This list of universal satisfier characteristics is derived from two principle scientific sources. First, there is the best available scientific/ technical knowledge articulating causal relationships between physical health or autonomy and other factors. Second, there is comparative anthropological knowledge about practices in the numerous cultures and sub-cultures, states and political systems in the contemporary world. Thus, to begin with it is the codified knowledge of the natural and social sciences that enables us to determine the composition of intermediate needs. This knowledge changes and typically expands – today often at dizzying speeds – through time. We are comfortable to acknowledge that humans as a species have made and continue to make progress in their capacity to understand and satisfy their needs (*THN* 111). The concept of human need we develop is historically open to such continual improvements in understanding.

This approach must, however, be complemented by the appeal to the experientially grounded knowledge of people. If need satisfaction is to be optimised, all groups must have the ability to participate in research into need satisfiers and to contribute to policy-making. Utilising Habermas, we argue that any rational and effective attempt to resolve disputes over needs 'must bring to bear both the codified knowledge of experts and the experiential knowledge of those whose basic needs and daily life world are under consideration. It requires a *dual strategy of social policy formation* which values compromise, provided that it does not extend to the general character of basic human needs and rights' (*THN* 141).

Thus, our theory is essentially 'iterative': universal and objective needs can be shown to exist but the ongoing growth of knowledge continually modifies and improves our understanding of intermediate needs and how they can best be satisfied. The appropriate indicators of intermediate needs are continually open to question and improvement as a result of the growth of codified and experientially grounded knowledge (*THN* 168). The practical solution to the problem of relating these two types of knowledge may be achieved through various forms of focus groups and deliberative democracy, as we recognised when discussing the assessment of disability (*THN* 174–176) and poverty (*THN* 323, fn. 5).

Step 4. Societal preconditions

Concerned lest our emphasis on autonomy suggests an individualised conception of human agency, we spend Chapter 5 of our book expounding the social dimension of autonomy. Following Braybrooke

(1987: 48–50), we identify four societal preconditions – production, reproduction, cultural transmission and political authority – which have to be satisfied by all collectives if they are to survive and flourish over long periods of time (*THN* 80–90). Yet, though individual needs can never be satisfied independently of the social environment, we continue to insist that they must be conceptualised independently of any social environment. It is on this basis that we go on to identify positive and negative freedoms as essential pre-requisites for the exercise of critical autonomy.[11]

Aside from these societal preconditions, we may summarise our approach in two steps (consider Gasper 1996):

(a) First, neo-Kantian reasoning is deployed to derive two universal basic needs: health and autonomy. At this stage, normative/ethical theories are deployed to determine which pre-requisites carry a priority status.

(b) Codified and experiential knowledge is then drawn on to provide, at any point in time, the best available evidence on universal satisfier characteristics. This stage uses instrumental, positive analysis of the prerequisites for various types and levels of capacity or functioning (Gasper 1996: 12).

Comparing and evaluating the two approaches

I will compare the two approaches under the following headings: components, derivation, and levels and thresholds. In the process I begin to evaluate the two and offer some defence of our own approach.

Components

Table 14.1 brings these two lists together within the framework of our hierarchical model. In *THN* we caution that our list, like all taxonomies, is in one sense arbitrary (*THN* 159). The groups are 'verbal wrappings' or 'labels' designed to demarcate one collection of characteristics from another. Moreover, the word-labels used will be ambiguous – they will 'not contain or exhaust the meaning of the need identified'. Ambiguity can be reduced by increasing the numbers of characteristics or 'need categories'. Yet the larger the set, the greater the problems in comprehending the totality of human needs. We believe that this dilemma is

---

[11] The procedural and material preconditions for individual need-satisfaction are discussed at length in Gough 2000, Chapter 2. They are not pursued here.

Table 14.1 *Comparing the lists*

Needs: Doyal and Gough		Central human functional capabilities: Nussbaum
Universal goals	Avoidance of serious harm	Bodily integrity
	Social participation	Affiliation A: social interaction, compassion and justice
	Critical participation	Control over environment A: political
Basic needs	Survival	Life
	Physical health	Bodily health
	Cognitive and emotional capacity	Senses, imagination, thought
		Emotions
		Affiliation B: the social bases of self-respect and freedom from discrimination
	Cultural understanding: teachers	Senses, imagination, thought
	Opportunities to participate	Affiliation A and B
	Critical autonomy	Practical reason
		Senses, imagination, thought
Universal satisfier characteristics	Nutrition and water	Bodily health
	Protective shelter	Bodily health
	Non-hazardous environment	?
	Safe birth control and child-bearing	Bodily health and bodily integrity
	Appropriate health care	?
	Security in childhood	Bodily integrity
		Emotions
	Significant primary relationships	Emotions
	Physical security	Bodily integrity
	Economic security	Control over environment B: material
	Basic education	Senses, imagination, thought
Societal preconditions	Civil/political rights and political participation	Affiliation B: protection against discrimination
		Control over environment A: political
		Also features in:
		Senses, imagination, thought
		Practical reason
	Social/economic rights	Control over environment B: material
		Also features in:
		Affiliation A: institutions that nourish affiliation
(Other)	?	Affiliation A: others
	?	Other species
	?	Play

encountered by Nussbaum, too, and indeed by anyone engaged in identifying components of well-being. The two lists must be compared bearing this in mind.

Table 14.1 shows that there is considerable overlap between the two lists, notwithstanding differences in 'labels'. This overlap is to be expected and is a notable finding of other comparisons of components of well-being using a wider range of lists.[12] Moreover, it is interesting that of the three CHFCs that Nussbaum identifies as central, affiliation is similar to our central goal of participation, whereas bodily integrity and practical reason are closely related to our two basic needs of health and autonomy. This is an encouraging indication of the close parallels between our two projects. Yet Nussbaum does not theoretically privilege these three components, as we do.

Another difference is that Nussbaum's CHFCs often include within them their societal preconditions. For example, after the component Affiliation A is introduced, there follows in parentheses: 'Protecting this capability means protecting institutions that constitute and nourish such forms of affiliation, and also protecting the freedom of assembly and political speech' (*WHD* 79). Is it appropriate to include welfare and political rights of this sort within a list of human capabilities?[13] We believe that our strict distinction between, in a different language, human needs and the societal preconditions for their realisation is more helpful. The former are attributes of individuals, the latter of collectivities. This builds on our distinction between basic autonomy or agency and critical autonomy, the latter served by political rights and freedoms. The intermingling of these within Nussbaum's list reflects the normative political conception and derivation of basic capabilities, at least since the early 1990s.

There are other differences. On the one hand, there are CHFCs which do not appear in our matrix of needs: certain aspects of Nussbaum's 'affiliation' do not appear to be covered by our universal goal of minimally disabled participation in one's social form of life. Similarly, 'play' and 'the ability to live in a fruitful relationship with animals and the world of nature' are absent. Nussbaum comments frankly on the present lack of consensus the last achieved in her project (*WHD* 157). In which case,

---

[12] For comparisons of these and other lists see Saith (2001), Clark (2002) and Alkire (2002). However, Alkire inexplicably includes only our intermediate needs and omits our basic needs from her summary table.

[13] Nussbaum addresses this by distinguishing between basic, internal and combined capabilities (*WHD* 84–85). Internal capabilities are those personal states that are 'sufficient for the exercise of the requisite functions'. Combined capabilities are internal capabilities combined with suitable external conditions for the exercise of the function. Yet little is made of this important distinction in what follows.

why include it? It is a stretch to consider that this component ranks on a par with bodily integrity or practical reason.[14]

On the other hand, using the concept of universal satisfier characteristics we can identify more instrumental need components which are also universal but which do not figure in Nussbaum's list: for example, the intermediate needs for a non-hazardous environment and for appropriate health care. Our second-order list enables us to get closer to the real basic unmet needs confronting poor peoples across the globe.[15]

Derivation

We clearly adopt very different approaches in constructing and deriving the two lists. Nussbaum claims that hers is two-stage and iterative: a core philosophical idea derived from Aristotle is examined in cross-cultural dialogues, revised and resubmitted in an iterative fashion. Putting aside for the moment the question of whether this accurately describes the derivation of her list, let me examine some of the implications.

First, does not the Aristotelian stance ('the noble shines through') conflict with the plurality and humility of the consensual method? In particular, how can a reliance on the preferences of actors at the second stage be squared with the 'independently justified list of substantive goods' at the first stage? Does not the way that social contexts shape preferences and the way that individuals adapt their preferences to social imperatives militate against the likelihood of convergence between the two stages?[16]

Second, and following on from this, if the method is genuinely open-ended, what are the limits to the list? Nussbaum claims at the end of her book that her approach is intended as 'the systematization and theorization of thoughts that women are pursuing all over the world, when they ask how their lives might be improved' (*WHD* 301). For Garagarella (2001), this is too sweeping a conclusion, given that her country, the US, does not represent the whole of the western world, and India, her case study, does not represent the rest of the world. When 200-odd other countries are included in the process, not to speak of countless other sub-cultures and language groups, what is to stop the list of CHFCs expanding and dissipating?

---

[14] Of course, this is not to deny the contemporary role of environmental degradation in undermining livelihoods. But this is captured via its harm to health or autonomy, not via a separate capability to live in relation to the world of nature.

[15] Compare Clark's survey of a township and a village in South Africa, enquiring of poor people's own conceptions of their well-being and capabilities (Clark 2003: 15–16).

[16] The problem of the circularity of preferences and preference evaluation was one of the starting points of our work (*THN*: 22–24).

Nussbaum is aware of these concerns, and in Chapter 2 of *WHD* ('Adaptive preferences and women's options') she presents an insightful analysis of adaptive preferences and the obstacles these pose to securing agreement on minimum standards let alone conditions for a flourishing life. This fascinating chapter deserves more attention than we can offer here, but some comments are in order to illustrate how she conceives of reconciling wants and needs.

Nussbaum argues against two extreme positions, subjective welfarism and Platonism, and develops her thinking on the general Aristotelian concept of 'desire'. Contrasting the concepts of desire and preference, she asks, what is the contribution of desire in the process of reaching such a 'reflective equilibrium' (*WHD* 151)? Her answer is that desire plays two roles: epistemic and political. First, 'when people are respected as equals, and free from intimidation, and able to learn about the world, and secure against desperate want, their judgments about the core of a political conception are likely to be more reliable than judgments formed under the pressure of ignorance and fear and desperate need' (*WHD* 152). Second, desire plays an ancillary role in justifying and buttressing the political support necessary for a reflective equilibrium to be sustained. She claims that once people learn new capabilities, they don't want to go back. Even when women choose to return to traditional lives, such as a return to veiling, this is almost always 'a change in their mode of *functioning*, not in their level of political *capability* as citizens' (*WHD* 153). In other words, they rarely insist, once experiencing the choice, that all women should be forced to veil. Nussbaum suggests that the epistemological and political roles of desire apply more strongly in subsequent generations.

Thus desires, in contrast to preferences, are not totally adaptive, for two reasons. On the one hand, 'the human personality has a structure that is at least to some extent independent of culture' (*WHD* 155) – a nod towards some universal conception of human capacities. On the other hand, 'by promoting education, equal respect, the integrity of the person, and so forth, we are also indirectly shaping desires' (*WHD* 161). Thus desire informed by (rarely achieved) conciousness-raising can play a subsidiary and confirmatory role in political justification. This suggests that there exists a potential bridge between the normative and the consensual stages in the shaping of an agreed list of human capabilities, though this must always be subsidiary to independent normative argument.[17]

---

[17] I am grateful to Martha C. Nussbaum for clarification of this point.

Of course, professional doomsters like John Gray decry as utopian any attempt to achieve consensus and coordinated action around eradicating poverty, let alone around broader emancipation. 'The combination of rising human numbers, dwindling natural resources and spreading weapons of mass destruction is more likely to unleash wars of unprecedented savagery. If we can bring ourselves to look clearly at this prospect, we will lay aside utopian fantasies of global co-operation. We will see our task as staving off disaster from day to day' (Gray 2002). This benighted vision is unconvincing as well as morally abhorrent, but it should caution against the over-optimistic alternative that wants and needs can be easily reconciled.[18]

More importantly, Nussbaum has not in practice utilised the method she advocates. She has made some revisions to her earlier approach in response to discussions in India, the work of Martha Chen (1986) and other writers. However, this does not amount to systematically confronting her conception of the good with the values and experiences of the poor.[19]

Our goal in developing a different, hierarchical approach was similar to Nussbaum's: to recognise cultural variety but to avoid subordinating the identification of needs to it. Our approach was, as we have seen, to develop a two-stage procedure. The first stage uses neo-Kantian arguments to develop a *thin* theory of human need. When focusing on health and autonomy of agency it is explicitly designed to fit all human societies. It deliberately seeks, so to speak, the lowest common denominator of universalisable preconditions for human action and social participation. In this way, we would claim, the potential for cross-cultural consensus is heightened. At the second stage, we appeal to collective knowledge, from both the natural and the social sciences, to identify the pre-requisites for healthy and autonomous persons across different cultures (consider the remarks in the first section above concerning cross-cultural agreement on health). Against much post-modern scepticism we retain a belief in the potential of the scientific community to approximate an (ever-moving) consensus on the pre-requisites for human flourishing.

---

[18] We certainly align ourselves closely with Nussbaum here: 'The potential for rationality to dominate the political process is linked to a moral vision which Habermas shares with Rousseau. It is a belief in the basic goodness of ordinary people and their potential to live, work, create and communicate together in harmony and to use practical reason peacefully to resolve their disputes and to optimise their need-satisfaction' (*THN* 124).

[19] This has been a major goal of our research in the ESRC Research Group on *Wellbeing in Developing Countries* at the University of Bath, where we have addressed this issue both conceptually and in practice in twenty-four sites in four developing countries. See Gough and McGregor 2007, and the website: www.welldev.org.uk/research/research. htm.

Does not our approach risk the accusation of being paternalist? We believe not, because we recognise the role of wide participation and experiential knowledge in understanding needs and need satisfiers. Drawing on Habermas's theorisation of communicative competence and the 'ideal speech situation', we stress that common rules of debate are required.[20] 'Insofar as participants in such debates conform to the above standards, Habermas contends that the most rational solutions ... will be those which achieve the widest consensus' (*THN* 123). In the real world of dominant systems and interests, this entails at the least that 'the codified knowledge of professionals must confront the rationalised life-world – the "experientially-grounded knowledge" – which ordinary citizens develop through such self-reflection' (*THN* 125). Notwithstanding her rejection of Habermas's proceduralism, there are some intriguing parallels with Nussbaum here, for example the idea of rationality as consensus and the assumption of the goodness of ordinary people.

However, what is underplayed in our approach is Sen's valuable distinction between functionings and capabilities. Nussbaum embraces this, as when she writes: 'Where adult citizens are concerned, *capability* not *functioning* is the appropriate political goal' (*WHD* 87). This permits universal goals to be identified yet individuals' rights not to pursue them to be given due weight. Fasting is not the same as starving, nor is celibacy the same as enforced sexual abstinence. This enables her to argue for both civil/political and social/economic rights. (By contrast, children may require enforced protection of and stimulation of their capabilities, for example through compulsory education.) The functioning–capability distinction would help us to diminish lingering charges of paternalism (see Gough 2000, Chapter 1).

Levels and thresholds

A third point of comparison between our two approaches concerns the scope of the universalisable interests which underlie our list of CHFCs/ needs. Both Nussbaum and we endorse a broad view of human flourishing *and* wish to focus on minimal standards. Thus, on the one hand, Nussbaum continually speaks of 'a fully human life', of 'a life truly worthy of a human being'. In a similar vein we speak of 'human liberation', 'human flourishing', 'critical autonomy' as a basic need, and the

---

[20] That all participants possess the best available understanding concerning the technical issues of the problem, that they possess relevant methodological and communicational skills, and that the communication is as democratic as possible.

right to 'optimal fulfilment' of basic needs. On the other hand, Nussbaum identifies a lower threshold level of capability, a basic social minimum which should be secured for all citizens (*WHD* 73, 75). Similarly, we focus much of our attention on a lower standard: on avoidance of serious harm and on minimally disabled uncritical participation in one's form of life.[21] Thus both works have a dual agenda:

	Nussbaum	Doyal and Gough
Minimal standard	Basic social minimum	Avoidance of serious harm
Broad human flourishing	Fully human life	Human liberation; optimal need fulfilment

Seizing on this, Gasper (1996) has criticised our own work for both 'over-reach' and 'parsimony'. 'Over-reach' because the original derivation of basic needs in terms of harm-avoidance is then used to do too much work. The issues raised by critical autonomy are wide-ranging and deserve different and stronger forms of defence. Similarly, claiming optimal fulfilment of health care needs raises severe problems of a moral, not just a resource allocation, kind, in an age where medicine can keep elderly people alive at vast cost. 'Parsimony', because our single-minded focus on health and autonomy excludes all aspects of life, such as sex and religion, which are not universally necessary for effective participation. This echoes Soper's (1993a: 119) description of our 'somewhat puritanical and limited' list of basic and intermediate needs.

Gasper concludes: 'Doyal and Gough (are) drawn towards a broader conception of needs than seems implied by a criterion of avoiding serious harm. They formalize this by the extension to include critical autonomy, and their theory then has two versions, narrower and broader ... We should accept that there are various criteria possible in needs discourse, each of which may be appropriate for different purposes. For pursuing a consensual priority for minimum requirements for decency, a narrower picture of needs is more appropriate than when trying to ... prescribe for "human flourishing" or "the good life" ... Both these major policy roles of needs analysis will be weakened by not clearly distinguishing between them' (Gasper 1996: 31–32).

This criticism is well taken. Towards the end of a long chapter I merely offer two assertions and a comment in reply. First, the same verdict would seem to apply *a fortiori* to Nussbaum's conceptualisation

---

[21] Much of the detailed argument in our respective books concerns this second, lower level.

of central human functional capabilities. Second, I believe that our distinction between autonomy of agency and critical autonomy provides a more rigorous foundation for our two-fold approach than Gasper claims.[22] Here, Sen's arguments for the value of 'unrestrained participation' in political and social activities help flesh out the meaning of critical autonomy and the broader agenda. The 'constructive' role of political freedom is necessary to comprehend and conceptualise economic needs, he argues: 'A proper understanding of what economic needs are – their content and their force – requires discussion and exchange' (Sen 1999: 153). This applies not only to the myriad decisions about need satisfiers, but to future, richer understandings of intermediate needs themselves.

Turning to the related and final issue of thresholds, I would claim that we go further than Nussbaum. While she promises to address this question, she delivers little, mainly because her politically liberal approach would leave the setting of minimum thresholds to national or local decision-making procedures. Our approach to the question of standards and thresholds (*THN* 159–164) is again hierarchical, but begins conceptually at Gasper's highest level of human flourishing.

At the stage of basic needs, we endorse neither absolute minimum nor culturally relevant standards, but an optimum standard. In line with the two levels of autonomy we identify two such levels: a participation optimum and a still higher, critical optimum. The latter comprises those levels of health and cognitive, emotional and social capacities which permit critical participation in one's chosen form of life. In practice, however, we endorse as a practical measure of this 'the most recent standards achieved by the social grouping with the highest overall standards of basic need-satisfaction'. We concluded that in the late 1980s, the best performing nation was Sweden. This also suggested a 'constrained optimum' standard for poorer countries: the highest achieved by countries at lower levels of development. We suggested these standard-setters were then Costa Rica for middle-income countries and Sri Lanka for poor nations. This could provide an empirical measure for assessing, for example, shortfalls in women's capabilities in the developing world, but it hardly constitutes the independently derived normative threshold with which we began.

Considering intermediate needs, we argue for a minimum optimorum or minopt threshold. This is the minimum quantity of any given intermediate need-satisfaction required to produce the optimum level of basic

---

[22] But see Soper 1993a and 1993b for critical comments on this distinction.

need-satisfaction. The underlying assumption here is that the relationship is asymptotic: additional increments of a satisfier characteristic generating decreasing increments of basic need satisfaction until at the minopt point no additional benefit is derived.

However, Soper and Wetherly criticise our basic need standard on related grounds. Soper contends that this standard may actually be too high, in that the extravagance of Swedish energy use and socio-economic institutions is not generalisable to all other peoples in the world or to future generations. Insofar as this is true, it is accommodated within our definition of constrained optimum. But this raises a difficult issue. We have narrowed our focus from a concern with the universal requirements for social participation to whatever is universalisable across time and place in practice (Soper, 1993a: 78). This raises more issues than can be dealt with here, but at the end of the day 'ought' must imply 'can'. If, due to past industrialism, population growth, environmental degradation and climate change, we can achieve less than optimal generalisable satisfaction of basic needs, then so be it. We will be forever living in a world of constraint. Wetherly goes on to claim that this reintroduces relativism. The constrained optimum standard remains 'historically – and so socially, culturally – relative' (Wetherly, 1996: 58). But the 'and so' does not follow. The concept of human need we develop is historically open to the continual improvements in understanding that have characterised human progress. But at any one time, there is a body of best knowledge to which international appeal can be made. Put starkly, our theory is relative in time but absolute in space.

Conclusion

This chapter has concentrated on one aspect of Martha C. Nussbaum's recent book – the derivation and identification of 'central human functional capabilities' – itself just one small part of her total *oeuvre*. My purpose has been to compare her approach with that developed by Len Doyal and myself in our theory of human need. The two works have much in common, including endorsement of a fully universal conception of human capabilities/needs, a critique of relativism and a case for the constitutional rights of all peoples for their needs/capabilities to be met. Both works articulate a conception of the good which aspires to be universal yet which is dynamic and open-ended. Both are also richer than Sen in their conception of human flourishing, for example in recognising the role of emotional capacities (consider Gasper 2002).

How convincing are the two works in specifying and justifying a conception of human flourishing of relevance to policy across the developing world? Nussbaum derives her CHFCs from Aristotle's writings on 'spheres of experience' and their corresponding virtues. Following her deep engagement with 'the hard practical reasoning of law' and her extended research visits to India, she claims that her latest account expresses an overlapping consensus of people from differing cultures, but there is little evidence that this has in fact happened, or that, if it did, the result would be the same. The potential of informed desire to bridge the gulf between, in our language, wants and needs is unproven. Paradoxically, I believe that little of this harms her central argument, as expressed for example in the powerful and insightful chapters on religion and love, care and dignity. However, a stronger conceptual foundation for her list would give added strength to the thrust of her book.

The Doyal–Gough theory, meanwhile, provides a more parsimonious and logical derivation of a thick conception of human flourishing and an equally detailed list of basic and intermediate needs. Beginning with a common human interest – to participate in one's social form of life – we derive two basic human needs. We then call on codified and experiential knowledges to flesh out the universal pre-requisites for meeting basic needs at optimum and lower levels. This permits need satisfiers to be identified in a dynamic yet objective way. However, the exact way that codified and experiential knowledges are to be reconciled in our approach remains to be tackled – especially in a closely bound world of startling inequality and persistent cultural conflicts. I look forward to further debate on these issues.

Nussbaum's thick approach to human capabilities embraces a wide range of human activities and extols a broad vision of human flourishing, but its foundations are shaky and its potential for securing cross-cultural consensus is unproven and probably weak. Sen's thin theory of capabilities has greater potential for identifying priority capacities and has a proven record in underpinning an international consensus on human development, but it provides little systematic or comprehensive guidance on components of human functioning or well-being. Our theory of human need, we would claim, combines the merits of both. By expounding a thin derivation, and by carefully distinguishing autonomy of agency from critical autonomy, it recognises cultural differences within a universalist framework, but by positing universal satisfier characteristics and recognising our collective understanding of these it provides a richer framework for conceiving, measuring and – conceivably – improving human well-being.

380   *Ian Gough*

REFERENCES

Alkire, Sabina (2002) Dimensions of human development, *World Development* 30(2): 181–205.

Braybrooke, David (1987) *Meeting Needs*. Princeton University Press.

Chen, Martha (1986) *A Quiet Revolution: Women in Transition in Rural Bangladesh*. Cambridge, Mass.: Schenkman Publishing Company.

Clark, David (2002) *Visions of Development: A Study of Human Value*. Cheltenham: Edward Elgar.

Doyal, Len and Ian Gough (1991) *A Theory of Human Need*. London: Macmillan.

Garagella, Roberto (2001) Women and human development: review, *Idea Newsletter*, June, www.carleton.ca/idea/newsletter/reports_062001_2.html

Gasper, Des (1996) Needs and basic needs – a clarification of foundational concepts for development ethics and policy. ISS Working Paper 210. The Hague.

(1997) Sen's capability approach and Nussbaum's capability ethic, *Journal of International Development* 9(2): 281–302.

(2001) Women and human development: review, *Idea Newsletter*, June, www.carleton.ca/idea/newsletter/reports_062001_7.html

(2002) Is Sen's capability approach an adequate basis for considering human development? ISS Working Paper 360. The Hague.

Gough, Ian (2000) *Global Capital, Human Needs and Social Policies: Selected Essays*. London: Palgrave.

Gough, Ian and J. Allister McGregor (eds) (2007) *Wellbeing in Developing Countries: From Theory to Research*. Cambridge University Press.

Gray, John (2002) The unstoppable march of the clones, *New Statesman*, 24 June: 29.

Max-Neef, Manfred *et al.* (1989) Human scale development: an option for the future', *Development Dialogue 1*, Upsala, Sweden.

Nussbaum, Martha C. (1988) Nature, function and capability: Aristotle on political distribution, *Oxford Studies in Ancient Philosophy*, Supplementary Volume 1: 145–184.

(1990) Aristotelian social democracy. In Bruce Douglass *et al.* (eds) *Liberalism and the Good*. London: Routledge: 203–252.

(1992) Human functioning and social justice: in defense of Aristotelian essentialism, *Political Theory* 20(2): 202–246.

(1993) Non-relative virtues: an Aristotelian approach. In Nussbaum and Sen (eds): 242–269.

(1995a) Introduction. In Nussbaum and Glover (eds): 1–34.

(1995b) Human capabilities, female human beings. In Nussbaum and Glover (eds): 61–104.

(2000) *Women and Human Development: The Capabilities Approach*. Cambridge University Press.

Nussbaum, Martha C. and Amartya Sen (eds) (1993) *The Quality of Life*. Oxford: Clarendon.

(2006) *Frontiers of Justice: Disability, Nationality, Species Membership*. Cambridge, Mass.: Harvard University Press.

Nussbaum, Martha C. and Jonathan Glover (eds) (1995) *Women, Culture and Development: a study of human capabilities*. Oxford: Clarendon.

Saith, Ruhi (2001) Capabilities: the concept and its operationalisation, QEH Working Paper 66, University of Oxford, February.

Sen, Amartya (1984) *Resources, Values and Development*. Oxford: Blackwell.
   (1985) *Commodities and Capabilities*. Oxford: Elsevier Science Publishers.
   (1992) *Inequality Reexamined*. Oxford: Clarendon.
   (1999) *Development as Freedom*. Oxford: Clarendon.

Soper, Kate (1993a) A theory of human need, *New Left Review* 197: 113–128.
   (1993b) The thick and thin of human needing. In Glenn Drover and Patrick Kerans (eds) *New Approaches to Welfare Theory*. Aldershot: Edward Elgar: 69–81.

Wetherly, Paul (1996) Basic needs and social policies, *Critical Social Policy* 16(1): 45–65.

15 Nussbaum, Rawls, and the ecological limits of justice: using capability ceilings to resolve capability conflicts[*]

Breena Holland

Introduction

On March 6, 2001, President George W. Bush issued a letter to several national-level senators publicly defending his decision to oppose committing the United States to the Kyoto Protocol, an international treaty regulating greenhouse gas emissions. Bush claimed that meeting the treaty's goals would "cause serious harm to the U.S. economy" and emphasized his strong commitment "not to take actions that could harm consumers." In the environmental policy debate, such references to the relationship between the benefits of economic productivity and the legitimacy of environmental protection are common. Like Bush, anti-regulatory advocates often emphasize the economic impacts of environmental policies and how these might bear on various dimensions of human well-being. For example, as one critic of highly precautionary regulatory regimes claims, "by slowing economic growth and/or increasing energy prices, regimes could, in the final analysis, decrease overall access to food which could lower health status and increase death and disease in the poorer segments of society, especially in the developing world" (Goklany, 2000, p. 221).

In this chapter I want to consider a normative question that bears on the rise of economic goals to this position of prominence in the environmental debate. Specifically, I want to consider how we ought to evaluate environmental protection policies when they come into conflict with economic goals that also play a key role in furthering human well-being. In answering this question, I argue that we should evaluate policy goals in

[*] This chapter was first prepared for presentation at the 2007 International Conference of the Human Development and Capability Association at the New School for Social Research in New York City. I am grateful to the participants in the panel session (Jennifer Clare Heyward, Jeremy Bendik-Keymer, Victoria Kamsler, Martha C. Nussbaum, and David Schlosberg) as well as to three anonymous reviewers from the *Journal of Human Development and Capabilities* for helpful questions and comments. Thanks also to Amy Linch, John Martin Gillroy, Rick Matthews, and Jennifer Rubenstein for their input and suggestions.

terms of their impacts on the environmental dimensions of human capabilities – that is, on the environmental resources and ecological conditions that enable people to do and be different things. To justify and develop this approach to evaluating policy goals, I rely on the "partial theory of justice" that Martha C. Nussbaum advances.[1] Nussbaum's capabilities approach provides a helpful and illuminating framework for reasoning about what justice requires in the context of relationships in which the activities of citizens in distant places impact each other through large-scale ecological interactions. However, in order to fully account for this relationship between citizens, global economic and ecological processes, and justice, Nussbaum's capabilities approach will require further theorizing. In particular, I focus on the need to establish "capability ceilings" – in addition to "capability thresholds" – as conditions of justice.

This chapter will proceed in the following way. As a practical reference point for developing my theoretical argument, I will first discuss a brief example of how complicated interactions between economic and ecological processes can produce troubling environmental inequities. Second, I will argue that Nussbaum's capabilities approach to justice provides a better framework for addressing environmental inequities than a framework that relies on John Rawls's political theory, which she seeks to complement and extend. Third, I will discuss some limitations in Nussbaum's theory and how they might be addressed through establishing "capabilities ceilings" within her broader theory of justice. Throughout this discussion I treat the capabilities approach as a framework for evaluation that can guide and offer suggestions in deliberation among citizens in a democratic society. However, in the final section of the chapter, I briefly sketch the components of a democratic politics that allows the theory to play a more authoritative or prescriptive role.

Habitat change and environmental inequity

A key feature of many contemporary environmental problems is that they are the product of complicated interactions between economic and ecological processes. Consider, for example, the interactions producing a new variant of cholera – Vibrio Cholerae – that spread

---

[1] Nussbaum's capabilities approach is a "partial" theory of justice because she does not advance it as an "exhaustive account of political justice." Instead, Nussbaum maintains that there may be other important political values closely connected with justice that her theory does not include (Nussbaum 2000a, pp. 75–76).

through India and Bangladesh in January of 1993 (Colwell, 1996, pp. 2026–2027). Aided by a previously undetected antigen, by mid-April this new strain of cholera had invaded Calcutta, infecting 15,000 people, killing 230, and it soon spread to Thailand, Pakistan, and 10 other Asian nations. During the peak of its attack, Vibrio Cholerae was infecting 600 people per day in the city of Dhaka, Bangladesh (Epstein, 1995, p. 169).

Public health experts attributed the 1993 cholera outbreak to several factors resulting from changing ecological conditions.[2] First, an increase in nitrogen-rich wastewaters, fertilizers, and acid rain prompted growth in the aquatic weeds and algae – free-floating phytoplankton and zoo-plankton – that can harbor a certain form of the cholera bacteria that is either directly consumed after being absorbed by estuary waters, or indirectly consumed through contaminated seafood (Colwell, 1996, pp. 2026–2028; Colwell and Spira, 1992; Islam *et al.*, 1994). Second, wetlands and mangroves that normally do the work of filtering out these nitrogen-rich stimuli are being lost to coastal development, aquaculture, diking, and drilling. Third, certain fish, which are the natural predators of the plankton that harbor the cholera bacteria, are in severe decline due to overfishing (Epstein, 1995, p. 170). Fourth, the warmer sea surface temperatures believed to be brought on by climate change augmented algae growth by boosting photosynthesis in algal metabolism, increasing nutrient-rich coastal upwelling, and shifting the community of organisms toward more toxic species (e.g. "red tides"); consequently coastal algae became less palatable to their natural predators (Colwell, 1996, p. 2027; Epstein, 1992, pp. 1167–1168).

These kinds of habitat change exemplify how complicated interactions between economic and ecological processes can amplify human vulner-ability to environmental threats.[3] As Paul Epstein emphasizes in explain-ing the prevalence of opportunistic pests, "Environmental change and pollutants stress individuals and populations [of plant and animal species], and this may be reflected in the global resurgence of infectious disease as these stresses cascade through the community assemblages of species" (Epstein 1995, p. 168). In the cholera case, industrial agricul-ture, coastal land-use development, commercial fishing, and greenhouse

---

[2] The ecological conditions affecting the 1993 cholera outbreak are summarized by Paul Epstein (1995, p. 170), but also see Siddique *et al.* (1991, p. 1126) for a discussion of how ecological changes (resulting from increased flooding caused by dams) may have contributed to cholera outbreaks in Bangladesh prior to the 1993 outbreak.

[3] For a discussion of various case studies relating human health problems to degradation of ecological conditions, see Grifo and Rosenthal (1997).

gases produced by fossil-fuel based economies all combined to affect ecological systems in ways that undermined human health. While these activities may benefit both the poor and the rich in different ways, the costs of the 1993 cholera outbreak were most significant for two relatively impoverished groups: those without access to water not penetrated by cholera organisms, and those dependent on eating fish that contained the mutated forms of cholera. Thus, the 1993 cholera outbreak illustrates that just as the poor are most vulnerable to environmental changes that will result from global warming, such as flooding, they are also especially vulnerable to various diseases that result from other kinds of large-scale ecological change.

Because the burdens of these ecological changes are both severe and unequally distributed, they raise important questions about the justness of environmental disparities that result from interaction between economic and ecological processes. The most prominent liberal theories of justice have done little to address these questions (Bell, 2004, p. 289; Miller, 1999, pp. 151–153); they often treat economic activity as a neutral or benign condition of societal well-being that will improve the material conditions of the rich and poor alike. As such, environmental problems are commonly treated merely as cases in which externalities need to be internalized. For example, in his original formulation of *A Theory of Justice*, John Rawls refers to the environment as a special kind of economic good, one that is public in nature, and therefore subject to the dangers of underproduction and unsustainability. From this economic perspective, to address environmental problems we merely need to apply taxes and subsidies that force polluters to pay for the (true) social cost of their negative impacts on the environment (Rawls, 1971, p. 268).

However, in a world connected by large-scale ecological processes, the external effects of economic activities can be distant and difficult to identify before their disastrous consequences occur. Maximizing food production in croplands and grazing lands, for instance, can alter ecological processes in ways that severely impact natural services (e.g. water purification) in places distant from the agricultural land itself (Galloway et al., 2003). Likewise, creating levees and channels to reduce natural flooding and protect farmland in fertile areas can lead to the loss of wetlands far downstream, and hence can reduce the capacity of wetlands to mitigate storm surges in coastal areas (Day et al., 2007). Furthermore, it is difficult to quantify the losses that result from these kinds of humanly induced changes in ecological systems (O'Neill, 2007, pp. 85–88). For example, if people cannot put a monetary value on the loss of identity and security that follows their evacuation from areas deluged by coastal flooding, then it will be excessively difficult to internalize the costs of economic activities that produce the ecological changes causing floods.

In light of these complications, addressing environmental inequities will require a theory of justice that accounts for how interactions between economic and large-scale ecological processes shape the distribution of individual advantage in society. I will argue that Martha C. Nussbaum's capabilities approach is appropriate for this purpose. However, because her theory emerges in critical dialogue with John Rawls's approach to justice, I will first explain why her theory is better than Rawls's for addressing questions about the environment's role as a condition of justice.

It is important to note that in identifying limitations in Rawls's theory, I focus on Rawls's theory of domestic justice rather than his theory of international justice. At one level, the domestic theory might seem like a misguided choice, since the kinds of environmental problems I focus on in this chapter cross state borders. But Rawls's theory of international justice is famously a theory about justice between *peoples*, not individuals (see Rawls, 1999), and as I argue below it is necessary to focus on individuals when addressing questions of environmental justice.[4] There are some ways in which Rawls's domestic theory is still problematic in this respect; specifically, his "difference principle" focuses on the position of the worst-off *class* in society. I explore the domestic theory nonetheless, because it can more easily accommodate this problem, and because Rawls's more recent work on his domestic theory of justice at least references environmental protection in relation to health care, which he claims can be included in his theory as a "primary good" (Rawls, 2001, pp. 168–176). The domestic theory, in short, provides a more sophisticated basis for critically engaging the potential of Rawls's political theory to address injustices that result from the distribution of environmental resources (e.g. Bell, 2004). The next section of this chapter discusses how Rawls's early work addresses the environment; the following section then turns to his more recent reference to the environment as a dimension of public health.[5]

[4] Beitz (1979) argues that Rawls's domestic theory could be applied as an international theory of justice that deals with individuals at the global level rather than the national level. I do not consider this option here because of the excessive institutional demands that would be involved in applying Rawls's "difference principle" at the international level, i.e. in identifying and reshaping all international economic inequalities such that they provide the greatest benefits to the least advantaged.

[5] In the present discussion I do not address the potential for Rawls's theory to address questions of *inter*generational justice – justice across generations – such as the argument that Marcel Wissenberg advances (1999). For present purposes I am concerned with how

Justice and the environment in Rawls's early political theory

In addressing how the institutional mechanisms of a liberal-democratic society bear on environmental inequities, the political theory of John Rawls seems like an obvious starting point. Rawls provides a systematic account of justice for modern liberal democracies, and because he treats economic institutions as part of the "basic structure" of society – and therefore, as subject to evaluation according to his two principles of justice – his theory also makes it possible to bring economic institutions under the lens of justice (Rawls, 1971, p. 259). However, as I argue below, Rawls's early work errs in treating environmental problems merely as a matter of internalizing externalities. Specifically, he fails to recognize the relevance of the environment to the basic liberties protected by his first principle of justice, a failure that is especially problematic when addressing environmental impacts that occur at the intersection of economic activities and ecological processes. Furthermore, even if Rawls were to account for functioning ecological systems as a precondition of the advantages that his principles of justice protect – an extension some defend based on Rawls's discussion (in his later work) of public health as a primary good – his theory of justice would still lack particular features of Nussbaum's capabilities approach that make it better for addressing the relationship between the environment and basic conditions of justice. As a preface to this argument, let us first consider some key features of Rawls's approach to justice.

Rawls advances the following two principles for determining how a just society ought to allocate the benefits of social and economic cooperation. First, each person is entitled to the most extensive scheme of equal basic liberties consistent with like liberties for all. Second, the benefits of social and economic cooperation must be (a) attached to offices and positions open to all under conditions of fair equality opportunity, and

Rawls's theory might be used to address questions of *intra*generational justice, by which I mean justice within a single generation. I also do not consider David Miller's (1999) discussion of Rawls's theory of justice, primarily because I am interested in how environmental resources and conditions can be directly attached to protections for existing primary goods. Miller recognizes this as one categorization of the environment's value, but the majority of his analysis concerns how to engage in more informed and democratic valuations of the natural environment's subjective value to citizens, which he treats as value that is additional to whatever baseline might be established as a minimum condition of justice. In this discussion, I am interested in evaluating policy impacts independent of people's subjective valuations, even if that evaluation ultimately serves only to further democratic reasoning. For a summary of additional efforts to apply Rawls's theory to environmental issues, and the problems with those efforts, see Daniel Thero (1995).

(b) distributed such that the greatest benefits go the least advantaged members of society (Rawls, 1971, p. 302; 1993, p. 291). The liberties relevant to the first principle consist of basic civil and political freedoms, such as freedom of speech, assembly, thought, and association (Rawls, 1971, p. 61; 1993, p. 291). These liberties have no particular priority among themselves, but Rawls does assign them priority with respect to the second principle (Rawls, 1971, p. 61). As he explains, "By priority of liberty I mean the precedence of the principle of equal liberty over the second principle of justice. The two principles are in lexical order, and therefore the claims of liberty are to be satisfied first" (Rawls, 1971, p. 244). Put differently, the political liberties protected under the first principle of justice "cannot be denied to certain social groups on the grounds that their having these liberties may enable them to block policies needed for economic efficiency and growth" (Rawls, 1993, p. 295). Rather, if policies needed for economic efficiency and growth do not violate the liberties that the first principle of justice protects, then they are acceptable so long as the constraints of the second principle guide the resulting distribution of benefits.

The second part of Rawls's second principle – commonly referred to as the "difference principle" – requires that projects producing inequalities (e.g. of power, income, status, etc.) make life better for the worst-off members in society, and that access to the more privileged or prestigious positions are not blocked (e.g. by racial or gender-based discrimination). Consequently, Rawls's difference principle "requires that the higher expectations of the more advantaged contribute to the prospects of the least advantaged" (Rawls, 1971, p. 95).

Rawls understands his two principles of justice as operating within a constitutional structure that secures the liberties of equal citizenship protected under the first principle (see Rawls, 1971, p. 197). Toward this end, governmental interventions in institutional activities are justifiable on two grounds: as a means to prevent the kind of wealth accumulation that can radically distort political power, and as a means to equalize basic liberties and opportunities. For example, in order to prevent distortions in political power, Rawls allows government to block monopolistic barriers that would undermine equality of opportunity in economic activities and in the free choice of occupation (Rawls, 1971, p. 275). Likewise, government may impose various levies and regulations in order to prevent a distribution of wealth that concentrates power in a way that is detrimental to political liberty and fair equality of opportunity (Rawls, 1971, p. 277). These purposes also justify using taxes to raise revenues for funding a public school system that provides equally endowed and motivated citizens an equal chance to attain educational and cultural experiences. Finally, government may also use these tax revenues to make transfer payments that otherwise satisfy the difference principle (Rawls, 1971, p. 278).[6] Taken together, the civil and political freedoms that Rawls's first principle secures (e.g. freedom of assembly and expression), and the social and economic conditions that Rawls's second principle distributes (e.g. equal opportunity and income redistribution), make up a list of "primary goods."

As I have mentioned, Rawls's *Theory of Justice* treats environmental protection as a form of governmental intervention that is necessary due to the public and indivisible nature of environmental goods (Miller, 1999, p. 156). Specifically, he views environmental resources as available to all if they are available to anyone, and as goods that cannot be divided up according to people's private preferences for more or less (see Rawls, 1971, pp. 266–268). Thus, Rawls's early political economy suggests that government should internalize externalities so that law and government can make polluters pay the true social cost of the waste they produce.

Although internalizing externalities is an important part of correcting for market failures, this original treatment of the environment is limited. Specifically, in *A Theory of Justice*, Rawls fails to recognize the environment's significance as a condition of social justice that is instrumental to the basic liberties and opportunities his principles of justice seek to protect. Furthermore, because addressing environmental problems puts the goals of his two principles of justice in tension with each other, the lexical priority of Rawls's first principle would require giving priority to considering how environmental resources bear on the basic liberties that his first principle secures. Let us consider this problem and then turn to the less obvious problem that remains in Rawls's later effort to treat health care as a primary good to which the environment is instrumental.

First, it is important to note that Rawls's early work errs in treating the environment as a mere public good that can be accurately valued by internalizing externalities. Many environmental resources indeed are indivisible in the sense that "the quantity produced cannot be divided up as private goods can and purchased by individuals according to their preferences" (Rawls, 1971, p. 206). However, this understanding of their indivisibility does not mean that their contribution to individual

---

[6] Although Rawls (1971, p. 277) does claim that beyond this suitable minimum provided by wealth transfers, "it may be perfectly fair that the rest of total income be settled by the price system, assuming that it is moderately efficient and free from monopolistic restrictions, and unreasonable externalities have been limited."

advantage is made equally available to everyone if made available to anyone. Primarily this is because environmental resources as well as larger ecological systems can exist in qualitatively different conditions. For example, preservation of the ozone layer is a good made available to everyone, but the advantages such preservation provides will be of greater benefit to those who are most threatened by its destruction, such as people living closer to the north and south poles of the earth. Likewise, wetland ecosystems involved in the process of water purification can exist in states of greater or less ecological health, and therefore they can be more or less effective at purifying water. It follows that the advantages of protecting wetland ecosystems will be greater for those who are more likely to rely on these systems for their water resources or for their nutritional inputs from fish living in wetland ecosystems.

Second, because the quality of environmental goods can in these ways make them unequally available, Rawls also errs in treating the environment as if it does not confer fundamental advantages of wealth and power to some and not to others. The environmental circumstances one is born into do affect one's initial chances in life, and like the social and economic circumstances that one is born into, appeal to notions of desert or merit do not justify them (Rawls, 1971, p. 7). For example, the children of poor and minority communities are often born into neighborhoods with more severe air pollution problems (American Lung Association, 2001). One consequence of exposure to air pollution is childhood asthma, a common and chronic health condition that affects 4.8 million children under the age of 18 in the United States. The prevalence rate of asthma attacks are 32 percent higher in African Americans than the rates for whites. Similarly, African American children are four times more likely to die from asthma than white children and three times more likely to be hospitalized for asthma (Sze, 2007, p. 95). Aside from hospitalization and death, asthma can have significant negative effects on work and school attendance, as well as on one's social life and emotional well-being (Nocon and Booth, 1989–1990). As a case in point, victims of asthma as well as their families and their communities often experience a loss of control that leads to family-wide and community-wide depression (Nossiter, 1995).

These problems demonstrate that environmental circumstances can have profound effects from the start of life. High levels of polluted air can have health impacts that close off the normal channels through which one would otherwise pursue important personal and career goals. Exposure to ultraviolet light that passes through a thinned ozone layer can produce skin cancer that leads to premature death. Eating fish from polluted water can involve ingesting toxins that affect the mental abilities of one's unborn children (Cone, 2005, pp. 153–167). In short, because the condition of the natural environment confers fundamental advantages to some and not to others, Rawls errs in not addressing its importance as a matter of basic justice, alongside other basic protections, such as equal opportunity and free expression.

In light of these limitations in Rawls's existing account of environmental problems, it would improve his theory to incorporate an account of the environment's instrumental value to basic conditions of justice. However, addressing the environment's instrumental value in a Rawlsian theoretical framework would demand much stronger environmental protections than Rawls's early political theory admits. Specifically, because protecting the environmental preconditions of basic liberties protected by the first principle of justice might conflict with economically productive uses of the environment that are necessary for satisfying the goals of the difference principle, the lexical priority of Rawls's first principle would require protecting the environment as a precondition of basic liberties.

Let us consider how this tension between Rawls's principles arises by returning to the Cholera outbreak (discussed above) that struck India and Bangladesh in January of 1993. This case demonstrates how complicated interactions between economic activities (that produce fertilizers, waste, acid rain, over-fishing, etc.) and ecological processes (such as those that filter water and control free-floating plankton) can function to undermine human health and well-being. Like air pollution, habitat changes fostering the spread of diseases such as cholera can indeed have a profound effect on one's initial chances in life, determining not just whether or not one is able to live a life but also whether one will have the physical capacity to take advantage of basic civil and political freedoms as well as opportunities for personal and professional advance. In a case such as this, then, in which economic activities produce environmental impacts that undermine some individuals' capacity to enjoy basic liberties, Rawls's commitment to the priority of liberty limits the scope his theory allows for pursuing economically productive uses of the environment that will improve the prospects of the least advantaged. In other words, environmental impacts require protections that conflict with the goals of the difference principle.

More fundamental than the priority Rawls accords to the civil and political freedoms that his first principle protects is his separation of them from the social and economic protections the second principle allocates. As Nussbaum has noted, this separation makes it difficult for Rawls adequately to address the extent to which political and civil freedoms have material prerequisites, or to recognize that social and economic protections are necessary preconditions for realizing these liberties.[7] Contemporary efforts to address this problem make progress with some aspects of Rawls's theory, but as I discuss below, they do this by adopting the concepts descriptive of human capabilities, which therefore only illuminates why a capabilities approach to justice offers a better framework for dealing with questions about the distribution of environmental goods and harms.

Justice and the environment in Rawls's later political theory

In his later work, Rawls briefly acknowledges that there may be material prerequisites to the protections that allow people to be "fully cooperating members of society" (Rawls, 2001, p. 169), and he suggests that if necessary, the basic liberties and opportunities included in the "index of primary goods" can include these prerequisites (see Rawls, 2001, p. 172). Insofar as these prerequisites pertain to basic liberties and opportunities, however, an adequate articulation of them points us toward capabilities. Insofar as they pertain to the distribution of other advantages, they remain, in the Rawlsian theory, insufficiently individualistic to cope with the environmental problems addressed here.

Most important to the present discussion, in *Justice as Fairness: A Restatement*, Rawls sketches what an extension of his theory of justice would entail if health care were considered among the primary goods that his second principle of justice distributes. Here, Rawls explicitly references clean air and unpolluted water as "in-kind" benefits that the government ought to provide:

[T]he primary goods of income and wealth are not to be identified only with personal income and private wealth ... As citizens we are also the beneficiaries of the government's providing various personal goods and services to which we are entitled, as in the case of health care, or of its providing public goods (in the economist's sense), as in the case of measures ensuring public health (clean air and unpolluted water, and the like). (Rawls, 2001 p. 172)

Derek Bell draws on this reference to argue that an extension of Rawls's theory of justice to include health care as a primary good can incorporate protection and provision of basic environmental goods (Bell, 2004). For

---

[7] Rawls (1993, p. 7) briefly addresses this point, granting that certain basic needs might need to be met in order for citizens to understand and exercise their basic civil and political liberties. But as Nussbaum notes, Rawls grants this point with "tantalizing brevity," and says little about what it might mean to satisfy basic needs. See Nussbaum (2006, p. 289).

Bell, "The inclusion of basic environmental goods on the list of primary goods is justified because of their role in maintaining the 'minimum essential capacities for being [a] normal and fully cooperating [member] of society'" (2004, p. 298). In other words, without basic environmental protections people might lack the conditions of bodily health necessary for executing the "two moral powers" – a capacity for a sense of justice and a capacity for a sense of the good – necessary for maintaining their status as free and equal citizens (Rawls's, 2001, pp. 18–19, 168–169).

Bell's effort to build on Rawls's brief discussion of health care in order to account for the distribution of environmental goods is illuminating. While he follows Rawls in identifying the needs of the least advantaged group in society, he also adopts the language of human capabilities in determining the environmental priorities a Rawlsian framework would arrive at. Consider, for example, the following quote from Bell's argument:

If the goal is to ensure that all members of the least advantaged group are normal and fully cooperating members of society, the "basic structure" of society must be designed (as far as possible) to maintain (and restore) for everyone a complex of physical and mental capacities that equips them to function (e.g. work, pursue a conception of the good) in their society ... In effect, we are choosing among alternative policy packages (available at any particular level of resources) and their guarantees of primary goods to members of the least advantaged group by considering their likely effects on the essential capacities of the members of the least advantaged group. (Bell, 2004, pp. 300–301)

I include this quote from Bell's argument because it demonstrates how quickly a discussion about practical issues of policy involves reasoning about the capacities that enable people to function, first, and how primary goods bear on them, second. To put this point differently, Bell's argument raises the question of whether Rawls's primary goods should be the basis for policy evaluation when what really matters is how those goods bear on the physical and mental capacities that enable people to function with and toward a sense of justice and a sense of the good.[8] Indeed, identifying injustice in the distribution of environmental goods and harms will ultimately involve going beyond the Rawlsian conception of individual advantage to assess how environmental conditions impact people's capacities or capabilities to function. Because this argument from the essential capacities of citizens thus moves us towards a capabilities account, I set it aside, below, when returning to Rawls's views.

---

[8] Of course, this is a primary point made in Amartya Sen's original critique of Rawls's theory of justice (Sen, 1982).

Rawls's later work also gestures at how his second principle might indirectly address environmental problems, but this approach also is limited in its potential environmental policy applications. Rawls associates the provision of health care – and by extension the environmental conditions that good health requires – with the primary goods of income and wealth. This is evident in the last extended quote from Rawls (cited above), where Rawls groups health care with the primary goods of "personal income and private wealth" rather than with the basic liberties (Rawls, 2001, p. 172).[9] Because income and wealth are subject to distribution according to Rawls's second principle of justice (i.e. the difference principle), the distribution of health care – and by extension the provision of environmental resources that enables individual health – can be unequal, so long as the greatest benefits go to the members of the least advantaged group or class in society. Here, it is the non-individualist focus of Rawls's theory that is problematic.

Specifically, although environmental justice advocates frequently point out that people in certain racial groups and classes of income face the worst environmental burdens, we cannot accurately evaluate the justness of a given distribution without looking at the environmental burdens that threaten people irrespective of their group or class association. In particular, poorer classes or minority groups do indeed face more extreme exposure to environmental risks and harms, but there can be important variations within these groups and classes – variations that make some individuals within a given group or class much worse off in relation to those exposures. Thus, in focusing on a group or a class – or their representative member – Rawls's theory of justice is in danger of supporting policies that improve aggregate environmental conditions, rather than promising that specific environmental conditions are met for each individual. Put differently, just as a region can in aggregate meet a given environmental standard (e.g. of air quality) while particular neighborhoods within that region can fail to meet that standard, a low-income group or class might experience environmental exposures at an aggregate level that differs substantially from the exposures faced by individuals within that group.

For this reason, and in addition to the problem with Rawls's conception of individual advantage discussed above, Nussbaum's capabilities approach is superior as a theory of justice for addressing inequities in the

---

[9] I have already discussed (in the section "Justice and the environment in Rawls's early political theory) why environmental protections should be attached to the basic liberties protected by Rawls's first principle of justice, so I will now focus on other problems with Bell's elaboration of Rawls's theory.

distribution of environmental goods and harms. As I will now argue, not only does Nussbaum provide a conception of individual advantage that can better account for the ways in which environmental benefits and burdens bear on basic conditions of justice, she also seeks to establish absolute protections for the social and economic conditions that are prerequisites for realizing each person's liberties. After explaining why these features of Nussbaum's capabilities approach make it easier to see the obstacles to equality that environmental problems pose, I will argue that in order to address these problems in a way that meets her conditions of justice, Nussbaum's approach will need to establish limits – or ceilings – on capability protections, in addition to threshold levels of capability protection which she already seeks to protect as constitutional entitlements. In this context, by 'capability protection' or 'capabilities protections' I refer to the legal, social, or political means through which a society protects any or all of the central human functional capabilities.

Advantages of a capabilities approach to environmental justice

Like Rawls, Nussbaum does not systematically theorize the multiple ways in which the natural environment bears on conditions of justice (Holland, 2008). However, because her theory of justice requires protecting people's capabilities to do and be different things, it is able to accommodate a broader and more accurate account of the environment's instrumental value to basic conditions of justice. Specifically, Rawls's theory of justice treats social "primary goods" as the basis on which to evaluate relative social position. As I have discussed, these goods consist of rights and liberties, powers and opportunities, and income and wealth (Rawls, 1971, p. 62). In contrast, Nussbaum bases evaluation of relative social position on a list of central human functional capabilities (Nussbaum, 2000a, 78–80).[10]

---

[10] Nussbaum's list of central human functional capabilities includes the following: *(1) Life.* Being able to live to the end of a human life of normal length; not dying prematurely, or before one's life is so reduced as to be not worth living. *(2) Bodily health.* Being able to have good health, including reproductive health; to be adequately nourished, to have adequate shelter. *(3) Bodily integrity.* Being able to move freely from place to place; having one's bodily boundaries treated as sovereign, i.e. being able to be secure against assault, including sexual assault, child sexual abuse, and domestic violence; having opportunities for sexual satisfaction and for choice in matters of reproduction. *(4) Senses, imagination, and thought.* Being able to use the senses, to imagine, think, and reason – and to do these things in a "truly human" way, a way informed and cultivated by an adequate education, including, but by no means limited to, literacy and basic mathematical and scientific training. Being able to use imagination and thought in connection with experiencing and producing self-expressive works and events of one's own choice, religious, literary, musical, and so forth. Being able to use one's mind in

Capabilities are conditions or states of human enablement that make it possible for people to achieve things, such as "being able to have good health" and being able "to move freely from place to place" (Nussbaum, 2000a, pp. 78–79; 2006, pp. 76–78). Some of Nussbaum's capabilities do establish protections for the same rights, opportunities, and material holdings that Rawls's two principles of justice distribute, e.g. Nussbaum's list of central capabilities includes "being able to use one's mind in ways protected by guarantees of freedom of expression with respect to both political and artistic speech, and freedom of religious exercise."[11] However, in Nussbaum's theory, income and wealth do not play such a central role in evaluating relative social position, for many things besides income and wealth contribute to individual advantage, and many of these things are not commensurable with income and wealth (Nussbaum, 2006, pp. 283–284). Furthermore, a person's capabilities indicate whether a person's circumstances allow her to translate the things she has into actual achievements (Sen, 1992, p. 110; 1982, pp. 357–358).

ways protected by guarantees of freedom of expression with respect to both political and artistic speech, and freedom of religious exercise. Being able to search for the ultimate meaning of life in one's own way. Being able to have pleasurable experiences, and to avoid non-necessary pain. *(5) Emotions.* Being able to have attachments to things and people outside ourselves; to love those who love and care for us, to grieve at their absence; in general, to love, to grieve, to experience longing, gratitude, and justified anger. Not having one's emotional development blighted by overwhelming fear and anxiety, or by traumatic events of abuse or neglect. (Supporting this capability means supporting forms of human association that can be shown to be crucial in their development.) *(6) Practical reason.* Being able to form a conception of the good and to engage in critical reflection about the planning of one's life. (This entails protection for the liberty of conscience.) *(7) Affiliation.* A. Being able to live with and toward others, to recognize and show concern for other human beings, to engage in various forms of social interaction; to be able to imagine the situation of another and to have compassion for that situation; to have the capability for both justice and friendship. (Protecting this capability means protecting institutions that constitute and nourish such forms of affiliation, and also protecting the freedom of assembly and political speech.) B. Having the social bases of self-respect and non-humiliation; being able to be treated as a dignified being whose worth is equal to that of others. This entails at a minimum, protections against discrimination on the basis of race, sex, sexual orientation, religion, caste, ethnicity, or national origin. In work, being able to work as a human being, exercising practical reason and entering into meaningful relationships of mutual recognition with other workers. *(8). Other species.* Being able to live with concern for and in relation to animals, plants, and the world of nature. *(9) Play.* Being able to laugh, to play, to enjoy recreational activities. (10) *Control over one's environment.* A. *Political.* Being able to participate effectively in political choices that govern one's life; having the right of political participation, protections of free speech and association. B. *Material.* Being able to hold property (both land and moveable goods), not just formally but in terms of real opportunity; and having property rights on an equal basis with others; having the right to seek employment on an equal basis with others; having the freedom from unwarranted search and seizure.

[11] See the fourth capability listed in the previous footnote.

Thus, in the capabilities approach, it is the goods and resources people have, as well as their abilities, that determine relative social position.

A conception of individual advantage that focuses on people's capabilities rather than on their primary goods has important advantages when it comes to addressing environmental problems. This is because the variation in individual circumstance that a focus on capabilities illuminates is especially important when the quality of a given standard of environmental protection varies dramatically across geographical space. Consider, for example, a regulation controlling pollutants that harm the atmosphere's ozone layer, which filters out harmful ultra-violet radiation from the sun. As discussed in my critique of cost internalization, a regulation limiting pollutants that damage this layer of atmospheric protection does not provide equal protection to all people, primarily because ozone depletion poses bigger threats to people living close to the earth's northern pole (where the layer of atmospheric protection is thinnest). What matters in this instance is whether one is able to translate a given level of pollution control into the achievement of avoiding cancer, given one's geographical circumstance. In other words, people in different geographical locations will be able to do different things with an existing level of pollution control. Because the capabilities approach thinks about individual advantage in terms of people's conditions or states of enablement, it can more easily observe how these variations in individual circumstance pose barriers to the kinds of equal protection that justice requires.

The capabilities approach also insists on securing a threshold level of capability protection for each person, treated as an end in their own right (Nussbaum, 2000a, pp. 5–6; 2006, p. 71, p. 78, and pp. 166–167). This gives it advantages in comparison with Rawls's early effort to address environmental problems through cost internalization, and in comparison with later elaborations of Rawls's theory of justice, which seek to address environmental impacts on well-being through the second principle of justice. With respect to cost internalization, if justice requires a threshold level of capability protection for each person, then the externalized costs of activities that deplete the ozone layer cannot be internalized in a way that satisfies the conditions of justice. For to merely make polluters pay more for damage to the ozone layer would be to treat the consequences of that damage to capabilities – i.e. damage to human life and health – as if those consequences are something for which it is possible to compensate people. Likewise, treating ozone depletion as a threat to the Rawlsian primary good of health care will involve remedying unequal impacts at the level of income and wealth, and according to a group- or class-based analysis of disadvantage (Wolff and De-Shalit, 2007, pp. 31–34). Yet, here again, it is unlikely that giving certain classes of people more income and wealth can make up for the health consequences of ozone depletion, for these consequences are not commensurable with income and wealth, and they may track geographical distributions that do not correspond to class distributions, such that important individual impacts are overlooked.

Nussbaum's capabilities approach need not attempt any such commensuration. Her capabilities approach does not permit such tradeoffs (between money and health) to occur below a minimum threshold level of human health enablement. As Nussbaum explains, "If people are below the threshold on any one of the capabilities, that is a failure of basic justice, no matter how high up they are on all the others" (2006, p. 167). It follows that if damage to the ozone layer pushes some people's capabilities for life and health below the threshold, then the activities that produce those damages are unjust.

Thus, whether we are considering Rawls's early effort to address environmental problems through cost internalization, or trying to draw on more recent work endeavoring to connect environmental protections to Rawlsian primary goods distributed by the second principle of justice, his theory has a limited capacity to identify the obstacles to equality that environmental problems pose for particular individuals, especially when cash transfers cannot eliminate or compensate for these problems (Wolff and De-Shalit, 2007, p. 26). In contrast, Nussbaum's capabilities approach is more likely to recognize the environmental barriers to social justice. I have argued that this is partly because an evaluative focus on each individual's capabilities can account for how variation in individual circumstance shapes well-being.

In addition to the advantages of this evaluative focus, Nussbaum's theory is more likely to recognize a wide range of barriers to social justice because it systematically incorporates the idea that political and civil liberties may have social and economic prerequisites. In particular, the mandate to protect the full list of capabilities for each person is not governed by distinct principles, one protecting civil and political freedoms, the other regulating the distribution of social and economic protections. For Nussbaum, the demand to attain social and economic protections is absolute: she does not subject social and economic protections to the distributive constraints of the Rawls's difference principle; rather, certain social and economic guarantees must be met regardless of where one falls with respect to the least advantaged group or class in society (Nussbaum, 2006, pp. 288–289). Consequently, if the environmental preconditions of a social protection such as bodily health conflict with the economic preconditions of a political protection such as free expression, then the capabilities approach registers a failure to attain equally important basic capability thresholds (i.e. of "bodily health" and "senses, imagination, and thought"). In this respect, Nussbaum's capabilities approach recognizes that the environmental preconditions of health for each person matter. It is not enough to protect only those environmental conditions that ensure the least advantaged group or its representative members are getting the majority health benefits, for depending on the existing distribution of health benefits, such a mandate may not even get each person in the least advantaged group up to an adequate bodily health capability threshold.

A theory of justice that in this way helps to clarify conflicts between different capability protections and identify when a given distribution of benefits remains inadequate for attaining minimum capability thresholds can make important contributions to deliberative politics. For example, a theory of justice that helps to clarify rather than conceal the environmental obstacles to achieving threshold levels of capability protection would usefully force society to face what Nussbaum refers to as the "tragic question." The tragic question arises when it is not possible to push one capability above the threshold that justice requires without simultaneously pushing another capability below the threshold that justice requires. Thus, the tragic question concerns whether any of the alternatives available in a choice situation are morally acceptable (Nussbaum, 2000b, p. 1007). It is important for individuals to face this question because doing so registers the fact that prioritizing one capability over another denies important moral commitments. Furthermore, as Nussbaum explains, squarely facing the tragic question "keeps the mind of the chooser firmly on the fact that his action is an immoral action, which it is always wrong to choose." It also "informs the chooser that he may owe reparations to the vanquished in an effort to rebuild their lives after the disaster that will have been inflicted upon them." When recognition of the loss of tragedy is public, this also constitutes an acknowledgement of moral culpability, which has expressive importance. Finally, facing the conflict also "reminds the chooser that he must not do such things henceforth, except in a very similar tragic circumstance" (Nussbaum, 2000b, p. 1009).

In these ways, recognizing the tragedy that a capability conflict implies can have the practical implication of pushing society toward justice. In part this is because the tragic question provides an occasion for public deliberation in which citizens try to understand a situation with important public consequences (Nussbaum, 2000b, p. 1011). Deliberation can, in turn, lead to some instructive thinking about how a society might govern better. It may, for example, motivate us to "imagine what a world would be like that did not confront people with such choices"

(Nussbaum, 2000b, p. 1013). It may give us a moment to pause and ask whether there is way of rearranging our social practices so that we can avoid the tragedy (Nussbaum, 2000b, p. 1016). For Nussbaum, when a conflict puts one capability in conflict with another, it is indeed a sign that society has probably gone wrong somewhere, that it is probably not well designed (Nussbaum, 2006, p. 401). Thus, the occurrence of a tragic conflict should initiate long-term planning efforts that will allocate resources away from supporting entitlements that are not fundamental and toward supporting threshold level of capabilities that define the conditions of justice (Nussbaum, 2006, p. 403). Conflict between the capabilities that Nussbaum seeks to protect as fundamental entitlements could be the basis for planning a future society that minimizes or eliminates conflicts.

Despite these advantages of the capabilities approach in revealing the conflicts among the preconditions required for achieving a threshold level of a single set of basic protections, this account of how to deal with these conflicts only takes us so far. In part this is because Nussbaum's discussion of tragic tradeoffs treats the capabilities approach as a tool to guide public deliberation and reasoning about the tradeoffs that public policies imply. In this context the capabilities approach offers a framework to guide the logic and reasoning of debate (within institutions and among the public), after a list of fundamental entitlements has been established; Nussbaum does not propose prioritizing some subset of the central capabilities, and she does not provide independent moral argument for why some people's capabilities are more worthy of protection when their capabilities conflict with each other. Thus, for the present purpose, which is to address degradation of aquatic ecosystems as a specific policy issue that requires the specification or interpretation of an existing entitlement or protection, I will follow Nussbaum's discussion of tragic tradeoffs in assuming this more deliberative and less prescriptive role for the capabilities approach. However, because Nussbaum's method for justifying her list of central human capabilities has components that are less procedural and more consequentialist, I will sketch one approach to defending a more prescriptive application of the capabilities approach in the final section of this chapter. In the meantime, let us return to Nussbaum's discussion of tragic tradeoffs in order to identify why the capabilities approach must theorize a role for capability ceilings.

First, Nussbaum envisions that a deliberative process, involving the public as well as legislative and judicial actors, will determine the rearrangement of practices necessary for removing tragic tradeoffs (Nussbaum, 2000b, p. 1027). As I suggest above, such a process would seem to draw on the capabilities approach to shape and guide deliberation among institutional actors but would not promise to protect capabilities in the way those actors propose, especially if doing so conflicts with other goals emerging from public deliberation about the policy in question (Nussbaum, 2000b, p. 1028). Second, it is through such a deliberative process that Nussbaum also seeks to establish the appropriate threshold levels of the central human functional capabilities. In establishing these thresholds, Nussbaum argues that the level of protection for each capability should be set with an eye to the other capabilities. As she explains:

In framing the education capability, for example, it is sensible to ask what we can expect to deliver compatibly with delivering all the other capabilities. On the one hand, the threshold of each should not be set in a utopian or unrealistic way: so we must ask what combination we can hope to deliver to people under reasonably good conditions. On the other hand, we should not set our sights too low, deferring to present bad arrangements. Thus it would have been wrong to conclude that universal primary and secondary education of children is not a good goal for a just public policy, on the grounds that right now it is not feasible in some badly managed states. (Nussbaum, 2006, p. 402)

In this way, the capabilities approach seeks to make a deliberative society attentive to how providing a high threshold for one capability might diminish the resources that can be put to providing similarly high thresholds for the other capabilities. Additionally, the capabilities approach seeks to make a society aspirational in setting thresholds at a level that is not held hostage by the appearance of its current possibilities (Nussbaum, 2000b, p. 1026).

As I will discuss later in this chapter, this deliberative theme in Nussbaum's capability approach may appear to be in tension with less procedural positions she sometimes holds in justifying protections for her list of capabilities as constitutional entitlements. However, let us assume for present purposes that a deliberative process should be the way in which society resolves tragic tradeoffs and determines the appropriate threshold of central human capabilities. Even in this context, when we consider how the environmental preconditions that produce tragic capability conflicts bear on social goals, it becomes clear that capability thresholds cannot be the only focus of our deliberation.

Why Nussbaum's conditions of justice require capability ceilings

Because protecting the environmental preconditions of some capabilities can undermine the economic conditions that enable other capabilities, adequate protection of all capabilities will require establishing capability ceilings in addition to capability thresholds. As I conceive them, capability ceilings establish maximum levels of capability protection. Their purpose is to limit the amount of resources that can be put to protecting capabilities that are in conflict with each other. Most importantly, capability ceilings force us not merely to face but constructively to spell out this conflict in our deliberations about what a society can realistically accomplish in its effort to provide protection of a threshold level of central human functional capabilities for each person. Specifically, our deliberations will have to address questions about *whose* capabilities have to be limited and *why*.

Thus, a capabilities approach that establishes capability ceilings would not just involve deliberation about what people should be able to do, it would also require establishing the limits of those capabilities. Nussbaum already implies the importance of establishing such limits (or ceilings), albeit in a less direct way. For example, in posing the problem that protecting the health of animals might require lowering the threshold for human health capabilities, she states:

> I believe that we should think about the whole set of capabilities together when facing such questions, rather than thinking that health costs must always be traded off against other costs. There are very likely other costs not associated with fundamental entitlements that could be trimmed way back before we would have to cut anyone's health care ... surely support for luxury items would be our first target. If, for example, people stopped driving SUVs there would be many gains, not the least of which would be decreased spending on gasoline, which would free up money to be used in other ways, connected with fundamental entitlements – and health would be the gainer, on both sides. (Nussbaum, 2006, p. 403)

We can understand this proposal to put a limitation on use of luxury items, such as SUVs, as an indirect way of establishing capability ceilings. Suppose this limitation were not voluntary but mandatory. Decreasing the use of SUVs would effectively divert monetary resources to health care that would improve some people's capabilities, but for those who drive SUVs this would put a limit (or ceiling) on two of their central capabilities: bodily integrity and material control over one's environment.

Specifically, to stop people from driving SUVs is to limit the ways people can move freely from place to place, which is one component of Nussbaum's bodily integrity capability. Of course, the threshold level of this mobility component may not be so high that it includes being able to move freely from place to place in SUVs, and Nussbaum clearly would not see this extent of mobility as a fundamental entitlement. Yet that is precisely why a capability ceiling is needed. For if some people do have the capability for this extent of mobility, then not only will their realization of that capability promote competitive tendencies that artificially inflate others' valuation of the capability to drive SUVs, it will also divert resources that could otherwise go to protecting threshold levels of more fundamental capability protections. Without a ceiling on the mobility component of one's bodily integrity capability, moving freely from place to place in an SUV, regardless of the purpose and lower impact alternatives, is treated as equivalent to achieving a threshold level of bodily health capability for those who lack it.

A similar implication follows if we treat driving SUVs as a component of the capability to have material control over one's environment. This capability enables people to hold property in both land and moveable goods, not just formally but in terms of real opportunity. If driving an SUV is understood as a condition of one's real opportunity to do what one wants with one's property, then to stop people from driving SUVs is to limit the ways in which people can pursue the opportunities that holding property currently makes available. Even if the threshold level of control over one's material environment is not set so high as to include being able to put one's property (i.e. SUV) to the uses one chooses, a capability ceiling is necessary for freeing up the resources involved in driving SUVs so that they can be put toward achieving threshold levels of capability protection for each person.

Nussbaum makes a similar argument in discussing the similarities between her position and that of non-liberal green theorists. Specifically, both she and the non-liberal green theorist "will support a good deal of government control over such matters as product safety, drug testing, medical licensing, housing codes, and the protection of individuals from harms caused by pollution and environmental contamination" (Nussbaum, 1998, p. 334). The reason Nussbaum and the non-liberal green theorist find agreement in this area is because "their rationale is not primarily to prevent risky personal choices but, rather, to prevent harm to others (the ignorant general public, the poor) that would be caused by the absence of such regulation" (Nussbaum, 1998, p. 335). In other words, for Nussbaum, what matters in determining whether to establish a capability ceiling through legal regulation of individual choice is whether the individual behavior being limited can be shown to cause harm to others.[12]

---

[12] The non-liberal green position that Nussbaum (1998) criticizes differs from her liberal position with respect to "the specific limits of state action, not in the support for the fact of such action" (p. 331). Thus, she might insist on stronger protection for personal property and possessions than the non-liberal green, as well as for stronger protections

These examples illustrate why capability ceilings are useful as a tool for instructing deliberation about capability thresholds and conflicts: when combined with the thresholds, ceilings make it possible to use conditions of justice as the criterion for determining the extent to which a society ought to limit capability protections having harmful effects. For example, Nussbaum has noted that, "Some capabilities are actually bad, and should be inhibited by law (the ability to discriminate on grounds of race or sex or disability, the ability to pollute the environment)" (Nussbaum, 2006, p. 166). But in order to determine and justify the extent to which law should limit these non-fundamental capabilities (such as the ability to pollute), it is necessary, first, to identify the more fundamental source of their justification, and second, to clarify why the limitation on capability protection – the ceiling – is necessary for protecting something equally fundamental.

For example, within a threshold-ceiling framework, we can understand the ability to pollute as a property right protected by one's capability to have material control over one's environment. Perhaps each of us should be assured some capability of polluting; however, to protect this capability far above a threshold level allows for polluting activities that undermine equally fundamental basic entitlements, such as life and bodily health. Thus, when our deliberations are guided by a threshold-ceiling framework, we can determine and justify the extent to which a society ought to limit property rights that constitute one's capability to have material control over one's environment by relating these limits to the equally fundamental entitlements they enable (e.g. bodily health).

In some instances it may seem that the ceiling for a capability should be set at the same level as the capability threshold. For example, to build on the preceding point, it may be that in order to provide adequate protection for the life and bodily health capabilities (threatened by polluting activities), the ceiling for the capability to control one's material environment should be set at or near the threshold level of that capability, especially when some people are below a threshold on any of the central human capabilities that polluting activity threatens. In other words, in such instances, it may seem that a ceiling is unnecessary, because for all intents and purposes, the capability threshold is also operating as the capability ceiling.[13] I contend, however, that maintaining the threshold-ceiling framework is important for two reasons.

---

against unwarranted search and seizure (see pp. 335–556). However, my effort to further theorize the liberal green position here is in part a response to her claim that this green dimension of the capabilities approach needs further elaboration (p. 331 and p. 336).

[13] Although I cannot fully address this issue here, I am grateful to an anonymous reviewer for bringing it to my attention.

First, the framework is necessary for making finely tuned policy judgments about the conditions required for protecting a central capability. In particular, there are many dimensions or specifications of any central human capability, and a ceiling that matches a threshold should be put only on those dimensions of a capability that operate to undermine other central capabilities. For example, the ability to pollute – as a dimension or specification of the capability to have material control over one's environment – may need to be restricted such that pollution above the threshold is not permitted. However, this is because polluting activity above the threshold harms other capabilities, pushing them below their thresholds. If protecting a different dimension or specification of the capability for control over one's material environment above the threshold is harmless, then there would be no reason to require that a ceiling be set at the threshold. Instead, the ceiling would need to be set only if or when an above-threshold level of capability protection has the potential to undermine other capabilities.

Thus, although it would seem reasonable to set the ceiling on one's ability to pollute at the same level as the threshold, a different dimension or specification of the capability to control one's material environment might allow for a ceiling that is set far above the threshold. Consider, for example, that the ability to extract groundwater from one's property (as a dimension or specification of the capability for material control over one's environment) might need to be set at a threshold level that ensures each property owner has enough water to irrigate the crops necessary for survival. For a variety of other uses, some property owners may extract water above what this threshold ensures. A ceiling that is above the threshold would allow this extraction up to the point at which further extraction starts to undermine other central capabilities. Being attentive to this difference between a threshold and a ceiling will allow for public policies that provide a wider range of functioning opportunities along those dimensions or specifications of a central capability for which capability protection above the threshold is harmless. Put differently, by allowing for threshold and ceilings to be set at different levels, we open up a wider range of choice among functioning possibilities. In this way, the threshold-ceiling framework is an instructive device for making fine-tuned policy judgments, such as those that allow for levels of protection to vary along different dimensions or specifications of any given capability.

There is a second reason why the threshold-ceiling framework is instructive, even in light of instances in which the threshold and ceiling are set at the same level: it can help us to identify when a seemingly tragic tradeoff is not really tragic. This is the case if it is possible to avoid a capability conflict without pushing anyone's capability below a threshold. For instance, technological optimists commonly present such solutions in response to those who favor stronger environmental protections, for there is always the hope and the possibility that a technological solution can prevent society from having to face tragic tradeoffs. If we make suitable investments in nuclear power or hydrogen cars, for example, then we can reduce the production of greenhouse gases such that there will be no need for people to stop driving SUVs. In light of such claims, deliberating about a capability ceiling remains important because it calls on those who view the conflict as non-tragic to demonstrate that their proposed solutions do in fact avoid pushing some people below the threshold. To return to the present example, reliance on nuclear power or hydrogen cars may simply create new problems that undermine capability thresholds. In this way, identifying ceilings is one way of getting those who wish to pursue activities that might undermine people's capabilities to demonstrate that activities do not have these effects.

Let us now consider how establishing capability ceilings might bear on solutions to the cholera outbreak that struck India and Bangladesh in January, 1993. In this case, various economically productive human activities led to habitat changes fostering the survival and spread of the Vibrio Cholera bacteria. In particular, agricultural activities, coastal land-use development, over-fishing, and activities producing greenhouse gases changed aquatic ecosystems by increasing weeds and algae harboring the cholera bacteria. It is important to note three important things about these activities. First, they were most likely a consequence of some people's existing capability protections, such as control over one's material environment, practical reason, life, and bodily integrity. Second, these activities might have led to improvements in some people's capabilities, such as those of bodily health, affiliation, control over one's political environment, and senses, imagination, and thought. Third, and in contrast, it is equally important to note that the activities produced ecological impacts that led to capability decline, most notably in some people's capabilities for life and bodily health. In this respect, a conflict of basic capabilities rests at the center of the conflict between goals of economic productivity and environmental protection.

Nussbaum's capabilities approach requires, first and foremost, that a threshold level of each capability be guaranteed for each person. The activities producing the cholera outbreak violate this requirement because they leave some people's life and bodily health capabilities below an obvious threshold of acceptability. However, as I suggest above, to halt these activities would be to violate various capability protections and to forgo various capability improvements.

Amidst this kind of tragic tradeoff, capability ceilings can help to establish the extent to which a society ought to limit capabilities in conflict with each other. Specifically, determining the appropriate capability ceilings requires that deliberators address the extent of capability protection society can realistically promise while simultaneously protecting a threshold of the central human functional capabilities for each person. Since capability ceilings establish maximum levels of capability protection, our deliberations will have to focus on establishing these ceilings for those people who already experience a level of capability protection that exists above the threshold of what justice requires.

For example, in the cholera case, the limitations on activities that foster a decline in aquatic ecosystems should involve constraining (or putting ceilings on) the capabilities of beneficiaries that already experience a threshold level of all the central human functional capabilities. This may mean establishing ceilings on the capabilities of those in distant locations who release greenhouse gases; to return to an earlier point, perhaps society ought to limit protection of people's capabilities to move freely from place to place in SUVs. Likewise, some people benefitting from the agricultural and coastal development projects may experience levels of capability protection far above the threshold level of capabilities that justice requires. Therefore, we might establish capability ceilings that limit the extent of protection of their bodily health capability or of their capability to have control over their material environment. For example, a ceiling might limit the extent to which a beneficiary can reasonably claim that his capability for bodily health is violated if regulations protecting aquatic life prevent him from making the kinds of profits that allow for extravagant nourishment, by which I mean nourishment that is far beyond what is necessary for protecting a threshold level of bodily health capability. In this way, a threshold-ceiling framework can help deliberators to arrive at solutions to the conflict between economic development and environmental protection that are justified directly in terms of their implications for capability protections that define the basic conditions of justice.

Environment and capabilities as preconditions of democratic functioning

To use the capabilities approach in this way is to treat it as a framework that guides public reasoning about the tradeoffs that public policies imply. As such, the capabilities approach helps to reveal conflicts between different preconditions required for achieving a threshold level of capabilities protection and it also calls for certain kinds of justification for public action. To advance the capabilities approach in a more prescriptive way – that is, as more than a tool for improving public reasoning and deliberation about capability specification and interpretation – would involve assigning its recommendations greater weight in policy decisions. Specifically, it would involve treating the conditions of justice that the capabilities approach demands as more important and therefore as more worthy of protection than conflicting outcomes emerging from public deliberations in a democratic political community.

Elsewhere I discuss how Nussbaum's method for justifying her capabilities as basic entitlements assumes this more prescriptive role (Holland, 2008, pp. 325–327). Specifically, in elaborating her method of political justification, she has argued that when the priorities implied by the list of capabilities come into conflict with the desires and preferences that emerge from people meeting and deliberating in the real world of political choice, a constitutional democracy should not in the short run conclude that those priorities are negotiable (Nussbaum, 2004). This is why she argues that a deliberative decision by a majority of people in India to replace their pluralistic constitution with one that declares India a Hindu state "should not lead us to conclude that equal freedom of conscience is a negotiable item for a decent pluralistic democracy" (Nussbaum, 2004, p. 201). In such a situation, declaring India a Hindu state would violate the fourth capability on Nussbaum's list of central human functional capabilities, which involves "being able to use one's mind in ways protected by guarantees of freedom of expression with respect to both political and artistic speech, and freedom of religious exercise" (Nussbaum, 2000a, p. 79). Denying the legitimacy of this violation, Nussbaum asserts that at least in the short run "we ought to say, 'what the majority desires here is wrong'" (Nussbaum, 2004, p. 201).

Because the present argument has been concerned with how the environment bears on specifying or interpreting capabilities that are otherwise treated as fundamental entitlements, I have not drawn on Nussbaum's method for justifying her list of basic capabilities. However, even without appealing to Nussbaum's method of political justification, it is possible to treat the environmental protections that the capabilities approach implies as conditions of democratic functioning rather than as a hopeful outcome of public reasoning that merely is guided by the principles and logic of the capabilities approach. For example, as a condition of democratic functioning, protecting the environmental preconditions necessary for attaining threshold levels of the central human capabilities is not something that a democratic society can disregard because that is preferred by a deliberative body. Instead, deliberative outcomes warrant respect insofar as they do not threaten to violate the fundamental capability thresholds and ceilings that define basic conditions of justice.

To apply the capabilities approach in this way would be to treat capabilities, and the environmental conditions that are instrumental to them, as preconditions of democratic deliberation. James Bohman has argued, for example, that capability protections are necessary for people to engage as full and equal participants in public dialogue and reasoning about what is good for society (Bohman, 1997, pp. 321–325). Extending this line of argument, environmental protections matter because of their instrumental value to individual health and identity, which people must experience at some minimal level in order to engage as equals in democratic deliberation. Thus, conceiving of environmental protections as preconditions of democratic deliberation could mean that levels of pollution interfering with the normal brain and respiratory functioning of children are impermissible, even if deliberators agree such pollution levels should be allowable because the aggregate gains they produce outweigh the resulting unequal capacity of those children to grow into adults who are able to speak and be heard in deliberative settings. Likewise, land use activities that forcibly push people off land that is used for subsistence, or that effectively destroy relationships to natural places that are deeply constitutive of individual identity, would be impermissible even if deliberators agree to pursue such activities (e.g. after determining that the aggregate gains produced by severing these people from their land outweigh the resulting unequal capacity of those people to participate as equals in political deliberation).

Putting such constraints on deliberative outcomes requires a form of deliberative democratic politics that admits there are circumstances in which it is justifiable to accept the claims of those able to make judgments about the relationship between environmental conditions and human capabilities necessary for full and equal participation in democratic deliberation. More specifically, this form of deliberative politics would acknowledge that those who make these claims are educated within a practice that gives them a unique competence in understanding certain areas of knowledge (O'Neill, 2007, pp. 159–160). With respect to the examples given above, these claims might come from those with training that gives them competence to understand the relationship between pollution and people's neurological and respiratory functioning, between subsistence lifestyles and a particular geographical region impacted by a development activity, or between particular places, individual identity, and the capacity for "voice" in political deliberation.

In admitting that citizens may lack the training and competence necessary for judging the adequacy of evidence supporting authoritative judgments about the relationship between the natural environment and human capabilities, this form of democratic politics need not adopt a conception of political reasoning that relies solely on logic or evidence as the basis of authority. Rather than knowing whether a given body of scientific evidence supports a certain level of environmental protection, citizens instead must be skilled in judging the credibility of those putting forth particular knowledge claims about the environment. Here, as John O'Neill explains, what matters is whether a person has skills to know "when and where it is reasonable to trust claims that call on authority" (O'Neill, 2007, p. 163). Toward this end, a person must be able to reason well while also recognizing the insufficiency of his or her own reasoning. Furthermore, because citizens are therefore dependent on the knowledge of others, they must have skills of skepticism that allow them to identify when they ought to be suspicious of those who claim authoritative knowledge. For example, when those claiming authority have a strong alliance with the views of special interests, or of those with power and wealth, then there are good grounds for scrutinizing and challenging the judgments that issue from their expertise (O'Neill, 1993, p. 137). In order to assess knowledge claims in this way, citizens must have the capacity to identify the conditions under which it is rational to trust and under which it is rational to scrutinize the institutions and claims of authority advanced by those with expertise and competence that they themselves lack.

A form of democratic politics that assigns citizens this role is especially attractive for dealing with environmental problems. As the brief references above suggest, there are many instances in modern life in which citizens must rely on the authoritative judgments of those with requisite expertise to determine the truth or falsity of scientific statements about how the natural environment relates to a given capability (O'Neill, 1993, pp. 124–126). In protecting the environmental basis of human capabilities as preconditions of democratic functioning, it is possible for the capabilities approach to play a more prescriptive role in policy decisions. Rather than merely offering proposals as part of public reasoning and dialogue about policy decisions, the capabilities approach would help to identify when democratically determined policy decisions undermine the preconditions of democratic functioning. In this context, the capabilities approach would be determinative of policy actions, for it would provide the criterion for ruling out policies detrimental to democracy, even if they are arrived at through purportedly democratic processes.[14]

---

[14] For further development of this argument, see Holland, 2014, Chapter 6.

Conclusion

The capabilities approach allows us to design policies that will achieve threshold levels of basic capabilities. Dialogue about capability ceilings can help us to identify and put limits on the capabilities of those who experience high levels of capability protection that make it unrealistic for society to achieve basic conditions of justice for others. I have argued that Nussbaum's capabilities approach is valuable in revealing capability conflicts that arise at the intersection of economic and ecological processes. Nussbaum does not follow Rawls in treating environmental problems as a matter of correcting externalities, and her approach to justice is more sensitive to how variation in each individual's situation can and should alter levels of environmental protection. For these reasons, Nussbaum's capabilities approach more easily observes what and why environmental inequities create conflicts that threaten social justice. Although Nussbaum's theory cannot avoid addressing these conflicts, with the addition of capability ceilings, her theory could help structure democratic dialogue about those conflicts or take a more prescriptive role in crafting policies that push society toward justice.

REFERENCES

American Lung Association (2001) "Urban Air Pollution and Health Inequities: A Workshop Report", *Environmental Health Perspectives*, 109 (June), pp. 357–374.

Beitz, C. (1979) *Political Theory and International Relations*, Princeton University Press.

Bell, D. (2004) "Environmental Justice and Rawls' Difference Principle", *Environmental Ethics*, 26 (3), pp. 287–306.

Bohman, J. (1997) "Deliberative Democracy and Effective Social Freedom: Capabilities, Resources, and Opportunities", in J. Bohman and W. Rehg (Eds.), *Deliberative Democracy: Essays on Reason and Politics*, MIT Press, Cambridge, MA.

Colwell, R. (1996) "Global Climate and Infectious Disease: The Cholera Paradigm", *Science*, 274 (5295), pp. 2025–2031.

Colwell, R. and Spira, W. (1992) "The Ecology of Vibrio Cholerae", in D. Barua and W. Greenrough (Eds.), *Cholera: Current Topics in Infectious Disease*, Plenum Medical Book Company, New York.

Cone, M. (2005) *Silent Snow: The Slow Poisoning of the Arctic*, Grove Press, New York.

Day, J., Donald, B., Clairain, E., Kemp, G., *et al.* (2007) "Restoration of the Mississippi Delta: Lessons from Hurricanes Katrina and Rita", *Science*, 315 (5819), pp. 1679–1684.

Epstein, P. (1992) "Cholera and the Environment", *The Lancet*, 339, pp. 1167–1168.

412   *Breena Holland*

(1995) "Emerging Diseases and Ecosystem Instability: New Threats to Public Health", *American Journal of Public Health*, 85 (2), pp. 168–172.

Galloway, J., Aber, J., Erisman, J. and Seitzinger, S. (2003) "The Nitrogen Cascade", *Bioscience*, 53 (4), pp. 341–356.

Goklany, I. (2000) "Applying the Precautionary Principle in a Broader Context", in J. Morris (Ed.), *Rethinking Risk and the Precautionary Principle*, Butterworth-Heinemann Press, Oxford.

Grifo, F. and Rosenthal, J. (Eds.) (1997) *Biodiversity and Human Health*, Island Press, Washington, DC.

Holland, B. (2008) "Justice and the Environment in Nussbaum's 'Capabilities Approach': Why Sustainable Ecological Capacity Is a Meta-Capability", *Political Research Quarterly*, 61 (2), pp. 319–332.

(forthcoming) *Allocating the Earth: A Distributional Framework for Protecting Capabilities in Environmental Law and Policy*. Oxford University Press.

Islam, M., Hasam, M., Miah, M., Yunus, M. and Albert, M. (1994) "Isolation of Vibrio Cholerae O139 Synonym Bengal: Implications for Disease Transmission", *Applied and Environmental Microbiology*, 60 (5), pp. 1684–1686.

Miller, D. (1999) "Social Justice and Environmental Goods", in A. Dobson (Ed.), *Fairness and Futurity: Essays on Environmental Sustainability and Social Justice*, Oxford University Press.

Nocon, A. and Booth, T. (1989–1990) "The Social Impact of Asthma: A Review of the Literature", *Social Work and the Social Sciences Review*, 1 (3), pp. 177–200.

Nossiter, A. (1995) "Asthma Common and on the Rise in the Crowded South Bronx", *New York Times*, September 5, p. 1.

Nussbaum, M. C. (1998) "The Good As Discipline, the Good As Freedom", in D. Crocker and T. Linden (Eds.), *The Ethics of Consumption: The Good Life, Justice, and Global Stewardship*, Rowman & Littlefield, Lanham, MD.

(2000a) *Women and Human Development: The Capabilities Approach*, Cambridge University Press.

(2000b) "The Costs of Tragedy: Some Moral Limits of Cost-Benefit Analysis", *Journal of Legal Studies*, 29 (2), pp. 1005–1036.

(2004) "On Hearing Women's Voices: A Reply to Susan Okin", *Philosophy and Public Affairs*, 32 (2): 193–205.

(2006) *Frontiers of Justice: Disability, Nationality, Species Membership*, Belknap Press of Harvard University Press, Cambridge, MA.

O'Neill, J. (1993) *Ecology, Policy and Politics: Human Well-Being and the Natural World*, Routledge, New York.

(2007) *Markets, Deliberation, and Environment*, Routledge, New York.

Rawls, J. (1971) *A Theory of Justice*, Belknap Press of Harvard University Press, Cambridge, MA.

(1993) *Political Liberalism*, Columbia University Press, New York.

(1999) *The Law of Peoples*, Harvard University Press, Cambridge, MA.

(2001) *Justice as Fairness: A Restatement*, Belknap Press of Harvard University Press, Cambridge, MA.

Sen, A. (1982) "Equality of What?", in *Choice, Welfare, and Measurement*, Harvard University Press, Cambridge, MA.

(1992) *Inequality Reexamined*, Harvard University Press, Cambridge, MA.

Siddique, A., Baqui Abue Eusof, A., Haider, K., *et al.* (1991) "Survival of Classic Cholera in Bangladesh", *The Lancet*, 337, pp. 1125–1127.

Sze, J. (2007) *Noxious New York: The Racial Politics of Urban Health and Environmental Justice*, MIT Press, Cambridge, MA.

Thero, D. (1995) "Rawls and Environmental Ethics: A Critical Examination of the Literature", *Environmental Ethics*, 17 (1), pp. 93–106.

Wissenburg, M. (1999) "An Extension of the Rawlsian Savings Principle to Liberal Theories of Justice in General", in A. Dobson (Ed.), *Fairness and Futurity: Essays on Environmental Sustainability and Social Justice*, Oxford University Press.

Wolff, J. and De-Shalit, A. (2007) *Disadvantage*, Oxford University Press.

16 Social justice and Nussbaum's concept of the person*

John M. Alexander

Introduction

In the wake of Rawls's influential work (1973; 1993), the concept of the person in contemporary political philosophy has become controversial. The various dimensions of this controversy can be clarified by taking note of two prominent positions on the issue. The first position tries to understand the human person in the light of some religious, moral or philosophical doctrines, and advocates that the aim of political philosophy is to promote such a conception. It is not that the proponents of this view deny that individuals vary and would have different ends, but they consider it best both for individuals and for society to unify the differences under some comprehensive conception. The second position totally rejects such a view. The proponents of the second view point out that a political philosophy centred on a particular comprehensive conception of the human person would legitimize paternalism and tyranny. If the aim of political philosophy were to promote individual freedom and human dignity on the one hand and inspire social stability on the other, it must be then independent of any comprehensive conception. It is true that some of people's ends might be related to their religious, moral or philosophical doctrines. Nevertheless, the purpose of political philosophy is not to concern itself with these comprehensive conceptions.

Nussbaum, as a moral and political philosopher, has often refused to be drawn into these kinds of extreme paradigms and her views on these issues are much more complex and nuanced than some of her critics are willing to admit.[1] Drawing inspiration from Aristotle's ethics and political philosophy, she has proposed a capabilities-centred approach to social justice. Accordingly, political theory and practice, in her view,

---

* This chapter is a revised version of a paper presented at conferences in Bristol, Cambridge, Leuven, and Pavia. I am grateful to the participants for their responses on these occasions and to Herman De Dijn, Toon Vandevelde, P. Van Parijs, John Baker, Martha C. Nussbaum, Ronald Tinnevelt and Stefan Rummens for their valuable comments.
[1] Among others, see Ackerly (2000); Hurka (2002); Menon (2002); Kekes (2003: Chapter 7).

should focus on providing citizens fundamental entitlements in the form of a list of (ten) basic capabilities as a required minimum of social justice. A life without a threshold level of basic capabilities such as nutrition, health, education, emotional health, affiliation, self-respect and political participation, Nussbaum would say, cannot even be considered a properly human life. And yet, Nussbaum has also tried to show that the vision of human being that underlies the capabilities-based political theory involves neither a comprehensive conception nor a paternalistic approach to human well-being.

Here we will not focus on the issue of paternalism partly because Nussbaum has already made an excellent rebuttal and partly because I believe that, as with most political theories, the capability approach does embrace a weak form of paternalism.[2] How weak it is or weaker it should become is both a matter of judgement and the point of comparison chosen. Instead, the discussion here will be more fundamental and philosophical: to critically elaborate and examine whether Nussbaum's theory of capabilities involves a comprehensive conception, especially in the light of the fact that it espouses a good-based approach to social justice and is willing to identify and take a stand on what ought to be the components of the good human life.

The following two sections outline in detail the concept of the person underpinned in Nussbaum's capability approach vis-à-vis Rawls's theory. I try to show that Nussbaum's theory of capabilities possesses the potential to address issues of social justice precisely because it blends certain liberal doctrines with a broader and more inclusive view of human being. At the same time, I argue that Nussbaum's hybrid theory cannot be equated with Rawls's political liberalism, as the later Nussbaum sometimes claims. The third section highlights that the challenge for the capability theorist is to develop the capability approach as a public conception on the basis of a non-contractarian model of political psychology.

The capability approach and the limits of Rawlsian theory

Nussbaum develops the theoretical foundations of the capability approach, and particularly the idea of human being it envisages, in response to the limitations of Rawls's political conception of the person. It is important to see to what extent such a project helps in furthering our understanding of social justice. An essential feature of Rawls's political

---

[2] See Nussbaum (2000a: 51–59; 2000b).

philosophy is that it is based not on any comprehensive conception but rather on a 'political' conception of the person. Utilitarianism, in Rawls's view, would be a classic example of a comprehensive conception because all that matters for this theory are consumer preferences, and hence politics should aim at maximizing citizens' preferences. Neither individual rights nor plurality of motivations are intrinsically valued. Also, a teleological or theological political theory, as was prevalent for instance in the Medieval period, can be considered a comprehensive conception because it advocates that society's institutions should represent and promote a singular conception of human being determined in the light of some natural or divine ends.

By contrast, Rawls claims that a liberal political theory should make "reasonable pluralism" a fundamental principle. Given the fact that citizens have different and often incommensurable ideas on how best they can lead their lives, it would be inappropriate and even unfair to affirm or promote any particular comprehensive view as a normative criterion. The "strains of commitment", as Rawls would say, should not threaten or undermine social unity. If I were to be a believer in the theory of Reincarnation in a society where the state endorses only the doctrine of One Life, either I would have to suppress my faith or else I run the risk of being burned at the stake. Rawls is not the first one to argue for the necessity and centrality of pluralism in political theory. It has been advocated and defended in different forms by liberal philosophers such as John Locke, John Stuart Mill, T. H. Green and Isaiah Berlin, among others. Perhaps what distinguishes Rawls from other liberal philosophers is his "practical" suggestion that pluralism can be persevered by a fair distribution of a list of "primary goods" in accordance with the difference principle. The list of primary goods that Rawls suggests is heterogeneous. It contains a number of important basic rights and liberties as well as material and non-material resources required for the well-being of citizens: opportunities and powers, income and wealth, and the social bases of self-respect. According to Rawls's political philosophy, therefore, liberals must not try to impose a comprehensive moral view on their society; instead, they should view the primary goods and the two principles as terms on which persons who hold a plurality of different comprehensive views can live with one another.

The details of Rawls's theory are important, but more important for our purpose here is the justification of primary goods. Why would one think of primary goods as a useful way to approximate what individuals need in order to pursue different conceptions of the good? Put differently, in proposing that every citizen has a claim against society for a fair share of primary goods of basic rights as well as material and non-material resources required for a decent living, does Rawls himself not assume a definite view of the human person? Looking retrospectively at Rawls's writings, one can discern a change of emphasis in Rawls's answer to this. In *A Theory of Justice*, Rawls seems to envision a much broader scope for primary goods by advocating them as "all-purpose means" essential for citizens to pursue their different conceptions of the good.

Now primary goods ... are things which it is supposed a rational man wants *whatever else he wants*. Regardless of what an individual's rational plans are in detail, it is assumed that there are various things which he would prefer more of rather than less. With more of these goods men can generally be assured of greater success in carrying out their intentions and in advancing their ends, *whatever these ends may be*. (Rawls 1973: 92, emphasis added)

In *Political Liberalism*, however, Rawls considerably restricts the scope of primary goods by advocating them not as all-purpose means but specifically as the needs of citizens of a constitutional liberal democracy. Despite this change of emphasis, at least two conditions underwrite the justification of primary goods. The first one is the idea of social cooperation. In Rawls's theory, a person is primarily a citizen with the capacity for a full social cooperation over a complete life. The following passage makes this clear:

Beginning with the ancient world, the concept of the person has been understood, in both philosophy and law, as the concept of someone who can take part in, or who can play a role in, social life, and hence exercise and respect its various rights and duties. Thus, we say that a person is someone who can be a citizen, that is, a normal and fully cooperating member of society over a complete life. (Rawls 1993: 18)

Rawls does not claim that all citizens have equal capacities. But what he does presuppose and consider as an important prerequisite for his theory is that citizens possess at least a minimum level of moral, intellectual and physical capacities so that they can function as fully cooperating members of society. So, the underlying political conception of the person in Rawls's theory by definition excludes people who do not or cannot engage in economic and social cooperation. These people are, in Rawls's own words, more like "patients" or people "below the line" and their "unusual needs" need not be taken into account in designing basic political principles (Rawls 1993: 189). The second condition under which primary goods are discerned to be adequate for citizens' needs is based on Rawls's distinction between the conception of the "person" and "human nature" (Rawls 1980: 534–5). The conception of the person is primarily characterised by the two moral powers: the capacity for a sense of justice and conception of the good. On the contrary, a theory of human nature is one that takes into account people's needs, natural abilities, social positions, contingencies of luck and so on. It is not that Rawls opts for the former and rejects the latter. Instead, he treats them as distinct and allows them to enter at different stages, theoretical and practical. At the level of the Original Position where the parties formulate the principles of justice that would underwrite political principles and consequently shape the culture of society's vital institutions, it is the conception of the person with its two moral powers that is taken into consideration. At this theoretical stage, elements concerning human nature do not play any role. If that were to be the case, Rawls then, right from the start, would have given a normative consideration to 'natural primary goods' such as health, handicaps, natural talents and so on. It is only at the more practical levels, such as the constitutional, legislative and judicial stages, where the principles of justice are applied concretely to existing structures of society, that elements concerning human needs and diversities are taken into consideration.

From the perspective of the capability approach, two criticisms have been advanced against Rawls's political conception of the person, one by Amartya Sen and Eva F. Kittay, the other by Nussbaum. Sen (1980; 1992; 1993) pioneered the criticism of the capability shortfalls that come from human diversity. Human beings differ from one another in a number of ways. There are, first and foremost, differences in personal characteristics such as health, age, sex and genetic endowments. Furthermore, human beings also vary in the types of external environment and social conditions in which they live. These different elements of human diversity crucially affect the ways in which primary goods are transformed into relevant functionings and capabilities. The most obvious case that Sen puts forward is a person in a wheelchair. Equalizing the amount of primary goods between a handicapped and an able-bodied person ignores the fact that the former would be in need of more material and social resources to be mobile and to achieve other functionings, including overcoming social discrimination against disability.

The person in the wheelchair is only a paradigmatic case. Yet disadvantages can arise due to other personal characteristics and from variations in people's social conditions. For example, feminist philosophers in developing as well as developed societies point out how to varying degrees being a girl or woman can constrain one's access to careers, social space and political participation. Since Rawls identifies the society's well-off and worse-off in terms of the amount of resources they hold, his theory overlooks the fact that individuals vary in their needs for resources and in their capacities to convert resources into valuable functionings.[3] Nussbaum (1988a; 1990) philosophized Sen's capabilities-based objection by pointing out that it revisits the Aristotelian idea that in matters of distributive justice, it is more appropriate to distribute resources in terms of "valuable human functionings" of what they are able to do and be (proportionate equality) rather than blindly settle for a quantitative division (arithmetic equality). Yet, as discussed in the following sections, Nussbaum had to draw Aristotle within a liberal landscape for the reason that Aristotle himself was inclined to read proportionality in favour of merit and class and the modern liberal idea of original equality of every human being is conspicuously absent in his thought.

In the spirit of Sen's capabilities-oriented critique, Kittay (2003) advances a "dependency critique" against Rawls's theory, focusing on the "human condition" of dependency and on the problems of people who provide care to the dependants. "It is my view that liberal political theory and Rawls's theory, in particular, are flawed in that they do not take the issue of dependency to be central. All of us are dependent in childhood; most of us are dependent for long periods of time (sometimes throughout a life) because of ill health. Dependency is thus a matter for us all in our lives as social beings" (Kittay 2003: 169). Kittay's critique draws attention to the fact that "dependency is a feature of our human condition" and that people who are dependent require care and caring persons to meet their needs. A theory of social justice cannot ignore the capability shortfalls of dependants. Further, Kittay also calls attention to the problems of justice with regard to "dependency workers" – people who attend to dependency needs of others, whether full or part time and through paid or unpaid work. These, by virtue of their attention to dependants, become vulnerable to a condition of "derived" dependence, particularly when society does not duly recognize or reward their work economically or otherwise so that they can offer an effective and fulfilling service. According to Kittay, this is an issue of gender justice since most care for the dependants is provided by women, and most of this care might not be recognized by the market as work.

While endorsing Sen–Kittay's point about capability shortfalls, Nussbaum (2006) traces the inadequacy of Rawls's theory to be structurally

[3] Even though Rawls (1971: 83) concedes that a certain amount of arbitrariness cannot be avoided in identifying members who would belong to this group, he nevertheless gives two indications as to how one may proceed in identifying the least advantaged. First, giving the example of an "unskilled worker", Rawls says that we may define the least advantaged as all those with approximately the income and wealth of the unskilled worker or similar categories. Second, Rawls also suggests that we can define the least advantaged as all those with less than half of the median income and wealth. These two suggestions further confirm Sen's point that Rawls omits the cases of people with physical disabilities.

linked to its contractarianism and the corollary idea of justice as mutual advantage. Rawls's theory, like most social contract theories, assumes citizens to be fully cooperating members of society over a complete life and the partnership envisaged is on the basis of mutual advantage of the contracting parties. This in effect implies that provisions for the needs of people who cannot either economically or socially cooperate are not seen as part of the basic political principle to which they agree. According to Nussbaum, a society modelled purely on the social con- tract doctrine encourages an instrumental attitude towards people: people are respected as human beings only insofar as they are able to "contribute" and be "productive" to society. On a deeper level, Nuss- baum (2006: 127–45, 159–60) finds the Kantian conception of the person that Rawls deploys to be narrow and insufficiently rich to address the needs of people with low level of capabilities, despite the fact that Rawls sees justice as fairness giving expression to the Kantian principle of treating every person as an end. Kant makes a division between the realm of nature on the one hand and the realm of reason on the other. He associates all non-human animals as well as the natural and non-rational part of human life with the former. In contrast, he elevates the human capacity for rationality to be different from and superior to the realm of nature. In fact, morality and moral freedom for Kant consist in acting in accordance with the pure good will untainted by elements of nature. In *Metaphysics of Morals* (1997: 393– 405), Kant refers to the good will as that which "shines like a jewel" and is superior to any of the other human characteristics such as needs, desires, talents and temperaments. Only when the good will excludes and harnesses all desires, inclinations and needs, and any forms of external influences, would it be able to freely determine itself and act autonomously. Rawls does not accept the metaphysical baggage of the Kantian personhood, but he nevertheless retains the Kantian concept of the person insofar as rationality and reciprocity become the fundamen- tal basis for deriving political principles.

Nussbaum takes the Kant–Rawlsian conception of the person to be misrepresenting and consequential for issues of justice. By making a division between what is rational and natural and privileging the former over the latter, it gives the impression that our rationality is something independent of our human vulnerability and dependency. We are moral and rational, but we cannot ignore the fact that our rationality and morality are deeply intertwined with human needs, dependency, disease and so on. Furthermore, the Kant–Rawlsian idea of the person seems to suggest that only those who possess a certain threshold level of rationality and reciprocity are eligible for social cooperation, and hence have claims of justice. Those who are seen not to be reaching up to the threshold – people with learning or physical disabilities, for example – might have claims of charity or benevolence, but not justice.

Rawls is a great philosopher and his theory has emerged to be among the most influential in contemporary political philosophy. Yet when it is confronted with the intuitive underpinning of the capability approach the need for correcting it in the light of citizens' basic capabilities becomes compelling. In *Political Liberalism*, Rawls writes: "I agree with Sen that basic capabilities are of first importance and that the use of primary goods is always to be assessed in the light of assumptions about those capabilities" (Rawls 1993: 83). In *Justice as Fairness: A Restatement*, his acknowledgement is even more sympathetic:

> The more extreme cases I have not considered, but this is not to deny their importance. I take it obvious, and accepted by common sense, that we have a duty towards all human beings, however severely handicapped. The question concerns the weight of these duties when they conflict with other basic claims. At some point, then, we must see whether justice as fairness can be extended to provide guideline for these cases; and if not, whether it must be rejected rather than supplemented by some other conception ... If Sen can work out a plausible view for these, it would be an important question whether, with certain adjustments, it could be included in justice as fairness when suitably extended, or else adopted to it as an essential complementary part. (Rawls 2001: 176, n. 59)

While these statements may suggest a natural extension of Rawls's theory in the direction of the capability approach, the question however is whether such extension can be done without violating the core claims of Rawls's political liberalism. The greatest concern for Rawls and a Rawlsian is whether the switch over to the capability paradigm would conflict with certain liberal claims and revert to some form of a comprehensive conception.

Varieties of comprehensive conceptions

The metaphor of the "thick vague conception" of the good that Nussbaum used in her earlier writings throws light on the broader and more inclusive view of human beings implied in the capability approach and underlines the contrast between the capability approach and dominant liberal theories, including that of Rawls.[4] The capability approach is a species of good-based approaches to justice. As Nussbaum realizes, this

---

[4] In the late 1980s and later, Nussbaum introduced this metaphor in order to distinguish the theoretical foundations of the capability approach from that of Rawls's theory of justice. See Nussbaum (1988a; 1988b; 1990).

requires that a capability theorist "must show what her concept of the good is, how much determinate content it has, how (using what background concepts) it is derived, and what political work it can do" (Nussbaum 1990: 217). However, a theory of the human good or well-being is not equivalent to a theory of justice. We might consider, for instance, a wide range of things to be valuable for human well-being – from a hunger-free life to a life of expensive banquets and exotic holidays, to immortality. And yet we might not enlist all of them among what we owe to each other in the name of justice. Judgements regarding claims of justice often demand identifying and delineating certain aspects of well-being. This is the underlying theoretical motivation behind Nussbaum's list of capabilities: it is supposed to function as a checklist for governments and other collective bodies for probing into their conscience as to whether or not they meet the demands of justice.

As some critics (e.g. Menon 2002; Kekes 2003) have pointed out, one may be put out by the "thickness" of the conception exhibited by the nature and number of capabilities involved. Governments and policy-makers might well wonder what exactly is expected of them in respect of capabilities such as emotional health, being able to experience justified anger, having opportunity for sexual satisfaction, being able to search for the ultimate meaning in life and so on. Is it legitimate and helpful to get involved in such matters in the first place? Economists are often concerned about the problem of scarcity of resources in order to be able to meet the ambitions of the list, but along with that political theorists are apprehensive about the possibility of obtaining consensus on so many disparate items. The capability theorist, however, adopts an optimistic view that the thickness of the conception is tempered by its accompanying vagueness: most of the items on the list are defined at such levels of abstractness and generality that they make room for multiple specifications in different cultural contexts through subsequent legislative and judicial procedures. Moreover, the list is not intended to be a dogmatic pronouncement but a blue-print that would serve as provisional fix-points for public discussion and democratic deliberation. As Nussbaum (2000a: 69, 76) remarks, the list is not evolved on the basis of being "dictatorial about the good" but instead on the basis of years of "cross-cultural discussions" and "input of other voices". There is obviously some tension between the thickness of the conception supporting the list on the one hand and the universalism it aims to represent on the other. But even here the capability theorist might choose to focus less on the tension than on the possibility of attaining some appropriate level of equilibrium.

In contrast to a capabilities-oriented theory, Rawls and Rawls-inspired liberals favour a different point of departure. As pointed out earlier,

Rawls is clear about the fact – this much more emphatically in *Political Liberalism* than in *A Theory of Justice* – that primary goods are the means that facilitate citizens' freedom to pursue their own conceptions of the good. In Rawls's theory, there is neither an attempt to define the good nor an endeavour to pursue it. The most stated liberal reason for this is pluralism and social unity of the political society – namely, that if we began to focus on the good, we would not succeed in obtaining an overlapping consensus among citizens with different and conflicting conceptions of the good. As Korsgaard (1993) points out, there is also another reason, perhaps not so explicitly stated. This is what might be called the scepticism of the good.[5] According to this view, there is no best life, or anyway we cannot prove that there is, so we have no solid ground for compelling people to lead or choose to lead one kind of life rather than another. Moreover, it is also important to note that often the unknowability of the good is combined with epistemological individualism. Consequently, the goodness of a life essentially depends on its being chosen by the person who lives it; as a matter of fact, it is the individual, and the individual alone, who is best placed to find out for herself what the best life is.

Only with these theoretical presuppositions can we begin to understand that the central aspiration of Rawls's political liberalism is to free the idea of what is right and just from the idea of what is good or advantageous for a person, exemplified in his well-known claim about "the priority of the right over the good". Rawls points out that what makes his theory "politically liberal" and attractive is that it gives priority to the right over the good. That is, it has an account of people's rightful claims that is not derived from any particular idea or conception of the good. Principles of right – equal basic liberties, fair equality of opportunity and the difference principle – are prior to and constrain the pursuit of the good. In contrast, what makes utilitarianism or Aristotelian or Medieval theories unattractive and disqualifies them as liberal theories is that they give priority to the good over the right. That is to say, they have an independent account of the good (happiness, virtues, or Kingdom of

---

[5] Raz (1990) makes a parallel criticism by noting that Rawls's theory embraces epistemic abstinence in order to defend pluralism as part of a theory of justice. He writes: "Rawls's epistemic abstinence lies in the fact he refrains from claiming that his doctrine of justice is true. The reason is that its truth, if it is true, must derive from deep, and possibly nonautonomous, foundations, from some sound comprehensive moral doctrine. Asserting the truth of the doctrine of justice, or rather claiming that its truth is the reason for accepting it, would negate the very spirit of Rawls's enterprise. It would present the doctrine of justice as one of many competing comprehensive moralities current in our society, and this would disqualify it from fulfilling its role of transcending the disagreement among these many incompatible moralities" (Raz 1990: 9).

God, for example) and the right is defined as maximization of that good. People's rightful claims (basic rights and opportunities, for example) are entirely dependent on what best promotes the good. This is what leads Rawls (1993: 178–86) not only to be reluctant about Sen's capabilities-based criticism of his theory but also to place the capability approach as among the comprehensive theories. Any capabilities-based theory that is concerned with identifying people's basic capabilities would have to appeal to a particular conception of the human good and value judgements and as a consequence turns out to be politically illiberal.

Nussbaum's writings on the capability approach have gone through development, refinement and change of positions. In some of her recent writings, Nussbaum no longer refers to the earlier metaphor of the thick vague conception, and even takes distance from it.[6] In order to circumvent a possible charge of being illiberal and comprehensive, she is keen to highlight the liberal base of the capability theory and even claims that the capability theory can be aligned with Rawls's political liberalism. First and foremost, central to the capability approach is the claim that as far as adult citizens are concerned, what citizens owe to each other as claims of justice is a set of basic capabilities and not functionings. While the latter refers to people's *achieved* doings and beings, the former refers to the extent of *freedom* that people have in order to achieve certain basic valuable functionings. Thus, individual choice is given a prominent place insofar as the capability approach as a political objective aims at equalizing citizens' life prospects for basic capabilities (opportunities) rather than what they do with these opportunities, namely functionings. As Nussbaum (2000a: 87) characteristically puts it: "Capability, not functionings, is the appropriate political goal." This means that having access to food, a person might prefer to fast, whether as a political protest or as part of religious beliefs or for some other reason; having adequate opportunities to get educated, a person might decide on what and how long to study; having required facilities for play and recreation, a person might decide to be a workaholic, taking no advantage of relaxation opportunities; having the necessary opportunities to actively participate in politics, a person might decide not to play a public role; and so on. In all of these instances, the basic idea is that social justice would be violated if people are in want of the capability to be adequately nourished, to be educated, to enjoy leisure and to participate in politics. In contrast, it would be no social injustice if functionings of nourishment, education, play and political participation are not achieved.

---

[6] See particularly Nussbaum (2000a; 2001) for continuity as well as changes in her views on the capability approach.

Another crucial way in which Nussbaum avoids incrimination of being illiberal and comprehensive is to make a broad range of civil and political rights as well as property rights as part of the list of basic capabilities. Civil and political rights create the required social and political institutions that would enhance the development of people's innate powers and capacities. Practical reason, for instance, is identified as a key human capability which Nussbaum defines as "being able to form conception and to engage in critical reflection about the planning of one's life. (This entails protection for the liberty of conscience.)" (Nussbaum 2000a: 79). In a similar vein, the capability of affiliation is also valued to be an important basic capability. According to Nussbaum, protecting this capability implies not only "protecting institutions that constitute and nourish such forms of affiliation, and also protecting the freedom of assembly and political speech" but also "protections against discrimination on the basis of race, sex, sexual orientation, religion, caste, ethnicity, or national origin" (Nussbaum 2000a: 79). Rights are not the same as capabilities, but nevertheless without the possession of some basic capabilities it would not be possible to make effective use of the existing rights recognized in a political community. Similarly, some capabilities are so basic and vital to a decent human life that it is important to formulate them in the language of rights. For example, the rights to free speech and political participation would make no meaning and will remain purely nominal when citizens are illiterate or inadequately educated. At the same time, citizens' educational capabilities can be enhanced when they can have recourse to appropriate environment and institutions and when they can freely and without fear criticize government policies and programmes. Nussbaum's list tries to epitomize this interdependence between capabilities and rights.

Finally, Nussbaum elevates the capability approach to the liberal mode by claiming that it can be aligned with Rawls's political liberalism, particularly by using the Rawlsian idea of overlapping consensus. She affirms that "although this list of central capabilities is somewhat different in both structure and substance from Rawls's list of primary goods, it is offered in a similar political-liberal spirit" (Nussbaum 2000a: 74). Furthermore, just like Rawls she is hopeful of arriving at a consensus on the list: "By 'overlapping consensus' I mean what John Rawls means: that people may sign on to this conception as the freestanding moral core of a political conception, without accepting any particular metaphysical view, or even any particular view of the human nature" (Nussbaum 2000a: 76). By this, Nussbaum means to say that whether a citizen is a Hindu or Christian, Aristotelian or Kantian, in his or her comprehensive conception of the good, he or she could endorse the necessity of representing these capabilities in the political sphere.

On account of these liberal properties, the capability theory can be differentiated and set apart from other comprehensive conceptions such as utilitarianism or other monistic theories. The human good it aims to distribute among citizens is irreducibly plural. Moreover, there is neither a suggestion for the maximization of the good nor any recommendation for the sacrifice of individual entitlements for the sake of the common good. As Nussbaum has emphatically stated, the capabilities on the list are non-negotiable fundamental entitlements and hence no cost-benefit analysis may be applied to them. But do all these, as Nussbaum claims, make the capability approach the same as Rawls's political liberalism? Can the Rawlsian overlapping consensus perform the same work for the capability approach as it does for the Rawlsian theory? At the outset, Rawls's political liberalism, as pointed out earlier, not only has a different point of departure than the capability approach, it is also founded on the scepticism of the good. While the capability approach starts from an inquiry about the components of the good life, such questions are irrelevant for Rawlsian political liberalism. It would also be conceptually odd to add the primary good of income and wealth to the list of capabilities. And not least, the scope of Rawls's political liberalism and its overlapping consensus are restricted to concepts of political justice implicit in the public culture of a constitutional liberal democracy. Rawls does not talk of consensus across cultures and different political spectrums. Nor does he envisage the type of universal aspiration and application that Nussbaum wishes to embrace.

Given these differences, grafting the capability approach on to Rawls's theory not only seems implausible but also does not bring any additional advantage. Alternatively, as I argue elsewhere,[7] the capability approach might be seen as a non-Rawlsian project in political philosophy and its conceptual framework can further be strengthened by working on its own strong points: while for a Rawlsian the requirements of justice are conceived as disconnected from, and accompanied by a degree of scepticism about the human good and well-being, for a capability theorist they are related to the reflection on the human good and well-being. To the extent that there is an adequate and public conception of the human good and well-being which delineates what is truly worth caring about and what makes a life really go better for the person who is living it, it makes sense to hold that what people in a society fundamentally owe to each other is a fair distribution of the human good.

---

[7] See Alexander (2008). Here I outline some of the characteristics of the capability approach that support a non-liberal interpretation and develop the capability approach as an independent and non-Rawlsian project in political philosophy.

An adequate and public conception of the good need not turn out to be comprehensive like utilitarianism or any of its allies that Rawls and others are seriously concerned about. Most surely, it would be pluralistic, taking cognizance of the fact that there are many distinct components of well-being and valuable ways of life, and will not strive for more than a partial consensus among the citizens. Furthermore, the capability theorist also needs to show that in the realm of political philosophy of what motivates human beings to cooperate, a political theory must espouse a richer conception.

A different kind of political psychology

The social contract theorists of the seventeenth and eighteenth centuries challenged the hegemony of the teleological and naturalistic theories in political philosophy. Until then, most philosophers appealed to a naturalistic vision of society, and attempted to derive political principles based on such a vision. Naturalism also often meant justification of a hierarchical conception of humans and society. We can find this to varying degrees in Aristotle, Plato and other ancient philosophers. Later, this continues to find prominent expression in theistic or deistic theories of the medieval period. In contrast, philosophers of the social contract tradition tried to justify political principles and institutions based not on natural or divine laws but on the idea of original equality of every human being and on the fact that people could make contract with one another to live in a political society. Therefore, the crucial question for the social contract philosophers was the following: how can we legitimize the existence and organization of the state, its coercive laws and institutions, the rights and duties of individuals, without resorting to any naturalistic or religious explanations? Since most philosophers belonging to the social contract tradition come up with somewhat different answers to this question, and there are also traditional and modern variants among them, it is difficult to refer to this tradition as one uniform group.[8] Nevertheless, for our purpose here, at least two features of this tradition can broadly be identified in order to demonstrate how Nussbaum's theory of capabilities is developed in response to the limitations of the idea of social contract.

The first is related to the state of nature and the idea of contract. Society in general, and particularly a political entity such as the state, does not come about through some natural process – as for example, Aristotle tried to explain it[9] – but instead is an *artefact*, distinctively

---

[8] See Freeman (1990).   [9] See Alexander (2005).

created by human beings through contract. In order to explain this, social contract thinkers invoke the idea of the "state of nature" – a kind of fictitious pre-political situation where there was no sovereign, government, laws, courts, property rights, etc. Hobbes describes it as state of "war of all against all". Locke and Rousseau do not describe it as a state of war; for them even in the state of nature human beings have some moral values. Nevertheless, in the absence of a proper political society there is really nothing to prevent the state of nature from turning into a state of war. People could continue to live in the state of nature, but it will be besieged by insecurity, distrust, violence and chaos. So, people leave such volatile states by making contracts with one another. The state of nature that these thinkers imagine is therefore not a historical moment or reality. Rather, it is a counterfactual, hypothetical situation in order to legitimize contemporary state and society: the reason why rational persons would agree to live together and socially cooperate and why they would surrender themselves to a legitimate authority such as the state, its laws and institutions.

The second feature concerns the motivations for contract. Why would free, equal and independent individuals agree to enter into a social contract? The parties are envisaged as doing so mainly in order to secure a mutual benefit which otherwise would not be available if they lived alone and without social cooperation. However, there are variations from one social contract thinker to another regarding the motivations for contract. For Hobbes, it is chiefly self-interest and mutual advantage: people would forgo some advantages in the state of nature only in exchange for some other advantage for their own well-being. Locke, however, does not paint such a pessimistic picture. People are motivated to enter into contract to protect themselves and their property, but they also have concern for others.

Rawls works out a contemporary version of the contractarian theory. He remains a contractarian philosopher in as much as he shares some aspects of these two elements.[10] Yet Rawls emerges to be a rather different type of contractarian theorist because he diverges from the traditional theories in some important ways, sifting ideas and authors of this tradition. He shows distaste for the Hobbesian version of contract

---

[10] Rawls explicitly acknowledges and sees his project as part of the social contract tradition: "My aim is to present a conception of justice which generalizes and carries to a higher level of abstraction the familiar theory of the social contract as found, say, in Locke, Rousseau and Kant" (Rawls 1971: 11). Furthermore, he compares the Original Position in his theory to the state of nature in the traditional social contract: "In justice as fairness the original position of equality corresponds to the state of nature in the traditional theory of social contract" (Rawls 1971: 12).

and keeps his distance from it: "For all its greatness, Hobbes's *Leviathan* raises special problems" (Rawls 1973: 11, n. 4). He is more attracted to the Kantian version, particularly its constructive approach to moral values and justice, and as pointed out earlier, the Kantian conception of the person. More importantly, Rawls's political psychology – the reasons and motivations why people socially cooperate – differs from that of his contractarian predecessors. Rawls achieves this by introducing a completely new idea into the notion contract, namely, the veil of ignorance. Through this he emphasizes that the contracting parties, in drawing up the principles of justice, are motivated not only by mutual advantage but also by impartiality (Barry 1989: 145f.). In other words, there is a calculation of self-interest behind the veil of ignorance embodied in impartiality. In traditional social contract theories, particularly those of Hobbes and Locke, we have neither the Rawlsian veil of ignorance nor anything indicative of the motive of impartiality.

If attraction to liberal doctrines and the effort to elevate the capability approach to political liberalism can be identified as the key distinguishing traits between the earlier and later Nussbaum, then embeddedness in Aristotle's philosophy is what provides continuity in Nussbaum's corpus of thinking. Sometimes Nussbaum's allusion to a legion of thinkers as different as Plato, Kant, Mill, Marx, Rawls and Sen in order to support her various claims of the capability approach might make it difficult to see where precisely her allegiance lies. Yet her critique of the contractarian idea of reciprocity, the Kant–Rawlsian conception of personhood and above all the hermeneutical detours that she makes to preserve as well as to purify certain of pertinent Aristotelian insights for modern political purposes makes it apparent that the source of her justification in the last instance is Aristotelian. In fact, Nussbaum's claim that a list of (ten) capabilities should provide the basis for fundamental political principles such as might be enshrined in the human rights charter or a country's constitution can be seen as a reconstruction of Aristotle's philosophy. Nowhere is the philosophical connection between Aristotle and Nussbaum's capabilities approach clearer than in her persistent inquiry and interpretation of Aristotle's "human-function argument" found in *Ethics* I.7. Aristotle here raises the question of whether human beings *as such* have a function or activity (*ergon*) that can be called typically their own:

But is it likely that whereas joiners and shoemakers have certain functions or activities, man as such has none, but has been left by nature a functionless being? Just as we can see that eye and hand and foot and every one of our members has some function, should we not assume that in like manner a human being has function over and above these particular functions? What, then, can this possibly be? (*Ethics* I.7; Aristotle 2000: 75)

Aristotle's answer to this question is not straightforward. The prelude to the answer, starting already in *Ethics* 1.5, consists in the rejection of different possible candidates. He argues against the view that human function can be identified with seeking of physical pleasure or wealth or honour and so on. In contrast to this, Aristotle's own answer to the question is a life of practical reason (*Ethics* I.7; Aristotle 2000: 75–6). Nussbaum (1988a: 181) envisages practical reason both as an architectonic principle that organizes the whole life, providing for its many activities, and as an infusing principle that makes each activity human rather than merely vegetative or animal. She holds the view that a flourishing human life and well-being should have many components, some of which will certainly be basic functionings related to being nourished, healthy, educated and so on. However, what makes them distinctively human functionings is the fact that they are done as parts of a life organized and infused by practical reason. Hence, in Nussbaum's view, political institutions should be arranged in such a way that citizens are able to live in accordance with practical reason.

The central task of the city [polis] will, then, be to give its people the conditions of fully human living: living in which the essential functionings according to practical reason will be available. This means don't just give food and allow people to 'graze': make it possible for people to choose to regulate their nutrition by their own reason. Don't just take care of their perceptual needs in a mechanical way, producing a seeing eye, a hearing ear, etc. Instead, make it possible for people to use their bodies and senses in a truly human way. And don't make all this available in a minimal way: make it possible to do these things well. (1988a: 183)

Not only does Nussbaum underscore the political import of the human-function argument, she also reworks and corrects Aristotle's conservative non-egalitarian stance. Aristotle was inclined to endorse the already prevailing view that certain categories of people such as slaves, women and craftsmen do not have the capacity or qualifications necessary to fully participate in the polis. Nussbaum's task in this regard is to show the inconsistencies in Aristotle's stance and to point out that Aristotle's thought can still be used for constructive political purposes.

Aristotle at times shrinks back from what might be the *revolutionary implications* of some of his statements into the position that we owe this treatment only to those who have already managed to get a certain part of the way towards capability. But it seems to me that a political theory that developed the implications of these statements without shrinking could justifiably call itself Aristotelian. (Nussbaum 1988a: 184, emphasis mine)

Nussbaum points out the possibility of deploying an 'Aristotelian argument' to counteract the kind of elitism that Aristotle himself seemed to have easily accepted. She argues that because the general thrust of Aristotle's ethics and political philosophy is to find out the "valuable" human functionings and capabilities, it is only legitimate that an appropriation of Aristotle for today's purpose focuses on the capabilities of every citizen in the political community rather than just on the capabilities of those who are already better off in terms of social position and education.

Furthermore, in comparison to the social contract-inspired political theories, Nussbaum's theory of capabilities is supported by a more complex political psychology of what motivates people to live together and socially cooperate. Sometimes people tend to cooperate because of what they in turn can get out of cooperation. At other times people cooperate for other motives such as sense of justice, justice for justice's sake, compassion and benevolence, without keeping an account of what they get out of cooperation. Sen (1977) makes a similar point in his critique of the traditional economic model of rationality, *homo economicus*. He criticizes utilitarianism for assuming that people behave solely on the basis of self-interest. Instead, he points out that human beings are not "rational fools" acting only on self-interest. Human beings are moved to act not only because of self-interest but also because of other-regarding interests such as sympathy and commitment. Rawls's revised contractarianism has certainly come quite far from the utilitarian model and the traditional social contract model which appeal only to self-interest or mutual advantage. Reasonableness as differentiated from rationality is central to Rawls's political psychology. Human beings are not only rational in the sense of looking for what is advantageous from their viewpoint, they are also reasonable insofar as they are willing to honour fair terms of cooperation and justify their support for principles and policies with arguments and reasons that other reasonable persons can acknowledge and endorse. Also, Rawls considers that citizens possess the capacity for a sense of justice, along with the capacity to form a conception of the good, to be essential for justice as fairness theory. Nonetheless, Rawls does not go to the extent of considering moral sentiments such as sympathy, commitment and benevolence as part of motivations for social cooperation.

Nussbaum, by contrast, suggests that social cooperation should be envisaged as originating from a plurality of motivations which includes not only mutual advantage and impartiality but also benevolence, compassion and commitment. The hybrid theory that she advocates envisions a public role for compassion. Thus, when other people suffer capabilities failure, the citizen she imagines will not simply feel the sentiments required by moral impartiality, viewed as a constraint on her pursuit of self-interest; instead, she will feel compassion for them *as* a part of her own good. Indeed, this makes the capability approach in contrast to most modern liberal theories – not the least to Rawls's. These have been rather careful to avoid talking about compassion or other related emotions as having a role in understanding the demands of justice. These theories hold the view that what we owe to each other in the name of justice is one thing, and what we, like the Good Samaritan, might be motivated to do for others by compassion or pity is totally another. Arguments from the standpoint of justice should be differentiated from obligations of humanitarianism, altruism or compassion. It is best that we do not mix these different intuitions.

Nussbaum (1996), however, points out that although we do not have to mix up justice with compassion, the latter can play a crucial 'public' role in informing and shaping the reasoning and judgements of individuals and political communities, personal and public rationality in recognizing the obligations of justice, particularly relating to people with capability shortfalls. Compassion, for Nussbaum, provides the required link between the individual and the community, and hence can be thought of as "our species' way of hooking the interests of others to our own personal goods" (Nussbaum 1996: 28). While most contemporary moral and political theories dismiss compassion as an irrational force in human affairs, one that has no use, or is likely to mislead or distract us when we try to think about the nature and scope of just social institutions and policies, Nussbaum thinks of it as an emotion entailing a complex "cognitive structure" and a particular sort of "reasoning", and therefore having normative influence in our public life. As she puts it: "Compassion is not the entirety of justice; but it both contains a powerful, if partial, vision of just distribution and provides imperfect citizens with an essential bridge from self-interest to just conduct" (Nussbaum 1996: 57).

In attending to the interests of people with capability shortfalls which Sen, Kittay and other capability theorists have been highlighting, and in realizing the obligations of justice that society may have in addressing them, it is indeed important to seek support for one's views in a richer understanding of human motivations, solidarity and social cooperation than a standard social contract political theory would admit. However, this richer conception brings with it its own strains and runs the risk of conflating justice and compassion and, as Boltanski (1999) points out, between what is required of "politics of justice" and "politics of pity".

Among other things, one distinctive characteristic of justice is the notion of reciprocity.[11] We can meaningfully talk about justice and the

---

[11] As Nagel (2005) points out, traditionally such reciprocity has been understood in "political" terms in the sense that questions of justice arise between people who are subject to the same coercive sovereign authority or between citizens who are subject to a

obligations implied thereby only when there are certain forms of inter-action and reciprocity between the parties involved. In contrast to this, compassion or pity arises in the context of non-reciprocity. In fact, the vulnerability and weakness of the sufferer or victim make it inappropriate to invoke any form of reciprocity. Of course, when displaying compassion-ate feelings or translating them into action, one can do it keeping in mind the dignity and agency of the sufferer. But even then it is not the same type of reciprocity that would be required for justice. Neither the people with capability shortfalls themselves nor a capability theorist who argues in their favour would be cheered that their grievances are addressed on grounds of compassion alone. Hence, if and when the issues are raised as demands of justice, some kind of reciprocity should be involved in order to obtain a wider moral and political endorsement, although the kind of reciprocity envisaged need not be direct, immediate and purely economic.

Furthermore, justice invariably invokes the idea of desert. An act or gesture may be said to be unjust only if it can be shown that the person concerned has been denied of what he deserves. There would be, of course, different criteria of desert, depending on the types of goods distributed. For example, the criterion of desert is different for academic positions, political offices and athletic honours. Nonetheless, demands of justice often involve some form of meritocratic judgement. Compassion, in contrast, works not on the basis of desert but rather on the idea of "luck". Instances of (bad) luck can make the life and well-being of some people exposed and vulnerable. Thus, while compassion focuses on the opposition between the fortunate and unfortunate, justice concentrates on the distinction between the deserving and the undeserving. Recogniz-ing this distinction requires on the part of the capability theorist further thinking as to what sort of specific principles and patterns of distribution are required in realizing basic capabilities for all. Strictly speaking, the ideal of realizing basic capabilities for all so that people would have the required economic, social and political freedoms to lead the type of life they have reason to value need not necessarily be viewed as a social justice claim. It can very well be the consequence of a judgement that certain absolute forms of poverty and capability deprivation are bad and even scandalous, and that no decent society should tolerate them, par-ticularly when it has the material and human resources to overcome

common set of coercively imposed laws and institutions. In modern times, particularly after Rawls's influential justice as fairness theory, reciprocity has also been understood more broadly to include "economic" interactions and interdependence. Consequently, obligations of justice would arise not only because the concerned parties are under common political institutions but also because they are more generally engaged in cooperative ventures for mutual benefits.

them. Therefore, in order to make her argument more convincing, a capability theorist should be able to show her counterparts that what makes the capability shortfalls of people precisely a social justice claim is the moral judgement that all capability inequalities in life prospects meted out to people by the basic structure of society and for which they are not responsible are *prima facie* unjust.

Conclusion

The strength of Nussbaum's hybrid theory of capabilities lies in its ecumenism. It brings together traditions and philosophers which were previously thought to be antagonistic and incompatible, thus making possible a renewed and refreshing type of approach in political philosophy. It is also important to note that the type of ecumenism that emerges is not ecumenism-mongering – ecumenism for its own sake – but one which always keeps in view the crucial problems of justice in the contemporary world and attempts to seek the most effective conceptual resources to tackle them. Moreover, after Rawls's influential theory, it was not uncommon among moral and political philosophers to think of a conceptual stand-off between good-based theories of justice on the one hand and those which take distance from the human good and well-being on the other. Nussbaum's work on the capability approach has shown how this can in effect be overcome by infusing liberal tenets into Aristotle's moral and political concern with valuable human functionings and capabilities.

In retracing the development of Nussbaum's hybrid theory, this chapter has particularly argued for the idea that the capability approach embraces a richer vision of political psychology which is not only embodied and visibly stated in the list of (ten) capabilities but is also conceptually supported by a more inclusive view of human beings and a complex account of moral sentiments and motivations for social cooperation. Such a vision is especially valuable in extending the scope of justice in order to address issues that have not received central attention in other theories. However, the chapter has also pointed out that in extending the scope of what can be achieved through a mixed theory, we cannot overlook the possible tensions that may arise in theory as well as in practice.

REFERENCES

Ackerly, B. A. 2000. *Political Theory and Feminist Social Criticism*, Cambridge University Press.
Alexander, J. M. 2004. "Capabilities, Human Rights and Moral Pluralism", *The International Journal of Human Rights*, 8/4 (Winter), 451–469.

2005. "Non-Reductionist Naturalism: Nussbaum between Aristotle and Hume", *Res Publica: A Journal of Legal and Social Philosophy*, 11/2, 157–183.

2008. *Capabilities and Social Justice: The Political Philosophy of Amartya Sen and Martha Nussbaum*, Aldershot: Ashgate Publishing Company.

Aristotle. 2000. *Nicomachean Ethics*, ed. R. Crisp, Cambridge University Press.

Barry, B. 1989. *Theories of Justice*, Berkeley, CA: University of California Press.

Boltanski, Luc. 1999. *Distant Suffering: Morality, Media and Politics*, trans. G. Burchell, Cambridge University Press.

Freeman, S. 1990. "Reason and Agreement in Social Contract Views", *Philosophy and Public Affairs*, 19/2, 122–157.

Hurka, T. 2002. "Capability, Functioning, and Perfectionism", *Apeiron*, 35/4, 137–162.

Kant, I. 1997. *Groundwork of the Metaphysics of Morals*, ed. M. Gregor, Cambridge University Press.

Kekes, J. 2003. *The Illusions of Egalitarianism*, New York: Cornell University Press.

Kittay, E. F. 2003. "Human Dependency and Rawlsian Equality" in *John Rawls: Vol. III*, ed. C. Kukathas, London: Routledge, 167–211.

Korsgaard, C. M. 1993. "Commentary" in *The Quality of Life*, eds. M. C. Nussbaum and A. Sen, Oxford: Clarendon Press, 54–61.

Menon, N. 2002. "Universalism Without Foundations?" *Economy and Society*, 31/1, 152–169.

Nagel, T. 2005. "The Problem of Global Justice", *Philosophy and Public Affairs*, 33/2, 113–147.

Nussbaum, M. C. 1986. *The Fragility of Goodness* [Updated Edition, 2001], Cambridge University Press.

1988a. "Nature, Function, and Capability: Aristotle on Political Distribution", *Oxford Studies in Ancient Philosophy*, Oxford University Press.

1988b. "Non-Relative Virtues: An Aristotelian Approach", *Midwest Studies in Philosophy*, 13/1, 32–53.

1990. "Aristotelian Social Democracy", in *Liberalism and the Good*, eds. B. B. Douglass *et al.*, New York: Routledge.

1995. "Aristotle on Human Nature and the Foundations of Ethics", in *World, Mind and Ethics*, eds. J. Altham and R. Harrison, Cambridge University Press.

1996. "Compassion: The Basic Social Emotion", *Social Philosophy and Policy*, 13/1, 27–58.

2000a. *Women and Human Development*, Cambridge University Press.

2000b. "Aristotle, Politics and Human Capabilities", *Ethics*, 111/1, 102–140.

2001. "Preface to the Revised Edition", in *The Fragility of Goodness*, Cambridge University Press.

2006. *Frontiers of Justice: Disability, Nationality and Species Membership*, Cambridge, MA: Harvard University Press.

Rawls, J. 1973. *A Theory of Justice*, Revised Edition, Oxford University Press.

1980. "Kantian Constructivism in Moral Theory", *The Journal of Philosophy*, 77/9, 515–572.

1993. *Political Liberalism*, New York: Columbia University Press.

2001. *Justice as Fairness: A Restatement*, Cambridge, MA: Harvard University Press.

Raz, J. 1990. "Facing Diversity: Epistemic Abstinence", *Philosophy and Public Affairs*, 19/1, 3–46.

Sen, A. 1977. "Rational Fools: A Critique of the Behavioural Foundations of Economic Theory", *Philosophy and Public Affairs*, 6/4, 317–344.

1980. "Equality of What?" in *Tanner Lectures on Human Values, Volume I*, ed. S. McMurrin, Cambridge University Press.

1992. *Inequality Reexamined*, Oxford University Press.

1993. "Well-being and Capability", in *The Quality of Life*, eds. M. Nussbaum and A. Sen, Oxford University Press.

17 God and Martha C. Nussbaum: towards a Reformed Christian view of capabilities

Jonathan Warner

Introduction

In *Women and Human Development*, Martha C. Nussbaum presents a normative and, she claims, a universal, theory of human capabilities. She argues for a list of what she calls central human functional capabilities, and defends this list (or some modified version of it that captures the same core capabilities) against charges of paternalism and cultural insensitivity. The items on this list, she believes, enjoy widespread support from people with a large number of differing perspectives and views as to what constitutes human flourishing and living the Good Life. In her view, the capabilities she lists are necessary conditions for being able to pursue the goals that people actually believe to be valuable, regardless of their differing "metaphysical" beliefs about the nature of reality. The overlapping consensus between people of widely differing views of the Good is what gives the list (a form of) universal applicability.

Nussbaum defends her list largely through an appeal to political liberalism and individual autonomy, based on the importance of regarding people as ends-in-themselves and of extending toleration to others who see things differently. She examines arguments that claim to show that the exercise of these capabilities would not in fact be seen as valuable, and counters that her concern is with capabilities – the potential to function, the ability to choose to function – rather than with functionings – the realisation of capabilities. She also argues that it is inappropriate that religious belief should impose limitations on the capabilities of people. People might, indeed, freely choose to adopt a religious system and practices that compromised their functionings, but they should not be denied the ability of making the opposite choice; nor should they seek to deny that contrary choice to others. "Other-regarding" preferences, then, have no place in her theory.

In this chapter I seek to develop a grounding to capabilities based on a Reformed understanding of the Judaeo–Christian Scriptures. While Nussbaum recognises (indeed, stresses) that hers is a normative theory, she seems to see capabilities as a neutral arbitrator in cases where beliefs conflict. She is particularly concerned with questions of the appropriate role of the State: when does the State have the right (and, perhaps, the obligation) to restrict religious activities when there is an overriding interest of the State in doing so? Specifically, this overriding interest would be the guaranteeing of capabilities, where religious beliefs would seem to restrict them. But in this case, the list of capabilities has become a standard of judgement – what Roy Clouser (1991) would call a religious idea itself. As Nussbaum is aware, the standard of judgement – recognising when the State's interest really is overriding – is problematic.

The capabilities approach is incomplete, in at least two senses. First, not all possible capabilities are included in the list, which is always provisional and subject to revision. Second, the capabilities approach does not provide a complete theory of how society ought to be, although upholding of capabilities has implications for the types of societal structure and institutions that there should be. One difference between a Reformed Christian approach and that of Martha C. Nussbaum is that the latter starts with individuals (the possessors of capabilities) and then works outwards towards a consideration of society, whereas a Reformed Christian approach starts with God, His creation and the relationship between the two. Further, Nussbaum argues that all items on her list enjoy the status of being irreducibly distinct aims. She attempts no ordering of them (although others have suggested that the claim that being able to play is of as great a value as bodily integrity is rather odd) and does not allow for a possibility of trade-offs between the items on the list. For Nussbaum, there is no higher court of appeal than the capabilities list itself. Yet an approach that takes a unitary principle as ultimate (such as "submission to God's will" – the ultimate good for a Moslem; or the building of *shalom* peace-with-justice) will rank capabilities in accordance to their importance in achieving this goal. Where there are perceived conflicts between capabilities (or, as is more likely to be the case, where resources are inadequate to implement all capabilities), the way these will be resolved will be in an appeal to the ultimate principle.

Of course, there needs to be a way of assessing religious claims from cultural (or political) claims, as Nussbaum points out (2000, p. 193). Jesus, in the tradition of the Hebrew prophets, attacked religious practices that were separated from a true understanding of religion, but rested instead on the opinions of men (see *Mark* 7:1–13, where Jesus quotes the prophet Isaiah to this effect). An established hermeneutic (such as the principles derived from Scripture and expounded by Reformed theologians) provides some of the criteria for making the distinction.

Judaeo–Christianity takes seriously the idea of men and women being created in the image of God (*Genesis* 1:26). It is this in which their value is grounded, not in being ends-in-themselves. This image, and much else in human nature, has been perverted as the result of sin. The primary purpose of men and women is to live in fellowship with God – true flourishing is seen in this light. From this starting point, a list of capabilities similar to Nussbaum's could be developed. However, there will be differences: toleration of divergent views will play a less central role, for example, and certain types of other-regarding preferences would be accommodated. I shall attempt to develop the criteria for drawing up such a list, and shall examine differences between this and Nussbaum's list.

In what follows I provide a brief sketch of the capabilities approach and Nussbaum's arguments for the existence of universal values. After a short account of what I understand by "Reformed Christianity", I develop an account of the Biblical concept of *shalom* as the overriding principle of a normative account of society. I then highlight four areas of possible difference between a Reformed Christian account of capabilities and Nussbaum's account.

The capabilities approach

Development is more than just economic growth. While improvements in the material standard of living of poor people are important, the ability to consume ever-increasing quantities of goods and services is not the sole determinant of a full and meaningful life. Indeed, excessive income growth can lead to impoverishment in other areas, a phenomenon that might be dubbed "overdevelopment" (Goudzwaard, 1975).

The capabilities approach offers a fruitful alternative to the traditional approach of viewing poverty and impoverishment solely in terms of inadequate income, by drawing attention to the fact that there is more to living a fulfilled life than being in possession of an adequate income. Over the past twenty-five years this point has become well accepted within the field of development economics: the United Nations Development Programme has adopted the Human Development Index as a measure of what constitutes development; leading textbooks also argue that development is more than just economic growth accompanied, perhaps, by income redistribution. For example, one of the major textbooks of development economics (Todaro, 2000, 2006) identifies three core values (the ability to meet basic needs, self-esteem, being able to choose) which the author sees as foundational to a fully fledged theory of development.

The capabilities approach takes the broader conception of development a stage further by emphasising the importance of various forms of positive freedoms – the ability, or potential, to do certain things, or pursue their own conception of the good life. As Martha C. Nussbaum (Nussbaum, 2000, pp. 1 ff.) points out, women, especially in poorer countries, have traditionally been denied opportunities available to men. When family resources are limited, it tends to be the sons rather than the daughters who receive the bulk of attention and opportunities. While boys are viewed as an asset to the family, girls are seen as a liability – their adult working lives will be spent in the service of their future husband's family rather than their own. And then there is the question of providing an appropriate dowry . . . In short, in many societies, women are, or have traditionally been, treated as second-class citizens or, worse, as chattels of their fathers or husbands, giving them little or no opportunity to flourish as human beings.

Capabilities can be regarded as a claim: as a certain level of capability-possession is necessary for living a fulfilled life and, as such, a theory of development needs to address this claim. As Nussbaum writes, "The basic intuition from which the capability approach begins, in the political arena, is that certain human abilities exert a moral claim that they should be developed" (Nussbaum, 2000 p. 83).

Amartya Sen's version of the capabilities approach stresses the primary importance of freedom – the freedom to be able to lead the life one wants and to pursue the goals that one sees as valuable (Sen, 1999). Martha C. Nussbaum has developed the capabilities approach in a somewhat different direction in producing her list of central human functioning capabilities that, she argues, are necessary for leading a worthwhile life.

The source of universal values

Enumerating a list has problems. Nussbaum argues that her list has universal applicability; that is, that everyone, whatever their religious, social, ethnic or cultural background, could agree that these capabilities are valuable. Or, at least, in the absence of distorting influences on the reasoning powers of individuals and inappropriately moulded ideas of the good (adaptive preferences), everyone should be able to agree on these things.

She defends the list from several types of attack: from the charges of paternalism, lack of cultural sensitivity and lack of respect for diversity. Nussbaum rebuts these charges by arguing that the capabilities on the list are aspirations consistent with all cultures. She agrees that cultural diversity, like biological diversity, is, in general, good, but that support for diversity alone is a weak argument: beating one's wife is not the sort of cultural diversity that should be encouraged. The justification of Nussbaum's form of liberalism can be found in a version of the Kantian Categorical Imperative – all persons are ends-in-themselves, autonomous human beings, with the right to make decisions about their own conception of the Good Life and how it should be lived.

Perhaps the biggest challenge to this approach comes from religion-based conceptions of the good that would deny that certain capabilities should be granted (especially to women). Nussbaum has no problem with a woman who voluntarily decides to submit to a religious code that denies her certain capabilities (e.g. to adopt a traditional style of dress, as Hamida Khala wished to do (Nussbaum, 2000, pp. 236–8)), but she argues that the woman should have the ability to choose *not* to submit. She is concerned that some decisions might be coerced (as Shah Bono probably was, pp. 239–40), or that the decision might be the result of inappropriately adapted preferences: that the woman might claim to prefer a mode of dress because lack of opportunity to see and comprehend the advantages of an alternative means that her preferences are not genuinely freely formed but have adapted to cohere to the culture within which she is living.

Further, Nussbaum argues that, in general, it is not essential to any (major) religious faith that capability-denying behaviour is admitted. Men do beat their wives, but no religion requires this. Of course, there are difficult cases; Nussbaum constructs a set of tests to shed light on the problem, and to point the way to possible resolution (2000, pp. 198–206).

Undergirding Nussbaum's approach is an idea of moral worth: that every person is valuable and entitled to (equal) respect. Her preferences should be respected and restricted only insofar as they deny equal opportunities to others. In the political arena, this is to be cashed out as a respect for genuinely equal human rights for all. Thus any religious or other viewpoint that seeks to deny the central capabilities of Nussbaum's list to groups of people is to be judged unacceptable. As she says, "What is ruled out by the type of focus on the person for which I have argued is any approach that seeks a good for Hinduism or Judaism, let us say, by denying the liberty of conscience of individual Hindus or Jews" (Nussbaum, 2000, p. 189).

There are two ways in which this claim of universal applicability of the capabilities approach might be related to religious belief. One could argue, first, that the recognition of capabilities is, in fact, consistent with the teachings of the various religions (correctly interpreted). That is, each person would find, on reflection, that the value of personhood, and therefore of the desirability of the listed capabilities, is taught by the

Scriptures of her religion; and further, that there is nothing in the capabilities list that contradicts the teachings of the religion. For example, the Golden Rule ("Do unto others as you would have them do unto you") is a teaching found in at least thirteen of the world's religious and spiritual traditions (Beversluis, 2001) and is, of course, a guiding principle of much thinking on moral philosophy. On this view, then, tenets of a religion that seem to deny capabilities to some are errors, due either to a faulty understanding of the religion, or to a faulty exegesis of the religion's sacred texts.

The second way is to claim that the capabilities approach transcends religion: that the recognition of the value of the capabilities in the list is prior to the claims of any religion. One could then use the list as a test by which to compare and critique religious teaching. This second alternative makes the list of capabilities, or the undergirding assessment of moral worth, as "divine", in Roy Clouser's sense, as the standard by which any other idea, religion or tradition is to be judged (Clouser, 1991). On this account, the true word of God to humankind is embodied in the capabilities that He wishes all His creation to enjoy, and therefore anything contradicting this taught by a religion must come from man, not from God. This line of argument, however, is unlikely to be fully convincing to believers in any revealed religion, as it places human reasoning above divine revelation. Although, as the history of Christianity has demonstrated, there is much scope for differing traditions within a particular religion, and in the application of revealed religious principles to particular situations, for Reformed (and almost all other) Christians the Word of God (as expressed in the Bible), not a set of tenets derived from human understanding, is the ultimate source of authority.

Nussbaum is ultimately committed to taking this second route. A religion that, as part of its structure, denies freedom of conscience (and perhaps the right of exit) to its adherents in the name of promoting that religion and the welfare of believers would thereby compromise the capabilities of the adherents. In a case of this type, Nussbaum would judge the religion at the bar of capabilities and find it wanting. For her, central human functional capabilities must always trump the dictates of religion in any case where a religion would deny a capability.

But she treats religious belief and practice seriously. She sees religious belief as an important component of seeking the Good, and wishes to allow a broad degree of latitude to religious practice. For many people, religious belief provides meaning and value to life, and so it is right to take religion-derived values seriously. Nussbaum also points out that religions are not, in general, monolithic; they have different strands of thought within them, different traditions, some of which, at least, are likely to value human worth and autonomy to the extent that they are *de facto* validating the capabilities approach. In what follows, I give a brief sketch of what I think a Reformed Christian account of capabilities would entail. The account is very much under-specified; in general, it leads to a vindication of the capabilities approach, but on a slightly different basis. I then try to see what differences, if any, my Christian version has with Martha C. Nussbaum's account.

Reformed Christianity

Reformed Christianity is most generally applied to that part of the Christian church that emerged from the Protestant Reformation following the views of John Calvin (1957) rather than those of Luther or the English reformers. For Reformed Christians, just as for most believers in a revealed religion, the starting point must be God. The purpose and value of human beings must be seen in their relationship to God. The Judaeo–Christian scriptures start with God, who is the creator of everything, and who said that the completed creation was very good (*Genesis* 1:31). Humankind is the peak of creation – the only part that bears the image of God. Creation was of a world of peace and harmony, of right relationships between the parts of creation, and between the Creator and what he had made.

This idyll was shattered by the entry of sin into the world. The result of Adam and Eve's rebellion against God's command was a world of disharmony, war, injustice and death. The relationship between God and man was impaired. Humankind was infected by an innate tendency to do wrong – the taint of original sin. The result is the world we see today – a world of beautiful and delightful things, yet spoilt by lust, oppression, crime and a whole host of other evils.

For Christians, there is good news. The hope of a better world is rooted in the Incarnation – God's coming to earth in the person of the Lord Jesus Christ, whose sacrificial death by crucifixion paid the penalty for that original sin. Christians, those who trust in Christ for salvation, can enjoy the peace that a right relationship with God brings, but full restoration has to wait: the created world still groans (*Romans 8:22*), awaiting the final consummation at Christ's return to earth.

Reformed Christian thinkers have developed the Gospel story of redemption into a fully fleshed-out philosophy of life. The Dutch Prime Minister and theologian Abraham Kuyper (1931) argued that Calvinism offered a hermeneutical key to life and provided the basis for an overall account of human purpose and existence. Calvin and Kuyper both resisted the type of dualism that draws a sharp division between the realm of the "secular" and that of the "sacred", stressing instead the unity of human life and calling. André Biéler has spelled out the social consequences of Calvin's thought (Biéler, 1961, 1964).

Redemption is not solely for the immaterial parts of human beings (their souls) but for all creation. The role of those who have become disciples of Christ is to work for the coming of God's kingdom, to work towards the restoration of harmony, of *shalom*. Part of the vision of *shalom* is a view of human flourishing – for which capabilities are a prerequisite.

A Reformed Christian alternative?

One might ask the question, "To what extent is the Nussbaum list of capabilities consistent with the teachings of Christianity?" A Christian, though, would be more likely to phrase the question thus: "What does my religion teach about God, and man, and how then should I live?" What God-given talents, rights, capabilities have I been given in order to allow me to live out my life as God intended?

Reformed Christianity, like other strands within the mainstream of Christian tradition, and indeed like any religion or worldview, has a substantive account of what constitutes the Good Life. In a sense, this presents a narrowing of perspective: Nussbaum's capabilities list is supposed to be consistent with any (reasonable) way of living the Good Life, whereas any substantive account of the Good Life will tend to value certain of the capabilities over others. For example, a religious account that takes the idea of sin seriously (and recognises the tendency in human beings to go astray) will view capabilities that can be misused (that can easily turn a good into an evil) rather more sceptically. The good of personal responsibility and freedom of choice will not necessarily always trump the desire to remove temptations. Jesus said, "If anyone causes one of these little ones who believe in me to sin, it would be better for him to have a large millstone hung around his neck and to be drowned in the depth of the sea. Woe to the world because of the things that cause people to sin! Such things must come, but woe to the man through whom they come" (*Matt. 18:6–7*). While sin is inevitable in a fallen world, the freedom to lead others, or oneself, into sin is not part of the Good Life.

A conception of the Good Life is broader than a list of capabilities, as Nussbaum acknowledges. Not only will it have an account of individual freedoms and responsibilities, it will also have an account of the appropriate role of institutions and other organs in bringing it to fruition. It would, for example, have at least a sketch of a theory of justice. A religious worldview produces a framework for living the Good Life: a structure providing the setting for capabilities. From this perspective, the capability approach is incomplete. The problem is that, as a fuller theory is developed, there is no guarantee that a substantive theory of justice and of the role of institutions would necessarily endorse all of the items on the list of capabilities.

Some form of Rawlsian "reflective equilibrium" might be necessary to work out an appropriate balance between the requirements of justice and the type of capabilities that might be endorsed. A just society with a widely embraced collective goal may need to deny individual capabilities in order to achieve that goal. For example, Hare demonstrated that, given highly unlikely but nevertheless reasonable assumptions, even the institution of slavery might allow more people to live out a certain conception of the Good Life than a system guaranteeing freedom from servitude (Hare, 1979).

This being said, the chief difference between a Christian account of capabilities and Martha C. Nussbaum's account is more at the level of justification than content. It would not be surprising if most of Nussbaum's list were consistent with the teachings of the Bible, given both the influence of Judaeo–Christian ideas on western civilisation and Nussbaum's own Jewish faith.

More fundamentally though, consistency between the Bible and Nussbaum's approach is to be expected if God really is a beneficent deity: how could the Father want the withholding of the good gifts of capabilities from His children (*Matt 7:11*) and, especially, from His daughters? Although the starting points and views of the nature of ultimate values are different, the instrumental or subordinate ends (such as a list of capabilities) are likely to be very similar. Nussbaum's belief that it is hard to deny that the values embodied in the list are genuinely universal also supports this conclusion.

But the starting points, and underlying presuppositions, differ. A Christian account of capabilities would start not by looking at an anthropocentric account of the Good Life but by looking at the nature of God, and God's plans for, and concerns about, the human race.

Reformed Christianity stresses God's ultimate sovereignty: there are no external constraints on what He can do. So the question posed by the Puritan theologian Jonathan Edwards needs to be asked: "Why did God create the universe?" He answers, arguing both from the Bible and by natural theology, that "the glory of God is the last end for which he created the world" (Edwards, 1765). The purpose of creation is to glorify God. Human beings, unique among the visible creation, were made to have fellowship with God. As the Westminster Catechism says, "Man's chief end is to glorify God (*1 Cor. 10:31; Rom. 11:36*), and to enjoy him for ever (*Ps. 73:25–28*)." If that is indeed the "chief end" of humankind, then the value of human capabilities rests in their promoting this end rather than in their ability to promote ends of each person's own devising.

It might be objected that this approach leads to an extreme form of Platonism (in the way Nussbaum uses the word); that is, individuals' preferences are ultimately irrelevant, all that matters is God's glory. Certainly, throughout human history various groups have claimed a monopoly on understanding what God has to say, and have used that supposed monopoly to restrict the functionings of people. But this is really a perversion of Christianity, at least to Protestants, in that the Holy Spirit indwells all followers of Christ and, as promised by Jesus, leads them in the ways of truth (*John 16:13*). If a believer seeks to live in accordance with God's will, then his or her own preferences will increasingly mirror what God wants and thereby bring glory to Him. (This one might term appropriately adaptive preferences.)

The Bible teaches that God is benevolent and cares about His creation. He created the resources necessary for the creatures, both human and non-human, to flourish. David says, "The Lord is compassionate and gracious, slow to anger, abounding in love" (*Ps 103:8*). God desires the happiness of His creatures. Indeed, John Piper (1987) argues that Jonathan Edwards was a Christian Hedonist, in that the pursuit of God's glory is part and parcel of what leads to happiness. "If we try to deny or mortify or abandon that pursuit of happiness, we set ourselves against virtue. And that would mean we set ourselves against the good of man and the glory of God."

For Reformed Christians, true flourishing and happiness – blessedness – consist in living in right relationships with God, other people and the non-human part of creation. This state of affairs is what the Hebrew authors call *shalom*. In a world characterised by *shalom*, justice and peace would prevail, people can flourish, developing the gifts and talents with which they have been endowed, to reach their potential as fully human creatures. Nicholas Wolterstorff (1983, pp. 69–71) puts it this way:

Shalom at its highest is *enjoyment* in one's relationships ... To dwell in shalom is to *enjoy* living before God, to *enjoy* living in one's physical surroundings, to *enjoy* living with one's fellows, to *enjoy* life with oneself.

[J]ustice ... is indispensable to shalom. That is because shalom is an *ethical* community. If individuals are not granted what is due them, if their claim on others is not acknowledged by those others, if others do not carry out their obligations to them, then shalom is wounded. ... Shalom cannot be secured in an unjust situation by managing to get all concerned to feel content with their lot in life. Shalom would not have been present *even if* all the blacks in the United States had been content in their state of slavery.

But … shalom is more than an ethical community. Shalom is the *responsible* community in which God's laws for the multifaceted existence of his creatures are obeyed.

Shalom goes beyond even the responsible community. We may all have acted responsibly and yet shalom may be wounded, for delight may be missing.

He concludes (p. 72):

Shalom is both God's cause in the world and our human calling. Even though the full incursion of shalom into our history will be a divine gift and not merely human achievement, even though its episodic incursion into our lives now also has a dimension of divine gift, nonetheless it is shalom that we are to work and struggle for. We are workers in God's cause, his peace-workers. The *missio Dei* is *our* mission.

Reaching this potential is glorifying to God. Thus a list of capabilities would stress these factors and would mostly coincide with Nussbaum's list. But note that it goes further: the transcendence of God is explicitly recognised, and the need for joy in all our relationships, not just ethical and responsible behaviour.

Of course, not all religious practices are good – not all glorify God. Through His prophets, God frequently rebuked the Israelites for holding religious meetings and making animal sacrifices when they were failing to do justice and mercy. (See, for example, *Isaiah 1:10 ff.*, where Israel is berated for honouring God through their forms of worship but not in the way they act.) As Nussbaum points out, "If we're agreed that God is just and good, and if we can show you that a certain form of conduct is egregiously bad, then it follows that this conduct … must be a form of human error" (Nussbaum, 2000, p. 197). The Christian's basis for believing that God is just and good, though, comes from what He has revealed of His nature. Nussbaum makes a similar point about Islam. The equality of the sexes taught in the Koran, treating women worse than the household dog, is inconsistent with the claims of the book that is the ultimate authority for Moslems (Nussbaum, 2000, pp. 227–8).

Christian theology sees the world, and the internal life of each person, as a war between good and evil. Although God pronounced His creation to be very good (*Genesis 1:31*), the entry of sin into the world has affected relationships and *shalom*. This tension will continue to exist until the Messiah, Jesus, comes again to inaugurate the new order pictured in *Revelation 21*. The apostle Paul writes of the internal tension: the recognition that certain things are right (God's commands in the Old Testament law) and the desire to do those things, while at the same time being unable to do what he wants to do: "In my mind I am a slave to God's law, but in the sinful nature a slave to the law of sin" (*Romans 7:25b*). The history of Christianity certainly demonstrates the effects that sin has had on individuals and on the institutions of society. This should make us wary, again, of attempts to restrict capabilities on the ground of religion. Taking the fall into sin seriously, however, requires an acknowledgement of not only institutional and structural sin, but also of the warping effects of sin on individual choices. Capacities which are good can be used for evil.

Further, it is doubtful that the Christian church has ever successfully articulated the vision in all its fullness. Wolterstorff's analysis of the content of *shalom* leaves unanswered the question of how this vision is to be cashed out, and the role of individuals, structures and institutions in that process. The hermeneutical question – how does this apply today? – remains after the exegesis of Biblical texts is finished. It is not clear, for example, how one should treat difficult Old Testament pronouncements: to what extent are the prescriptions of the Law binding on us today, and to what extent relevant solely to a particular period in history? One promising approach is the redemptive movement hermen-eutic (Webb, 2001) – the idea that the Bible (from Genesis Chapter 3 onwards) is primarily an account of redemption, and demonstrates and enjoins a movement from the bad practices of pagan culture to a fully fledged vision of *shalom*. Thus the Law regulated the way in which slaves might be treated (setting a standard far higher than that of the surround-ing nations); only much later was the whole idea of slavery successfully challenged on Biblical grounds. The ultimate ethic (a necessary compon-ent of *shalom*) is the elimination of all slavery and, in Webb's view, "improved working conditions; wages maximized for all; harmony, respect, and unified purpose between all levels in an organizational structure" (Tennant, 2002).

In terms of a list of basic capabilities, there is little difference between a Judaeo–Christian view of capabilities as a means for human beings, made in God's image, to glorify God, and Nussbaum's approach of deriving capabilities from each person's value as a person. Does the explicit recognition of a Creator really make a difference at the level of capabilities?

Nussbaum argues for a type of political liberalism that is "a form of liberalism not grounded in divisive religious or metaphysical principles" that allows for an overlapping consensus on matters of public policy: that people from differing metaphysical and religious views can accept common principles and goals regardless of their beliefs (Nussbaum, 2006, p. 6). While this is probably true in many cases, differences in beliefs about the nature of human beings may lead to different conclu-sions. Thus, if one believes that human life begins at conception, one's views on public policy towards abortion will probably differ from those who believe that personhood develops later. Further, if what constitutes personhood depends on a metaphysical assertion that is not shared by the non-human world (the image of God), then the nature of human relationships with, and duties towards, the rest of creation will be affected by this belief.

In her more recent work, Nussbaum has sought to extend the scope of the capabilities approach to provide guidance for the treatment of animals (Nussbaum, 2006, Chapter 6). Both Kantian social contract accounts of political interactions and other theories influenced by traditional Judaeo–Christian beliefs are deficient in that they fail to provide a basis for a respect for non-human life. Animals are seen as either complicated machines (and so incapable of feeling pain) or soulless beings (and so of no value other than their instrumental value to human beings), or incapable of having rights because they are incapable of understanding and carrying out duties. Nussbaum rightly believes that this view of animals is insufficient, that they are worthy of more respect and entitled to enjoy certain (modified) capabilities.

The Biblical mandate to humankind to "have dominion" or "rule over" the animal kingdom has tended to make Christians unresponsive to the pain and suffering of animals. The command to "take care of" creation (to *shamar* it, bless it) in *Genesis 2:15* has been widely ignored, resurfacing only in the past fifty or so years. But the basis of concern about creation is different: for Nussbaum it is an entitlement to a flourishing life based on justice (2006, p. 392); for Christians, animal flourishing is good on the basis that animals, along with people, form part of a creation that God pronounced to be very good. Part of the human task is to model the image of God to all creation. But as animals do not bear that image, their role, function and relation to God and to people are fundamentally different from the relationship between God and human beings. Cruelty towards animals is wrong, but animal rights or entitlements can be trumped by genuine human needs. Again, a metaphysical difference (the *Imago Dei*) makes a difference to the ground on which the right treatment of animals rests and, potentially, to what constitutes right treatment. As eating animals is explicitly permitted (*Genesis 9:3*), any *compulsory* vegetarianism would be rejected.

One would expect, then, that there would be differences in the form of capabilities between a Reformed Christian approach and that of Martha C. Nussbaum. The next four sections of the chapter attempt to examine what differences there might be and how these differences might be cashed out in the political arena. I then suggest a slightly revised list of capabilities or, rather, an annotated version of Nussbaum's list.

Differences I – the extent of individual liberty

Nussbaum's theory is strongly individualistic in that the unit of analysis (the possessor of capabilities) is always an individual person. Capabilities cannot be denied simply because their denial brings an apparent good to the community, whereas the building of *shalom* might place constraints on what individuals ought to do because of the effects of their actions on others.

Bodily integrity is the third item on Nussbaum's list. It seems that each person has sovereignty over one's own body. Certainly, the right not to be interfered with, not to be raped, struck or otherwise physically abused is basic to one's value as a person. But are there limits to this sovereignty? May one abuse one's own body; may one commit suicide?

Nussbaum's argument against suicide is in terms of the irreversibility of the act and the uneasiness that the suicide's decision is not truly thought out: of those who talk of committing suicide, only a tiny minority actually make a serious attempt (Bascom and Tolle, 2002). But there are cases where suicide is a premeditated, rational response to circumstances. (See, for example, BBC, 2002 and links for a British case.)

A Christian response would start by denying our complete sovereignty over our own bodies. God, as creator, has rights over what we do with our bodies. Also, our moral duty to be concerned about others means that the potential suicide is obligated to consider the effects of his action on others in the community. Thomas Aquinas, following Augustine, argued that suicide was, in effect, self-murder and so a sin. Aquinas also argues that suicide is contrary to man's nature (his self-love) and is a sin against the community (Aquinas, *Summa Theologica II-II Q64 Art. 5*). Paul, speaking against sexual immorality, stresses that, as Christians "bought at a price" by God are not their own: the body belongs to God, and therefore ways that treat it with contempt are sinful (*1 Cor. 6:19–20*).

"Choice in matters of reproduction" may also be problematic. Sexual morality has long been a concern of the Church. Jesus, quoting *Genesis*, reaffirmed teaching on the sanctity of marriage. Paul castigated the abuse of freedom by means of illicit sexual relations in the Corinthian church. Homosexual relationships, fornication and adultery are all condemned. Considerations of this sort mean that Nussbaum's third item, bodily integrity, would read a little differently: "having opportunities for sexual satisfaction and for choice in matters of reproduction" would be modified to take into account the appropriate limits of sexual activity (within a marriage) imposed by Scripture.

Women's access to appropriate methods of birth control, to limit the number of children they have, has been a contentious issue. New human life is good, and children are a blessing from the Lord (*Ps 127:3–5*). But a woman's life can be impoverished by continually bearing child after child, and pregnancy can be used as a means of male domination. At the very least, the wider implications of childbearing need to be considered. Both the would-be father and the would-be mother have a legitimate interest in family-planning decisions. If resources are limited, the welfare of the community needs to be considered as well. So must the interests of the unborn child: Christian respect for human life means that abortion (at least after the first few weeks) is seen as sinful. So is deliberately choosing to conceive a handicapped child (Dowling, 2002). Metaphysical views on the nature of personhood and the commencement of human life do make a difference.

Differences II – establishment, the State and public policy

In general, Nussbaum's approach seeks to give broad latitude to differing religious beliefs and practices; she feels that the US Constitution's freedom of religion/non-establishment clause provides the basis for an appropriate political framework for the status of religion. When religious practices and what the State wants conflict, the State is to interfere only when there is a compelling interest to do so. Within the framework of the US Constitution, the Religious Freedom Restoration Act (RFRA) sought to do this.

The problem is in cashing out "compelling state interest." Ultimately, for Nussbaum, this has to be in terms of capabilities. If a religion systematically restricts the functionings of adherents in such a way as to impair their basic capabilities, then the State has a duty to step in and regulate that behaviour. One challenge for the capabilities approach is the question of how to deal with hard cases, where some action deemed necessary for the practice of a religion runs up against other ends that the State considers to be good. Nussbaum considers the examples of smoking narcotics, racial and sexual discrimination, education, and the denial of certain opportunities to women and children. These cases do much to flesh out her approach – she sympathetically considers the religious case for the restriction of functioning and, with reservations, is prepared to support religious freedoms against the state in more cases than the US courts have (Nussbaum, 2000, pp. 202 ff.; see also Nussbaum 2008).

The Reformed Christian would approach cases rather differently. The criteria would be: does this behaviour truly lead to the building of *shalom*? Does it violate God's laws? As noted above, not all activity that claims to glorify God actually does; there are good *prima facie* grounds for saying that capacity-denying ordinances are not in accord with the will of a benevolent God. Thus one could give good *religious* reasons, as well as humanist ones, why suicide bombers and the hijackers of September 11, 2001 were not, despite their opinion, carrying out God's will.

Since Constantine made it the preferred religion of the Roman Empire, Christianity has had an unfortunate history of intolerance to those of other faiths, and to those who saw the True Faith differently. One needs think only of the Crusades and the persecutions of the Reformation to see the truth of this. Jesus's claim in *John 14:6* to be the sole way to God came to be interpreted by the institutionalised Church as granting it a monopoly on access to the deity, and as a duty on the State to impose what it viewed as True Religion. (See, for example, article 36 of the Belgic Confession, which gives a duty to civil magistrates to "countenance the preaching of the Word of the gospel everywhere, that God may be honoured and worshipped by every one, of what state, quality, or condition so ever he may be.") The United States adopted Constitutional non-establishment of a particular Church at least in part because groups of different religious traditions had founded the various colonies, so that religious orthodoxy varied from place to place. The separation of church and state has generally served the US well, both in avoiding conflicts between Christian groups, and in protecting the churches from State interference. It is significant, though, that religious toleration was argued for by some Christians on the basis of the Bible and their Christian beliefs. Nussbaum (2008) elevates Roger Williams, the seventeenth-century founder of the Rhode Island colony, as the prime example of early belief in liberty of conscience, but, as Richard Neuhaus (2008) points out in his review of the book, Williams's defence of Quakers, Jews and dissenters of various types was based explicitly on his reading of the Bible (and his suspicion, based on this, that existing churches were largely apostate; see Chupack, 1969; Garrett, 1970).

In addition, it must be remembered that religious belief is not just a set of outward observances; at core, it is an internal disposition. Although it is possible for a government to achieve limited outward compliance with religious practices, insisting on compliance of this sort is likely to be counterproductive in producing a nation of genuine believers.

The devastating effects of intolerance in the history of Christianity, and the success of the US system of separating church and State, together provide strong grounds for religious toleration rather than endorsement of any one denomination or belief set as the only correct version. Toleration is desirable for the same reason that democracy is good: it diffuses power and prevents the unhealthy concentration of power without accountability that leads to abuses. Similarly, toleration of differing religious beliefs and practices recognises that human beings are corrupted by sin and prone to misinterpret what God has said. The humility of recognising that a particular interpretation of Scripture (even if it's our own!) might be wrong, having become so encrusted by human traditions that the original meaning has been lost, is a healthy corrective to dogmatism.

But toleration, while a virtue, is not the highest virtue. Toleration of systems, institutions and actions that are inimical to building *shalom* will be limited. Just as democracy is not always conducive to genuine freedom and capability enhancement and, unrestrained, can degenerate into the tyranny of the majority over the minority, so toleration of all religious practice can lead to oppression for adherents of certain religions, as Nussbaum documents.

When she discusses the potential for conflict between deeply held sincere religious beliefs and the ability to exercise capabilities, Nussbaum suggests that something like the US Constitution can act as arbitrator between the two. The twin principles of non-establishment and free exercise between them, she feels, define the appropriate space in which religion and capabilities can be reconciled (Nussbaum, 2000, p. 189). Nussbaum wants to allow freedom of religious belief but rule out any religion that seeks the good of an individual by denying the liberty of conscience of individual adherents of the religion (ibid.). Nussbaum is, of course, aware that there are difficult cases. She examines, for example, the case of Bob Jones University's discriminatory racial practices and concludes that the State had an overriding interest in demanding amendments to that policy. But using the US Constitution, or something similar, as the arbitrator of public policy makes it "divine" in Clouser's sense: "overriding public policy imperatives" overrule religious beliefs.

The US doctrine of separation of Church and State, while conducive to liberty and guaranteeing (most) capabilities, does leave open the problem of identifying what is and what is not a religion, and where to draw the line when claims of religious believers conflict with the dictates of (secular) law. There are various financial incentives for a group to claim religious status (donations to it can then be written off against US income taxes, for example), which encourages new groups to do so. Few countries outside the United States would accept the Church of Body Modification as a legitimate religious entity (CBM, 2004). More contentious is the case of Scientology. While L. Ron Hubbard's organisation has the status of a religion in the United States, authorities in Germany have had the tendency to see it as a cover for commercial business activity, and other European countries, such as Belgium and Austria, deny the organisation any official recognition (and consequent tax advantages) as a religion.

Abraham Kuyper, in his work on Calvinism, developed what came to be called the theory of sphere sovereignty: that the various structures and institutions of human society would have sovereign authority (to make rules, conduct their business) within their appropriate area, or sphere, of activity (Kuyper, 1880). The idea is simple: a school is not a church, is not a business; they have different roles in society. What is appropriate for one is not necessarily appropriate for the others. Parents are sovereign over their families, churches over their members (*qua* members of the church). The source of this authority is God: the State, like other institutions of society, has certain rights and obligations, a role assigned to it by God. The church has a different role: it has a different focus from the state, a different agenda and different tools by which to carry out that mandate. For example, the mandate Jesus gave to the Church was to make disciples of all nations – to preach the Gospel to every creature (*Matt. 28:19* – the Great Commission); the Old Testament gives a mandate to parents to educate their children. Similarly, businesses, schools and even sports clubs can be seen as deriving authority for their mandates directly from God. Ultimate sovereignty belongs to God alone; all human institutions derive their authority from Him.

The problem, though, is to delineate the appropriate boundaries between the spheres. If sovereignty comes directly from God, so that there is no hierarchical structure, who decides where the boundaries lie? For Kuyper, like Clouser, and like Nussbaum, the final arbiter must be the State, but the way in which the State is to act as arbiter is different. With Nussbaum, "compelling state interest" is cashed out in terms of protection of capabilities. By adopting this standard, it appears that certain religions are favoured over others: capability-affirming religions will find they have more *de facto* freedom to operate than capability-denying beliefs. The Christian alternative approach would make the building of *shalom* as the ultimate criterion; the State has the authority to decide the appropriate bounds and sphere of activity of religion but not to dictate what religious practices take place within those bounds.

While generally supportive of the US version of the separation of Church and State, Nussbaum is prepared to concede that the establishment of a particular religion may be a better protection of the capabilities of followers of other religions than a secularised State. In the US, religious influence, though strong, has no official role in the government. In Britain, an official role is preserved by the access of selected Anglican bishops to the political process. Archbishop William Temple saw that the (institutionalised) Church should act as a sort of conscience, as a constraint on the actions of government (Temple, 1976). It is not up to the Church to make specific policy recommendations, he said (in Kuyperian language, that would be a violation of sphere sovereignty), but the Church does have the obligation to point out cases of injustice, problems where "something must be done." Where *shalom* is compromised, action needs to be taken. It may be that it is the role of government to take action, but perhaps some other institution more appropriately takes the remedial action.

In addition, the establishment of religion will serve to delineate the appropriate limits to toleration of divergent behaviour. "Compelling state interest" could be cashed out slightly differently. Using the building of *shalom* as the political outworking of the glorification of God, as the appropriate principle, the question to ask of a religious practice is: is this activity consistent with those principles? Thus different Christian traditions, as diverse as Quakers and Roman Catholics, would be free to operate their own educational systems, including the teaching of critical thinking skills (and even a critique of the churches themselves); a diversity of religious views within the Christian tradition reduces the inherent problems of a religious monopoly, a view with which Roger Williams would no doubt have sympathised, if for rather different reasons.

Differences III – other-regarding preferences

Other-regarding preferences are preferences that one person has about the behaviour of others. The capabilities approach, with its strong emphasis on individualism, declares illegitimate any preference of mine that others' capabilities be restricted. The only legitimate other-regarding preference is a type of benevolence: respect for others' capabilities.

Certain religious preferences, though, will attempt to place restrictions on others' behaviour and deny opportunities that they otherwise might want. The Taliban regime in Afghanistan denied that many of the capabilities on Nussbaum's list were appropriate for women. The chief purpose of women, apparently, was to bear children (preferably male). Education of girls was deemed to be unnecessary and inappropriate; women were denied opportunities to work, and were required to cover themselves from head to foot when they went out. As these preferences require the denial of capabilities to women, they are given no weight.

Religions involve a conception of the Good – a way to salvation, perhaps. These conceptions tend to be "paternalistic" in one sense: they tend to impose some of the outward implications of the belief system on non-believers. This may be the result of legislation, or the result of social pressure or custom. Some non-adherents might even see the restrictions as good – their preferences adapt to the expectations of the community.

A community in which I once lived is mainly Reformed Christian and takes the Judaeo–Christian idea of a weekly rest seriously. On Sunday most shops are closed; one does not work, or even mow one's lawn. The story goes that one person who did mow his lawn on Sunday was prosecuted for "disturbing the peace." My freedom to affiliate with others is in effect constrained – I need to live in accordance with the expected norms of the society in which I live if I am to form deep relationships within it. I could, of course, choose to live elsewhere; what I cannot do is to stay put and disregard the Sabbath observance customs of the town. As it is for Nussbaum's Orthodox Brooklyn Jews (2006, p. 185), exit from the community is easy, but geographical separation might be necessary for the remaining community to continue to flourish.

Other-regarding preferences are problematic in ethical theory. One objection to utilitarianism is that it seems to require people to do things they do not wish to do and which reduce their utility, because the gain to overall utility is greater than the converse. Amartya Sen has shown that a utilitarianism that validates other-regarding preferences conflicts with a basic notion of liberty – in his example, the freedom to choose whether or not to read a book one considers pornographic (Sen, 1970). Similarly, a utilitarian defence of the Taliban could claim (implausibly) that the denial of basic functionings to women increased the happiness of the men by more than the loss of happiness of the women.

Because of the danger of reaching conclusions of this type, many philosophers, including Martha C. Nussbaum, are wary of giving weight to other-regarding preferences. One alternative is to disregard all other-regarding preferences entirely: a form of libertarianism that says that any act is morally permissible if it does not cause direct harm to another person. Reducing another's utility by indulging in actions that he deems to be wrong is not a "direct harm." Benevolence towards others, and a desire that they, too, tolerate the choices of others, is the only legitimate other-regarding preference.

There are good reasons for rejecting this approach. First, there are cases where freedoms, even when indulged in from the best of motives, can cause indirect harm. Hardin drew attention to the "Tragedy of the Commons" (Hardin, 1968), where individual choices may result in disaster if they involve the unsustainable use of a resource. It is also possible to produce examples where doing what, individually considered, is best leads to a situation that is worse for all, including the actor: the familiar Prisoners' Dilemma cases fall into this category. Parfit has shown that it is possible also to produce examples where what seems right, morally, can produce a worse result for the actor, even in terms of his own ethical theory (Parfit, 1984: Chapters 23 and 24).

Second, the democratic process is at least partially an exercise in forming community preferences, which involve preferences about what other people do and how they behave. In general, these are not going to conflict with capabilities, but they may conflict with certain functionings. Expecting, or requiring, a particular type of Sabbath observance does limit the choices of those who wish to do otherwise. So do constraints on what constitutes appropriate sexual behaviour. Perhaps of more consequence politically is the decision as to how to allocate medical resources, which directly impacts the ability of people to live a life of normal length.

Third, a conception of the Good will have, as a consequence, substantive and not just procedural preferences about the lives of other people. For a Reformed Christian, this should be governed by a principle of generosity – the desire that others, too, might flourish. Positively, this means accepting the desires of others, but also, negatively, discouraging wrongful, sinful behaviour. The Christian claim is that, even though certain things you might want to do are prohibited, it is better for you if they are. The justifications for this type of prohibition need to be made carefully: Nussbaum is rightly concerned that this kind of argument has been used to try to justify unequal treatment of women. The onus, then, would be on the proposer of the restraint to justify it.

We are accustomed to such constraints being placed on children, and, to a lesser extent, on adults for their greater good and protection. The conflicts inherent in compulsory education and use of seatbelts illustrate this point. A further example in Britain and Canada has been the conflict for motorcycling Sikhs between the law's requirement for a crash helmet and the religious requirement to wear a turban. Laws against drugs, illicit sexual relationships and the like tend to be justified on this ground.

Probably what is at issue is more the placing of restraints on the way that the capabilities are exercised (the particular mode of functioning) rather than on the denial of any of the capabilities. This is, I think, analogous to Nussbaum's point that it is sometimes necessary to insist on a functioning to prevent the loss of a capability: restraining the way in which a capability is used may be necessary to prevent damage to oneself, or to others. Thus, for example, one might limit the freedom of speech to discourage slander (modelling the relevant law on the British rather than the American standard), just as some countries have found it necessary to prohibit Holocaust denial.

Differences IV – religious freedom

Perhaps the toughest challenge for the Reformed Christian-based view that I am suggesting is the degree of freedom to be granted to other religions or, indeed, to other Christian denominations. Can an established Church genuinely support religious pluralism? Can a religion that believes it has some conception of absolute truth permit people to propose ideas that are contrary to that revealed truth?

I want to make two points here. First, the apostle Paul says that God wants all people to be saved and to come to a knowledge of the truth about Jesus and His atoning sacrifice for the human race (*1 Tim 2:3–6*). The way that this is to be achieved is by the preaching of the Gospel message (*Romans 10:14–15*). The Good News of the redemption of all things by Jesus Christ needs to go forth unhindered.

Second, the ability to form a conception of the good is not something that can be done in a vacuum: it will be shaped by the person's experiences and education, including religious education. "Train a child in the way he should go, and when he is old he will not depart from it," says Solomon (*Prov. 22:6*). One's conception of the good will be shaped by the religious (or other) tradition to which one belongs.

These two points suggest that exposure to the teachings of Christianity would be of great importance. But this need not exclude teaching on other religions: if Christianity is, indeed, the truth, then, providing it is well taught, it should have little to fear from teachings from other religions. Again, it is apposite to draw a comparison between Britain and the United States. In the US, attempts to have children in state schools read the Bible (or the Koran, for that matter) have been resisted as a violation of the principle of the separation of Church and State. This means that, for most children, there is no school teaching of religion: children in state schools do not hear about God. In Britain, children study several world religions. This gives them some information on the way that previous generations and different religious traditions have perceived God, but it also allows them to compare the different traditions and so helps them form a conception of the Good. (This supports Nussbaum's point that countries with state-sponsored, established churches are not necessarily more inimical to different religious traditions than are avowedly secular states, which tend to elevate humanism to divine status, in Clouser's sense.)

Freedom for other religious traditions is consistent with a Reformed Christian view of capabilities, just as it was for Roger Williams. The restraints would be only that the Christian gospel would not be impeded and the practices of other faiths that are inimical to the Gospel message would be restrained. In practice, this would allow a good deal of freedom. Muslim girls in France (and women in Turkey) would be allowed to wear headscarves. Perhaps even Mormon polygamy would pass as acceptable under this heading. But wife-beating and suicide-bombing would not, and Williams vehemently denounced the antics of Quakers "who thought nothing, for example, of running naked through the streets to proclaim their beliefs" (Chupack, 1969, p. 134).

A revised capabilities list

Table 17.1 shows the modifications of Nussbaum's list that a Reformed Christian view might make. In addition, taking the building of *shalom* to be the aim of life, capabilities would be ordered according to their ability to increase *shalom*.

Conclusion

In sketching out and defending a list of basic human capabilities, Martha C. Nussbaum has produced a most useful tool to aid thinking about the meaning of human development. Her emphasis on examining the actual living conditions and opportunities available to real women is also a helpful corrective to abstract thinking on human rights – all too often an account of the rights of, and opportunities open to, the male of the species.

The theory in its present form is incomplete as a normative account of society, but certainly the foundation is here for a full-blown moral theory, giving an account of matters of justice, obligation and duty and with a notion of the Good.

The flexibility of the capabilities approach is sometimes seen as a liability – attempts to "operationalise" the approach (to come up with a maximisable equation) have proved difficult, as the approach is unhappy dealing with trade-offs between different types of capability, and many of the elements are either unmeasurable or all-or-nothing concepts. Nussbaum's idea of a threshold level is helpful here, and defining a (Pareto) improvement in capability-satisfaction is possible without the need for the cardinality of a metric.

Yet the flexibility of the approach is also an asset. People from many different religious traditions, as well as the western individualist tradition in philosophy, can agree on the value of a set of capabilities. While lists of what capabilities are important will differ (depending on the perspective or worldview of the compiler), there is likely to be substantial overlap and agreement between the lists of people from many different religious (and non-religious) traditions. My critique from a Reformed Christian perspective has attempted to show that the differences between it and Nussbaum's approach would be relatively minor at the level of application, although the justification of capabilities, and their status, is rather

Table 17.1 *Central human functional capabilities*

Nussbaum's list	Reformed Christian perspective
1. *Life*. Being able to live to the end of a human life of normal length; not dying prematurely, or before one's life is so reduced as to be not worth living.	
2. *Bodily health*. Being able to have good health, including reproductive health; to be adequately nourished; to have adequate shelter.	
3. *Bodily integrity*. Being able to move freely from place to place; having one's bodily boundaries treated as sovereign, i.e. being able to be secure against assault, including sexual assault, child sexual abuse, and domestic violence; having opportunities for sexual satisfaction and for choice in matters of reproduction.	Limitations on opportunities for sexual satisfaction to marriage. Choice in matters of reproduction not unlimited: abortion not endorsed.
4. *Senses, imagination and thought*. Being able to use the senses, to imagine, think, and reason – and to do these things in a "truly human" way, a way informed and cultivated by an adequate education, including, but by no means limited to, literacy and basic mathematical and scientific training. Being able to use imagination and thought in connection with experiencing and producing self-expressive works and events of one's own choice, religious, literary, musical, and so forth. Being able to use one's mind in ways protected by guarantees of freedom of expression with respect to both political and artistic speech, and freedom of religious exercise. Being able to search for the ultimate meaning of life in one's own way. Being able to have pleasurable experiences, and to avoid non-necessary pain.	To include religious education; the basis of shalom, God's commandments; to hear the Gospel of Jesus Christ. Not all "speech" deemed to be protected under the US Bill of Rights need be endorsed, e.g. inciting racial hatred, denigrating religion, advocating unjust/shalom-destroying activities, blasphemy not supported.
5. *Emotions*. Being able to have attachments to things and people outside ourselves; to love those who love and care for us, to grieve at their absence; in general, to love, to grieve, to experience longing, gratitude, and justified anger. Not having one's emotional development blighted by overwhelming fear and anxiety, or by traumatic events of abuse or neglect. (Supporting this capability means supporting forms of human association that can be shown to be crucial in their development.)	Demonstrations of the love of God.

6. *Practical reason.* Being able to form a conception of the good and to engage in critical reflection about the planning of one's life. (This entails protection for the liberty of conscience.) — To be informed by Christian teaching.

7. *Affiliation.* A. Being able to live with and toward others, to recognize and show concern for other human beings, to engage in various forms of social interaction; to be able to imagine the situation of another and to have compassion for that situation: to have the capability for both justice and friendship. (Protecting this capability means protecting institutions that constitute and nourish such forms of affiliation, and also protecting the freedom of assembly and political speech.) — ... but restraining speech that tends to destroy societal harmony.

B. Having the social bases of self-respect and non-humiliation; being able to be treated as a dignified being whose worth is equal to that of others. This entails, at a minimum, protections against discrimination on the basis of race, sex, sexual orientation, religion, caste, ethnicity, or national origin. In work, being able to work as a human being, exercising practical reason and entering into meaningful relationships of mutual recognition with other workers. — Discrimination only on basis of "fitness for office"; certain roles may be limited to one gender. "Sexual orientation" not supported.

8. *Other species.* Being able to live with concern for and in relation to animals, plants and the world of nature.

9. *Play.* Being able to laugh, to play, to enjoy recreational activities.

10. *Control over one's environment.* A. *Political.* Being able to participate effectively in political choices that govern one's life; having the right of political participation, protections of free speech and association. — With the limitations noted above. The right to have one's point of view heard.

B. *Material.* Being able to hold property (both land and movable goods), not just formally but in terms of real opportunity; and having property rights on an equal basis with others; having the right to seek employment on an equal basis with others; having the freedom from unwarranted search and seizure. (Nussbaum, 2000, 78–80) different. Because of this, the details of the list may well require some modifications, but the underlying assumption of the value of capabilities remains.

REFERENCES

Bascom, Paul, and Susan Tolle (2002) Responding to requests for physician-assisted suicide, *Journal of the American Medical Association* Vol. 288 No. 1 (3rd July) pp. 91–98.

BBC (2002) Woman welcomes "right to die" ruling, http://news.bbc.co.uk/hi/english/health/newsid_1887000/1887281.stm, accessed 22/7/02.

Beversluis, Joel (2001) Teaching the Golden Rules, *Christian Educators Journal* Vol. 41 No. 2 (December) pp. 8–9.

Biéler, André (1961) *La pensée économique et sociale de Calvin*, Geneva: Georg & Cie.

(1964) *The Social Humanism of Calvin*, Richmond, VA: John Knox Press.

Calvin, John (1957) *Institutes of the Christian Religion*, Grand Rapids, MI: Eerdmans (originally published in 1559).

CBM (2004) Church of Body Modification website, www.uscobm.com/, accessed 5/7/04.

Chupack, Henry (1969) *Roger Williams*, New York: Twayne.

Clouser, Roy (1991) *The Myth of Religious Neutrality*, University of Notre Dame Press.

Dowling, Tim (2002) Deaf babies by design, *Saga* (July) pp. 10–11.

Edwards, Jonathan (1765) *A Dissertation Concerning the End for Which God Created the World*, edited by Samuel Hopkins, www.biblicaltheology.com/classics/Jonathan%20Edwards/edwards105.html, accessed 22/07/02.

Garrett, John (1970) *Roger Williams: Witness Beyond Christendom 1603–1683*, London: Macmillan.

Goudzwaard, Bob (1975) *Aid for the Overdeveloped West*, Toronto: Wedge Publishing.

Hardin, Garrett (1968) The tragedy of the commons, *Science* Vol. 162 No. 3859 pp. 1243–1248.

Hare, R.M. (1979) What is wrong with slavery, *Philosophy and Public Affairs* Vol. 8 No. 2 (Winter) pp. 103–121.

Kuyper, Abraham (1880) *Souvereiniteit in Eigen Kring* (Sovereignty in its circle), address at the opening of the Free University of Amsterdam, 20 October.

(1931) *Lectures on Calvinism*, Grand Rapids, MI: Eerdmans (originally published 1898).

Neuhaus, Richard John (2008) Freedom for religion, *New York Sun 27th February*, www.nysun.com/article/71945, accessed 17/3/08.

Nussbaum, Martha C. (2000) *Women and Human Development*, Cambridge University Press.

(2006) *Frontiers of Justice*, Cambridge, MA: The Belknap Press.

(2008) *Liberty of Conscience: In Defense of America's Tradition of Religious Equality*, New York: Basic Books.

Parfit, Derek (1984) *Reasons and Persons*, Oxford: Clarendon Press.

Piper, John (1987) Was Jonathan Edwards a Christian Hedonist? www. desiringGod.org, accessed 22/7/02.

Sen, Amartya (1970) The impossibility of a Paretian liberal, *Journal of Political Economy* Vol. 78 No. 1 pp. 152–157.

(1999) *Development as Freedom*, New York: Random House.

Temple, William (1976) *Christianity and Social Order*, London: Shepheard-Walwyn.

Tennant, Agnieszka (2002) Stretch pants, beer, and other controversies (review of Webb, 2001), *Christianity Today* (8th July) pp. 66–67.

Todaro, Michael (2000) *Economic Development*, Reading, MA: Addison-Wesley, 7th edition; 9th edition (with Stephen C. Smith) 2006.

Webb, William J. (2001) *Slaves, Women and Homosexuals*, Downers Grove, IL: IVP.

Wolsterstorff, Nicholas (1983) *Until Justice and Peace Embrace*, Grand Rapids, MI: William B. Eerdmans.

Index

Printed in the United States
By Bookmasters